INNOVATION PROJECT MANAGEMENT

INNOVATION
PROJECT
MANAGEMENT

Methods, Case Studies, and Tools
for Managing Innovation Projects

Second Edition

HAROLD KERZNER, PH.D.

WILEY

Library of Congress Cataloging-in-Publication Data
Names: Kerzner, Harold, author.
Title: Innovation Project Management : Methods, Case Studies, and Tools for Managing Innovation
   Projects/Harold Kerzner
Description: Hoboken, NJ: John Wiley & Sons, 2023. | Includes bibliographical references and index.
Identifiers: LCCN 2022063043 (print) | LCCN 2022063044 (ebook) | ISBN 9781119931249 (hardback) |
   ISBN 9781119931263 (pdf) | ISBN 9781119931256 (epub) | ISBN 9781119931270 (ebook)
Subjects: LCSH: Art and Architecture.
Classification: LCC QR111. P333 2023 (print) | LCC QR111 (ebook) | DDC 579/.1757--dc23/eng/20230304
LC record available at https://lccn.loc.gov/2022063043
LC ebook record available at https://lccn.loc.gov/2022063044

Set in 10/12.5pt Times LT Std by Integra Software Services Pvt. Ltd, Pondicherry, India

SKY10038606_111822

To
my wife, Jo Ellyn,
for years of ongoing love,
support, and understanding

Contents

Preface   *xv*

1   INTRODUCTION TO INNOVATION PROJECT MANAGEMENT   1

Introduction   1
Definitions for Innovation   2
The Business Need   4
Innovation Literature   6
Project Management Literature   7
Innovation Benchmarking   8
Value: The Missing Link   10
Innovation Targeting   12
Timeline for Innovation Targeting   13
Innovation in Small Companies   14
Seven Critical Dimensions for Scaling Project Management Innovation   14
Implications and Issues for Project Managers and Innovation Personnel   16

2   TYPES OF INNOVATION   19

Introduction   19
Continuous Versus Discontinuous Innovation   20
Incremental Versus Radical Innovation   21
Understanding Innovation Differences   22
Incremental Innovation Versus New Product Development   23
Product Development Innovation Categories   23
Closed and Open Innovation   25
Crowdsourcing   27
Co-Creation Innovation   29
Open Innovation in Action: Airbus and Co-creation Partnerships   35

Value (Or Value-Driven) Innovation   37
Agile Innovation   38
Agile Innovation in Action: Deloitte   40
Government Innovation   47
Financial Innovation   50
Healthcare Innovation   51
Brand Innovation   53
Sustainable Innovation   53
Humanitarian/Social Innovation   54
Social Innovation in Action: Hitachi   55
Educational Innovation   57
Manufacturing Innovation   58
A Case Study   60
Nontechnical Innovation in Action   60
Other Categories of Innovation   62
Role of the Board of Directors   66
Finding an Innovation Project Sponsor   66
Implications and Issues for Project Managers and Innovation Personnel   67

3   INNOVATION AND STRATEGIC PLANNING   69

Introduction   69
Role of the Innovation Project Manager in Strategic Planning   70
Role of the Portfolio PMO   70
Business Impact Analysis   71
Innovation Maturity Models   71
Types of Strategies   73
Role of Innovation in Strategic Planning   74
Role of Marketing in Strategic Innovation Planning   75
Product Portfolio Analysis   76
Identifying Core Competencies Using SWOT Analysis   82
Innovation Project Management Competency Models in Action: Eli Lilly   84
Marketing's Involvement with Innovation Project Managers   95
Product Life Cycles   97
Classification of R&D Projects   97
Research Versus Development   98
The Research and Development Ratio   99
Offensive Versus Defensive Innovation   100
Modeling the R&D Planning Function   101
Priority Setting   105
Contract R&D   107
Nondisclosure Agreements, Secrecy Agreements, and Confidentiality Agreements   108
Government Influence   108
Sources for Innovation Technology   109
Sources of Ideas   110

The Project Manager's Role in Developing Innovation Skills and Ideas in People   112
Establishing a Project Selection Criteria   114
Project Selection Issues   115
Economic Evaluation of Projects   116
Role of the Project Manager in Project Selection   119
Project Selection and Politics   124
Project Readjustments   126
Project Termination   127
Implications and Issues for Project Managers and Innovation Personnel   127

4   INNOVATION TOOLS AND PROCESSES   129

Introduction   129
New Product Development   130
The Fuzzy Front End   131
Prioritizing Product Features   133
Line of Sight   134
Misalignment Issues   135
Risk Management   137
The Innovation Culture   140
Innovation Functional Units   145
Innovative Cultures and Corporate Leadership   145
Idea Generation   146
Spinoff Innovations   147
Understanding Reward Systems   148
Innovation Leadership in Action: Medtronic   149
IPM Skills Needed   152
Design Thinking   155
Brainstorming   157
Whiteboarding   163
Mind Maps   163
Active Listening   165
Pitching the Innovation   167
Cognitive Biases   167
Prototypes   168
Creativity and Innovation Fears   170
Innovation Governance   170
Corporate Innovation Governance Risks   171
Transformational Governance   174
Balanced Scorecard   175
Strategy Maps   176
Innovation Portfolio Management   177
Innovation Sponsorship   179
The Innovation Team   180
Virtual Versus Co-Located Innovation Teams   181

Artificial Intelligence and IPM   182
The Need for PM 2.0 and PM 3.0   184
Implications and Issues for Project Managers and Innovation Personnel   187

5   FROM TRADITIONAL TO INNOVATION PROJECT MANAGEMENT THINKING   191

Introduction   191
Information Warehouses   193
Innovation Planning Overview   197
Innovation Methodologies   200
Methodology Gates   202
Innovation Assumptions   202
Validating the Objectives   204
Differing Views of the Project   206
Life-Cycle Phases   206
Life-Cycle Costing   210
Work Breakdown Structure   211
Budgeting   212
Scheduling   212
Scope Change Control   213
Technology Readiness Levels   214
Lean Project Management: Kanban   216
Communication   217
Enabling Innovation Success in Solution Design and Delivery in Healthcare Business   218
Innovation in Action: Dubai Customs and the Accelerated Exploratory Lab   229
Innovation in Action: Merck KGaA, Darmstadt, Germany   234
Innovation in Action: Repsol   237
Staffing Innovation Projects   241
Implications and Issues for Project Managers and Innovation Personnel   243

6   INNOVATION MANAGEMENT SOFTWARE   245

Introduction   245
Origin and Benefits of Innovation Software   246
Software Innovation in Action: IdeaScale   248
Software Innovation in Action: Hype Innovation   251
Software and Open Innovation   260
Implications and Issues for Project Managers and Innovation Personnel   261

7   VALUE-BASED INNOVATION PROJECT MANAGEMENT METRICS   263

Introduction   263
Value Over the Years   265
Value and Leadership   266
Combining Benefits and Value   268

Recognizing the Need for Value Metrics   269
The Need for Effective Measurement Techniques   271
Measuring Intangible Assets   276
Customer/Stakeholder Impact on Value Metrics   278
Customer Value Management Programs   279
The Relationship between Project Management and Value   282
Creating an Innovation Project Management Baseline   284
Selecting the Right Metrics   286
The Failure of Traditional Metrics and KPIs   288
The Need for Value Metrics   288
Creating Value Metrics   289
Industry Examples of Innovation Value Metrics   295
Alignment to Strategic Business Objectives   296
Metrics for Innovation Governance   298
Innovation Metrics in Action: InnovationLabs   299
The Dark Side of Innovation Metrics   309
Establishing a Metrics Management Program   310
Implications and Issues for Project Managers and Innovation Personnel   312

8 BUSINESS MODELS   315

Introduction   315
From Project Manager to Designer   317
Business Models and Value   318
Business Model Characteristics   318
Strategic Partnerships   319
Business Intelligence   319
Skills for the Business Model Innovator   320
Business Model Enhancements   322
Types of Business Models   324
Business Models and Strategic Alliances   326
Identifying Business Model Threats   327
Business Model Failure   328
Business Models and Lawsuits   328
Implications and Issues for Project Managers and Innovation Personnel   330

9 DISRUPTIVE INNOVATION   333

Introduction   333
Early Understanding of Disruption   334
Innovation and the Business Model Disruption   335
Categories of Disruptive Innovations   337
The Dark Side of Disruptive Innovation   338
Using Integrated Product/Project Teams   339
Disruptive Innovation in Action   341
Implications and Issues for Project Managers and Innovation Personnel   342

10   INNOVATION ROADBLOCKS   345

Introduction   345
The Failure of Success   346
One Size Fits All   346
Insufficient Line of Sight   346
Failing to Search for Ideas   347
Sense of Urgency   347
Working with Prima Donnas   347
Lack of Collaboration   348
Politics   348
Project Workloads   348
Intellectual Property Rights   348
Not Understanding the Relationship between Creativity and Innovation   349
Too Many Assumptions   350
Innovation Funding   350
Cash Flow and Financial Uncertainty   350
Control, Control, and Control   350
Analysis–Paralysis   351
Innovation in Action: Naviair   351
Innovation in Action: Overcoming the Roadblocks   363

11   DEFINING INNOVATION SUCCESS AND FAILURE   367

Introduction   367
The Business Side of Traditional Project Success   368
Defining Project Success: The Early Years   370
Redefining Project Success: Approaching the Twenty-First Century   371
Degrees of Success and Failure   372
Defining Success at the Beginning of the Project   374
The Role of Marketing in Defining Innovation Success   374
The Business Side of Innovation Success   377
Prioritization of the Success Factors   379
Innovation Project Success and Core Competencies   380
Innovation Project Success and Business Models   381
Causes of Innovation Project Failure   381
Identifying the Success and Failure Criteria   384
Post-Failure Success Analysis   385
Sensemaking   386
The Need for New Metrics   387
Learning from Failure   387
The Failure of Success   388
Conclusion   390
Implications and Issues for Project Managers and Innovation Personnel   390

12   INNOVATION IN ACTION   393

Introduction   393
Innovation in Action: Apple   393
Innovation in Action: Facebook   395
Innovation in Action: IBM   396
Innovation in Action: Texas Instruments   399
Innovation in Action: 3M   401
Innovation in Action: Motorola   403
Innovation Project Management: The Case of KAUST Smart   404
Key Characteristic of KAUST Smart Projects (What makes KAUST Smart Projects Unique)   405
Recent and Ongoing Project Examples   408
Innovation in Action: Samsung   410
Agile Innovation in Action: Integrated Computer Solutions, Inc   411
Innovation in Action: COMAU   418
Innovation in Action: Tokio Marine and Nichido Systems   425
Innovation in Action: GEA   427
Innovation Management at GEA – The Strategic Parts   432
Innovation in Action: Wärtsilä Energy Solutions   435
Critical Issues   437

13   CASE STUDIES   439

Disney (A): Innovation Project Management Skills at Disney   439
Disney (B): Creating Innovation: Disney's Haunted Mansion   449
Disney (C): Impact Of Culture On Global Innovation Opportunities   464
Disney (D): The Partnership Side Of Global Business Model Innovation   482
Case Study: Boeing 787 Dreamliner: Managing Innovation Risks with a New Business Model   494
Case Study: The Sydney Australia Opera House   501
Case Study: Ampore Faucet Company: Managing Different Views on Innovation   508
Case Study: The Innovation Sponsors   510
Case Study: The Rise, Fall, and Resurrection of Iridium: When an Innovation Business Model Fails   512
Case Study: Zane Corporation: Selecting an Innovation Framework   540
Case Study: Redstone Inc.: Understanding Innovation Cultures   544
Case Study: The Government Think Tank: The Failure of Crowdsourcing   546
Case Study: Lego: Brand Management Innovation   548

INDEX   565

Preface

All companies desire growth. But without some innovations, the opportunities may be limited. And even if the firm does have a few successful innovations, failure can still occur if the company focuses on past successes without developing a culture for continuous and sustainable innovations. Today's industry leaders can become tomorrow's failures without constantly challenging results.

If continuous and sustainable innovation is to occur, then innovation leadership and project management must be married together and with a clear understanding of each other's roles. Innovation defines what we would like to do, and project management determines if it can be done. The marriage also may require that both parties learn new skills and create a corporate culture that supports idea management practices. As discussed in several of the chapters in the book, companies are developing organizational units dedicated to innovation activities and idea management.

Understanding each other's roles is the first step in making a company more innovative. This requires that the project managers and other innovation personnel understand what they do not do now but must do for long-term successful innovation. This also includes understanding the interfacing with marketing personnel and customers.

The book is broken down as follows:

- **Chapter 1:** Discusses why innovation and project management are often not discussed together and some of the links that are needed to bridge innovation, project management, and business strategy.
- **Chapter 2:** Discusses the different types of innovation. This is essential because each type of innovation may require a different form of project management.
- **Chapter 3:** Discusses how business strategy may determine the type of innovation required and links together project management with the different types of innovation.
- **Chapter 4:** Discusses the tools that traditional project managers need to learn in order to manage innovation projects. Many of these tools are not discussed in traditional project management programs.
- **Chapter 5:** Discusses why some of the processes used in traditional project management activities may not work within innovation projects without some degree of modification.

- **Chapter 6:** Discusses the growth in innovation management software that project managers are now using in the front end of projects for idea management, alternative analyses, and decision making.
- **Chapter 7:** Discusses the new metrics that project managers and innovation personnel are using for the monitoring and controlling of innovation projects.
- **Chapter 8:** Discusses innovations related to business models rather than products and services.
- **Chapter 9:** Discusses how disruptive innovation requirements may need a completely new form of project management and the need to interface closely with the consumer marketplace.
- **Chapter 10:** Discusses the roadblocks affecting the working relationship between project management and innovation.
- **Chapter 11:** Discusses how some projects, including innovation activities, have degrees of success and failure rather than complete success and failure as defined by the triple constraints.
- **Chapter 12:** Discusses the innovation culture that several companies have developed as well as the functional units they created to support innovation creation.
- **Chapter 13:** Case studies that discuss issues with innovation.

Companies mentioned in this book include:

- 3 M
- Advanced Micro Devices
- Airbus
- Amazon
- Apple
- Blockbuster
- Boeing
- Booz, Allen and Hamilton
- Boston Consulting Group
- Comau
- Daimler-Chrysler
- Dell Computer
- Deloitte
- Dubai Customs
- eBay
- Eli Lilly
- Facebook
- GEA
- General Electric
- Google
- Hewlett-Packard
- Hitachi
- Home Depot
- HYPE Innovation
- IBM
- IdeaScale
- Implement Consulting Group
- Industriens Fond
- InnovationLabs
- Integrated Computer Solutions
- Intel
- Iridium
- KAUST
- Kodak
- Lego
- Lenovo
- Logitech
- Medtronic
- Merck KGaA, Darmstadt, Germany
- Microsoft
- Motorola
- Naviair
- NEC
- Netflix
- Nike
- PayPal
- Philips
- Repsol
- Samsung
- Southwest Airlines
- Starbucks
- Texas Instruments

- Tokio Marine & Nichido Co, Ltd.
- Toyota
- Toys R Us
- Transmeta

- UNICEF
- Walt Disney
- Wärtsilä

The author is indebted to all the companies that were willing to share information on innovation to help better prepare the next generation of innovation project managers. Special thanks to Dr. Luigi Morsa for his input and constructive criticism throughout the preparation of this book.

Seminars, webinars, e-learning courses, and workshops in innovation project management that use this book are available by contacting:

Lori Milhaven, Executive Vice President, IIL
Phone: 800-325-1533 or 212-515-5121
Fax: 212-755-0777
E-mail: lori.milhaven@iil.com

Harold Kerzner
International Institute for Learning

Introduction to Innovation Project Management

Learning Objectives for Project Managers and Innovation Personnel

To understand the differences between traditional and innovation project management

To understand that there are new skills, responsibilities, and expectations for managing innovation activities

To understand the strategic/business importance of innovation

To understand the importance of measuring innovation business value

INTRODUCTION

> *"The future is a direction, not a destination."*
>
> — Edwin Catmull

Over the past three decades, there has been a great deal of literature published on innovation and innovation management. Converting a creative idea into reality requires projects and some form of project management. Unfortunately, innovation projects may not be able to be managed effectively using the traditional project management philosophy we teach in our project management courses. Innovation varies from industry to industry, and even companies within the same industry cannot come to an agreement on how innovation project management should work. Part of the disagreement

Innovation Project Management: Methods, Case Studies, and Tools for Managing Innovation Projects,
Second Edition. Harold Kerzner.
© 2023 John Wiley & Sons, Inc. Published 2023 by John Wiley & Sons, Inc.

comes from the fact that there are several forms of innovation, each one with different characteristics and possibly requiring different tools.

It is inevitable that, over the next several years, professional organizations such as the Project Management Institute (PMI) will recognize the need to begin setting some standards for innovation project management and possibly partner with organizations, such as the Product Development and Management Association (PDMA), which offers a certification program related to innovation. There may also appear an Innovation Project Management Manifesto like the Agile Manifesto. The greatest innovation in the next decade may be the recognition and advancement of innovation project management as a specialized project management career path position.

There are differences between traditional and innovation project management. People have avoided using the words "innovation" and "project management" in the same sentence because of these differences. Even some organizations that offer certification in innovation practices do not use the words "project management." There is limited research on examining the link between innovation and project management.

Innovation is often unstructured and requires people to utilize those portions of the brain that focus on free thinking, creativity, brainstorming, and alternative analyses. Project management, on the other hand, is very structured, with a well-defined scope, and often with a very low tolerance for any creativity or brainstorming that is believed to be out of scope.

There are several types of innovation, ranging from small, incremental changes to a product to totally new products and processes that are the result of a breakthrough in technology that disrupts the market. Incremental innovation may follow some of the standard project management processes. Radical or disruptive innovation may require playing by a different set of rules. All assumptions must be challenged, even if they appear in a business case. Innovation requires the identification of the right problems and thinking about elegant solutions. All of these factors may require that the organizational culture change.

DEFINITIONS FOR INNOVATION

"If you want something new, you have to stop doing something old."

— Peter Drucker

"Innovation = Ideas + Execution + Adoption"
— Jag Randhawa, *The Bright Idea Box: A Proven System to Drive Employee
Engagement and Innovation*

There are conflicting views on what innovation means. Some people argue that innovation is standing in the future (rather than the present) and helping others see it. Another view of innovation (to paraphrase Martha Graham) states that innovation teams, and innovators, are not ahead of their time in what they see. They are in real time, and the rest of the world hasn't caught up to them yet because they are still focusing on the past.

There is no universally agreed-on definition for innovation, but two common definitions are:

1. Innovation is the transformation of knowledge or intellectual property into commercialization.
2. Innovation is not necessarily invention; it can be the creation of something new, as in a new application. Innovation is finding a new or better solution to market needs in a manner that creates long-term shareholder value. Externally, it is seen by customers as improved quality, durability, service,

and/or price. Internally, it appears as positive changes in efficiency, productivity, quality, competitiveness, and market share.

To understand the difficulty in defining innovation, we will look first at the reasons for performing innovation:

- To produce new products or services with long-term profitable growth potential
- To produce long-term profitable improvements to existing products and services
- To produce scientific knowledge that can lead to new opportunities, better ways to conduct business (i.e., process improvements and new business models), or improved problem solving

There are many forms of process or operational innovation. Process innovation is needed to run the business. Capturing and implementing best practices, whether project management or business related, is a form of process innovation. Process innovation can also include changing some of the key operations such as in manufacturing to reduce cost, add business value, or speed up time-to-market. Process innovation overcomes the misbelief that innovation occurs only with technical solutions for designing a new product.

Strategic innovation is needed to grow the business. The output from strategic innovation can create sustainable business value in the form of:

- New products
- Enhancements in brand value
- Additional services
- Efficiencies and/or improved productivities
- Improvements in quality
- Reduction in time-to-market
- An increase in competitiveness
- An increase in market share
- New processes
- New technologies
- Reduction in labor or material costs
- Reduction in energy consumption
- Conformance to regulations
- New platforms
- New strategic partnerships or acquisitions

The long-term benefits of innovations include an increase in market share, greater competitiveness, greater shareholder satisfaction, and so on. Many of these outputs are not the traditional, tangible deliverables or outcomes that most project managers are accustomed to seeing. These outputs can be more business related and intangible. Therefore, deliverables may take on a new meaning during innovation.

There are several types of innovation that can be used for these products, services, and processes, each with unique requirements and different life-cycle phases. Therefore, there is no single path to innovation, making it impossible to establish a uniform approach for all types of innovation projects.

Today, academia is differentiating between R&D and innovation. R&D departments are usually needed for breakthrough innovations that generally involve new technologies. If the R&D group develops a new technology or a new way of doing something that is substantially different from the way it was done before, then it could be turned over to the innovation team to find applications.

THE BUSINESS NEED

"Vulnerability is the birthplace of innovation, creativity, and change."

— Brene Brown

"Normal is where innovation goes to die."
— Richie Norton, *The Power of Starting Something Stupid: How to Crush Fear,*
Make Dreams Happen, and Live without Regret

Global business is susceptible to changes in technology, demographics, a turbulent political climate, industrial maturity, unexpected events, and other factors that can affect competitiveness. Taking advantage of these changes will be challenging. Companies need growth for long-term survival. Companies cannot grow simply through cost reduction and reengineering efforts that are more aligned to a short-term solution. Also, companies are recognizing that brand loyalty accompanied by a higher level of quality does not always equate to customer retention unless supported by some innovations.

According to management guru Peter Drucker, there are only two sources for growth: marketing and innovation (Drucker 2008). Innovation is often viewed as the Holy Grail of business and the primary driver for growth. Innovation forces companies to adapt to an ever-changing environment and to be able to take advantage of opportunities as they arise. Companies are also aware that their competitors will eventually come to market with new products and services that will make some existing products and services obsolete, causing the competitive environment to change. Continuous innovation is needed, regardless of current economic conditions, to provide firms with a sustainable competitive advantage and to differentiate themselves from their competitors.

The more competitive the business environment, the greater the investment needed for successful innovation. Companies with limited resources can take on strategic business partners and focus on co-creation. Co-creation innovation project management can result in faster time-to-market, less risk exposure, greater customer satisfaction, a greater focus on value creation, and better technical solutions (DeFillippi and Roser 2014). With co-creation, the project manager must learn how to manage group diversity not just of race, religion, ethnic background, or sex, but also the diverse personal interests in prestige, benefits they might gain, and the degree of importance attached to the project.

Investors and stockholders seek information on the innovation projects in the firm's pipeline. This gives them an indication of possible success in the future. Influential stockholders and stakeholders can put pressure on innovation activities by asking for:

- Shorter product development life cycles
- An increase in product competitiveness
- Faster time to market
- Execution with fewer resources
- Higher performance requirements than the competitors
- Better product quality

Stockholder pressure to shorten development time must not be at the expense of product liability.

For years, project management and innovation management were treated as separate disciplines. Innovation requires an acceptance of possibly significant risk, fostering of a creative mindset, and collaboration across organizational boundaries. Innovation management, in its purest form, is a combination of the management of innovation processes and change management. It refers to products, services, business processes, and accompanying transformational needs whereby the organization must change the way they conduct their business. It includes a set of tools that allow line managers, project managers, workers, stakeholders, and clients to cooperate with a common understanding of the innovation processes and goals. Innovation management allows the organization to respond to external or internal opportunities, and use its creativity to introduce new ideas, processes, or products (Kelly and Kranzburg 1978). It requires a different mindset than the linear thinking model that has been used consistently in traditional project management practices. Innovation management tools allow companies to grow by utilizing the creative capabilities of its workforce (Clark 1980). However, there are still industries and types of projects that require linear thinking.

Project management practices generally follow the processes and domain areas identified in the Project Management Institute's *PMBOK® Guide*.* Strategic innovation follows other processes such as strategizing, entrepreneurship, changing, and investing (de Wit and Meyer 2014). But now, companies are realizing that innovation strategy is implemented through projects. Simply stated, we are managing our business as though it were a series of projects. Project management has become the delivery system for innovation, but only if the rigidity of some project management processes is removed. Without some degree of flexibility, creativity and brainstorming may suffer.

Today's project managers are seen more as managing part of a business rather than managing just a project. Project managers are now treated as market problem solvers and expected to be involved in business decisions as well as project decisions. End-to-end project management is now coming of age. In the past, project managers were actively involved mainly in project execution, with the responsibility of providing a deliverable or an outcome. Today, with end-to-end project management, the project manager is actively involved in all life-cycle phases including idea generation and product commercialization. The end of the project could be a decade or longer after the deliverables were created.

For decades, most project managers were trained in traditional project management practices and were ill-equipped to manage many types of innovation projects. Projects with a heavy focus on achieving strategic business objectives were managed by functional managers. Project managers handled the more operational or tactical projects and often had little knowledge about strategic plans and strategic objectives that required innovation activities. Project management and innovation management are now being integrated into a single profession, namely, innovation project management (IPM), whereby project managers are provided with strategic information. Project managers are now the new strategic leaders. IPMs now focus heavily on the long-term business or strategic aspects rather than the operational aspects that encourage a mindset of "getting the job done."

Several years ago, a Fortune 500 company hired consultants from a prestigious organization to analyze its business strategy and major product lines, and to make recommendations as to where the firm should be positioned in 5 and 10 years, and what it should be doing strategically. After the consultants left, the executives met to discuss what they had learned. The conclusion was that the consultants had told them "what" to do, but not "how" to do it. The executives realized quickly that the "how" would require superior project management capabilities, especially for innovation. The marriage between business strategy, innovation, and project management was now clear in their minds.

Figure 1-1 illustrates how strategic planning was often seen in the C-suite. All the boxes in Figure 1-1 were considered important, except often not the last box, namely the implementation of the strategy. Therefore, senior management did not see the link between project management and

---

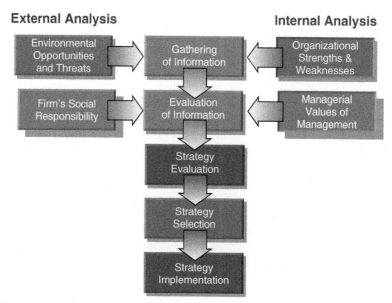

Figure 1–1. Traditional Strategic Planning Activities.

strategic planning activities because it was not recognized as part of their job description. Project management is now recognized as the delivery system by which an organization meets it strategic business objectives. If innovation activities are required, then project managers must undergo training in innovation project management.

Innovation project management is now being recognized as a career path discipline that may be more complex and challenging than traditional project management practices. Innovation projects have a high degree of risk because of the unpredictability of the markets, unstable economic conditions, and a high impact on human factors that may force an organization to change the way that it does business (Filippov and Mooi 2010). Innovation project managers may need a different skill set than traditional project managers.

Organizations need the ability to manage a multitude of innovation projects concurrently to be successful, and therefore innovation project management is being supported by corporate-level portfolio management practices. IPM cannot guarantee that all projects will be successful, but it can improve the chances of success and provide much-needed guidance on when to "pull the plug," reassign resources, and minimize losses.

INNOVATION LITERATURE

There exists an abundance of literature on innovation. One of the reasons for this is that competitiveness is increasing the number of business objectives, thus mandating more innovation (Crawford et al. 2006). Some of the literature focuses on empirical studies, whereas other publications address mainly traditional product innovation. However, some of the projects that may appear as sole product innovation may have significant complexity and include multiple innovations. Examples would be the design of Boeing's 787 Dreamliner (Shenhar et al. 2016); the Opera House in Sydney, Australia (Kerzner 2014); the Iridium Project; the Construction of Denver International Airport; and Disney's theme parks (Kerzner 2017). Because of the divergent nature of innovation from industry to industry, there are publications that focus on industry-specific innovations such as the auto industry (Lenfle and Midler 2009), the pharmaceutical industry (Aagaard and Gertsen 2011), the manufacturing industry (Calik and Bardudeen 2016), and the construction industry (Brockmann et al. 2016; Ozohorn and Oral 2017). These publications also address academic studies toward finding solutions to innovation problems.

Some researchers try to add structure to innovation by identifying categories of innovation according to elements such as complexity, life-cycle phases, levels of risk, strategic business importance, and information available (Garcia and Calantone 2002; O'Connor and Rice 2013). There are also articles that question whether such classifications are realities or myths because to date there is no consistent definition for innovation (Frankelius 2009).

There is also a human behavior side to innovation that appears in the literature. Examples include the ability to motivate people involved in innovation project management (Pihlajamma 2017) and reducing the tension and stress created by innovation ambiguity (Stetler and Magnusson 2014).

PROJECT MANAGEMENT LITERATURE

There exists a plethora of literature on project management. Unfortunately, most of the literature focuses on linear project management models with the assumption that "one size fits all." While this may hold true in some industries and for some projects, the concept of "one size fits all" does not apply to projects involving innovation.

Today, more than ever before, companies are realizing that business strategy, including innovation needs, is being implemented using project and program management concepts (Lenfle 2008). Although project management has matured into a strategic competency for some firms, not all project managers possess innovation management skills. What is missing in the literature is articles that identify innovation competencies that project managers must possess as well as articles that bridge the gaps between innovation, project management, and business strategy. There is no simple model in existence that bridges these gaps. But what most articles seem to agree on is the need to manage innovation for sustained performance.

There are published articles now appearing that discuss the management of innovation considering the relationship between project management and innovation (Špaček and Vacík 2016; Kenny 2003; Marin 2011; Midler 2019). Most of the published literature provides helpful guidance on the new metrics that should be used for innovation project management.

Špaček, M. and Vacík, E. (2016). Management of innovation projects in SMEs in the Czech Republic. *Journal of Economics & Management* 24, 14–30.

Kenny, J. (2003 March). Effective project management for strategic innovation and change in an organizational context. *Project Management Journal* 34 (1), 43–53.

Marin, A. (2011 June). On innovation through access to technology in project management. Case study. *Managerial Challenges of the Contemporary Society* (2), 169–172.

Midler, C. (2019). Crossing the valley of death: Managing the when, what, and how of innovative development projects. *Project Management Journal* 50 (4), 447–459.

Traditional project management is often seen as standardized processes for planning, scheduling, controlling, and sometimes risk management. The standardized processes are based on rigid policies and procedures that everyone must follow regardless of the unique characteristics of the projects. Some people regard traditional project management as obedience to regulations, policies, and authority (Geraldi et al. 2008).

The discipline of traditional project management may not work well when innovation is required. Project managers need flexibility in their ability to select the appropriate tools for their projects and customize the processes to fit the needs of the projects. This holds true even for many projects that do not require innovation. The future for some types of innovation and for some industries will be flexible project management models such as those used in agile and Scrum projects.

Some industries still have requirements and a valid need for traditional project management practices. But there is a change taking place. "Managers need to recognize the type of project at the start, resist institutional pressure to adapt traditional 'rational' approaches to all projects and apply an appropriate approach—one tailored for the type of project" (Lenfle and Loch 2010). Traditional project management does not distinguish between types of projects. Articles are appearing in the literature that propose a methodology to classify projects to guide the design of a suitable project management model (Geraldi et al. 2011). Even with flexible project management approaches, there may be issues such as those identified by Coombs et al. (1998):

> Thus we have seen that the literature suggests that there may be a need for different project management styles according to a number of distinguishing characteristics between innovations. The major distinctions are the level of technological uncertainty, the extent to which the technology is novel to the firm, the extent to which the technologies and products involved cause market disruption, and the size and complexity of the product or system involved. The implication here is that one generic model would lead to an over simplified view of project management. However, it is also clear that all these dimensions, if combined in all their possible permutations, could lead to the generation of a large and unwieldy number of different possibilities for project management styles. There is therefore a need for a compromise between the inflexibility dangers of "one-best-model," and the excessive costs of tailoring project management approaches for each project. (p. 177)

INNOVATION BENCHMARKING

Literature on innovation and project management does not always provide enough information for companies to improve their innovation practices. Many firms find benchmarking to be the best approach. Benchmarking is part of the continuous improvement process whereby we recognize that others, such as those considered as best in class, might be better at doing something and we wish to learn how to equal and/or surpass them. We measure the gap between us and the reference organization and decide how to compress it.

Benchmarking is more than just looking at products or services or the forms, guidelines, templates, and checklists that others are using. Benchmarking also promotes an understanding of the business processes, the business model under investigation, and the firm's strategy and strategic objectives. This knowledge is critical for continuous improvements for innovation activities.

There are several types of benchmarking activities. The two most common are process and strategic benchmarking:

- *Process benchmarking* focuses on critical steps such as the components of a project management methodology.
- *Strategic benchmarking* analyzes the strategies and core competencies used to create products and services.

In traditional organizations, project managers and the PMOs are usually active in performing process benchmarking. In highly innovative organizations, the focus is on strategic benchmarking.

Several years ago, a division of a Fortune 100 company decided to perform project management process benchmarking against their competitors in the same industry. At the end of the benchmarking process, management patted itself on the back, stating "Boy, are we good compared to our competitors."

After the gloating period was over, the PMO decided to benchmark against world-class project management organizations that were not in their industry. The results showed that the firm was quite poor in their project management capabilities. Recognizing the need for action, the company created the position of vice president for innovation. The VP's role was to perform strategic benchmarking against any company in the world that would share information and discover what best practices could be brought into the company as part of a continuous improvement effort. This included capturing best practices on innovation management.

The previous example makes it clear that innovation benchmarking must be properly targeted to extract the information needed that contributed to success. While companies may be willing to share the processes, forms, guidelines, templates, and checklists they use in managing innovation projects, they may be reluctant to provide strategic information on how they link innovation objectives to corporate business strategy, their culture, employee motivation practices, their commercialization practices, and how they determine the needs of their customers. The information they are reluctant to share may be critical for determining how to tailor their successes to your organization.

Knowing what questions to ask during strategic innovation benchmarking is important. There are published articles that can provide some guidance (Dembowski 2013; Pages and Toft 2009; Coombs et al. 1998; Berg et al. 2006).

Innovation benchmark targeting can also focus on innovation systems that nations use and support rather just individual companies (Ruu Lin et al. 2008; Manjón 2010; Burz and Marian (2016). How a country, geographical region, or business sector, views innovation practices could act as an attraction or deterrent for your company to open a plant, an innovation center, or seek out strategic partners in their area. Some national factors to consider include:

- What special policies and regulations might exist in the country related to patent protection and control of intellectual property?
- Are there special health and safety policies that can hinder innovation activities?
- Is there a national culture that supports innovation practices, perhaps by providing workforce assistance?
- Is there a technical infrastructure supported by technical courses and degrees taught at local universities and available to the workforce?

Dembowski, F. L. (2013 Winter). The role of benchmarking, best practices & innovation in organizational effectiveness. *International Journal of Organizational Innovation* 5 (3), 6–20.

Pages, E. R. and Toft, G. S. (2009 Winter). Benchmarking innovation. *Economic Development Journal* 8 (1), 22–27.

Coombs, R., McMeekin, A. and Pybus, R. (1998 July). Toward the development of benchmarking tools for R&D project management. *R&D Management* 28 (3), 175–187.

Berg, P., Pihlajamaa, J., Poskela, J. and Smedlund, A. (2006). Benchmarking of quality and maturity of innovation activities in a networked environment. *International Journal of Technology Management* 33 (2–3), 255–278.

Ruu Lin, G. T., Shen, Y.-C., Yu, H.-C. and Sun, C.-C. (2008 September). Benchmarking evaluation of national innovation policy implementation. *Journal of Global Business & Technology* 4 (2), 1–23.

Manjón, J. V. G. (2010). A proposal of indicators and policy framework for innovation benchmark in Europe. *Journal of Technology Management & Innovation* 5 (2), 13–23.

Burz, G. and Marian, L. O. (2016). Benchmarking study on Romanian innovation system. *Review of Management & Economic Engineering* 15 (2), 276–295.

VALUE: THE MISSING LINK

"Innovation is the creation and delivery of new customer value in the marketplace."
— Michael J. Gelb, *Innovate Like Edison: The Success System of America's Greatest Inventor*

The literature most commonly identifies three reasons for innovation: to produce new products or services for profitable growth, to produce profitable improvements to existing products and services, and to produce scientific knowledge that can lead to new opportunities or problem solving. But what about the creation of business value? Both innovation and project management literature are now stressing the importance of business value creation as the true measure of success.

The ultimate purpose of performing innovation activities should be the creation of long-term, sustainable shareholder value. Value, whether business or shareholder, may be the most important driver in innovation management and can have a profound influence on how we define success and failure. Suitability and exit criteria must have components related to business value creation. Examples include the following:

- Innovation suitability criteria:
  - Similar technology
  - Similar marketing and distribution channels
  - Can be sold by the current sales force
  - Purchased by the existing customer base
  - Fits company philosophy, profit goals, and strategic plans
  - Can be produced within current production facilities
- Innovation exit criteria:
  - Unexpected occurrences and uncertainties
  - An update or improvement in processes
  - Industry and market changes
  - Demographic changes

However, it must be realized that financial value is just one form of value. Other forms of value appear in Figure 1-2.

Any company can make financial numbers look good for a month or even an entire year by sacrificing the company's future. Companies that want to be highly successful at innovation should resist selecting board members who focus mainly on financial numbers. From a strategic perspective, the primary goal for innovation should be to increase shareholder value over the long term rather than taking unnecessary risks and trying to maximize financial value in the short term.

There can be primary and secondary types of values created. As an example, a company creates a new product. This could be a primary value to the firm. If the company must modernize its production line to manufacture the product, then the modernization efforts could be a secondary value that could be applied to other products.

While the goal of successful innovation is to add value, the effect can be negative or even destructive if it results in an unfavorable cultural change or a radical departure from existing ways of doing work. The impact that innovation can have on the way that a firm runs its business is often referred to as disruptive innovation. We must remember that many process innovations result in disruptive changes to the processes and the way we conduct business rather than sales. The failure of an innovation project can lead to demoralizing the organization and causing talented people to be risk-avoiders rather than risk-takers.

There are numerous case studies and theories on product innovation, but not from the perspective of the project manager. In this book, we will focus on the challenges faced by project managers involved in innovation projects, and the solution to some of the challenges.

Project management is the delivery system for innovation. Project management makes innovation happen. Innovation project management (IPM) is more than creating inventions and technology. It is a way to compete and run a business in an ever-changing environment. With IPM, we act proactively rather than reactively, and offensively rather than defensively. With IPM, we recognize that best practices that were captured in the past with traditional project management may be of little value if we use them to rest on our laurels.

Figure 1–2. Forms of Value.

INNOVATION TARGETING

"Our wretched species is so made that those who walk on the well-trodden path always throw stones at those who are showing a new road."

— Voltaire, *Philosophical Dictionary*

"Throughout history, people with new ideas—who think differently and try to change things—have always been called troublemakers."

— Richelle Mead, *Shadow Kiss*

Successful innovation must be targeted, and this is the weakest link because it requires a useful information system and knowledge about the company's long-term business strategy. Innovation targeting requires the answering of two questions:

- How well do we understand the problem?
- How well do we understand the domain?

The answer to these questions, which may be dependent upon a good knowledge management system, can help determine the risk and the type of innovation project to be undertaken. In most cases, only some of the information is available and the innovation team must fill in the knowledge gaps to justify an investment.

Creating the business strategy requires the interactions shown in Figure 1-3.

The organization identifies the need for innovation and provides funding and competent people with the necessary skills. Marketing provides insight about consumers' needs and what they might be willing to pay for the product or service. Marketing also provides insight into what market segments should be targeted. Innovations require technology.

In the past, business needs focused on repetitive tasks, improving efficiencies, and productivity. There was a heavy focus on these factors:

- Profitability
- Elimination of variations
- Maintaining authority through command and control
- Overreliance on utilization of business metrics
- Six Sigma to improve quality

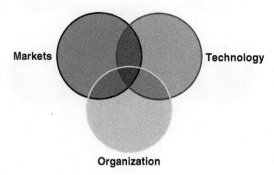

Figure 1–3. Three Critical Interactions for Innovation.

Today, we face challenges and crises due to competition, unstable economies, disruptive technologies, and sustainability. "Business as usual" is no longer an option. "We will build it and they will come" does not work. We must be willing to break away from traditional thinking. There are greater risks, but greater opportunities. We must work closely with our customers using prototypes or risk that the idea will be a loser.

We must focus on long-term spending, which requires the answering of critical linkage questions:

- In what direction should we grow?
- Should we change our image and, if so, what should it be?
- How well do we understand the customers' needs and wants?

We must listen to the voices: the voice of technology and the voice of the customers. Three questions must be answered:

- What do the customers need?
- What will they pay for?
- What value will they receive?

TIMELINE FOR INNOVATION TARGETING

"Implementing best practice is copying yesterday; innovation is inventing tomorrow."

— Paul Sloane

Although we cannot establish the exact date when innovation will happen, we must still consider the need to somehow recover our innovation costs. This is shown in Figure 1-4.

Innovation targeting must include reasoned expectations for possible outcomes, break-even timing, and cash flow generation. Of course, market conditions can change, forcing the acceptance of the exit criteria.

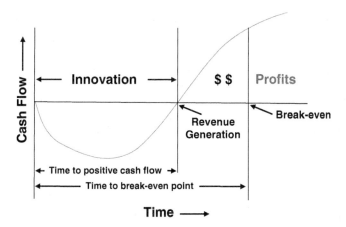

Figure 1–4. Typical Innovation Cash Flow.

INNOVATION IN SMALL COMPANIES

There is a common misconception that innovation occurs only in large companies. However, Tidd and Bessant (2013, 69) believe that small companies tend to have more innovation than large companies. They identify advantages and disadvantages for small companies. The advantages include:

- Faster decision making
- More of an informal culture
- Higher-quality communications
- Shared and clear vision
- Flexible and agile structure
- Entrepreneurial environment
- Acceptance of more risks
- Passionate about innovation
- Good at networking

The disadvantages include:

- Lack of a formal earned value measurement control system
- Poor cost and schedule control
- Perhaps a lack of qualified resources or their availability
- Focus on short-term strategy above long-term strategy
- Poor risk management

Large companies can finance a multitude of projects, often more than they need to, accept a great deal of risk, and write off millions of dollars in innovation project failures. Small companies cannot afford this luxury and therefore work on fewer projects, especially those with a higher probability of success. Small companies often perform better at innovation than large companies because a failure of as little as one project could have a significant impact on the business.

SEVEN CRITICAL DIMENSIONS FOR SCALING PROJECT MANAGEMENT INNOVATION

If project management and innovation are to be "married" with the goal of creating a synergistic organic organization, then it should be obvious that organization change will be needed and that it begins at the C-suite who are the architects of the organizational culture. Dr. Zeitoun describes the seven critical dimensions for project management innovation scaling:

This section was provided by Dr. Al Zeitoun, PgMP, PMI Fellow. Dr. Zeitoun, Global Business Strategist, is an organizational transformation and operational excellence expert with global experiences in strategy execution, operational excellence, portfolio, program, and project management. His experience includes serving on PMI's global board of directors, PM Solutions president, Emirates Nuclear Energy Corporation executive director, Booz Allen Hamilton portfolio management leader, and International Institute for Learning's chief projects officer. He can be reached at zeitounstrategy@gmail.com. © 2022 by Al Zeitoun. All rights reserved. Reproduced with permission.

1. *The role of executive leadership.* One of the most critical dimensions for projects success over the years has always been executive support. The way by which that tier of organizational leaders champions projects, sponsors the cause of their mission, and provides the necessary backing to the project managers and their teams tends to consistently make the difference between success and failure. In scaling innovation, more and more organizations are finding that it is critical to start at the top. Boards of directors and executive leaders of the future are not going to be sitting around a fancy table in order to steer the ship. They are going to play a very different role. They are becoming a working group and their number one role will center on changing the business for the better, improving, innovating, and strengthening the excellence of execution that comes from innovative project management. Boardrooms are becoming workrooms with white boards all around and are becoming the place where the right degree of risk is taken every day to ensure that organizations of the future use and execute projects more creatively.

2. *The achievement of the right balance between alignment and autonomy.* Innovation in project management requires a good degree of autonomy. In the everchanging dynamics of today's workplace, teams are fortunately becoming more self-directed. This is advantageous, and even a necessity, for enhancing the chance for creativity, the flow of ideas, and the assurance that the teams will produce the innovations needed for the approach taken to run projects. The key becomes finding the right balance. Specifically, we do need alignment across project teams, but with a light hand; it should be just enough to ensure the right focus on the project's goals and the anticipated benefits. The road to get there is enriched by the autonomy, and the more the teams are authorized to chart their own course, the better the innovation opportunities will be.

3. *The development of the innovation culture.* Without the safety that is needed to innovate, organizations miss out on the right amount of innovation enablement. The culture to support innovation in project management must be adaptive. No longer would a classic view of the slow buildup of phases of a given project be suitable for generating and testing the best ideas. Much higher iteration would be needed. Teams must be encouraged to take risks and the organization must have a high tolerance for mistakes that can occur at a higher rate than ever before. Fail fast and learn will become part of the new DNA of most organizations. The learning culture that this creates is priceless. This appetite for risk taking and the courage that is required to fail and learn is the new normal. Executive leadership will play a big role here too, as they will have to walk the talk frequently and will have to use a high level of emotional intelligence to manage the stress related to the risk taking required. Leaders will have to relate to their project managers differently to instill a new sense of trust.

4. *The use of projects as innovation labs.* More than any time in history projects will become the best opportunity to innovate. By nature, projects are designed to change the business. They are no longer merely operational activities. They now enable a change from a current state to a future state. The right organizational focus will be looking at projects as labs to test innovation in all dimensions. Innovation will include selecting the right mix of team members, experimenting with the right balance of virtual and collocated teams, testing new ways of working, experimenting fast with outcomes, innovating the use of data analytics in making faster and more effective decisions, and sensing very differently while engaging with the customers often and fast for best creative outcomes.

5. *The development of future innovation competencies.* As we look ahead to 2030 and beyond, collaboration is becoming the top competency of the future project managers. This directly links with success in innovation. No longer will the project manager of the future be focused on controlling the work. The time spent in reporting, policing, or managing conflicts, will be replaced with a different set of priorities. Amongst these top priorities will be the role of a coach. This will be fundamental in allowing the autonomous teams to experiment fast, try new ideas, and execute more dynamically, while the project manager guides, integrates, connects the dots, and creates the opportunities for the enhanced and continual exchange of innovative ideas.

6. *The need to block off time to think again.* If there is one dimension that will support innovation in projects the most, it would be this one. Noise has been the main challenge and even a roadblock in accomplishing project work for the last 20 years. We have continued to focus on new techniques for managing projects, gotten ourselves into increasingly busy work schedules, mastered the hype around getting things done, all without giving ourselves the chance to make reflection part of our daily routine. We have got to find a way to think again about constructive change management opportunities. Blocking off daily calendar time to reflect on what we have learned directly strengthens the innovative muscles we need to plan and execute our projects differently. Without that ability to be holistic again and see things from the right distance via continual reflection, we would struggle to enable new innovative habits and the associated flow of creativity in our project work.

7. *The new ways of working.* The workplace of the future is here and is not! It is becoming obvious that what we have been accustomed to does not lend itself to the right degree of innovation. The silos of the physical space, the organizational verticals, and the rigid views, all must be broken down, and quickly. We have been reflecting that in the changing physical design of our offices, in the ways we create the small teams, running daily scrums, or collaborating differently. For innovation to flow, this way of working needs to be like a river. It must flow smoothly. Ideas must envision no barriers, fast execution will have to be encouraged, and seamless access will be key. This requires us to adapt and continually welcome the changes needed for the way we work as we welcome machine intelligence and use Internet of Things to connect us in ways we never thought possible.

As innovation in project management continues to drive the priorities in the C-suite, these seven critical dimensions for scaling innovation show a natural cascading effect, from the intelligent messages and guidance of the executive leadership, to the elements required for igniting the hearts and motivation of adaptive teams, and finally to executing faster while getting things done innovatively, and finding new opportunities for improving and operating with excellence.

IMPLICATIONS AND ISSUES FOR PROJECT MANAGERS AND INNOVATION PERSONNEL

Project managers that are asked to manage innovation projects must understand that the environment they must now work in can be significantly different than the traditional environment. Some of the critical issues and challenges that may be new for some project managers include:

- Benefits of success may appear differently than in traditional project management.
- A focus on long-term rather than short-term thinking might be needed.
- There might need to be heavy focus on alignment of the project and decision making toward business strategy and strategic business objectives.
- Many of the team members may be made up of consumers and partner organizations, especially if co-creation is being used.
- Project managers may be expected to make a significant number of business decisions.
- There are differences between traditional and innovation project management.
- Innovation project management is a strategic competency.
- There is a linkage between IPM and strategic planning.

Many of these issues will require new tools and a new way of thinking. Some of these issues may be managed using traditional processes based on where the project resides in the investment or product life cycle.

REFERENCES

Aagaard, A. and Gertsen, F. (2011). Supporting radical front end innovation: Perceived key factors of pharmaceutical innovation. *Creative Innovation Management* 20, 330–346. DOI: 10.1111/j.1467-8691.2011.00609.x.

Brockmann, C., Brezinski, H. and Erbe, A. (2016). Innovation in construction megaprojects. *Journal of Construction Engineering Management* 142 (11), 040160591. DOI: 10.1061/(ASCE)CO.1943-7862.00011168.

Calik, E. and Bardudeen, F. (2016). A measurement scale to evaluate sustainable innovation performance in manufacturing organizations. *13th Global Conference on Sustainable Manufacturing*, 449–454.

Clark, C. H. (1980). *Idea Management: How to Motivate Creativity and Innovation.* New York: AMACOM.

Coombs, R., McMeekin, A. and Pybus, R. (1998). Toward the development of benchmarking tools for R&D project management. *R&D Management* 28 (3), 175–183.

Crawford, L., Hobbs, B. and Turner, J. R. (2006). Aligning capability with strategy: Categorizing projects to do the right projects and to do them right. *Project Management Journal* 37 (2), 38–50.

de Wit, B. and Meyer, R. (2014). *Strategy: An International Perspective* (5th ed.). Andover, MA: Cengage Learning.

DeFillippi, R. and Roser, T. (2014). Aligning the co-creation project portfolio with company strategy. *Strategy and Leadership* 42 (1), 30–36. DOI: 10.1108/SL-10-2013-0075.

Drucker, P. F. (2008). *The Essential Drucker.* New York: HarperCollins.

Filippov, S. and Mooi, H. (2010). Innovation project management: A research agenda. *Journal on Innovation and Sustainability*, 1(1), 1–15.

Frankelius, P. (2009). Questioning two myths in innovation literature. *Journal of High Technology Management Research* 20 (1), 40–51.

Garcia, R. and Calantone, R. (2002). A critical look at technological innovation typology and innovativeness terminology: A literature review. *Journal of Product Innovation Management* 19 (2), 110–132.

Geraldi, J. G., Maylor, H. and Williams, T. (2011). Now, let's make it really complex (complicated): A systematic review of the complexities of projects. *International Journal of Operations and Production Management* 31 (9), 966–990.

Geraldi, J. G., Turner, J. R., Maylor, H., Söderholm, A., Hobday, M. and Brady, T. (2008). Innovation in project management: Voice of researchers. *International Journal of Project Management* 26 (5), 586–589. DOI: 10.1016/j.ijproman.2008.05.011.

Kelly, P. and Kranzburg, M. (1978). *Technological Innovation: A Critical Review of Current Knowledge.* San Francisco: San Francisco Press.

Kerzner, H. (2014). *Project Recovery.* Hoboken, NJ: John Wiley and Sons, 265–273.

Kerzner, H. (2017). *Project Management Case Studies* (5th ed.). Hoboken, NJ: John Wiley and Sons, 255–286, 467–506 and 583–654.

Lenfle, M. and Loch, C. (2010). Lost roots: How project management came to emphasize control over flexibility novelty. *California Management Review* 53 (1), 32–55.

Lenfle, M. and Midler, C. (2009). The launch of innovative product related services: Lessons from automotive telematics. *Research Policy* 38 (1), 156–169.

Lenfle, S. (2008). Exploration and project management. *International Journal of Project Management* 26 (5), 469–478.

O'Connor, G. C. and Rice, M. P. (2013). A comprehensive model of uncertainty associated with radical innovation. *Journal of Product Innovation Management* 30, 2–18.

Ozohorn, B. and Oral, K. (2017). Drivers of innovation in construction projects. *Journal of Construction Engineering and Management* 143 (4), 1–9. DOI: 10.1061/(ASCE)CO.1943-7862.0001234.

Pihlajamma, M. (2017). Going the extra mile: Managing individual motivation in radical innovation development. *Journal of Engineering and Technology Management* 43, 48–66. DOI: 10.1016/j.jengtecman.2017.01.003.

Shenhar, A. J., Holzman, V., Melamed, B. and Zhao, Y. (2016, April-May). The challenge of innovation in highly complex projects: What can we learn from Boeing's Dreamliner experience? *Project Management Journal*, 62–78. DOI: 10.1002/pmj.21579.

Stetler, K. L. and Magnusson, M. (2014). Exploring the tension between clarity and ambiguity in goal setting for innovation. *Creativity and Innovation Management* 24 (2), 231–246.

Tidd, J. and Bessant, J. (2013). *Managing Innovation: Integrating Technological, Market and Organizational Change* (5th ed.). Hoboken, NJ: John Wiley and Sons.

2 Types of Innovation

Learning Objectives for Project Managers and Innovation Personnel
To understand the different types of innovation and their characteristics
To understand that, in some forms of innovation, many team members can be external
  to the company
To understand the importance of measuring "value-in-use"

INTRODUCTION

"Innovation is an evolutionary process, so it's not necessary to be radical all the time."

— Marc Jacobs

"Of the top 10 sources of innovation, employees are the only resource that you can control and access that your competitors cannot. Employees are the one asset you have that can actually be a sustainable competitive advantage."

— Kaihan Krippendorff

Over the years, our view of innovation, and its importance, has changed. Table 2-1 illustrates how our view has changed:

Innovation Project Management: Methods, Case Studies, and Tools for Managing Innovation Projects,
Second Edition. Harold Kerzner.
© 2023 John Wiley & Sons, Inc. Published 2023 by John Wiley & Sons, Inc.

TABLE 2–1.   CHANGING VIEWS OF INNOVATION

Old View	New View
Incremental changes to existing products	Development of new or radical products
Focus on existing customer base	Expansion to new markets
Perform innovation in house and without any strategic partners	Offshore partners may be necessary
Capture knowledge from internal workers	Seek out worldwide knowledge from a variety of sources

As our view of innovation has changed, so has the definition of innovation.

According to Webster's Dictionary, innovation can be defined simply as a "new idea, device or method." However, innovation is also viewed as the application of better solutions that meet new requirements, unarticulated needs, or existing market needs (Maryville 1992; Frankelius 2009). This is accomplished through more effective products, processes, services, technologies, or business models that are readily available to satisfy market needs.

From an organizational perspective, innovation may be linked to positive changes in efficiency, productivity, quality, competitiveness, and market share. Research findings highlight the importance of the firm's organizational culture in enabling organizations to translate innovative activities into tangible performance improvements (Salge and Vera 2012). Organizations can also improve profits and performance by providing workers with adequate resources and tools to innovate, in addition to supporting the employees' core job tasks.

CONTINUOUS VERSUS DISCONTINUOUS INNOVATION

Defining the types of innovation has been challenging to both academia and industry. In simple context, innovation can be classified as continuous or discontinuous. Within each category can be several other types of innovation. Continuous innovation is also referred to as incremental innovation and is characterized by small changes in quality, additional features to a product, and/or the reduction in cost to the consumer. Incremental innovation most often occurs in a business-as-usual environment where all outcomes are predictable, and the business risks are relatively low.

Discontinuous innovation is when the direction of the project might have to change because of changing conditions. This could occur any time during the execution of the project. There are several sources that can cause the discontinuity. According to Bessant (2005[1]), the sources can be contributed to: (1) the emerging of new markets, (2) the emerging of new technology, (3) new political rules, (4) industrial maturity, (5) changes in market sentiment and behavior, (6) deregulation, (7) changes in social attitudes toward an issue or a particular product, (8) business model innovation, (9) shifts in techno-economic paradigm, (10) architectural innovation, and (11) unthinkable events.

There is some confusion when discussing types of innovation as to whether the title refers to the management of the innovation process or the outcome. Discontinuous innovation generally refers to the management of the discontinuous process. The output of discontinuous innovation can be radical or

---

1. Bessant, J. (2005). Enabling continuous and discontinuous innovation: Learning from the private sector. *Public Money and Management* 25 (1), 35–42.

disruptive innovation. Radical innovation could be the outcome of a discontinuous innovation project resulting from a technical breakthrough. However, the technical breakthrough may not disrupt the way you conduct your business and your relationship with your customers. If there is a disruption, the outcome is often referred to as disruptive innovation rather than discontinuous innovation.

Radical outcomes become disruptive when the discontinuity causes some existing products to be obsolete, the closing of obsolete product lines, having to lay off workers and/or hire other workers with different skill sets, or possibly creating a new business model. Radical innovation outcomes that negatively impact the survival of existing products and services are called creative destruction.

There are several risks and uncertainties associated with discontinuity based upon the source of the discontinuity. Some of these risks and uncertainties include:

- Uncertain competitive advantage
- Uncertainty as to how customers will respond
- Unproven new technology
- Slower time to market
- Impact on existing products and services
- Possibly new policies and procedures
- Possibly a new business model
- The need for a new supplier network
- The need for organizational restructuring

Because of the number of risks and uncertainties, there is a preference to maintain several different types of innovations rather than to narrow them down into smaller categories.

INCREMENTAL VERSUS RADICAL INNOVATION

Companies have been struggling with ways to classify the different forms of innovation. In one of the early studies on innovation, Marquis (1969) differentiated between two types of innovation, incremental and radical. Many authors today consider these as the two primary forms of innovation.

Incremental innovation consists of small, and often continuous, improvements to existing products and services to maintain support for customers in existing market segments and hopefully attract some new customers. The intent may be to extend the life of a product or service. The improvements may or may not be technical improvements. Investments in incremental technology improvements can occur with the intent of lowering production costs. Nontechnical incremental improvements may be the addition of a new feature or functionality, improvements in quality, or even changes in color and design to make a product more aesthetically appealing. The amount of flexibility provided to the innovation team may be limited because the organization has a reasonably good idea as to where they are heading.

Radical innovation is the use of new technologies to create new products and services for new markets. The resulting product might be new to the company, new to the national market, or new to the international market. Radical innovation is characterized by search, discovery, experimentation, and risk taking. The innovation project team may have some degree of flexibility but within the confinement of more formal ideation methods. The innovation may be driven by dreams or a vision of what might be possible.

There are risks with successful radical innovation. The result might be the loss of some customers that are not ready for the new technology. The new products and services may lead to creative destruction, whereby some of your existing products and services are now obsolete and the new products cannot be produced within the existing manufacturing facilities. There can also be radical changes in the relationships with your suppliers, distributors, and other partnerships. Similar arguments can be made regarding making too many incremental innovations while consumers and partners are looking for technical breakthroughs.

Scholars like to compare incremental and radical innovation. Incremental innovation is a slight change to an existing product, whereas radical innovation is a change based on a completely new idea. Incremental innovation focuses on existing markets and enhancements of existing products and services as well as refinements to production and delivery services (Danneels 2002; Jansen et al. 2006). Radical innovation focuses on the development of new technologies, usually targeted for new markets, which adds a great deal of uncertainty and risk (Garcia and Calantone 2002; O'Connor and Rice 2013).

UNDERSTANDING INNOVATION DIFFERENCES

All form of innovation can have their own characteristics. The characteristics are often used to define the type of innovation. For example, if we compare incremental versus radical or disruptive innovation as shown in Table 2-2 we may find that:

From a project manager's perspective, these two types of innovation projects have different and often-competing strategic objectives, which must be managed differently. Radical innovation creates long-term profits for a firm. However, the cash flow needed for radical innovation may depend on the firm's success with incremental innovation. The "hidden" strategic objective, as seen by the project manager, is therefore to get the change made as quickly as possible to generate cash flow for radical innovation. Trying to develop the perfect incremental change to a product is not as important as time-to-market. Making incremental changes every year may be a better decision than trying to make a perfect change every three years and run the risk that competitive products will enter the market, causing you to lose cash flow opportunities. Incremental changes can be made quickly if the changes are made within the core competencies of the team.

Another difference between the competing objectives of incremental versus radical innovation is the opportunity for creative destruction. With incremental innovation, the project manager knows that the product will be commercialized using existing technology and existing manufacturing processes. With radical innovation, the project manager must consider that the new product will displace older products and the production technologies used in manufacturing will also need to be updated. Therefore, there can be disruptive changes to the commercialization process because of new products.

TABLE 2–2.   INCREMENTAL VERSUS RADICAL INNOVATION

Characteristic	Incremental Innovation	Radical Innovation
Business Case	Can be developed in detail prior to the start of the project	Must evolve throughout the project using discovery and learning
Life cycle phases	Waterfall approach may be acceptable	Use of frameworks such as agile and Scrum
Technology	Using existing technology	Exploring new technologies
Emphasis	Lowering of cost or feature improvements	Launch new business or new product opportunities
Resources and competencies	Exists within the capabilities of the assigned staff	Unknowns may exist requiring hiring of new workers

Just from these two types of innovation activities, it should be obvious that project managers must have a good understanding of the type of innovation being undertaken. Each type of innovation has strategic business objectives that compete with other forms of innovation. Also, project managers must know the core competences of the assigned team members rather than just if the functional managers assigned the right people. With traditional project management, we may not worry as much about core competencies. With innovation, core competencies have a significant impact on strategic business objectives, time-to-market, and other commercialization activities.

INCREMENTAL INNOVATION VERSUS NEW PRODUCT DEVELOPMENT

The decision between incremental innovation and other types of innovation that can be included in new product development (NPD) involves several factors, the most important usually considered is whether you have an incumbent firm or a new market entrant. Incumbent firms focus on technological improvements in existing products and reducing production costs. Most improvements generally appear using lower-cost production technologies. Market entrants focus on new products and new technologies to capture market share from vintage products.

It is a mistake to believe that a one-size-fits-all approach can be utilized in both forms of innovation. There are different risks and different decisions that must be made. As an example, NPD may occur in an environment that fosters creative destruction of some existing products. Even though the potential rewards arc greater, the decisions and risks in this environment are different than in incremental innovation because of new customer uncertainties and perhaps uncertain commercialization costs. Song and Montoya-Weiss (1998) identified six sets of activities that impact project management and appear more critical in NPD than incremental innovation:

- Strategic planning
- Idea development and screening
- Business and market opportunity analysis
- Technical development
- Product testing
- Product commercialization

PRODUCT DEVELOPMENT INNOVATION CATEGORIES

Figure 2-1 shows some typical categories for product development innovation. There are four general types of product innovation. Each type comes with advantages and disadvantages:

1. *Add-ons, enhancements, product/quality improvements, and cost-reduction efforts.* This type of innovation may be able to be accomplished quickly and with the existing resources in the company. The intent is to solve a problem and add incremental value to the result. The disadvantage is that this may have to be done frequently.

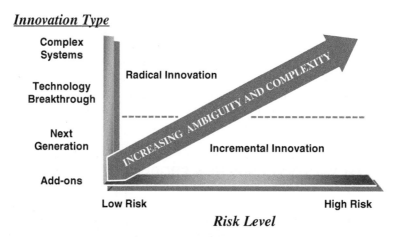

Figure 2–1. Typical Types of Innovation for Products.

2. *New family members or next generation.* This is the creation of totally new products or possibly to complete a product line and may require a technological breakthrough. The risk is in market acceptance.
3. *Radical breakthrough in technology.* This type of innovation has risks. You may not be able to determine when the breakthrough will be made and what the accompanying cost will be. Even if the breakthrough can be made, there is no guarantee that the client will receive added value from this solution. If the breakthrough cannot be made, the client may still be happy with the partial solution. This type of innovation may require the skills of only one or two people.
4. *Totally complex system or platform.* This is the solution with the greatest risk. If the complex system cannot be developed, then the project will probably be considered a total loss. Many highly talented resources are needed for this form of innovation.

Incremental innovation includes add-ons and next-generation products that may simply be the result of the add-ons. Radical innovation is based on new technology that could lead to a totally new complex system.

As we go from add-ons to complex systems, ambiguity and complexity will usually increase. Project managers may find it difficult to define requirements, understand changes in the marketplace, estimate time and cost, perform risk management, and deal with extensive meddling by stakeholders. Project managers may not be qualified to manage each type of product innovation project, and this does not include other company innovation projects such as service-related projects, new processes, and transformational projects.

Some projects can begin as incremental innovation and then expand into radical innovation. This can lead to a change in project leadership because not all project managers possess the skills to manage each type of innovation project. Project teams responsible for incremental innovation respond to changes in market conditions, whereas radical innovation teams perform in a more proactive manner. Radical innovation teams are multidisciplinary and self-managed. They must have open communication channels to share ideas and solve problems rapidly. This may require that project managers possess a different skill set.

For innovation to occur on a repetitive basis and for a firm to retain its competitive advantage, the organization must create and nurture an environment conducive for innovation. Executives and managers need to break away from traditional ways of thinking and use change to their advantage. Executives must adopt an innovation mindset. There is a great deal of risk, but with it comes greater opportunities. Innovations may force companies to downsize and re-engineer their operations to remain competitive. This may affect employment as businesses may be forced to reduce the number of people employed while accomplishing the same amount of work if not more (Anthony et al. 2008). The impact that innovation can have on the way that a firm runs its business is often referred to as disruptive innovation. We must remember that many process innovations result in disruptive changes rather than sales.

CLOSED AND OPEN INNOVATION

"True innovation and disruption happens outside of the accepted playing field, outside of the court, outside of the battleground. Disruption breaches the field and changes the game."
— Tony Curl

"To measure market needs, I would watch carefully what customers do, not simply listen to what they say. Watching how customers actually use a product provides much more reliable information that can be gleaned from a verbal interview or a focus group."
— Clayton M. Christensen, *The Innovator's Dilemma*

Wheelwright and Clark (1992) were among the first to identify how diverse types of innovation projects can impact the way a firm is managed, and that organizational change may occur frequently to maintain an innovation environment. The authors argue that companies are challenged with linking innovation projects to the company's strategy and that, although each project may have its own business strategy, there must still exist a linkage to the firm's overall business strategy. In an earlier work (Abernathy and Clark 1985), projects were classified according to the firm's technical and marketing capabilities, which became the basis for identifying competence-enhancing versus competence-destroying innovations.

The innovation environment in a firm can be defined as closed or open concerning idea generation and sources of information.

Closed innovation is based on the premise that successful innovation requires control. Particularly, a company should control the generation of their own ideas, as well as production, marketing, distribution, servicing, financing, and supporting. This way, it is left up to the corporations to take the new product development cycle into their own hands. In this approach, the company assumes that there is not enough time to wait for other companies to start producing some of the components that are required in their final product. These companies become relatively self-sufficient, with little communication directed outward to other companies or universities.

With closed innovation, companies must rely on their own people and events to gather ideas. Typical sources for ideas might include:

- Unexpected occurrences, whether a success or failure
- Incongruities
- Process needs
- Observed industry and market changes
- Observed changes in demographics

- Changes in perception
- New knowledge

Open innovation argues that companies cannot rely entirely on their own research but should solicit ideas from outside the firm, including consumers, rival companies, academic institutions, licensing, and joint ventures. The boundaries between the firm and its environment are now permeable.

Throughout the years several factors have emerged that paved the way for open innovation paradigms:

- The increasing availability and mobility of skilled workers
- The growth of the venture capital market
- External options for ideas sitting on the shelf
- The increasing capability of external suppliers

Open innovation offers several benefits to companies operating on a program of global collaboration:

- Reducing the cost for idea generation
- Reduced the cost of conducting research and development on their own
- Incorporating customers early in the development process to get buy-in and possibly partial ownership
- A more accurate understanding of the targets market segments and customers
- Potential for productivity and efficiency improvements

Implementing a model of open innovation is naturally associated with risks and challenges, including:

- Possibility of revealing information not intended for sharing
- Potential for the hosting organization to lose its competitive advantage by revealing intellectual property
- Increased complexity of controlling innovation and regulating how contributors affect a project
- Devising a means to properly identify and incorporate external innovation

Typical sources for ideas with open innovation include:

- Customers, competitors, and suppliers
- Purchasing or licensing of technology
- Private inventors
- Academic institutions and academic research reports
- Government agencies and government-funded research
- Journals and other publications such as working papers
- Technical fairs and trade fairs
- Open innovation fairs

Both buying or licensing inventions and patents from others and forming joint ventures bring with them additional risks. First, you may be revealing too many technical details not found in publications. Second, there is always the risk of willful patent infringement. Third, you are informing people that someone believes there are opportunities here by the justification of costs and negotiations and accompanying financial obligations.

Converting ideas to reality requires technology. There are four levels of technology for innovation:

- Level I: The technology exists within the company.
- Level II: The technology can be obtained from other sources within the country
- Level III: The technology can be obtained from other sources outside of the country.
- Level IV: Technology must be researched outside of the country and brought back to the parent company.

Regardless of whether we use open or closed innovation, techniques must be established for the capturing and storage of information. Typical idea handling techniques include:

- Idea inventories
- Idea clearinghouses
- Idea banks
- Screening or review teams

The greater the number of creative ideas generated, the greater the chance of selecting the types of innovation projects that will maximize the business value. If the organization is risk averse, then high-risk projects with the potential of delivering high levels of value may never surface.

CROWDSOURCING _____

> *"This is not the wisdom of the crowd, but the wisdom of someone in the crowd. It's not that the network itself is smart; it's that the individuals get smarter because they're connected to the network."*
> — Steven Johnson, *Where Good Ideas Come From: The Natural History of Innovation*

> *"Customers often know more about your products than you do. Use them as a source of inspiration and ideas for product development."*
> — David J. Greer, *Wind in Your Sails*

Crowdsourcing is often associated with open innovation and is the act of a company or institution taking a function once performed by employees and outsourcing it to an undefined (and generally large) network of people. Crowdsourcing is one of the ways that a company can organize a group of people that are familiar with your product or strategic intent to think up ideas for the future and to solve problems. Although each person may be able to contribute ideas to only a part of the problem, the collective gathering of ideas can generate viable alternatives and solutions.

There is usually a greater number of creative and innovative people outside of a company than within it. Open innovation focuses on idea generation, whereas the intent of crowdsourcing is to solve a potential problem and then share the information freely with all contributors. The challenge is determining the size of the crowd, its ability to be productive, and whether its members understand their role.

Some of the risks can be minimized by asking critical questions even before the crowdsourcing begins:

- Is the problem defined well enough to be fully understood?
- Can we expect solutions that can solve the problem?
- Will the expected solutions be able to take advantage of the existing opportunity?

Collecting information from crowdsourcing can be accomplished through formal channels of communication and/or informal social media networks. However, there are risks in both cases as to the value of the information received.

Abrahamson et al. (2013, 15) identify five possible outcomes from crowdsourcing:

1. *Getting ideas.* Obtaining many ideas that would otherwise be beyond the scope of what is possible with an internal team or traditional partners.
2. *Evaluating ideas.* Efficiently receiving feedback and interpretations from a wide range of stakeholders to determine where to make future investments.
3. *Finding talent.* Through the proposals, identify new individuals, teams, and organizations to work with.
4. *Causing conversation.* Generating content and often provocative ideas that in turn lead to conversations and media coverage.
5. *Transforming relationships.* Enabling stakeholders to participate in generating and selecting ideas can positively change the relationship between the organization and stakeholders.

There are several limitations and controversies about crowdsourcing:

- Crowdsourcing might negatively affect product quality due to the considerable number of participants that may be involved, many of whom may be unqualified.
- A great deal of time and money can be spent evaluating low-quality contributions because little information is available currently about the desired product.
- Crowdworkers may not communicate with one another, and the results could be suboptimal.
- Increased number of funded ideas may make the evaluation process complex, resulting in good ideas not being considered.
- Trustworthiness of the information and the decision-making process can be open for debate.
- Determining who controls copyright information, patents, etc. can create legal headaches.

One often overlooked crowdsourcing item during the early innovation stages is the control of intellectual property (IP). Competitors will most likely act in a predatory manner based upon the importance of the IP created. If the competitors have a significant cash flow, they can drag out the legal issues in court for a considerable time, thus creating havoc for poorer, smaller companies that wish to protect their rights.

One way a small company may be able to protect themselves is to team up with strategic partners that have ample resources to protect the IP rights. This partnership could then provide some degree of protection for licensing and royalty agreements as well. The partnership agreement could also contain information on how the IP rights will be disposed of in case one of the partners exits the business.

Issues with the control of intellectual property will always exist but the risks are usually greater when crowdsourcing is considered. Some of the issues are shown in Table 2-3.

When we refer to crowdsourcing, we generally think about people external to our company. However, the same crowdsourcing concepts can be applied internally to a company's workforce that is distributed, especially if people are located across the globe. More companies are allowing people to work

TABLE 2–3.   ISSUES WITH INTELLECTUAL PROPERTY

Issue	Using Employees	Using Crowdsourcing
Access to needed expertise	Limited to internal knowledge	Access to much more expertise and feedback options
Ownership	Owned and patented by the company	May need legal/licensing agreements and partnerships agreements
Transactional costs including nondisclosure agreements and employment agreements	Minimal filing and control costs	High transactional costs
Potential for leakage of business strategy	Low	Very high
Potential for leakage of intellectual property	Low	Very high
Product development cost	Perhaps very high	Perhaps very low using strategic partners
Ability to block or counteract competitive actions	High	Low
Access to talent	Limited	Very high
Financial rewards for contributors	Cash or prizes to individuals	Contracts, partnership agreements, licensing agreements, revenue sharing, and equity investment options

from home. Generally, the advantages outweigh the disadvantages. People can still provide ideas and, if face-to-face interaction is necessary, computer technology will allow it to happen.

CO-CREATION INNOVATION

"It takes people from the outside to change things on the inside. Innovation happens from outsiders."
— Richie Norton

"To go from Bitter, to BETTER, means you need to turn your I onto an E, by embracing WE."
— Tony Dovale

Most companies have limited resources and cannot undertake all the innovation activities they desire. Other reasons for resource restrictions might include:

- In-house technical resources have insufficient knowledge/skills.
- In-house resources are committed to higher-priority projects.
- In-house talent exists but work can be done externally for less money and in less time.

Companies may then wish to take on strategic business partners and focus on co-creation. Co-creation is a management initiative or strategy that brings different parties together, such as a company and a group of customers, to jointly produce a product or service that has value-in-use to all parties. Co-creation brings a blend of ideas from direct customers or viewers (who may not be the direct users of the product), which in turn brings innovative ideas to the organization. However, the project manager must decide in which phases, early or late, in the life cycle to involve the co-creation team.

Co-creation is a much better tool than market research for determining consumer behavior because it provides some degree of power and decision making to the participants for brand identification and future direction. Co-creation is an excellent way to identify opportunities because "none of us are as smart as all of us." Co-creation teams that involve leading-edge users generally provide more ideas than a company could generate internally. The size of a co-creation team can vary from a few participants to hundreds.

For novelty products, co-creation teams may have an easier time thinking out of the box than using just internal personnel. The co-creation team may also provide ideas for value chain efficiency, especially if they are part of the value chain.

Co-created value arises in the form of personalized, unique experiences for the customer (value-in-use) and ongoing revenue, learning, and enhanced market performance drivers for the firm (loyalty, relationships, customer word of mouth). Value is co-created with customers when a customer can personalize his or her experience using a firm's product-service proposition to create greater value. The result can be faster time-to-market, less exposure to risks and uncertainty, greater customer satisfaction, lower cost, better product quality, higher revenues/profitability, superior brand value/loyalty, and better technical solutions. A major value for the firm sponsoring co-creation is better fulfillment of customer needs that increases the likelihood of new product/service success.

Co-creation is a form of "open" innovation, as seen in Figure 2-2. The six arrows in the top portion of Figure 2-2 are the characteristics of a closed innovation process where the firm does everything by themselves. When co-creation takes place, the boxes in the bottom portion of Figure 2-2 are added in to form an open innovation environment.

The purpose of innovation is to create value. As seen in Figure 2-3, companies are investing heavily in customer value management programs. According to a study by the American Productivity and Quality Center (APQC 1998, 8):

> Although customer satisfaction is still measured and used in decision-making, the majority of partner organizations (used in this study) have shifted their focus from customer satisfaction to customer value.

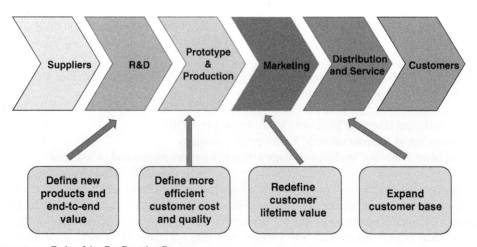

Figure 2–2. Role of the Co-Creation Partners.

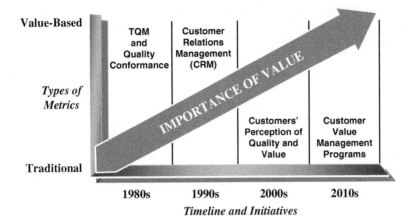

Figure 2–3. Growth in the Importance of Value.

Customer value management programs are replacing customer relations management (CRM) programs. Traditionally, CRM activities focused on handling customer complaints and product returns. This provided information related to existing products only with little or no information related to future products and services, and a rather informal approach to listening to the voice of the customer.

Companies must establish repeatable processes to listen to the voice of the customer, not just to discover the customer's needs, but to understand the customer's definition of value, especially value-in-use. The only way to deliver value to the customer is to understand how their perception of value motivates them. Companies must also listen to stakeholders other than customers because these stakeholders may buy into your products/services later and increase your chances for finding successful innovations.

Most companies have customer relationship management (CRM) systems and have the mistaken belief that this is how to determine the customer's definition of value. Most CRM systems have their primary role as getting customers to accept the products and services they are offering. The focus is most often on collecting customer comments, listening to complaints, and handling returns. The focus is not on extracting information related to value or value-in-use. When this happens, companies may end up committing vast resources to short-term innovation projects to make it easier for customers to accept existing offerings rather than targeting future needs that can lead to a sustainable competitive advantage.

Co-creation is a critical component of customer value management programs because it allows you to get closer to the customers and understand their perception of value and their needs. Companies need to know how their customers interpret value and create their own value. Customers and the ultimate consumers provide the sources of competitive advantage. Companies therefore need customer-driven innovation to unlock the sources of competitive advantage. This will require new forms of relationships with customers for activities other than innovation as well.

The importance of value creates an innovation focus that is not just on cost and quality. It also includes beauty, safety, comfort, pride, aesthetic value, and so on. Financing is not a critical issue for innovation in most firms, especially when value is the ultimate goal.

The project manager and his/her IPM team must have a clear understanding of value and its importance to the innovation process. This is different than what most PMs are used to when they work with internal personnel only. This includes:

- Customers will co-create with you if they perceive the value-in-use of buying your goods and services.
- Value is usually a personal judgment, and the focus must be on value-in-use.
- Customers must perceive the value before integrating their own resources into a co-creation effort.
- Determining value-in-use requires marketing and the IPM team to get closer to the customer.
- It is the customer that determines what is valuable.
- There is a difference between perceived and actual value in the innovation life cycle.
- Value-in-use focuses on lifetime value.
- Value can appear as financial value, organizational value, and strategic value.

Customer co-creation can be looked at from a business-to-consumer (B2C) perspective or from a business-to-business (B2B) perspective. Customer co-creation for innovation in B2B contexts is relatively mature, whereas B2C settings are only now being studied. In both cases, customer co-creation is described as a network or "ecosystem" involving several types of actors. There are different actors for each case as well as different boundary conditions and requirements. There can also be different forms of co-creation logic used, such as:

- Goods-dominant logic (G-D)
- Service-dominant logic (S-D)

A critical component in customer co-creation is the identification of "appropriate" customer co-creators for specific outcomes. Some publications make a distinction between ordinary/mainstream customers and advanced customers/lead user innovators that possess superior knowledge and/or have advanced market needs. Both types of customers must be able to think outside the box and provide original ideas.

Co-creation offers firms and their network of "actors" significant opportunities for innovation, as each actor offers access to untapped resources through a process of resource integration. Actors can come from a variety of sources including suppliers, customers, strategic and nonstrategic partners, competitors (with similar offerings), and influencers (indirect collaborators such as media, government, and regulatory agencies). Customers are often considered as the most important actors because they can provide new sources of competitive advantage in value creation that can lead to enhanced consumer loyalty, consumer satisfaction, and higher purchases.

The output of a co-creation effort can be a product or a platform. A platform is a core design from which customers can customize the result with features or amenities specifically designed for their markets. This approach involves developing and introducing a partially completed product, for the purpose of providing a platform, framework, or tool kit for contributors to access, customize, and exploit. The goal is for the contributors to extend the platform product's functionality while increasing the overall value of the product for everyone involved.

As an example of platform co-creation, Boeing allowed eight airlines to have a role in the development of the Boeing 777 aircraft. The eight airlines were All Nippon Airways, American Airlines, British Airways, Cathay Pacific, Delta Air Lines, Japan Airlines, Qantas, and United Airlines. This was a departure from industry practice, where manufacturers typically designed aircraft with minimal customer input.

The eight airlines that contributed to the design process became known within Boeing as the "Working Together" group. At the first group meeting, a 23-page questionnaire was distributed to the airline representatives, asking what each wanted in the design. Two months later, Boeing and the airlines had decided on a basic design configuration that included flexible interiors to satisfy the needs of each airline. Part of the co-creation effort was also to look at ways of designing an aircraft such that maintenance costs could be lowered. At one point, Boeing had 240 design teams, with up to 40 members each, addressing almost 1,500 design issues with individual aircraft components. The fuselage diameter was increased to suit Cathay Pacific, the baseline model grew longer for All Nippon Airways, and British Airways' input led to added built-in testing and interior flexibility, along with higher operating weight options.

Most customers usually welcome participation in co-creation efforts because they view it as beneficial to their organization and possibly themselves personally. Some potential benefits include:

- Partial ownership in the result
- Excitement
- Creating and collecting intellectual property
- Possibility of obtaining a competitive advantage and competitive leadership for their own firm
- Possibility of enriching their portfolio and introducing new products and services

The customers and the parent company must be two equal problem solvers rather than just the company listening to the voice of the customer. Dialogue is needed in order to identify:

- Each party's vision and sense of urgency
- What each party sees as a competitive advantage
- New customers

Selecting co-creation partners is difficult even if it is for a specific outcome. Critical questions that must be considered include:

- Who are the actors—end users, extreme end users, suppliers, distributors?
- Should we look at a mass crowd of users? (i.e., crowd-sorting)
- Do we select actors that are ordinary users or those who have some proficiency in product development?
- Do we select ordinary/mainstream customers or advanced customers (lead users) that have superior knowledge and advanced needs?
- Should we select lead users in the idea generation stage and ordinary users in the testing stage?
- Does it make a difference in actor selection if we have incremental or radical innovation?
- Does the expected innovation outcome make a difference in actor selection?
- Can ordinary customers think out of the box?
- What are the pros and cons of each group of actors?
- Can customer involvement vary based upon the life-cycle phase?
- How much freedom should we give the lead firm to design the architecture of participation and determine who makes decisions?
- How should we plan for situations where some partners are unwilling to share information if they are already participating in co-creation?

Selecting partners can create challenges for the parent company, especially behavioral issues that could impact relationships in the future. Some questions that the enterprise must consider before seeking partners include:

- What are the reasons for the partnerships?
- Will all partners be working with the same goals and objectives?
- Will all partners have the same levels of technology?
- How do we recruit and find actors/customers?
- Will the actors function in a support role or will it be joint innovation?
- Do we understand the cost and risks of co-creation activities?
- Who will own the intellectual property rights?
- Will there be a sharing of revenue and/or proprietary knowledge?
- Will any of the customers be unhappy and not agree to participate in the future?
- How should we handle irrational behavior by some of the partners?
- How will partners react to each other's behavior?
- What are the potential conflicts among the partners and how should they be resolved?
- Will all partners have the same vision for the time and cost of the venture?

IPMs must participate in discussions involving answers to these questions. Unlike traditional project management practices where issues like these are handled by the project sponsor, these issues may require direct involvement by the innovation project manager and possibly team members.

There are numerous benefits to using co-creation. They include:

- Supplanted innovation
- Better alignment to the customer's needs and the customer's business model
- Maintaining technical leadership and skills
- More new business opportunities
- Maintaining a defensive posture to meet competition
- Balancing work loads and maintaining better asset allocation
- Maintaining customer goodwill
- Improvements to existing products
- Reduction in commercialization time
- Faster time-to-market
- Lower risk of failure
- Early identification of market reaction
- Better focus on value creation
- Reduction in innovation costs
- Make company more competitive in the future and lower market entry barriers
- Repeatable elsewhere

Some companies prefer to identify the benefits of co-creation by the following:

- Co-design
- Co-production
- Co-promotion
- Co-pricing

- Co-distribution
- Co-maintenance
- Co-consumption
- Co-disposal
- Co-outsourcing

Companies that are highly successful at co-creation build co-creation activities into their business model. The result can be better customer relations management practices, quicker compliance to regulatory and social needs, identification of better ways to restructure the organization, better strategic planning options by identifying future needs, and more predictable financial considerations.

Sometimes we start out with the best intentions and then discover that things went wrong. Some of the factors that can destroy co-creation initiatives include:

- Participants working toward different goal and objectives
- Partner problems
- A landlord–tenant relationship between parties
- Unrealistic expectations
- Lack of senior management support and commitment
- Being close-minded about ideas
- Mismatched cultures
- Personality clashes
- Failing to keep creative people engaged and challenged
- Bringing the wrong people on board
- Too large a group
- Not listening to everyone
- Allowing time pressure to force you to make rapid decisions based on partial information
- Criticizing ideas perhaps without justification
- Failing to focus on lifetime value

Perhaps the greatest risk with co-creation occurs when the outcome is creative destruction. Creative destruction occurs when the team develops a product that is new and revolutionizes the marketplace to a point where their other products are now obsolete. This could result in a loss of revenue from past customers, having to lay off people, and the need for a completely new business model.

OPEN INNOVATION IN ACTION: AIRBUS AND CO-CREATION PARTNERSHIPS

Airbus was formed in 1970 as a consortium of aerospace manufacturers from four countries in Europe. Airbus designs, manufactures, and sells civil and military aerospace products worldwide. The company has three divisions: commercial aircraft, defense and space, and helicopters. In the commercial aircraft division, which is the older division, manufacturing is shared as follows: the wings are made in the United Kingdom, the fuselage and the vertical part of the tail in Germany, the horizontal part of the tail in Spain, and the plane is assembled in Toulouse, France. Considering the heterogeneity of the involved companies, Airbus is inherently a laboratory of "open innovation." According to Chesbrough (2003), who coined the term, open innovation is the cooperation between several companies that share resources, knowledge, and skills in a creative goal. This is exactly what has been done at Airbus, namely four aerospace companies in Europe put together the efforts, knowledge, and experiences in order to be competitive with the US aviation companies. However, it has to be noticed that, especially in the case of product innovation and in the high-tech field, the effort of a "single" company (even of a consortium like Airbus) could be not enough to promote the development of new technologies or, to cite Schumpeter (1942), to induce the *creative destruction* process.[2] As observed by Chesbrough, in order to better create the conditions to make easier the development of new technologies, it is extremely advantageous to cooperate with other firms in the same sector, with suppliers, with universities, with research centers, and so on. Figuratively, the continuous line that ideally defines the boundaries of a firm must become a dash line, allowing the knowledge to be shared freely among the partners. As pointed out by Park et al. (2014) the sharing of resources promotes innovation and generates collective competitive advantages to distance competitors who are not involved in the partnership. In addition, the cooperating networks of actors create synergies, multiply the ability to innovate, and all involved partners benefit from each other's expertise (Chesbrough 2003).

At Airbus, open innovation is not only a concept used to create and compete but also a way to provide very advanced products that include new technologies. In accordance with Chesbrough's theory, the idea generation and the creation of new products is reached by the constant collaboration between Airbus and suppliers, and with universities and research centers. An example is the advanced center for composite materials research, Technocampus EMC[2]. Located near Nantes (France) Technocampus EMC[2], which includes in its name Einstein's most famous equation, is a technological research center dedicated to composite manufacturing. It encompasses industrial and academic players who work on developing innovative manufacturing technologies for high-performance composite materials. Opened in September 2009, it offers pooled equipment and resources, encourages an interdisciplinary approach, collaborative R&D, and technology transfer. With the Technocampus EMC[2] Airbus has established efficient means of research and development in technologies of impregnated composites and thermoplastic resin infusion. These technologies have been widely used in the design of the latest long-haul aircraft in its class: the A350 XWB.[3] Airbus develops materials with Technocampus EMC[2] for airplanes of tomorrow in collaboration with academic partners: the Ecole Centrale Nantes, the Ecole des Mines, ICAM, and Polytech; industrial partners such as CETIM, Aerolia, CIMPA, Composite Tool, Daher-Socata, and Euro Engineering. The involvement of all these actors represents the contribution of skills and technological knowledge needed when the priority is to develop a revolutionary innovative product or a killer technology (Allal-Chérif 2015).

---

2. Creative destruction refers to the incessant product and process innovation mechanism by which new production units replace outdated ones. This idea was introduced by the Austrian-American economist Joseph Schumpeter in 1942.

3. The Airbus A350 XWB (eXtra Wide Body) is a family of long-range, twin-engine wide-body jet airliners developed by European aerospace manufacturer Airbus. The A350 is the first Airbus aircraft with both fuselage and wing structures made primarily of carbon-fiber-reinforced polymer. Its variants seat 280 to 366 passengers in typical three-class seating layouts. It was introduced to the market on January 15, 2015 with the delivery to Qatar Airways.

VALUE (OR VALUE-DRIVEN) INNOVATION _____

"Focus on innovating at value, not positioning against competitors."
— W. Chan Kim, *Blue Ocean Strategy: How to Create Uncontested Market Space and Make the Competition Irrelevant*

"When organizations fail to register the difference between value innovation and innovation per se, they all too often end with an innovation that breaks new ground but does not unlock the mass of target buyers."
— W. Chan Kim, *Blue Ocean Strategy: How to Create Uncontested Market Space and Make the Competition Irrelevant*

When companies embark on a quest for innovation, they often use conventional logic. In this approach, products and services are introduced into the marketplace with the hope that customers and end users see some value in the use of the product or service. Companies can invest billions of dollars on just a hunch that the end user will accept the product rather than taking the more realistic approach of talking first to end users. Decisions may be made to expand a product line, add more features to a product, or possibly disrupt the markets with radical innovation. But regardless of what decisions are made, real success is measured by value.

Companies today appear to prefer using value-in-use rather than just value. Value-in-use is a term commonly attributed to accounting, real estate, or investments. It represents the net present value (NPV) of a cash flow or other benefits that an asset generates for a specific owner under a specific use. Value-in-use is useful for evaluating the utility of an asset to determine whether it should be retained, repaired, or taken out of service.

Value-in-use can also be used to determine the present or future market value of a product created through innovation. Innovation requires a commitment of costly resources. Executives may believe in pressuring the innovation team to get the job done quicker and reduce time to market and time to achieve profitability. What executives often fail to realize is that the customer's perception of value or value-in-use, not time to market, shortens the payback period and drives profitability.

Some people believe that value-in-use is determined exclusively by the customer. Companies therefore commit resources to observe how the customers use their products and to solicit feedback on value-in-use and recommendations for product improvements.

What is often overlooked is the value of the contributions made by the firm's employees during the innovation project and even thereafter. The insights made by the employees, regardless of whether they observe the customers using the product, can offer unique perspectives for improvements that may prove more beneficial than recommendations by the customers. Therefore, successful strategic alignment for the marketplace demand for new or improved products should strike a balance between competing interpretations of value and/or value-in-use between in-house talent and customers.

When customers recognize value-in-use of the products, the results translate into value for your company that can then be measured in economic or financial terms. The focus therefore should be on the customer's perception of value rather than just creating another product. This thinking has led to a new form of innovation—namely, value or *value-driven innovation*. Some people use the term *customer-driven innovation* as a form of value-driven innovation.

With this approach, there is a heavy emphasis on capturing the true voice of the customer. Customer-perceived value may appear in incremental rather than radical changes, improvements in quality, speed to market, and customer support. Value may also be insensitive to price.

Value innovation possesses many of the following characteristics that are not part of conventional logic:

- You must go beyond just listening to customers; ask them what their needs are now and in the future.
- You must observe the customers using your products and services; put yourself in your customers' shoes.
- Carefully watch how your customers use your products or services to discover opportunities for further improvements or innovations.
- Involve customers in testing your prototypes and products.
- Make value-driven innovation activities part of your firm's culture.

There are several benefits to value-driven innovation:

- Having products targeted toward customer value rather than sales or marketing goals
- An easier time targeting market segments
- Development of an innovation product portfolio that focuses on the delivery of value to the customers rather than just deliverables
- Better focus on developing a meaningful business strategy and aligning thinking with strategic business objectives.[4]

Innovation researchers and academia have recognized the importance of value-driven innovation for some time, but private industry was slow in responding because of the lack of knowledge in establishing value-based metrics as part of managing innovation projects. Value-based metrics, as will be discussed in Chapter 7, have opened the door for use of value-driven innovation.

AGILE INNOVATION

Shifting customer needs are common in today's marketplace. Businesses must be adaptive and responsive to change while delivering an exceptional customer experience to be competitive. Traditional development and delivery frameworks such as waterfall are often ineffective. In contrast, Scrum is a value-driven agile approach which incorporates adjustments based on regular and repeated customer and stakeholder feedback. And Scrum's built-in rapid response to change leads to substantial benefits such as fast time-to-market, higher satisfaction, and continuous improvement—which supports innovation and drives competitive advantage."

— Scott M. Graffius, *Agile Scrum: Your Quick Start Guide*
with Step-by-Step Instructions

Products in the marketplace are becoming obsolete at a faster rate than ever before. Combining this with an increase in new competitors entering the marketplace, companies are being pressured to shorten

---

4. Additional benefits of value innovation activities will be discussed in the Samsung section in Chapter 12.

the product development life cycle for a speedy, time-to-market product launch. This has led to the introduction of a new form of innovation, namely, *agile innovation*, that allows teams to launch new products quickly and at a lower risk than with other more traditional innovation practices.

Agile innovation is an approach that companies take to achieve optimal efficiency and effectiveness in their innovation activities. The objective is to obtain the best solution to a problem through a collaborative effort. The solution must solve the conflicting requirements of time, cost, scope, quality, and innovation. The underlying principle is that rapid access to the required knowledge makes it easier to organize and manage the agile innovation team. Speed is a critical attribute of agile innovation.

Agile techniques have been used for some time in IT organizations for software development projects. Today, the principles of agile have spread to other corporate functions such as innovation. Rigby et al. (2018) state:

Agile teams are best suited to innovation—that is, the profitable application of creativity to improve products and services, processes, or business models. They are small and multidisciplinary. Confronted with a large, complex problem, they break it into modules, develop solutions to each component through rapid prototyping and tight feedback loops, and integrate the solutions into a coherent whole. They place more value on adapting to change than on sticking to a plan, and they hold themselves accountable for outcomes (such as growth, profitability, and customer loyalty), not outputs (such as lines of code or number of new products).

The authors then continue by stating how agile teams may impact governance:

Agile teams work differently from chain-of-command bureaucracies. They are largely self-governing: Senior leaders tell team members where to innovate but not how. And the teams work closely with customers, both external and internal. Ideally, this puts responsibility for innovation in the hands of those who are closest to customers. It reduces layers of control and approval, thereby speeding up work and increasing the teams' motivation. It also frees up senior leaders to do what only they can do: create and communicate long-term visions, set and sequence strategic priorities, and build the organizational capabilities to achieve those goals.

While there are significant benefits in using agile teams, not all types of projects are well suited for this approach. However, agile does make it easier for a company to work in a more dynamic rather than static environment.

Some activities, such as with incremental innovation, may be done in weeks. As such, companies are now using the term "short-sprint innovation" rather than agile or Scrum innovation. Examples of short-sprint innovation might include, replacing the material on a product with higher-quality material, changing the design of a software screen, or testing a new material.

Practitioners use the term short-sprint innovation because these innovation projects generally use an agile or Scrum framework that is based upon the use of sprints. The characteristics of a short-sprint innovation are closely aligned to agile and Scrum, namely:

- The objectives are reasonably well understood
- The objectives are realistic and attainable within the team's expertise and within the imposed constraints
- The budget and schedule are realistic
- The objectives can be achieved with existing technology

AGILE INNOVATION IN ACTION: DELOITTE _____

Introduction

For a company such as Deloitte Central Europe (hereafter referred to as Deloitte), stating that employees are the most valuable assets is not just a cliché. Deloitte creates value for its clients by delivering professional services in the areas of audit, consulting, financial advisory, legal, and tax based on the skills and knowledge of its employees. Recently, Deloitte has broadened its scope of services, which means that its appetite for talent is even bigger than before. No wonder that recruiting at Deloitte is a strategic process in its value creation chain.

Nevertheless, the legacy recruiting system that Deloitte has been using for years became seriously outdated, as it did not keep up with standards that we are used to in the new digital world. In order to apply, candidates had to go through 11 screens and 18 data fields entailing 30 mouse clicks. And, as if that were not bad enough, the candidate could encounter several critical errors, which would make it impossible to successfully complete the application process.

Being so far behind the pace set by the digital leaders, Deloitte was experiencing the loss of nearly half of the candidates who began the application process. Qualitative research showed that many of those who dropped out of the process were in fact exactly the type of talent that was needed for the new suite of digital services Deloitte was beginning to offer. Faced with such a difficult application process and knowing that there were dozens of other companies, which in many instances were the primary choice for such employees, many candidates abandoned their applications or declined to apply to Deloitte. Therefore, a substantial part of the company's employer branding effort was wasted due to poor candidate experience in the application process. That was a serious impediment for implementing the organization's strategy of attracting and retaining top talent. In addition, from the recruiter's point of view the legacy system did not meet basic expectations such as the ability to easily search for candidates and quickly screen their profiles.

Having realized the inability to deliver its strategy using the legacy recruiting solution, Deloitte leaders decided to build a new, custom-made solution. On the one hand, it was a risky decision in that there were quite a lot of off-the-shelf solutions that could improve the situation. On the other hand, within the organization there was a group of individuals passionate to build an innovative application, tailored to meet the needs of candidates and recruiters alike. Fortunately, leadership trusted the team and decided to run an experiment by building the system from scratch, created in close collaboration with candidates and recruiters, in a cloud environment, using agile practices. The project, which received the acronym "CEX," which stood for Candidate Experience Platform, was born.

Body

Project Manager Duties

Why should the project sponsor invest in such a role as the project manager for the "CEX" project? On the one hand, there was a feeling that building a new digital product in an agile approach, based on the values and principles of agile rather than on the traditional command and control elements of a waterfall approach, would create an environment for creative thinking and unobstructed working.

On the other hand, since it was one of first agile projects delivered in the organization, it was met with some expectations, fears, and worries. Most notably, the sponsors wanted a single point of contact for the project, one person responsible for managing progress and the budget, provide coaching, and cultivating an open environment for sharing ideas. It didn't matter if this person was called the "agile coach" or "project manager," the expectations were that someone was responsible for planning, delegating, monitoring, and controlling the project. So how was the traditional role of "project manager" applied across these areas to such an innovative initiative as CEX?

Plan

The project was envisioned and delivered in four subsequent phases: discover, define, develop, and deploy, following the "double diamond," a creative process created by the Design Council, a nonprofit organization promoting the concept of inclusive design, depicted in Figure 2-4.

In the "discover" and "define" phases, there was no agile coach or project manager role present. These phases were not conducted according to the traditional project delivery methodology, but rather in the so-called "magic time," meaning somewhere in between all other tasks. In these first two phases, there was just a single "management" role—the product owner, who was responsible for gathering insights as well as understanding the problems and needs of candidates and recruiters. The understanding of the underlying problems to be solved provided the foundation to develop the interactive prototype and subsequently define the initial product backlog of the future recruiting solution.

The third phase of "develop" required significant capital investment, and as such, the sponsors asked for the project manager (PM) or agile coach (AC) role. The first task for the appointed PM/ AC and PO working in tandem was to prepare the statement of work and the pitch presentation to the

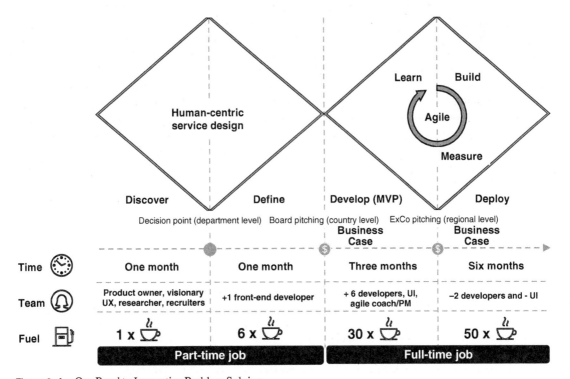

Figure 2–4. Our Road to Innovative Problem Solving.

management board, which included project approach, timeline, scope, budget, and team structure. This required proper traditional planning. An iterative approach for the delivery of the new recruitment platform was selected as the preferred project management approach. This decision was made by one of the sponsors (let's call him the *visionary*) based on his intuition rather than experience. PM/AC/PO together with the visionary explained to other stakeholders, that using the iterative approach would minimize risk and waste.

Regarding the timeline, from the beginning of the project it was clear that there was no hard deadline for launching the new recruitment platform. "Hard deadline" was understood to mean a date resulting from business, technical, or compliance reasons. Nevertheless, a deadline was set, the date when the team will run out of money (budget). Other points on the timeline were more indicative and were presented in order to depict the team's ideas for subsequent stages of the project delivery, from demos, to UATs, RITE tests, friends and family testing, and security testing, to potential release dates. These points of time were not treated as milestones, as they did not define the critical path (this expression was never used during the project), and moreover, the changing of initially defined dates did not require acceptance from the sponsors. These activities were not regarded as "project deliverables." The only agreed deliverable was the business value to be delivered, meaning an improved candidate experience, enhanced recruiter experience, and reduced time needed to process candidates through the recruiting cycle.

The scope was defined in a few iterative steps starting with an interactive prototype created during the "define" phase of the project. The prototype was discussed with almost all business users (around 20 individuals) during a full-day workshop. The prototype covered key user interactions and flows across the entire recruitment journey. That was a very helpful tool for the product owner and UX designer—the facilitators of the workshop tasked to engage future users in the co-creation process. For the candidates, recruiters, and the business, it was also much easier to point out key recruiting activities that should be enabled and simplified based on the prototype. In the second step, based on the workshop outcomes, the product owner, with support from PM/AC, wrote the product backlog with MoSCoW (must have, should have, could have, and won't have) priorities, along with the DEEP technique. Next, during a two-day workshop the development team estimated in man-days the required work effort, which was taken as the baseline for the project budget to be agreed with the sponsors. So far, the role of the PM/AC was focused more on facilitation of meetings and elimination of impediments, so he acted more like the agile coach. Regarding the team structure, sponsors expected to see who would be responsible for specific project areas such as business requirements, architecture, and quality assurance, and so the DSDM (dynamic systems development method) team structure was used to define such roles as business visionaries, business ambassadors, technical coordinators, solution developers, and so on. In subsequent stage of the project, the team worked much closer to a traditional Scrum framework with three key roles: product owner, development team, and agile coach.

Monitor and Control

Costs

Since the key project constraint was the budget, not the timeline, the PM/AC did not focus much on tracking on how well the work was progressing against the project schedule. The most important item that was tracked was the ratio between investment (tracked at the sprint level) and business outcome (verified after production releases). In order to manage the investment and keep track of project costs, two key cost management measures were introduced. First, all project purchases, such as SaaS licenses for Heroku (development platform), Lucidchart or Atlassian (project support tools), were made directly by the PM/

AC. This ensured that opex costs were under control and could be easily tracked. As the PM/AC was working very closely with the team (same location, almost every day), he did not constitute a bottleneck in this case. Second, everyone on the team reported work time in JIRA (project support tool) on user story level, even time spent on Scrum ceremonies. It was agreed with the team in the definition of "done" that a user story could be treated as done, among other criteria, only once all hours have been reported. This allowed the PM/AC to control the budget and present biweekly updates of budget consumption to the team and sponsors. This act of transparency turned out to be very useful in discussions about changes to product backlog and priorities.

Deadlines

As already stated, the only hard deadline the development team faced was the date the budget would be exhausted. The role of the project manager was to closely monitor the budget in order to know when to start user acceptance tests (UATs), which were not conducted as part of each sprint due to recruiters' time limitations. Every two weeks the project manager presented to the team, sponsors, and other stakeholders the expected kickoff date of UATs, as well as the target end date of the project based on past budget consumption and planned team capacity, which varied because of vacations, public holidays and sometimes other duties assumed by project team members. Such an approach allowed the team to appropriately plan their sprints, and the product owner to effectively manage priorities.

One additional deadline that was important to the project team was the end of each sprint. Every two weeks the team had to present to the product owner (and sometimes also to other stakeholders) the product increment. This allowed the team members to keep their focus on the goal of each sprint. It was also a useful mechanism that enabled the team and the project manager to monitor the progress made and check whether the project was going in the right direction, taking into consideration the scope that had been agreed on with the sponsors and stakeholders.

Scope

Before the official start of the project and just after the prototyping phase, there was a need to create an initial list of features of the product. The idea was to conduct a whole-day workshop with business users (around 20 individuals) in order to create a list of features that would be included. Therefore, the team decided to print all screens of the prototype in the form of mockups and hang them on the walls of the conference room. The task of invited guests from the business side was to mark various functionalities with self-adhesive colored cards, where the color reflected the perceived importance. Initial prioritization of backlog items was possible with the use of MoSCoW priorities (must, should, could, won't), as per the DSDM methodology. The joint workshop provided a great opportunity to gather feedback from the actual users of the future system as well as a chance to engage them in the co-creation of future functionalities.

It is worth highlighting that business users initially believed that all the proposed functionalities were equally important for the functioning of the application and all features should or even must be included in the final version of the product. Such thinking is typical of the traditional waterfall model, where the requirements are collected at the beginning of the project and making subsequent changes to the preliminary scope is difficult. Because of these habits and experiences, the selection of key functionalities turned out to be at first very difficult. The solution was to limit the number of "must" and "should" cards, which brought up a dialogue between business users and project team members. It was crucial that business users understood the basic limitation, which was the budget. The main challenge for the product owner during the workshop was to guide business decisions and raise awareness that they were creating a product for the end users (in this case, candidates that were being recruited to Deloitte) and therefore should be guided by their expectations and not by what seemed to be important business users and team members at the time.

This was also the reason why the team decided to show the MVP (minimal viable product) during the software development process to end users (i.e., students at Warsaw universities), who agreed to take part in RITE (rapid iterative testing and evaluation) tests. At the beginning of the week, UX designers conducted tests with users in a room behind a Venetian mirror. Provided feedback was incorporated into the application during the week and the next round of RITE tests took place on Friday. The increase in end-user satisfaction in the second round was truly outstanding.

The product owner's focus on scope management played a key role in the subsequent iterations of the project. The person acting in this role is always under pressure from two sides—the business and the team. We can describe this phenomenon as *product-oriented dual personality*. The product owner always required from the team that they deliver valuable increments of working software while at the same time he was responsible for identifying unfeasible requirements presented by the business side. For that reason, the product owner had to know the limitations and capacity of the team in order to be able to effectively negotiate the scope of a sprint with the sponsors, to make sure that it was both feasible and valuable.

At the end of the project, the development team had yet to integrate the application with LinkedIn, integrate the back office with the provider of preliminary test results (SHL) for the organization, create report panel for recruiters with statistics of the ongoing job applications, and adapt the application to mobile devices through full responsive web design (RWD). The budget would only allow for the delivery of two of the four functionalities that were originally categorized as "should have." The product owner facilitated a business meeting during which it was decided that the key functionalities required of the final product were a reporting module and access from mobile devices. The remaining "should haves" had to be de-scoped.

The last verification of the product's scope of functionalities before deployment was the launch of friends and family tests, during which the final feedback on what else should be included in the scope of the solution was collected from a group of over 80 candidates and 10 recruiters. A benefit of running tests for many users at the same time was the discovery of new bugs on the production environment before the final release.

Quality

At every stage of product development, the product owner felt fully responsible for the produced software and the value delivered to future users. Appropriate empowerment within the organization, responsibility for management of the entrusted product budget, an entrepreneurial and innovative personality, as well as the ability to pay special attention to detail, made the product owner identify with the product very closely. She made her best effort to present the expected product before the organization, so she never compromised on quality. During sprint reviews, the product owner always made sure that the user story complied with the definition of done and the acceptance criteria. Moreover, the product owner challenged the development team on a daily basis to make any given functionality easier, faster, and better. A few weeks after the project startup, the members of the development team started to identify themselves with the brand of the product and ambitiously wanted to create an innovative product at the highest level of quality.

Risks

Agile delivery philosophy (of which the most popular method—Scrum—was chosen for this project), allowed the project manager to identify and help the team mitigate risks very quickly. Each day, at the daily Scrum event, all developers discussed whether anything was preventing them from completing the tasks to complete a sprint. The project manager's task was to help remove the impediments identified by the team members. Additionally, during the sprint review, by presenting the product increment and using the definition of done, the team could verify with the product owner how much closer they were to delivery of the agreed scope. Each review ended with an update to the burndown chart, which made demonstrating progress transparent to the team and stakeholders. If the team's velocity was lower than expected, it was the project manager's duty to explain the situation to the sponsors and the stakeholders, as well as help the product owner collaborate with them to reprioritize the backlog. Furthermore, the use of another Scrum event, the sprint retrospective—which focused on inspecting and adapting the delivery process—allowed the project manager to discuss with the team how to avoid and manage certain risks.

Iterative delivery was itself a great risk mitigation solution. For example, since developers working in an iterative way merge code more often, this allows for discovery of inconsistencies much earlier. Each sprint included rigorous testing, which again contributed to lower implementation risk at the time of release. The project manager's duty in this case was to make sure that each developer committed code at least once a day and the functionalities were developed accordingly to the agreed criteria of the definition of done, including automated testing code coverage.

All risks not associated with developing the system, such as legal or compliance issues, were reported to the sponsors every two weeks during the status meeting. Where matters needed the immediate attention of sponsors or other stakeholders, a quick escalation path was designed for the project manager to bypass the biweekly meeting and organize another call to make the proper decisions as soon as possible.

Benefits

The product owner's role is to build a product that provides a specific business value. However, in the case of the recruitment platform, it was extremely difficult to calculate and depict measurable business benefits that flow directly from the implementation of such a solution. From the organization's point of view, the entire project was treated as an investment that had to pay back.

To create a point of reference, the team measured the conversion rate of the previous recruitment application. It turned out that of users who visited the recruiting website and started the application process the number who actually completed and submitted it was significantly low. That meant that a lot of effort and money invested into employer branding was being wasted. The overwhelming number of screens and irrelevant questions annoyed applicants and as a result they abandoned the application process. Even those who completed the process were annoyed by the amount of time required to submit the application, which in turn negatively influenced their perception of the entire company. Therefore, the business case for the project was based on the simple assumption that we should significantly increase the conversion rate and make the application process for the candidates as easy and convenient as possible.

The product owner must have a good understanding of the value the product brings to the organization; he must prove it, set a clear and measurable target, and regularly show how the value increases over time.

Agile Coach Duties (Scrum Methodology)

Expect High Performance

What is not clearly defined in PRINCE2[5] (but was very important on the CEX project) is focus on the team's performance. It clearly resulted from making the project budget central not only in discussions with sponsors, but also during reviews, plannings, and refinements. As the daily cost of the project team was quite significant, there was pressure to make sure the team had the right working conditions and that it was not distracted by external factors. The team was also aware of the importance of improving its productivity. From the value stream map perspective, there was very little space for any kind of waste, so in accordance with the principles of Lean management, the team eliminated these potential time-wasters:

- Partially done work. Everyday code commitments, team reviews of documents.
- Extra processes. The team was self-organizing; project processes were set up by the team not imposed by external parties so extra processes were avoided.
- Extra features. No budget for extra features so this was avoided.
- Task switching. Individuals dedicated to one project, cross-functional team.
- Waiting. Multidisciplinary team members were limiting queues.
- Motion. No need for handoffs, all tools and skills present in the team.
- Defects. Defects were limited due to definition of done and acceptance criteria.

Another method for improving the efficiency was the adoption of development approach and architecture based on the DevOps concept. The team was responsible and empowered not only for developing, but also for maintaining of the new recruitment platform.

Inspiration for the Team

The uttermost inspiration for the development team was the awareness that their work can change the reality around them. The first time the product owner read the opinions of students who had the opportunity to try out a new recruitment platform, he was extremely happy, because nobody expected such positive feedback.

The entire team was also in close contact with recruiters, who used the platform every single day. As it turned out, the new solution significantly improved the comfort and efficiency of their work. Browsing through the applications of potential candidates had become a pleasant, easy and intuitive task. Furthermore, the product improved the ease of applying to Deloitte for about 20,000 candidates who send applications to our organization every year.

Observing the real impact of the product on the life and behavior of users was a very rewarding experience. Over the course of time, the team not only drew inspiration from feedback, but also set itself the challenge of better and better insights.

Protecting the Team

One of the most important decisions made was to locate the entire team in a place separated from the headquarters building, which limited random involvements in different projects. However, it was not

---

5. PRINCE2 (Projects in Controlled Environments) is a structured project management methodology, a process-based method for effective project management.

enough to guarantee that team members would be fully dedicated to project work. Very often, line managers tried to engage developers in different projects as SMEs or event part-time developers. It was the role of PM/AC to inform line managers about the consequences of disrupting the team and sometimes to escalate those issues to sponsors. The PM/AC was not popular among line managers, as the main key performance indicator (KPI) of the PM/AC was team efficiency in the long term while line managers' KPI was new sales.

Summary and Takeaways

The initial conversion of users completing the application process increased from 60 percent (average between June 2016 and October 2016) to almost 100 percent in the period after application release. In the first four months the platform collected 14,574 applications for advertised jobs and 11,787 candidate CVs. On average, 30 percent of candidates viewed job offers via mobile devices, so the decision taken in the last sprints to make the product compatible with mobile devices was crucial for the achievement of the eventual outcome.

At the beginning of the project, the established Scrum team did not have enough knowledge about the expectations of end users. Working in short iterations and regularly collecting feedback from both sponsors and the market made it possible to develop custom-made solution that met the expectations of all stakeholders. The experience has shown that in the case of innovative projects with a high probability of changes in scope, an agile approach works perfectly. Although it might seem that Scrum in a large corporation does not make sense, that it will not succeed, and that the whole project is doomed to failure due to numerous procedures, rules, and excessive documentation, we managed to prove that nothing is impossible. Adequate management support and the necessary trust in the team has enabled us to deliver in five months a very mature product, which is currently in use by recruiters in 16 countries across central Europe. The development costs have been fully paid back and the platform will continue to serve the organization for many years to come.

GOVERNMENT INNOVATION _____

> *"…it is the public sector I find more interesting, because governments and other non-market institutions have long suffered from the innovation malaise of top-heavy bureaucracies. Today, these institutions have an opportunity to fundamentally alter the way they cultivate and promote good ideas. The more the government thinks of itself as an open platform instead of a centralized bureaucracy, the better it will be for all of us, citizens and activists, and entrepreneurs alike."*
>
> — Steven Johnson, *Where Good Ideas Come From: The Natural History of Innovation*

The need for innovation in the public sector has grown in many cases faster than in the private sector. The public sector does not have a profit motive but still needs innovation to take place. Public service innovations are evolutionary and dynamic, not radical. If significant population diversity exists, it is more difficult to satisfy the needs of an entire population with the innovation.

Examples of public-sector innovations include:

- Social responsibility innovations
  - Reducing poverty
  - Providing low-cost housing
  - Providing startup capital
  - Reducing unemployment
  - Reducing resource depletion
- Marketing innovations
  - Contracting and outsourcing
- Organizational innovations
  - Decentralization and delayering
- Service innovations
  - New services to existing users
  - New services to new users
  - Existing services to new users

As more and more government agencies adopt the project management approach, we discover that public-sector projects, including innovation, can be more complex than private-sector projects and more difficult to manage. According to David Wirick (2009, 8–10):

> Private-sector project managers like to assume that their work is more demanding than projects in the public sector. They assume that their projects are more complex, subject to tougher management oversight and mandated to move at faster speeds. Although private-sector projects can be tough, in many cases, it is easier to accomplish results in the private sector than in the public sector.

Public-sector projects can be more difficult than many private-sector projects because they:

- Operate in an environment of often-conflicting goals and outcomes
- Involve many layers of stakeholders with varied interests
- Must placate political interests and operate under media scrutiny
- Are allowed little tolerance for failure
- Operate in organizations that often have a difficult time identifying outcome measures and missions
- Are required to be performed under constraints imposed by administrative rules and often-cumbersome policies and processes that can delay projects and consume project resources
- Require the cooperation and performance of agencies outside of the project team for purchasing, hiring, and other functions
- Must make do with existing staff resources more often than private-sector projects because of civil-service protections and hiring systems
- Are performed in organizations that may not be comfortable or used to directed action and project success
- Are performed in an environment that may include political adversaries

If these challenges were not tough enough, because of their ability to push the burden of paying for projects to future generations, public-sector projects have a reach deep into the future. That introduces the challenges of serving the needs of stakeholders who are not yet "at the table" and whose interests might be difficult to identify.

Some also cite the relative lack of project management maturity in public organizations as a challenge for public-sector projects. In addition to these complications, public projects are often more complex than those in the private sector. For some projects, the outcome can be defined at the beginning of the project. Construction projects are one example. For other projects, the desired outcome can only be defined as the project progresses. Examples of those are organizational change projects and complex information technology projects. Although the first type of project can be difficult and require detailed planning and implementation, the second type, those whose outcomes are determined over the course of the project, are regarded as more challenging. They require more interaction with stakeholders and more openness to factors outside of the control of the project team. Because of the multiple stakeholders involved in public-sector projects, the types of projects the public sector engages in, and the difficulty of identifying measurable outcomes in the public sector, more public-sector projects are likely to be of the latter variety and more difficult.

The public sector generally does a better job identifying causes of failure than the private sector. The following are causes of failure on public-sector projects, including innovation (Wirick 2009, 18–19):

- Cannot identify the stakeholders
- Optimistic schedules and no plan for late deliverables
- Insufficient or unqualified resources
- Restrictions on use of resources
- Turf issues arise when sharing resources
- Not enough time for project planning
- Inability to prioritize projects
- Poor risk management practices (fear of exposing risks)
- No revalidation of assumptions
- Lack of repeatable project management processes
- Inexperienced project managers
- Fail to benefit from, or capture, lessons learned and best practices
- Political changes due to elections
- Changing (political) priorities
- Resistance to changes
- Policy conflicts
- Legislative issues
- Unclear goals and objectives

The criticism of the lack of public-sector innovations has waned over the past decade as successes have increased and been publicized. Government agencies worldwide are now embracing advances in technology to lower operating costs, eliminate excessive red tape, and remove outdated systems. This acted as a profit motive like in private-sector innovations. But perhaps the biggest reason for the growth in public-sector innovations is the growth in government project management practices. Government project managers are no longer seen as just issuing a statement of work and then acting as a project monitor tracking the performance of contractors. Government project management is now a career path position and treated as a strategic competency like the private sector.

FINANCIAL INNOVATION _____

All industries undergo changes due to advances in technology and the financial industry is no exception. The revolution in financial technologies can be attributed to advances on the Internet of Things (IoT) applications, cloud computing, blockchain technology, and mobile devices such as cell phones and tablets. According to Vlad BRĂTĂȘANU:[6]

[The] Internet of Things created new data analytics models, capable [of optimizing] decision processes, impacting technology-based financial products and services:

(i)   Operational processes that create a new type of customer experience through the use of digital platforms, offering financial services such as payments, lending and asset management.
(ii) Big data algorithms to automate financial services decision-making processes, thus increasing efficiency and building new risk management tools.
(iii) The use of cryptocurrency and blockchain technology, creating real-time global payment systems.
(iv) Peer-to-peer lending models (e.g., crowdfunding) based on marketplace lending, creating new channels in the existing lending services landscape.

Financial technology (FinTech) firms are becoming the major players is applying new technologies to assist customers in the way they pay their bills, make purchases, and control their assets. This is resulting in changes in the way we do banking, commerce, and trade. The result is often new business models for the FinTech firms. Companies that are not able to recognize and accept the FinTech revolution may find their future bleak.

The FinTech revolution has resulted in new financial institutions, products, and processes. Financial institutions are those companies that specialize in financial instruments such as specialty credit cards. Online brokerage houses can also be included in this category where your entire portfolio of stocks, bonds, and other assets can be managed from your cell phone or computer. FinTech products can include derivatives, mortgages, and loans. FinTech processes relate to the way that FinTech companies conduct their business, such as online banking, telephone banking, and online portfolio management from internet brokerage house trading platforms.

The FinTech processes may require that the firm changes its traditional business model to a customer-centric business model. An example would be the growth in branchless banking which gives consumers access beyond the bank's normal business hours. As stated by Gomber et al. (2018):

Traditionally, physical bank branches have served as the primary point of contact for facilitating retail banking and customer transactions. As technology improves, customers are switching from in-person to digital transactions through a complementary effect delivered by the enhanced access to digital banking services, and an enhanced experience of new digital access products, services, and functionality. For example, many banks now allow for physical checks to be deposited through a mobile application on a smartphone with a camera. The transition has also opened up the market for nonbank firms to offer financial services.

---

6. Adapted from BRĂTĂȘANU, V. (2017). Digital innovation the new paradigm for financial services industry. *Theoretical & Applied Economics*. Special Issue, 24, 84.

Some companies that are nonfinancial players but have made innovations in payments, lending, and personal finances include Apple, Starbucks, Disney, Facebook, Google, and Samsung.

There have been many breaches in security that have forced companies, especially some retailers, to take additional precautions at the point-of-sale (POS). Some of the precautions include the ability to make mobile payments, encryption of information and tokenization. FinTech firms are using the new technologies to make it easier for people to make payments in a manner that satisfies their individual needs and possibly time constraints. One such example would be the use of digital wallets. As stated by Margaret Weichert,[7]

> Adoption statistics suggest that the key to digital wallet success is how well the digital wallet experience improves on the status quo end-to-end shopping and buying experience. PayPal and Amazon built strong customer usage by dramatically simplifying commerce and payment, removing the need to enter payment, shipping and other data repeatedly. By contrast, some mobile wallets designed for POS checkout do not materially improve the customer POS experience, but simply replace a card swipe with a mobile tap.

It may be too early to predict who the winners will be in the FinTech revolution. But we can be relatively sure that the leaders will have new business models that provide consumers with 24 hours a day service and relatively safe from a risk perspective.

HEALTHCARE INNOVATION

Perhaps the most important innovations that will occur this decade, or innovations that people hope will occur, will be in healthcare. The healthcare industry has been criticized for possible misdiagnoses, the usage of unnecessary or improper healthcare treatments, high prices for drugs, and high administrative costs. Bringing engineering and technology into healthcare and medicine should allow us to increase the quality and speed of healthcare services, and hopefully make them more affordable.

Healthcare innovations are significantly broader and more complex than just the introduction of new drugs. As stated by Omachonu and Einspruch:[8]

> Healthcare innovations concern "the introduction of a new concept, idea, service, process, or product to improve treatment, diagnosis, education, outreach, prevention and research with the long-term goals of improving quality, safety, outcomes, efficiency and costs."

The technical side of healthcare innovation will include handheld diagnostic machines with superior sensing capabilities where diagnostics may be done in your home. There will also be 3D bioprinters that can analyze diseases by making it appear that the examination is being performed from within the body.

---

7. Weichert, M. (2017 Spring). The future of payments: How FinTech players are accelerating customer-driven innovation in financial services. *Journal of Payments Strategy & Systems* 11 (1), 29–30.

8. Omachonu, V. K. and Einspruch, N. G. (2010). Innovation in healthcare delivery systems: A conceptual framework. *Innovation Journal*. 15, 2.

There are several articles published on the need for innovation in home healthcare including telemedicine applications. Kyle Schruder believes that:[9]

> By all measures, the home is the future of healthcare. Not only will more people receive care in their homes, but many medical procedures that have historically been carried out in institutional settings will be administered in patients' living rooms. This shift is being accelerated by improvements to automation and artificial intelligence (AI) such as chatbots, enabling the notion of "care anywhere."
>
> The growing appetite for home care is a response to three main drivers: increasing access problems (wait times), growing patient and family expectations (choice, convenience, quality) and society's inability (or unwillingness) to continue to pay for the costs of delivering healthcare in formal institutions, which are being outstripped by demand.

Healthcare innovations, including diagnostics, will require "big data," which is extensive amounts of healthcare information. Creating these databases will require support from vast resources throughout the healthcare community. As stated by Raghupathi, W. and Raghupathi, V.:[10]

> These databases exist of structured and unstructured data. Structured data include instrument readings, health and medical records. Unstructured data concern handwritten notes, hospital admission and discharge records, paper prescriptions and medical imaging documents.

There are several challenges associated with creating and using healthcare databases. Three of the challenges include:

- Complexities in the design of the database, how the data will be analyzed, and how it will be integrated with decision-making criteria
- Ethical and legal challenges associated with confidentiality of the information, informed consent, data sharing and privacy regulations
- Organizational challenges as to who will build the data bases, manage them, and how they will be used for healthcare decision making

Effective healthcare database management innovation based upon information and communicational technologies will lead to intelligent decision support systems for healthcare professionals. Most of the healthcare facilities have neither the time nor the available resources to construct and maintain these large databases. The result will be public–private partnerships (PPPs) that share resources, ideas, expertise, and costs for the beneficial mission of both public- and private-sector organizations.

Managing these innovation projects in healthcare facilities are expected to create initially an environment of chaos and instability. Traditional forms of project management that healthcare firms had used in the past may not work. New skills such as design thinking will be necessary accompanied by new forms of executive leadership and governance. As stated by Koomans and Hilders:[11]

> As design thinking continues to evolve in its application for value creation, organizational change, and culture setting, the quest for value in healthcare has just begun; value-based healthcare as the foundation for patient-focused and outcome-driven value creation. Unfortunately, this process needs acceleration. We

---

9. Schruder, K. (2019 Fall). The next frontier in healthcare innovation. *Rotman Management*, 74.

10. Raghupathi, W. and Raghupathi, V. (2014). Big data analytics in healthcare: Promise and potential. *Health Information Science and System* 2, 3.

11. Koomans, M. and Hilders, C. (2016 October). Design-driven leadership for value innovation in healthcare. *Design Management Journal* 11 (1), 43.

claim that it is necessary to adopt and learn from design thinking practices to identify meaning, purposeful thinking, and patient-oriented innovation. We need to use design to structure culture and organizations to continue the healthcare value journey. Effective leadership in these uncharted territories is necessary. Comparing design capabilities and leadership capabilities presents us with a whole new viewpoint: interdisciplinary leadership design, as a basis for the formulation of options to enhance value creation and the outcome-based management of change and innovation. Lessons can also be learned for the needed evolution of design leadership in healthcare.

BRAND INNOVATION

One of the most difficult types of innovation projects to manage are those that must support brand management activities. A brand could be the company, a product or family of products, specific services, or people. Successful brands may take years to develop, and continuous innovation is necessary to maintain brand awareness, credibility, and consumer loyalty. Companies with strong brand awareness include Apple, Google, Disney, Microsoft, Coca-Cola, Facebook, and Lego.

Brand management practices are heavily oriented around marketing activities that focus on the target markets and how the product or family of products look, are priced out and are packaged. Brand management must also focus on the intangible properties of the brand and the perceived value to the customers. An intangible property might be the value your customers place on your products such that they are willing to pay more than the cost of a generic brand that may function the same.

Almost all brand innovations involve governance by the brand manager whose responsibility is to oversee the relationships that the consumers have with the brand thus increasing the value of the brand over time. Innovations should allow for the awareness and pricing of the brand to grow as well as maintaining or improving consumer brand loyalty. However, the cost and associated risks of maintaining and expanding the brand must be evaluated.

Unlike other forms of innovation where project teams have the freedom to explore multiple options and ideas and go off on tangents, brand innovation may have restrictions established by brand management. Brand management is responsible for not only managing and promoting the brand, but also deciding what new products or innovations could fall under the brand umbrella. This could generate changes in the firm's business model. Brand innovation is a marriage between the brand's core values, the target market, and management's vision. The difference between the long-term success and failure of a brand rests with brand innovation.

SUSTAINABLE INNOVATION

Companies today maintain a self-regulated strategy called corporate social responsibility (CSR) that is integrated into the firm's business model and identifies the ethically oriented activities the firm will undertake for the benefit of consumers, society, ecology, and government regulations. Included in the description of a firm's CSR is usually the term "sustainability" which may be defined as improving human life without impacting the capacity of the supporting ecosystems. This leads us to the term "sustainable innovation" which is the creation of products and services that support sustainability and CSR. The outcomes of sustainable innovation must support the economy environment and society. However, before a firm invests heavily in sustainable innovation activities, it must understand, possible tradeoffs between short-term profitability, pressure from investors for a reasonable ROI, and social and environmental goals. Companies believe that, by creating a social value proposition that supports sustainability efforts, they will gain consumer loyalty and trust.

Sustainable innovation has traditionally been used in reference to business innovation sustainability which is the continuous development of new products and services to increase the firm's financial objectives such as market share, revenue, profitability, and shareholder value. However, sustainable innovation can also be aligned with social innovation and environmentally friendly innovation activities that are part of business innovation sustainability.

Social innovation involves more than just improving the quality of life and human well-being. The social activities that the firm can consider as part of CSR include philanthropy, volunteer work, the way it markets and sells its products and services, and the products it creates using natural or renewable resources that do not impact the environment.

Environmentally friendly sustainability includes the consumption of certain natural and renewable resources such as water, energy, and other materials. Environmental innovation activities might force us to consider the impact that our innovation and commercialization decisions can have on global warming, depletion of the ozone layer, land use, and human health considerations resulting from the use of toxic pollutants.

HUMANITARIAN/SOCIAL INNOVATION

Humanitarian or social innovations are most frequently a subset of public-sector innovations but can occur in the private sector as well based on a firm's commitment to its social responsibility program. There are also organizations that are committed to humanitarian concerns such as GAHI, the Global Alliance for Humanitarian Innovation.

The innovations created by these organizations are driven by humanitarian needs, usually involving health and safety concerns, and are designed to save lives and reduce human suffering of vulnerable people. Innovation projects can involve disaster sanitation, saving children and refugees, disease control and reduction, emergency relief possibly from weather concerns, sanitized water, medicines, electricity generation, and refrigeration.

Humanitarian innovations depend heavily on private donors and usually have spokespeople who are well-known actors, actresses, and/or professional athletes. The choice of spokesperson is based on the target audience for the humanitarian innovation, and possibly the geographical area where the spokesperson may be well known and has proven ability to promote donations.

As an example of a humanitarian need, many developing countries suffer from severe acute malnutrition, which is a life-threatening condition that requires urgent treatment. Until recently, severely malnourished children had to receive medical care and a therapeutic diet in a hospital setting. With the advent of ready-to-use therapeutic food (RUTF), large numbers of children who are severely malnourished can now be treated successfully in their communities, which has the potential to transform the lives of millions of malnourished children.

UNICEF Kid Power is a philanthropic initiative that began in 2014 as a division of the US Fund for UNICEF to help solve this humanitarian need using the RUTF innovation. During the launch, UNICEF Kid Power was sponsored by the George Harrison Fund for UNICEF and backed by mayors from New York, Boston, and Dallas, and supported by local sports teams and players, including the Boston Celtics, Boston Bruins, Brooklyn Nets, and Dallas Mavericks. Sports teams and players help encourage kids to stay active by cheering them on with classroom visits, recognizing the young philanthropists at home games and more. Some athletes that have acted as spokespersons include:

- Alex Morgan (soccer)
- Tyson Chandler (men's professional basketball)
- Maya Moore (women's professional basketball)
- Aly Raisman (gymnastics)
- Dartanyon Crockett (judo)
- Meryl Davis (ice dancing)
- David Ortiz (baseball)

SOCIAL INNOVATION IN ACTION: HITACHI

Background

Hitachi, Ltd., headquartered in Tokyo, Japan, delivers innovations that answer society's challenges, combining its operational technology, information technology, and products/systems. The company's consolidated revenues for fiscal 2017 (ended March 31, 2018) totaled 9,368.6 billion yen ($88.4 billion). The Hitachi Group is an innovation partner for the Internet of Things (IoT) era, and it has approximately 307,000 employees worldwide. Through collaborative creation with customers, Hitachi is deploying social innovation business using digital technologies in a broad range of sectors, including power/energy, industry/distribution/water, urban development, and finance/social infrastructure/health care.

Lumada

Lumada is Hitachi's advanced digital solutions, services, and technologies for turning data into insights to drive digital innovation.

Co-Creation

Hitachi helps customers with everything from discovering latent problems to devising new strategies and methodologies. Hitachi has a complete palette of services to facilitate efficient co-creation with customers.

Domain Expertise

Hitachi has a rich portfolio of customer cases that demonstrate the company's swift delivery of reliable digital solutions to customer's management issues.

Platform Products and Technologies

Lumada consists of a core of platform services, architecture, and technologies that enable the quick development and implementation of advanced digital solutions. Lumada is composed of six main layers that form the architecture of the Lumada IoT platform: edge, core, data management, analytics, studio, and foundry. Together they serve as a software platform that is intelligent, composable, secure, and flexible.

Integrating proven commercial technologies from across Hitachi's portfolio, Lumada is a comprehensive, enterprise-grade IoT core platform with an open and adaptable architecture that simplifies IoT solution creation and customization. It incorporates expansive expertise in operational technology (OT) and information technology (IT), blending powerful and proven data orchestration, streaming analytics, content intelligence, simulation models, and other Hitachi software technologies. Lumada accelerates synthesizing of actionable insights, delivering faster time to value, and supporting better decisions that lead to real-world outcomes, like increased productivity and safety, streamlined processes, reduced operational costs and carbon footprint, and improved quality of life. The platform will serve as the core foundation on which all of Hitachi's IoT solutions are built and will enable the creation of IoT business ecosystems.

Case Study: Training at Daikin's Shiga Plant

The Problem

Daikin developed Japan's first packaged air conditioner in 1951. The company now operates in more than 150 countries. The skills of plant workers underpin its high quality. To pass on skills, the company launched Daikin Group Succession Committee and its meister program in 2001. Other initiatives have included creating skill maps and securing more experts.

Despite these efforts, the increasing need for speed in training became even more important as the number of overseas production plants surged. One particular necessity was to train workers in brazing. This accounts for around 30 percent of air conditioner production processes, making it a strategic skill requirement for an air conditioner manufacturer.

Tooru Inazuka, senior associate officer, deputy general manager of the Technology and Innovation Center, says, "Around 2,000 workers companywide are involved in brazing. But we had only a few workers who are named experts or meisters, and they provide the training. It was really hard to pass on these skills because know-how of brazing is transferred in person."

Mr. Inazuka says, "We previously produced training manuals for brazing. But it's hard for workers to acquire brazing skills from such documentation. Thus, expert workers ultimately had to visit workplaces around the world to teach one worker at a time."

Brazing entails applying a gas torch to an alloy (wire feeding) with a lower melting point than copper pipes (work piece). The wire feeding bonds with the base material without melting it. A worker applies the wire feeding with one hand to the work piece, applying torch heat with the other hand. Here, it is important to maintain consistent joint and wire feeding temperatures. Workers must therefore move both hands simultaneously to carefully position the torch and wire feeding. While these actions are instinctive for expert workers, it is very hard to convey skills that can only come from experience.

Air conditioners have become more compact and sophisticated in recent years. The piping inside this equipment has thus become more complex, requiring more precise brazing. Mr. Inazuka says, "We had to standardize brazing expertise and deploy a framework so that workers could quickly master the process."

The Solution

Daikin decided to overcome these challenges by partnering and co-creating with Hitachi. Hitachi had integrated operational technology and information technology (OT and IT) amassed over the years through its IoT platform "Lumada." It was also already developing a production process efficiency initiative based on "3M" data of man-machine-materials data, that it combined with image analysis and sensor technology. Impressed, Daikin decided to co-create and draw on both companies' know-how. Although machines will continue to evolve, some tasks will always need a worker's expert touch. This is the reason that Daikin decided to transfer manufacturing skills for maintaining its manufacturing expertise.

The solution would necessitate visualization. Visualizing the motions of expert workers enables trainees to master skills quickly, as they can compare their work with that of expert workers.

Hitachi's project members undertook brazing themselves to clarify issues for digitization and to evaluate the sensors needed to measure changes in movements, distances, and temperatures. In the course of this effort, Hitachi communicated extensively with Daikin employees and conducted more than 10 discussion sessions. It was through these processes that Hitachi analyzed brazing processes and combined digital perspectives with the analog perspectives of expert workers and trainees.

Hitachi drew on knowledge amassed through these processes to determine 18 elements of brazing skills. It collected data from around 50 people, including expert workers, trainees, and overseas workers. After extensive repetition and verification over just under a year, Hitachi completed the Brazing Training Support System in October 2017. The system was deployed at a training facility at Daikin's Shiga Plant for setting up advanced production models.

The system collects time-series data to digitally capture expert hand motions, angular speeds of torches, supply angles, wire feeding distances, and workpiece temperature differences. Huge volumes of data go to Lumada for evaluations and analysis. Visualizing the motions of experts enable trainees to compare their own motions with that of experts to quickly master skills.

Results

The visualization of expert worker's motions made passing down skills easier. Mr. Inazuka says, "Once, there was time when even expert workers were unable to see their motions. That is no longer the case." He notes that multidirectional visualization has made it possible to standardize basic motions. He adds, "It is easier for trainees to learn because they can see clearly how their motions differ from those of experts. And by deploying this system overseas we no longer have to send expert workers abroad to teach trainees one by one."

The new setup has also overcome the language barrier as it uses images and numeral values. Previously, training took a lot of time when instructors visited overseas plants because they could not teach directly in local languages.

With this system, Daikin looks to halve the time needed to ready a newly hired worker for work tasks. Daikin values globally consistent levels of quality, and when new plants open, the system will shorten the time needed to train workers.

Daikin plans to gradually roll out the system at manufacturing sites in Japan and abroad. It also plans to use this system for training in other skills, enabling the company to sustainably enhance its human resources worldwide.

EDUCATIONAL INNOVATION _____

Universities are now being asked by both the public and private sectors to change the way that many courses are taught and include more information and student exercises on innovative thinking and ways to implement the innovative ideas. This is now a necessity because the nature of work in most companies has changed and includes a greater need for innovation. Innovation activities must be included in courses for undergraduates and graduate students as well as continuing education courses for mid-career professionals that believed that their careers were ensured. The COVID-19 pandemic has made many professionals feel insecure and handicapped by skills obsolescence due to technological innovations needed for the job and working from home. Part of the problem is that new technologies can and will result in organizational changes that remove people from their comfort zones.

The need for more innovative thinking that focuses on digitalization and different human skills has resulted from the growth on the internet of things (IoT), artificial intelligence practices, cloud computing, machine learning, and robotics. Students need to be taught the value of these new knowledge sources compared to traditional textbook learning. Simply putting computers and video projectors in a classroom is not the solution to teaching innovation practices. Educators must recognize that effective innovation learning goes beyond the confines of the four traditional classroom walls. Students must learn by "experiencing" the innovation process that industry requires.

Industry would like to see more university courses focus on an innovative work behavior (IWB) environment where students are exposed to the complete innovation process. This requires faculty members to give student the opportunity to participate in innovation projects, not just idea identification, but idea implementation as well. This will show the students the conceptual and practical value of the activities needed to potentially address unsolved problems and, from a behavioral perspective, learn from one another.

Not all university courses can develop a "creative classroom" and provide students with the exposure to an IWB environment. Sustainability or social innovation projects seem to be the preferred choice for the types of classroom innovation projects in many educational institutions. Some universities have created an organization or focal point within the universities that identifies local or national sustainability or social innovation projects and then provides guidance to faculty members and students for project implementation. This benefits the students as well as the community. An excellent example of this is in Chapter 12.

Courses in innovation practices may become part of a university's core competency requirements for all students. There will be a growing need for universities to attract faculty members knowledgeable in innovation practices and to educate the existing faculty in these practices.

MANUFACTURING INNOVATION

Not all innovative actions have to be difficult. Many simple actions can be taken that will greatly improve efficiency, productivity, and quality. Take for example, reducing Set-up Time. We are all aware that frequent set-up changes to machinery or processes are necessary in most manufacturing operations. In such instances the machine tool or die, the process, or the material being used must be shut down to accomplish the change. During the time that this shut down and changeover occurs there is no production taking place, or no product being produced. Therefore, such time is totally wasted time. By reducing the amount of this down time, both efficiency and productivity can be improved. However, accomplishing such a reduction involves changes to the current equipment and/or methods being used in the process.

Such changes may sometimes meet with resistance from several different sources such as the machine or process operator, Product Engineers or financial personal. We have all encountered the initial response to change which is; "We've always done it this way." That may have been satisfactory in the past. But there may be a better way now and for the future. Therefore, we must find innovative ways to overcome such resistance, and get the change implemented.

Now, some given facts are: People are naturally and inherently resistant to change. It upsets their routines or causes disruptions in their normal operations. However, there are several soundly proven methods that can be applied to overcome resistance to the innovative implementation of change that works in almost any area: People will accept change if it is their idea. There will be immediate acceptance, with no resistance. So, when change is required, talk to the people involved. Explain the change and the reasons why. Try to get their: "By-In." ahead of time. Then there will be no resistance to the change itself.

People will accept change if there is something in it for them. For example, a financial or job position improvement. If the change results in such circumstances. Be sure to explain such benefits when explaining the change.

People will accept change if there is benefit to them in their current position. Will the change make their job easier, cleaner, less physical, or similar improvement? Include these benefits when explaining the change.

Lastly, people will accept change if it is mandated or required by a higher authority, either from corporate offices or outside forces, such as governmental authorities. Then the change will have to be implemented. Here is where the most resistance to change will occur. In some cases, operators or set-up operators will sometimes even take actions to make sure that the change, once implemented, doesn't work.

Now, let's talk about machine set-up reduction. Set-up time begins from the last good piece to the first good piece of a part on any machine. It is pure down time, wasted nonproductive time, and all efforts must be exercised to eliminate as much of it as possible in all operations.

Back in 1988 Dr. Shigeo Shingo, working for Toyota, authored a book outlining a process for reducing machine and tool change over entitled; "Single Minute Exchange of Die", which won a Nobel Prize. "Single Minute of Exchange of Die" meant that all machine tool or die changes in any manufacturing operation should be able to be changed over from one part being produced to the new part to be made in less than one minute. Now, that may seem like a very short period. But just look at your wristwatch and see how long it takes for the second hand to go all the way around the dial. You probably couldn't hold your breath for that long.

Not only did Shingo propose such a feat, but he also explained how it could be accomplished. Some of his methods involve: Having tools or dies re-located from tool cribs, sometimes located far away from the machines they served, to a rack directly adjacent to the machines that used them, greatly reduced change over times. Modifying tools or dies making them easier to remove and re-install by using large clamps instead of bolts, studs, and nuts. If such fasteners are absolutely required, employing breakaway bolts that will fold over after loosening just one turn of the nut. Modifying tools or dies to facilitate quick accurate insertion employing dowel pins or adding insert tracks to eliminate any adjustments to the tool or die once it is inserted. Having duplicate tools or dies available that can be preset-up prior to the need to changeover the current set-up. Teaching machine operators to make their own set-ups. Most of these simple innovative changes can be accomplished for very little money and the modifications can usually be made in-house.

Shingo's books and methods are still actively being applied in manufacturing operations worldwide, now combined with the Just-In-Time manufacturing methods also established by Toyota.

A CASE STUDY

At an electronic device manufacturing factory in Singapore there was a bank of 20 winding machines winding gold wire thinner than a human hair around a ceramic core. There were many different codes being produced, each having a different number of turns or layers of wire that would designate the code number of the device and the function it served in the end product. At the end of each run of a particular code, the center section of the winding machine had to be removed by a set-up operator, taken to his bench, and the center section adjusted to accommodate the winding requirements of the next code to be manufactured. Then returned and reinstalled into the winding machine. Set-up times ranged from 12 to 15 minutes during which time the winding machine stood idle, and the operator just sat and waited for the center section of the machine to be returned and reinstalled.

After a review of the operation, the question was asked, "How much does a new center section for a winding machine cost?" The first reply was "A lot." Which was typical of the oriental mindset. Additional inquiries resulted in a price of approximately US$1,000 each, obtained from the US machine manufacturer. A request was made to purchase five new winding machine center sections for the additional cost of approximately $6,000 delivered. Once received, a master schedule system of tracking which codes were scheduled to be produced on each machine allowed the set-up operators to pre-set-up a duplicate center section for that winding machine before the run of that code was completed. Then the exchange of the center section of that particular machine could be made in less than one minute, and production of the new code begun. In addition, dowel pins were installed on the back of each winding machine center section to provide for immediate lock-in of the section upon reinstallation thereby eliminating any adjustments needed after the initial instillation. Both set-up times and production efficiency increased tremendously for a very minimal investment.

This is an example of simple innovative action taking place.

NONTECHNICAL INNOVATION IN ACTION

When discussing innovation, our first thoughts usually involve technical innovation such as with cell phones, computers, and other mobile devices. But there are other forms of innovation, some very simple and without technology, and the results can be outstanding.

As a young engineer I accepted a position working on a Finnish Aid project that encompassed the entire Kenyan Western Province. The project's objective was to provide the rural population in Western Kenya with clean water by dug or drilled wells. All of these wells were equipped with manually operated hand pumps. When I became involved in the project, there were over 1500 wells and pumps already installed throughout the province. My job designation was a hand pump engineer with a role to maintain and further develop these pumps, their durability, serviceability, and usage. As expected, the pumps were subject to breakage quite often since the pumps were utilized day and night.

The first innovation was to change the mechanical lever-operated pumps to a so-called direct-action lever with two different-sized polyethylene pipes, one inside the other, and both reaching to bottom of well. The outer pipe had a one-way valve at the end. When pulling the bottom-end-closed inner pipe up, with handle on top, it sucked up water into the outer tube thru the bottom valve. Then, pushing the inner

Material in this section provided by Seppo Halminen, vice president, the International Institute for Learning. ©2022 by Seppo Halminen. All rights reserved. Reproduced with permission.

pipe down, water rushed up between the pipes and out of the spout. The design and operation were simple enough, and the only breaking/malfunctioning part was the bottom valve. These pumps were lasting far longer than any other hand pumps in the market. But even with the new design, it was inevitable that the pumps would break now and then.

The project had two pump mechanic teams traveling around Kenya's most populous and large province. My predecessors had started training bicycle repairmen in each village with pumps, giving them the responsibility to find and fix broken pumps. Everyone seemed to believe that when the Finns left and the project was handed over the local repairmen, they would use the equipment for personal projects. Sure enough, after a while we started getting reports that pumps were not being repaired. Where were the repairmen–bicycle mechanics? Moved to cities, where there were more customers!

I needed to find a solution to the dilemma. It was obvious who would suffer the most if the pump was not working—the women. The women, who were responsible for bringing home the water, had to travel vast distances to fetch water from alluvial creeks and rivers. The result was often disease and sickness, making their husband and rest of their family very unhappy.

From a westerner's point of view, my next innovation was maybe not that brilliant. But from the local point of view, it was next to impossible to even envision what was about to happen. I told my Kenyan team, most of whom were opposed to my idea and were doubtful that it would work, to announce to the population that we needed 10 women to come to the first pump repair training program. Only two women came. Why? Their husbands did not let them attend.

Back in the 1980s, gender equality was not what it is nowadays. This was especially true in rural areas such as the one where I was located back then, where women were considered as property of their husbands. Thus, it is now easy to understand the feelings of insecurity among the men; they feared what might change.

Some rather brutal rumors started spreading about us foreigners as well. Today one might call the rumors "fake news."

Then came my small innovative idea. Let's call all the men of a geographical area to a meeting. We knew that the most important pastime of a typical African village man is to discuss pertinent matters and drink home-brewed beer with his colleagues. What usually happens when the water to the beer is not clean? An inconvenient diarrhea occurs, badly disturbing one's pastime! Since it was the task of the women to brew this beer, they often took the blame if the beer made their husbands sick. But think, we argued, if the water is clean then you won't get sick and you do not need to blame your woman. Look, your women can give you that! Ye-es, good, came the first hesitant response, but then it became unanimous.Eleven women, instead of invited ten, turned up in the following morning—one extra was sent by a man inspired by the palaver.

After we conducted the first training, we wanted to have some official recognition for the women we had trained. So, we printed certificates of "Certified Pump Repair Woman" to be handed to them by a section supervisor, a government employee. After two hours of waiting under a mango tree for a government employee, finally there appeared a young, uniformed man with his bicycle, the youngest in the administration and probably with no one to delegate further. He shoved the certificates to these women, not even glancing into their eyes, and then rushed away when he was done with the last one.

Fast forward to some six months later....

By this time, some 300 village women had been trained and received their already highly praised professional certifications. I then received a call. "This is the provincial governor" (from one of six provinces, each reporting directly and only to the country's president) announced the speaker. "I understand that you are training women to fix pumps." "Yes sir," I replied. "When and where is the next event of handing out the certificates?" I told him. "I want to be there to hand those certificates to those women; can I?" "Of course, sir, it will be a great honor," I responded. At this certificate handing ceremony there were more than 3000 spectators, including all governmental and provincial dignitaries. The governor hosted a lunch with 200 guests. The governor seated me opposite him. I felt honored, not because of my seat, but by having created something sustainable that probably helped a large number of people—women, men, and children alike. The aid project had had some remarkable results.

What I learned was that thinking out of the traditional or local box might yield more than one can imagine. Maybe thinking globally, mixing people intentionally from different cultures could inspire novel ideas and solutions to projects and products. And as this story has shown, innovation can occur without technology, with as little as one piece of paper depending on how we use it.

OTHER CATEGORIES OF INNOVATION

There are several other generic categories for innovation projects. Many of these definitions are like other forms of innovation but are looked at slightly differently by scholars because of minor differences and applications.

Value-added innovation involves refining and revising an existing product or service. It is often compared with incremental innovation. Value-added innovation typically requires minimal risk taking compared to other forms of innovation such as exploratory innovation, which often involves taking an appreciable risk. Value-added innovations in the automotive sector would include making improvements on existing cars by making them faster, more comfortable, and with better gas mileage.

Occasionally, a value-added innovation may require a completely new way of thinking and possibly taking new risks. In this example, the usage of an existing product was reworked and introduced into a new market. While an existing product is being changed and/or improved upon, characterizing it as a value-added innovation, outside-the-box thinking, research, and risk taking may still be required since it is being introduced into a new market.

Financial innovation, as discussed previously, is the act of creating new financial instruments as well as new financial technologies, institutions, and markets. There are three categories of innovation—institutional, product, and process. Institutional innovations relate to the creation of new types of financial firms such as specialist credit card firms, discount brokerage firms, and Internet banks. Product innovation relates to new products for investments and financing. Process innovations relate to new ways of doing financial business such as consumer lending. This also includes the growth in financial technologies such as online banking and telephone banking that focus on ease of payments.

Hidden innovation, invisible innovation, or *stealth innovation* refers to innovation that is done under the radar screen and not captured or reported by traditional indicators or metrics. The term generally refers to innovation that takes place outside the traditional R&D organization because of a lack of R&D funding. If a discovery is made, the project may then become a fully funded project so that the innovation research can continue.

All forms of innovation have risks. One of the important roles of innovation governance is determining when innovation has progressed enough to begin commercialization. In stealth innovation, formalized governance may not exist, and senior management may not be aware of the existence or status of the innovation activities. The person working on the innovation may be a technical expert who is in love with his/her project and seeks perfection, perhaps for personal gratification, before letting anyone know that the deliverable(s) of the project could be available for commercialization.

Service innovation includes new or improved ways of designing and producing services. This may include innovation in the client interaction channel and service delivery systems. The innovation may be based on technology, expertise, or a combination of both.

Most companies have limited resources and must decide the best way that the scarce resources should be allocated between the firm's products and services offerings. Although companies will still provide both products and services, emphasis is being placed upon service innovations. The service innovations can be either business-to-business service innovations (B2BSIs) or business-to-consumer service innovations (B2CSIs). Many companies have found that the B2CSI approach is best whereby the firm can satisfy the complex demands of its individual consumers by providing them with new benefits and unique value propositions. The belief is that this approach makes it easier for a firm to defend themselves against marketplace competition.

Eco-innovation is the development of products and processes that contribute to sustainable development, applying the commercial application of knowledge to elicit direct or indirect ecological improvements. This includes a range of related ideas, from environmentally friendly technological advances to socially acceptable innovative paths toward sustainability.

Companies will invest in eco-innovation if they believe it will give them a competitive advantage and social legitimacy concerning environmental resource management. There are several factors that encourage companies toward eco-innovation:

- Government regulations and subsidies for innovations
- Public pressure
- Business opportunities and a competitive advantage
- Improved image and reputation
- Having adequate technical knowledge and environmental problem-solving skills
- Location in the production chain

Some companies believe that eco-innovation is more important in the later stages of the production/ commercialization chain because they have more direct contact with the end-product consumers.

There are also factors that can impede eco-innovation:

- Believing that eco-innovation is an additional cost that could harm their business
- Lack of management support
- Believing that eco-innovation does not enhance managerial practices
- Believing that eco-innovation should be used solely to comply with laws
- Adopting a reactive rather than proactive strategy for eco-innovation

Open sustainability innovation is the use of open innovation in the development of sustainable products, services, and initiatives. This approach to marketing may prove to be advantageous as it is not point-of-sale based, but rather, offers consumers information they have previously never been exposed to.

Social innovations are new strategies, concepts, ideas, and organizations that aim to meet social needs resulting from working conditions, education, community development, and health. These ideas, which are related to public-sector innovations discussed above, are created with the goal of extending and strengthening civil society. Social innovation includes the social processes of innovation, such as open source methods and techniques, and also the innovations that have a social purpose, such as activism, online volunteering, microcredit, or distance learning.

Crisis-driven innovation is often regarded as a subset of social innovation depending on the cause of the crisis. It is needed when unexpected events occur that can threaten the firm's survival, the outcome of the project, or the health and well-being of your customers or the general population. Other than actions by your competitors, the unexpected events might include product tampering, product misuse, or global health issues such as with a pandemic. Crisis response must be done rapidly such as designing a new package to prevent product tampering or misuse.

The pandemic environment with COVID-19 created a global crisis. Companies had disruptions to their supply chain which resulted in a reduction in the workforce. Flextime was used in many companies to keep workers safe and allow employees to work from home.

Many companies responded with rapid innovation practices such as retailers manufacturing face masks, companies manufacturing sanitizers, companies manufacturing ventilators, government agencies creating two-person ventilators, and telemedicine.

The pandemic environment also led to innovations in education by using technology for distance learning activities. New techniques were developed on how teachers, students, and administrators interact with each other. Universities had been using videoconferencing software for some time, but all of this was new to teachers and students in grades K-12. Students must learn from home using self-study techniques and teachers must learn innovative ways of presenting material so that learning takes place.

Lessons learned and best practices from past crises have provided us with actions we must consider during crisis-driven innovations. Some actions include:

- Be prepared to respond quickly
- Be prepared to continuously rethink innovation strategies
- Aggressively involve both public- and private-sector stakeholders
- Use past and present data for decisions
- Make decisions based upon reliable data rather than assumptions
- Encourage stakeholders to interact and quickly develop solutions
- Use technology such as digital platforms for rapid communications
- If necessary, lock down the business, allow people to work from home, limit or eliminate travel, and cancel events
- Consider the need for immediate "innovative" changes in hygiene factors such as distancing between people and use of telemedicine
- Rapidly create and safely test medications if necessary
- As a precaution, continue the innovation process both during and after the crisis

Offensive innovation projects are designed to capture new markets or expand market share within existing markets. Offensive projects mandate the continuous development of new products and services using innovations.

Defensive innovation projects are designed to extend the life of existing products or services. This includes add-ons or enhancements geared toward keeping present customers or finding new customers for one's existing products or services. Defensive projects are usually easier to manage than offensive projects and have a higher probability of success.

Discontinuous innovation projects must change direction in midstream because of changing conditions; rules of the game have changed quickly.

Disruptive innovation causes some products to be removed from the market immediately and replaced with new products.

Followership innovation, unlike leadership innovation, requires a good understanding of the competition's skills and trying to produce it cheaper and at a higher quality without having to incur the competition's innovation costs.

Pulled (or inbound) innovation involves finding customer areas not met and finding solutions to their needs.

Pushed (or outbound) innovation involves finding profitable applications for newly invented technology.

Innovation classifications can be made in the way that innovation data is collected and interpreted (OECD 2005). In this regard, innovations are represented as related project activities that can be classified as:

- Product/service innovations
- Process innovations
- Organizational innovations
- Marketing innovations

Innovation can also be classified by application. Keeley (2013) defines 10 categories of innovation by application:

- Profit model (How do we make money?)
- Networks (Do we have collaboration or partnerships with others?)
- Structure (Does our organizational structure help us and attract talent?)
- Process (Do we have knowledge, skills, and patents to sustain our processes?)
- Product performance (Do we have superior offerings?)
- Product system (Do we have products that are connected or distinct?)
- Service (Arc customers happy with our service?)
- Channel (Do we have the right channels of distribution?)
- Brand (Do we have distinct brand identification?)
- Customer engagement (Are our products part of our customers' lives?)

There are many other classification systems for innovation. Saren (1984) suggested classifying innovation projects according to five types; departmental-stage models, activity-stage models, decision-stage models, conversation process models, and response models. Pich et al. (2002) characterize projects based on information available up front to the project team:

- *Instructionalist project.* The information needed for innovation is available.
- *Selectionist project.* Not enough information is available and there is an elevated level of uncertainty.
- *Learning project.* The project is susceptible to unforeseen events.

Shenhar and Dvir (2004, 2007) identify innovation project categories as novelty, technology, complexity, and pace using their "diamond of innovation." These were some of the first articles that bridged innovation and project management. Another way to classify innovations is according to a complexity factor. One such approach identified five different dimensions of complexity: structural, uncertainty, dynamics, pace, and sociopolitical (Geraldi et al. 2011).

If any form of standardization is to be established for innovation project managers, the starting point must be in the way that we classify innovation projects. The number of different types, and the way the types can overlap, makes it clear that innovation project management practices may be different based on the type of innovation project. Each type of innovation can have its own unique success criteria and unique metrics for tracking performance.

ROLE OF THE BOARD OF DIRECTORS ———————————————————

"Innovation is too important to leave solely in the hands of the management team without any Board oversight or guidance."

— Pearl Zhu, *Digitizing Boardroom:*
The Multifaceted Aspects of Digital Ready Boards

A critical question facing many companies involves the role of the board of directors when it comes to innovation considerations. In a recent *Harvard Business Review* article by Cheng and Groysberg (2018), the authors conducted a survey of 5,000 companies and found that innovation was not a top boardroom priority. While innovation was on the list, it was not considered as important as hiring the right talent, competitive and regulatory analysis, shareholder relations, and strategic and financial planning.

The role of innovation, as stated previously, is to create long-term shareholder value. Yet members of the board, and senior management, appear in many companies to be more occupied with short-term rather than long-term thinking and the accompanying results. Board members and executives seem more interested in ways to exploit the innovations created than in active innovation management practices.

While board members may remain distant from actual innovation practices, the same will not work for senior managers who are looking for sustainable, long-term innovations. Senior managers are the architects of the innovative corporate culture. They can be active participants, and function as innovation project sponsors, or provide their support by creating innovation centers[12] that maintain some degree of control over innovation ideas, track innovation project performance, and make briefings to senior management and the board of directors.

Part of the innovation challenges that companies must overcome is that not all executives have the same view or strategic objectives for seeking innovations. For some, the focus is on market share. For others, it is the revenue stream from new product introduction. There are also executives that are interested more so in obtaining patents and intellectual property rather than the financial impact from innovations.

Corporate innovation governance also plays a critical role in defining project success and the success/failure criteria. Due to the diversity in membership in the board of directors and corporate innovation governance, each person may see the project differently. IPMs may find it necessary to deal with multiple definitions of success on a project that are subject to change.

FINDING AN INNOVATION PROJECT SPONSOR ———————————————

Innovation projects rarely become fully funded projects without a project sponsor or champion. Without a sponsor, a promising idea could be scrapped. The greatest risk is with pure research and bootlegged innovation projects, where innovators cannot recognize the need for seeking out a sponsor even in the early stages of innovation.[13]

---

12. Innovation centers are functional units committed to innovation activities. Innovation centers will be discussed in Chapter 12.

13. The Iridium case study discussed in Chapter 13 illustrates the benefits of early identification of a sponsor on a bootlegged innovation project.

Innovators must play the unfamiliar role of a salesperson. This involves identifying the person to become the sponsor, selling them on the idea, and then following up periodically to keep the sponsor involved so that his/her influence in making this a fully funded project is not diminished.

The right sponsor is not merely the person who can write out a check or fund the project, but someone who can influence others to see the value of the project. If there is a choice of people to function as sponsor, preference usually goes to that person who can authorize more resources to be committed to the project. The sponsor should have some vested interest in the intellectual property that will be forthcoming and fully understand the scope of the project.

The natural tendency is to seek out a sponsor at the senior-most levels of management. While this seems like the best approach, it comes with risks. When you bypass middle levels of management, you risk turning them into enemies. Middle managers are the people you may need to work with daily for project staffing, and their support may be critical for success.

Selling the innovation concept requires focusing on the benefits and value that will be forthcoming, namely revenue, profits, or cost-reduction opportunities. The benefits and value must be linked to the long-term interests of both the company and the sponsoring organization.

IMPLICATIONS AND ISSUES FOR PROJECT MANAGERS AND INNOVATION PERSONNEL

Project managers who are asked to manage innovation projects must understand the different types of innovation and the fact that a different project management leadership style may have to be used for each type. Some of the critical issues and challenges that may be new for some project managers include an understanding of the following:

- Each type of innovation is different.
- Different forms of innovation can have competing strategic objectives.
- Individuals have their own internal strengths and weaknesses, and they may not be able to perform as expected in some types of innovation.
- They may need to use a different form of project management leadership when working with a co-creation team.
- External team members may provide better ideas and more out-of-the-box thinking than internal personnel.
- The goal for innovation is not just the creation of a deliverable, but a value-in-use product and/or service as defined by the customer.
- Success may be defined by the customer as value-in-use.

REFERENCES

Abernathy, W. and Clark, K. (1985). Innovation: Mapping the winds of creative destruction. *Research Policy* 14 (1), 3–22.

Abrahamson, S., Ryder, P. and Unterberg, B. (2013). *Crowdstorm: The Future of Innovation Ideas, and Problem Solving*. Hoboken, NJ: John Wiley and Sons.

Allal-Chérif, O. (2015). The way towards open innovation: Airbus multi-functional teams. *European Scientific Journal* (December), 129–139.

American Productivity and Quality Center (APQC). (1998). *Customer Value Management: Gaining Strategic Advantage.* Houston, TX: American Productivity and Quality Center.

Anthony, S. D., Johnson, M. W., Sinfield, J. V. and Altman, E. J. (2008). *Innovator's Guide to Growth: Putting Disruptive Innovation to Work.* Boston, MA: Harvard Business School Press.

Cheng, J. Y. and Groysberg, B. (2018). Innovation should be a top priority for boards. So why isn't it? Harvard Business Review, September 21.

Chesbrough, H. W. (2003). *Open Innovation: The New Imperative for Creating and Profiting from Technology.* Boston, MA: Harvard Business School Press.

Danneels, E. (2002). The dynamics of product innovation and firm competences. *Strategic Management Journal* 23 (12), 1095–1121.

Frankelius, P. (2009). Questioning two myths in innovation literature. *Journal of High Technology Management Research* 20 (1), 40–51.

Garcia, R. and Calantone, R. (2002). A critical look at technological innovation typology and innovativeness terminology: A literature review. *Journal of Product Innovation Management* 19 (2), 110–132.

Geraldi, J. G., Maylor, H. and Williams, T. (2011). Now, let's make it really complex (complicated): A systematic review of the complexities of projects. *International Journal of Operations and Production Management* 31 (9), 966–990.

Gomber, P., Kauffman, R. J., Parker, C., and Weber, B. W. (2018). On the FinTech revolution: Interpreting the forces of innovation, disruption and transformation in financial services. *Journal of Management Information Systems* 35 (1), 230.

Jansen, J. P., Van Den Bosch, F. A. and Volberda, H. W. (2006). Exploratory innovation, exploitative innovation, and performance: Effects of organizational antecedents and environmental moderators. *Management Science* 52 (11), 1661–1674.

Keeley, L. (2013). *Ten Types of Innovation.* Hoboken, NJ: John Wiley and Sons.

Marquis, D. (1969). The anatomy of successful innovations. *Innovation Newsletter* 1 (7), 29–37.

Maryville, S. (1992). Entrepreneurship in the business curriculum. *Journal of Education for Business* 68 (1), 27–31.

Organisation for Economic Cooperation and Development (OECD). (2005). *Oslo Manual: Guidelines for Collecting and Interpreting Innovation Data.* Paris: OECD and Eurostat.

Park, B.-J., Srivastava, M. K. and Gnyawali, D. R. (2014). Walking the tight rope of coopetition: Impact of competition and cooperation intensities and balance on firm innovation performance. *Industrial Marketing Management* 43 (2), 210–221.

Pich, M. T., Loch, C. H. and De Meyer, A. (2002). On uncertainty, ambiguity and complexity in project management. *Management Science* 48 (8), 1008–1023.

Rigby, D. K., Sutherland, J. and Noble, A. (2018). Agile at scale. *Harvard Business Review* 96 (3), 88–96.

Salge, T. O. and Vera, A. (2012). Benefiting from public sector innovation: The moderating role of customer and learning orientation. *Public Administration Review* 72 (4), 50–60.

Saren, M. A. (1984). A classification and review of models of the intra-firm innovation process. *R&D Management* 4 (1), 11–24.

Schumpeter, J. (1942). *Capitalism, Socialism, and Democracy.* New York: Harper and Bros.

Shenhar, A. J. and Dvir, D. (2004). *Project management evolution: Past history and future research directions.* PMI research conference proceedings, PMP, (2), July, London, England.

Shenhar, A. J. and Dvir, D. (2007). *Reinventing Project Management: The Diamond Approach to Successful Growth and Innovation.* Boston, MA: Harvard Business School Press.

Song, X. M. and Montoya-Weiss, M. M. (1998). Critical development activities for really new versus incremental products. *Journal of Product Innovation Management* 15, 124–135.

Wheelwright, S. C. and Clark, K. B. (1992). *Creating Project Plans to Focus Product Development.* Cambridge, MA: Harvard Business School Publishing.

Wirick, D. W. (2009). *Public-Sector Project Management: Meeting the Challenges and Achieving Results.* Hoboken, NJ: John Wiley & Sons.

3

Innovation and Strategic Planning

Learning Objectives for Project Managers and Innovation Personnel

To understand the different types of business strategies and how they impact innovation decision making

To understand the differences between project and product life-cycle phases

To understand the differences between innovation and R&D

To understand the importance of a close working relationship between project management, marketing, and consumers

INTRODUCTION

"Innovation basically involves making obsolete that which you did before."
— Jay Abraham, *The Sticking Point Solution: 9 Ways to Move Your Business from Stagnation to Stunning Growth in Tough Economic Times*

For years, innovation project management has been regarded as some type of mystique. Companies even went so far as to develop enterprise project management methodologies that did not include innovation or R&D. One of the reasons for this was the belief that, if you can develop a schedule and budget for an innovation project, you do not have innovation.

Innovation Project Management: Methods, Case Studies, and Tools for Managing Innovation Projects,
Second Edition. Harold Kerzner.
© 2023 John Wiley & Sons, Inc. Published 2023 by John Wiley & Sons, Inc.

ROLE OF THE INNOVATION PROJECT MANAGER IN STRATEGIC PLANNING

"As an innovator, you need to be aware of how traditions, habits and bias can act as barriers to accepting new ideas."

— Max McKeown, *The Innovation Book: How to Manage Ideas and Execution for Outstanding Results*

In traditional project management, which focuses heavily on operational projects, we start out each project with a well-defined business case outlining the project's objectives. Project managers expect that the team will have the correct core competencies and that the projects can be completed with the existing human and nonhuman resources of the firm. Project managers most likely were not involved in the strategy sessions that formulated these projects nor were they involved in project selection activities. Finally, it is expected that the project managers can execute these projects using the firm's one-size-fits-all methodology.

Executives have refused to allow project managers to participate in strategic planning activities, arguing that it's not their job and they do not have a need to know. Then, without giving careful thought as to who should be assigned, someone is arbitrarily chosen as the project manager. There are several types of project managers, just as there are types of projects, and each type of project manager has his or her own strengths and weaknesses. Then, if a project gets in trouble or even fails, postmortem analysis never blames the executives for contributing to the problem by their failure to match the individual project manager's skills against the project's needs.

Bringing project managers on board early does not mean that they are performing strategic planning, although their contributions and ability to answer questions about resources required, timing, risks, and pricing would be beneficial. They can also demonstrate their understanding behind the strategic intent of the project and ask questions to assist their decision-making efforts during project execution. Executives may then be able to better assess if they have the right innovation project manager assigned.

ROLE OF THE PORTFOLIO PMO

Very few people in the company seem to understand the process by which innovation projects were selected and prioritized. Some people believe it is just a guess or the whims of management. Today, all these beliefs are slowly going by the wayside, thanks to the establishment of a portfolio or strategic project management office (PMO). The strategic PMO is responsible for participating in the portfolio selection of projects, and this includes involvement in innovation-type projects as well as noninnovation projects. The strategic PMO is also responsible for developing an innovation strategy approach that is aligned with the firm's business strategy including alignment to short-term as well as long-term business objectives.

The PMO brings to the table a more structured process for the portfolio selection of projects. However, not all innovation projects require PMO involvement. Companies can be working on hundreds of innovation projects, but the portfolio PMO generally provides governance for those projects that are the most critical for long-term success. Typically, the portfolio PMO will have governance responsibility for only 10–20 strategic projects at one time.

The PMO may be able to support executives in selection of the right project manager for the job. The project manager may still be assigned to a functional area but report on a dotted line relationship to the PMO.

BUSINESS IMPACT ANALYSIS

There always exists the risk that a project will face a potential crisis once the innovation process begins thus requiring additional business analyses. The primary purpose of business impact analysis (BIA) is to determine the threats to the business whether the threats are operational or financial. In the past, BIA was performed in response to a crisis such as a natural disaster, act of terrorism, or consumers getting hurt using the firm's products. Today, the trend is for BIA to be a more proactive than reactive process and to develop contingency plans that can minimize the recovery time due to adverse events. Based upon the risks, BIA may be treated as an ongoing activity. Many of the recovery decisions made by innovation governance personnel will apply to current and future innovation activities.

Adverse events can also occur in the use of the firm's business model. The failure of a business model often appears as a staged disease. The company may look healthy on the outside but be quite sick internally. The earlier the sickness is detected, the greater the chances for business model recovery.

Reacting to adverse events is the choice of reducing costs or increasing revenue or a combination of both. The goal is to keep the business going by identifying the critical processes. BIA activities are generally performed by corporate governance, the IPM, the portfolio PMO, and possibly members of the board of directors, all working together. Innovation governance generally finds more options for lowering costs than increasing revenue. Corporate governance can tell IPMs to:

- Outsource components if feasible rather than to manufacture them internally
- Carefully analyzing all outsourcing contracts and partnership agreements before any commitments are made
- Design products and components that use the existing commercialization systems
- Use less costly and possibly lower-quality materials
- Accelerate the commercialization process while maintaining reasonable levels of risk

Innovation governance and IPMs will then work together performing detailed risk analyses to help protect the critical processes.

INNOVATION MATURITY MODELS

One of the ways to orient a company to better innovation practices is to use an innovation maturity model. Innovation maturity models are road maps or frameworks that indicate the steps a company should undertake for continuous improvements toward maturity and help an organization determine where they stand competitively from an innovation perspective. Most innovation maturity models focus on the existence and use of people, processes, and tools necessary to support a continuous innovation capability and the accompanying improvements.

Metrics can be established to show that improvements are being made. Metrics can measure improvements in quality, use of resources, project management, business process management, governance, alignment to core values, effectiveness of the corporate culture, use of knowledge management systems, change management, and marketing.

There are numerous maturity models that can be used based upon the discipline. Some of these include:

- Capability Maturity Model Integration (CMMI)
- Performance Management Maturity Model
- OPM3 (Organizational Project Management Maturity Model)
- P3M3 (Portfolio, Program, and Project Management Maturity Model)
- Quality Maturity Model
- Strategic Management Maturity Model
- Change Management Maturity Model
- ITIL Maturity Model
- Big Data Maturity Model

There are maturity models that focus entirely upon innovation. Examples include:

- Hype's High Involvement Innovation Maturity Model
- Planview's Innovation Management Maturity Model
- Credera's Growth Life-Cycle Model

Innovation maturity models focus heavily upon the creation of a culture that fosters free thinking, alignment to strategic goals and objectives, market orientation, and effective use of resources. Most models are generic, and the application is based upon the types of products offered and markets served. Each organization must build its own unique innovation capability rather than relying on someone else's approach that may not be in alignment with their products, services, and processes. The model should be built around the firm's core values.

Even with the use of an innovation maturity model, companies often struggle in determining which life-cycle phase they are in regarding maturity. Most models provide questions such as shown below to ease the pain:

- Does the company have an innovation strategy?
- Does the company have the correct resources for innovation to take place?
- Are the correct resources allocated to innovation activities?
- Does the company have a culture that supports innovation activities?
- Does the company monitor changes in the marketplace?
- Does the company react in a timely manner to the marketplace changes?

What appears to be lacking in the literature is the integration of project management into the innovation maturity models. The solution could be the development of an innovation project management maturity model that clearly identifies the processes and tools that project managers must use in each life-cycle phase of the innovation maturity models. Innovation projects do not always follow the same path as traditional projects because of the new skills needed and innovation project management maturity models should help.

Project management maturity models generally focus on creating high-performance project teams. What companies are now realizing is that the strategic focus should be on creating a high-performance organization (HPO) rather than just high-performance teams. Innovation maturity models serve this purpose. The rationalization is as follows: If we believe that we are managing our entire business by projects, then the organization rather than individual teams should be driven to high-performance outcomes. This will then lead to a potential sustainable competitive advantage.

HPOs can eliminate barriers that may hinder the achievement of strategic goals by responding and adjusting quickly to environmental changes. High levels of mutual trust and clear and open communications exist allowing for cross-functional collaboration and the flattening of organizational hierarchies.

HPOs have cultures that focus on knowledge, collaboration, shared visions, and the right worker skill sets. Workers are empowered, asked for their opinions, and willingly accept responsibility and accountability. They are provided with the necessary information to meet customer and stakeholder needs to ensure business success.

TYPES OF STRATEGIES

> *"The main benefit of innovation for your organization is not competitive advantage. It is survival."*
> — Paul Sloane, *The Leader's Guide to Lateral Thinking Skills: Unlocking the Creativity and Innovation in You and Your Team*

Today, there is no haven from which a company can safely protect its market share. This holds true for all companies. Companies are using innovation practices to remove not just small niches, but large chunks of successful businesses from the competition. The more successful the business, the greater the threat from competitors. Companies that survived in the past by doing things "The Same Old Way" are doomed to failure. Unless a company can continuously innovate, they risk seeing their business shrivel and possibly disappear. The solution is to develop continuously updated strategies that include innovation activities.

A strategy is the company's plan for a sustained competitive advantage. It is based on assumptions about the future. The future of a company is heavily dependent on the innovation strategy they select. The innovation strategy then dictates the type of innovation that should be used. Typical innovation strategies include:

- *Co-creation strategy*: Working with one or more customers, stakeholders, and/or partners to design a product that meets all their needs.
- *Brand value strategy*: Adding features or functionality, possibly using incremental innovation, to keep meeting customers' present and future expectations.
- *Alliance strategy*: The formulation of strategic partnerships or joint ventures to meet competitive pressure.
- *Platform strategy*: Creating a set of products that share a common technology and allow users to customize the platform for their use.
- *Time-to-market strategy*: Reducing the cycle time to get to the market ahead of the competitors.
- *Technology usage strategy*: Using existing or new technology to perform better than the competition. With new technology, this could lead to a disruptive innovation strategy.
- *Lean manufacturing strategy*: This could be a form of incremental innovation attempting to lower the manufacturing costs or reduce waste.

One of the reasons for early involvement of PMs is so that they have a clear understanding of the real business strategy. Some strategies can have conflicting objectives and it is best for these to become visible early on. Without fully understanding the strategic intent, the project manager can make poor decisions that lead to ineffective risk management.

ROLE OF INNOVATION IN STRATEGIC PLANNING

"For the most part, the best opportunities now lie where your competitors have yet to establish themselves, not where they're already entrenched. Microsoft is struggling to adapt to that new reality."

— Paul G. Allen, *Idea Man: A Memoir by the Cofounder of Microsoft*

Strategic planning and innovation have a common bond in that both deal with the future profits and growth of the organization. Without a continuous stream of new products, the company's strategic planning options may be limited. Today, advances in technology, growing competitive pressures, and the necessity to compress time, cost, and performance gaps are forcing companies to develop novel and innovative products while the life cycle of existing products appears to be decreasing at an alarming rate. Yet, at the same time, executives may keep research groups in a vacuum and fail to take advantage of the potential profit contribution that can result from effective innovation project management. The PMO appears to be making it easier to integrate innovation into the ongoing business while at the same time provide valuable information during the portfolio management of projects.

Previously, we stated that there are three primary reasons why corporations conduct innovation activities:

1. To produce new products or services for sustainable profitable growth
2. To produce profitable improvements to existing products and services for long-term growth
3. To produce scientific knowledge that can improve processes and assist in identifying new opportunities or in "fighting fires"

Each of these can require a different form of project management if a firm uses a flexible project management methodology, but they all require innovation project management of some sort.

Successful innovation projects are targeted toward the accomplishment of specific strategic objectives but targeting requires a knowledge management system where information is shared. Unfortunately, this is the weakest link in most companies. Innovation information systems must include assessments of customer and market needs, product and service pricing information, and other data to support project selection. The PMO may provide valuable assistance, but other groups, such as marketing, must also be involved.

Assessing customer and market needs involves opportunity-seeking and commercial intelligence functions. Most companies delegate these responsibilities to the marketing group, and this may result in a detrimental effort because marketing groups appear to be overwhelmed with today's products and near-term profitability. They simply may not have the time or resources to adequately analyze other innovation activities that have long-term implications. Also, marketing groups may not have technically trained personnel who can communicate effectively with the innovation groups of the customers and suppliers. Another problem is that marketing may have a "wish list" of projects they would like to see accomplished but resource limitations can exist. The PMO often has the responsibility to perform capacity planning activities, thus providing valuable information on how much additional work can be undertaken without overburdening the existing labor force.

The success and possible direction of a corporate strategic plan may be dependent solely on that point in time where marketing tests the new products or features in the marketplace. Quite often, senior management will attempt to shorten the innovation time to increase earnings at a faster rate. This could increase product liability risks that may be overlooked in the executives' haste to produce results due to the stockholder pressure. In times of trouble, executives cut innovation and R&D funding in the mistaken belief that cost reductions will occur. The long-term impact on the organization may prove unhealthy. Innovation project managers are often not provided with all the market research data during project initiation, and this sometimes causes the innovation project manager to make suboptimal decisions.

Budgeting for all types of projects, including innovation and R&D, must begin with a solid foundation based on effective strategic planning. Companies cannot afford to work on all the projects they would like. Developing detailed plans for innovation and R&D is very difficult. Only when there are well-defined and agreed-to innovation goals and objectives, which is the starting point for innovation planning, can project managers improve their chances of success. These projects, once approved, generate the need for an effective method of budgeting, feedback, and control to verify that the work is progressing according to the strategic direction. Unlike other traditional projects that appear more as operational, every innovation project can be viewed as part of the executives' strategic plan.

Innovation activities, regardless of where they are performed within the organizational structure of the firm, can be viewed as a strategic-planning system with an input of money and an output of products. Furthermore, as with most systems, a feedback mechanism must exist such that the flow of money can be diverted from less promising projects to those with the greater potential. This implies that the innovation system must be continuously monitored, perhaps more so than the other systems. Once again, this justifies the need for involvement by some type of PMO.

ROLE OF MARKETING IN STRATEGIC INNOVATION PLANNING _____

Marketing plays the dominant role in strategic innovation planning. Marketing understands the customers' needs and wants, is a good listener, and collects data from the lead users of the products and services. Marketing provides the critical factors to be considered during project selection, namely:

- The long-range company position in the industry
- Overtaking specific competitors
- Maintaining market share
- Having a lead or lag position technically
- Growth in certain market segments

Marketing also provides categories of customers because the innovation might be targeted to a specific customer audience, such as:

- Satisfied customers
- Unsatisfied (not happy with offerings)
- Wannabes (appeals but out of reach)

- Refusers (aware but cannot see relevance)
- Unexplored (unconsidered audience)

The role of marketing is more than just looking at the product-market element in strategic planning, namely the products offered and the markets served. Marketing's close contact with customers provides an insight into new features that customers believe will add value to the products. When marketing provides feature information to brainstorming teams, the time needed to come up with, and evaluate good ideas, is reduced.

Marketing can also enhance the company's competitiveness through marketing innovations in the way that products are designed, packaged, and promoted. Unfortunately, organizations do not consider these types of marketing innovations as important as product or technical innovations.

PRODUCT PORTFOLIO ANALYSIS

"The hybrid nature of innovation is a combination of something old with something new, with a mixed portfolio of incremental innovations and radical innovations."
— Pearl Zhu, *Digital Hybridity*

When a corporation develops its strategic plan for innovation, the plan must be aligned with the corporation's strategic business unit and portfolio of products or services. Innovation projects are selected to enhance the portfolio of products or services by either adding new products or continuous improvements to existing products. A corporation should have a balanced mix of products, and the projects selected should support each type of product or product line.

There are several ways by which a portfolio of products can be represented. The three most common methods are Boston Consulting Group (BCG) model, the General Electric (GE) model, and the product life-cycle model.[1] Each model brings with it advantages and disadvantages, but all three models can be used to assist in the selection of projects. Companies may use more than one model as part of strategic planning.

The first model is the BCG model and is shown in Figure 3-1.

In the BCG model, the product mix consists of stars, cash cows, dogs, and question marks as shown in Figure 3-1. For simplicity sake, we can classify each product as follows:

- *Stars*: These products represent the company's best opportunity for long-term growth and profitability. These stars are supported by innovation projects to enhance quality, and find other potential uses for the products, spin-offs, and continuous improvement efforts. The focus of the innovation projects includes increasing market share and finding new uses/customers for the products. Because of the heavy investment in innovation projects, stars are often cash-users rather than cash-generators because of their potential for long-term growth and profitability. However, most stars are generally low-risk investments in incremental innovation and most of the investment funds eventually get recovered.
- *Question marks*: These products, often called problem children, eventually become either stars or dogs. To convert a question mark into a star requires a very heavy investment in innovation

---

This section ("Product Portfolio Analysis") has been adapted from Rea and Kerzner (1997). *Strategic Planning: A Practical Guide*. New York: Van Nostrand Reinhold; chapters 1 and 3.

1. Most textbooks on strategic planning and strategic management cover these models in detail. The intent here is simply to show some of the models that are used to help select innovation projects.

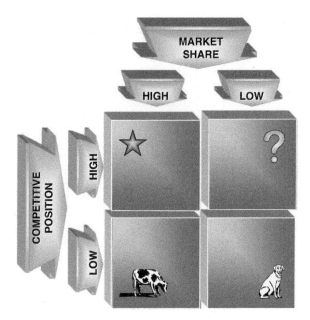

Figure 3–1. The BCG Model.

with the focus on creating product features that will enhance new market penetration and increase market share. The innovation may require a breakthrough in technology. Innovation investment in question mark products is risky because, if the product becomes a dog rather than a star, the funds invested in innovation will never be recovered.

- *Cash cows*: These products have a relatively high share of the market, but the growth opportunities are limited or declining. The focus of innovation is getting the cash cow to live as long as possible for milking purposes. Typical innovation projects would include quality improvements, upgrades, and enhancements.
- *Dogs*: These products are either liquidated or divested because they consume a great deal of effort with very limited return. For a dog to become a question mark or star, a significant technical breakthrough would be required. This could necessitate a heavy investment in basic or applied research along with relatively unknown time frames. Significant luck may be required to recover innovation costs related to dogs.

Some products generate cash, while others use cash. Obviously, in order to manage the company in the short term, cash cows are required. On the other hand, in both the short and long term, a company needs stars coming into the marketplace for future growth. It is doubtful that a company would want to invest very heavily in innovation projects for the development of new products in a declining mature market. In this example, a company may choose to emphasize cost-reduction projects associated with existing products.

Similar to the BCG model is the GE model shown Figure 3-2. The GE model has a grid of nine boxes, whereas the BCG model had only four boxes.

The selection of R&D projects for each box in the grid is based on the desired competitive position and market attractiveness. Items that are looked at in these areas are shown in Figures 3-3 and 3-4.

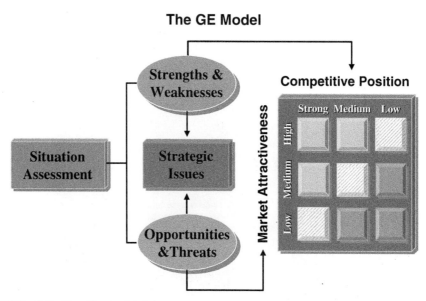

Figure 3–2. The GE Portfolio Classification Model.

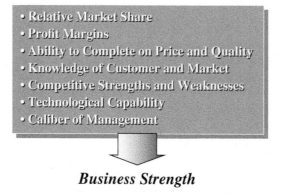

Figure3–3. CompetitivePosition.

Some companies select innovation projects and determine the size of the investment according to the product line life cycle. This is illustrated in Figure 3-5. A continuous product improvement program is necessary to remain ahead of the competition.

In Figure 3-5, the circles represent the size of the industry, and the pie-shaped wedge illustrates the product's market share. Using Figure 3-5, we can select innovation projects related to a product's life-cycle phase and competitiveness.

There are several types of product life-cycle portfolios, as shown in Figures 3-6–3-8. Figure 3-6 shows a growth life-cycle portfolio. Since several of the projects are approaching the maturity life-cycle phase, the company may prefer to spend significantly more money on new product or radical innovation than incremental innovation. Figure 3-7 shows a profit portfolio similar to the cash cows in the BCG model. Once again, significant investment must be made in new product development. Figure 3-8 shows

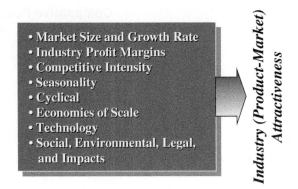

Figure 3–4. Market Attractiveness.

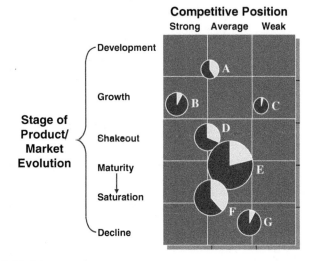

Figure 3–5. The Life-Cycle Model.

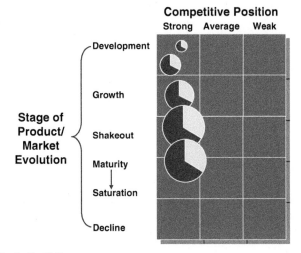

Figure 3–6. Growth Life-Cycle Portfolio.

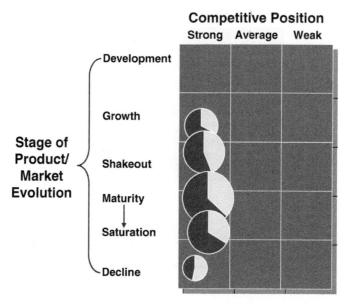

Figure 3–7.   Profit Life-Cycle Portfolio.

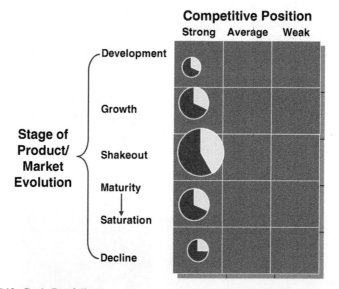

Figure 3–8.   Balanced Life-Cycle Portfolio.

a balanced portfolio. In this case, it may be best to invest heavily in incremental innovation to extend the life of the products.

Whenever market-share analysis is combined with market-growth analysis, as seen in the portfolio models, executives are provided with excellent tools to determine whether there exists an investment opportunity, a source of cash, or an item that should be removed from service, such as was shown with the BCG model for product portfolio analysis. The general terminology for these elements of the market-share/market-growth matrix or BCG model is cash cows, stars, dogs, and either question marks or problem children. In portfolio planning, each of these, as discussed previously, has a bearing on the direction of the innovation thrust, which is either to maintain market share, build market share, harvest, or simply withdraw:

- *Maintain market share.* This strategy represents a stable market and is ideal for stars or cash cows. In this case, the accompanying strategy should stress a defensive posture and applications engineering rather than diversification.
- *Build market share.* This strategy is ideal for selected stars and problem children. The strategy to support this would include methods for lowering production costs, improving quality, and applications engineering. This build-market-share strategy can also be used for dogs, provided that the company sees a technological breakthrough that will drastically increase market share and perhaps some degree of patent protection that will guarantee a profitable life cycle.
- *Harvest market share.* This strategy is used for a cash cow probably because the funds are needed for other activities. A reasonable strategy here would be to improve the quality of the product or lower the production cost.
- *Withdraw market share.* This strategy is used with dogs, where the troublesome product has a very low market share and is marginally profitable or operating at a loss. The innovation strategy, if employed at all, should be to look for spinoffs, specialized applications if profitable, or minimal defensive innovation to support future activities that may need this technology as a base.

Another issue is how to balance the investment in innovations across the major portions of the business, such as the need to:

- Improve internal efficiencies such as processes and business models.
- Generate cash flow to support operations.
- Create products for future cash flows.
- Satisfy the needs for client-specific innovations.

This is shown in Figure 3-9. Innovation investments may be needed in each of the four quadrants to make sure that the innovation portfolio is balanced. This approach can also be used to determine the financial investment for each quadrant. In each quadrant there can be a different type of innovation and different strategic objectives. The product portfolio analysis models can then be used in each quadrant.

Organizations that undertake many projects have found it beneficial to develop a categorization system such as shown in Figure 3-9. The benefits of categorization include:

- Easier prioritization of projects
- Ability to rebalance the projects in each category
- Identification of core competencies needed in each category which makes it easier for resources allocation

The four quadrants in Figure 3-9 are generic quadrants for types of innovation projects. Within each of these quadrants, the projects can be further subdivided into traditional and/or strategic projects monitored and supported by different types of PMOs.

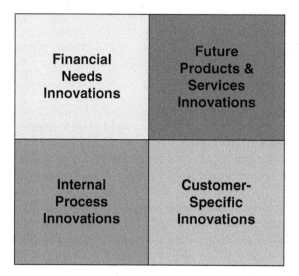

Figure 3–9. Categories of Innovations.

IDENTIFYING CORE COMPETENCIES USING SWOT ANALYSIS

"With age brings wisdom, with youth brings innovation. Combine the two and they are unstoppable."

— Ocian Hamel-Smith

The purpose of innovation is to improve a firm's long-term competitiveness. To encourage this to happen, organizations examine their strengths, weaknesses, opportunities, and threats, otherwise known as a SWOT analysis. This is a straightforward and effective tool that can be used to identify an organization's ability to match its core competencies against strategic opportunities. Strengths and weaknesses, which include internal factors such as marketing, finance, human resources, leadership, facilities, equipment, and so on, tell a firm about its core competencies. Opportunities and threats refer to external factors such as social, technical, economic, political, and legal trends and issues. The use of SWOT analysis was shown in Figure 3-2.

The fundamental goal of a SWOT analysis is to assess the fit between the organization and its environment. It allows the organization to examine the gap between where the enterprise is today and where it needs to be. A SWOT analysis formulates the problems confronting an organization before moves are made to resolve these problems by introducing new products and services or changing the business model.

Assessing a firm's external threats and opportunities is referred to as *environmental scanning*. The goal of environmental scanning is to educate decision makers about external issues that influence the firm's ability to fulfill its mission. The process should identify demographic, economic, political, and technical forces and trends that affect an organization's success or survival. Central to the process is the assessment of the organization's customers and competition. Are the preferences of current and potential customers stable or shifting? What are the firm's competitive advantages? What advantages do competitors possess? In other words, is the firm or its competitors best positioned to serve current and potential customers?

Examining the organization's internal strengths and weaknesses uncovers what the organization does particularly well or where it is vulnerable. In the jargon of strategy, the process should identify the organization's distinctive competencies.

Clearly the strategic issues that have the greatest appeal, and where most innovation activities are selected, are combinations of strengths and opportunities. In these instances, the organization is positioned well to take advantage of the opportunities and may focus on disruptive innovation. In contrast, issues that are combinations of weaknesses and threats are obviously disturbing since the organization will be in a poor position to defend itself against these threats. This would require defensive innovation activities.

Internal strengths and weaknesses for various groups include:

Marketing
- Competitive position
- Market share
- Sales-forecasting ability
- Price-value analysis
- Quality and ability of the sales force
- Budgets allocated for sales, promotions, advertising, and research
- Size and location of sales offices and warehouses
- Size and location of service facilities
- Turnaround time of service facilities
- Completeness of product lines
- Life-cycle phases of each product
- Degree of forward integration
- Brand loyalty
- Patent protection
- Turnover of key people

Manufacturing
- Efficiency of the operation
- Proximity to channels of distribution
- Proximity to other strategic corporate offices
- Raw material availability and cost
- Maintenance capability
- Downtime
- Vertical integration abilities
- Flexibility in operations should the need arise (i.e., changeover to other products)
- Inventory-control system
- Quality-assurance system
- Relationship with marketing and R&D
- Magnitude of the capital budgets
- Age of the equipment
- Turnover of personnel
- Relationship with unions
- Precision machinery availability
- Ability to perform tradeoffs and lower costs
- Learning-curve applications
- Subsystems integration
- Tight scheduling

Finance and Accounting
- Dividend policy
- Cash flow (present and future projections)
- Returns on assets
- Debt to equity ratio
- Corporate stock activity
- Corporate credit rating (equity and capital markets)
- Working capital requirements
- Quality of the information system
- Skills in feasibility studies/cost–benefits analyses
- Investment-management skills
- Consumer financing capability
- Size of customer base
- Turnover of customers
- Cyclical or noncyclical business

Human Resource Management
- Corporate image
- Turnover rate of key personnel
- Promotion opportunity (multiple career paths)
- Recruitment ability
- Relationship with unions
- Effectiveness of information systems
- Salary structure
- Opportunities for training/education
- Tuition reimbursement plan
- Health and benefit programs
- Relationship with government/regulatory agencies
- Strength of board of directors
- Quality of management at all levels
- Public relations policies
- Social consciousness

INNOVATION PROJECT MANAGEMENT COMPETENCY MODELS IN ACTION: ELI LILLY

Thirty years ago, companies prepared job descriptions for project managers to help clarify their roles and responsibilities. Unfortunately, the job descriptions were usually abbreviated and provided very little guidance on what educational skills were required that could lead to promotions or salary increases. Twenty years ago, we still emphasized the job descriptions, but it was now supported by coursework, which was often mandatory. By the turn of the century, companies began emphasizing core competency models, which clearly depicted the skill levels needed to be effective as a project manager. Training programs were instituted to support the core competency models. Unfortunately, establishing a core competency model and the accompanying training is no easy task especially for people involved in innovation and R&D.

Eli Lilly has perhaps one of the most comprehensive and effective competency models in industry today. The model was developed more than 15 years ago and remains today as one of the best competency models developed for innovation and R&D project management. The model encompasses many of the core competencies that will be discussed individually and in depth in later chapters.

Martin D. Hynes, III, formerly director, pharmaceutical projects management (PPM), was the key sponsor of the initiative to develop the competency model. Thomas J. Konechnik, formerly operations manager, pharmaceutical projects management, was responsible for the implementation and integration of the competency model with other processes within the PPM group. The basis for the competency model is described here.

Lilly Research Laboratories project management competencies are classified under three major areas: scientific/technical expertise, process skills, and leadership.

Scientific/Technical Expertise

- *Knows the business.* Brings an understanding of the drug development process and organizational realities to bear on decisions.
- *Initiates action.* Takes proactive steps to address needs or problems before the situation requires it.
- *Thinks critically.* Seeks facts, data, or expert opinion to guide a decision or course of action.
- *Manages risks.* Anticipates and allows for changes in priorities, schedules, and resources and changes due to scientific/technical issues.

Process Skills

- *Communicates clearly.* Listens well and provides information that is easily understood and useful to others.
- *Pays attention to details.* Maintains complete and detailed records of plans, meeting minutes, agreements.
- *Structures the process.* Constructs, adapts, or follows a logical process to ensure achievement of objectives and goals.

Leadership

- *Focuses on results.* Continually focuses own and others' attention on realistic milestones and deliverables.
- *Builds a team.* Creates an environment of cooperation and mutual accountability within and across functions to achieve common objectives.
- *Manages complexity.* Organizes, plans, and monitors multiple activities, people, and resources.
- *Makes tough decisions.* Demonstrates assurance in own abilities, judgments, and capabilities; assumes accountability for actions.
- *Builds strategic support.* Gets the support and level of effort needed from senior management and others to keep project on track.

We next examine each of these competencies in more detail.

Scientific/Technical Expertise

Knows the business. Brings an understanding of the drug development process and organizational realities to bear on decisions.

Project managers/associates who demonstrate this competency will:

- Recognize how other functions in Eli Lilly impact the success of a development effort.
- Use knowledge of what activities are taking place in the project as a whole to establish credibility.
- Know when team members in own and other functions will need additional support to complete an assignment/activity.
- Generate questions based on understanding of nonobvious interactions of different parts of the project.
- Focus attention on the issues and assumptions that have the greatest impact on the success of a particular project activity or task.
- Understand/recognize political issues/structures of the organization.
- Use understanding of competing functional and business priorities to reality test project plans, assumptions, time estimates, and commitments from the functions.
- Pinpoint consequences to the project of decisions and events in other parts of the organization.
- Recognize and respond to the different perspectives and operating realities of different parts of the organization.
- Consider the long-term implications (pro and con) of decisions.
- Understand the financial implications of different choices.

Project managers/associates who do not demonstrate this competency will:

- Rely on resource and time estimates from those responsible for an activity or task.
- Make decisions based on what ideally should happen.
- Build plans and timelines by rolling up individual timelines and so on.
- Perceive delays as conscious acts on the part of other parts of the organization.
- Assume that team members understand how their activities impact other parts of the project.
- Focus attention on providing accurate accounts of what has happened.
- Avoid changing plans until forced to do so.
- Wait for team members to ask for assistance.

Selected consequences for projects/business of not demonstrating this competency are:

- Project manager or associate may rely on senior management to resolve issues and obtain resources.
- Proposed project timelines may be significantly reworked to meet current guidelines.
- Attention may be focused on secondary issues rather than central business or technical issues.
- Current commitments, suppliers, and so on, may be continued regardless of reliability and value.
- Project deliverables may be compromised by changes in other parts of Lilly.
- Project plans may have adverse impact on other parts of the organization.

Initiates action. Takes proactive steps to address needs or problems before the situation requires it. Project managers/associates who demonstrate this competency will:

- Follow up immediately when unanticipated events occur.
- Push for immediate action to resolve issues and make choices.
- Frame decisions and options for project team, not simply facilitate discussions.
- Take on responsibility for dealing with issues for which no one else is taking responsibility.
- Formulate proposals and action plans when a need or gap is identified.
- Quickly surface and raise issues with project team and others.
- Let others know early on when issues have major implications for project.
- Take action to ensure that relevant players are included by others in critical processes or discussions.

Project managers/associates who do not demonstrate this competency will:

- Focus efforts on ensuring that all sides of issues are explored.
- Ask others to formulate initial responses or plans to issue or emerging events.
- Let functional areas resolve resource issues on their own.
- Raise difficult issues or potential problems after their impact is fully understood.
- Avoid interfering or intervening in areas outside own area of expertise.
- Assume team members and others will respond as soon as they can.
- Defer to more experienced team members on how to handle an issue.
- Selected consequences for projects/business of not demonstrating this competency are:
- Senior management may be surprised by project-related events.
- Project activities may be delayed due to "miscommunications" or to waiting for functions to respond.
- Effort and resources may be wasted or underutilized.
- Multiple approaches may be pursued in parallel.
- Difficult issues may be left unresolved.

Thinks critically. Seeks facts, data, or expert opinion to guide a decision or course of action.
Project managers/associates who demonstrate this competency will:

- Seek input from people with expertise or first-hand knowledge of issues and so on.
- Ask tough, incisive questions to clarify time estimates or to challenge assumptions and be able to understand the answers.
- Immerse self in project information to quickly gain a thorough understanding of a project's status and key issues.
- Focus attention on key assumptions and root causes when problems or issues arise.
- Quickly and succinctly summarize lengthy discussions.
- Gather data on past projects, and so on, to help determine best future options for a project.
- Push to get sufficient facts and data in order to make a sound judgment.
- Assimilate large volumes of information from many different sources.
- Use formal decision tools when appropriate to evaluate alternatives and identify risks and issues.

Project managers/associates who do not demonstrate this competency will:

- Accept traditional assumptions regarding resource requirements and time estimates.
- Rely on team members to provide information needed.

- Push for a new milestone without determining the reason previous milestone was missed.
- Summarize details of discussions and arguments without drawing conclusions.
- Limit inquiries to standard sources of information.
- Use procedures and tools that are readily available.
- Define role narrowly as facilitating and documenting team members' discussions.

Selected consequences for projects/business of not demonstrating this competency are:

- Commitments may be made to unrealistic or untested dates.
- High-risk approaches may be adopted without explicit acknowledgment.
- Projects may take longer to complete than necessary.
- New findings and results may be incorporated slowly only into current Lilly practices.
- Major problems may arise unexpectedly.
- Same issues may be revisited.
- Project plan may remain unchanged despite major shifts in resources, people, and priorities.

Manages risks. Anticipates and allows for changes in priorities, schedules, resources, and changes due to scientific/technical issues.
Project managers/associates who demonstrate this competency will:

- Double-check validity of key data and assumptions before making controversial or potentially risky decisions.
- Create a contingency plan when pursuing options that have clear risks associated with them.
- Maintain ongoing direct contact with "risky" or critical path activities to understand progress.
- Push team members to identify all the assumptions implicit in their estimates and commitments.
- Stay in regular contact with those whose decisions impact the project.
- Let management and others know early on the risks associated with a particular plan of action.
- Argue for level of resources and time estimates that allow for predictable "unexpected" events.
- Pinpoint major sources of scientific risks.

Project managers/associates who do not demonstrate this competency will:

- Remain optimistic regardless of progress.
- Agree to project timelines despite serious reservations.
- Value innovation and new ideas despite attendant risks.
- Accept less experienced team members in key areas.
- Give individuals freedom to explore different options.
- Accept estimates and assessments with minimal discussion.

Selected consequences for projects/business of not demonstrating this competency are:

- Projects may take longer to complete than necessary.
- Project may have difficulty responding to shifts in organizational priorities.
- Major delays could occur if proposed innovative approach proves inappropriate.
- Known problem areas may remain sources of difficulties.
- Project plans may be subject to dramatic revisions.

Process Skills

Communicates clearly. Listens well and provides information that is easily understood and useful to others.

Project managers/associates who demonstrate this competency will:

- Present technical and other complex issues in a concise, clear, and compelling manner.
- Target or position communication to address needs or level of understanding of recipient(s) (e.g., medical, senior management).
- Filter data to provide the most relevant information (e.g., does not go over all details but knows when and how to provide an overall view).
- Keep others informed in a timely manner about decision or issues that may impact them.
- Facilitate and encourage open communication among team members.
- Set up mechanisms for regular communications with team members in remote locations.
- Accurately capture key points of complex or extended discussions.
- Spend the time necessary to prepare presentations for management.
- Effectively communicate and represent technical arguments outside own area of expertise.

Project managers/associates who do not demonstrate this competency will:

- Provide all the available details.
- See multiple reminders or messages as inefficient.
- Expect team members to understand technical terms of each other's specialties.
- Reuse communication and briefing materials with different audiences.
- Limit communications to periodic updates.
- Invite to meetings only those who (are presumed to) need to be there or who have something to contribute.
- Rely on technical experts to provide briefings in specialized, technical areas.

Selected consequences for projects/business of not demonstrating this competency are:

- Individuals outside of the immediate team may have little understanding of the project.
- Other projects may be disrupted by "fire drills" or last-minute changes in plan.
- Key decisions and discussions may be inadequately documented.
- Management briefings may be experienced as ordeals by team and management.
- Resources/effort may be wasted or misapplied.

Pays attention to details. Maintains complete and detailed records of plans, meeting minutes, agreements.
Project managers/associates who demonstrate this competency will:

- Remind individuals of due dates and other requirements.
- Ensure that all relevant parties are informed of meetings and decisions.
- Prepare timely, accurate, and complete minutes of meetings.
- Continually update or adjust project documents to reflect decisions and changes.
- Check the validity of key assumptions in building the plan.
- Follow up to ensure that commitments are understood.

Project managers/associates who do not demonstrate this competency will:

- Assume that others are tracking the details.
- See formal reviews as intrusions and waste of time.
- Choose procedures that are least demanding in terms of tracking details.
- Only sporadically review and update or adjust project documents to reflect decisions and other changes.
- Limit project documentation to those formally required.
- Rely on meeting notes as adequate documentation of meetings.

Selected consequences for projects/business of not demonstrating this competency are:

- Coordination with other parts of the organization may be lacking.
- Documentation may be incomplete or difficult to use to review project issues.
- Disagreements may arise as to what was committed to.
- Project may be excessively dependent on the physical presence of manager or associate.

Structures the process. Constructs, adapts, or follows a logical process to ensure achievement of objectives and goals.

Project managers/associates who demonstrate this competency will:

- Choose milestones that the team can use for assessing progress.
- Structure meetings to ensure agenda items are covered.
- Identify sequence of steps needed to execute project management process.
- Maintain up-to-date documentation that maps expectations for individual team members.
- Use available planning tools to standardize procedures and structure activities.
- Create simple tools to help team members track, organize, and communicate information.
- Build a process that efficiently uses team members' time, while allowing them to participate in project decision; all team members should not attend all meetings.
- Review implications of discussion or decisions for the project plan as mechanism for summarizing and clarifying discussions.
- Keep discussions moving by noting disagreements rather than trying to resolve them there and then.
- Create and use a process to ensure priorities are established and project strategy is defined.

Project managers/associates who do not demonstrate this competency will:

- Trust that experienced team members know what they are doing.
- Treat complex sequences of activities as a whole.
- Share responsibility for running meetings, formulating agendas, and so on.
- Create plans and documents that are as complete and detailed as possible.
- Provide written documentation only when asked for.
- Allow team members to have their say.

Selected consequences for projects/business of not demonstrating this competency are:

- Projects may receive significantly different levels of attention.
- Project may lack a single direction or focus.

- Planning documents may be incomplete or out of date.
- Presentations and briefings may require large amounts of additional work.
- Meetings may be seen as unproductive.
- Key issues may be left unresolved.
- Other parts of the organization may be unclear about what is expected and when.

Leadership

Focuses on results. Continually focuses own and others' attention on realistic project milestones and deliverables.

Project managers/associates who demonstrate this competency will:

- Stress need to keep project-related activities moving forward.
- Continually focus on ultimate deliverables (e.g., product to market, affirm/disconfirm merits of compound, value of product/program to Lilly) (manager).
- Choose actions in terms of what needs to be accomplished rather than seeking optimal solutions or answers.
- Remind project team members of key project milestones and schedules.
- Keep key milestones visible to the team.
- Use fundamental objective of project as means of evaluating option driving decisions in a timely fashion.
- Push team members to make explicit and public commitments to deliverables.
- Terminate projects or low-value activities in timely fashion.

Project managers/associates who do not demonstrate this competency will:

- Assume that team members have a clear understanding of project deliverables and milestones.
- Approach tasks and issues only when they become absolutely critical.
- Downplay or overlook negative results or outcomes.
- Keep pushing to meet original objectives in spite of new data/major changes.
- Pursue activities unrelated to original project requirements.
- Trust that definite plans will be agreed to once team members are involved in the project.
- Allow unqualified individuals to remain on tasks.
- Make attendance at project planning meetings discretionary.

Selected consequences for projects/business of not demonstrating this competency are:

- Milestones may be missed without adequate explanation.
- Functional areas may be surprised at demand for key resources.
- Commitments may be made to unreasonable or unrealistic goals or schedules.
- Projects may take longer to complete than necessary.
- Objectives and priorities may differ significantly from one team member to another.

Builds a team. Creates an environment of cooperation and mutual accountability within and across functions to achieve common objectives.

Project managers/associates who demonstrate this competency will:

- Openly acknowledge different viewpoints and disagreements.
- Actively encourage all team members to participate regardless of their functional background or level in the organization.
- Devote time and resources explicitly to building a team identity and a set of shared objectives.
- Maintain objectivity; avoid personalizing issues and disagreements.
- Establish one-on-one relationship with team members.
- Encourage team members to contribute input in areas outside functional areas.
- Involve team members in the planning process from beginning to end.
- Recognize and tap into the experience and expertise that each team member possesses.
- Solicit input and involvement from different functions prior to their major involvement.
- Once a decision is made, insist that the team accept it until additional data become available.
- Push for explicit commitment from team members when resolving controversial issues.

Project managers/associates who do not demonstrate this competency will:

- State what can and cannot be done.
- Assume that mature professionals need little support or team recognition.
- Limit contacts with team members to formal meetings and discussions.
- Treat issues that impact a team member's performance as the responsibility of functional line management.
- Help others only when explicitly asked to do so.
- Be openly critical about other team members' contributions or attitudes.
- Revisit decisions when team members resurface issues.

Selected consequences for projects/business of not demonstrating this competency are:

- Team members may be unclear as to their responsibilities.
- Key individuals may move onto other projects.
- Obstacles and setbacks may undermine overall effort.
- Conflicts over priorities within project team may get escalated to senior management.
- Responsibility for project may get diffused.
- Team members may be reluctant to provide each other with support or accommodate special requests.

Manages complexity. Organizes, plans, and monitors multiple activities, people, and resources. Project managers/associates who demonstrate this competency will:

- Remain calm when under personal attack or extreme pressure.
- Monitor progress on frequent and consistent basis.
- Focus personal efforts on most critical tasks: apply 80–20 rule.
- Carefully document commitments and responsibilities.
- Define tasks and activities to all for monitoring and a sense of progress.
- Break activities and assignments into components that appear doable.
- Balance and optimize workloads among different groups and individuals.

- Quickly pull together special teams or use outside experts in order to address emergencies or unusual circumstances.
- Debrief to capture "best practices" and "lessons learned."

Project managers/associates who do not demonstrate this competency will:

- Limit the number of reviews to maximize time available to team members.
- Stay on top of all the details.
- Depend on team members to keep track of their own progress.
- Let others know how they feel about an issue or individual.
- Rely on the team to address issues.
- Assume individuals recognize and learn from their own mistakes.

Selected consequences for projects/business of not demonstrating this competency are:

- Projects may receive significantly different levels of attention.
- Projects may take on a life of their own with no clear direction or attainable outcome.
- Responsibility for decisions may be diffused among team members.
- Exact status of projects may be difficult to determine.
- Major issues can become unmanageable.
- Activities of different parts of the business may be uncoordinated.
- Conflicts may continually surface between project leadership and other parts of Lilly.

Makes tough decisions. Demonstrates assurance in own abilities, judgments, and capabilities; assumes accountability for actions.
Project managers/associates who demonstrate this competency will:

- Challenge the way things are done and make decisions about how things will get done.
- Force others to deal with the unpleasant realities of a situation.
- Push for reassessment of controversial decisions by management when new information/data become available.
- Bring issues with significant impact to the attention of others.
- Consciously use past experiences and historical data to persuade others.
- Confront individuals who are not meeting their commitments.
- Push line management to replace individuals who fail to meet expectations.
- Challenge continued investment in a project if data suggest it will not succeed.
- Pursue or adopt innovative procedures that offer significant potential benefits even where limited prior experience is available.

Project managers/associates who do not demonstrate this competency will:

- Defer to the ideas of more experienced team members.
- Give others the benefit of the doubt around missed commitments.
- Hold off on making decisions until the last possible moment.
- Pursue multiple options rather than halt work on alternative approaches.
- Wait for explicit support from others before raising difficult issues.

- Accept senior managers' decisions as "nonnegotiable."
- Rely on the team to make controversial decisions.
- Provide problematic performers with additional resources and time.

Selected consequences for projects/business of not demonstrating this competency are:

- Projects may take longer to complete than necessary.
- Failing projects may be allowed to linger.
- Decisions may be delegated upward.
- Morale of team may be undermined by nonperformance of certain team members.
- "Bad news" may not be communicated until the last minute.
- Key individuals may "bum out" in effort to play catch-up.

Builds strategic support. Gets the support and level of effort needed from senior management and others to keep projects on track.
Project managers/associates who demonstrate this competency will:

- Assume responsibility for championing the projects while demonstrating a balance between passion and objectivity.
- Tailor arguments and presentations to address key concerns of influential decision makers.
- Familiarize self with operational and business concerns of major functions within Lilly.
- Use network of contacts to determine best way to surface an issue or make a proposal.
- Push for active involvement of individuals with the experience and influence needed to make things happen.
- Pinpoint the distribution of influence in conflict situations.
- Presell controversial ideas or information.
- Select presenter to ensure appropriate message is sent.
- Ask senior management to help position issues with other senior managers.

Project managers/associates who do not demonstrate this competency will:

- Meet senior management and project sponsors only in formal settings.
- Propose major shifts in direction in group meetings.
- Make contact with key decision makers when faced with obstacles or problems.
- Limit number of face-to-face contacts with "global" partners.
- Treat individuals as equally important.
- Avoid the appearance of "politicking."
- Depend on other team members to communicate to senior managers in unfamiliar parts of Lilly.

Selected consequences for projects/business of not demonstrating this competency are:

- Viable projects may be killed without clear articulation of benefits.
- "Cultural differences" may limit success of global projects.
- Decisions may be made without the input of key individuals.
- Resistance to changes in project scope or direction may become entrenched before merits of proposals are understood.

- Key individuals/organizations may never buy in to a project's direction or scope.
- Minor conflicts may escalate and drag on.

MARKETING'S INVOLVEMENT WITH INNOVATION PROJECT MANAGERS

From previous sections in this chapter, it should be obvious that marketing often provides the greatest input in identifying the critical variables for innovation project selection. Marketing's involvement provides project managers information related to:

- Market attractiveness for each product/product line
- Relative market share (and trend)
- Sales growth rate (and trend)
- Current business strength
- Forecasted market-share trend
- Recommend investment strategy

For the selection of an innovation project designed to create new features or a totally new product, additional factors considered during project selection include marketing's policy toward first to market, follow the leader, applications engineering, and "me too." It should be evident that innovation project managers must have a good knowledge about the business in general, especially a window into the future.

First to Market

This risky but potentially rewarding strategy has several important ramifications for the business:

- A research-intensive effort supported by major development resources
- Close downstream coupling in product planning and moderately close coupling thereafter
- High proximity to the state of the art
- May need a major technical breakthrough
- High innovation investment
- A high risk of failure for individual products

Taken together, they outline a clear philosophy of business. The company must recruit and retain outstanding innovation personnel who can win leadership positions in the industry with their competencies. The company must see that these technical people and the project managers are in close and useful communication with marketing planners to identify potentially profitable markets. The company must often risk large investments of time and money in technical and market development without any immediate return. It must be able to absorb mistakes, withdraw, and recoup without losing its position in other product lines. As the nature of the market clarifies, initial plans may need to be modified quickly.

Perhaps most important, top management must be able to make important judgments of timing, balancing the improved product development stemming from a delayed introduction against the risk of being second into the market. Such a company must have more than its share of long-range thinkers who can confidently assess market and competitive trends in their earliest stages and plan with both confidence and flexibility.

Follow the Leader

This marketing strategy implies:

- Development-intensive technical effort
- Moderate competence across the spectrum of relevant technologies
- Exceptionally rapid response time in product development and marketing based on completed research
- High downstream coupling of innovation with marketing and manufacturing
- Superior competitive intelligence so that the firm can duplicate the competitors' products without patent infringement
- Innovation personnel that are knowledgeable about the competitors' products

The company that follows this strategy is—or should be—an organization that gets things done. It uses many interfunctional techniques, responds rapidly to change, and often seems to be in a perpetual fire drill. It has few scientists on its payroll but some of the best development engineers available. Its senior executives are constantly concerned with maintaining the right balance of strengths among the technical, marketing, and manufacturing functions so that the company can respond effectively to the leader's moves in any of these three areas.

Application Engineering

This strategy requires:

- Substantial product design and engineering resources, but no research or innovation and little real development
- Ready access to product users within customer companies
- Technically perceptive salespeople and sales engineers who work closely with product designers
- Good product-line control to prevent costly proliferation
- Considerable cost consciousness in deciding what applications to develop
- An efficiency-oriented manufacturing organization
- A flair for minimizing development and manufacturing cost by using the same parts or elements in many different applications.

The applications engineering strategy tends to avoid innovative efforts in the interest of the economy. Planning is precise, assignments are clear, and any new technology is introduced cautiously, well behind the economic state of the art. Return-on-investment and cash flow calculations are standard practice, and the entire management team is profit oriented.

"Me Too"

This strategy, which has flourished in the past decade as never before, is distinguished by:

- No innovation, research, or development
- Strong manufacturing function and dominating product design team
- Strong price and delivery performance
- Ability to copy new designs quickly, modifying them only to reduce production costs

Competing on price, taking a low margin, but avoiding all development expense, a company that has adopted this strategy can wreak havoc with competitors following the first-to-market or follow-the-leader strategies. This is because the "me-too" strategy, effectively pursued, shortens the profitable period after introduction when the leaders' margins are most substantial. The me-too strategy requires a low-overhead approach to manufacturing and administration and a direct hard sell on price and delivery to the customer. It does not require any technical enthusiasm, nor does it aim to generate any.

PRODUCT LIFE CYCLES

The length of the product life cycles has a bearing on how much risk the company should take and how much money should be invested, and this risk is then transferred to the innovation project managers for risk mitigation. This provides them with a rough idea of how much time they have and the approximate budget. Long product life cycles may generate enough cash flow and lead time for new product introduction. Innovation project managers may then be under very little pressure to develop new products in a short time frame. However, with short product life cycles, companies are under pressure to reduce the time to market without sacrificing quality or other needs of the customers.

Unfortunately, many companies put the emphasis in the wrong place. As the product life cycle grows, emphasis shifts from a competitive position, based on product performance, to product variations (i.e., incremental innovation) and ultimately lower costs due to learning curve effects. Instead of having the innovation project managers focus on the development of new products, emphasis is on the continuation of existing products perhaps through enhancements.

Many companies prefer taking the low risk (cost-wise) of developing "line extension" or "flanker" products, which are simply the same product in a different form. Bringing out something new is a risky business, and some companies simply prefer to develop cheap imitations.

Many small companies thrive on short product life cycles, even in fragmented markets. As an example, consider that if the top executive of a small engineering company is also the founding genius and top scientist, new products are developed quickly and move rapidly from innovation to commercialization and then to the marketplace. This company has learned to cope well with short product life cycles.

CLASSIFICATION OF R&D PROJECTS

From the previous sections, it should be obvious that there are numerous ways for innovation projects to be classified based on the relationship between innovation and marketing personnel. Some companies prefer to classify projects according to the type of R&D required; the following are categories commonly found in books on R&D management:

Grass roots projects. This type of project can be simply an idea with as few as one or two good data points. Grass roots projects are funded with "seed money," which is a small sum of money usually under the control of the R&D project manager. The purpose of the seed money is to see if the grass roots project is feasible enough to be developed into a full-blown, well-funded R&D project to be further incorporated into the strategic plan.

Bootlegged projects. This type of project is one in which funding does not exist either because the selection team did not consider this project worthy of funding or because funding had been terminated (or ran out) and funding renewal was not considered appropriate. In either event, a bootlegged project is done on the sly, under the radar screen, using another project's budgeted charge numbers. Bootlegged projects run the complete spectrum from conceptual ideas to terminated, well-defined activities.

Basic research projects. Basic research projects may include grass roots and bootlegged projects. Basic research activities are designed to expand knowledge in a specific scientific area or to improve the state of the art. These types of projects do not generally result in products that can be directly sold by marketing and, as a result, require special handling.

Applied research projects. The applied research project is an extension or follow-on to the basic research project and explores direct application of a given body of knowledge. These types of projects hopefully result in marketable products, product improvements, or new applications for existing products.

Advanced development projects. These types of activities follow the applied research or exploratory development projects with the intent of producing full-scale prototypes supported by experimental testing.

Full-scale development projects. This activity includes a completed working drawing design of the product together with a detailed bill of materials, exact vendor quotes, and specification development. This type of R&D activity requires strong manufacturing involvement and may result in a new business model.

Production support projects. This category can include either applications engineering to find better uses of this product for a customer or internal operations support to investigate limitations and feasibility of a given system with hopes of modification or redesign. Projects designed to find ways of lowering production costs or improving product quality are examples of internal production support projects.

Even though we consider these seven types and categories of R&D, the results can be fruitful enough to become fully funded as innovation projects and then reclassified.

RESEARCH VERSUS DEVELOPMENT

Although most people consider R&D project management as a single entity, there are critical differences between research and development. Some project managers are excellent in managing research projects, while others excel in development projects. Basic differences include:

- **Specifications.** Researchers generally function with weak specifications because of the freedom to invent, whereas development personnel are paid not to create new alternatives but to reduce available alternatives to one hopefully simple solution available for implementation.
- **Resources.** Generally, more resources are needed for development work rather the pure research. This generates a greater need for structured supervision, whereas research is often conducted in a campus-like work environment.
- **Scheduling.** Researchers prefer very loose schedules with the freedom to go off on tangents, whereas developmental schedules are more rigid. Research schedules identify parallel activities whereas in development, scheduled activities are sequential.

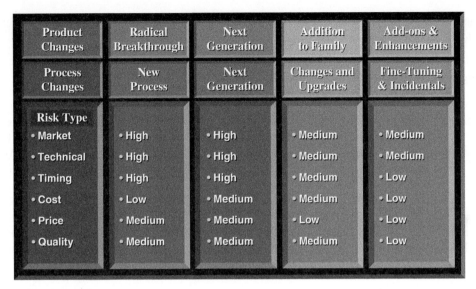

Product Changes	Radical Breakthrough	Next Generation	Addition to Family	Add-ons & Enhancements
Process Changes	New Process	Next Generation	Changes and Upgrades	Fine-Tuning & Incidentals
Risk Type				
• Market	• High	• High	• Medium	• Medium
• Technical	• High	• High	• Medium	• Medium
• Timing	• High	• High	• Medium	• Low
• Cost	• Low	• Medium	• Medium	• Low
• Price	• Medium	• Medium	• Low	• Low
• Quality	• Medium	• Medium	• Medium	• Low

Figure 3–10. Risk Intensity.

● **Engineering changes.** In the research stages of a project, engineering changes, specification changes, and engineering redirection (even if simply caused by the personal whims of management) may have a minor cost impact compared to the same changes occurring in the development stage.

A different form of innovation can be used whether the project is for research or development. There can also be different types of risks and different risk intensities, as shown in Figure 3-10.

THE RESEARCH AND DEVELOPMENT RATIO

A company must determine the balance or ratio of basic research, applied research, product development, and other forms of innovation with project managers specially trained in each area. Basic research may or may not respond directly to a specific problem or need, but it is selected and directed into those fields where advances will have a major impact on the company's future core businesses.

Applied research is the next step in using a technology to accomplish business objectives that may include innovation in processes, cost reduction, and so on. Product development uses all technologies available to it to develop a product that is consistent with the direction of the company.

An industrial company needs to determine the ratio of the above-mentioned areas when determining its strategy for short- and long-term decisions. Basic research is generally a long-term commitment that must be made and driven by top management. Marketing, sales, and manufacturing do not have the incentive to sponsor applied research and more product-development research for short-term programs. Therefore, it is the responsibility of top management to provide direction to the research and development effort within the corporation.

Functional groups must work closely with the PMO in the strategic selection of projects. Each group brings to the table different ideas that usually favor its own functional area.

Manufacturing and Sales

These two groups must be included in the portfolio selection of projects for innovation, research, and development. This is particularly true for the development of new products and technologies. It is essential to know if manufacturing has the capability to make the product using existing manufacturing facilities and equipment. Will the existing manufacturing plants have sufficient capacity to meet demand? Will they be able to manufacture the product and be cost effective? If new equipment and plants are needed, this information needs to be factored into the overall innovation plan, so they will be prepared when the new product is ready to be launched. Just as important is the sales force. Is the present sales force adequate? Adequacy must be evaluated in terms of numbers, training, location, and so on. Will the new product require different selling skills than the company's present product line? Another factor that must be evaluated is the possible reduction in sales force due to a new product. What adverse effect might that have on the morale of the sales group? What are the behavioral ramifications of such a move?

Human Behavior

One of the key factors in project management is the ability to communicate effectively with a great deal of emphasis placed on teamwork, interaction between groups, managing group diversity, and knowing your customer. Obviously, the more top management and project management understand human behavior, the better they can control productivity and the management of limited human resources.

One of the many problems associated with innovation management is ownership. Top management may feel that they have the need and the right to constantly control an innovation project. Management must relinquish control to allow innovation project managers to inject the degree of creativity needed to make the project successful. On the other hand, the individual or team within innovation or R&D that is working on the project also needs to relinquish control once the project is ready to be released to manufacturing and marketing. Unlike other forms of project management, innovation project managers may not be involved throughout the complete life cycle of the project. However, new corporate initiatives such as with benefits realization and value management are keeping part of the project team involved even after product commercialization.

OFFENSIVE VERSUS DEFENSIVE INNOVATION _____

"Having a me-too brand is a death sentence."

— David Brier, *The Lucky Brand*

Should a company direct its resources toward offensive or defensive innovation? Offensive innovation is product innovation/R&D, whereas defensive innovation is process innovation/R&D. In an offensive posture, the intent is to penetrate a new market as quickly as possible, replace an existing product, or simply satisfies a customer's need. Offensive innovation stresses a first-to-market approach. The ultimate decision can be related to some of the models discussed previously such as the General Electric nine-square grid, as shown in Figure 3-11.

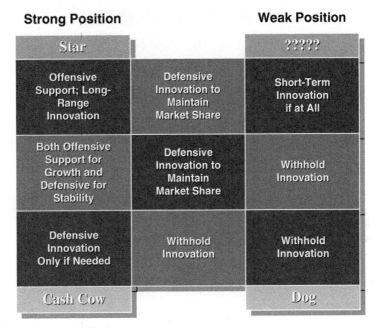

Strong Position **Weak Position**

Star		?????
Offensive Support; Long-Range Innovation	Defensive Innovation to Maintain Market Share	Short-Term Innovation if at All
Both Offensive Support for Growth and Defensive for Stability	Defensive Innovation to Maintain Market Share	Withhold Innovation
Defensive Innovation Only if Needed	Withhold Innovation	Withhold Innovation
Cash Cow		Dog

Figure 3–11. Positioning the Innovation Strategy.

Defensive innovation, on the other hand, is used to either lengthen the product life cycle or to protect existing product lines from serious competitive pressures. Defensive innovation is also employed in situations where the company has a successful product line and fears that the introduction of a new technology at this time may jeopardize existing profits. Defensive innovation concentrates on minor improvements rather than major discoveries and, as a result, requires less funding. Today, with the high cost of money, companies are concentrating on minor product improvements, such as style, and introduce the product into the marketplace as a new, improved version when, in fact, it is simply the original product slightly changed.

This approach had been used by several companies in copying someone else's successful product, improving the quality, changing the style, and then introducing it into the marketplace. A big advantage to these companies was that the product could be sold at a lower cost, because the selling price did not have to include recovery of expensive innovation or R&D costs.

Defensive innovation is a necessity for those organizations that must support existing products and hopefully extend the product's life span. A firm's strategic posture in the marketplace is, therefore, not restricted solely to new-product introduction. Companies must find the proper technological balance between offensive and defensive innovation.

MODELING THE R&D PLANNING FUNCTION

Schematic modeling of innovation project management requires an understanding of how innovation fits into the total strategic plan. Figure 3-12 illustrates the integration of innovation into the total strategic planning function. Once the business is defined, together with an environmental analysis of strengths,

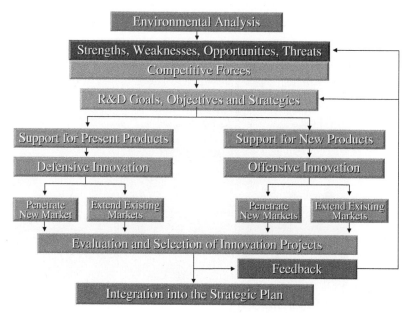

Figure 3–12. Integrating Innovation into Strategic Planning.

weaknesses, opportunities, and threats, the corporate strategic goals and objectives are defined. Unfortunately, the definition of the strategic goals and objectives is usually made in financial terms or through the product/market element. This type of definition implies a critical assumption: innovation/R&D can and will develop the new products or product improvements within the required specifications in order to meet target goals and objectives. Unfortunately, many companies have not realized the importance of soliciting input from innovation and/or R&D personnel into the objective-setting stage and, therefore, treat innovation and R&D simply as service organizations. Once the objectives are set, marketing will identify the products and approach (tactics) to achieve the strategies. Here again, innovation and R&D may be treated as service organizations.

The portfolio PMO, along with the appropriate senior managers, will manage the portfolio selection process for the projects. It is not uncommon for the innovation selection process to be controlled by marketing or for the entire innovation budget to be part of the marketing budget. The reason for this is because marketing wants to be sure that it can sell successfully what the innovation team produces.

In mature organizations, however, innovation/R&D personnel can express their concerns over the feasibility of the goals and objectives and of the probability of successfully achieving the strategic objectives. In such a case, there exists a feedback loop from project selection to objective setting, as shown in Figure 3-12.

The box in Figure 3-12 titled "Support for New Products" requires that the project selection process accounts for the management of innovation and entrepreneurship and can be modeled as shown in Figure 3-13. Not all companies have entrepreneurship strategies like 3M, Texas Instruments, or Apple because of a slow and tedious permeation process into the corporate culture. The successful companies consider entrepreneurship as "business" and marry it to the mainstream of the company. In this case, innovation project managers are expected to possess some degree of entrepreneurship skills.

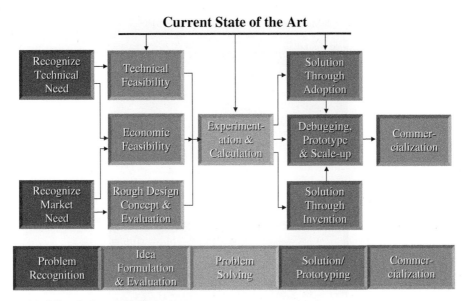

Figure 3–13. Modeling the Innovation Process.

Figure 3-13 also shows that successful integration of innovation into the strategic plan requires that the innovation team understands the firm's production process, distribution process, market research, and market distribution channels. This requires that the team understand marketing's decision to introduce a new product by either being first to market, second to market, application engineering, or "me too" (i.e., copycat).

When a company has perceived a strategic need to enter a new market, increase growth, or improve an existing product, the company is faced with the problem of how to acquire the technical skills necessary for integration in the strategic plan. The alternatives are:

- Innovation/R&D with existing resources that have the technical capability
- Innovation/R&D with existing resources through internal technical training
- Innovation/R&D through newly hired employees
- Innovation/R&D through consultants
- Acquisition of a company with the required technology
- Joint ventures
- Buying technology through licensing

Innovation is impacted by the length of the product life cycle. For short product life cycles, project managers must be willing to respond rapidly, especially if the environment is ever-changing. Adaptability to short product life cycles is characteristic of flat organizational structures with a wide span of control. Because decision making must be quick in short product life cycles, organizational coupling must be high between marketing, R&D, and manufacturing. Weak coupling can result in the late introduction of new products into the marketplace.

Figures 3-14–3-16 illustrate the degrees of coupling. Figure 3-14 represents an incremental innovation project where only small changes are expected and there will be no impact on manufacturability.

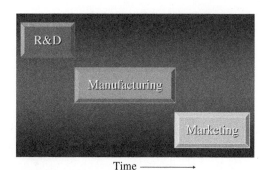

Figure 3–14. Low-Risk Coupling.

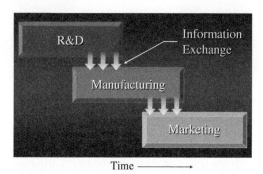

Figure 3–15. Moderate-Risk Coupling.

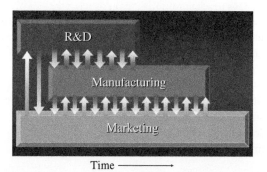

Figure 3–16. High-Risk Coupling.

Figure 3-15 represents moderate-risk coupling. In this case, there may be small changes needed to manufacture the product and marketing may need to change how they approach customers. Figure 3-16 represents high risk, where R&D, manufacturing, and marketing must be in constant communication. This would occur with radical innovation.

Several years ago, an oil drilling company developed an innovative way to drill for oil. The cost of drilling was more than $30,000 per hour. A component in the drilling apparatus kept fracturing after a certain number of hours. Management was furious that the costly drilling process had to stop periodically for maintenance. The reason for the problem was that engineering designed the component without involving manufacturing. The manufacturing personnel stated that had they been involved during the innovation design effort, rather than just being handed drawings and told to build it, this problem would have come to the surface rapidly and been resolved. This is an example of the risks in an uncoupled R&D–manufacturing environment.

The shorter the product life cycle, the greater will be the involvement of senior management. Strategic planning at the strategic business unit (SBU) level may be cumbersome with short product life cycles. The shorter the product life cycle, the greater the number of new products needed to sustain a reasonable growth. As a result, shorter product life cycles have a greater need for superior innovation talent.

The strategic-marketing approach to the product life cycle can vary based on the size of the company. Small companies that compete in short product life-cycle markets must be first-to-market to reap profits. In short product life cycles, large companies can commit vast resource to take advantage of experience curves, thus creating a barrier to entry for smaller companies that try to employ a follow-the-leader approach.

PRIORITY SETTING

Priorities create colossal management headaches for the R&D project manager because R&D projects are usually prioritized differently from all other projects. Functional managers who must staff R&D projects as well as ongoing work must now supply resources according to two priority lists. Unfortunately, the R&D priority list is usually not given proper attention.

As an example of this, the director of R&D of a Fortune 25 corporation made the following remarks:

> Each of our operating divisions has their own R&D projects and priorities. Last year, corporate R&D had a very high R&D project geared toward cost improvement in the manufacturing areas. Our priorities were based upon the short-run requirements. Unfortunately, the operating division that had to supply resources to our project felt that the benefits would not be received until the long run and, therefore, placed support for our project low on their priority list.

Communication of priorities is often a problem in the innovation/R&D area. Priorities set at the divisional level may not be passed down to the departmental level, and vice versa. We must have early feedback on priorities so that functional managers can make their own plans. Portfolio PMOs often prioritize projects as must be done, should be done, and can be backlogged.

Working with Marketing

In most organizations, either R&D drives marketing or marketing drives R&D. The latter is more common. Well-managed organizations maintain a proper balance between marketing and R&D. Marketing-driven organizations can create havoc, especially if marketing continuously requests information faster than R&D can deliver it and if bootleg R&D is eliminated. In this case, all R&D funding comes out of the marketing budget.

To stimulate creativity, innovation/R&D should have control over at least a portion of its own budget. This is a necessity, because not all innovation activities are designed to benefit marketing. Some activities are simply to improve technology or create a new way of doing business.

Marketing support, if needed, should be available to all innovation/R&D projects regardless of whether they originate in marketing or R&D. An R&D project manager at a major food manufacturer made the following remarks:

> A few years ago, one of our R&D people came up with an idea and I was assigned as the project manager. When the project was completed, we had developed a new product, ready for market introduction and testing. Unfortunately, R&D does not maintain funds for the market testing of a new product. The funds come out of marketing. Our marketing people did not understand the product and placed it low on their priority list. We in R&D tried to talk to them. They were reluctant to test the new product because the project was our idea. Marketing lives in its own little world. To make a long story short, last year one of our competitors introduced the same product into the marketplace. Now, instead of being the leader, we are playing catch-up. I know R&D project managers are not trained in market testing, but what if marketing refuses to support R&D-conceived projects? What can we do?

Several organizations today have innovation project managers reporting directly to a new business group, business development group, or marketing. Engineering-oriented R&D project managers continuously voice displeasure at being evaluated for promotion by someone in marketing who really may not understand the technical difficulties in managing an innovation/R&D project. Yet, executives have valid arguments for this arrangement, asserting that these high-technology project managers are so in love with their projects that they don't know how and when to cancel a project. Marketing executives contend that projects should be canceled when:

- Costs become excessive, causing product cost to be noncompetitive
- Return on investment will occur too late
- Competition is too stiff and not worth the risk

Of course, the question arises, "Should marketing have a vote in the cancellation of each R&D project or only those that are marketing-driven?" Some organizations cancel projects on consensus of the project team.

Companies are either R&D dominated, marketing dominated, or balanced. In R&D-dominated companies, the R&D staff researches fundamental problems, looks for major breakthroughs, and strives for technical perfection in product development. R&D expenditures are high, and the new-product success rate tends to be low, although R&D occasionally comes up with major new products.

In marketing-dominated companies, the R&D staff designs products for specific market needs, much of it involving product modification and the application of existing technologies. A high ratio of new products eventually succeeds, but they represent mainly product modifications with relatively short product lives.

A balanced R&D/marketing company is one in which effective organizational relationships have been worked out between R&D and marketing to share responsibility for successful market-orientation innovations. The R&D staff takes responsibility not for invention alone but for successful innovation. The marketing staff takes responsibility not for new sales features alone but also for helping identify new ways to satisfy needs. R&D/marketing cooperation is facilitated in several ways:

- Joint seminars are sponsored to build understanding and respect for each other's goals, working styles, and problems.
- Each new project is assigned to an R&D person and a marketing person who work together through the life of the project.

- R&D and marketing personnel are interchanged so that they have a chance to experience each other's work situations (some R&D people may travel with the sales force, while some marketing people might hang around the lab for a short time).
- Higher management, following a clear procedure, works out conflicts.

CONTRACT R&D

Contract (or outsourced) R&D is another form of strategic planning for R&D project management that can be used with any of the different classifications for projects. Contract R&D is generally used for the development of a new technology rather than for innovations that use this new technology. There are other reasons for conducting contract R&D, depending on whether you are the customer or the contractor. Companies subcontract out R&D because they may not have the necessary in-house technical skills; have in-house skills, but the resources are committed to higher-priority activities; and/or may have the available talent, but external sources have superior talent and may be able to produce the desired results in less time and for less money.

The benefits to the company doing the outsourcing include:

- Maintaining technical leadership
- Targeted, specific R&D and innovation from qualified firms
- Creates new business opportunities
- Maintain a defensive posture, if needed, to meet the competition
- Helps balance internal workloads
- Maintains customer goodwill
- Generates improvements in existing products

From a subcontractor's point of view, contract R&D project management is a way to develop new technologies at someone else's expense. Subcontractors view contract R&D as a way to:

- Minimize the internal cost of supporting R&D personnel.
- Develop new technologies to penetrate new markets/products.
- Develop new technologies to support existing market/products.
- Maintain technical leadership.
- Improve resource utilization by balancing workloads.
- Maintain customer goodwill.
- Look for spinoffs on existing products.

There also exist disadvantages to contract R&D. From the customer's point of view:

- How dependent should I become on a subcontractor to produce the desired results within time and cost?
- What criteria are used to evaluate subcontractors?
- What type of communication network should be established?
- How do I know if the subcontractor is being honest with me?
- If tradeoffs are needed, how will decisions be made?

- Who controls patent rights resulting from the research under contract?
- Will project failures impact strategic planning process?

From the subcontractor's point of view:

- What influence will the customer try to exercise over my personnel?
- Will project success generate follow-on work?
- Will project success enhance our goodwill image?
- Will project failure damage our image?

NONDISCLOSURE AGREEMENTS, SECRECY AGREEMENTS, AND CONFIDENTIALITY AGREEMENTS

"The need for security often kills the quest for innovation."

— Haresh Sippy

In the course of doing business, few companies can develop and market a new product without some help from outside their company. Innovation/R&D project managers, perhaps more so than any other type of project manager, must have some knowledge about nondisclosure agreements, secrecy agreements, and confidentiality agreements. When it is necessary to secure outside help, it is essential to protect the proprietary nature of the information being transmitted to the outside party. To do this, an agreement is drawn up between the two parties and signed by a corporate office from each firm.

Top management must develop a policy on how to handle the transfer of confidential information and intellectual property regarding technological developments to outside sources involved in the project. There are two types of agreements: one-way and mutual. The one-way agreement is exactly what the name implies in that the company with the confidential information is transferring that information to the second party with nothing coming back. The mutual agreement calls for the transfer of confidential information between both parties.

GOVERNMENT INFLUENCE

Foreign and domestic governments play a significant role in the strategic-planning process for R&D and can therefore influence the way that innovation and R&D projects are managed. The laws and policies set forth by government can encourage or discourage R&D. This effect can be direct or indirect. The government may have tax incentives that will foster a climate for innovation and R&D to flourish. Governments can also impose regulations or standards that will encourage the development of new products to meet those standards. The behavior and posture of foreign governments can influence licensing agreements, the competitive edge on new products, the ability to market new products, and so on.

The three interactions in Figure 1-3 can be impacted by government policy toward innovation. Regulated environments can require higher R&D and innovation costs, lengthen the time from R&D and innovation to product introduction, force companies to work on fewer R&D and innovation projects, and transfer more work to countries with fewer health and safety regulations. It is not uncommon for a pharmaceutical company to perform clinical testing in a country that has fewer restrictions or for a manufacturing company to open plants in a country that has less safety requirements than in their parent country.

The following list is but a sampling of how government can control and influence industrial research and development:

- Fiscal and monetary policies
- International operations and control
- Technology transfer restrictions
- Patents
- Policy impact on technological corporations
- Taxes; monetary flow restrictions
- Labor/management relations
- Worker rights
- Safety during manufacturing
- Risks
- Regulations on disposal of hazardous materials
- Regulations on environmental hazards
- Sponsor of technological advance, with corporate involvement
- Contract types such as cost and cost sharing contracts

SOURCES FOR INNOVATION TECHNOLOGY

Contract research, licensing, joint ventures, acquisitions, and the luxury of hiring additional personnel are taken for granted in the United States. Other countries may not have these luxuries, and additional classifications may be needed, usually by the level of technology. According to one country, the following levels are used:

- **Level I.** Technology exists within the company.
- **Level II.** Technology can be purchased from companies within the country.
- **Level III.** Technology can be purchased from outside the country.
- **Level IV.** Technology must be researched in other countries and brought back into the parent country.

Because a great many countries fall into Levels III and IV, several foreign corporations have established employee sabbatical funds. Each month the company withholds 3 percent of the employee's salary and matches this with 7 percent of company funds. Every five or six years, each participating employee is permitted to study abroad to bring technical expertise back into the country. The employee draws his or her full salary while on sabbatical in addition to the sabbatical fund.

For strategic innovation planning, this type of sabbatical leave creates a gap in the organization. Management can delay a sabbatical leave for an employee for one year only. What happens if the employee is in a strategic position? What if the employee is working on a critical project? What if the employee is the only person with the needed skills in a specific discipline? Who replaces the employee? Where do we put the employee upon his or her return to the organization? What happens if the employee's previous management slot is no longer vacant? Obviously, these questions have serious impact on the strategic-planning process.

SOURCES OF IDEAS _____

"The best way to get a good idea is to have a lot of ideas."

— Linus Pauling

Unlike other types of planning, strategic R&D project planning must be willing to solicit ideas from the depths of the organization and from outside the organization. Successful companies with a reputation for continuous new-product introduction have new-product development teams that operate in a relatively unstructured environment to obtain the best possible ideas. Some companies go so far as to develop idea inventories, idea banks, and idea clearinghouses.

These idea sessions are brainstorming sessions and not intended for problem solving. If properly structured, the meeting will have an atmosphere of free expression and creative thinking, an ideal technique for stimulating ideas. Arguments against brainstorming sessions include no rewards for creators, attack of only superficial problems, possibility of potentially good ideas coming out prematurely and being disregarded, and lack of consideration for those individuals who are more creative by themselves.

Principles that can be used in brainstorming sessions include:

- Select personnel from a variety of levels; avoid those responsible for implementation.
- Allow people to decline assignments.
- Avoid evaluation and criticism of ideas.
- Provide credit recognition and/or rewards for contributors.
- Limit session to 60 minutes.

Ideas are not merely limited to internal sources. There are several external sources of new product ideas such as:

- Customers
- Competitors
- Suppliers
- Purchase of technologies
- Licensing of technologies
- Unsolicited ideas from customers or others
- Private inventors
- Acquisitions
- Trade fairs
- Technology fairs
- Private data banks
- Technical journals
- Trade journals
- Government-funded research programs
- Government innovation/technology transfer programs
- Government agencies

Innovation is expensive and the more ideas you have the greater the chance for a commercially successful product to emerge. In a study of new-product activities of several hundred companies in all industries, Booz, Allen, and Hamilton (1984, 180) defined the new-product evolution process as the time it takes to bring a product to commercial existence. This process began with company objectives, which included fields of product interest, goals, and growth plans, and ended with, hopefully, a successful product. The more specific these objectives were defined, the greater the guidance given to the new product program. This process was broken down into six manageable, clear sequential stages:

1. **Exploration.** The search for product ideas to meet company objectives.
2. **Screening.** A quick analysis to determine which ideas were pertinent and merit more detailed study.
3. **Business analysis.** The expansion of the idea, through creative analysis, into a concrete business recommendation, including product features, financial analysis, risk analysis, market assessment, and a program for the product.
4. **Development.** Turning the idea-on-paper into a product-in-hand, demonstrable and producible. This stage focuses on R&D and the inventive capability of the firm. When unanticipated problems arise, new solutions and tradeoffs are sought. In many instances, the obstacles are so great that a solution cannot be found, and work is terminated or deferred.
5. **Testing.** The technical and commercial experiments necessary to verify earlier technical and business judgments.
6. **Commercialization.** Launching the product in full-scale production and sales; committing the company's reputation and resources.

In the Booz, Allen, and Hamilton study, the new-product process was characterized by a decay curve for ideas, as shown in Figure 3-17. This showed a progressive rejection of ideas or projects by stages in the product-evolution process. Although the rate of rejection varied between industries and companies, the general shape of the decay curve is typical. The curve shows that it generally took close to 60 ideas to yield one successful new product.

The process of new-product evolution involves a series of management decisions. Each stage is progressively more expensive, as measured in expenditures of both time and money. Figure 3-18 shows the rate at which expense dollars are spent as time accumulates for the average project within a sample of leading companies. This information was based on an all-industry average and is therefore useful in

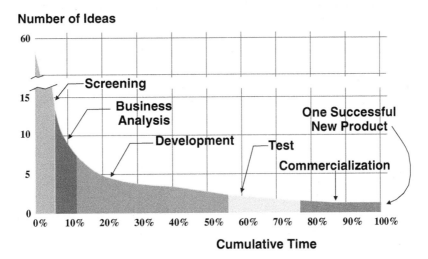

Figure 3–17. Mortality of New Product Ideas.

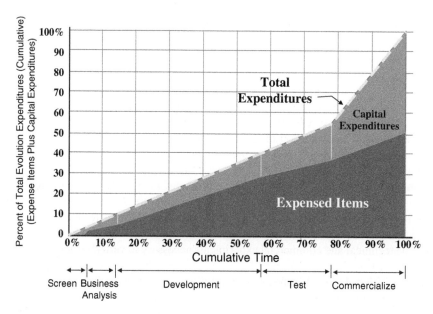

Figure 3–18. Cumulative Expenditures and Time.

understanding the typical industrial new-product process. It is significant to note that most capital expenditures are concentrated in the last three stages of evolution. It is therefore very important to do a better job of screening for business and financial analysis. This will help eliminate ideas of limited potential before they reach the more expensive stages of evolution.

THE PROJECT MANAGER'S ROLE IN DEVELOPING INNOVATION SKILLS AND IDEAS IN PEOPLE

The role of the project manager is no longer limited to just participation in project selection and innovation project execution. In many of today's companies, especially those actively pursuing innovation, the new project opportunities must be stimulated or induced inside the company. This includes bringing new ideas to the surface followed by a selection of the most promising ones. In this framework, the role of the innovation project manager can be crucial. The reason relies in the fact that he/she has the privilege to deal with workers, technicians, and the upper management level. Therefore, in this vertical path, he/she can see a concept at initial level and to persuade the higher levels to provide funding.

To efficiently pursue this task, companies have adopted several tools, procedures, and strategies that help the birth of new ideas—in addition to adopting the classical Research and Development Department (especially if we are speaking about product innovation).

Ideas are clearly generated by people and therefore companies must realize that the secret to obtain as many new ideas as possible is to create the "ideal condition" to allow people to bring their contribution

This section was prepared by Luigi Morsa, Ph.D., aerospace engineer and project manager. ©2022 Luigi Morsa, Ph.D. All rights reserved. Reproduced by permission.

to the surface. One interesting way to accomplish the task is represented by so-called "Innovation Management Software (IMS)". This has been developing during the last two decades and it can be seen as the latest evolution of the "suggestion box", introduced more than 100 years ago and still present in some offices.

The Innovation software programs are usually conceived in a way that there is a common platform where all the users (basically employees of the company) have access and can freely leave their proposals or opinions about a possible new idea. Then, each new proposal generates an online debate or discussion with the effect to improve it. Once a certain number of ideas is reached, the selection phase starts. This is conducted by innovation project managers with the support of sector experts and business unit people. Their intent is to evaluate the feasibility from a technical and business point of view, respectively. Finally, this committee selects the ideas which are worthy of an investment and makes recommendations to decision makers.

In most cases, even though the IMS is very fascinating to work with, a good percentage of employees are reluctant to contribute their ideas to the company. Possible reasons may be because they have not developed a sense of belonging, they simply do not believe in the company, or they think that an idea given to the company is a kind of gift without some form of repayment. To avoid such inefficiencies, tools like IMS should be supported by an additional software that we could baptize as "People Innovation Software (PIS)". The starting point is the slight change in the philosophical approach between the IMS and PIS. We can say that the innovation management software assumes that the main heritage of a company that wants to innovate lies on the ideas of the people within the company. Therefore, the software "simply" helps the development of ideas. In the case of PIS, the basis goes further. The software helps people to innovate among themselves and, consequently, the company.

If the company believes in the employees, the employees feel more engaged and motivated to give their contribution to the company and, finally, to innovate.

The weak side of the IMS is, on one hand, it favors peoples' connections and discussions to help generate ideas. On the other hand, it does not care about how an employee can develop himself or herself during this time. How can a sense of belonging or the desire to participate in the innovation process of a company be generated in employees? The answer is the following: through the idea that a company wants to take care of its employees, wants to bet on them, wants to donate a future vision and wants to provide professional development opportunities for them.

Using the PI software, we could have a special section where all the employees' profiles are stored, the possible career paths are shown based upon their work experience, the courses needed to achieve some additional opportunities, and how their innovative ideas can be supported or promoted.

The other important aspect is: who are the players that ensure PIS works properly? In this regard, we are talking about people in Human Resources, the project innovation managers, and the line managers. All these players must have access to the PIS shell, and they must help employees in their development innovation ideas and career path opportunities. In general, HR could monitor if an employee is satisfied and understand all of his/her needs; the line manager could define what can be done for their professional development; and the project innovation manager could stay alert in case of new potential ideas.

The software could be a powerful tool to motivate employees. One of the biggest challenges in organizational management is how to provide recognition (and possibly rewards) to workers that make a significant contribution to the business. There are two critical issues with recognition systems.

● First, not all employees are in a position where their performance can be directly related to business success. This can alienate workers who believe they are missing out on these opportunities because of their current work assignment or position.

- Second, the company must decide if the recognition will be done monetarily or non-monetarily. Believe it or not, having a diagram with visible professional development, with the past achievements and above all with the future targets for an employee is priceless. People could believe that regular meetings with HR and managers of various kinds are enough, but they are not. Software is needed since it is important to have a visible, professional practice with clear prospects.

In conclusion, we observe that PIS' purpose is not to replace traditional innovation software management. On the contrary, PIS completes the IMS by enlarging potential. The IMS encourages cooperation for the development of an idea, creates the useful connections and improves the concepts promoting discussions. PIS accompanies and encourages the employees to find out the best way to be motivated and to better express themselves. It creates more suitable conditions to generate ideas. It is something that a company (devoted to innovation) should have and develop according to its needs.

To convince the company to invest in people it is useful to ponder the following statement:

The effort that a company can spend to support on personal/professional employee development and to facilitate the fulfillment of his/her ideas is not a gift to the employee, but a precondition for the INNOVATION.

We can finally underline that in the innovation process that brings to project selection the role played by the project manager is crucial. He/she has the possibility to function as the "patron" of ideas and to implement the company strategies by inducing, thanks to his/her strategic position in the company, top management to follow some promising paths.

ESTABLISHING A PROJECT SELECTION CRITERIA

Companies can come up with a multitude of ideas for potential innovation projects, but funding limitations necessitate that not all projects can be authorized for implementation. The decision of what to work on and the timing must be based upon not just what you want, but also on what you can deliver within limits. Therefore, there must exist some idea selection criteria to simplify the process.

Some companies prefer to use feasibility studies, benefit-to-cost analyses, and voting. But the more common approach is to use the company's core values as the main component in the selection criteria. The core values are also the driving force for the company's culture. Typical core values that a company may strive for can include:

- Feasibility
- Product quality
- Customer focus and desirability
- Profitability
- Desire to be recognized as an industry pioneer
- Desire to use leading edge technology
- Creation of patents, trademarks, and copyrights to protect the intellectual property
- Availability of necessary skilled resources
- Risks

The weighing factors of each core value can change from company to company. When the same core values, regardless of the weighing factors, are used for project selection and creation of an innovation culture, the outcome is usually a highly innovative organization.

The core values used for the selection of projects also serves as the basis for establishing project success and failure criteria. Both tangible and intangible metrics can be established to track that the performance of the project supports the core values.

PROJECT SELECTION ISSUES

Project selection should be aligned with the company strategy. This often requires a description of the product strategy assuming the necessary information is available. Product strategies can simplify the project selection process and increase worker motivation.

There are numerous factors that must be considered during the selection process. First, there is information that we may know when evaluating a project, such as:

- Relationships with other projects
- Funding limitations and cash flow
- Strategic importance
- Prioritization within the portfolio of projects
- Resources available and accompanying skill levels
- Availability of qualified innovation project managers

There will be limitations that need to be considered such as:

- Having less information than we would like
- Unknown likelihood of success especially if a technical breakthrough is necessary
- Unknown market response
- Unknown cost and time for completion (possibly due to resource availability)
- Needed critical resources to be released from ongoing projects

Consideration must be given to how much innovation the firm can absorb. Each organizational unit can have a different opinion on what innovation projects to support. The final solution must be acceptable to the entire organization. Behavioral limitations that come into play during project selection include:

- Departmental loyalties
- Differences in perspectives
- Conflicts in desires
- Impact of success or failure on one's career
- Unwillingness to share information and surrender intellectual property (i.e., information is power)
- Unwilling to trust opinions of others
- Using a subjective rather than objective selection criteria

Although companies prepare lists of what the "wish" to do, they must consider during selection of what they "can" do. There may be asset specificity or assets that they must use, and the assets are not a good fit for certain projects. The organization may not have workers with project-specific skills needed and/or experience curve data for this type of project.

Selecting more projects than you can handle can create an environment where all projects take longer than anticipated and perhaps nothing gets done correctly or as planned. Some companies prioritize innovation projects and even limit the number of projects that can be prioritized, such as only 20 projects. All other projects are then staffed only if qualified resources are not needed on the prioritized projects.

Some large innovation projects may require significant funding and then the decision becomes whether the funding should come from debt or equity. Debt funding is a risk if the project fails, and it leads to a high probability of financial distress due to uncertain returns.

ECONOMIC EVALUATION OF PROJECTS

There are several methods available for the economic evaluation of a single R&D project. According to Martino (1995, 192), these methods include the following:

Ranking Methods
- Pairwise comparison
- Scoring models
- Analytic hierarchy procedure

Economic Methods
- Net present value
- Internal rate of return
- Cash flow payback
- Expected value

Portfolio Optimization Methods
- Mathematical programming
- Cluster analysis
- Simulation
- Sensitivity analysis

Ad hoc Methods
- Profiles
- Interactive methods
- Cognitive modeling

Multistage Decisions
- Decision theory

Martino (1995, 193) also identifies factors that can be used for evaluating R&D projects one against another:

Factors that Can Be Included
- Cost
- Payoff

- Probability of technical success
- Probability of market success
- Market size
- Market share
- Availability of required staff
- Degree of organizational commitment
- Strategic positioning for project
- Degree of competition
- Favorability of regulatory environment

Special Input Requirements
- Requires precise cash flow information
- Requires precise life-cycle information
- Requires probability of technical success
- Requires probability of market success

Special Features
- Considers resource dependencies
- Considers budget constraints
- Considers technical interactions
- Considers market interactions
- Incorporates program considerations
- Can be used for large numbers of projects
- Allows comparison with other investments
- Suited for research stage
- Suited for development stage

Typical rating models adapted from Souder (1984, 66–69) are shown in Figures 3-19–3-21. These models can be used for both strategic selection and prioritization of innovation/R&D projects.

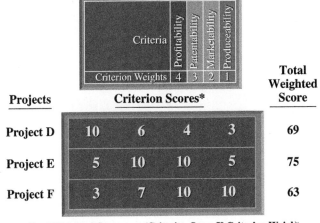

Projects	Criteria	Profitability	Patentability	Marketability	Produceability	Total Weighted Score
	Criterion Weights	4	3	2	1	
	Criterion Scores*					
Project D		10	6	4	3	69
Project E		5	10	10	5	75
Project F		3	7	10	10	63

Total Weighted Score = (Criterion Score X Criterion Weight)
* Scale: 10 = Excellent; 1 = Unacceptable

Figure 3–19. Illustration of a Scoring Model.

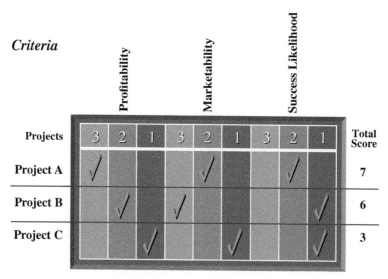

Figure 3-20. Illustration of a Checklist for Three Projects.

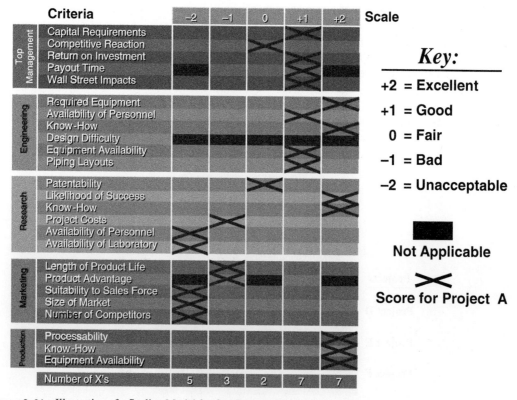

Figure 3-21. Illustration of a Scaling Model for One Project; Project A.

There are other costs that must be considered during project selection. Typical innovation costs include:

- Personnel
- Laboratory equipment and supplies
- Consultants
- Library and literature research
- Facilities and space
- Computer services
- Statistical services
- Marketing research activities

ROLE OF THE PROJECT MANAGER IN PROJECT SELECTION

Project selection is the process of outlining and choosing the next series of projects for the organization. Most organizations have several potential projects in their pipeline at any given time, and all the projects typically compete for the limited available resources. Criteria are established, often with templates, for defining the critical attributes of each project. Quantitative and qualitative models are available for assisting decision makers on ways to compare and then prioritize the projects. Organizations find themselves challenged with numerous ways to determine if they are working on the right projects.

In the past, project managers rarely participated during an organization's project selection process even though their expertise could be of value in decision making. There are textbooks dedicated to project selection practices. Some books are industry-specific, such as IT, construction, or product innovation. Unfortunately, most project management books, including the *PMBOK® Guide*, focus on traditional project management practices and do not discuss the different project selection techniques which leads people to believe that the PM's involvement may be unnecessary this early in the project's life cycle. However, the same books do discuss the financial measures established during the project selection process that might define project success factors.

Introduction to Project Selection

During the initiation stage of a project, executives and managers make decisions on what projects are needed for the business to grow and survive. Most often, business cases and statements of work (SOWs) are prepared, and the projects are prioritized and added to the queue. Then project managers are assigned, usually based upon availability, and often pressured to undertake something that may be unrealistic or even impossible. For fear of punishment, project managers undertake the assignments, and then we wonder why projects do not deliver the expected results or even fail. Project managers may end up taking the blame even though stakeholders may have approved the project based upon their own often hidden agenda.

The root cause of the problem is the timing when project selection decision makers bring project managers onboard. While it is true that strategic planning is done by senior management rather than having others doing it for them, early assignment of project managers can significantly improve project selection efforts. Experienced project managers often possess skills that executives may lack such as estimating project risks due to uncertainties, success and failure factors of past projects, resource competencies needed, selecting potential contractors and partners, and identification of information needs for project decision making.

Execution of a business strategy is accomplished by the selection of the correct projects. Project selection decision makers may be doing a disservice to their company when they believe that "information is power" and project managers do not have a "need to know" until after the project is approved.

Simply stating that a project is aligned to a strategic business objective does not mean that this is the correct project to be executed. Without participation in the project selection process, project managers must make both technical and business decisions based upon just the information in the business case and SOW, both of which may be incomplete. This can result in suboptimal project decisions where project teams have only partial information and not privileged to the full thought process and variables that went into the selection of the project. This can then limit the project manager's ability to be innovative.

The path to a company's sustainable business future will require the execution of more strategic and innovation projects than in the past. The pathway for these nontraditional projects goes from idea generation to idea development and then to market entry. In the idea development stage, on some projects, SOWs and business cases may be replaced by just an idea or a short statement defining strategic goals and objectives. This can create severe migraine headaches for decision making during project execution unless project managers are active participants in the idea generation stage.

The Fuzzy Front End

The fuzzy front end (FFE) is generally part of the initiation phase of a project where ideas are approved for development. Typical life-cycle phases that may be part of the FFE include:

- Identifying needs, ideas, or potential projects
- Choosing the selection criteria for each project considered
- Comparing projects using multiple methods both quantitative and qualitative
- Analyzing the findings
- Selecting a project

Each of these life-cycle phases struggle with imprecise information, uncertainties, and risks. This is the reason for the fuzziness. There are templates and mathematical models to assist decision makers in each life-cycle phase, and they are often used differently in each company.

The expression, FFE, was seldom used in the early years of project management which resided in project-driven organizations that survived on competitive bidding practices. Sales and marketing personnel often made the decision on whether to bid on a job and made sure that the contractual SOW was reasonably well-defined. Sometimes, project managers were asked to participate in preparing the bidding package, but generally project managers were not assigned until the contract was awarded and the requirements were well-understood.

The growth of the FFE also appeared in non-project-driven organizations where the projects were designed for the creation of new products or services and improvements in the way that the firm conducts business. Most of these projects started out as just ideas. Detailed requirements appeared as the projects progressed through project execution. Unlike traditional projects designed for a single customer, these non-traditional projects focused upon the problems and issues of all customers as well as future business opportunities.

The challenge with the FFE during project selection activities is in minimizing risks and maximizing opportunities given the number of project possibilities and the limited number of available resources. The situation is further complicated because much of the needed information on the attributes of each project considered is incomplete or imprecise, thus creating a great deal of risk and uncertainty. There is also uncertainty in determining the importance of each project attribute and the impact or relationship between attributes.

Even though there are tools and techniques for project selection, decisions are often based upon intuition rather than facts or partial information when dealing with threats and opportunities. Bringing project managers onboard during FFE activities, accompanied by effective use of project selection models, can make the difference between organizational success and failure.

Understanding Project Attributes

Even though every organization may have unique characteristics, there are some general attributes common to most project selection models. The attributes may appear as forms, guidelines, templates, or checklists and identify factors that should be considered for the evaluation and comparison of each project.

Attribute #1: Core Values and Management's Vision

Most companies have core values for products and services such as a specific customer age group, a specific price range, and perhaps a desire to stay within a certain geographical market segment. The core values, which are senior management's vision of the organization's future, establish broad boundaries for project selection. If management's vision for the project involves new opportunities that fall outside of the core values, project managers must be made aware of this because of the impact on project execution decisions.

Attribute #2: Alignment to Strategic Business Objectives

The projects selected must be aligned to strategic business objectives. For simplicity's sake, strategic projects can be defined under two categories:

- Business growth projects which focus on expanding the products and services of the business
- Business model improvement projects focus on improvements in the efficiency and effectiveness of the organization's business model that describes how the firm will interact with its customers, suppliers, and distributors.

Typical strategic objectives within the two generic categories in this attribute are shown in Exhibit 3-1. There are different paths and different decisions to be made in each category and possibly for each strategic objective.

Management must ensure that these business objectives are visible to project teams. Project managers must understand the rationale for establishing a specific strategy to maintain continuous alignment of project decisions to support strategic objectives. Even though the project manager may participate during the project selection process, there must still exist a line-of-sight between the project team and senior management during project execution in case business objectives change or the alignment of the project to the business objectives has issues.

The growth in metrics measurement techniques has allowed project teams to establish business, intangible and strategic metrics for project measurement, and reporting. The metrics can be used to measure business value created and alignment to strategic business objectives. Sometimes, small changes in the creation of strategic business goals and objectives makes it easier for project teams to report alignment and creation of business value.

EXHIBIT 3–1. GENERIC ATTRIBUTE CATEGORIES

Business Growth Projects	Business Model Improvement Projects
Revenue growth	Products can be sold by current sales force
Market share growth	Use similar marketing and distribution channels
Image and reputation	Purchased by existing customer base
Brand awareness	Reduction in time-to-market and product cycle times
Business importance	Cost reduction opportunities
Strategic partnerships	Improvements in customer satisfaction

By participating in FFE activities, project managers have a better understanding of the strategic information that is important to senior management and the board of directors. The PM can then select the appropriate strategic metrics that focus on business benefits and value being created and report this information to the senior levels of management and possibly even the board of directors.

The information presented in Exhibit 3-1 can be considered as suitability criteria for selecting projects. Approving projects that fall outside of the suitability criteria can delay time to market, increase the cost associated with a product launch, and incur additional costs associate with product redesign efforts. Project managers must understand the relationship between a project's deliverables and the suitability criteria.

Attribute #3: Core Competencies

The selection of projects should be aligned with the firm's core competencies, which can include use of existing technologies, and can be manufactured using existing production facilities. Experienced project managers usually have a better understanding of the firm's core competencies than do senior managers and can make this information available during FFE activities.

Attribute #4: Resource Requirements

Perhaps the most significant contribution project managers can make to the project selection processes is in the determination of the resources needed for the undertaking. Resources include people, time, money, and possibly facilities. Executives often select and prioritize projects without considering the resources needed. Project managers have a good grasp on human resource needs such as full-time or part-time, worker ramp up and ramp down time, additional training needs if necessary, and risks associated with the untimely removal of highly skilled workers to satisfy the needs of other projects. The result can be a stalled project and a financial drain.

Attribute #5: Using a Knowledge Management System

When working on strategic or innovation projects, having the right resources with the necessary competencies may not be enough. The organization may also need access to an information warehouse or knowledge management system.

Project managers may have expertise in working with the organization's knowledge management systems on previous projects. By knowing the contents of the system, PMs can provide advice on the need to hire contractors, proprietary information restrictions, control of intellectual property, and knowledge needed about customers' purchasing decisions that may impact project selection.

Attribute #6: Establishing Failure Criteria

Another important reason for project managers to participate in FFE activities is to work with senior management in deciding upon the project failure criteria. Every organization has its own tolerance threshold for risk and the threshold limit of unacceptable risk can be different for each project. Without an established failure criterion, it can be hard for a project team to know when to pull the plug and minimize the potential damage. Some examples of failure criteria include:

- Insurmountable obstacles (business or technical)
- Inadequate know-how and/or lack of qualified resources
- Legal/regulatory or product liability uncertainties
- Too small a market or market share for the product; dependence on a limited customer base
- Unacceptable dependence on some suppliers and/or specialized raw materials

- Unwillingness to accept joint ventures and/or licensing agreements
- Costs are excessive, and the selling price of the deliverable will be noncompetitive
- Return on investment will occur too late
- Competition is too stiff and not worth the risks
- The product life cycle is too short
- The technology is not like that used in our other products and services
- The product cannot be supported by our existing production facilities
- The product cannot be sold by our existing sales force and is not a fit with our marketing and distribution channels
- The product/services will not be purchased by our existing customer base

Growth of the Portfolio Project Management Office

For more than 20 years, companies have used the concept of a project management office (PMO) as the organization's knowledge repository of project management practices, guardian of the best practices library, and control point for continuous improvements in project management. In some organizations, all project managers are solid line reporting to the PMO.

As companies began embarking on more strategic and innovation projects, senior management recognized that they could not commit the amount of time necessary for project selection activities without sacrificing their other duties. The solution appeared as establishing a portfolio PMO with the responsibility of selecting and managing a group of projects. The PMO became the organization's lifeblood for identifying ideas and turning them into successful projects. The portfolio PMO relied heavily upon participation of project managers for the identification, selection, and execution of the projects within the portfolio.

As the use of project managers increased in the portfolio PMOs, PMs began developing additional skills in project selection and execution under higher degrees of uncertainty, determining the maximum level of resources needed, mapping of critical labor skills needed, and identifying effective ways for splitting or interrupting projects due to resource scarcity.

Project managers are now recognizing the skills needed to work in the FFE environment. Decision making for portfolio project selection activities requires an understanding of how to apply fuzzy logic when dealing with uncertainty.

The Growth of Fuzzy Logic

There are several project selection methods as discussed in the previous section. Some methods use complex mathematical concepts involving hard numbers to turn real-world problems into solvable equations. Other models which use fuzzy logic principles attempt to reduce uncertainty, such as in project selection activities (Demircan Keskin 2020; Kuchta 2001; Mohagheghi et al. 2019; Tolga 2008; Zolfaghari et al. 2021).

The fuzzy logic concept, which was introduced in 1965, allows us to make decisions based upon vague or imprecise information by providing weights to each attribute element. In fuzzification, the value of each variable or attribute element is represented by a real number between 0 and 1. The number 0 may represent a completely false situation unlikely to occur and not applicable whereas the number 1 may mean completely true. Numbers between 0 and 1 represent partial truths to help us make project selection decisions based upon imprecise or non-numerical information.

Fuzzy logic application can also be integrated with other mathematical formulations. Fuzzy logic mathematics allows us to manage project selection uncertainties and make decisions that would normally be just a best guess. Examples where fuzzy logic has been shown to be of value include:

- Resource dependencies attributed to multiple projects
- Minimizing scheduling issues when starting and stopping projects intermittently due to a scarcity of resources
- Determining the maximum number of resources needed for all projects
- Erratic supply dates for raw materials
- The interaction between project selection attributes

Nonfinancial Factors

There are nonfinancial reasons for selecting some projects. Examples might include supporting an organization's corporate social responsibility vision on environmental impact, usage and depletion of scarce natural resources, customer impact, maintaining a certain market share, keeping a product line open and workers employed, and maintaining the correct image and reputation. The nonfinancial factors are usually not quantified and are often difficult to compare against other projects with financial factors but may have significant strategic importance.

REFERENCES FOR ABOVE SECTION

Demircan Keskin, F., (2020). A two-stage fuzzy approach for Industry 4.0 project portfolio selection within criteria and project interdependencies context. *Journal of Multi-Criteria Decision Analysis* 27, 65–83.

Kuchta, D. (2001). A fuzzy model for R&D project selection with benefit, outcome and resource interactions. *Engineering Economist* 46 (3), 164–180.

Mohagheghi, V., Mousavi, S. M., Antucheviciene, J. and Mojtahedi, M. (2019). Project portfolio selection problems: A review of models, uncertainty approaches, solution techniques, and case studies. *Technological and Economic Development of Economy* 25 (6), 138.

Tolga, A. (2008). Fuzzy multicriteria R&D project selection with a real options validation model. *Journal of Intelligent and Fuzzy Systems* 19, 359–371.

Zolfaghari, S., Mousavi, S. M. and Antucheviciene, J. (2021). A type-2 fuzzy optimization model for project portfolio selection and scheduling by incorporating project interdependency and splitting. *Technological and Economic Development of Economy* 27 (2), 493–510.

PROJECT SELECTION AND POLITICS

There are several factors that are changing the landscape for project management. Some of the factors include:

- We are now working on significantly more projects, especially strategic and innovation projects that have more unknowns
- The direction of the strategic and innovation projects can change over the life cycle of the projects, thus increasing the number of decisions that must be made
- The projects are longer than in the past
- There is a greater likelihood that workers will be assigned full-time rather than part-time
- We have a growth in the development of flexible methodologies and each project can have a different methodology and different decisions to be made
- Stakeholder involvement in project decision making is increasing

All six of these factors have a common characteristic: they require much greater collaboration with and between team members, stakeholders, and customers than in the past. Increases in the need for collaboration will most certainly be accompanied by an increase in project politics.

Many people believed that project politics were mainly restricted to multinational projects where we may have to deal with political instability in governments. The outcome of a political risk might be that a new political party takes control of the government and project funding is cut or there is a significant change in the direction of the project. Political risk could also alter the raw materials you must use, the sources of the materials (countries from which the materials come), and which contractors you must use.

On traditional projects, project politics were often misunderstood and avoided with the belief that it was self-serving and would lead to negative results. In the past, we relied heavily upon the project sponsor or the governance committee to resolve the political risks. Today, the responsibility for political risk management falls on the shoulders of the project managers because many of the causes of political risk are the result of actions or requests made by the people empowered to provide project governance. Every project has some form of political issues. It can also come from customers as well as stakeholders trying to redirect the project because of personal agendas.

We now live in a VUCA environment where the impact of enterprise environmental factors (EEFs) is growing. Project political risks are no longer attributed just to multinational projects. Project politics is most frequently treated in project management as part of risk management practices as a political risk. The result of a political risk can alter the outcome of a project by changing the probability of meeting the original business objectives.

The longer the project and the less information you have (i.e., such as on strategic or innovation projects) the greater the need to understand as quickly as possible if people have personal or political agendas. The more ambiguity and uncertainty you have during project selection activities, the greater the risk of political decision making. When politics becomes important, people selecting the projects may not express all their real concerns for fear of exposing their true agenda.

When political risks materialize, you can classify people as supporters, fence-sitters, and challengers. Supporters will align themselves to your way of thinking, fence-sitters haven't made up their minds yet, and challengers will do everything possible to make you believe that their political position is correct. Successful project management occurs when PMs can resolve the political conflicts and convert the issues to project success.

Most project managers do not have authority to conduct performance reviews, and this limits their ability to resolve political risks. They rely heavily upon whatever informal power base they may have as well as their skills in conflict management, negotiations, and influencing people. The good news is that project management training programs are now including models on politicking and mitigating political risks.

Another topic that is being covered in depth in project management courses is stakeholder relations management. Project managers must know who the key stakeholders are and whether they are supporters, fence-sitters, or challengers. Making this identification should occur even before the project manager organizes the project and begins planning. This is yet another reason why project managers should be in attendance in project selection meetings. For project success to happen, PMs must know where they have support and where they have resistance. Knowledge about the key stakeholders can impact the way that the project is organized and establishes the political boundaries for a smooth decision-making process. This becomes extremely important when risks appear that, if not mitigated, can lead to project failure.

Project managers must learn how to manage projects in a political environment. They must be willing to understand who the stakeholders and decision makers are and develop a stakeholder management or political plan as part of the project's communications plan.

PROJECT READJUSTMENTS _____

"Think back to the Apollo 13 story. The astronauts and engineers had spent years planning for the launch. They had built a core team inspired by the vision of another flight to the moon. Despite all of that planning, they hit that gut-wrenching moment and said the famous words 'Houston, we have a problem.'"

— John Spencer and A. J. Juliani

Many innovation and R&D projects are managed by overly optimistic prima donnas who truly believe that they can develop any type of product if left alone and provided with enough funding. Unfortunately, such projects never end because the innovation/R&D managers either do not know when the project is over (poor understanding of the goals and objectives) or do not want the project to end (because they want to exceed the objectives). In either event, periodic project review or readjustment action must be considered. The primary reason for periodic review is to reassess the risks based on current strategic thinking and project performance. Souder (1984, 66–69) has identified several types of project risks:

- Technical failure
- Market failure
- Failure to perform
- Failure to finish on time
- Research failure
- Development failure
- Engineering failure
- Production failure
- User acceptance failure
- Unforeseen events
- Insurmountable technical obstacles
- Unexpected outcomes
- Inadequate know-how
- Legal/regulatory uncertainties

Project risks generally result in project selection readjustment. Typical readjustment actions might include:

- Replanning the project
- Readjusting the portfolio of projects
- Reallocating funds
- Rescheduling the project
- Backlogging the project
- Reprioritizing the projects
- Terminating the project
- Replacement with a backlogged project
- Replacement with a new project

PROJECT TERMINATION

Previously, we stated that innovation/R&D projects should be periodically reviewed so that readjustment actions can be taken. One technique for readjustment is to terminate the project. The following are the most common reasons and indications that termination is necessary:

- *Final achievement of the objectives*. This is obviously the best of all possible reasons.
- *Poor initial planning and market prognosis*. This could be caused by a loss of interest in the project by the marketing personnel or an overly optimistic initial strategy.
- *A better alternative has been found*. This could be caused by finding a new approach that has a higher likelihood of success.
- *A change in the company interest and strategy*. This could be caused by a loss of the market, major changes in the market, development of a new strategy, or simply a lack of commitment and enthusiasm of project personnel.
- *Allocated time has been exceeded.*
- *Budget costs have been exceeded.*
- *Key people have left the organization*. This could be caused by a major change in the technical difficulty of the project with the departure of key scientists who had the knowledge.
- *Personal whims of management*. This could be caused by the loss of interest by senior management.
- *Problem is too complex for the resources available*. This could be caused by an optimistic initial view when, in fact, the project has insurmountable technological hurdles that did not appear until well into the project.

Executives normally employ one or more of the following methods to terminate the innovation/R&D projects:

- Orderly planned termination
- The hatchet (withdrawal of funds and cutting of personnel)
- Reassignment of people to higher-priority projects
- Redirection of efforts toward different objectives or strategies
- Bury it or let it die on the vine

Innovation/R&D project managers are highly motivated and hate to see projects terminate in midstream. Executives must carefully assess the risks and morale effects of project termination.

IMPLICATIONS AND ISSUES FOR PROJECT MANAGERS AND INNOVATION PERSONNEL

If innovation project management is the delivery system for meeting strategic business goals and objectives, then innovation project managers must have more than just a cursory knowledge of business strategy. Some of the critical issues and challenges that may be new for some project managers include:

- An understanding of their own capabilities and willingness to say, "I am not qualified to manage this type of innovation project"
- An understanding of the different types of strategies and how innovation fits in
- An understanding of product portfolio analysis and the role of innovation
- Identifying the core competencies of the team early in the project, possibly by using SWOT analysis
- Understand the need for information on consumers and be able to work closely with marketing to obtain this information

REFERENCES

Booz, Allen, and Hamilton. (1984). *Management of New Products*. New York: Booz, Allen, and Hamilton, 180–181.
Martino, J. (1995). *R&D Project Selection*. Hoboken, NJ: John Wiley & Sons.
Souder, W. (1984). *Project Selection and Economic Appraisal*. New York: Van Nostrand Reinhold.

4 Innovation Tools and Processes

Learning Objectives for Project Managers and Innovation Personnel

To understand the characteristics of the innovation environment and how they differ from a traditional project management environment

To understand that there will be new tools that project managers and innovation personnel must use in an innovation environment

To understand that the organizational reward system may influence team members to work differently on innovation projects

INTRODUCTION

> *"Problem-insight precedes solution insight. Someone has to recognise a problem before they start to solve the problem."*
> — Max Mckeown, *The Innovation Book: How to Manage Ideas and Execution for Outstanding Results*

For innovation to take place on a repetitive basis, there must be an environment that fosters creativity and free thinking. Environments that focus on rigid policies and procedures generally have one

Innovation Project Management: Methods, Case Studies, and Tools for Managing Innovation Projects,
Second Edition. Harold Kerzner.
© 2023 John Wiley & Sons, Inc. Published 2023 by John Wiley & Sons, Inc.

and only one approach to managing projects and tend to reward people for obeying the requirements of the methodology. Innovation is often limited, and good ideas may never make it to the surface for examination.

The situation gets worse if senior management dwells on past successes and cannot envision the future. While governance of innovation is a necessity, it cannot be the same as governance of the day-to-day operations. Executives must understand that innovation leadership and governance may have to follow different practices than we use in traditional hierarchical leadership.

In this chapter we will look at some of the topics taught in traditional project management courses and how some of these topics may have to be looked at differently in an innovation environment. Emphasis will be placed on the new tools that innovation project managers must use. Most of the traditional project management tools still apply to innovation projects but may have to be supported by other tools such as brainstorming, prototype development, product or investment life cycles rather than the stage-gate approach, design thinking, and idea management.

NEW PRODUCT DEVELOPMENT

"Dreamers are mocked as impractical. The truth is they are the most practical, as their innovations lead to progress and a better way of life for all of us."

— Robin Sharma

Most innovations in business are in the form of incremental changes to existing products or totally new products resulting from discontinuous innovation efforts. The product can be tangible (something physical that one can touch) or intangible (like a service, experience, or belief), though we tend to separate services and other processes from products.

In business and engineering, new product development (NPD) covers all activities necessary to bring a new product to market. A central aspect of NPD is product design, along with various business considerations. NPD requires an understanding of customer needs and wants, the competitive environment, and the nature of the market. Although cost, time, and quality are the main variables that drive customer needs, the management of innovation covers significantly more variables. Aiming at these three variables, companies develop continuously improved practices and strategies to better satisfy customer requirements and to increase their own market share by a regular development of new products. There are many uncertainties and challenges that companies must face throughout these activities.

The product development process typically consists of several activities that firms employ in the complex process of delivering new products to the market. A process management approach is used to provide structure. Product development often overlaps much with the engineering design process, particularly if the new product being developed involves application of math and/or science. Every new product will pass through a series of stages/phases, including ideation among other aspects of design, as well as manufacturing and market introduction. In highly complex engineered products (e.g., aircraft, automotive, machinery), the NPD process can be likewise complex regarding management of personnel, milestones, and deliverables. Such projects typically use an integrated product team approach. The process for managing large-scale complex engineering products is much slower (often 10-plus years) than that deployed for many types of consumer goods.

THE FUZZY FRONT END _____

The product development process can be broken down in several ways, many of which often include the following phases/stages:

1. *Fuzzy front end* (FFE) is the set of activities employed before the more formal and well-defined requirements specification is completed. Requirements speak to what the product should do or have, at varying degrees of specificity, to meet the perceived market or business need.
2. *Product design* is the development of both the high-level and detailed-level design of the product: which turns the *what* of the requirements into a specific *how* this particular product will meet those requirements. This typically has the most overlap with the engineering design process but can also include industrial design and even purely aesthetic aspects of design. On the marketing and planning side, this phase ends at the pre-commercialization analysis stage.
3. *Product implementation* often refers to later stages of detailed engineering design (e.g., refining mechanical or electrical hardware, or software, or goods or other product forms), as well as test processes that may be used to validate that the prototype actually meets all design specifications that were established.
4. *Fuzzy back end* or commercialization phase represents the action steps where the production and market launch occur.

The front end of the innovation is the greatest area of weakness in the NPD process. This is mainly because the FFE is often chaotic, unpredictable, and unstructured. Unfortunately, this is where many of the decisions are made for later development and commercialization. It includes all activities from the search for new opportunities through the formation of a germ of an idea to the development of a precise concept. The FFE phase ends when an organization approves and begins formal development of the concept.

Although the FFE may not be an expensive part of product development, it can consume 50 percent of development time, and it is where major commitments are typically made involving time, money, and the product's nature, thus setting the course for the entire project and final product. Consequently, this phase should be considered as an essential part of development rather than something that happens "before development," and its cycle time should be included in the total development cycle time.

There has been a great deal of research on the FFE in incremental innovation but limited research regarding radical or disruptive innovation. With incremental innovation, which tends to reinforce existing core competencies, information regarding technology and the markets are known and many of the ideas that come forth are internally generated. Therefore, a business case can be developed where strategic business objectives drive the decision-making process in the FFE. With radical innovation, the reverse is true. Technology and competition may be unknown, and therefore the outcome of the FFE can drive the strategic planning process from which the business case is then prepared. Knowledge about the technology and the technology trajectory selected may come from just one individual, or perhaps a small team, and personal desires may affect his/her decisions. The decisions must still be approved by senior management, but the decision-making process can be significantly different than with incremental innovation. The organization may not understand the FFE process. A great many more assumptions must be made during the FFE in radical innovation, and less information is normally available.

De Brentani and Reid (2012) identify three characteristics of networking and information sharing that are important during FFE activities:

- Quality of the information
- Speed of the information
- Variables impacting effectiveness of information flow

Koen et al. (2001) distinguish five different front-end elements (not necessarily in any order) that must be considered:

1. *Opportunity identification.* In this element, large or incremental business and technological chances are identified in a structured way. Using the guidelines established here, resources will eventually be allocated to new projects—which then lead to a structured NPPD (new product and process development) strategy.
2. *Opportunity analysis.* It is done to translate the identified opportunities into implications for the business and technology specific context of the company. Here, extensive efforts may be made to align ideas to target customer groups and perform market studies and/or technical trials and research.
3. *Idea genesis.* This is described as an evolutionary and iterative process progressing from birth to maturation of the opportunity into a tangible idea. The process of the idea genesis can be made internally or come from outside inputs, such as a supplier offering a new material/technology or from a customer with an unusual request.
4. *Idea selection.* Its purpose is to choose whether to pursue an idea by analyzing its potential business value.
5. *Idea and technology development.* During this part of the front-end process, the business case is developed based on estimates of the total available market, customer needs, investment requirements, competition analysis, and project uncertainty. Some organizations consider this to be the first stage of the NPPD process (i.e., Stage 0).

A universally acceptable definition for fuzzy front end or a dominant framework has not been developed so far. The reason is that the FFE for incremental innovation appears to be easier to understand than for radical innovation, and there is significantly more literature on incremental than radical innovation. However, the outcomes of FFE in both types of innovation are the following:

- Mission statement
- Customer needs
- Details of the selected idea
- Product definition and specifications
- Economic analysis of the product
- Development schedule
- Project staffing and the budget
- Business plan aligned with corporate strategy

PRIORITIZING PRODUCT FEATURES _____

Innovation project management can be very costly and time-consuming. One of the ways to possibly reduce cost and time-to-market while satisfying customers is to reduce the fuzziness in the fuzzy front end by identifying the features of the product or service to be created. Highly technical team members may want to develop sophisticated products regardless of user needs. Marketing's desire may be to satisfy a customer's minimum requirements. Management often focuses on innovation in terms of profitability. The production team wants products and services that are easy and quick to produce using existing facilities. Given these different views, how does an innovation project management team know in what direction to go with the selection of features? How does a team determine the prioritization of features?

IPM teams must rely upon what customers say and do to fully understand what they want now and possibly in the future. Asking customers to vote on features, possibly using a ranking system, does not always provide the necessary deeper understanding of the features needed. Without this information, it is difficult to bring all of the different functional organizations into alignment on features.

Product features can range from those that might disappoint customers to those that satisfy or even delight the customer base. Selecting the right features requires the creation of a product roadmap to help identify what appeases your customers and makes them prefer your products/services over others. To help select from the many features options, road maps must identify factors for measuring *satisfaction* and also how to go beyond satisfaction into *delight*. There are several road maps that can be used. Most are based upon questionnaires with scales that range from *not important* to *extremely important*. The road maps allow a firm to prioritize the features for the products. Some road maps ask questions such as:

- How would you feel if you had this feature?
- How would you feel if this feature were not included?

There are several types of road maps such as a customer journey, a spaghetti diagram, and an affinity diagram. A customer journey map is a visual representation of their experience through each of the phases of interaction with your products and services. It includes all the steps from awareness of your product, visualizing their needs and perceptions, to the purchase and feedback following usage. It helps you understand the steps you see and do not see to take advantage of future opportunities and feature selection with this customer. This approach allows you to select and add features that can improve customer satisfaction.

A spaghetti diagram is a visual representation of a continuous flow line of an activity through a process. When used as an analysis tool, it enables the innovation team to identify opportunities to expedite process flow by eliminating redundancies. This method was first used to track routing and quality issues through factories. Today, this approach is used to determine the effort needed to implement the innovation features and deciding what to prioritize. It helps eliminate unnecessary features and steps that consume resources.

Affinity diagrams are bundling of ideas based upon similarities and differences in terms of value to the customers. It is beneficial when there are many ideas and helps you to organize your notes and insights from customer interviews. By understanding what your customers expect from your products, you can identify the features as must-have, nice-to-have, and not-needed. This approach, as well as other approaches, are beneficial during brainstorming and design thinking sessions as well as during the fuzzy front end of a project.

Other methods used for product/feature prioritization include:

- RICE Scoring Model
- Cost of delay prioritization method
- PriX method prioritization method
- Story mapping prioritization method
- Value vs. Effort prioritization method
- Kano Model prioritization method
- Opportunity scoring prioritization method
- The Product Tree prioritization method
- Cost of Delay prioritization method
- Buy a feature prioritization method

LINE OF SIGHT

Strategic planning is an activity usually performed at the senior-most levels of management. Executives establish the company vision and mission statement, and then roll it out to all levels of the organization to get their support. As stated by Jack Welch, former chairman and CEO of General Electric,

> Good business leaders create a vision, articulate the vision, passionately own the vision and relentlessly drive it to completion.
>
> (Tichy and Charan 1989)

The execution of the plan is performed at various lower levels through a series of projects. Not all projects require detailed knowledge about the strategic plan. For those projects where this information is critical for decision making, such as in the FFE innovation activities for new product development, there must be a line of sight between the executives, strategic planners, and the innovation team for information sharing to make sure that innovation decisions are aligned with strategic business objectives. Some executives believe that information is power and refuse to share. If then sharing is done, it generally varies according to the need to know, hierarchical level, tenure, and type of project.

Without knowing the strategy, innovation team members can be at a loss on how to contribute effectively. They may develop conflicting goals and objectives that can interfere with expected innovation success. Free thinking may then be replaced by simply following the commands given to them by others. Line of sight creates not only the correct decision-making mindset for the workers, but also provides them with more knowledge about the company, thus reducing the chance for ineffective behavior. It also makes workers believe that they are contributing to the success of the company and increases motivation. Line of sight can also make it easier to develop the proper risk management mindset especially if there exists a fuzzy front end.

Strategic planning and portfolio management must be aligned with project planning and execution. If the alignment does not exist, we may end up canceling potentially successful projects or wasting precious resources on projects that provide little business value. Line-of-sight is critical for this alignment to occur and assists in risk-mitigation activities.

MISALIGNMENT ISSUES _____

Strategies and the achievement of strategic goals and objectives are achieved through the execution of the right projects. As project management practices began transitioning from just traditional projects to the execution of strategic projects including innovation activities, the linkage between the words "strategy" and "projects" became apparent. Innovation project management practices must now deal with strategy formulation and implementation as well as the execution of strategic projects. Innovation project managers are becoming organizational strategists. Unfortunately, as with any new management practices, what also appears are serious issues that could prevent strategic success. If corporate-wide adoption of innovation project management techniques is to become relevant for achieving strategic objectives, the alignment issues between project management, business strategy, and innovation activities needs to be addressed.

Misalignment is the incorrect positioning or use of something in relation to something else. In traditional project management practices, misalignment commonly appears when project management execution techniques do not appear to fully support the project's objectives as stated in the business case.

Misalignment does not necessarily result in project failure. The result could be less than optimal achievement of strategic objectives, unexpected outcomes, or the need for additional time to correct possible problems.

Successful alignment increases the chances that organizations will select the right projects to achieve strategic objectives. Proper alignment will provide organizations more opportunities for making the necessary adjustments to match resources availability to strategic objectives. Effective alignment of innovation project management to business strategy can result in improved organizational communications especially between senior management and business units, better alignment of project priorities to business strategies, improved synergies between the business units, better monitoring and reporting of project performance, and successful execution of strategies.

The biggest challenge with misalignment involves senior management. Senior management are the architects of the corporate strategy. Unfortunately, they often just establish strategic goals and objectives without fully understanding how projects can be used to achieve these strategic goals and objectives. Strategies are implemented using projects. Senior management must understand how project management can impact business strategies. Misalignment occurs when management has a poor understanding of how to translate strategy into projects [Ansari et al. (2015) and Young and Grant (2015)].

Senior management often delegate the responsibility for innovation project identification to others but retain the authority for project approval. Innovation projects may be approved without careful consideration of their alignment to strategic issues. Managers asked to identify innovation projects may select those projects that are aligned more so to their functional unit strategies rather than critical corporate business strategies.

Senior management often create alignment issues when they believe that "information is power," are reluctant to support a line-of-sight between senior management and project teams, and refuse to bring innovation project managers on board early to understand the thought processes that were the background to establishing the strategy. Project managers are then assigned to the innovation projects after approval and without understanding the justification for the project, the reasoning behind the assumptions and constraints, and the priority for the project. Project teams may then select an incorrect set of metrics and KPIs for reporting project performance because of different interpretations of the strategy.

Selecting the right metrics is critical for senior management to know that the innovation projects are correctly aligned to strategic objectives and that innovation project managers continuously realize that projects related to corporate strategy may be of a higher level of importance than other projects they are managing. This may require the creation of alignment metrics that are reported as part of line-of-sight performance measurement and reporting practices. Relying on commonly used traditional metrics is a mistake. According to Bhasin (2008), problems with the use of traditional metrics on innovation and R&D activities include:

- Traditional metrics are not suited for strategic decisions
- Traditional metrics do not measure and report the creation of business value
- Traditional metrics are not very effective for the evaluation of intangible assets
- Traditional metrics provide little information on the root cause of problems impacting strategy execution

Simply because we understand the existence of misalignments is no guarantee that the problems will be resolved. There are steps however that can be taken:

- Senior management must develop a framework to ensure that selected projects are in line with business strategies.
- Senior management must recognize that innovation projects may not be able to be managed with the same standardized project management practices used on traditional type projects.
- PMOs can develop their own distinct methodologies and frameworks for the projects under their supervision and governance. They can also develop their own protocols for project selection and prioritization if it correctly supports the organization's strategic direction.
- PMOs must develop business-related and strategic metrics that measure the ongoing alignment of PMO projects to organizational strategic goals and objectives. Senior management must understand the importance of these metrics.
- Metrics must be established that measure business benefits and business value created throughout the life cycles of the projects. These metrics must measure and predict both tangible and intangible business value being created.
- Senior management must continuously remind project managers, program managers, and PMOs that they are expected to make decisions that are in the best interest of corporate strategy first rather than other criteria such as functional unit objectives and goals.

REFERENCES FOR THIS SECTION

Ansari, R., Shakeri, E. and Raddadi, A. (2015). Framework for aligning project management with organizational strategies. *Journal of Management in Engineering* 31 (4), 1–8.

Bhasin, S. (2008). Lean and performance measurement. *Journal of Manufacturing Technology Management* 19 (5), 670–684.

Young, R. and Grant, J. (2015). Is strategy implemented by projects? Disturbing evidence in the State of NSW. *International Journal of Project Management* 33 (1), 15–28.

RISK MANAGEMENT

Effective risk management practices are critical in an innovation environment, and quite often people do not realize the importance. As an example, a company began losing market share because of a performance gap that existed between what they could deliver and what their customers expected. This is shown in Figure 4-1.

The company put together an innovation team to solve the problem and close the gap. The innovation team eventually solved the problem, but much later than they desired, resulting in lost revenue and a smaller market share than they anticipated.

The company debriefed the innovation team after the project was over to find out what lessons were learned and any accompanying best practices. Initially, everyone believed that the problem was the result of having the wrong technical people assigned to the project. What the interviews showed was that the right team was assigned, but the team did not understand that risk management in innovation and the accompanying complexities were not the same as risk management in traditional project management. The result, as shown in Figure 4-2, was that ineffective risk management practices had prevented certain

Figure 4–1. The Performance Gap.

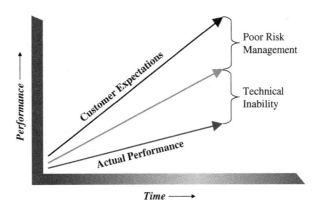

Figure 4–2. The Need For Risk Management.

critical decisions from being made in a timely manner, thus missing strategic opportunities. Effective risk management is a critical skill in innovation.

Sometimes, innovation risk management suffers because of the team's desire to get involved in detail that can hinder effective risk-taking. As Douglas Bowman (2009), a former visual designer at Google, explained:

> When a company is filled with engineers, it turns to engineering to solve problems. Reduce each decision to a simple logic problem. Remove all subjectivity and just look at the data.... (For example) a team at Google couldn't decide between two blues, so they're testing 41 shades between each blue to see which one performs better. I had a recent debate over whether a border should be 3, 4 or 5 pixels wide, and was asked to prove my case. That data eventually becomes a crutch for every decision, paralyzing the company and preventing it from making any daring design decisions.

The innovation environment can be characterized by five words: ambiguity, complexity, uncertainty, risk, and crisis. Some authors prefer to just use the terminology of a "VUCA" environment, which is volatility, uncertainty, complexity, and ambiguity. In Figure 2-1, we showed that certain types of innovation are accompanied by very high levels of ambiguity and complexity, thus increasing the need for effective risk management practices. While these words also apply to some degree to traditional project management practices and are considered during risk management activities, they may not have the severity impact as in innovation project management (Pich et al. 2002).

Ambiguity is caused by having unknown events. The more unknowns you have, the greater the ambiguity. As shown in Table 4-1, there are unknowns in the innovation environment that are treated as knowns in traditional project management. There are several other differences that could have been listed in Figure 4-1. It is important to understand that the way we taught project managers in the past was by promoting the use of an enterprise project management methodology that had forms, guidelines, templates, and checklists often designed to minimize the ambiguity on a project. These tools may not be applicable on innovation projects. Other tools will be necessary.

TABLE 4–1.　DIFFERENCES BETWEEN TRADITIONAL AND INNOVATION PROJECT MANAGEMENT PRACTICES

Factor	Traditional Project Management	Innovation Project Management
Cost	Reasonably well known except for possible scope changes.	Generally unknown.
Time	Reasonably well known and may not be able to be changed.	Generally unknown; cannot predict how long it will take to make a breakthrough. Innovators prefer very loose schedules, so they can go off on tangents.
Scope	May be well-defined in a statement of work and the business case.	Generally defined through high-level goals and objectives rather than a detailed scope statement. Innovators prefer weak specifications for the freedom to be creative.
Work breakdown structure	May be able to create a highly detailed WBS.	May have only high-level activities identified and must use rolling wave or progressive elaboration as the project continues.
Resources needed	Skill level of resources are generally predicable, and the resources may remain for the duration of the project.	Skill level of the required resources may not be known until well into the project and may change based on changes in the enterprise environmental factors.
Metrics	Usually the same performance metrics are used, such as time, cost, and scope, and fixed for the duration of the project.	Both business-related and performance metrics that can change over the life of the project must also be included.
Methodology	Usually an inflexible enterprise project management methodology.	Need for a great deal of flexibility and use of innovation tools.

Traditional project management focuses heavily on well-defined business cases and statements of work, whereas IPM relies on goal setting. Tension can exist when setting IPM goals (Stetler and Magnusson 2014). There is no clear-cut path for identifying IPM goals. Some people argue that improper goal setting can change the intended direction for an innovation project, whereas others prefer to recognize the need for some ambiguity with the argument that it creates space for innovative ideas, more fallback options are available, and the team may have an easier time converting ideas to reality.

Complexity deals with the number of components the project managers must monitor and the relationship between components. In innovation, many of the components are not known even with experimentation. If the technology is new and the product being developed is considered novel, then the company may have little historical experience and must therefore plan for cost and schedule uncertainties during innovation activities.

Complexity also increases when the project team must interface with a large stakeholder base or co-creation team, all of whom may have their own ideas about the project. With a large stakeholder base, the PM must deal with:

- Multiple stakeholders, each from a different culture and perhaps with hidden agendas
- Political decisions that become more important than project decisions
- Slow decision-making processes
- Conflicts among stakeholders
- Stakeholders that do not know their own role
- Frequent changes to the stakeholder base

Most innovation projects, which by nature are complex projects, generally have several components. The integration of these components requires an understand of the relationships between the project, the company's business strategy, management practices, processes, and the organizational process assets. (Gann and Salter 2000) and (Hobday and Rush 1999). Although the complexity in innovation projects may be no different than complexity in traditional projects, the impact it can have on risk management practices can be severe. Standard project management methodologies that often use linear thinking tend to evaluate risks on an individual risk basis without considering the human ramifications associated with each risk (Williams 2017). Without considering the human ramifications, marketing may have issues downstream in dealing with customers.

Ambiguity, complexity, and the accompanying risks are characterized and assessed using the amount of information available. If too little information is known, as is the case in the early stages of innovation activities, the payoff table for decision making becomes ambiguous or there may be too many interacting parameters that create complexity. In both cases, risk management becomes complicated.

As the complexity and ambiguity increase, so does the uncertainty. In traditional project management practices, project managers can assign a probability of occurrence to the uncertainty so that we can create a payoff table and perform risk management activities. But with innovation, there most likely will not be any historical data from which to assign probabilities to the uncertainties, thus increasing the risks and hampering risk mitigation efforts.

If we now include the impact on human factors, the situation can become even worse. When complexity, ambiguity, and uncertainty affect human factors, as it often does in innovation projects, risks can increase because the rational basis for decision making may no longer exist. "In projects, bad things tend to happen in groups, not individually… Events that affect projects in many ways … tend to go together. Even when one of those things occurs individually, it tends to trigger a cascade of problematic effects" (Merrow 2011). The combination of risks, accompanied by management's actions and team reactions, can create vicious circles of disruption (Williams 2017).

The fifth element characterizing the innovation environment is the need for crisis management. A crisis is an element of surprise that can occur unexpectedly and threaten the organization, the project, the customers, or the general population. Some authors prefer to use volatility rather than crisis. A crisis comes from a slowdown in the economy, recessions, making wrong decisions, or unexpected events that can lead to bodily harm such as product tampering, product misuse, or a pandemic. In general, there are no contingency plans in place because of the number of different crises that can occur. However, the innovation team must have a crisis mindset, which requires rapid response and an ability to consider the worst-case scenario while simultaneously coming up with alternatives and solutions. Organizations must continuously use risk-mitigation and crisis-management practices when there is a chance for significant unexpected events to occur, especially if the events are unfavorable.

The five elements characterizing the environment can have a serious impact on how a firm runs its business and the changes that may be needed for survival. As projects become more complex, the integration of components such as the firm's strategy, management practices, and organizational processes can and will change. We must understand the internal dynamics within the company. (Gann and Salter 2000) and (Hobday and Rush 1999).

There are options or approaches that innovation project managers can take to minimize the impact of these five elements. Examples include:

- *Complexity*: Understand the connectivity and dependencies between elements of work and staff the project with highly qualified resources that can perform in a complex environment.
- *Ambiguity*: Have a willingness to conduct meaningful experimentation and understand cause and effect relationships.
- *Uncertainty*: Continuously seek information that can support or negate the assumptions and constraints that might change the direction of the project.
- *Risk*: Continuously monitor and evaluate risks and their probability of occurrence; understand available risk mitigation strategies.
- *Crises(volatility)*: Closely monitor the enterprise environmental factors using a worst-case scenario approach and build in slack if possible.

THE INNOVATION CULTURE

"The key is to build a continuous learning culture of experimenters versus specialists, where it's everyone's job to be accountable toward creating and capturing customer value."
— Ash Maurya, *Running Lean: Iterate from Plan A to a Plan That Works*

All companies sooner or later may come up with a few brilliant ideas that lead to successful innovations. But the companies that are highly successful have a continuous stream of brilliant ideas largely due to their culture which supports innovation and creative problem-solving.

A culture is the shared values, beliefs, and performances that define a group of people and their behavior. Value includes the attitudes, beliefs, needs, and desires that people perceive as being important. Organizational cultures are intangible assets that can lead a firm to success or failure.

Some cultures thrive on free-thinking and encourage people to think outside of the box and outside of their area of expertise. It is not uncommon for people to then come up with elegant solutions that may not

EXHIBIT 4–1. FOUR DIMENSIONS OF AN INNOVATIVE CULTURE

Dimension	Description
Vision	Team members share clear and valued objectives aligned to the business strategy
Participative safety	A non-threating environment where team members can participate freely in discussions and decisions
Task orientation	A focus on achieving excellence through high quality work and acceptance of constructive criticism
Support for innovation	Recognition of the value of innovation and supporting the activities needed to achieve the innovation

be aligned to the strategic goal that was established, are more costly and require more time than simpler solutions when people think inside the box. This can lead to chaos if not controlled. Good innovation cultures strike a balance between order and chaos. There are tools and software to help reduce the chaos. As an example, mind maps and concept maps are diagrams that can be used to visualize information that focus on words or ideas. They often appear in the form of a spider diagram during brainstorming to help us visualize how ideas relate to the strategic goal.

Much has been written over the years about the importance of the right type of culture for innovation to succeed. With the correct culture, not only does a firm achieve better results, but they also have a faster time-to-market. In one of the early studies on innovation cultures, West (1990) identified four dimensions of an innovative team culture as shown in Exhibit 4-1. The four dimensions look at culture from a high level.

There are several possible causes for organizational resistance to convert to an innovation culture. Innovation cultures are subject to frequent change as new products and services are created or due to a change in the firm's business model. Some people fear change since it may remove them from their comfort zones. The longer someone spends in project management using a one-size-fits-all methodology, the more likely it is that they may become protective of the standard tools, techniques, and processes they have been using and resist change.

Cultural resistance can occur when innovation makes people nervous about new roles and expectations. Many people believe they are not creative. Many also conclude that it is not part of their job description, and that innovation is the sole responsibility of research and development (R&D) people. Some are not even persuaded that innovation is important enough to justify a major initiative.

Effective innovative cultures must allow for:

- Risk taking
- Curiosity
- Failure tolerance
- Everyone to tap into their own level of creativity
- Freedom to follow one's intuition
- Avoid or defer from rapid judgment
- Collaboration (informal)
- Active listening
- Being team players
- Managing tensions rather than just tradeoffs

The importance of an organization's and/or project's culture is often underestimated. Companies that aspire for continuous innovation must create an organizational culture that allows people to freely contribute ideas. In the same regard, creativity alone is not sufficient for achieving the goals of innovation; organizational initiative is a necessary condition for creativity to affect innovation. In a project environment, the PM must encourage people to have a sense of curiosity, to have the freedom to bring forth ideas as well as alternative solutions and to demonstrate their own commitment to the project. This also includes a visible willingness to accept the risks necessary to make the impossible possible. Executives are the architects of the corporate culture and the support they provide must be visible.

While the PM may be able to create a project culture, it must be supported by a similar corporate culture that also encourages ideas to flow freely, understands the strengths and weaknesses of the innovation personnel, and has confidence in their abilities.

Today, most companies have innovation cultures that are based upon the company's core values. Unfortunately, not all innovation cultures are easy to embrace because of a poor understanding of what the components of an innovation culture should be and the accompanying risks. As an example, consider the information in Exhibit 4-2 which shows the components of the culture from a more detailed level and some of the risks to consider.[1]

Some companies actively support innovation but only for its core businesses. Even though a firm has a strong culture, disaster can still occur if technology changes. Kodak was reluctant to accept the oncoming digital revolution because it did not want to deviate significantly from its legacy business.

Not all cultures foster an innovative environment. McLean (1960) describes nine practices that some cultures use that can destroy creativity and squelch genius:

1. *Coordinate work carefully to avoid duplication.* Everything new can be made to look like something we have done before or are now doing.
2. *Keep the check reins tight.* Define mission clearly; follow regulations: Nothing very new will ever get a chance to be inserted.
3. *Concentrate on planning and scheduling and insist on meeting time scales.* New, interesting ideas may not work and always need extra time.
4. *Ensure full output by rigorous adherence to scheduled workday.* Don't be late. Creative people sometimes remember their new ideas, but delay in working on them helps to dissipate them.

EXHIBIT 4–2. RISKS WITH INNOVATION CULTURES

Component	Risks to Consider
Tolerance for failure	The cause of the failure must be explained and not be the result of incompetence. There must be a willingness to refocus if necessary.
Safe to speak one's mind	This requires that management demonstrate a willingness to hear the truth. Hopefully, this is based upon competent ideas.
Willingness to experiment	This mandates that right people are making the decisions and know what experimentation should be conducted based upon sound judgment.
Highly collaborative team	Even though the team works closely together, they must be willing to accept confrontation and criticism as well as ask peers for help when necessary. They must also accept accountability for their actions.
A nonhierarchical organization	Even though the team may function in a self-directed environment, there must still exist strong and disciplined leadership.

1. For additional information, see Pisano, G. P. (2019 January/February). The hard truth about innovative cultures. *Harvard Business Review* 97 (1), 62–71.

5. *Insist that all plans go through at least three review levels before starting work.* Review weeds out and filters innovation. More levels will do it faster, but three is adequate, particularly if they are protected from exposure to the innovator's enthusiasm. Insist on only written proposals.
6. *Optimize each component to ensure that each, separately, be as near perfect as possible.* This leads to a wealth of "sacred" specifications that will be supported in the mind of the creative person by the early "believe teacher" training. The creator will the reject any pressure to depart from the envisioned specifications.
7. *Centralize as many functions as possible.* This will create more review levels, and it cuts down on direct contact between people.
8. *Strive to avoid mistakes.* This increases the filter action of review.
9. *Strive for a stable, successful productive organization.* This decreases the need for change and justifies the opposition to it.

One of the more serious risks that can prevent effective innovation cultures from forming is when internal competition becomes unhealthy. If management allows rewards for individual achievements to significantly outweigh team rewards, workers may make decisions in their own best interest rather than the best interest of the company. Information may not be shared, and sub-optimal decision-making may occur.

Some companies provide financial rewards or prizes for workers that come up with good ideas. This can set a bad example if implemented incorrectly and limit the interaction of brainstorming teams. Most workers are interested more so in receiving recognition for their contributions rather than financial remuneration. Some companies have created societies within the company to recognize achievements in innovation. Examples include:

- Disney: Imagineering Legends
- Apple: Apple Fellows
- 3M: Carlton Society

Companies can maximize the abilities of the innovation personnel by providing workers with a "line of sight" to the organization's strategic objectives and establishing processes to make this happen. When employees have a sense of awareness of the organization's direction and strategic goals, they make decisions based on the greatest importance to the firm. (Boswell 2006) and (Crawford et al. 2006).

Effective decision making is an important characteristic of the innovation culture. Decision making should be structured and based on evidence and facts rather than seat-of-the-pants guesses. Employees should have a decision-making mindset, not just on making decisions but on how to contribute. Positive reactions and favorable results will occur when people understand the expectations.

Executive involvement in decision making may be essential because innovation isn't predictable. Management must demonstrate a willingness to support trade-offs and adjustments when necessary. Management must also make it clear to innovation teams that they have a willingness to cancel projects when certain criteria are not met. The cultural environment must be failure-tolerant and without punishing people for their willingness to accept a great deal of risk and uncertainty.

Some cultures focus on command and control of the hierarchy. The result is that only the executives can initiate innovation activities and make critical decisions. The frontline workers have little or no authority and/or power to solve customers' problems in a novel way. Executives that are rewarded for meeting budgets and deadlines may be afraid of disruptions from innovation. Executives may not know how to overcome resistance to change resulting from an innovation.

Executives must decide which organizational structure would be best for the type of innovation. Typical options include:

- Functional teams
- Strong matrix teams
- Weak matrix teams
- Hybrid matrix teams
- Full-time co-located teams
- Virtual teams

The decision on what organizational form is best becomes more complicated when co-creation is taking place as well as with partnerships and joint ventures. Based on the organizational structure selected, executives may participate in selecting individuals for key positions. Some questions that need to be addressed include:

- How do we determine which people in a company have the mindset of an innovation project manager?
- How do we determine which workers have the mindset of an innovator?
- How do we determine if employees are in a comfort zone because they have been doing the same job continuously, are possibly technically obsolete, and are not in tune with the big picture?
- How do we know if workers near the bottom of the hierarchy know the strategic goal and objectives that can influence their decisions?

Miles and Snow (1978) identify the types of people that are commonly assigned to project teams. They include:

- Technical enthusiasts: appreciate innovation and can tolerate glitches
- Visionaries: focus on high-reward opportunities
- Pragmatists: risk-averse and want to see proven applications
- Conservatives: risk-averse, price sensitive, and want bulletproof solutions
- Skeptics: want status quo and resist new technologies

The meaning of "value" plays a critical role in establishing a culture. Good cultures create a mindset that value considerations are integrated in the way that project decisions are made. Some firms have value-driven cultures that focus on the delivery of business value rather than simply outcomes or deliverables from an innovation project.

There are, however, risks that need to be considered in any value-driven culture. They include possibly endless changes in requirements if the definition of value is not controlled, unnecessary scopes creep while attempting to maximize value, having the definition of value made by different people over the project's life cycle, and stakeholders not believing the forecasted value.

The innovation culture thrives on the free flow of information. Some cultures struggle with information overload and have difficulty in evaluating the trustworthiness of the information. The more widely dispersed the project team is, the greater the need for effective communications and coordination. Effective communication and sharing of information create synergy. In the project culture, the PM must communicate with senior management as well as stakeholders. This must be done within a climate of trust.

INNOVATION FUNCTIONAL UNITS

Companies have long recognized the need for innovation for corporate growth. But only recently have companies seen the need for functional units, such as innovation labs, dedicated to innovation activities and superimposed upon existing organizational structures as mentioned previously. One of the main purposes of the innovation unit is to make sure the company continuously innovates to remain competitive and that potential ideas for new products and services are not forgotten or confined to the back burner.

The innovation units usually do not do brainstorming but may take the lead in conducting brainstorming sessions. The innovation units observe how products are being used, collect and evaluate ideas for new products, and then work with other functional units for support to come up with a plan for commercialization of the best ideas.

Innovation units are more than just vaults to store ideas. There must be an idea evaluation process that is easy to use and transparent to all to encourage employee engagement. There are several techniques that can be used to encourage employee participation and feedback. The ideas can be evaluated using a ranking method from a predetermined scale, a yes–no questionnaire, or a pass–fail analysis based upon criteria established in an idea evaluation template or checklist.

The evaluation process may address several of the following issues:

- What are the strengths, weaknesses, opportunities, and threats to this idea?
- How sensitive is this idea to the enterprise environmental factors and the VUCA environment?
- To what business strategy or strategic business objective is this idea most likely linked?
- Is this idea limited to certain business units?
- Does the company have qualified and available resources to make this idea a success?
- What barriers could prevent this idea from being achieved?
- What is your best guess that this idea can succeed?

There may also be regional functional units rather than just a single corporate unit because each geographical area may have its own culture for creativity and the units must account for the cultural differences to maximize the innovation potential. Some cultures focus on individualism whereas other cultures emphasize teamwork. The individuals assigned to these units are committed to innovation activities rather than traditional business activities and look for ways to bring unique value to its customers. By separating the innovation units from traditional business units, it is easier to collect, evaluate, and bring good ideas to market.

Regional innovation departments are in constant communication with the customers in their general region of responsibility to assess their present and future needs. They also communicate with stakeholders and potential future customers. Their responsibilities include soliciting feedback from customers, combining ideas, maintain an idea inventory, providing information to the company's information warehouse, and selecting or developing the processes, tools, and techniques to support innovation management activities.

INNOVATIVE CULTURES AND CORPORATE LEADERSHIP

"As our business grows, it becomes increasingly necessary to delegate responsibility and to encourage men and women to exercise their initiative. This requires considerable tolerance.

Those men and women, to whom we delegate authority and responsibility, if they are good people, are going to want to do their jobs in their own way. Mistakes will be made. But if a person is essentially right, the mistakes he or she makes are not as serious in the long run as the mistakes management will make if it undertakes to tell those in authority exactly how they must do their jobs. Management that is destructively critical when mistakes are made kills initiative. And it's essential that we have many people with initiative if we are to continue to grow."

— William L. McKnight

Executives are the architects of the corporate culture and drive innovation leadership. As stated by Roland Bel (2010):

In surveys of most innovative companies, firms like Apple, Google, Microsoft, or Virgin regularly top the ranks, and stories of their emblematic leaders are recurring topics for management books and magazines. But what do Steve Jobs, Larry Page and Sergey Brin, Bill Gates, and Richard Branson have in common? What do they do that steers innovation in their companies? Are they the sole drivers of innovation leadership? And is there a direct link between the innovation capability of a firm and the charisma of its leader? After all, companies such as Toyota, 3M, Samsung, and Logitech are also recognized for their innovation capabilities, even though it would be more difficult to put a face on their innovation leadership.

Innovation leadership involves different roles and abilities across organization levels and strategic orientations, and along the organization and innovation life cycle. In most companies, the leadership is through an executive team rather than in the hands of one individual who may appear frequently in the media and the eyes of the public.

There are two critical activities that innovation leadership must consider: when to start and stop innovation without impacting the corporate culture. First, they must balance short- and long-term strategies. The intent of innovation is to create a long-term sustainable competitive advantage. However, this must be balanced without sacrificing short-term economic performance to appease investors. There must be a prioritization system for projects based on both short- and long-term strategic objectives. Not all strategic innovation projects can be funded.

Second, executives must be willing to cancel or place plans on the backburner. Pulling the plug on a potentially promising project is difficult. But it must be done if there are other more promising projects that require certain critical resources. Reasons for project termination must be explained to the workers so that the desire to be innovative is not dampened.

Project managers must understand that project termination is a way of life. In traditional project management, PMs tend to focus on the present rather than the future. In innovational project management, PMs must understand that executive leadership needs to balance the present with the future. Executives must make sure that the culture understands the reasons behind the decision and that project termination will not impact workers' performance reviews and career path opportunities.

IDEA GENERATION

"Steve Jobs gave a small private presentation about the iTunes Music Store to some independent record label people. My favorite line of the day was when people kept raising their hand saying, 'Does it do (x)? Do you plan to add (y)?' Finally Jobs said, 'Wait, wait—put your hands down. Listen: I know you have a

thousand ideas for all the cool features iTunes could have. So do we. But we don't want a thousand fea-
tures. That would be ugly. Innovation is not about saying yes to everything. It's about saying NO to all but
the most crucial features.'"

— Derek Sivers

Some cultures spend more time collecting and analyzing ideas than using them. This happens if the ideas lack supporting data. As a result, not all projects are brought forth immediately. Most people know that the more information they discover to support their idea, the greater the likelihood that the idea can become a fully funded innovation project. One way to get the supporting information, at least internally, is to begin with a bootlegged or stealth project. These projects are not recognized as "official" projects and do not have established budgets. The person with the idea tries to generate the supporting data while working on his/her other duties. If additional resources are needed, then the person with the idea must find people he/she knows and trusts to assist while keeping the project under the radar screen.

Bootlegged projects are done in secrecy because in most companies there is competition for funding and resources for other innovation projects. There may also be turf wars. Companies cannot fund or support all the ideas that come forth. Timing is everything. If the idea is released too early or if word leaked out about the idea, and without supporting data, there is a risk that the idea would be smothered by naysayers. These projects start in the stealth mode because you can delay or postpone the moment that the clock starts ticking for your idea (Miller and Wedell-Wedellsborg 2013).

When a project is done in secrecy, you may still need a sponsor to assist with getting resources and possibly some disguised funding. Generally, during the secrecy stage, you may be able to attract sponsors from middle management positions. Once the project is known, getting executive-level support may become essential because it gives you legitimacy, funding, and human resources. However, there is also a downside risk that your project is now in the spotlight and your career may be at risk.

SPINOFF INNOVATIONS

Regardless as to whether an innovation project appears as a success or failure, IPMs must look for possible spinoffs for the technology and intellectual property discovered. It is not uncommon for another innovation project to start up just for spinoff opportunities. A spinoff is an application for a product that is different from the original intent or original statement of work. The spinoff may be discovered immediately or even years later.

PMs must understand that spinoffs are part of innovation project management. Looking for spinoffs is often less costly than starting other projects and trying to reinvent the wheel. PMs must perform idea generation, creativity, and brainstorming for spinoff products even while they are managing a project. It is an ongoing process, not something that occurs just at project startup.

At one of 3M's innovation forums, an employee was speaking about how he was trying to invent a super-strong adhesive for the aircraft industry. But instead, he accidentally created a weak adhesive, but could not find an application for it. In the audience was another 3M employee, Arthur Fry. Fry sang in the church choir and had a habit of losing the bookmark in his hymn book. He soon discovered that the weak adhesive could replace the bookmark. The weak adhesive could be peeled away after use without leaving any adhesive substance on the page. Fry applied for and received funding for an innovation project to develop a product—which later became the Post-it Notes.

Companies that painted cars used a tape that either left some type of adhesive residue on the car or reacted chemically with the type of paint used. Richard Drew, an engineer at 3M, believed that he could solve the problem. Two years later, Scotch tape hit the marketplace.

A pharmaceutical company conducted a study on the 292 R&D projects they worked on over a 10-year period. A typical project had three life-cycle phases:

- Discovery or R&D: innovation project management
- Development: program management
- Commercialization: product management

Out of the 292 projects, the company developed 24 products, and 8 products were considered to be "home runs," which generated more than $500 million each year in revenue. A typical project that completes the discovery and development phases can cost between $750 million to $1 billion and can take 3,000 days or 10 years to complete. With the amount of time and money invested in pharmaceutical R&D, it is expected that all possible spinoff avenues for other applications would be investigated before a project is considered as a failure.

UNDERSTANDING REWARD SYSTEMS

When workers get assigned to a project, their first concern is "What's in it for me?" They expect to be rewarded for the work they do. The fairness of the reward system can change behavior and affect risk taking. Unfair reward systems can destroy an innovation culture.

Historically, reward systems were linked to cost-cutting efforts rather than innovations. This has now changed. There has been considerable research done on reward systems for product innovations (Jansen et al. 2006) and (Chen 2015). Reward systems generally follow two approaches. In a process-based reward system, which is often used in traditional project management practices, teams are rewarded based on how well they follow internal policies, procedures, and expected behaviors to achieve the desired outcome. In an outcome-based reward system, teams are rewarded based on the outcome of the project and the impact it may have on the bottom line of financial statements. There is significantly more pressure placed on the workers in an outcome-based reward system.

If compensation is tied to project outcomes, companies still seem to prefer to use existing well-established methods rather than seeking out new alternatives by trial and error. A better approach might be to tie the reward system to the risks that the project team must accept rather than entirely on the outcomes.

In radical innovation, workers are under a great deal of pressure to create innovative technologies for new markets using a highly uncertain development process that is accompanied by a multitude of risks. Individual motivation under these circumstances is critical (O'Connor and McDermott 2004). Employees must be trusted and given the freedom to experiment. However, boundaries must be set, and this can be done through goal setting (Pihlajamma 2017).

Regardless of the reward system chosen, there are fears that workers may perceive. In innovation project management, there is the chance that people might resign if the reward system is unsuitable, if they do not receive recognition for their performance, if there is jealousy from the rest of the organization and if the company has a low tolerance for failure. Reward systems must focus on retention of talent and the ability to renew the firm's competencies. The downside risk is that a linkage to reward systems may limit one's desire to take risks.

The rewards need not be monetary rewards but monetary equivalents such as giving team members gifts from a catalog, theater tickets, or a dinner at a nice restaurant. Some companies give people additional days of vacation or use of a company car. One company created a "wall of fame" display as people entered the company cafeteria showing pictures of the team members and describing their innovations. Companies such as 3M, Apple, and Disney have created societies to recognize the achievements of some of their talented and innovative employees.

In traditional project management, the PMs generally have no responsibility for wage and salary administration. This may change in IPM.

INNOVATION LEADERSHIP IN ACTION: MEDTRONIC _____

Background

In today's fast-changing world, we need leadership more than ever to increase innovation; to seize opportunities to make an impact; to inspire; to raise up voices that have been ignored; create beauty, and to continue learning. Leadership can be found in everything that we do at work and home. It is important to be a leader that can improve others. Leadership will create innovation in products and services. Leadership is an important part of innovation project management. Innovation project management is an area that is new in thought, and I believe will need to better define this area as leaders to move the next generation of project leaders and into future success.

Organizational Leadership

Our organization is creating an enterprise-wide innovation project management toolbox focused on the technical community, but this would also be available to the rest of the corporation. We have a dedicated career track focused only on program management and this would also be a great partnership for this type of career. We also know that there are different medical device headwinds which are having an impact on our businesses; for instance, enterprise excellence, European medical device regulation (MDR), pressures to reduce cost and improve quality, and access to our products in more regions around the world, just to name a few. We believe improved innovation project management will help improve the efficiency and productivity across the enterprise and present patients with more solutions to improve their health.

Working in an organization that creates many innovative products and services, innovation project management is very important to us. Creating efficiency and productivity in each project in the company will need to be the norm not on the nice-to-have list. We must now think of how we can become more efficient and productive during the project life cycle and after the project and the product or service that is the output of the project. Four generations are now working together, and many more innovative project managers will be added to new roles in the next couple of years. Many people are being moved into or

Material in this section ("Innovation Leadership in Action: Medtronic") provided by Michael O'Connor, Ph.D., MS, MBA, PMP, PgMP, IPMA-B, CPD, Director, Strategy and Project Management, Medtronic. ©2022 by Medtronic. All rights reserved. Reproduced with permission.

drafted into a project manager role before ever having any formal training. This change is also creating a need for traditional and innovation project managers to become improved leaders, change agents, and receive more training in this new and important area.

I believe that there is and will be a significant need for effective innovation project management. The innovation project manager role should be an easy-to-remember architecture that can improve the success of an organization. It can create a sustaining and strategic opportunity in innovation. With health care changing and moving toward value-based health care, it is important that we are able to change and lead with innovation and a framework to deliver a sustainable consistent cadence of projects into the organization that add value for the business need, align with the strategy, adhere to defined practices, and create a strong and robust portfolio. The successful innovation project manager will be able to build a model that businesses will pursue to effectively compete in today's rapidly changing business environment.

There should be internal/external training centered around innovation project management and a potential career path, perhaps even a certification program to align the innovation project managers of the future. The traditional approach to project management will most likely not fit the more up-front innovative projects of the future. This new type of innovation project management will need to be more flexible, increase speed, create trust, and add accountability. The impact that this could have on the organization could be large and should be considered as a potential new career path for these current and future leaders.

Leadership in innovation project management can mean many different things to many people. It is much more than just being a manager or supervisor. Leaders step up and create innovation, and a direction, vision, or strategy for others to follow. I believe strong leadership creates successful innovative projects. Project, program, and PMO management need leaders that have this direction, vision, or strategy. Leadership is the basic building block for successful innovative projects and improved successful outcomes.

Effective leadership requires skills that can be applied to the workplace and advance the organization. These are very important to create innovation and support innovation project management. I have four general areas that I believe will be important to innovation project management. First, I believe that one must know their strengths and weaknesses to be a more effective leader. Being able to know your Myers-Briggs or MBTI is a good start to understanding your personality type.[2] I have taken these three times and I come out with the same result as an ENTJ. The framework focuses in four key areas: energy, information, decisions, and approaching the outside world. I have taken this information and built my career and leadership style with this framework in mind. Since we utilize this in my organization, it better helps me understand the work I am preforming and how others get their work completed, and it creates a more effective leadership stance for myself and the team.

The second area I believe a leader should know and be in touch with how they score in the strength finder assessment. This is a tool that identifies your personal talent and skills. Again, I have taken this twice and scored nearly the same. It is very simple to apply the results. You first complete an assessment that is straightforward, and it takes less than an hour. You will then get a customized set of results and a report to better understand your talents. Once you have your report, you can review the leadership opportunities and work with your teams to improve how you all create effective leadership skills and improve innovation project management. This will empower you as a leader and will also create more efficiency among your group and the organization.

---

2. Myers-Briggs Type Indicator is a personality tool that provides an individual with his or her preferences based on a series of questions that focus on people preferences. ENTJ stands for Extraverted, Intuition, Thinking, and Judging. Only about 3% of people make up an ENTJ. These types of people typically assume leadership positions.

The third area is soft skills that a leader needs that can be applied appropriately to the group and organization. For innovation project management to be successful, I believe that the soft skills need must be fully understood and applied. This is where, from my experience, things can get difficult. A leader and innovation project management practitioner must navigate these soft skills to become solid leaders. Soft skills as a leader and in innovation project management can be difficult to learn from a book, online, or in the classroom. Many of these skills need to be experienced in a work setting. I have worked to create many different soft-skill leadership experiences in many different functional groups within my organization and career. By having these experiences and being able to see soft skills applied through many different lenses has made me a better leader and helped me also better understand the innovation cycle and how innovation project management can be improved by applying soft skills. This is also where being connected as a leader in your organization can help you find these types of different experiences.

Connecting, networking, and collaboration are also important leadership activities that will improve innovation project management and can be a part of the soft skills needed. Not only as a leader do you need to execute your strategy, tactics, and deliverables you also need to interface with new people in various groups and functions to build your brand and work with other leaders across the organization. I think this is one of the most impactful areas in which leaders can quickly improve their ability to lead in the organization and be able to work across many different groups to help implement innovation project management successfully throughout the organization. It takes time to meet with leaders and work with them to better understand their wants and needs. This activity, even performed at 5 percent a week, will have a large payback in the short and long run.

Finally, the fourth area is communication as a proactive leadership skill that will tie many of the skills a leader needs to be fully effective and move the needle in a positive direction. Communication is also another area that becomes much more important as the speed of business moves more rapidly. With improved technology you can keep a project alive and moving 24/7/365, which can be great for the project but not always for an innovation project manager that needs to get some rest and downtime. There are also many more different types of communication media such as with email, IM, texting, cell phones, tablets, and connection to the internet almost any place in the world. What is the best method, most consistent, and standard cadence of information for a project is a question that each PM needs to answer. Communication comes in many forms today. To be a successful leader in innovation project management, you need to understand the communication needs of your stakeholders and have a plan to utilize to create the highest leadership value. Communication is the heart and soul of an effective leader and innovation project management also requires these skills. While new generations turn to different modes of communication, good leaders will change their style or methods to accommodate others and create the highest value for overall organization success.

Innovation project management at my organization is relatively new and mostly focused in the research and technology areas. We have in the past set up projects/programs that have been larger in size than usual and hoped for success, with limited innovative project management training, coaching, and mentoring. We are now working with outside organizations to deliver project management training with face-to-face, virtual, and on-demand training. We believe this is a good first step but one that will require more investigation, changes, and ability to apply to our ever-changing environment. We believe now that to find successful technology or markets, we will need to apply many ideas and projects in something we call the smallest executable step. In other words, we would like to place as many bets as possible with our resources and finances and see which ones we can move to the next feasible step. We also need to be able to bring out information on technology and research projects into a dashboard format and will need to apply a technology tool that will enable us to quickly add and access information. This will be important to the overall sustainability of the innovation project management life cycle.

Our organizational innovative project management community is engaged in new ideas on how we can improve our workaround innovation project management companywide. We will need leaders in the innovation project management discipline to continue the success of our products and services. We also need leaders with the passion of dedicated professionals that see the value in innovation project management to speak with other leaders in the value this brings to the organization. The complexity of innovation project management will make it important to continue to educate and train current and future innovative projects managers.

IPM SKILLS NEEDED

In traditional project management, our actions rely heavily on company policies and procedures. We may also have an enterprise project management methodology where the project manager simply instructs the team to fill in the boxes in the forms and checklists. With IPM, there will be different skills needed because the innovation project managers will be involved end to end in all the life-cycle phases.

IPM skills are normally discussed as core competencies. Competencies are the roles, knowledge, skills, personal characteristics, and attributes that someone must have to fulfill a position. Competencies for managing traditional or operational projects are reasonably well-defined in documents such as PMI's *PMBOK® Guide* and IPMA's Competency Baseline, Version 3.0. However, for innovation projects, there is no universal agreement on the content of the competencies. Many of the traditional project management competencies are also components of innovation project management competencies, but there are others related to the types of decisions that must be made based upon the company's core competencies for managing operational work and the type of innovation project at hand.

When projects are well-defined from the start, as with traditional projects, we can define the skill sets needed with reasonable accuracy. It may be possible to define a skill set for incremental innovation where the goal is to get better at what we are already doing. But for disruptive innovation strategies, we may need to develop unconventional skill sets.

Most companies, especially large firms, have operational core competencies that are burdened with formal procedures that often make it difficult to react quickly to take advantage of opportunities that can lead to a sustainable competitive advantage. These companies are generally risk averse and perform as market followers rather than leaders.

If a company wants an entrepreneurial environment, then there must exist some degree of autonomy and flexibility in the operational core competencies that impact innovation activities for both product and process improvements. Typical core competencies for an entrepreneurial environment include:

- Inventiveness
- Understanding business strategy
- Understanding value propositions
- Having a business orientation
- Having knowledge about markets and customer behavior
- Working with high degrees of risk, uncertainty, and complexity
- Working with project success and cancellation criteria
- Managing diverse cross-functional teams
- Team building skills
- Design thinking

- Emotional intelligence
- Communication skills including active listening techniques
- Innovation leadership
- Possess good conflict resolution skills
- Coordination and control over activities

Competencies can vary from company to company in the way that the characteristics of the competencies are combined and the relationship to the firm's business model. Competencies are also dependent on the type of projects and corporate leadership exhibited.

Leadership must include allowing for some autonomy accompanied by the acceptance and support of taking on risky ventures often in reaction to technological changes in the marketplace. Autonomy is usually measured by the speed by which the firm's cross-functional activities are integrated to take advantage of opportunities for delivering innovative products. For entrepreneurship to work, there must be a corporate culture that supports risk-taking and experimentation without fear of reprisal if the results are not what was expected.

When the right skills exist, the success of an innovation corporate culture is measured by:

- The number of new products created
- The number of new products created that were first to market
- The speed by which commercialization took place

As seen in Figure 4-3, many of the skills needed by innovation project managers are not the core skills or tools discussed in the *PMBOK® Guide*, but are unique to an innovation project management environment.

Everyone understands the importance of "leadership" in IPM, but there is not much published on how it is impacted by the different types of innovation. In radical innovation for example, technical expertise may be needed to determine the viability of the project and to identify possible derailments. Technical expertise may also be needed to coordinate the efforts of diverse technical groups. Technical expertise is needed for product innovations, whereas organizational expertise is needed for process innovations.

Figure 4–3. Core Versus Specialized Skills.

Innovation leadership must include the ability to provide directions to many diverse groups. Managing group diversity is not just coordinating the efforts of a team based on different race, religion, sex, or ethnic background. This is critical when considering co-creation efforts.

Creative problem solving is another critical skill and is used to direct the efforts of the team, encourage ideas, and provide alternatives and possible solutions. The person acting as the creative problem-solver directs the efforts but is not necessarily the key player.

There are three additional skills that both PMs and team members should possess, in an ideal situation involving innovation:

1. *Emotional intelligence (EI)*. Recognize one's own and other people's emotions and use this information to guide thinking and behavior. Innovation environments can be highly stressful. If the IPM is unable to help manage the emotions of the team, then less than optimal results may occur. IPMs that understand emotional intelligence use emotional management techniques in their leadership style to reduce team stress. The result is usually better decision making.
2. *Business intelligence (BI)*. BI comprises the strategies and technologies used by the firm to provide historical, current, and predictive views of business operations and for decision making.
3. *Data discovery*. This is a user-driven process of using data mining and searching for visualized BI data patterns or specific items in a data set.

We tend to hire or assign technically competent candidates to fill innovation PM positions, even though they have no EI skills. This can create a serious problem with innovation projects where EI skills are necessary. Technical expertise is not the only ingredient for project success.

There have been articles that try to classify the types of innovation project managers according to skills needed. For example, Pedersen and Ritter (2017) identify innovation PMs as gamblers, prophets, executors, and experts. Each category has specialized skills that, when known, make it easier to align people to projects.

One of the challenges facing executives is the amount of technical knowledge that an IPM should possess. In many R&D organizations, the project manager is the person with the greatest amount of expertise about the technology of the project. However, the PM in this organization may not need all the other skills that IPMs might need because there may not be any customer or stakeholder interfacing. There may be no life-cycle phases that require gate reviews and written reports. PMs may have the freedom to deviate from the original objective or to discard the effort and investigate other alternatives without management's approval.

With IPM activities outside of the R&D group, it may be best to utilize professional project managers trained in innovation activities and follow the organization's protocols for innovation. The IPM may spend the bulk of his/her time communicating with marketing, stakeholders, and potential customers. If the IPM is actively involved in open innovation, the time commitments can be quite large and the IPM must then rely heavily upon the expertise within the team for understanding and applying the technology.

Organizations must have a firm grasp of the innovation-capable resources needed for competitive survival as well as the resources needed in the future for a competitive advantage. This can be accomplished by human resources using a talent pipeline that recognizes the competencies that are needed and their readiness to step in on short notice as backup talent.

The importance of the human resources group is often hidden, but it does have an impact on creating a corporate image and reputation that promotes innovation. This is accomplished by attracting talented technical people, giving them the opportunity to be creative, and ultimately increasing the public's confidence in the value and quality of the innovations.

DESIGN THINKING

Perhaps the most important skill for innovation project managers is design thinking. Design thinking is a structured process for exploring ill-defined problems that were not clearly articulated, helping to solve ill-structured situations, and improving innovation outcomes. The focus of design thinking is generally finding solutions to a problem rather than identifying the problem. Design thinking can help resolve innovation challenges. "Design thinking helps structure team interactions to cultivate greater inclusiveness, foster creativity, deepen empathy, and align participants around specific goals and results" (Mootee 2013, 63).

Design thinking is a collaborating approach to creative problem solving in rapidly changing markets where breakthrough ideas may be necessary. Design thinking also mandates a close and trusting relationship with the team members and the stakeholders throughout the life of the innovation. The focus is on customer needs and "thinking outside of the box."

As part of design thinking, you must know who your customers are or will be. This information may come from an understanding of competitive research such as a SWOT (strengths, weaknesses, opportunities, and threats) analysis and may include identification of:

- The most profitable and demanding customers
- The less demanding customers
- The new customers that are willing to accept a "good enough" product or service

Interviewing customers may be highly advantageous. The information can then be mapped as shown in Figure 4-4.

The team and the PM must also have a line of sight as to what are the strategic goals and growth objectives. There are no clear-cut tools or paths for identifying IPM goals. Some people argue that improper goal setting can change the intended direction for an innovation project, whereas others prefer to recognize the need for some ambiguity with the argument that it creates space for innovative ideas, more fallback options are available, and the team may have an easier time converting ideas to reality using

Customers

Customer Concerns		Customer #1	Customer #2	Customer #3	Customer #4	Customer #5
	Product Quality	A	C	B	B	B
	Product Safety	A	C	A	C	C
	Product Features	A	C	C	C	B
	Product Cost	B	A	C	A	C
	Delivery Date	A	B	C	A	A

A = High Customer Importance
B = Somewhat Important to Customer
C = Low Customer Importance

Figure 4–4. Customer Mapping According to Needs.

design thinking. When deciding to "kill" an idea because the value is not there, you must first put your-self in the users' shoes and think about the first user, not yourself. Innovation PMs must know the firm's tangible and intangible assets (capabilities and resources). The design thinking approach to redefine value for the customers begins with people, not products.

Design thinkers seek to understand the cultures not only of others but also of themselves, recognizing that their own emotions, practices, and belief systems inform what, how, and why they do what they do.

Embedding design thinking into a business means embedding it into the company's strategy, corporate culture, processes and practices, systems, and structures. According to Mootee (2013, 60):

> Applied design thinking in business problem solving incorporates mental models, tools, processes, and techniques such as design, engineering, economics, the humanities, and the social sciences to identify, define, and address business challenges in strategic planning, product development, innovation, corporate social responsibility, and beyond.

Unfortunately, most of these topics are not covered in traditional project management training pro-grams but are a necessity for IPM activities.

There are several benefits to design thinking:

- Greater focus on the customers' needs
- Discover new customer insights (i.e., with engagement project management)
- More creativity through idea generation and prototyping
- Solutions created as quickly as possible
- Creates a culture of learning
- Better handling of ambiguity
- Better understanding of complex connections
- Incrementally little bets as we go along rather than big bets

There are also causes for design thinking failure:

- Not understanding the problem and/or lack of definition
- Lack of information
- Poor communication channels, especially with stakeholders
- Rushing into prototype development
- Expecting a final solution from using one prototype
- Looking for a quick solution
- Team members being closed-minded to the ideas of others
- Relying too much on history and past customer behavior
- Overthinking the information at hand
- Failing to consider parallel paths
- Corporate gravity (i.e., removal from comfort zones)
- Cynicism

Project managers face several challenges, beginning with the FFE. A well-managed FFE usually leads to better innovation outcomes. Unfortunately, because of up-front uncertainty and a need to make quick choices, especially based on incomplete information, managing the FFE is a challenge.

Prototyping is another challenge. In linear prototyping, which occurs in traditional project manage-ment, the prototype is developed near the end of the project. In nonlinear prototyping, which is most common in innovation, several prototypes are developed, beginning upfront during design thinking. "Fail fast, fail cheap, and fail early" must be replaced by "learn fast, learn cheap, and learn early." Full validation of an innovation may require several prototypes and possibly world testing.

Organizational friction will occur during design thinking and can be advantageous and create internal competition surrounding intangible assets, such as the interpretation of intellectual property and the rationale for some decisions. People may then bring additional information to the table to support their position.

If the outcome of a project is to create customer value through innovation, then there is a need to bring design principles, methods, and these new tools into organizational management and business strategy development (Brown 2008). "Design thinking activities and project management are both evolving rapidly as transformation factors and processes in firms and the economic landscape change. Both fields are anchored in a practice characterized by methods and tools, but they are moving beyond that operational perspective toward a strategic one" (Ben Mahmoud-Jouini et al. 2016). A primary reason for this is because an output of design thinking may not be a product but instead a new business model that includes significant changes in customer management practices, innovation activities for the future, regulatory and social considerations, and organizational and financial considerations.

There are more than 100 tools that can be used as part of design thinking (see Kumar 2013). Some common design thinking tools include:

- Storytelling (providing narrative info rather than dry facts)
- Storyboards (depicting the innovation needs through a story with artwork)
- Mind maps (connecting all the information and relationships among the pieces)
- Context maps (uncover insights on user experience)
- Customer journey maps (stages customers go through to purchase the product and use it)
- Stakeholder maps (visualizing stakeholder involvement)
- Personas (who are the users and nonusers)
- Metaphors (comparison with something else)
- Prototyping (testing different ideas)
- Generative sessions (looking at stakeholder experience)

There are numerous textbooks that go into detail on each of these tools. See, for example, Keeley (2013), Kumar (2013), Tidd and Bessant (2013), and Luchs et al. (2016). Only a few of these tools will be discussed in detail later in this chapter.

BRAINSTORMING

Brainstorming capability is another critical IPM skill, but some researchers disagree. The argument is that creativity usually precedes innovation, and the innovation project manager may not be involved this early on. Creativity is where brainstorming takes place, and the role of innovation is to bring the creative ideas to life. Innovation ideas can come from several sources such as industry and market changes, demographic changes, new knowledge, and unexpected events. Innovation requires people to use both sides of their brain to take advantage of an opportunity. The people must demonstrate diligence, persistence, and commitment regardless of their knowledge and ingenuity.

Creativity is the ability to think up ideas to produce something new through imaginative skills, whether a new solution to a problem or a new method or device. Innovation is the ability to solve the problem by converting the idea into reality, whether it is a product, service, or any form of deliverable for the client. Innovation goes beyond creative thinking. Creativity and innovation do not necessarily go hand in hand. Any problem-solving team can come up with creative solutions that cannot be implemented. Any engineering team can design a product (or a modification to a product) that manufacturing cannot build.

Innovation is more than simply turning an idea into reality. It is a process that creates value. End-of-the-line customers are paying for something of value. Whatever solution is arrived at must be recognized by the customer as possessing value. The best of all possibilities is when the real value can be somehow shared between the customer's needs and your company's strategy. The final alternative selected might increase or decrease the value of the end deliverables, as seen by the customer, but there must always be some recognizable value in the solution selected.

Because of constraints and limitations, some solutions to a problem may necessitate a reduction in value compared to the original strategic objectives of the project. This is referred to as negative innovation. In such cases, innovation for a solution that reduces value can have a negative or destructive effect on the team. People could see negative innovation as damage to their reputation and career.

If the innovation risks are too great, the project team may recommend some form of open innovation. Open innovation is a partnership with those outside your company by sharing the risks and rewards of the outcome. Many companies have creative ideas for solving problems but lack the innovative talent to implement a solution. Partnerships and joint ventures may be the final solution.

It is possible that after evaluating the alternatives the best approach might just be a combination of alternatives. This is referred to as a hybrid alternative. Alternative A might be a high risk but a low cost of implementation. Alternative B might be a low risk but a high cost of implementation. By combining alternative A and B, we may be able to come up with a hybrid alternative with an acceptable cost and risk factor.

Sometimes, creativity is needed to develop alternatives. Not all people are creative, even if they are at the top of their pay grade. People can do the same repetitive task for so long that they are considered subject matter experts. They can rise to the top of their pay grade based on experience and years of service. But that alone does not mean that they have creativity skills. Most people think that they are creative when, in fact, they are not. Companies also do not often provide their workers training in creative thinking.

In a project environment, creativity is the ability to use one's imagination to come up with new and original ideas or things to meet requirements and/or solve problems. People are assigned to project teams based on experience. It is impossible for the project manager, and sometimes even the functional managers, to know whether these people have the creativity skills needed to solve problems that can arise during an innovation project. Unless you have worked with these people previously, it is difficult to know if people have imagination, inspiration, ingenuity, inventiveness, vision, and resourcefulness, all being common characteristics of creativity.

All ideas discussed during brainstorming sessions should be treated as intellectual property and recorded as part of a larger knowledge management system. Idea management is a component of knowledge management. Even if a company has idea screening criteria, all ideas should be recorded. What might appear as a bad idea today could end up as a great idea tomorrow. The drawback for a long time has been that innovation is a stand-alone process and not seen as part of any knowledge management system.

There is a valid argument that everyone assigned to the innovation team should possess brainstorming skills. Walt Disney's Imagineering division, which has the responsibility for designing theme parks around the world, is an example of how everyone throughout the life of the innovation project is expected to have brainstorming skills. At Disney, the term *"Imagineering"* is used, and it is defined as a combination of IMAGINation and enginEERING. Everyone in the Imagineering division, from executives to janitors, call themselves Imagineers and can participate in brainstorming sessions (Kerzner 2017). The culture in the Imagineering division is totally supportive of brainstorming and innovation. Titles and silos are not considered during brainstorming efforts.

With projects requiring traditional project management practices, brainstorming may be measured in hours or days. The membership of the brainstorming group may be large or small and may include marketing personnel to help identify the specific need for a new product or enhancement to an existing product, and technical personnel to state how long it will take and the approximate cost. Quite often, in traditional project management, a mistake is made whereby the innovation project managers may not be assigned and brought on board until after the brainstorming sessions are over, the project has been approved and added to the queue, and the goals established. At Disney's Imagineering division, brainstorming may be measured in years and a multitude of Imagineering personnel will participate, including the innovation project managers.

Brainstorming can be structured or unstructured. Structured brainstorming could entail thinking up an attraction based on a newly released animated or non-animated Disney movie. Unstructured brainstorming is usually referred to as "blue sky" brainstorming. Several sessions may be required to come up with the best idea because people need time to brainstorm. Effective brainstorming mandates that we be open-minded to all ideas. And even if everyone agrees on the idea, Imagineers always ask, "Can we make it even better?" Unlike traditional brainstorming, it may take years before an idea comes to fruition at the Imagineering division.

Disney is an exception whereby everyone in the Imagineering division may participate in brainstorming. This is not the case in all companies. There may be industry-specific skills that may be difficult to teach in a classroom. The skills needed by the Imagineers can include:

- The ability to envision a story
- The ability to brainstorm
- The ability to create a storyboard and build mock-ups in various stages of detail
- A willingness to work with a multitude of disciplines in a team environment
- An understanding of theme park design requirements
- Recognizing that the customers and stakeholders range from toddlers to senior citizens
- An ability to envision the attraction through the eyes and shoes of the guests
- An understanding of the importance of safety, quality, and aesthetic value as additional competing constraints
- A passion for aesthetic details
- An understanding of the importance of colors and the relationship between colors and emotions
- An understanding of how music, animatronics, architecture, and landscaping must support the story (Kerzner 2017)

The purpose of storytelling in innovation is to help the team visualize the need for innovation from the perspectives of other people and have the team build a shared meaning and understanding for the situation.

According to Luchs et al. (2016, 89–90):

In a design thinking product development process, stories allow concepts to be visualized and experienced before they have been designed and developed. Initially, the development team builds the stories and then shares them with the other stakeholders in the product development process. Stakeholders may include end users and potential partners.

The function of stories within the product development process is to create shared definitions of the types of problems to be solved, the contexts in which the problems occur, and the types of solutions that could resolve the problems. Stories allow quick communication within the complete product development team, its intended customers, and its extended stakeholder chain.

The user's or customer's point of view is the basis of the story narrative. Stories told from the viewpoint of the end user of the product are the foundation of business-to-consumer concepts. Business-to-business stories require creation of many variations of a story, each from the narrative points of view of the various customers within a value chain.

A good product development story informs its audience about the functional activities and interactions among people, products, and systems. It also reveals the emotional and rational needs of the people in it. Understanding these things allows the audience of the story to feel empathy for the people within it and develop a "feel" for how credible interactions within the described context could work.

When companies want innovation or to solve a problem, they quickly focus on setting up brainstorming sessions. Brainstorming sessions may not be necessary. A study conducted at the University of Amsterdam showed that, when people work alone, they tend to come up with more ideas than when working in a group. Most brainstorming sessions simply do not work despite starting out with admirable intentions. In some sessions, people show up not knowing what to expect, just to vent their emotions or with the belief that the session is just to support a decision already made by senior management. It is not because the brainstorming process does not work, but because the sessions are conducted poorly. Understanding the reasons for brainstorming failure often serve as a motivational force for corrective action. Some of the most critical reasons for failure include:

- *Lack of training for the facilitators and attendees:* Most project management training programs discuss brainstorming but never fully train people on the right way for the session to be conducted.
- *People spend too much time on solutions:* People tend to focus heavily upon solutions without fully understanding the problem, goal, or question presented. While having people come prepared with ideas and solutions seems a good idea, the focus must be on the right question or problem before generating ideas. Sufficient time must be allowed for people to understand why the meeting was called. Otherwise, people might have no idea what the solution should look like or how to arrive at a solution.
- *Poorly trained facilitators begin the meeting by asking for ideas immediately:* The meeting should begin with an understanding of the ground rules (such as no distractions or interruptions), creating the right mindset, the expectations on behavior of the participants (following directions), how the meeting will be conducted, and a clarification of the purpose of the meeting.
- *Failing to consider the fears and apprehensions of the participants:* Some people have an inherent fear of brainstorming sessions, and this includes experienced personnel. The apprehensions might include fear of being criticized, fear of being drawn into a conflict, and fear of change if the implementation of some of the ideas might remove one from their comfort zone.
- *Too long of a meeting:* Brainstorming sessions in some companies may be as short as 15 minutes. Meetings that go beyond 1–2 hours make people edgy and looking at the clock hoping for adjournment.
- *Large groups stifle creativity:* There is a valid argument that small groups of 5–10 people yield better results than large groups. Jeff Bezos, Amazon's CEO, calls it the two-pizza rule: If the

group can eat more than two pizzas, it is too big. The sessions may be composed of subject matter experts and may not include employees that might later be assigned to the project. Having a large group does not mean that more ideas will be forthcoming. Some people may feel intimidated by the size of the group and contribute only a limited number of ideas. With large groups, people worry about how others will view their ideas and may be afraid to contribute for fear of criticism. People tend to contribute better when in small groups. If the group is large, it may be best to break the participants into smaller groups at the start of the session and then reconvene into a large group near the session's end. Strong leadership is necessary to prevent the loudest voices and largest groups from drowning out the smaller voices and individualism.

- *Not building on the ideas of others:* Sometimes combining ideas may generate the best possible solution. For this to work correctly, people must be given ample time to digest what they heard and to express their thoughts. This is the reason why smaller groups are often best. Brainstorming sessions put people under pressure. A second brainstorming session may be necessary to give people a chance to think how they can build on the ideas of others.
- *Having the wrong balance of experience and knowledge in the session:* People should be invited to attend based upon the contribution that they can make rather than simply because of their rank, title, or availability.
- *Not having a diverse group:* Having a diverse brainstorming team may be advantageous. More information may come forth that leads to a different and better solution to a problem. Diverse teams usually do a better job challenging the assumptions, looking at problems and solutions differently, and dividing up the work requirements. Diverse teams generally do a better job looking at each of the individual components of a problem and then figure out a way to combine them into a solution.
- *Premature evaluation:* Some groups tend to quickly jump on the first acceptable idea and run with it without proper evaluation.

Some of the things that a company can do include:

- Send out an agenda early clearly stating the purpose of the meeting, the ground rules, and the topic(s) to be discussed
- If handouts are necessary, provide the handouts with the agenda so people can review it prior to the meeting and then come prepared to ask the right questions and possibly make decisions
- Clearly articulate the goal and make sure that it is reachable in a reasonable time frame
- While asking people to "think outside of the box" seems like a good idea, the best solution may be when the participants think "inside the box" instead
- It may be best to have a professionally trained facilitator conduct the brainstorming session to get people to contribute ideas and limit distractions
- Invite participants that may have an interest in the topic because they may look at the topic differently
- Ask people not to bring distractions such as cell phones, notepads, or laptops
- Make sure all attendees know that their ideas will be heard. Encourage everyone to come prepared to share their ideas, whether good or bad
- Document all ideas because some ideas may be valuable later
- Do not criticize any ideas no matter how bad they sound

- If research is required such as for a new or modified product, ask the participants to obtain information from consumer end-users rather than the middle people
- If the people that participated in the fuzzy front end prioritized the features, be sure that all participants have the information

The term "thinking outside the box" is a metaphor that relates to thinking differently, unconventionally, or looking at a situation from a different perspective. It is commonly used with brainstorming and creative thinking sessions. Companies prefer to use diverse teams when thinking outside of the box is required. Diversity is more than just race, gender, age, and personal values. It is also the way that people address a problem. Diverse teams often look at problems differently and may come up with ideas and solutions that others did not see.

While excellent results can occur, there are significant risks that must be considered. Some of the risks include:

- The "box" was most likely created by management based upon their vision and values they expect for growth. Thinking outside of the box may not be in management's interest.
- Diverse teams may have different meanings for certain words and expressions, thus creating misunderstanding.
- Diverse teams may look at the enterprise environmental factors differently.
- Diverse teams may make different assumptions and assume different constraints.
- There are significant risks (as well as rewards) with out-of-the-box thinking, and the risks must be understood right from the start.

Thus far, we assumed that the people attending the brainstorming session were in the same building or location. Today, workers generally spend a minimum of 25 percent of their time in virtual communications. This percentage is increasing as companies are now embarking upon virtual brainstorming sessions because more people are working from home because of several factors including COVID-19, the cost of office rental space, and the workers needed for the sessions may be dispersed geographically across multiple continents.

Virtual brainstorming is somewhat more difficult than onsite brainstorming because the virtual environment may require a different set of tools and software for communication, viewing, recording and displaying of ideas, and interaction among participants. Professional facilitators are trained in emotional intelligence and how to read body language. They can observe the expressions on people's faces and watch what they do with their hands or the way they are sitting as an indication of whether they are upset or in agreement with the discussion. Their fears and apprehensions can be visible by how they act. This is difficult to observe virtually.

If the group must be broken down in smaller groups, multiple concurrent virtual sessions may be necessary. The proper use of virtual brainstorming tools can overcome the productivity loss encountered in onsite brainstorming, bring out more creative ideas per person, and generate a higher degree of satisfaction among the team members.

Brainstorming sessions run the risk of information overload. This is particularly true if multiple brainstorming sessions are needed. Information overload can be demoralizing but can be controlled using idea management software or other tools.

The intent of a brainstorming session is to identify many workable ideas. This can become time-consuming since all ideas, whether good or bad, are usually heard and evaluated. A prioritization criteria, framework, or checklist can help filter out quickly ideas that should not be considered.

Prioritization criteria or framework is a list of rules or decision-making processes that the team should follow. The criteria do not prevent ideas from being heard but provides guidance in selecting the best idea and to make valuable use of the team's time. The criteria can be unique for each brainstorming session and prepared by senior management to keep the team focused on what is important to the company. The criteria can include items such as creating a product that can be produced entirely in the firm's manufacturing plants or the product must rely only on raw material from existing contracted suppliers to the firm.

There are other tools, models, and templates that can assist companies during brainstorming and creative thinking endeavors. TRIZ (see www.triz-journal.com) was developed in Russia as a systematic inventive problem-solving approach that contains 40 principles of invention and several templates. TRIZ is applicable to all industries. Synectics (see www.wikipedia.org;synectics) is a creative problem-solving model for harnessing creativity and invention.

WHITEBOARDING

Successful innovations using the tools and processes discussed previously in this chapter most frequently require a group of two or more individuals to collaborate to accomplish a common objective. Collaboration tools support the other innovation tools, encourage problem solving, and help the team remain focused using real-time meaningful discussions that can shorten the time needed to select the best idea. Collaboration tools can be non-technical such as flipcharts, post-it notes or whiteboards, whereas technical tools can include idea management software and specialized collaboration software. With the growth of virtual innovation teams, collaboration tools can eliminate the problem of making sure that all team members have the most recent versions of documents needed for decision-making.

Whiteboarding is one of the most used techniques and can be used virtually or in person. Whiteboarding is the most common collaborative tool used in brainstorming sessions. It allows team members to remain focused and be creative. Team members can express their ideas using sticky notes and move them freely around the board to see the connections with other ideas, thus adding structure to decision-making. All the ideas are captured, shared, and visible to all. Collaboration then allows for the orderly elimination of some ideas and the determination of a path to success through the remaining ideas on the whiteboard. The result is usually meaningful conversations either virtually or in person.

Collaboration tools allow team members to organize their thoughts, thus increasing their engagement, motivation, and productivity. The collaboration tools are used in conjunction with brainstorming, design thinking, and creative problem-solving processes.

Expecting workers to attend a brainstorming session and quickly grasp the concepts of collaboration tools such as whiteboarding is unrealistic. The tools should be taught either in separate workshops or perhaps in an introductory manner at the beginning of brainstorming, design thinking, or creative problem-solving sessions. There are exercises that can be used to teach these tools and maximize the ability of workers to think out of the box. Some of the exercises include mind mapping, storyboarding, and brainwriting.

MIND MAPS

Mind maps are mental maps of thoughts without having to worry about order or structure. When the mind maps are transferred to paper, flip charts, or white boards, the maps function as visual templates used to organize possibly monotonous information in an easily understandable manner.

Mind maps can make it easy to get information into and out of your brain. When used in meetings, mind maps make it easier to follow the conversation and make meaningful contributions. They are considered as tools for the brain by allowing you to collect knowledge, remember what you have collected, and map out meaningful ideas logically. They show the relationships among the pieces needed to fulfill the objective in a logical manner and create a better understanding by team members of what needs to be done and decisions to be made. Mind maps make it easier for one's brain to retain information and enhance innovation opportunities by overcoming potential roadblocks in the way we think. In a project management environment, mind maps are beneficial for:

- Preparing a work breakdown structure
- Preparing reports
- Conducting team meetings
- Conducting brainstorming sessions
- Participating in design thinking and creative problem-solving sessions
- Communicating with stakeholders
- Increasing team productivity

Mind maps are hierarchical. An image or central concept is drawn in the center of a blank page. Other ideas, images, lines, colors, and words are then branched out from the central concept. The mind map can appear as a spider's web. When the mind map is completed, it allows you to see all of the ideas at once and relationships between them in a logical and comprehensible way.

The amount of detail is based upon the needs of the user. Once the main or central concept is drawn, another pass through the network can create a second tier of detail, followed by a third or fourth tier of detail as necessary. Each tier shows the connection or relationship of ideas and information to the previous tier.

As an example, let's assume you want to purchase a new car. Therefore, new car purchase is the central theme. In the second tier, you create boxes with the names of each car manufacturer. In the third tier, you can include the different model cars that each manufacturer produces. In the fourth tier, you might include special features in each model, such as external or internal colors, seat comfort, amount of space, size of the trunk, etc.

These are several types of type of mind maps based upon the purpose, and they have become popular during innovation activities. One of the most used mind maps is the customer journey map. A customer journey map provides you with information on how your customers interact with your company and your products, why they make the choices they do, and possibly what features or parts of your products they like best. It includes the stages they go through from learning about your product, to purchasing it, to accessing customer service, and to providing feedback (favorable or unfavorable) using social media platforms. Customer journey maps are vital for sales and marketing personnel to understand the customer experience and provide innovation recommendations for updating your products with new features or creating new products.

Customer journey maps allow you to identify in which parts of the journey the customers may need the most help in deciding to purchase. It is important to understand the pain points those users face in each stage as well as the emotions they may feel that can impact their decision on interfacing with your products/services.

There can be several stages as part of a customer's journey and each stage may require significant data research. Typical customer journey stages might include:

- Product awareness
- Inquiry

- Comparison with other products
- Purchase
- Product use
- Customer experience and loyalty

In each stage, information is needed to understand the customer's experience. As an example, the information needed for customer awareness and inquiry might include:

- What is the customer's goal? Why are they interested in your product?
- How did they learn about your product?
- What were the touchpoints where the potential customer interacts with your company?
  - Advertisements
  - Internet browsing including user comments
  - Visiting stores that sell the products
  - Contacting your company

The next step is to determine what were the most likely customer emotions or friction they may feel at each stage and touchpoint and how might it have impacted their decision to become a product user. Typical emotions/feelings at each touchpoint might be:

- Anxiety
- Confusion
- Disenchanted
- Excited

Customer journey maps help you better understand the steps you see as well as the steps you do not see. They provide you with a much deeper insight into your customers. They help you identify innovation opportunities that can completely change the customer's experience. The same innovation opportunities exist with other mind-map applications to improve product and service desirability.

ACTIVE LISTENING

Design thinking skills must be accompanied by good communications skills, especially active listening skills. Improper listening can result in miscommunication, numerous and costly mistakes, having to repeat work, schedule delays, and the creation of a poor working environment. The result of poor listening is often more team meetings than originally thought and an abundance of action items. In brainstorming sessions, the result can be missed opportunities.

Active listening is a structured way of listening that focuses heavily upon the speaker and avoiding distractions. The result is usually a better understanding of what has been said. Active listening involves more than just listening to the words that the speaker says. It also involves reading body language. Sometimes, the person's body language provides the listener with a much more accurate understanding of the intent of the message.

All elements of communication, including active listening, may be affected by barriers that can impede the flow of conversation. Such barriers include distractions, trigger words, poor choice of vocabulary, and limited attention span. Listening barriers may be psychological (e.g., emotions) or physical (e.g., noise and visual distraction). Cultural differences including speakers' accents, vocabulary, and misunderstandings due to cultural assumptions often obstruct the listening process. Frequently, the listener's personal interpretations, attitudes, biases, and prejudices lead to ineffective communication.

Although we often talk about the listener when we discuss active listening barriers, it should be noted that sometimes the barriers to active listening are created by the speaker. This can occur when the speaker continuously changes subjects, uses words and expressions that confuses the listener, distracts the listener with improper or unnecessary body language and neglects to solicit feedback as to whether the listener truly understood the message.

Typical active listening barriers created by the speaker include:

- Creating a communications environment where excessive notetaking is required such that the listener never gets to digest the material or see the body language
- Allowing constant interruptions to take place which can lead to conflicts and arguments, or allowing the interruptions to get the actual subject of the communications way off track
- Allowing people to cut you off, change subjects and/or defend their positions
- Allowing for competitive interruptions
- Speaking in an environment where there may be excessive noise or distractions
- Talking without pauses or talking too fast
- Neglecting to paraphrase or summarize critical points
- Failing to solicit feedback by asking the right questions
- Answering questions with responses that are slightly off

Typical active listening barriers created by the listener include:

- Looking at distractions rather than focusing on the speaker
- Letting your mind wander and looking off in the distance rather than staying focused
- Failing to ask for clarification of information that you do not understand
- Multitasking: doing some tasks, such as reading, while the speaker is presenting his/her message
- Not trying to see the information through the eyes of the speaker
- Allowing your emotions to cloud your thinking and listening
- Being anxious for your turn to speak
- Being anxious for the meeting to be over

Some techniques for active listening effectiveness might include:

- Always face the speaker
- Maintain eye contact
- Look at the speaker's body language
- Minimize distractions, whether internal or external
- Focus on what the speaker is saying without evaluating the message or defending your position
- Keep an open mind on what is being discussed and try to empathize with the speaker even if you disagree
- Do not interrupt the speaker even though you have a different position or opinion

PITCHING THE INNOVATION _____

IPMs are often placed in positions where they must pitch the innovation to get initial or continued support. The IPM may or may not be the technical expert but is still responsible for seeking support. This requires strong communication skills accompanied by active listening skills.

Sometimes IPMs fall so much in love with technology that they forget what may be of critical importance to the audience where they are making a presentation. The pitch should address the five Ws, namely What, Why, When (if known), Where, and Who (if known). Senior management is, of course, interested in the return on investment, the risks, the cost of development, and the opportunity lost cost if the innovation is not undertaken. Marketing is interested in the time to market and how this innovation, if successful, will surpass the functionality of similar products from the competitors. Customers are concerned about the value they will receive and what they may have to pay.

If there are functional managers in the audience, they may be concerned about how the work will be done, namely the innovation development plan that they must staff. Innovators may have a great deal of knowledge about the technology but have limited experience in the creation of a technology development plan. In such a situation, it may be better to avoid addressing issues related to the plan.

COGNITIVE BIASES _____

Active listening and good communication skills require that the IPM possess a reasonable understanding of cognitive biases. A cognitive bias is a pattern of irrationality in judgment caused by the brain's attempt to filter information based upon personal experiences and preferences, and then make speedy decisions. The result is often poor judgment, illogical interpretation of information, perceptual distortion, and suboptimal decision-making.

Although all people have some biases, the type of project often dictates the impact of the biases. As an example, in traditional project management with a one-size-fits-all methodology based upon rigid policies and procedures, projects are well-defined at the start and the impact of the biases to influence faulty interpretation of information and decision-making is minimal. But in IPM, using flexible frameworks and with just an idea at project initiation, the opportunity for biases to exist is there. Innovation project managers must be able to identify the biases and minimize their impact.

Typical biases include:

- *Over-optimistic or over-confidence bias:* this occurs when you believe that you can perform better than you can because you have falsely assessed your abilities and intellect.
- *Confirmation or self-serving bias:* this occurs during decision-making when a team member analyzes and evaluates only the information that confirms his/her way of thinking about the problem. What's in the team member's best interest is seen as more important than the needs of the customers or stakeholders. If something bad were to happen, it is attributed to bad luck rather than bad judgment.
- *Misinterpretation bias:* this occurs when team members intentionally misinterpret what the data actually means to justify their position.
- *Herd mentality bias:* this occurs when you decide to follow the leader or group thinking rather than state your disagreement. This way, you can blame others if things turn out wrong.
- *Heuristics bias:* this occurs when people focus on what they believe are the most relevant components of the problem and make a quick decision based upon past similar experiences that were successful.

The risk occurs when they are wrong in identifying the most relevant components or falsely assume past experiences were similar.

- *Anchoring bias:* this occurs when you make a rapid decision or judgment based upon the first information you receive rather than evaluating all the information.
- *Mental accounting bias:* this occurs when team members may focus on and be enamored with the financial value of the outcome rather than the activities needed to get there.
- *Substitution bias:* this is when the team members may not recognize the complexity of the problem at hand or its solution, and may look at an alternative problem or solution, possibly unrelated to the project, that they think is the same and easier to understand and solve.
- *Naïve realism bias::* this is when team members believe that colleagues that disagree with them are uninformed or simply irrational in their understanding of the project.
- *Introspection illusion bias:* this occurs when people make false but confident predictions of how well they might perform when comparing themselves to other team members or possibly other projects they worked on.
- *Failure aversion bias:* this occurs when you look for an approach to the project that most likely cannot fail even though the result would most likely not be entirely what the customer wanted. You are worried more so what a failure could do to your career rather than completely meeting the client's expectations.

There are of course many other biases that could have been listed.

PROTOTYPES

A prototype is an early or incomplete model of a product built to test a concept or process. Prototypes are tangible communication tools that share information with everyone. Prototypes are most commonly used during product development innovation but can be used for service and process innovations as well. Over the life cycle of an innovation project there may be several prototypes built at different intervals. Prototyping serves to provide specifications for a real, working system rather than a theoretical one. In some design workflow models, creating prototypes are the steps between the evaluation of an idea and commercialization of a product.

There are several purposes for creating prototypes, six of which are identified below (Luchs et al. 2016, 131–133):

1. Initial explorations of an idea
2. Determining the appropriate direction
3. Attract funding
4. Garner feedback
5. Define patents
6. Facilitate the manufacturing process

Prototypes are used to explore different aspects of an intended design:[3]

- A *proof-of-principle prototype* serves to verify some key functional aspects of the intended design, but usually does not have all the functionality of the final product.
- A *working prototype* represents all or nearly all the functionality of the final product.

---

3. The remainder of this section has been adapted from *Wikipedia*; "Prototype" https://en.wikipedia.org/wiki/Prototype. Accessed May 15, 2019.

- A *visual prototype* represents the size and appearance, but not the functionality, of the intended design.
- A *form study prototype* is a preliminary type of visual prototype in which the geometric features of a design are emphasized, with less concern for color, texture, or other aspects of the final appearance.
- A *user experience prototype* represents enough of the appearance and function of the product that it can be used for user research.
- A *functional prototype* captures both function and appearance of the intended design, though it may be created with different techniques and even different scale from final design.
- A *paper prototype* is a printed or hand-drawn representation of the user interface of a software product. Such prototypes are commonly used for early testing of a software design, and can be part of a software walkthrough to confirm design decisions before more costly levels of design effort are expended.

In general, the creation of prototypes will differ from creation of the final product in some fundamental ways:

- *Material*. The materials that will be used in a final product may be expensive or difficult to fabricate, so prototypes may be made from different materials than the final product. In some cases, the final production materials may still be undergoing development themselves and are not yet available for use in a prototype.
- *Process*. Mass-production processes are often unsuitable for making a small number of parts, so prototypes may be made using different fabrication processes than the final product. For example, a final product that will be made by plastic injection molding will require expensive custom tooling, so a prototype for this product may be fabricated by machining or stereolithography instead. Differences in fabrication process may lead to differences in the appearance of the prototype as compared to the final product.
- *Verification*. The final product may be subject to several quality assurance tests to verify conformance with drawings or specifications. These tests may involve custom inspection fixtures, statistical sampling methods, and other techniques appropriate for ongoing production of a large quantity of the final product. Prototypes are generally made with much closer individual inspection and the assumption that some adjustment or rework will be part of the fabrication process. Prototypes may also be exempted from some requirements that will apply to the final product.

Engineers and prototype specialists attempt to minimize the impact of these differences on the intended role for the prototype. For example, if a visual prototype is not able to use the same materials as the final product, they will attempt to substitute materials with properties that closely simulate the intended final materials.

It is important to realize that by their very definition, prototypes will represent some compromise between the initial idea and the final production design. Due to differences in materials, processes, and design fidelity, it is possible that a prototype may fail to perform acceptably whereas the production design may have been sound. A counterintuitive idea is that prototypes may perform acceptably whereas the production design may be flawed, since prototyping materials and processes may occasionally outperform their production counterparts.

In general, it can be expected that individual prototype costs will be substantially greater than the final production costs due to inefficiencies in materials and processes. Prototypes are also used to revise the design for the purposes of reducing costs through optimization and refinement.

It is possible to use prototype testing to reduce the risk that a design may not perform as intended; however, prototypes generally cannot eliminate all risk. There are pragmatic and practical limitations to the ability of a prototype to match the intended final performance of the product, and some allowances and engineering judgment are often required before moving forward with a production design.

Building the full design is often expensive and can be time-consuming, especially when repeated several times—building the full design, figuring out what the problems are and how to solve them, then building another full design. As an alternative, rapid prototyping or rapid application development techniques are used for the initial prototypes, which implement part, but not all, of the complete design. This allows designers and manufacturers to rapidly and inexpensively test the parts of the design that are most likely to have problems, solve those problems, and then build the full design.

CREATIVITY AND INNOVATION FEARS

All workers are under some form of stress and pressure in the workplace; in some companies/industries more so than others. The stress creates fears such as doing things wrong, unpredictable events, not abiding by instructions, and possibly a loss of employment. These fears can be compounded in an innovation environment where people are asked to be creative but are afraid of the unknowns resulting from what they might say or do, such as being ridiculed or laughed at.

Sweeney and Imaretska (2016, 52–53) identify four symptoms of fear:

1. When an organization asks people to embrace a sense of frugality and expense reduction, I often see people fearfully translate that into drastically decreasing the number of ideas they produce—because they could cost money.
2. Sometimes I see leaders accidentally condemn the past when their intention is simply to energize and celebrate the future. That sometimes can affect the people they lead into thinking that all their previous hard work wasn't innovative.
3. There's the old standby that since the ultimate metric of whether our innovation was good or bad will be its return on investment, we should simply not waste any time considering ideas or innovations that won't make us money. That approach often blinds us to the benefits of the idea not associated with ROI, which could be very profitable in another form.
4. Many groups are frightened to learn what a truly different and perhaps conflicting set of ideas will do to their innovation. They simply dub themselves content experts, which allows them to be insulated from something that could drastically change their path or strategy. Voice of the customer (VOC) is a prime example of how listening to an outside perspective can help innovation.

Organizations must create a culture where people are not fearful of contributing their ideas, whether good or bad.

INNOVATION GOVERNANCE

Proper innovation governance can alleviate many of the fears described in the previous section. Unfortunately, assigning the right person to an innovation governance position has challenged executives for some time. The most common solution is to assign someone from the senior levels of management, most frequently from R&D or marketing. Many times, these individuals have progressed up the organizational hierarchy without ever having managed projects or been involved in innovation. These individuals then make the mistake in believing that innovation governance is the same as organizational governance and end up providing the wrong type of governance to innovation projects.

Innovation governance requires an understanding of the following:

- Governance personnel must understand that the way that governance is applied will vary from the fuzzy front end to commercialization at the speedy back end.
- The fuzzy front end focuses on exploring opportunities, idea generation, idea selection, and developing creative solutions. A knowledge of brainstorming practices may be mandatory.
- Governance personnel must create or support a culture where all ideas, whether good or bad, are valued. This may require the removal of cultural inhibitions and fears that can stifle innovation creativity.
- Governance personnel must make sure that all creative solutions are aligned with strategic corporate objectives. This may require the establishment of boundary conditions during brainstorming and alternative analyses. Governance personnel must keep the team focused and, at the same time, recognize that spinoff opportunities may exist outside of the boundary conditions.
- Governance personnel must demonstrate a willingness to pull the plug on projects that do not satisfy strategic requirements.
- Governance must create or support a culture where risk taking is encouraged and failure is acceptable without any form of punishment.
- Governance must demonstrate a passion for the innovation process and encourage team members to feel the same passion.
- Governance must be able to identify individuals with innovation capabilities and encourage them to perform at the best of their abilities. This may require identification of untapped talent.
- Governance personnel must demonstrate a willingness to experiment and test possibly multiple prototypes. This may involve new technologies.
- Governance personnel must interface with numerous groups outside of the company such as stakeholders, end-of-the-line customers, partners and open-source team members.
- Governance personnel must understand the importance of a speedy back end to commercialize the products and reap the benefits as soon as possible

CORPORATE INNOVATION GOVERNANCE RISKS

All innovation projects require some form of corporate governance. For incremental innovation, governance may be provided from lower or middle management levels. For the more complex projects that are considered as strategic and may end up as a radical or disruptive innovation effort, governance may be provided by the senior levels of management and may include members of the board of directors.

Companies recruit board members for a variety of reasons, many of which are related to the firm's desire to increase their innovative capabilities. Some of the reasons include:

- The ability to make strategic decisions for new products and services based upon unbiased assessments of opportunities and threats
- The ability to perform strategic risk management and reduce innovation uncertainties for the best interest of the shareholders
- Knowledge, education, and experience in new product development

- Knowledge, education, and experience in identifying new markets
- Finding ways to improve the marketing of products and services
- Building strategic alliances with suppliers, distributors, and consumers
- Providing support and networking for co-creation opportunities
- Assisting with providing sources of funds for large-scale innovation projects

Board members may be asked to provide governance on some innovation projects, and this is where unfavorable events may occur if the board members have hidden agendas or simply do not understand their role in innovation project governance. Corporate innovation governance is more than just assisting project managers with the daily decisions needed to produce successful innovations. It can also include dealing with ethical issues, corporate social responsibility, and managing relations with stakeholders and external investors. Governance decisions begin with the selection of innovation projects. Executives hire into companies with compensation contracts that are usually aligned to the stock price. This is motivation to align themselves with and support the best possible innovation projects that could impact their image, reputation, and career. Governance must also make decisions that provide some degree of protection that the financiers expect to receive for the capital they are providing for large-scale innovation.

Innovation governance personnel may include members of the board of directors that are shareholders. Pension and mutual funds with large equity positions often have seats on the board of directors and may be asked to assist in monitoring performance and providing governance.

There are numerous roadblocks impacting both the public and private sectors that must be considered when selecting the innovation governance team. Some of these roadblocks that innovation governance must deal with include:

- Organizational fragmentation and/or bureaucracy
- Slow decision-making processes
- Institutionalized mistrust
- Unclear financial incentives
- Unclear reward incentives for successful innovation
- Unstable time horizon
- Conflicting views between debt and equity holders

Appeasing everyone, including managers, investors, and shareholders, is not easy during project selection. Some people such as shareholders might prefer short-term profits resulting from low-risk innovation projects such as incremental innovation rather than long term and larger profits accompanied by higher risks that are associated with the best innovation project that may take years to come to fruition. Management may prefer long term and risky projects provided they are willing to burden the blame if the project fails. The project selection and approval process must consider the personal agendas of all parties. This is difficult to do if the personal agendas are hidden.

Selecting the best innovation project with the greatest expected returns may not be in the best interest of executives if the success of the company makes it a target for a takeover. Executives may then have to cede control of the company to a corporate raider. Some executives have compensation contracts that include golden parachutes in case of a takeover. The golden parachutes are usually aligned to the stock price and compensate the executive for loss of control and other benefits. Golden parachutes can and do influence executives in the degree of innovation they wish to support. Some countries have antitakeover laws that prevent outside corporate raiders from getting control of the firm's intellectual property rights for their own use using acquisitions.

Another challenge facing innovation governance is in deciding whether innovation should be internal or external to the firm. External innovation could come from the acquisition of a company or licensing rights to use their intellectual property. External innovation is faster than internal innovation creation because of proven technologies. There may also be advantages that come from faster introduction into new markets, having quicker earnings and brand recognition.

The decision between internal or external innovation opportunities is usually based upon the composition of the board of directors and their incentives and time horizons. As stated by Hoskisson et al. (2002):

> Examining the relationship between governance and corporate innovation strategies, we found, in opposition to the assumption that owners have a unified voice, differences among governance constituencies' preferences for corporate innovation strategies. The managers of public pension funds preferred internal innovation, but professional investment funds' managers preferred acquiring external innovation. The profiles of boards of directors also shaped these innovation strategies. Inside directors with equity emphasized internal innovation, and outside directors with equity emphasized external innovation. The two types of fund manager equally preferred boards composed of outsider representatives with equity. However, pension fund managers preferred inside directors with equity more strongly than did professional investment fund owners.

Corporate innovation governance personnel and board members with large equity positions are often reluctant to cancel innovation projects once started because of the negative effects it could have on the stock price. Instead, they tend to voice their opinion in hopes of encouraging people to improve efficiencies.

Innovation governance personnel do not always make decisions in the best interest of the firm. Sometimes they may believe that their decision and guidance is correct, but it can have a negative impact as shown in Exhibit 4-3.

EXHIBIT 4–3. POTENTIAL NEGATIVE IMPACTS FROM CORPORATE GOVERNANCE DECISIONS

Corporate Governance Decision	Potential Adverse Impact on Innovation
Falling in love with the project	Too proud to admit a mistake or unable to make necessary changes and risking a complete failure
Focus on short-term profitability	Perhaps unnecessary scope reduction and/or selection of the wrong projects
Focus on accelerating time-to-market	Increase in risks, scope reduction, and unpredictability of market acceptance
Reducing needed project resources	Lengthening of the project's schedule, poor product functionality, and scope reduction
Adding unnecessary project resources	Sacrifice day-to-day operations at the expense of innovation activities
Protecting project resources from non-core innovation projects	Fragmented and unhappy culture that may not support core innovation projects; possible staffing issues
Seeking the perfect innovation result	Lengthening of the schedule and changes in market demand and acceptance
Having too few innovation metrics	Making decisions based upon incomplete information and possibly going in the wrong direction
Having too many innovation metrics	Not knowing which metrics are necessary for decision-making and an invitation for corporate governance micromanagement

TRANSFORMATIONAL GOVERNANCE

There have been numerous books written on effective project management sponsorship and governance. Most books seem to favor situational governance and leadership, where the leadership style that is selected is based on the size and nature of the innovation project, the importance of the deliverables, the skill level of the innovation project team members, the project manager's previous experience working with these team members, and the risks associated with the project.

In the past, governance personnel were expected to provide leadership in a manner that improves the team's performance and skills and allows the employees to grow while working on project teams. Today, governance personnel are also being asked to function as the leaders of organizational change that may result from certain innovation projects, such as the creation of a new business model.

Organizational change may be a necessity resulting from the outcome of any innovation project whether it is a product, service, or new business model. Even the failure of an innovation project can induce organizational change that impacts the culture of the firm.

Organizational change requires that people change. This mandates that governance personnel possess a set of skills that may be different than what was appropriate for managing an organizational hierarchy. This approach is now being called *transformational governance*. Not all innovation projects will require transformational governance.

There are specific situations where transformational governance must be used and employees must be removed from their previous comfort zones. As an example, not all projects come to an end once the deliverables are created. Consider a multinational company that establishes an IT project to create a new, high-security company-wide email system. Once the software is developed, the project is ready to "go live." Historically, the person acting as the project manager to develop the software moves on to another project at "go live," and the responsibility for implementation goes to the functional managers or someone else. Today, companies are asking both the project manager and the governance personnel to remain on board the project and act as the change agent for full, corporate-wide implementation of the changeover to the new system or business model.

Transformational leadership and governance is heavily focused on the people side of the change and is a method for managing the resistance to the change, whether the change is in processes, technology, acquisitions, targets, or organizational restructuring. People need to understand the change and buy into it. Forcing change on people is an invitation for prolonged resistance, especially if people see their job threatened.

Effective communication practices can ease some of the pain when the organizational culture must change. As stated by Jessica Day:[4]

> Organizational culture is the substrate that "feeds" everything that everyone does in your company. Neglect it, and you neglect not only your employees but ultimately your clients and customers. Organizational culture is a living entity, wherein there is no endpoint. A strong, living, thriving culture is essential to innovation, and it's also essential to helping everyone be open to and ready for changes.
>
> People can't prepare for and implement change if they don't know about it and understand it. How far in advance you need to inform everyone will be unique to your organizational needs. However, people do need to know change is coming, and they need to be able to communicate their thoughts and questions about it. One of the biggest ways that organizations induce change fatigue is by pushing change onto people without informing them and allowing them to be part of the change process.

---

4. Extracted from Jessica Day, *Overcoming Organizational Change Fatigues: 5 Strategies That Work*, IdeaScale Newsletter, October 17, 2019.

Innovation and change are natural partners. Yet change is almost always stressful to some degree. Minding the big picture while prioritizing changes, developing a long-term strategy for change, tending to organizational culture, and keeping the lines of communication open are ways to prevent change fatigue and better deal with it when it happens.

BALANCED SCORECARD

The balanced scorecard, popularized by Kaplan and Norton (1996), is a performance management tool that tracks components of the business strategy which may include innovation. It is an essential tool for innovation portfolio governance. The balanced scorecard focuses more so on tracking performance than formulating strategy. It is a set of measures that provides a comprehensive view of the business based on actions taken. It complements other measurements such as customer satisfaction, financial measures, and innovation activities that drive future performance. The purpose of the report is to alert managers when performance deviates from expectations. It is not a replacement for traditional financial or operational reports.

The original thinking behind a balanced scorecard was for it to be focused on information relating to the implementation of a strategy, and over time there has been a blurring of the boundaries between conventional strategic planning and control activities and those required to design a balanced scorecard. This is illustrated by the four steps required to design a balanced scorecard included in Kaplan and Norton's writing on the subject:

1. Translating the vision into operational goals
2. Communicating the vision and linking it to individual performance
3. Business planning; index setting
4. Feedback and learning, and then adjusting the strategy accordingly

These steps go far beyond the simple task of identifying a small number of financial and nonfinancial measures but illustrate the requirement for whatever design process is used to fit within broader thinking about how the resulting balanced scorecard will integrate with the wider business management process or business model.

The first generation of balanced scorecard designs used a "four perspectives" approach to identify what measures to use to track the implementation of strategy, originally proposed by Kaplan and Norton (1992):

1. *Financial.* This perspective encourages the identification of a few relevant high-level financial measures. In particular, designers were encouraged to choose measures that helped inform the answer to the question, "How do we look to shareholders?" Examples: cash flow, sales growth, operating income, return on equity.
2. *Customer.* This encourages the identification of measures that answer the question, "What is important to our customers and stakeholders?" Examples: percent of sales from new products, on time delivery, share of important customers' purchases, and ranking by important customers.

Portions of the "Balanced Scorecard" and "Strategy Maps" sections have been adapted from *Wikipedia* entries, "Balanced Scorecard" and "Strategy Map."

3. *Internal business processes.* The third perspective encourages the identification of measures that answer the question, "What must we excel at?" Examples: cycle time, unit cost, yield, and new product introductions.

4. *Learning and growth.* This encourages the identification of measures that answer the question, "How can we continue to improve, create value, and innovate?" Examples: time to develop a new generation of products, life cycle to product maturity, time-to-market versus competition.

The idea was that managers used these perspective headings to prompt the selection of a small number of measures that informed on that aspect of the organization's strategic performance. There are now later generations of the balanced scorecard.

STRATEGY MAPS

A strategy map is a diagram used by innovation project managers to document the primary strategic goals being pursued by an organization or management team. It is most commonly associated with the balanced scorecard. The strategy map is important in innovation activities because traditional measurement of the success of an innovation strategy has been based on tangible assets that appear on the company's balance sheet. Today, tools such as the balanced scorecard and strategy maps exist by which we can measure intangible assets, such as knowledge-based assets, and their impact on the balance sheet. These tools allow us to better translate a strategy into operational terms and align performance against strategic business objectives. The strategy map is the architecture for designing the framework for the strategy. The strategy map shows how intangible assets can be converted into tangible outcomes. It is a flowchart of the business strategy.

The Kaplan and Norton approach to strategy maps has these features:

- An underlying framework of horizontal perspectives is arranged in a cause-and-effect relationship, typically financial, customer, process, and learning and growth.
- Objectives are within those perspectives. Each objective as text appears within a shape (usually an oval or rectangle). Relatively few objectives (usually fewer than 20) are used.
- Vertical sets of linked objectives then span the perspectives. These are called strategic themes.
- Clear cause-and-effect relationships exist between these objectives, across the perspectives. The strategic themes represent hypotheses about how the strategy will bring about change to the outcomes of the organization.

The balanced scorecard helps managers focus their attention more closely on the interventions necessary to ensure the strategy is effectively and efficiently executed. One of the big challenges faced in the design of balanced scorecard-based performance management systems is deciding what activities and outcomes to monitor. By providing a simple visual representation of the strategic objectives to be focused on, along with additional visual cues in the form of the perspectives and causal arrows, the strategy map has been found useful in enabling discussion within a management team about what objectives to choose, and subsequently to support discussion of the actual performance achieved.

The strategy map is a device that promotes three stages of conversation during the strategy development, implementation, and learning process:

1. Capture a strategy from a management team. To promote discussion among that team on the strategy, so they all leave the room telling the same story of their strategy.

2. Communicate the strategy, focus organization efforts, and choose appropriate measures to report on an organization's progress in implementing a strategy.
3. Provide a basis to review and potentially revise the strategy (not simply the measures or targets) and support conversations and decision making, as the team learn from the strategy's implementation.

Strategy maps align processes, people, systems, and innovation to shared strategic goals and objectives. The maps identify clear cause-and-effect relationships and how the strategy will bring about change to the outcomes of the organization.

INNOVATION PORTFOLIO MANAGEMENT

There is growth in the literature for an innovation portfolio project management office (IPPMO) dedicated just to projects requiring innovation. The IPPMO can exist along with other PMOs but may have the responsibility for just the twenty or so strategic innovation projects that are prioritized. The reason for the IPPMO is that innovation may require a different form of organization governance than is used to manage the day-to-day business. IPPMOs are critical for continuous innovations and can influence end-to-end IPM performance. There can be other project management offices (PMOs) dedicated to other functions, including strategic projects that may not require radical innovation of sorts. Unlike many other forms of portfolio management, innovation portfolio management is a complex decision-making process characterized by an elevated level of uncertainty. It deals with constantly changing information about opportunities internal as well as external to the firm (Meifort 2015).

The IPPMO provides the necessary governance to link projects to strategic objectives. Innovation benefits the entire company and therefore portfolio decision making should be emphasized over silo decision making. Analysis-paralysis situations should be avoided. Finally, the gaps between the project team, various functional groups, governance personnel, and stakeholders should be reduced through effective communications.

Almost all projects require tradeoffs, and in most cases the decisions about the tradeoffs are made by the project team. In innovation projects, the IPPMO may have a very active role and may be required to approve all tradeoffs as well as identifying the need for tradeoffs because of the impact it may have on the business strategy and the need for change management. The IPPMO may have a better understanding of the changes in the marketplace and possess proprietary data related to strategic planning. Typical reasons for tradeoffs on innovation projects include:

- Loss of market for the product
- Major changes in the market for the product
- Loss of faith and enthusiasm by top management and/or project personnel
- The appearance of potentially insurmountable technical hurdles
- Organizational changes (i.e., new leadership with different agendas)
- Better technical approaches have been found, possibly with less risk
- Availability or loss of highly skilled labor
- Risks involving health, safety, environmental factors, and product liability

Making tradeoffs involving ethical decisions is never easy because of the multitude of competing interests. Management should not encourage or coerce unethical behavior in dealing with employees, stakeholders, customers, or suppliers.

The IPPMO must insulate the innovation team from internal and external pressures. Some of the pressures include:

- Shortening development time at the expense of product liability
- Stockholder pressure for quick results
- Cost reduction
- Rushing into projects without a clear understanding of the need

Highly creative people thrive on recognition and want to show that their idea had merit and was achievable even if the market for their deliverable has changed. They do not like to be told to stop working or change their direction. As such, they may resist change and need to be monitored by the IPPMO if readjustments to the project are necessary.

The IPPMO's involvement in projects will be based on the type of project and the type of innovation. This is shown in Figure 4-5. The greater the unknowns, risks, and uncertainties, the greater the involvement by the IPPMO.

Existing PMO literature focuses on the execution of projects that are reasonably well-defined. Therefore, the roles and responsibilities of the membership in the traditional PMO can be reasonably defined. The IPPMO must serve as the bridge between innovation needs, business strategy, the organization's culture, and resource capabilities. Therefore, the roles and responsibilities of the IPPMO membership are more complex. Perhaps the most significant role of the IPPMO is in the front end of innovation where they must identify target markets, customer needs, value propositions, expected costs, and functionalities (Bonner et al. 2002; Wheelwright and Clark 1992).

As stated previously, culture often plays a significant role in how companies create a portfolio of projects that includes innovation. Some cultures try to minimize risk and focus on improvements or modifications to existing ideas whereas more aggressive cultures pursue fundamentally innovative ideas with the goal of becoming a market leader rather than a follower. There may also be a national-level culture that influences project portfolio development (Unger et al. 2014).

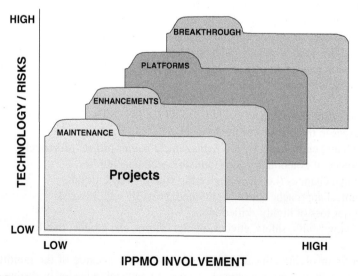

Figure 4–5.   IPPMO Involvement in Innovation.

Barreto (2010, 271) identifies four responsibilities for the IPPMO: (1) sensing opportunities and threats; (2) making timely decisions; (3) making market-oriented decisions; and (4) changing the firm's resource base. Sicotte et al. (2014, 60–61) add to the list topics such as intrapreneurship, proactive adaptability, strategic renewal, and value chain and technical leadership.

An important item that is frequently not discussed in the literature is the IPPMO's responsibility for nondisclosure, secrecy, and confidentiality agreements. This affects innovation project management more so than traditional project management. The IPPMO, working with top management, must develop a policy on how to handle transfer of confidential information regarding innovation and technological developments to outside sources, including stakeholders.

Some of the significant differences in the role of the IPPMO versus a traditional PMO include:

● Setting up boundaries related to the strategy so that reasonable goals can be established for the projects
● Dealing with constantly changing information and opportunities
● Monitoring the enterprise environmental factors
● Making sure that innovation specialists are assigned to the IPPMO to support opportunity-seeking behavior
● Supporting dynamic capabilities by determining if the organization must gain or release resources to match or create a change in the marketplace
● Looking for ways to renew and vitalize the firm's competencies
● Balancing the tension for resources between the ongoing business needs and the staffing for innovation projects
● Monitoring the slack in the firm's resources because there is an associated cost, and too much slack may allow bad projects to survive
● Understanding that resource allocation decisions are challenging because not all contingencies are known, and estimates and economic conditions are uncertain
● Monitoring the performance of the projects to avoid design drifts

Critical success factors (CSFs) can be identified for effective innovation cultures including IPPMO roles (Lester 1998). Typical CSFs include:

● Visible support and commitment by senior management
● Having an effective wage and salary program that rewards achievements by individuals and business units
● Proper staffing and training for innovation personnel and support teams
● Encouragement for new product ideas to be generated

INNOVATION SPONSORSHIP

The IPPMO exists for the management of a portfolio of projects. But sometimes, members of the IPPMO function as sponsors for individual projects in the portfolio. When this happens, the role of the project sponsor or project champion includes the following:

EXHIBIT 4–4.   DIFFERING VIEWS ON INNOVATION MANAGEMENT ACTIVITIES

Factor	Innovation Project Manager's Perspective	Executive Perspective
Deliverable	An outcome that exceeds expectations	A revenue-generating commercialized product
Product features	Brings recognition from peers	Recognized as value by the consumers
Schedule	As long as it takes, regardless of imposed constraints	Driven by time-to-market consideration
Cost	Desire to control all project funding	Balance cost against competition for funding other projects
Collaboration	Mainly with peers in technology development	With marketing, and co-creation partners
Governance	Micromanagement by the project manager	Structured methodology and decision making

- Demonstrates management's willingness and ability to assist in performing tradeoffs on time, cost, quality, and scope
- Assists with working relationships between innovation and other groups such as marketing
- Demonstrates management's willingness to cancel projects if necessary
- Explains management's attitude toward risk taking
- Assists in assessing opportunities and threats
- Knows the team's strengths and weaknesses
- Demonstrates confidence in the team's ability, trusting the talent assigned, and holding them accountable
- Assists teams with:
  - Assessment of customers' needs
  - Assessment of market needs
- Performs an economic evaluation of the project

Even though everyone appears to support innovation activities, there can be differing perspectives on what innovation is and how it should be managed and governed. Some of the characteristics of companies that may be considered as immature in IPM and lead to different perspectives are shown in Exhibit 4-4.

Companies need to develop a culture and framework for IPM to work successfully on a repetitive basis. This requires that everyone has the same understanding of the innovation being worked on.

THE INNOVATION TEAM

The six major players on an innovation team are shown in Figure 4-6. For innovation regarding products and services, the business owner could be internal to the firm, such as marketing, or customers. A co-creation team could be considered as part of the team and the future business owners.

Some projects will require a harvesting team and a sustainment team. The harvesting team has the responsibility or taking the outcome or deliverable created from the innovation project and extracting the expected benefits and value. The benefits and value may be defined in monetary terms. The harvesting team may be sales, marketing, and partners that have a financial interest in the outcome. Members of the innovation team can also be members of the harvesting team.

The sustainment team is usually assigned to process innovations. As an example, let's assume that a company develops a new business model. The harvesting team might be responsible for informing people about

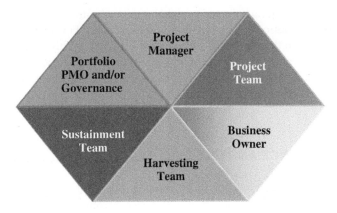

Figure 4–6. Major Categories of an Innovation Team.

the new business model. But if there is a risk that people will be removed from their comfort zone and may try to revert to the "old" way of doing things, then the sustainment team tries to prevent this from happening.

VIRTUAL VERSUS CO-LOCATED INNOVATION TEAMS

Much has been written about the use of virtual and co-located teams using traditional project management practices where the statements of work and other requirements are well-defined at the onset of the project. Project managers are reasonably comfortably working in both environments.

On innovation projects, the PMs are faced with new challenges which may dictate whether co-located teams may be favored over virtual teams or vice versa. Some of the questions that may influence the decision include:

- How complex is the innovation?
- Will the sharing of information by the team members be an issue?
- Will face-to-face communication be needed to enforce collaboration?
- Are trusted relationships between the team members an issue?
- Can the confidentiality of the information be safeguarded?
- Will the need for continuous prototyping and testing be a problem?
- Are there different union agreements at each location?
- How can we guarantee that all employees receive the same training if necessary?
- Can each location have a different wage and salary administration program and different incentives?
- Can each location have different reward systems?
- How close must the innovation be to supply chain partners?

Some companies establish worldwide R&D and/or innovation centers to create new products and services. These centers may have permanently assigned co-located teams but based on the type of innovation, may also use virtual teams.

The COVID-19 pandemic quickly forced companies to resolve the challenges posed from the previous questions. Opening innovation centers was a possible solution. For most companies, there was no choice but to quickly adapt to the use of virtual teams for innovation. This required a better understanding of virtual brainstorming practices, the use of virtual whiteboards, the use of innovation software, and experimentation with other innovation tools. Companies struggled with the transition to a virtual work environment but converted it into a learning experience.

ARTIFICIAL INTELLIGENCE AND IPM

As computer and information technology advances, pressure is being placed upon IPMs to manage innovation projects that include some aspects of artificial intelligence. A common traditional definition of artificial intelligence (AI) is intelligence exhibited by machines.[5] There have been advances in the use of AI for expert and knowledge-based systems that offer the promise of faster and possibly less costly data collection. AI systems can save the users a great deal of time and efforts as well as identifying trends in the data. This provides opportunities for use in information warehouses needed for IPM as well as IPM decision-making.

From a project management perspective, could a machine eventually mimic the cognitive functions associated with the mind of an innovation project manager such as decision making and problem solving? The principles of AI are already being used in speech recognition systems and search engines such as Google Search and Siri. Self-driving cars use AI concepts as do military simulation exercises and content delivery networks. Computers can now defeat most people in strategy games such as chess. It is just a matter of time before we see AI techniques involved in project management.

The overall purpose of AI is to create computers and machinery that can function in an intelligent manner. This requires the use of statistical methods, computational intelligence, and optimization techniques. The programming for such AI techniques requires not only an understanding of technology, but also an understanding of psychology, linguistics, neuroscience, and many other knowledge areas. The results can be highly beneficial to all forms of project management, including innovation.

The question regarding the use of AI is whether the mind of a project manager can be described so precisely that it can be simulated using the techniques described above. Perhaps there is no simple logic that will accomplish this in the near term, but there is hope because of faster computers, the use of cloud computing, and increases in machine learning technology. However, there are some applications of AI that could assist project managers, including IPMs, in the near term:

- The growth in competing constraints rather use of the traditional triple constraints will make it more difficult to perform tradeoff analyses. The use of AI concepts could make life easier for the project manager.
- We tend to take it for granted that the assumptions and constraints given to us at the onset of the project will remain intact throughout the life cycle of the project. Today, we know that this is not true and that all assumptions and constraints must be tracked throughout the life cycle. AI could help us in this area.
- Executives quite often do not know when to intervene in a project. Many companies today are using crisis dashboards. When an executive looks at the crisis dashboard on his/her computer, the display identifies only those projects that may have issues, which metrics are out of the acceptable

---

5. This definition and part of this section has been adapted from Wikipedia, The Free Encyclopedia: Artificial Intelligence.

target range, and perhaps even the degree of criticality. AI practices could identify immediate actions that could be taken and thus shorten response time to out-of-tolerance situations.

- Management does not know how much additional work can be added to the queue without overburdening the labor force. As such, projects are often added to the queue with little regard for (1) resource availability, (2) skill level of the resources needed, and (3) the level of technology needed. AI practices could allow us to create a portfolio of projects that has the best chance to maximize the business value the firm will receive while considering effective resource management practices.
- Although some software algorithms already exist, project schedule optimization practices still seem to be a manual activity using trial and error techniques. Effective AI practices could make schedule optimization significantly more effective by considering all the present and future projects in the company rather than just individual projects.

Project managers are often pressured to make rapid decisions based upon intuition rather than by step-by-step deduction used by computers. Nothing is simply true or false because we must make assumptions. Generally, the more information we have available, the fewer the assumptions that must be made. With a database of information, AI tools could perform reasoning and problem solving based upon possibly incomplete or partial information. AI can visualize the future and provide us with choices that can maximize the value of the decision.

If AI practices are to be beneficial to the project management community of practice, then "pockets" of project management knowledge that existed in the past must be consolidated into a corporate-wide knowledge management system that includes all the firm's intellectual property. The more information available to the AI tools, the greater the value of the outcome. Therefore, the starting point must be a consolidation of project management intellectual property and the AI tools must have access to this information. PMOs will most likely have this responsibility.

While all of this sounds workable, there are still some downside risks based upon which area of knowledge in the ***PMBOK® Guide*** where we apply the AI tools. As an example, using the Human Resources Knowledge Area, can AI measure and even demonstrate empathy in dealing with people? In the Integration Management Knowledge Area, can AI include additional assumptions and constraints that were not included in the business case when the project was approved? In the Stakeholder Management Knowledge Area, can the AI tools identify the power and authority relationships of each stakeholder? And with machine ethics, can an AI tool be made to follow or adhere to PMI®'s Code of Ethics and Professional Responsibility when making a decision?

While all of this seems challenging and futuristic to some, AI is closer than most people believe. Amazon, Google, Facebook, IBM, and Microsoft have established a non-profit partnership to formulate best practices on artificial intelligence technologies, advance the public's understanding, and to serve as a platform about artificial intelligence.[6] They stated: "This partnership on AI will conduct research, organize discussions, provide thought leadership, consult with relevant third parties, respond to questions from the public and media, and create educational material that advance the understanding of AI technologies including machine perception, learning, and automated reasoning."[7] Apple joined other tech companies as a founding member of the Partnership on AI in January, 2017. The corporate members will make financial and research contributions to the group, while engaging with the scientific community to bring academics onto the board.[8]

---

6. (Wikipedia footnote) "Partnership on Artificial Intelligence to Benefit People and Society." N.p., n.d. October 24, 2016.

7. Ibid.

8. (Wikipedia footnote) Fiegerman, Seth. "Facebook, Google, Amazon Create Group to Ease AI Concerns." CNNMoney. n.d. December 4, 2016.

Given the fact that Amazon, Google, Facebook, IBM, Microsoft, and Apple are all heavy users of project management, and by some are considered to have world-class project practices, it may be soon when they develop AI practices for their own project management community of practice. The implementation of AI practices to project management may very well be right around the corner.

THE NEED FOR PM 2.0 AND PM 3.0

The traditional approach to project management has worked well for decades and will continue to be used in certain industries and for certain types of projects. But for others, change to a more flexible approach where rigid methodologies are replaced with frameworks will take place. The change may not impact all forms of innovation. The greatest impact will most likely occur with process innovations, such as business model innovation.

The idea for PM 2.0 came primarily from those project managers involved in software development projects where adding version numbers to project management seemed a necessity because of the different tools now being used and different project needs. Over the years, several studies have been conducted to determine the causes of IT project failures. Common failure threads among almost all the studies included lack of user involvement early on, poor governance, and isolated decision making. These common threads have identified the need for distributed collaboration on IT projects, and eventually led to the development of agile and Scrum approaches. From an IT perspective, we can define PM 2.0 using the following formula: Distributed collaboration is driven by open communication. It thrives on collective intelligence that supports better decision making. Distributed collaboration is the driver for co-creation teams and open-source innovation practices. Traditional project management favored hierarchical decision making and formalized reporting, whereas PM 2.0 stresses the need for access to information by the entire project team, including the stakeholders and those people that sit on the project governance committee. This is a necessity for an effective innovation environment.

The need for distributed collaboration is quite clear:

- Stakeholders and members of governance committees are expected to make informed decisions based on evidence and facts rather than just any decisions.
- Informed decision making requires more meaningful metrics.
- The metrics information must be shared rapidly.

Collaboration through formalized reporting can be a very expensive proposition, which is why PM 2.0 focuses heavily on new project management metrics, key performance indicators (KPIs), and dashboard reporting systems. This increase in collaboration leads some people to believe that PM 2.0 is "socialized project management."

Agile project management is probably today's primary user of PM 2.0. However, there is criticism that the concepts of PM 2.0, accompanied by the heavy usage of distributed collaboration, cannot be used effectively on some large projects. This criticism may have some merit. There still exists a valid need for traditional project management, PM 1.0, but at the same time there are attempts to blend together the principles of PM 1.0 and PM 2.0.

Some people argue that PM 2.0 is just a variation of traditional project management. Table 4-2 shows many of the differences between PM 2.0 and PM 1.0. When reading over Table 4-2, we must keep in mind that not all projects, such as those utilizing an agile project management methodology for process innovations, will necessarily use all the characteristics shown in the PM 2.0 column.

TABLE 4–2.   DIFFERENCES BETWEEN PM 1.0 AND PM 2.0

Factor	PM 1.0	PM 2.0
Project approval process	Minimal project management involvement	Mandatory project management involvement
Types of projects	Operational	Operational and strategic
Sponsor selection criteria	From funding organization	Business and project management knowledge
Overall project sponsorship	Single-person sponsorship	Committee governance
Planning	Centralized	Decentralized
Project requirements	Well-defined	Evolving and flexible
Work breakdown structure (WBS) development	Top down	Bottom up and evolving
Assumptions and constraints	Assumed fixed for duration of project	Revalidated and revised throughout project
Benefit realization planning	Optional	Mandatory
Number of constraints	Time, cost, and scope	Competing constraints
Definition of success	Time, cost, and scope	Business value created
Importance of project management	Nice-to-have career path	Strategic competency necessary for success
Scope changes	Minimized	Possibly continuous
Activity workflow	In series	In parallel
Project management methodologies	Rigid	Flexible
Overall project flexibility	Minimal	Extensive, as needed
Type of control	Centralized	Decentralized
Type of leadership	Authoritarian	Participative (collaborative)
Overall communications	Localized	Everywhere
Access to information	Localized and restricted	Live, unlimited access, and globalized
Amount of documentation	Extensive	Minimal
Communication media	Reports	Dashboards
Frequency of metrics measurement	Periodically	Continuously
Role of software	As needed	Mandatory
Software tool complexity	Highly complex tools	Easy-to-use tools
Type of contract	Firm fixed price	Cost reimbursable
Responsibility for success	With project manager	With the team
Decision making	By project manager	By the team
Project health checks	Optional	Mandatory
Type of project team	Co-located	Distributed or virtual
Resource qualifications	Taken for granted	Validated
Team member creativity	Limited	Extensive
Project management culture within firm	Competitive	Cooperative
Access to stakeholders	At selected intervals	Continuous
Stakeholder experience with project management	Optional	Mandatory
Customer involvement	Optional	Mandatory

TABLE 4–2. (CONTINUED)

Factor	PM 1.0	PM 2.0
Organizational project management maturity	Optional	Mandatory
Life-cycle phases	Traditional life-cycle phases	Investment life-cycle phases
Executive's trust in the project manager	Low level of trust	Elevated level of trust
Speed of continuous improvement efforts	Slow	Rapid
Project management education	Nice to have but not necessary	Necessary and part of life-long learning

Project managers in the future will be given the freedom to select what approach will work best for them on their project. Rigid methodologies on some types of projects will be replaced by forms, guidelines, templates, and checklists. The project manager will walk through a cafeteria and select from the shelves those elements/activities that best fit his/her project. At the end of the cafeteria line, the project manager, accompanied by the project team, will combine all the elements/activities into a project playbook specifically designed for a given client or innovation project. Client customization will be an essential ingredient of PM 2.0. Rigid methodologies will be converted into flexible methodologies or frameworks.

PM 2.0 is not a separate project management methodology appropriate just for small projects. It is more of a streamlined compilation of many of the updated practices that were embodied in PM 1.0 to allow for a rapid development process. The streamlining was largely due to advances in Web 2.0 software, and success was achieved when everyone on the project team used the same tools.

Although PM 2.0 has been reasonably successful on small projects, the question still exists as to whether PM 1.0 is better for large projects. The jury has not delivered a verdict yet. But some of the publications that discuss how PM 1.0 and PM 2.0 can be combined offer promise. The expected benefits are proactive rather than reactive management, more rapid decision making, quicker problem resolution, and a better working environment.

PM 3.0 focuses heavily on project management as a recognized business process responsible for the delivery of outcomes necessary to meet strategic business objectives. Heavy emphasis is placed on benefits realization and value management practices with the expectation that bad projects either will not get into the portfolio or will be cancelled early on. Table 4-3 shows some of the differences with PM 3.0.

TABLE 4–3.   DIFFERENCES BETWEEN PM 1.0, PM 2.0, AND PM 3.0

Factor	PM 1.0 AND PM 2.0	PM 3.0
Project management areas of emphases	Project planning, measuring, and controlling	Benefits realization and value management
Project investment drivers	Cost and profitability	Alignment to strategic business objectives
Metrics selected	To track tangible elements only	To track tangible and intangible elements
Assumptions and constraints	Fixed over the project's life cycle	Can vary over the project's life cycle
Business case development	Unstructured and often with vague assumptions	Structured including benefits and value identification
Methodologies	Project methodologies; earned value measurement systems (EVMS) and enterprise project management (EPM)	Frameworks and value measurement methodologies (VMM) on certain projects and types of innovation
Project staffing	Misapplication of critical resources	Capacity planning and resource management

IMPLICATIONS AND ISSUES FOR PROJECT MANAGERS AND INNOVATION PERSONNEL

Perhaps the biggest challenge facing project managers, especially experienced project managers, is understanding that innovation projects may require a completely different set of tools than they have been accustomed to using. Project managers may have to undergo training in:

- Using design thinking tools
- Conducting brainstorming sessions
- Building different types of prototypes throughout a project
- Creating balanced scorecards and strategy maps

Project managers must understand that the way they managed and mitigated risks on traditional projects may not work as well on innovation activities because of increased levels of ambiguity, complexity, uncertainty, and the possibility of crises occurring. Risk mitigation may be more complex.

Project managers must understand the differences between the innovation and traditional project management environments. This includes an understanding of the following:

- There are different types of life-cycle stages and phases.
- The activities in the fuzzy front end of a project are important.
- There is a need for a line of sight to senior management.
- Organization reward systems can impact how people perform on a project.
- Organizations must have strategies to overcome the fears that people possess when assigned to innovation projects.
- If the culture does not support innovation, this can be detrimental to the chances of innovation success.
- There are differences between traditional and innovation project governance.

REFERENCES

Barreto, I. (2010). Dynamic capabilities: A review of past research and an agenda for the future. *Journal of Management* 36 (1), 256–280.

Bel, R. (2010). Leadership and Innovation: Learning from the Best. © 2010 Wiley Periodicals, Inc. Available at https://onlinelibrary.wiley.com/doi/abs/10.1002/joe.20308.

Ben Mahmoud-Jouini, S., Midler, C. and Silberzahn, P. (2016). Contributions of design thinking to project management in an innovation context. *Project Management Journal* (April–May), 144–156. DOI: 10.1002/pmj.21577.

Bonner, J. M., Ruekert, R. W. and Walker, O. C., Jr. (2002). Upper management control of new product development projects and project performance. *The Journal of Product Innovation Management* 19, 233–245.

Boswell, W. (2006). Aligning employees with the organization's strategic objectives: Out of line of sight, out of mind. *International Journal of Human Resource Management* 17 (9), 1489–1511.

Bowman, D. (2009). Goodbye, Google. *stopdesign* (blog) March 20, 2009. http://stopdesign.com/archive/2009/03/20/goodbye-google.html.

Brown, T. (2008). Design thinking. *Harvard Business Review* 86 (6), 84.

Chen, Y. J. (2015). The role of reward systems in product innovations: An examination of new product development projects. *Project Management Journal* 46 (3), 36–48.

Crawford, L., Hobbs, B. and Turner, J. R. (2006). Aligning capability with strategy: Categorizing projects to do the right projects and to do them right. *Project Management Journal* 37 (2), 38–50.

De Brentani, U. and Reid, S. (2012). The fuzzy front-end of discontinuous innovation: Insights for research and management. *Journal of Product Innovation Management* 29 (1), 70–87.

Gann, D. M. and Salter, A. J. (2000). Innovation in project-based, service-enhanced firms: The construction of complex products and systems. *Research Policy* 29 (7), 955–972.

Hobday, M. and Rush, H. (1999). Technology management in complex product systems (CoPS): Ten questions answered. *International Journal of Technology Management* 17 (6), 618–638.

Hoskisson, R.E., Hitt, M.A., Johnson, R.A. and Grossman, W. (2002). Conflicting voices: The effects of institutional ownership heterogeneity and internal governance on corporate innovation strategies. *Academy of Management Journal*, 45 (4), 697.

Jansen, J. P., Van Den Bosch, F. A. and Volberda, H. W. (2006). Exploratory innovation, exploitative innovation, and performance: Effects of organizational antecedents and environmental moderators. *Management Science* 52 (11), 1661–1674.

Kaplan, R. S. and Norton, D. P. (1996). *The Balanced Scorecard: Translating Strategy into Action*. Boston, MA: Harvard Business School Press.

———. (1992). The balanced scorecard: Measures that drive performance. *Harvard Business Review (January–February)*, 71–79.

Keeley, L. (2013). *Ten Types of Innovation*. Hoboken, NJ: John Wiley and Sons.

Kerzner, H. (2017). *Project Management Case Studies* (5th ed.). Hoboken, NJ: John Wiley and Sons, 255–286, 467–506, and 583–654.

Koen, P., Ajamian, G., Burkart, R., et al. (2001). Providing clarity and a common language to the "fuzzy front end.". *Research Technology Management* 44, 46–55.

Kumar, V. (2013). *101 Design Methods: A Structured Approach for Driving Innovation in Your Organization*. Hoboken, NJ: John Wiley and Sons, 197.

Lester, D. H. (1998). Critical success factors for new product development. *Research Technology Management* 41 (1), 36–43.

Luchs, M. G., Swan, K. S. and Griffin, A. (2016). *Design Thinking*. Hoboken, NJ: John Wiley and Sons.

McLean, W. (1960). Management and the creative scientist. *California Management Review* 3 (1), 9–11.

Meifort, A. (2015). Innovation portfolio management: A synthesis and research agenda. *Creativity and Innovation Management*. DOI: 10.1111/caim.12109.

Merrow, D. (2011). *Industrial Megaprojects: Concepts, Strategies and Practices for Success*. Hoboken, NJ: John Wiley and Sons, 327.

Miles, R. E. and Snow, C. C. (1978). *Organizational Strategy, Structure and Process*. New York: McGraw-Hill.

Miller, P. and Wedell-Wedellsborg, T. (2013, March). The case for stealth innovation. *Harvard Business Review*, 91–97.

Mootee, I. (2013). *Design Thinking for Strategic Innovation*. Hoboken, NJ: John Wiley and Sons.

O'Connor, G. C. and McDermott, C. M. (2004). The human side of radical innovation. *Journal of Engineering Technology Management* 21, 11–30.

Pedersen, C. L. and Ritter, T. (2017). The 4 types of project manager. Harvard Business Review (July 27). Available at https://hbr.org/2017/07/the-4-types-of-project-manager.

Pich, M. T., Loch, C. H. and De Meyer, A. (2002). On uncertainty, ambiguity and complexity in project management. *Management Science* 48 (8), 1008–1023.

Pihlajamma, M. (2017). Going the extra mile: Managing individual motivation in radical innovation development. *Journal of Engineering and Technology Management* 43, 48–66. DOI: 10.1016/j.jengtecman.2017.01.003.

Sicotte, H., Drouin, N. and Delerue, H. (2014). Innovation portfolio management as a subset of dynamic capabilities: Measurement and impact on innovative performance. *Project Management Journal* 58–72. DOI: 10.1002/pmj.21456.

Stetler, K. L. and Magnusson, M. (2014). Exploring the tension between clarity and ambiguity in goal setting for innovation. *Creativity and Innovation Management* 24 (2), 231–246.

Sweeney, J. and Imaretska, E. (2016). *The Innovation Mindset: 5 Behaviors for Accelerating Breakthroughs*. Hoboken, NJ: John Wiley & Sons.

Tichy, N. and Charan, R. (1989). Speed, simplicity, self-confidence: An interview with Jack Welch. *Harvard Business Review* (September–October). Available at https://hbr.org/1989/09/speed-simplicity-self-confidence-an-interview-with-jack-welch.

Tidd, J. and Bessant, J. (2013). *Managing Innovation: Integrating Technological, Market and Organizational Change.* Hoboken, NJ: John Wiley & Sons.

Unger, B. N., Rank, J. and Gemünden, H. G. (2014). Corporate innovation culture and dimensions of project portfolio success: The moderating role of national culture. *Project Management Journal* 45 (6), 38–57.

West, M.A. (1990). The social psychology of innovation in groups. In M.A. West and J.L. Farr (eds.) *Innovation and Creativity at Work: Psychological and Organizational Strategies.* New York: Wiley, 101–122.

Wheelwright, S. C. and Clark, K. B. (1992). *Creating Project Plans to Focus Product Development.* Cambridge, MA: Harvard Business School Publishing.

Williams, T. (2017). The nature of risk in complex projects. *Project Management Journal* (August–September), 55–66.

From Traditional to Innovation Project Management Thinking

5

Learning Objectives for Project Managers and Innovation Personnel

To understand that some traditional tools and processes may still apply but need to be used differently during innovation

To understand the impact that changing assumptions and enterprise environmental factors can have on innovation decisions

To understand the need for an information warehouse to support innovation decisions

INTRODUCTION

"Arming employees with the tools, know-how, and mindset needed to successfully innovate on a continual basis will be paramount to organizational survival."

— Kaihan Krippendorff

For more than 50 years, we have used traditional project management practices with a great deal of success. Unfortunately, this success did not occur on all types of projects. Everyone understood that different forms of project management should be used based on the type of the project, but there existed the mentality that "one size fits all."

The birth of modern project management was attributed to contracts with the Department of Defense (DOD) and the Space Program. Whenever upgrades to the project management approach took place, emphasis was on "command and control" with the belief that success of a project was based solely on

Innovation Project Management: Methods, Case Studies, and Tools for Managing Innovation Projects,
Second Edition. Harold Kerzner.
© 2023 John Wiley & Sons, Inc. Published 2023 by John Wiley & Sons, Inc.

time, cost, and scope. As long as the project manager got the job done within these three constraints, the project was considered as a success.

The private sector realized quickly that a project (such as with an innovation intent) could be managed within time, cost, and scope, and yet there were no customers interested in purchasing the product. The interface between project management, marketing, and the customers was not seen as critical. Marketing or senior management would act as the sponsor for the project and maintain the customer interface. In some situations, project managers did not interface at all with the customers.

By the turn of the century, four significant changes occurred. First, companies realized that the traditional approach to project management had limits and a more flexible project management way of creating results was needed. The introduction of agile and Scrum, both of which are flexible project management approaches, also called frameworks, solved this problem and forced proponents of traditional project management to think about changes.

Second, our definition of project success was changing. Project success is when the results of a project produce sustainable business value. Completing a project within time, cost and scope does not mean that business value was created. Now, using business value as the driving force, we can have different definitions of success on each project based on how we define business value. This now required marketing to be involved with the definition of innovation project success.

Third, we need metrics other than time, cost, and scope metrics to measure business value success and benefits realization. Now, projects can have a multitude of metrics, and this can lead to issues with competing constraints. Projects can have dozens of metrics, and companies are creating metric libraries the same way that we created and used best practices libraries.

Fourth, we are changing to some degree our definition of "project closure." Traditionally, when the deliverable or outcome of a project was completed, the project manager would complete the necessary administrative paperwork and move on to another assignment. The problem with this approach is that business value may not be measurable until sometime after the deliverables were completed. Business value may be measured by the customer's purchase of the product and its beneficial usage. Therefore, on innovation projects, some project team members may still be assigned to the project to measure the possibility of sustainable business value and to see if any adjustments or scope changes may be necessary.

Project managers must think differently when managing innovation projects. Schedules, budgets, work breakdown structures (WBS), and statements of work may not be able to be used the same way that we used them in traditional projects because of the ambiguity, complexity, and uncertainty issues discussed previously.

Even though many of the standard project management tools and techniques are applicable to innovation projects, there are still significant difference in their application which creates challenges. Some of the challenges facing project managers that are accustomed to managing traditional projects when asked to manage innovation projects include:

- Inability to predict exactly when an innovation will occur
- Inability to identify what the cost of innovation will be
- Inability to predict how the enterprise environmental factors will change over the life of the project
- Working with just an idea or goal rather than a formal statement of work
- Limited knowledge about what tasks are needed to support the idea
- Working with strategic/business objectives rather than operational/traditional objectives
- Inability to predict changes in consumer tastes, needs, and behaviors
- Inability to deal with extremely high levels of risk, uncertainty, complexity, ambiguity, and variability

- Having to use a new flexible methodology or framework based upon investment life cycle phases rather than traditional waterfall life cycle phases
- A need to focus on metrics related to business benefits and value rather than the traditional time, cost, and scope metrics

INFORMATION WAREHOUSES

For more than 20 years, the project manager's prime source of current information related to project management excellence came from the Best Practices Library managed by the PMO. Business related information was provided in the business case or by the project sponsor. We believe today that we are managing our business by projects and that project management is the delivery system for sustainable business value. Therefore, project managers are expected to make business decisions as well as project decisions and need direct access to a great deal of business information.

Throughout the life of a project, especially innovation projects, there is a significant amount of data that must be collected including information related to the project business case, project benefits realization plan, project charter, project master plan, customer interfacing, and market analyses. This information is necessary for innovation decision-making.

The knowledge contained in information warehouses provide companies with a source of competitive advantage. In simple terms, if we apply knowledge to tasks we already know how to do, we call it productivity, but if we apply knowledge to tasks that are new and different, we call it *innovation* so that knowledge management is a core component to the innovation process (Drucker 1999).

If the intent of the innovation is to create a commercially successful product, then the team members must understand the commercialization life cycle even though the IPM and many of the innovation team members may not be active participants during commercialization. Making the wrong decisions in the innovation stage can create havoc during commercialization efforts. Innovation teams should review commercialization data records of previously introduced products so that they understand the downstream impact of their decisions. This information should be included in information warehouses and provided decision-makers with the opportunity to perform innovation mapping.

Information warehouses must capture not only project-related best practices, but business best practices as well. All this information falls into the category of intellectual capital and is shown in Figure 5-1. However, most companies have significantly more categories than what is represented in Figure 5-1.

It can be extremely difficult to get people to use a knowledge management system correctly unless they can recognize the value in its use. With the amount of information contained in knowledge management systems, care must be taken in how much information to extract. This is critical during the FFE of an innovation project. According to Calabretta and Gemser (2016, 108):

> All FFE activities require significant information management. Given the unpredictability of innovation outcomes, managers tend to reduce FFE perceived uncertainty by collecting as much diversified information as possible (e.g., market intelligence, technological knowledge, financial information). However, given the limitations of human information processing capabilities, simply accumulating information does not necessarily reduce uncertainty. To increase the odds of successful innovation, information should be selectively retrieved, meaningfully organized, and effectively communicated.

A mistake is often made whereby the only information extracted relates to your company and the targeted, end-of-the-line customer base. While it is true that not all customers and stakeholders are equally

Figure 5–1. Components of a Knowledge Repository.

important, to increase the value created by the innovation, we must also consider new customers that might eventually buy into our products and services. Focusing on diverse needs of a larger customer base may prove rewarding especially if some customers no longer are important and new customers enter the market with needs that are different than current customers.

Companies invest millions of dollars in developing information warehouses and knowledge management systems. There is a tremendous amount of rich but often complicated data about customers, their likes and dislikes, and buying habits. This knowledge is treated as both tangible and intangible assets. But the hard part is trying to convert the information into useful knowledge.

Innovation personnel should first map out the mission-critical knowledge assets that are needed to support the strategy. The next step is to determine which knowledge assets to use and exploit. By mapping the knowledge assets, you put boundaries around what the innovation project is designed to do.

Unfortunately, the only true value of a knowledge management system is the impact on the business in areas such as revenue generation, increased profits, customer satisfaction, and improved business operations (Hanley 2014). Simply stated, we must show that the investment in a knowledge management system contributes to a future competitive advantage.

There are four activities that are part of knowledge management: knowledge creation, knowledge storage, knowledge transfer, and knowledge application. Organizational cultures can influence knowledge management practices by affecting employee behavior (Kayworth and Leidner 2003).

The growth in intellectual capital, knowledge repositories, and cloud computing has provided companies with the opportunities for data warehouses. According to Melik (2007, 238):

> Many organizations use diverse applications and information systems, each having their own database. The data from disparate systems can be merged into one single database (centralized data) in a process known as *data warehousing*. For example, a company could use a customer relations management (CRM) solution from Vendor A, a project management system from Vendor B, and an enterprise resource planning (ERP) or accounting system from Vendor C; data warehousing would be used to aggregate the data from these three sources. Business intelligence and reporting tools are then used to perform detailed analysis on all of the data. Data warehouse reports are usually not real time, since the data aggregation takes time to complete and is typically scheduled for once per week, month, or even quarter.

Knowledge management can increase competitiveness, allow for faster decisions and responses to disruptive changes, and rapid adaptation to changes in the environment. Knowledge management access is critical during design thinking. The growth in information, as shown in Figure 5-2, has created a need for cloud computing. There is also a great deal of research being done on establishing categories for knowledge management systems such as:

- Knowledge creation
- Collecting the information
- Information processing: identification, categorization, and codification
- Validate and evaluate
- Repository storage
- Distribution, transfer, and retrieval protocols (i.e., restricted viewing, etc.)
- Knowledge application

Intellectual capital, as shown in Figure 5-3, is considered as intangible assets categorized as human, product and structural capital. These are assets normally not identified on the balance sheets of companies, but they can be transformed into value that leads to a sustainable competitive advantage. Knowledge data bases and information warehouses are needed to support intellectual capital components. These intangible assets that are used to define intellectual capital could be strategically more important to the growth and survival of the firm than its tangible assets.

Peter Drucker (1999) said that "knowledge has become the key economic resource and the dominant and perhaps even the only source of competitive advantage." Over the past two decades, there has been considerable research that showed that the greater the firm's intellectual capital, the greater the ability of the firm to be innovative.

Converting intellectual capital to innovations requires a firm to have absorptive capacity. Zahra and George (2002) identify the two critical elements of absorptive capacity. First there is knowledge acquisition which "refers to a firm's capability to identify and acquire externally generated knowledge that is critical to its operations." This information could come from the firm's worldwide innovation labs or innovation offices. Second, there is assimilation capability which "refers to the firm's routines and processes that allow it to analyze, process, interpret and understand the information obtained from external sources."

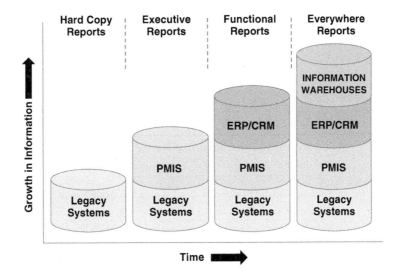

Figure 5–2. The Growth in Information.

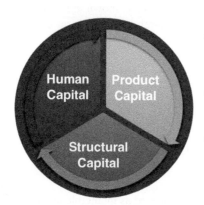

Categories

- **Human capital**
  - **Employee knowledge, competence, and innovativeness**
- **Product capital**
  - **Brand loyalty and customer relationships**
- **Structural capital**
  - **Company culture, patents, efficiencies, and knowledge data bases**

Figure 5–3. Three Critical Intangible Components of Intellectual Capital.

REFERENCES FOR ABOVE SECTION

Drucker, P. (1999). Managing in a Time of Great Change. New York: Harper Business.
Zahra, Shaker A. and George, Gerard. (2002). Absorptive capacity: A review, reconceptualization, and extension. *Academy of Management Review* 27 (2), 185–203.

As innovation grows, so does the need for easy access to the knowledge management or network system where employees can access the information they need. There are several ways the strategic knowledge network can be structured. One such way is identified by Ihrig et al. (2011, 2):

> To pursue a knowledge network strategy, you have to first map your critical knowledge assets, then decide how to deploy them strategically. Which will you hold on to as deep, tacit insights, which will you develop, protect and legally enforce, and which will you proactively share? Strategic knowledge mapping helps you decide which knowledge assets to share, and then how to connect these shared assets with the tacit knowledge only you possess.

There are several types of knowledge, and they are not mutually exclusive. Table 5-1 lists some ways to classify knowledge:

TABLE 5–1. TYPES OF KNOWLEDGE

Type of Knowledge	Description
Explicit	Encoded knowledge that can be found in books, magazines, and other documents.
Implicit (or Tacit)	Knowledge in the heads of people. Also, knowledge retained by suppliers and vendors. Knowledge may be difficult to explain.
Situational	Knowledge related to a specific situation, such as a specific use of a product.
Dispersed	Knowledge that is not controlled by a single person.
Experience	Knowledge obtained from experiences or observations of clients using the product; must understand user behavior.
Procedural	Detailed knowledge on how to do something.

INNOVATION PLANNING OVERVIEW _____

Planning in a traditional project environment may be described as establishing a predetermined course of action within a forecasted environment. The project's requirements set the major milestones. This assumes that we understand the forecasted environment, we have well-defined business objectives, an easily understood business case, and a detailed project plan. There is also the assumption that the business case will remain the same over the life of the project. In an innovation environment, we must think differently because none of these items may exist.

Decision makers must understand that, over the life cycle of an innovation project, circumstances can change requiring modification of the requirements, shifting of priorities, and redefinition of the desired outcomes. This can happen on any project, but it is more likely to occur during innovation activities due to changes in consumer behavior and new products being introduced by the competition.

Project managers monitor closely the enterprise environmental factors which are assumptions about external environmental conditions that can affect the success of the project, such as interest rates, market conditions, changing customer demands, and requirements, customer involvement, changes in technology, political climate, and even government policies. On innovation projects, enterprise environmental factors also include such items as:

- Geographical markets
- Market size
- Market share
- Company size
- Dependence on suppliers
- Dependence on a limited customer base
- Profitability and return on investment
- Bond market rating

Projects usually begin with the development of a business case for the project. This occurs most often well before the actual scope of the project is defined. A business case is a document that provides the reasoning why a project should be initiated. For example, if the project manager is expected to develop a new product, the intent may be to:

- Penetrate new markets across the world.
- Penetrate new national markets.
- Fill out a product line.
- Replace existing products in the marketplace with a new product that has improved features.
- Replace existing products in the marketplace with similar products that are cheaper to manufacture.

Each of these intentions could require a different type of innovation, have different budgets and schedules, and have a different form of governance. And to add in more complexity, the strategic goals and objectives can change over the course of the project.

Historically, business cases were small documents or presentations, and the decision to initiate the project was based on the rank of the person making the request. Today, business cases are well-structured written documents that support a specific business need. Each business case should describe the boundaries to the project in sufficient detail such that the decision makers can determine that the expected business value and benefits exceed the cost of performing the project.

The business case must contain both quantifiable and unquantifiable information that justifies the investment in the project. Typical information that can be part of a business case includes:

- *The business need.* This identifies the gap that currently exists and the need for the investment.
- *The opportunity options.* This identifies how the project is linked to strategic business objectives.
- *The benefit realization plan.* This identifies the value/benefits (rather than products or deliverables) that can be obtained whether they are cost savings, additional profits, or opportunities.
- *Assumptions made.* This identifies all of the assumptions that are made to justify the project.
- *High-level objectives.* This identifies the high-level or strategic objectives for the project.
- *Recommendation for evaluation.* This identifies what techniques should be used for evaluation such as a benefit-to-cost ratio, cash flow considerations, strategic options, opportunity costs, return on investment, net present value, and risks.
- *Project metrics.* This identifies the financial and nonfinancial metrics that will be used to track the performance of the project.
- *Exit strategies.* This identifies the cancellation criteria to be used to cancel the project if necessary.
- *Project risks.* This helps the decision makers evaluate the project by listing briefly the business, legal, technical, and other risks of the project.
- *Project complexity.* This identifies how complex the project might be, perhaps even from a risk perspective, if the organization can manage the complexity, and if it can be done with existing technology.
- *Resources needed.* This identifies the human and nonhuman resources needed.
- *Timing.* This identifies the major milestones for the project.
- *Legal requirements.* This identifies and legal requirements that must be followed.

The above information is used not only to approve the project, but also to be able to prioritize it with all of the other projects in the queue.

Templates can be established for most of the items in the business case. Sometimes, the benefits realization is a separate document rather than being included as part of the business case. A template for a benefits realization plan might include the following:

- A description of the benefits
- Identification of each benefit as tangible or intangible
- Identification of the recipient of each benefit
- How the benefits will be realized
- How the benefits will be measured
- The realization date for each benefit
- The handover activities to another group that may be responsible for converting the project's deliverables into benefits realization

Kaplan and Warren (2009, 98) have identified items that should be included in a business case specific to innovation projects:

- Details of the product or service
- Assessment of the market opportunity
- Identification of the target customers
- Barriers to entry and competitor analysis

- Experience, expertise, and commitment of the management team
- Strategy for pricing, distribution, and sales
- Identification and planning for key risks
- Cash flow calculation, including breakeven points and sensitivity
- Financial and other resource requirements

Not all types of innovation projects will require a business case. The details in the business case can vary, based on the type of innovation project. This requires PMs to think differently. Pure research and bootlegged innovation may have no business case until important results are discovered and the project becomes a fully funded innovation project. Sometimes, this information in the business case is considered proprietary, and preparing a business case lets everyone know what innovation activities the company is working on.

It is entirely possible that the business case and benefits realization plan, if they exist, can change to a point where the outcome of the project provides detrimental results and the project should be canceled or backlogged for consideration at a later time. Some of the factors that can induce changes in the business case or benefits realization plan include:

- *Changes in business owner or executive leadership.* Over the life of a project, there can be a change in leadership. Executives that originally crafted the project may have passed it along to others who either have a tough time understanding the benefits, are unwilling to provide the same level of commitment, or see other projects as providing more important benefits.
- *Changes in assumptions.* Based on the length of the project and potential changes in the targeted market segments, the assumptions can and most likely will change. Tracking metrics must be established to make sure that the original or changing assumptions are still aligned with the expected benefits.
- *Changes in constraints.* Changes in market conditions (i.e., markets served and consumer behavior) or risks can induce changes in the constraints. Companies may approve scope changes to take advantage of additional opportunities or reduce funding based on cash flow restrictions. Metrics must also track for changes in the constraints.
- *Changes in resource availability.* The availability or loss of resources with the necessary critical skills is always an issue and can impact benefits and customer value if a breakthrough in technology is needed to achieve the benefits or to find a better technical approach with less risk.

One of the axioms of project management is that the earlier the project manager is assigned, the better the plan and the greater the commitment to the project. Unfortunately, there is a trend today for not bringing the project manager on board early enough to participate in business case development.

There are valid arguments for assigning the project manager after the requirements are outlined and/or the business case is developed:

- The project manager may have limited knowledge and not be able to contribute to the project at this time.
- The project might not be approved and/or funded, and it would be an added cost to have the project manager on board this early.
- The project might not be defined well enough at this early stage to determine the best person to be assigned as the project manager.

While these arguments seem to have merit, there is a more serious issue affecting innovation in that the project manager ultimately assigned may not fully understand the assumptions, constraints, marketing's information on customer segments, and consumer behavior and alternatives considered. This could lead to less-than-optimal development of a project plan. It is wishful thinking to believe that the business case development effort, which may have been prepared by someone completely separated from the execution of the project, contains all of the necessary assumptions, alternatives, and constraints. The innovation PM must be brought on board as early as possible.

Business requirements, often established by marketing, may result in a highly optimistic approach with little regard for the schedule and/or the budget. Pressure is then placed on the innovation project manager to accept unrealistic arguments and assumptions made during business case development. If the project fails to meet business case expectations, then the blame may be placed on the project manager. There must be an understanding that is embedded in the corporate culture that not all innovation projects will be successful.

INNOVATION METHODOLOGIES

Shortly after the turn of the century, the introduction of an agile approach to project management gave companies a choice between a rigid one-size-fits-all methodology and a very flexible agile methodology or framework. Unfortunately, not all projects, including innovation projects, are perfect fits for an extremely rigid or flexible approach. Some projects are hybrid or middle-of-the-road projects that may fall in between rigid waterfall approaches and very flexible agile frameworks.

Some practitioners envision the future of project management methodologies as simply a decision between waterfall, agile, and Scrum as to which one will be a best fit for a given project. Others argue that new frameworks should be created from the best features of each approach and then applied to a project. What we do know with a reasonable degree of confidence is that new frameworks, with a great deal of flexibility and the ability to be customized, will certainly appear in the future. Deciding which framework is best suited to a given innovation project will be the challenge and project teams will be given the choice of which one to use.

Project teams of the future will begin each project by determining which approach will best suit their needs. This can be accomplished with checklists and questions that address characteristics of the project such as flexibility of the requirements and constraints, type of leadership needed, team skill levels needed, and the culture of the organization. The answers to the questions will then be pieced together to form a framework which may be unique to a given project. Typical questions might include:

1. **How clear are the innovation requirements and the linkage to the strategic business objectives?** On some projects, especially when innovation and/or R&D may be required, it may be difficult to come up with well-defined objectives for the project even though the line-of-sight to the strategic business objectives is well known. These projects may focus more so on big, hairy, audacious goals (BHAGs) rather than on more well-defined objectives.

   When the requirements are unclear, as they are in innovation activities, then the project may be tentative in nature and subject to cancellation. You must also expect that changes will occur throughout the life of the project. These types of projects require highly flexible frameworks and a high degree of customer involvement.

2. **How likely is it that changes in the requirements will take place over the life of the project?** The greater the expectation of changes, the greater the need for a highly flexible approach. Changes may

occur because of changing consumer tastes, needs, or expectations. Allowing for too many changes to take place may get the project off track and result in a failed project that produces no benefits or business value. The size of the project is also important because larger projects are more susceptible to scope changes.

In addition to the number of changes that may be needed, it is also important to know how much time will be allowed for the changes to take place. In critical situations where the changes may have to take place in days or weeks, a fast paced, flexible approach may be necessary with continuous involvement by stakeholders and decision-makers.

3. **Will the customer expect all the features and functionality as we approach the end of the project, or will the customer allow for incremental scope changes?** Incremental scope changes allow the project to be broken down and completed in small increments that may increase the overall quality and tangible business value of the outcome. This may also provide less pressure on decision-making.

4. **Is the team collocated or virtual?** Projects that require a great deal of collaboration for decision-making may be more easily managed with a collocated team especially when a large amount of scope changes are expected.

5. **If the project requires the creation of new features to a product, where will the information come from for determining which features are necessary?** The answer to this question may require that the project team interface frequently with marketing and end users to make sure that the features are what the users desire. The ease by which the team can interface with the end users may be of critical importance.

6. **Is there success (and/or failure) criteria that will help us determine when the project is over?** With a poor or lack of success criteria, the project may require a great deal of flexibility, testing, and prototype development.

7. **How knowledgeable will the stakeholders be with the framework selected?** If the stakeholders are unfamiliar with the framework, a great deal of wasted time may be needed to educate the customer on the framework selected and their expected role and responsibility in the framework. This may create a problem for stakeholders that exhibit a resistance to change.

8. **What metrics will the stakeholders and business owner require?** Waterfall methodologies focus on time, cost, and scope metrics. Flexible methodologies allow for other metrics such as business benefits and value achieved.

Selecting the right framework may seem like a relatively easy thing to do. However, all methodologies and frameworks come with disadvantages as well as advantages. Innovation project teams must then hope for the best but plan for the worst. They must understand what can go wrong and select an approach where execution issues can be resolved in a timely manner. Some of the questions focusing on "What can go wrong?" that should be addressed before finalizing the approach to be taken include:

1. Are the customer's expectations realistic?
2. Will the needs of the project be evolving or known at the onset?
3. Can the required work be broken down and managed using small work packages and sprints or is it an all-or-nothing approach?
4. Will the customer and stakeholders provide the necessary support and in a timely manner?
5. Will the customer and/or stakeholder be overbearing and try to manage the project themselves?
6. How much documentation will be required?
7. Will the project team possess the necessary communications, teamwork, and innovation/technical skills?

8. Will the team members be able to commit the necessary time to the project?
9. Is the type of contract (i.e., fixed price, cost reimbursable, cost sharing, etc.) well-suited for the framework selected?

Selecting a highly flexible approach may seem on the surface to be the best way to go since mistakes and potential risks can be identified early, which then allows for faster corrective action to take place and prevent disasters from occurring. But what people seem to fail to realize is that the greater the level of flexibility, more layers of management and supervision may need to be in place.

Today, there are several methodologies and frameworks available for project teams such as "Agile," "Waterfall," "Scrum," "Prince2," "Rapid Application Development," etc. In the future, we can expect the number of methodologies and frameworks available to increase significantly. Some type of criteria must be established to select the best approach for a given project.

METHODOLOGY GATES

As companies mature in project management, rigid methodologies are being replaced with frameworks or flexible methodologies that utilize different life-cycle phases. One of the most important differences when selecting an approach is in the gate review decisions that must be made at the completion of a life-cycle phase. As an example, traditional projects, especially for external clients, usually require decisions that have less complexity than in innovation project gate reviews as seen in Table 5-2.

INNOVATION ASSUMPTIONS

Quite often, the assumptions included in the project's business case are made by marketing and sales personnel, and then approved by senior management as part of the innovation project selection and approval process. The expectations for the final results are usually heavily based on the assumptions made.

TABLE 5–2.   TRADITIONAL VS. INNOVATION PROJECT GATE DECISIONS

Factor	Traditional Project Gates	Innovation Project Gates
Go or no-go decision	Continuation highly likely	Cancellation highly likely
Project redirection	Provided that it remains within original SOW	Can be redirection to new scope or completely new project
Scope changes	Usually small changes	Major changes
Schedule slippages	Small changes	Major changes
Cost increases	Small increases in budget	Major budgetary changes
Risk assessment and mitigation	Not often	Almost always
Evaluation of brainstorming ideas	Rarely	Frequently
Selection of best approach	Rarely	Frequently

There are several types of assumptions. The two most common categories are explicit and implicit assumptions, and critical and noncritical assumptions. Critical and noncritical assumptions are also referred to as primary and secondary assumptions. These two categories of assumptions are not mutually exclusive.

Explicit assumptions may be quantified and are expressed without any ambiguity. An example might be the ability to increase market share in a given segment. Implicit assumptions may be hidden and may go undetected, such as the ability to penetrate new market segments. Explicit assumptions often contain hidden implicit assumptions. As an example, we could make an explicit assumption that five people will be needed full time to complete the project. Hidden is the implicit assumption that the people assigned will be available full time and possess the necessary skills. Serious consequences can occur if the implicit assumptions are proven to be false.

Critical assumptions are those assumptions that can cause significant damage to a project if even small changes take place. Critical assumptions must be tracked closely, whereas noncritical assumptions may not be tracked and may not require any action as long as they do not become critical assumptions. A critical assumption might be that competitors will not beat us into the market with a new product. Project managers must develop a plan for how they will measure, track, and report the critical assumptions. Measurement implies that the assumptions can be quantified. Since assumptions predict future outcomes, testing and measurement might not be possible until well into the future or unless some risk triggers appear. Sensitivity analysis may be required to determine the risk triggers.

In an innovation environment, the project manager and marketing must work together to identify the assumptions. An agreement must be reached on the critical assumptions especially with regard to business value, risks, and costs. An understanding must also be reached on what changes to the critical assumptions may trigger the need for scope changes. This requires that the project manager and marketing remain in close collaboration throughout the life of the project as they monitor the marketplace.

There are some assumptions that innovation project managers may never see or even know about. These are referred to as strategic assumptions and are retained by decision makers when approving a project or selecting a portfolio of projects. These types of assumptions may contain company proprietary information that executives do not want the project team to know about.

Documenting Assumptions

All innovation assumptions should be documented at project initiation. Throughout the project, the project manager must revalidate and challenge the assumptions. Changing assumptions may mandate that the project be terminated or redirected toward a different set of goals and objectives.

Documenting assumptions is necessary in order to track the changes. Examples of assumptions that are likely to change over the duration of an innovation project, especially on a long-term project, might be that:

- The cost of borrowing money and financing the project will remain fixed.
- The procurement costs will not increase.
- The breakthrough in technology will take place as scheduled.
- The resources with the necessary skills will be available when needed.
- The marketplace will readily accept the product.
- Our competitors will not catch up to us.
- The risks are low and can be easily mitigated.
- The product can be manufactured using existing facilities.

TABLE 5–3.   ASSUMPTION VALIDATION CHECKLIST

Checklist for Validating Assumptions	YES	NO
Assumption is outside of the control of the project team.		
Assumption is outside of the control of the stakeholder(s).		
The assumption can be validated as correct.		
Changes in the assumption can be controlled.		
The assumed condition is not fatal.		
The probability of the assumption holding true is clear.		
The consequences of this assumption pose a serious risk to the project.		
Unfavorable changes in the assumption can be fatal to the project.		

Enterprise Environmental Factors

Assumptions about enterprise environmental factors

- Interest rates
- Market conditions
- Changing customer demands and requirements
- Changes in technology
- Government policies

Organizational Process Assets

Assumptions about organizational process assets are assumptions about present or future company assets that can impact the success of the project such as:

- The capability of your enterprise project management methodology
- The project management information system, including forms, templates, guidelines, and checklists
- The ability to capture and use lessons learned data and best practices

Faulty assumptions can lead to faulty conclusions, bad results, and unhappy customers. The best defense against poor assumptions is good preparation at project initiation, including the development of risk mitigation strategies. One possible way to do this is with a validation checklist, as shown in Table 5-3.

VALIDATING THE OBJECTIVES

"Vision without action is a daydream, but action without vision is a nightmare."
— Kaihan Krippendorff

When project managers are assigned to a project and review the requirements, they look first at the assumptions and objectives for the project. Traditional project management focuses heavily on well-defined business cases containing detailed objectives and statements of work whereas innovation project management is focused on goal-setting. Goals rather than objectives are frequently used at the beginning of an innovation project because the requirements may be ill-defined at this time.

A goal represents the end point or finish line that depicts where you wish to end up. Goals can have a window of 5–30 years. Objectives are long- or short-term activities or actions necessary to attain the goals. Many innovation projects start out with just goals, often "big hairy audacious goals" (BHAGs), and then the objectives are prepared as the project progresses.

A project's objectives, which are usually high-level objectives, provide an aim or desired end of action. Project managers must then prepare the interim objectives to satisfy the high-level objectives as well as the goals.

Clearly written and well-understood objectives are essential so that the project team will know when the project is over (i.e., the objectives have been achieved). Unfortunately, the objectives are usually imposed on the project manager, rather than having the project manager assigned early enough so as to participate in the establishment of the objectives.

Clearly written objectives follow the **SMART** rule: **S**pecific, **M**easurable, **A**ttainable, **R**ealistic or **R**elevant, **T**angible or **T**ime-bound.

- S = Specific: The objectives are clear and focused toward performance targets or a business purpose.
- M = Measurable: The objectives can be expressed quantitatively.
- A = Attainable: The objectives are reasonable and achievable.
- R = Realistic or Relevant: The objectives are directly pertinent to the work done on the project.
- T = Tangible or Time-bound: The objectives are measurable within a given time period.

Project managers may not be able to establish the objectives themselves without some assistance from perhaps the governance committee and marketing. Most project managers may be able to establish the technical components of the objectives but must rely heavily on others for the business components.

If the project manager believes that the requirements are unrealistic, then he may consider scaling back the scope of the objectives. While other techniques are available for scaling back the objectives, scope reduction is often the first attempt. According to Eric Verzuh (2016, 278):

> If the goals of the project will take too long to accomplish or cost too much, the first step is to scale down the objectives—the product scope. The result of this alternative will be to reduce the functionality of the end product. Perhaps an aircraft will carry less weight, a software product will have fewer features, or a building will have fewer square feet or less expensive wood paneling.
>
> *Positive.* This will save the project while saving both time and money.
>
> *Negative.* When a product's functionality is reduced, its value is reduced. If the airplane won't carry as much weight, will the customers still want it? If a software product has fewer features, will it stand up to competition? A smaller office building with less expensive wood paneling may not attract high-enough rents to justify the project.
>
> *Best application.* The key to reducing a product's scope without reducing its value is to reevaluate the true requirements for the business case. Many a product has been over budget because it was overbuilt. Quality has best been defined as "conformance to requirements." Therefore, reducing product scope so that the requirements are met more accurately actually improves the value of the product, because it is produced more quickly and for a lower cost.

Establishing goals requires forecasting. Forecasting what will happen may not be easy, especially if predictions of consumer reactions after commercialization are required. Forecasting is customarily defined as either strategic, tactical, or operational. Strategic forecasting is generally for five years or more, tactical can be for one to five years, and operational is the here and now of six months to one year.

Although most projects are operational, many forms of innovation projects can be considered as strategic, especially if spinoffs or follow-up work is promising or if the expectation is to disrupt the markets. Forecasting also requires an understanding of strengths and weaknesses in:

- The competitive situation
- Marketing
- Research and development
- Production
- Financing
- Personnel
- Governance

DIFFERING VIEWS OF THE PROJECT

All companies strive for innovation excellence and hope for a continuous stream of innovative products. Plans are approved by senior management, all assumptions are reviewed, and strategic objectives are established. Even then, there can be different perspectives on the importance of the project and the benefits associated with the outcome. Sometimes, the view is based upon the benefits to the person associated with the project. When different perspectives exist, the company may be considered as immature in IPM. Some of the characteristics of companies that may be considered as immature in IPM are shown in Table 5-4.

Companies need to develop a culture and framework for IPM to work successfully on a repetitive basis. This requires that everyone have the same understanding of the innovation being worked on and in agreement on the success and failure criteria that has been established.

LIFE-CYCLE PHASES

Project planning takes place at two levels. The first level is the corporate cultural approach; the second is the individual's approach. The corporate cultural approach breaks the project down into life-cycle phases. The life-cycle phase approach is *not* an attempt to put handcuffs on the project manager but to provide a methodology for uniformity in project planning and structured decision making for control. Many

TABLE 5–4.   DIFFERING VIEWS ON INNOVATION MANAGEMENT ACTIVITIES

Factor	Innovation Project Manager's Perspective	Executive Perspective
Deliverable	An outcome that exceeds expectations	A revenue-generating commercialized product
Product features	Brings recognition from peers	Recognized as value by the consumers
Schedule	As long as it takes, regardless of imposed constraints	Driven by time-to-market consideration
Cost	Desire to control all project funding	Balance cost against competition for funding other projects
Collaboration	Mainly with peers in technology development	With marketing, and co-creation partners
Governance	Micromanagement by the project manager	Structured methodology and decision making

companies, including government agencies, prepare checklists of activities that should be considered in each phase. These checklists are for consistency in planning. The project manager can still exercise his own planning initiatives within each phase.

Another benefit of life-cycle phases is control. At the end of each phase there is a meeting of the project manager, sponsor, senior management, and even the customer, to assess the accomplishments of this life-cycle phase and to get approval for the next phase. These meetings are often called critical design reviews, "on-off ramps," and "gates." In some companies, these meetings are used to firm up budgets and schedules for the follow-on phases. In addition to monetary and schedule considerations, life-cycle phases can be used for staffing deployment and equipment/facility utilization. Some companies go so far as to prepare project management policy and procedure manuals where all information is subdivided according to life-cycle phasing. They include:

- Proceed with the next phase based on an approved funding level.
- Proceed to the next phase but with a new or modified set of objectives.
- Postpone approval to proceed based on a need for additional information.
- Terminate project.

When we discuss life-cycle phases, it is generally understood that there are "go" or "no-go" milestones at the end of each life-cycle phase. These milestones are used to determine if the project should be continued, and if so, should there be any changes to the funding or requirements? But there are also other interim milestones that support the end-of-phase milestones or appear within certain life-cycle phases.

Scope Freeze Milestones

Scope freeze milestones are locations in the project's timeline where the scope is frozen and further scope changes will not be allowed. In traditional project management, we often do not use scope freeze milestones because it is assumed that the scope is well-defined at project initiation. But on other projects, especially in IT and innovation, the project may begin based on just an idea and the project's scope must evolve as the project is being implemented. This is quite common with techniques such as agile and Scrum.

According to Melik:

There will be resistance to scope freeze; if it is too early, you may have an unhappy customer, too late and the project will be over budget or late. Striking the right balance between the customer's needs and your ability to deliver on time and on budget is a judgment call; timing varies from project to project, but the scope should always be frozen before a [significant] financial commitment is made. (2007, 205–206)

What if the scope baseline cannot be agreed on? One of the following approaches may be helpful:

- Work more with the customer until scope freeze is achieved.
- Agree to work in phases; proceed with partial project execution, clarify and agree to the rest of the scope during the course of the project. Pilot, prototype, or fit-to-business-analysis mini-projects are helpful.
- Structure the project with many predetermined milestones and phases of short duration; such a project is far more likely to remain aligned with its ultimate objectives.

Scope freeze milestones are important in innovation projects because highly talented people may want to create a perfect product and continue designing and experimenting. There is a point where one must freeze the design, commercialize the product, and allow all further enhancements to be part of the next generation of this product. Scope freezes may be necessary to enter the marketplace quickly and generate revenue.

Design Freeze Milestones

In addition to scope freeze milestones, there can also be design freeze milestones. Even if the scope is well-defined and agreed to, there may be several different design options to meet the scope. Sometimes, the best design may require that the scope change and the scope freeze milestone must be moved out.

A design freeze milestone is a point in a project where no further changes to the design of the product can be made without incurring a financial risk, especially if the design must then go to manufacturing. The decision point for the freeze usually occurs at the end of a specific life-cycle phase. There are several types of freezes, and they can occur in just about any type of project. However, they are most common in new product development (NPD) projects.

In NPD projects with technical innovation, we normally have both a specification freeze and a design freeze. Innovation teams usually dislike specifications claiming it limits their freedom to be creative.

> I think that a lot of the most interesting and novel solutions come when you don't have a definite specification.
>
> **Dr. William McLean, Sidewinder project director, in hearings before the Committee on Armed Services, US Senate, December 1971, p. 233.**

However, specifications are often necessary and dictate the set of requirements upon which the final design must be made. There may be health and safety reasons for the specifications.

Following a specification freeze, we have a design freeze whereby the final design is handed over to manufacturing. The design freeze may be necessary for timely procurement of long lead items such as parts and tooling that are necessary for the final product to be manufactured. The timing of the design freeze is often dictated by the lead times and may be beyond the control of the company. Failing to meet design freeze points has a significantly greater impact on manufacturing than engineering design.

Design freezes have the additional benefit of controlling downstream scope changes. However, even though design changes can be costly, they are often necessary for safety reasons, to protect the firm against possible product liability lawsuits, and to satisfy a customer's specific needs.

Changes to a product after the product's design is handed over to manufacturing can be costly. As a rule, we generally state that the cost of a change in any life-cycle phase after the design freeze is 10 times the cost of performing the change in the previous life-cycle phase. As an example, let's assume that if a mistake is made prior to the design freeze point, the correction could have been made for $100. But if the mistake is not detected until the manufacturing stage, then the correction cost could be $1000. The same mistake, if detected after the customer receives the product, could cost $10,000 to correct a $100 planning mistake or a $1000 manufacturing mistake. While the rule of 10 may seem a little exaggerated, it does show the trend in correcting costs downstream.

Customer Approval Milestones

Some innovations may be designed for a specific customer base and may be done as part of co-creation. Project managers often neglect to include in the life-cycle phases timeline milestones and the accompanying time durations for customer approvals of the project's schedule baseline with the mistaken belief that the approval process will happen quickly. The approval process in the project manager's parent company may be known with some reasonable degree of certainly, but the same cannot be said for the client's or partners' approval process. Factors that can impact the speed by which the approvals take place can include:

- How many people are involved in the approval process
- Whether any of the people are new to the project
- When all the necessary participants can find a mutually agreed on time to meet
- The amount of time the people need to review the data, understand the data, and determine the impact of their decision
- Their knowledge of project management
- A review of the previous project decisions that were made by them or others
- How well they understand the impact of a delayed decision
- Whether they need additional information before a decision can be made
- Whether the decision can be made verbally or if it must be written in report format

Simply adding a milestone to a schedule that says "customer approval" does not solve the problem. Project managers must find out how long their customers need before making a decision, and it may be better to indicate customer approval as an activity rather than as a milestone.

Nontraditional Life-Cycle Phases

As stated earlier, innovation projects may not work well within the traditional life-cycle phases. Some companies use product development life-cycle phases in additional to traditional life-cycle phases on other projects. Techniques such as agile and Scrum are flexible approaches that set up their frameworks according to the unique requirements of each project. Once again, one size does not fit all.

Innovation can use nontraditional life-cycle phases, as shown in Figure 5-4. These life-cycle phases can still use scope freeze milestones, design freeze milestones, and customer approval milestones. There can be different nontraditional life-cycle phases on innovation projects based on whether we have product, service, or process innovation and whether the innovation is intended to be incremental or radical.

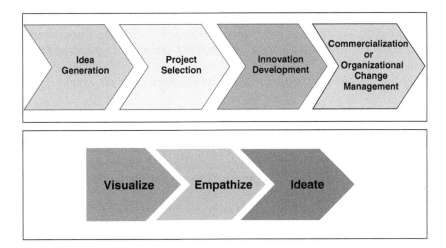

Figure 5–4. Nontraditional Life-Cycle Phases for Innovation.

LIFE-CYCLE COSTING

For years, many innovation (and R&D) organizations have operated in a vacuum where technical decisions made during innovation were based entirely on the innovation portion of the plan, with little regard for what happens after commercialization and production begins. Decisions made during innovation can have serious consequences during and after commercialization.

Today, industrial firms are adopting the life-cycle costing approach that has been adapted from military organizations. Simply stated, life-cycle costing (LCC) requires that decisions made during innovation be evaluated against the total life-cycle cost of the product or system. As an example, the innovation team has two possible design configurations for a new product. Both design configurations will require the same budget for innovation and the same costs for commercialization. However, the maintenance, support and disposal costs may be substantially greater for one of the products. If these downstream costs are not considered in the R&D phase, large unanticipated expenses may result at a point where no alternatives exist.

Life-cycle costs are the total cost to an organization for the ownership and acquisition of the product over its full life. This includes the cost of innovation, production, operation, support, and, where applicable, disposal or retirement. A typical breakdown description might include:

- *Innovation cost*: The cost of feasibility studies; cost-benefit analyses; system analyses; detail design and development; fabrication, assembly, and test of engineering models; prototypes; initial product evaluation; and associated documentation.
- *Production cost*: The cost of fabrication, assembly, and testing of production models; operation and maintenance of the production capability; and associated internal logistic support requirements, including test and support equipment development, spare/repair parts provisioning, technical data development, training, and entry of items into inventory.
- *Commercialization cost*: This can include the production costs and the necessary costs for advertising, marketing, and selling the product or service.
- *Construction cost*: The cost of new manufacturing facilities or upgrading existing structures to accommodate production and operation of support requirements.
- *Operation and maintenance cost*: The cost of sustaining operational personnel and maintenance support; spare/repair parts and related inventories; test and support equipment maintenance; transportation and handling; facilities, modifications, and technical data changes; and so on.
- *Product retirement and phaseout cost (also called disposal cost)*: The cost of phasing the product out of inventory due to obsolescence or wear-out, and subsequent equipment item recycling and reclamation as appropriate. This can also include the costs associated with non-compliance with social and environmental sustainability efforts and damage to the eco-system.

Life-cycle cost analysis is the systematic analytical process of evaluating various alternative courses of action, not just in the innovation phase of a project, but in all life-cycle phases. The objective is to choose the best way to employ scarce resources, especially those resources that can impact the firm's corporate social and environmentally friendly innovation activities. Successful application of LCC will provide downstream resource impact visibility, provide life-cycle cost management, influence innovation decision-making, and support downstream strategic budgeting.

There are several limitations to life-cycle cost analyses. They include:

- The assumption that the product, as known, has a finite life cycle
- A high cost to perform, which may not be appropriate for low-cost/low-volume production
- A high sensitivity to changing requirements

Life-cycle costing requires that early estimates be made. The estimating method selected is based on the problem context (i.e., decisions to be made, required accuracy, complexity of the product, and the development status of the product) and the operational considerations (i.e., market introduction date, time available for analysis, and available resources).

The estimating methods available can be classified as follows:

- Informal estimating methods
  - Judgment based on experience
  - Analogy
  - SWAG method
  - ROM method
  - Rule-of-thumb method
- Formal estimating methods
  - Detailed (from industrial engineering standards)
  - Parametric

Life-cycle cost analysis is an integral part of strategic planning since today's decision will affect tomorrow's actions. Yet there are common errors made during life-cycle cost analyses:

- Loss or omission of data
- Lack of systematic structure
- Misinterpretation of data
- Wrong or misused techniques
- A concentration on insignificant facts
- Failure to assess uncertainty
- Failure to check work
- Estimating the wrong items

WORK BREAKDOWN STRUCTURE

A work breakdown structure (WBS) is a product-oriented family tree subdivision of the hardware, services, and data required to produce the end product. The WBS is structured in accordance with the way the work will be performed and reflects the way in which project costs and data will be summarized and eventually reported. Preparation of the WBS also considers other areas that require structured data, such as scheduling, configuration management, contract funding, and technical performance parameters.

The WBS acts as a vehicle for breaking the work down into smaller elements, thus providing a greater probability that every major and minor activity will be accounted for. However, in innovation there may be no statement of work or listing of detailed requirements. As such, we may have only high-level activities identified in the WBS and need to use rolling wave or progressive elaboration as the project progresses.

In innovation, we tend to prepare a high-level WBS for activities that we are sure about over the next month or two. As we progress with design work, experimentation, and testing, we expand the WBS with more detail for the next two months. In this case, we are using a two-month moving window for updates to the WBS. The failure of as little as one test could result in a major change in the WBS as well as in the direction of the project.

The length of the moving window and the elaboration of the WBS with more details will vary based on the type of innovation and the amount of information available. Developing a detailed WBS for incremental innovation is much easier than for radical or disruptive innovation.

BUDGETING

There are three categories of estimates that most companies use. The decision of which category to use is based on the amount of information available at the time of the estimate. The first type of estimate is an *order-of-magnitude* analysis, which is made without any detailed engineering data. The order-of-magnitude analysis may have an accuracy of ±35 percent within the scope of the project. This type of estimate may use past experience (not necessarily similar), scale factors, parametric curves, or capacity estimates.

Order-of-magnitude estimates are top-down estimates usually applied to level 1 of the WBS, and in some industries, use of parametric estimates are included. A parametric estimate is based on statistical data.

Next, there is the *approximate estimate* (or top-down estimate), which is also made without detailed engineering data, and may be accurate to ±15 percent. This type of estimate is prorated from previous projects that are similar in scope and capacity, and may be titled as estimating by analogy, parametric curves, rule of thumb, and indexed cost of similar activities adjusted for capacity and technology. In such a case, the estimator may say that this activity is 50 percent more difficult than a previous (i.e., reference) activity and requires 50 percent more time, man-hours, dollars, materials, and so on.

The *definitive estimate*, or grassroots buildup estimate, is prepared from well-defined engineering data including (as a minimum) vendor quotes, fairly complete plans, specifications, unit prices, and estimate to complete. The definitive estimate, also referred to as detailed estimating, has an accuracy of ±5 percent. Another method for estimating is the use of *learning curves*. Learning curves are graphical representations of repetitive functions in which continuous operations will lead to a reduction in time, resources, and money. The theory behind learning curves is usually applied to manufacturing operations.

Each company may have a unique approach to estimating. However, for normal project management practices, the three estimating categories discussed would suffice as a starting point. Many companies try to standardize their estimating procedures by developing an *estimating manual*. The estimating manual is then used to price out the effort, perhaps as much as 90 percent. Estimating manuals usually give better estimates than industrial engineering standards because they include groups of tasks and take into consideration such items as downtime, cleanup time, lunch, and breaks.

Innovation projects, with limited information available at the onset, are generally forced to use order-of-magnitude estimating. As the work progresses, and more knowledge becomes available, companies can use different and more accurate estimating techniques for the remaining work.

SCHEDULING

Task duration estimates and schedule preparation suffer from the same issues as with budgeting. If you can prepare a detailed schedule for innovation and predict the exact date when you will make a technical breakthrough, you do not have innovation.

Researchers and innovators prefer very loose schedules with the freedom to go off on tangents, whereas developmental schedules, such as used in incremental innovation, are often more rigid. Research and innovation schedules identify parallel activities, whereas in development, scheduled activities may be sequential.

Schedules are usually prepared using moving window or rolling wave planning where a detailed schedule may be prepared for a short window of time, such as two or three months. The results of one or two tests could require that the schedule be changed significantly. Since the schedule is prepared from the activities in the WBS, it is understandable that the accuracy of the schedule is based on the levels of detail used in the WBS.

Executives and governance personnel often place pressure upon innovation teams to complete the project sooner and without any sacrifice to quality. This is not always possibly, but there are some things that can be done, such as:

- Work on the most difficult and/or the greatest value task first
- Increase the rate of experimentation when possible
- Build rapid prototype development models as often as necessary
- Eliminate or reduce the time spent on non-value-added activities

SCOPE CHANGE CONTROL

A critical tool employed by a project manager in traditional project management is configuration management or configuration/scope change control. As projects progress downstream through the various life-cycle phases, the cost of changes in the design of a product or service can grow boundlessly.

Innovators generally function with weak specifications because of the freedom to invent, whereas development personnel are paid not to create new alternatives but to reduce available alternatives to one, hopefully simple, solution available for implementation and commercialization. Unfortunately, weak specifications are an invitation for scope changes.

Configuration management is a control technique, through an orderly process, for formal review and approval of scope changes. If properly implemented, configuration management provides:

- Appropriate levels of review and approval for changes
- Focal points for those seeking to make changes
- A single point of input to contracting representatives in the customer's and contractor's office for approved changes

At a minimum, the configuration control committee should include representation from the customer, contractor, and line group initiating the change. Discussions should answer the following questions:

- What is the cost of the change?
- Do the changes improve quality?
- Is the additional cost for this quality justifiable?
- Is the change necessary?
- Is there an impact on the delivery date?
- Are resources available for the change?
- Will the approval of a change impact other projects?

Changes cost money, impact schedules, and can alter promises made by marketing to downstream customers. In the life-cycle stages of a research or innovation project, engineering changes, specification changes, and engineering redirection (even if caused simply by the whims of management) may have a minor cost impact compared to these same changes occurring in the development or commercialization life-cycle stages. Therefore, it is imperative that configuration management be implemented correctly. The following steps can enhance the implementation process:

- Define the starting point or "baseline" configuration that marketing expects for a product or service.
- Define the "classes" of changes since not all changes will need to be approved by a change control board (CCB).
- Define the necessary controls or limitations on both the customers and contractors.
- Identify policies and procedures, such as board chairman, voters/alternatives, meeting time, agenda, approval forums, step-by-step processes, and expedition processes in case of emergencies.

If co-creation is being used for innovation, determining the members of the CCB will be challenging because some of the scope changes can alter the baselines and accompany expectations of the co-creation team members. All members of the co-creation team must be made aware of the approved and denied changes. Marketing may wish to consult with product end users as well as to their opinion of the changes.

An important question that needs to be answered during a CCB meeting is whether resources with critical skills will be available for the scope change. The change may dictate the need for skills at a higher level than the project team possesses. If these resources must be removed from other ongoing projects, the other projects may incur significant slippages. Given this, some scope changes that are needed may be placed on the back burner for a later time.

As a final note, it must be understood that configuration/scope change control, as used here, is not a replacement for design review meetings or customer interface meetings. These meetings are still an integral part of all projects.

TECHNOLOGY READINESS LEVELS

Not all innovation activities require achievements in technology. But those that do have such a need, seem to struggle with many areas of innovation decision-making. This becomes critical when discussing scope changes. The critical issue is the readiness of the technology. Pressure is being placed upon organizations to shorten product development time as product life cycles are getting shorter. Predicting the maturity level of technology and when technology will be available for market launch is extremely difficult. This can impact how and when decisions are made affecting funding, manpower needs, risk mitigation activities, construction of new facilities, time-to-market factors, and product commercialization.

Background

Technology readiness levels (TRLs) were developed by NASA during the 1970s to assist in the making decisions during the acquisition phase of a space program activities. The creation of the levels was to provide some degree of standardization for discussions of technical maturity across programs that had different types of technology requirements.

By the early 2000s, the Department of Defense used TRLs for weapon system procurement activities. By 2008, the European Space Agency (ESA) also began using TRLs. The intent of the TRL was to develop some type of standard by which a government agency can examine the desired technology requirements of a program and compare them to demonstrated technology capabilities.

TRLs are based on a scale from 1 to 9 with 9 being the most mature technology. The current nine-point NASA scale is:

Level 1 – Basic principles observed and reported
Level 2 – Technology concept and/or application formulated
Level 3 – Analytical and experimental critical function and/or proof-of-concept
Level 4 – Component and/or breadboard validation in environment
Level 5 – Component and/or breadboard validation in relevant environment
Level 6 – System/subsystem model or prototype demonstration in a relevant environment (ground or space)
Level 7 – System prototype demonstration in a space environment
Level 8 – Actual system completed and "flight qualified" through test and demonstration (ground or space)
Level 9 – Actual system "flight proven" through successful mission operations

There have been attempts made in the public sector to integrate TRLs into program management activities requiring innovation using the principles of program management and systems engineering. The United States Army developed *The Technology Program Management Model* that provided some degree of guidance to program managers responsible successful technology transition on government programs.

In the private sector, attempts have been made to convert the traditional stage gate life cycle phases and enterprise project management life cycle phases to a technology development stage gate approach. As of now, no consensus has been reached as to whether it has worked as expected. Most companies seem to be risk adverse when it comes to changing the technologies in their product development pipeline. The difficulty is in applying it to the unique characteristics of products and services of each company.

Advantages and Disadvantages:

All techniques are accompanied by advantages and disadvantages that usually appear as the techniques are being used. The advantages of using TRLs are:[1]

- Identification of a common understanding/language of technical progress
- Better risk management practices on new technology projects provided that the organization is willing to use risk mitigation strategies when needed
- Better decision making on funding, strategic planning, portfolio management, and intellectual property protection strategy
- Better decision making on the cost and timing of commercialization activities

---

1. Some of the advantages /disadvantages have been adapted from Ben Dawson, *"The Impact of Technology Insertion on Organisations,"* October 31, 2007. The work described in this document was undertaken by the Human Factors Integration Defence Technology Centre and part funded by the Human Capability Domain of the UK Ministry of Defence Scientific Research Programme.

The disadvantages may include:

- Complexity in applying the model for all types of technology projects
- Does not account for some of the differences between public and private sector programs and projects
- Technical readiness for a product can be different than technical maturity
- The complexities of each project/product may make it difficult to compare TRLs between projects
- The impact that new technology can have on human factors can be severe especially if workers are removed from their comfort zones

Most private sector project management methodologies are designed to create deliverables based upon existing technologies and do not provide the support needed by advocates of inserting new technologies. Senior management can also act as roadblocks by having an overly optimistic or unrealistic expectation of how new technology insertion will impact their business model and how they provide governance. Being highly optimistic often results in providing additional funding to technology projects that should be cancelled. Being highly pessimistic has the opposite effect by underfunding or prematurely cancelling projects that had potential.

In the public sector, the use of TRLs has had some degree of success in space and weapons system technology projects and programs. In the private sector, the results are inconclusive because the environment is different. But, when TRLs can be shown to be effective on private sector industrial projects, the result could easily be the establishment of a critical metric that can be used to determine a product's readiness for commercialization.

LEAN PROJECT MANAGEMENT: KANBAN

Kanban isa lean methodology that can be used alone as Kanban project management or along with other frameworks such as the waterfall approach, agile or Scrum. It is now part of many innovation methodologies and is used to manage and improve work by balancing demands with available capacity, and by improving the handling of system-level bottlenecks. Work items are visualized to give participants a view of progress and process, from start to finish—usually via a Kanban board.

Kanban is used quite often used in software development projects but can also be used in innovation activities. The intent is to provide a visual process management system which aids decision-making about what, when, and how much effort to produce. Kanban is commonly used in software development in combination with other methods and frameworks such as traditional project management, agile and Scrum.

Kanban uses a story board approach, usually on one page or screen, and designed to show project features and user stories identified through workflow activities. The intent is to make the general workflow and the progress of individual items clear to participants and stakeholders. Kanban is easy to use and allows the viewers to see what each person is working on and its position in the project life cycle. This allows work to be performed faster and in smaller increments.

The two primary practices of Kanban are:

- Visualize your work
- Limit work in progress (WIP)

This workflow control works similarly for every step. Problems are visual and evident immediately, and re-planning can be done continuously. The work management is made possible by limiting work in progress in a way that team members can always visualize and track performance.

There are several benefits to using Kanban. They include:

- Allows for visualization of how strategy and project execution are aligned
- Allows for the elimination of waste and increases efficiency
- Allows for avoiding bottlenecks and pain points
- Easy to see where individuals are idle or overloaded with assignments
- Allows for clear assignment and accompanying responsibility of individuals to tasks
- Work is done faster and more efficiently by limiting the work in progress
- Changes that must be made are implemented quicker
- The process continues to improve over the life cycle of the project

When used with other frameworks, Kanban identifies continuous improvement opportunities and ways to reduce waste by eliminating activities that do not add value. Kanban works well with short cycle time activities such as sprints used in agile innovation. However, there are some limitations:

- Kanban is less rigid than other frameworks
- Kanban uses fewer tasks than other frameworks, but the tasks are more focused
- Team members that are experienced with the more inflexible frameworks might find it difficult at first to adapt to Kanban

COMMUNICATION

> *"It is critical to learn how to listen for what is not being said."*
> — Debra Kaye, *Red Thread Thinking: Weaving Together Connections for Brilliant Ideas and Profitable Innovations*

Many people argue that the most important skill that a project must possess is communications management. Yet at the same time, innovation in project communication management has been slow. We tend to focus primarily on the way that project managers communicate with the project team. In most cases, it is either with a collocated or virtual team where communication takes place using written reports, presentations, or videoconferencing.

In the early years of project management, all external communications to stakeholders, and in some cases the customers as well, were handled by the project sponsors. All of this has now changed, and the project managers have the responsibility of communicating with everyone.

As project management grows into a multinational environment, project managers are finding themselves in a different type of communication situation. As an example, a multinational project manager in the United States commented:

In the United States, when you have an issue on a project, you know that the communication path goes to the project sponsor, and many times it stops there for resolution. In some countries, when you escalate an issue, you are unsure where the issue will go. Suddenly you discover government ministers and other government and political figures that previously were not involved in the project are now becoming active stakeholders. They may even attempt to micromanage some of your activities and require different forms of communication.

We are now looking at ways to innovate communications management. We have more metrics on projects today than we had in the past. Companies are asking for real-time status reporting, perhaps daily, and with the use of dashboards. Project managers are now being asked to communicate with everyone, and this is adding complexity to the traditional project management processes. Innovation in communication is now a necessity and the growth in information warehouses supported by innovation software is helping.

ENABLING INNOVATION SUCCESS IN SOLUTION DESIGN AND DELIVERY IN HEALTHCARE BUSINESS

PHILIPS Hospital Patient Monitoring Business

HPM Services & Solution Deliverability, describe how Customer Success Management and Outcomes realization are successfully integrated with a Scalable Solution Design & Delivery Services framework.

Special thanks to Lisa Midttun (HPM R&D Program Manager) and Stacy Meyer (Philips Solution Delivery Program Manager) for their valuable contributions in the respective areas of Solution Innovation & Commercialization process and importance of Communities of Practice (CoP) & Social Learning for Solution Innovation success.

In the 4th Edition of *Project Management Best Practices Achieving Global Excellence*, Michael Bauer provided an overview of the Philips SOLiD Framework, along with key takeaways on how a scalable approach enables organizations to achieve Solution Implementation & Services Excellence.[2]

In this section, we review key trends in healthcare driving Solution Innovation, translation of these into customer needs and solution complexity, as well as enablers for achieving **Solution Design & Delivery Service Excellence**, including:

- **Solution Development** and **Commercialization**
- **Scalable and role-specific Solution Design & Delivery Services framework**
- **Solution Design & Delivery Services** and specific **Capabilities**
- Holistic and fully integrated approach for the **Customer Lifecycle**
- **Communities of Practice**
- **Process Harmonization and Standardization**
- **Continuous Improvement** of Capabilities

---

2. Kerzner, H. (2018). *Project Management Best Practices Achieving Global Excellence* (4th ed.). New York: Wiley, 448–457.

Enabling Innovation Success in Solution Design & Delivery in Healthcare Business

About Royal Philips

Royal Philips (NYSE: PHG, AEX: PHIA) is a leading health technology company focused on improving people's health and well-being and enabling better outcomes across the health continuum—from healthy living and prevention, to diagnosis, treatment, and home care. Philips leverages advanced technology and deep clinical and consumer insights to deliver integrated solutions. Headquartered in the Netherlands, the company is a leader in diagnostic imaging, image-guided therapy, patient monitoring and health informatics, as well as in consumer health and home care. Philips generated 2021 sales of EUR 17.2 billion and employs approximately 78,000 employees with sales and services in more than 100 countries. News about Philips can be found at www.philips.com/newscenter.

The **Hospital Patient Monitoring (HPM) Business** is a software and solutions business encompassing patient monitoring and its capabilities. Reaching over 500 million people every year, HPM solutions are advanced intelligence platforms, providing key insights and information to clinicians when and where they need it. The ultimate priority for the HPM Business Group is to enable smart decision-making for caregivers, administrators, and patients such that workflows are improved, costs are controlled, efficiency is increased, and, importantly, better health outcomes are supported.

Mega Trends in Healthcare Toward Innovative Solutions[3]

The healthcare industry is quickly evolving. Digital technology and innovative solutions are shaping the industry to support individuals taking charge of their own health.

There are four key trends driving disruptive change in healthcare technology. They include:

1. The shift from volume to **value-based care**, due to global resource constraints. The World Health Organization estimates that 18 million more healthcare workers are needed to close the gap to meet demands of the system in 2018.[4]
2. The growing population of **older patients** and increase in **chronic conditions** such as cardiovascular disease, cancer, and diabetes. The world's older population is forecasted to outpace the younger population over the next three decades.
3. Patients are exerting **more control over healthcare decisions** and choosing which healthcare organizations they utilize as consumers. With access to digital healthcare tools and the incentive of reducing out of pocket expenses, patients are making more carefully informed decisions regarding care (He et al. 2016, 6).
4. The initiation of **healthcare digitalization**, triggering growing demand for **integrated solutions** over discrete products. Physicians can now leverage digital and artificial intelligence solutions to automate data collection and translate it into useful information to make evidence based medical decisions (World Economic Forum 2017).

---

3. See www.results.philips.com/publications/ar17#/strategy.

4. See Health workers density and distribution: https://www.who.int/data/gho/data/indicators/indicator-details/GHO/community-health-workers-density-(per-10-000-population).

These trends have resulted in healthcare organizations striving to find solutions to reach the goals of improving clinical, patient and financial outcomes while also addressing the well-being and engagement of healthcare employees (Bodenheimer and Sinsky 2014).

Philips has adopted a solution-oriented approach in delivering value to customers via integrated solution offerings. Philips defines a Solution as a combination of Philips (and third-party) systems, devices, software, consumables and services, configured and delivered in a way that solves customer- (segment) specific needs.

Varying Customer Needs and Different Solution Complexities

Solutions address the customer need to cost effectively maximize speed and consistency of clinical decisions, actions, and usage of patient information for reduced clinical variation and improved clinical performance within their IT ecosystem.

Designing and Delivering Solution Projects is a local activity performed at hospital organizations in every country, often in the local language. Philips operates with both local and centralized resources to support this. This global/local organizational design often leads to virtual working environments with specific requirements to efficiently drive the Solution Project Delivery. The requirements and maturity levels in each country, market, and hospital customer greatly vary. Each project in a hospital is unique and varies in duration (from weeks to years), in size (up to multi-million euros/dollars) and in complexity (from stand-alone solution for one clinician to regional distributed solution for thousands of users). The range of size and complexity for Solution Projects in healthcare is broad, it includes simple products, highly configurable systems, as well as software and services including clinical consulting. It is influenced by different customer situations, demand and existing and new technologies. A Solution Design & Delivery Framework addresses customer needs and requirements, which vary from project to project (see figure 1):

- **From** Single Department **to** Multi-hospital deployment across country borders
- **From** Standalone solutions in group practice or small departments **to** Complex solutions with different systems, software, services fully integrated in the hospital infrastructure across multiple departments
- **From** Simple clinical processes **to** Highly designed workflows
- **From** "Greenfield" implementations across all modalities and applications **to** Customized solutions into an existing hospital environment

The variability in customer needs drives the Solution Commercialization process. Important elements considered include scalable solution requirements in product & service design, solution delivery readiness, and quality of execution in markets.

When designing and delivering low complexity, single solution projects in one hospital department on a simple, stand-alone network, the Project Manager will implement basic tasks within the five PMI[5] process groups. They include stakeholder identification, plan development, performing installation, controlling scope, and obtaining customer acceptance. When a high complexity solution is delivered within a health system, with many stakeholders and a variety of solutions, the Solution Design & Delivery model becomes much more detailed. The Project Manager and the multidisciplinary Project Team will execute additional tasks from the five PMI process groups. These include performing a customer expectation

---

5. PMI stands for Project Management Institute; see www.pmi.org for more information.

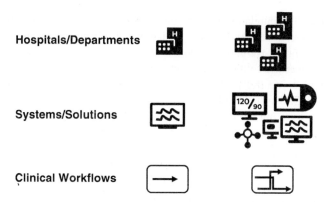

Figure 5–5. Healthcare Projects: Different Drivers influence Complexity.

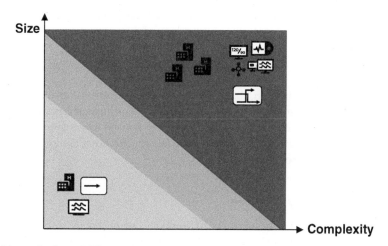

Figure 5–6. Healthcare Projects: Different Complexity Levels.

analysis, developing a Stakeholder RACI matrix, performing a workflow analysis, performing solution integration testing, controlling risk, cost & labor budgets, and conducting Lessons Learned reviews. See figure 2 to visualize the different complexity levels in healthcare projects.

Implications for Solution Innovation Development and Commercialization

Solution Innovation Development and Commercialization processes are key enablers for an effective and efficient Solution Design & Delivery process. These processes support the development and launch of new solutions, define new ways of working and drive necessary changes to supporting infrastructure.

In order to develop a solution that includes systems, devices, software, consumables, and services, first we rely on stellar project management for product and services realization and market launch.

Secondly, we build upon this foundation to add new capabilities (process, tool, content) as needed for a complete solution for a customer. An example is new ways of transacting business with Philips such as subscription services. Thirdly, we underpin both with the human resource capabilities (skill) required to design, deploy, and deliver the solution. This may include new roles, or new ways of working across the organization. Fourthly, as we transform into a solutions partner, we are assessing our organizational structure and ensuring an E2E systems approach is followed. Customer experience is driving all of our decisions regarding changes to our internal processes & organization.

Two processes developed in support of Solutions Transformation:

1. A process to de-risk innovation prior to Solution Commercialization
   - based on the industry proven process for managing venture investments
   - designed to incorporate learnings from previous experience
   - created and matured through a stage-gated approach
   - with multi-tiered governance
2. A new process for Solution Commercialization
   - drives customer solution requirements for consideration in product & service designs
   - ensures continued alignment & execution on accepted requirements
   - commercialized through a gated process that is scalable, repeatable, and leverages enabling realization processes
   - ensures delivery readiness and quality execution of solution in markets

Due to the nature of Solution Innovation, the traditional aspects of project management are needed but are not enough. Focus on the human aspects is necessary to help impacted parties (internal, partners, customers) to transition through change. It helps ensure adoption and to sustain the change. Key to this is strong, aligned messaging, delivered by all levels of leadership, articulating business and customer benefits and our contribution to that benefit.

Solution Design and Delivery Services

Solution projects need a specific combination of Services, executed by a multi-disciplinary team consisting of Project Managers, Solution Architects, Technical Consultants, Clinical Consultants, and Field Service Engineers in teamwork with Sales and other Professional Services team members. Some of the Solution related **Services** are specific to the Solution, some are more generic and independent of the Solution. For any Solution it is a combination of both (see figure 3).

Solution Design and Delivery Capabilities

A set of capabilities are required to provide Solution Design & Delivery Services. Philips considers the following important **Capabilities** with regard **to Solution Design and Delivery Services:**

- **Skills**: Well educated, certified, skilled (hard, soft) and continuously trained Solution Architects, Projects Managers, & Project Team, and Professional Services Consultants with a professional mindset, appearance, and behavior. This also includes recruiting the best talent.[6]

---

6. See as well for importance of Project Management talent management: PMI's Pulse of the Profession in Depth Study: Talent Management, March 2013.

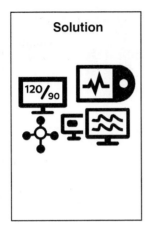
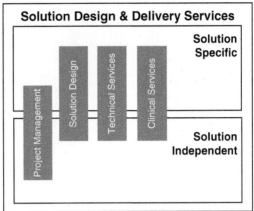

Figure 5–7. Solution Projects need Set of Services & Capabilities.

- **Processes/Methodology**: Highly efficient, standardized, lean, repeatable, and well-documented processes which are continuously improved.
- **Tools**: Highly integrated and efficient tools, templates, and applications from the project acquisition until the end of the project.
- **Content**: Role-specific content (templates, training material, diagrams) around the Solution Design & Delivery.

Some of the Solution related **Capabilities** are specific to the Solution, some are more generic and independent of the Solution. For any Solution it is a combination of both. The Solution specific capabilities are directly linked to the Solution Innovation. To be fully successful with Selling, Designing, Delivering Solution Projects these capabilities need to be prepared, designed, and deployed to executing organizations in the countries.

The SOLiD Design & Delivery Framework has an integrator function to combine a Solution specific and Solution independent capabilities for any Solution, which enables every role to contribute successfully to the project see figure 4 for the distinction between solution specific/independent capabilities and the integration aspect with the SOLiD framework.

Philips strives for Solution Design & Delivery Excellence. This is not seen as a static goal; the ambition is to continuously raise the bar for the overall Maturity & all Capabilities:

The following aspects are critical to build and improve Solution related Capabilities:

- **Solution Design & Delivery Services Excellence matters** – key aspect to value and improving skills, processes, and tools.
- **Change Management** – identify, drive, and implement improvements and changes in the organization.
- **Standardization** – enable standardized & lean practices and processes across product domains and regions.[7]

---

7. "High performing organizations are almost three times more likely than low-performing organizations (36 percent vs. 13 percent) to use standardized practices throughout the organization, and have better project outcomes as a result." Source: PMI's Pulse of the Profession™, March 2013, page 10.

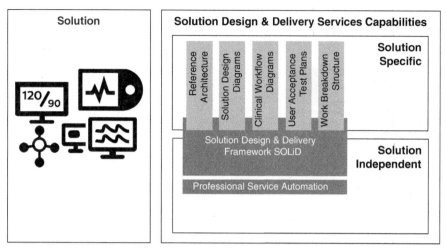

Figure 5–8. Solution Design & Delivery Services need Set of Capabilities.

- **Continuous learning** – train, review, and mentor as required.
- Facilitation of **Community of Practice** for all the different professions – key aspect to enable to Share, Learn, Leverage, Network and Communicate.[8]

Solution Services along the Customer Lifecycle

HPM Services strategized a fully integrated approach on how to offer and implement Solutions & Services from a process and methodology perspective. This is getting more important as the HPM portfolio transitions more and more into a Solutions and Services business. A more holistic approach is key for scoping & designing, delivering and servicing Solutions at the customer throughout the **Customer Lifecycle**.[9] (see figure 5).

The Customer Lifecycle begins with **Solution Discovery**. This involves intensive dialogue with the customer to fully understand the customer needs. It is followed by the **Solution Design** phase during pre-sales, where reference architectures and design guidelines help to shape a strong customer solution. This phase is essential for following Solution phases; it builds the real foundation. "Having a solid foundation is an essential element for delivering project excellence" (Martin 2010). The work performed in the Solution Design phase is captured and documented into a SOW (Statement of Work) which is referenced throughout the rest of the project. McKinsey emphasizes the importance of technical and commercial capabilities: "companies that invest in this capability are able to achieve win rates of 40 to 50 percent in new business and 80 to 90 percent in renewal business."[10] Following the Solution Design phase, a multi-year **Solution Lifecycle Plan** is aligned with the customer. Then the **Solution Delivery**

---

8. See wenger-trayner.com/Intro-to-CoPs for more information about Community of Practice (CoP).

9. Find more information about the Health Care Technology Life Cycle from the University of Vermont: its.uvm.edu/tsp.

10. McKinsey & Company. (2016 September). *Let's talk about sales growth* [Audio podcast].

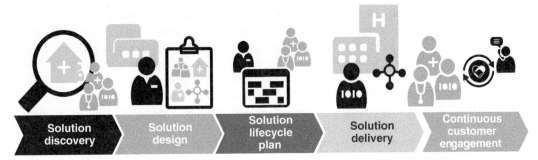

Figure 5–9. Solution Services along Customer Lifecycle.

phase is executed to implement the solution initially and additional services are provided over the life-cycle to fully create the customer value. **Continuous Customer Engagement** is key for full success and enablement of the desired customer outcome (including continuous partnership and collaboration going forward).

Out of the entire Customer Lifecycle several key areas need to be highlighted:

- **Solution Discovery**
  - understanding our customer's clinical, technical, and operational requirements
  - drive consensus with customer stakeholders on solution vision
- **Solution Design**
  - technically feasible and implementable
  - supportable by Philips and the customer
  - financially transparent and profitable
  - aligned with customer expectations
- **Solution Delivery**
  - successful implementation, in line with what was scoped
  - enabling a lean and scalable Project Management approach
  - provide the right tools to deliver an exceptional Customer Experience
  - align way of working across all markets
- **Service Management**
  - focus on the Service, not only the Technology or Products
  - standardize the way we define and add value to support Customer Experience
  - have flexible and responsive processes to support value creation
  - be service oriented internally and externally

Solution Services Lifecycle and Customer Experience

Philips is conscious that each organization leaves an imprint with the customer, an experience made up of rational and emotional aspects which determines what Healthcare customers associate with the Philips brand, and what Philips means to them. This is especially pronounced in a services business. Customer experience is at the heart of a relationship that translates into whether customers repeatedly rely upon the organization's capabilities and embrace them as a trusted advisor.[11] Therefore another important aspect is how the organization actively & holistically "design" the customer experience End to End (E2E) in terms of all capabilities, e.g. tools, processes and skills. Philips strives to apply this customer experience focused approach across the entire Customer Lifecycle from the point in time the customers share their vision through Solution Design, Delivery, and Continuous Engagement & Improvement.

In this context, **Solutions Design & Delivery Services Excellence** are key strategic ingredients to ensure Philips reliably and repeatedly delivers the desired customer experience. Hence, building and sustaining Project Solution Design & Delivery Services Excellence and reaching a high level of project management maturity with solution implementation projects is an adamant ambition of vital importance for both, the customer and Philips.

The SOLiD Framework

In close collaboration with the Philips Solutions & Services Community around the globe the SOLiD Framework was developed. The SOLiD Framework is now the Philips solution approach for designing, managing, executing, and servicing customer facing Solution Implementation Projects and Services. SOLiD is an abbreviation and stands for:

- **S**calable, which allows flexibility to meet the demands of our low, medium, and high complexity projects.
- **O**perationally agile, meaning a rapid, customer focused development approach was utilized and we will continue to build and improve via iterations over time.
- **L**ean, only including the tasks that would add value to the Project & Services Team and even more important to hospital customers.
- **i**T focused, including the structure, tools, and processes needed to successfully manage Projects & Services in an IT Solutions environment and lastly SOLiD will help to
- **D**eliver consistent results and bring business value by providing a standard & lean way of working.

The underpinnings of this framework are the process groups of Initiating, Planning, Executing, Monitoring/Controlling, and Closing as defined in the PMBOK (Project Management Body of Knowledge) by the Project Management Institute (PMI).[12] Each process group is then further broken down into more specific processes and procedures detailing the implementation of Solution Projects & Services. All project team member roles are included in the Framework, along with the related activities each is responsible for during the Solution Design and Delivery phases. This definition enables the organization to deliver high quality implementations and includes a holistic approach to Solution Design and Testing. An important element of the approach is the definition of a customer Reference Architecture for the Solution. This serves as the vision for the solution where use models, application/configuration, and infrastructure elements are defined. The Reference Architecture Specification is utilized to develop the system design and define the solution test plan.

Scalability in Project Implementations is key to allow the right, flexible, agile and efficient approach per project but to leverage from a rich tool set. Solution Projects are defined by their level of complexity. Typical factors when defining complexity are total cost of the project, number of team members involved,

---

11. Sources for customer experience concepts: www.temkingroup.com, www.beyondphilosophy.com.

12. See www.pmi.org/pmbok-guide-standards/foundational/pmbok for more information.

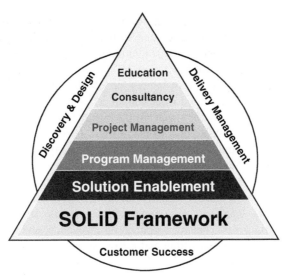

Figure 5–10.   Scalable Solution Design & Delivery Framework.

number and size of deliverables, complexity of deliverables and complexity of the customer environment and timeframes involved.

PMI defines a project as being different from other ongoing operations in an organization, because unlike operations, projects have a definite beginning and an end—they have a limited duration and bring value to the organization.

The SOLiD Framework (see figure 6) is designed to help offer guidance based on various complexity levels & modules:

- **Foundation**: Designed for low complexity projects with basic Project Management tasks required, e.g. basic testing and simple Statement of Work.
- **Advanced**: Incorporates the tasks in Foundation with additional activities/processes to help better scope, manage and execute medium complexity projects; includes Solution Design components.
- **Integrated**: Incorporates both Foundation and Advanced frameworks with additional activities needed to design, manage and execute more intricate, high complexity projects; usually more clinical workflow analysis, technical integration & testing activities, and different level of risk & stakeholder management needed.
- **Consultancy:** Includes activities that should be performed in the design and delivery of consultancy projects, such as clinical practice/outcomes consulting, operational improvement consulting, or technical architecture consulting.

Value of Social Learning in Solution Innovation

In developing the Solution Design & Delivery capabilities needed for customer success, it is imperative to ensure connections exist between Project Team members and their domain peers for the purpose of ongoing learning, knowledge sharing, continuous process improvement, and people development. In a multidisciplinary team environment, it is important for the Project team members to have access to a network of peers that share their experiences and lessons learned. Two specific approaches have been utilized in Philips: 1. Community of Practices and 2. Social Learning.

The basic model for a Community of Practice (CoP) includes three main parts—Domain, Community, and Practice. First, the shared domain of interest people identify with is defined. The community then determines who should be included and what kind of relationships they should form. Lastly, within the practice, members determine what they want to do together and how they can make a difference in practice. These elements are essential for a CoP to thrive. There are key differences between CoPs and formal work groups which should be recognized. The purpose of CoPs is to develop self-selecting members' capabilities and to exchange knowledge with one another whereas, a formal working groups' purpose is to deliver a product or service with everyone reporting to the group's manager. Both groups can be complimentary to each other and are essential for innovation to occur (Wenger and Snyder 2000).

The real value practitioners' gain from being part of a CoP is to help each other solve problems, reflect on practices to improve, keep up with change, cooperate on innovation, and find a voice to gain strategic influence.[13] As new communities emerge, within and across business groups, functions and markets, even more knowledge is shared. In today's world, knowledge sharing is simply not enough. To truly transform and innovate faster, social learning spaces are necessary to pay attention to the data, engage uncertainty and move people to make a difference. Learning partnerships created to cross boundaries can turn into valuable learning assets. Value-creation frameworks provide a structure for capturing the flow of events or ideas from social learning spaces (virtual or in person), through data and stories. The information learned together in the space, new ideas, methods, and tools flow back into the real world through the small and big actions taken as a result. When the findings are then brought back to the community, that is referred to as creating learning loops.

An example of how to develop learning loops is to facilitate open collaboration, between boundaries by bringing people together to share stories of both successes and failures and then to solicit feedback and allow time for questions and discussion. When people are open to share their struggle, it speeds up learning for others because they contribute to finding ways to help solve problems (Wenger et al. 2011).The results are impressive because not only does the person sharing get advice and new ideas, the community is also engaged in active problem solving which can be applied to their own struggles and challenges. Through active dialogue and problem solving, important learning can thrive.

Customers are increasingly looking for solution propositions that will help them add value and address their business challenges. Communities of Practice create environments where exchanges can happen in real-time between various functions that trigger new ideas leading to solutions customers really need. It is important for Community Moderators to be proactive in looking for relevant stories that can result in innovative successes when space is allowed for this to happen. Bringing failures forward in communities is an opportunity to apply the learning loop model while solving complex problems together. This is viewed as a very positive experience for members. Community Moderators in Philips have witnessed that applauding failure can create powerful learnings in the right environment.

A key takeaway from our ongoing community development experience is to ask the community first, before sharing what is already known, because this helps to build engagement by allowing the members to find the answers themselves through collaboration. Sharing value creation stories that come from their experiences, creates strong learning loops. Results are achieved by applying learnings to build on strengths. Innovation comes from finding something new out of a struggle, or failure which is shared, solutions are offered, then applied and new results are brought back into the community.

---

13. See thesystemsthinker.com/communities-of-practice-learning-as-a-social-system for more information.

Key Takeaways for Solution Innovation Excellence

The key takeaways for achieving **Solution Design & Delivery Service Excellence** could be summarized as follows:

- **Scalable and role-specific Solution Design & Delivery framework** enables success for different project complexities and all Project team members.
- **Solution Design & Delivery Services** require a specific **Set of Capabilities** at the organization & market. Some of the capabilities are solution specific, some capabilities are generic for any solution.
- Holistic and fully integrated approach for the **Customer Lifecycle** is key for scoping, designing, delivering, and servicing Solutions for healthcare customers.
- **Work intensively with Communities of Practice and the Experts around the Globe.** A Community of Practice for the different professions is a state-of-the art approach and recognized best-practice to Share, Learn, Leverage, Network, and Communicate together.
- **Process Harmonization and Standardization** is highly important for the success of an organization operating globally and reducing complexity. Tight integration in the upstream processes (e.g. sales, bid management) and downstream processes (e.g. entire lifecycle) are very important too. This has to be supported by solid change management and training activities.
- **Solution Design & Delivery Service Excellence is not a static objective**. It requires continuous improvement around all Capabilities. Even though it is not an absolute objective per se, it is considered a proactive way to anticipate and fulfill the needs of our customers with regards Solutions & Services.

INNOVATION IN ACTION: DUBAI CUSTOMS AND THE ACCELERATED EXPLORATORY LAB

Digital transformation and the fourth Industrial Revolution have been gathering momentum across all industry sectors, driven by a new wave of disruptive technologies forcing businesses to adapt to new ways of working. As organizations strive to harness the business benefits of digital disruption, the value of robust and more strategic project management practices continues to soar. Digital disruption brings huge challenges as well as major opportunities to drive business growth and competitive advantage across all diversified industries.

Challenges

Innovation in silos often posed a huge challenge at Dubai Customs, especially when business units and departments were running their own research and analysis to build prototypes of similar nature initiatives, limiting the transparency of opportunities addressed in dealing with disruptive technologies. As disruptive technology impacts the work we do, Dubai Customs sets out to explore a more collaborative solution that enables business owners, SMEs, and customers to be involved in every part of the exploratory process and find new ways to better enhance project management capabilities in innovation to gain a competitive advantage.

Approach

Dubai Customs, as an innovative organization, realized that these disruptions in the nature of new advancements in knowledge/technology, involving some level of uncertainty and having multiple dimensions (in terms of the kind of outcomes/cost and time), presented the opportunity to evolve our existing best practices. For this, the most important aspect was to create the culture within Dubai Customs that can support agility by embracing a new a design thinking-led approach (Figure 5-11) to better manage disruptive technologies, such as blockchain, artificial intelligence (AI), Internet of Things (IoT), augmented reality and virtual reality, relying on project success as a competitive advantage and succeed in a fast-paced and disruptive business environment to move quickly, decisively, and effectively to anticipate, initiate, and take advantage of change, yet remain robust enough to absorb any setbacks.

Accelerated Exploratory Lab Solution

Using the approach Dubai Customs further set out to create a collaborative accelerated exploratory environment which was a joint task force (Figure 5-12) formed between demand management, services innovations, project delivery, and customs IT development, which better served as an opportunity to advance, focus on the value delivery landscape for the business community, and enable project managers to play a more strategic role in managing disruptions and embrace the value delivery landscape. The lab offered a unique, collaborative environment specifically designed to facilitate idea exploration through research and development to seek the desired results focused in establishing a partnership from idea to impact by having all the concerned partners working together both internal and external to Dubai Customs exploring and prototyping the changes/potential solutions systemically through agile projects in rapid iterations.

The accelerated exploratory lab landscape (Figure 5-13) addresses three main areas; determining the strategic direction, then learning to determine if something works and finally scaling to growth the potential solutions that create value for the organization. In the figure, CDC is a governing body overseeing all technology related investments at Dubai Customs. The landscape helps teams quickly get on-boarded and encapsulates the complexities and challenges involved in testing and building a solution development overlooked by the innovation governance process. The entire governance process is integrated into the landscape with an innovation committee overseeing all the R&D initiatives and ensuring traceability with infused expertise in agile project management approaches wherein project managers are involved right from the start having more subject matter expertise creating more in the value delivery process.

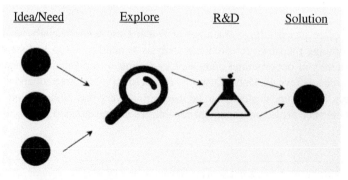

Figure 5–11. Design Thinking-Led Approach.

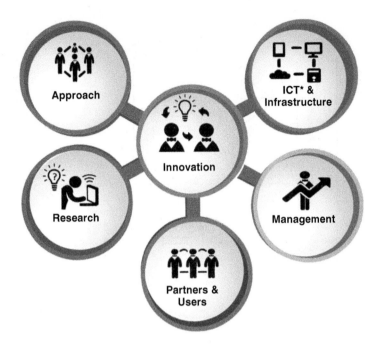

*ICT refers to information and communication technology.

Figure 5–12. Exploratory Lab Environment.

In dealing with all disruptive technologies project categories were categorized under the umbrella of innovation projects (Figure 5-14), such as hypothesis research projects, data research projects and new product / experimental development projects run in an agile approach with rapid iterations for all the exploratory initiatives to determine value delivery capabilities and differentiate our customer experiences.

Benefits

The benefits realized from all innovation engagements:

- Provides a collaborative environment where all partners collectively work together
- Helps to filter and focus on all the valuable ideas, based on the research results
- Accelerates discovery process
- Ensures better transparency and visibility across the organization

Lessons Learned

- It is always important to get support from senior management in the organization on the way we approach disruptive technologies vs. already established technologies.
- For disruptive technologies, start using the approach to prototype to know if a solution works for addressing specific challenges before we proceed with a full investment.

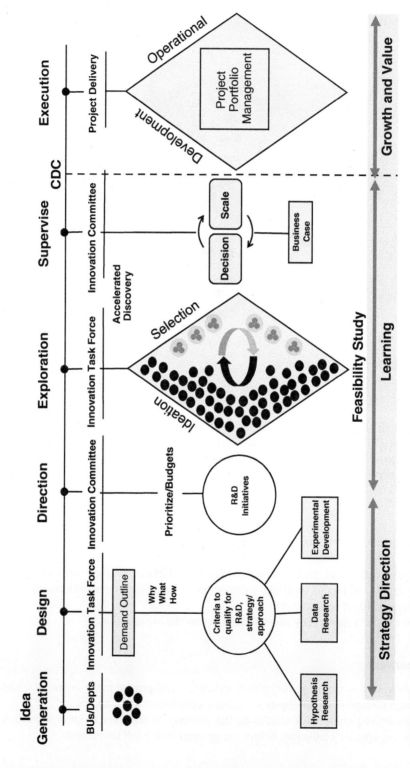

*CDC is a governing body overseeing all technology-related investments at Dubai Customs.

Figure 5–13. Accelerated Exploratory Lab Landscape.

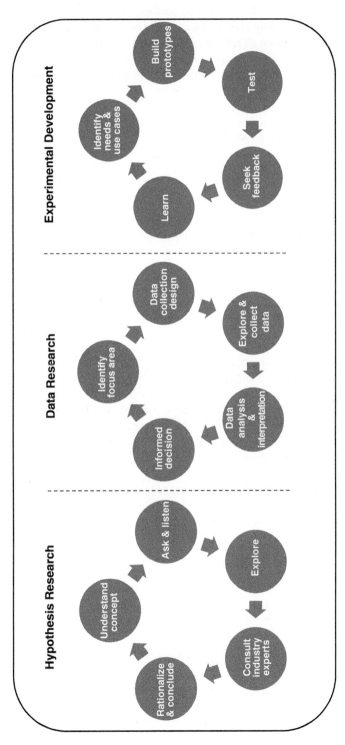

Figure 5–14. Innovation Project Categories.

- Test in small scale using chosen scenarios by inviting all the required participants (internal and external stakeholders) to jointly explore the potential of disruptive technologies.
- Radical collaboration between all relevant stakeholders is a must.
- An innovation governance process serves as a mechanism to help the organization provide a full visibility on all disruptive technology initiatives including every stage of the design process.
- Embed a culture of prototyping in the organization.
- Shift the mindset to show, don't tell.
- Display a bias toward action (focus more action-oriented then discussion-based to show if something works versus assuming something will work).

INNOVATION IN ACTION: MERCK KGaA, DARMSTADT, GERMANY

In the current economic worldwide context, a company can survive only if the following component are achieved:

- Having products to answer customer pain points and needs
- Addressing a growing market
- Having a competitive margin
- Having a strategy

In order to fulfill the first point, you need to be better than the competition and then, to have innovative products. Having a strategy is not enough by itself. But if you look on the process described here, you will see that this is the starting point of the "market pull" process to deliver new products on the market. To develop some market-pull products, a classic project management process is required with some stage gates, decision point, signatories, and so on, during the execution phase.

In parallel to this process, you have a "technology push" process, as shown in Figure 5-15, which is nurturing the above process. In fact, some new trends and technologies can influence your strategy, your defined product, and technology roadmaps.

These two processes should be different as they are not addressing the same topics.

What is important, as a lesson learned from past experiences, is to have two separate processes: one to address *new product development* and another one for *new technologies development*.

New Technology Development Process

For the new technology development process, the project management style should be different, as it requires more flexibility and agility. This process should focus on new technologies to be embedded into future new products but also to acquire knowledge.

Let me share with you some thoughts on this process.

Even if this process is flexible or agile to allow for creativity, you cannot let a team circle around for months or years knowing that you have limited resources and budget. You still must have some project management basics as, for example:

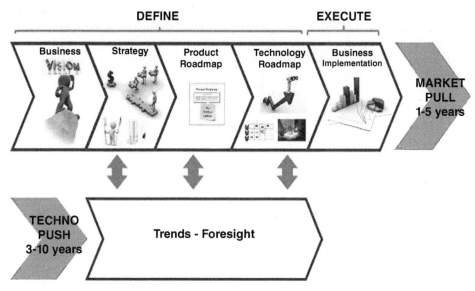

Figure 5–15. The Two Processes.

- Team charter with a clear scope and objectives for the project/activities
- As soon as you are going through a phase, you need to have an evaluation of time and budget needed to cover the next one
- Defined phases and deliverables
- Sponsors and signatories

You can have creativity, brainstorming, and so on during a phase, but at the end of the day, the team should know where to go and the desired end point. This has already been addressed, using design thinking in each phase where design thinking is necessary, while keeping in mind the original global goals and objectives of the project, as budget and resources are not unlimited, unfortunately.

This is where the project manager's role becomes important: Letting the team be creative but ensuring that the framework is well understood and managing the team within that framework. This is key for a project manager: the ability to drive the team within a defined framework to a defined goal but allowing for enough flexibility to "unchain" the team members.

We have encountered many situations where the project manager was following the defined process as is, without taking into account the situation or the personalities of the different team members. This is a recipe for failure. With this separate process, you then have the possibility of knowing exactly what the budget is you are investing in new technologies and potentially this budget may not be recoverable through future sales.

Product Development Process and Portfolio Management

One of the first steps in portfolio management activities a company must take is to build the definition of the innovation categories. Why? These definitions will be critical in order to implement portfolio management. Breakthrough innovations are at risk and you need to know how much money you want to be at risk.

A very reference is *Harvard Business Review*, "Managing your Innovation Portfolio," by Bansi Nagji and Geoff Tuff (2012). In this paper, they describe how to build the definition for three innovation categories—breakthrough, incremental, and sustaining—based on two axes: through the customer's lens and through your internal capability's lens. This way, we can define the different categories in such a way that they can be used in all types of industries.

With these definitions, you can tag your projects in your company and then have additional information to manage your portfolio. Keep in mind that a complete disruptive technology can be embedded or hidden in an incremental product. This is what we see in the automotive industry, for instance: cars are incremental, but with new features and breakthrough technologies. This is why multiple processes are needed: to maintain an efficient innovation portfolio and for project management.

When you are developing a new product, you can run in parallel the multiple processes described above: the product development process and the new technology development process. This can happen when you identify the need for a breakthrough technology during the development of your product. This technology will be then embedded into the product.

It is quite a challenge to run both activities through the same process and at the same time. The pace, the project management style, is not really the same for each. The project manager is responsible for driving decision making.

If the technology you are looking for is not part of your company's capabilities, you as project manager need to ensure that a clear decision is made by the sponsors whether to "make or buy." This happened on one of our projects; we wanted to develop our own technology, and after several month of work, project management personnel pushed for a clear decision. Then a compromise was formed because similar technology had already been developed.

One of the key terms in all situations, and whatever the process used, is *common sense*. A project manager's key skill is to be able to adapt and to lead the team through complex situations. This is where we can recognize an efficient project manager.

Case Study

Some time ago, based on our strategy and customer needs, it was decided to start working on new technologies that would be able to quickly detect microorganisms in different matrices for a dedicated market. The choice had been made to develop these technologies within the company instead of forming partnerships. At that time, new technology choices and evaluation were in the hand of the R&D group. We had a clear process with defined milestones and R&D was the only signatory for each step. Scope was defined by R&D and the work started. The team's status reports stated that we were progressing well and after two years, results were shared with and approved by the head of R&D.

Then we started a project to develop a new product using this promising technology. Marketing confirmed the customers' needs, the different matrices to be used, and the conditions for product usage. During one of the first project meetings, the R&D team started to compare the work already done on the technology with the product features and requirements. There was no, or little match! The technology defined had been tested on some topics that were not relevant for the future products at all. As a result, the R&D team was frustrated by the loss of time and money:

Question: How could the team have done better on this?

Answer: Following a lesson-learned session on this project, it was decided to review our process to develop a new technology. We still had some defined phases, but we included the following improvement:

- Marketing is now one of the signatories along with R&D for each stage.
- We have included a specifications list defined by marketing as a support for R&D and to ensure that the work done will answer future market needs.
- At the last stage of the process, a representative of the future team that will develop the new product will be part of the team meeting and stage gate review. During this meeting the focus will be on the features tested, results obtained, and expectations to ensure this new technology will answer our future needs.

INNOVATION IN ACTION: REPSOL

Repsol is a global and integrated company in the energy sector. We operate across 37 countries with a team comprising over 25,000 people who work on building a sustainable future. Our vision of being a global energy company based on innovation, efficiency, and respect sustainably creates value to promote progress in society.

Innovation is an important leverage in our vision and is also one of our company values, together with transparency, responsibility, results orientation, and collaboration. At Repsol, we believe that the key to our competitiveness and development resides in our ability to generate new ideas and put them into practice in a spirit of cooperation and continuous collective learning. It has been a long and arduous journey to get innovation as part of our DNA, and there are still many challenges to be overcome.

The following is how we are building the culture and capabilities for being the global and integrated energy company that we want to be and keep sustainably in the market.

First Phase: Acquiring Knowledge (2011–2012)

Until 2011, innovation at Repsol was focused on R&D activity. In 2011, the innovation program was launched in response to the strategic plan (2011–2014) about the quality control and knowledge management functions. The program was sponsored by upper management that decided to incorporate innovation as one of the corporate values since 2012. The main objective was to embed the innovation in our culture and day-to-day activities.

In addition, an organizational structure was created to support and encourage the innovation program. The corporate innovation unit, business innovation units, and the innovation committee were the organizational units in this structure. An innovation network was created including entrepreneurs, innovation teams, and facilitators.

Second Phase: Strengthening the Organization (2013–2015)

In 2013, the focus was to build the capacity for the organization. The first edition of the Facilitators Training Program was held to support continuous improvement processes with lean-based methodologies.

Besides that, a pilot within the chemical business started. This pilot is a successful case in our company, and it has become the lean transformation program for this business and other businesses and corporate areas where it has been deployed according to their needs.

The aim was to promote a culture of innovation in 2014. The strategic innovation reflection (SIR) was held with the participation of all the innovation units generating a company model to add more value from innovation. Meanwhile, the first edition of the IN awards was launched with the participation of +5,000 employees and +500 initiatives. In 2014, the innovation network continued growing until around 75 innovation and improvement teams.

In 2015, some KPIs were defined and put in place to measure the impact of innovation. A global corporate program called "Go" started with the aim to generate innovative proposals in order to improve the EBITDA. In addition, business units deployed the innovation model through specific roadmaps to leverage their strategic plans.

Figure 5-16 shows actions put in place to support and encourage innovation from the innovation units in corporation and business areas.

Third Phase: Leverages for Transformation (2016–2018)

Management Principles

Since 2016, an evolution of the operating model (processes, structure, policies and management criteria, work dynamic and decision making, knowledge management, etc.) is afforded by each business unit in accordance with the new strategic challenges. The innovation programs accompanying the new strategic update include the identification and prioritization of initiatives by the business units' committees.

The alignment and mobilization of the organization to attain a shared purpose and vision are essential in this transformation. Besides this, communication is a key element to ensure the final goals.

New Models of People and Organization Management: Agile Philosophy as the Engine of the Change

Some global initiatives foster a more flexible and efficient corporate environment, taking advantage of the new technologies:

- Development and implementation of policies and models to ensure that the culture of innovation is promoted
- Proposal of new ways of working to be implemented in the units depending on their own and global needs
- Promotion of continuous improvement projects in order to optimize processes (lean)
- Definition and proposition of the cultural change necessary to achieve a flexible and collaborative organization
- Development of leaders to ensure behaviors associated with innovation and entrepreneurship
- Recognition of entrepreneurs and innovation teams who develop initiatives
- Generation and development of capacity in the organization, both in project teams and units
- Surveillance, validation, and divulgation of new effective and replicable approaches with high potential impact in order to respond to the problems and opportunities of the businesses

The result, as shown in Figure 5-17, is a cultural transformation based on innovation and new ways of working that have provided Repsol some important leverages of this transformation toward becoming a lean company.

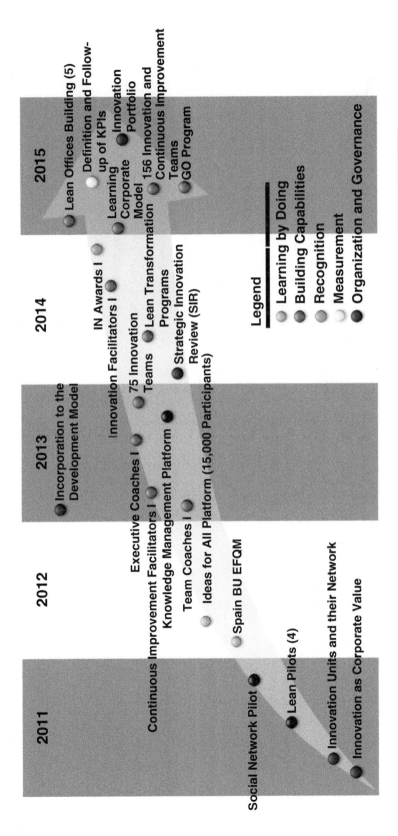

Figure 5–16.   Details of the Actions Accomplished.

REPSOL

Model

Model definition for innovation and new ways of working (NWW) across the company:

- Generation of models, methodologies and processes to promote new ways of working
- Deployment of the continuous improvement culture
- Participation in external networks within the innovation environment

Programs

Project development:

- Supporting the strategic programs in the company
- Managing projects in business and corporate areas based on new ways of working (NWW)

Culture

We accelerate the innovation culture:

- Managing the facilitators program
- Building capabilities in the organization
- Measuring through the innovation index
- Recognizing the innovation

Team mobilization

We support the teams with new ways of working in collaborative sessions focused on:

- Multidisciplinary team-building sessions
- Challenges and solutions identification
- Vision and strategy definition, and their deployment
- Providing tailor-made support depending on the needs.

Figure 5–17. The Cultural Transformation: A Lean Company with New Ways of Working.

STAFFING INNOVATION PROJECTS _____

Skill level of the resources needed is generally predictable if we have a well-defined SOW and detailed listing of the requirements. In innovation, the skill level of the resources required may not be known until well into the project and may change based on changes in the marketplace and enterprise environmental factors. Generally, more resources are needed for development work such as in incremental innovation rather than pure research or radical innovation. This generates a greater need for structured supervision in certain types of innovation, such as in pure research, which is often conducted in a campus-like work environment.

Having good intentions for and expectations from innovation activities is based on proper staffing. Resources can be obtained by:

- Using existing resources that have the necessary technical skills
- Using existing resources that must undergo technical training
- Using newly hired employees
- Using consultants
- Company acquisitions
- Sharing resources through joint ventures or licensing agreements
- Using resources as part of co-creation teams

Executives tend to select projects, add them to the queue, and prioritize them with little regard if the organization has available and qualified personnel. Even worse, most executives do not know how much additional work they can take on without overburdening the labor force.

Balancing resource availability and demand requires open dialogue. Innovation PMs need to be brought on board early. Project managers need to participate in staffing activities and seek out qualified resources that support the idea and are willing to work in a team environment. Some people may feel skeptical about the project. The PM must allay their fears and win their trust. Project staffing requirements may dictate that the PM works closely with human resources for the duration of the project if people with new skills must be hired.

Companies can be working on several different types of innovation concurrently. This poses a challenge as to which innovation projects should have the best resources:

- Should resources be reallocated from sustainment innovation that satisfies existing customers' needs to disruptive innovation targeted for future customers?
- If we reallocate resources, say from incremental to disruptive innovation projects, is there a risk that market leaders may lose their leadership positions?

In fast-changing organizations, the link between strategy formulation and strategy execution is based on the organization's understanding and use of dynamic capabilities. Dynamic capabilities theory concerns the development of strategies for senior managers of successful companies to adapt to radical discontinuous change. It requires reconfiguring assets to match a changing environment (O'Connor 2008). Organizations must have a firm grasp of the resources needed for competitive survival as well as the resources needed in the future for a competitive advantage. This can be accomplished using a talent pipeline that recognizes the competencies that are needed and their readiness to step in on short notice as backup talent. Specialized resources may also be needed because of deficiencies resulting from organizational change management.

There are shortcomings in resource management practices, as shown in Figure 5-18, which can prevent organizations from achieving their strategic goals and allow bad projects to survive. Executives may

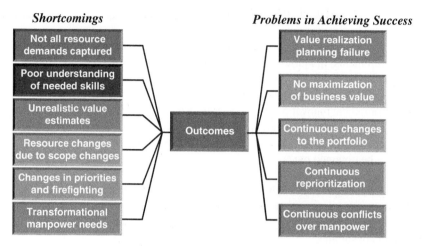

Figure 5-18. Resource Management Issues and Outcomes.

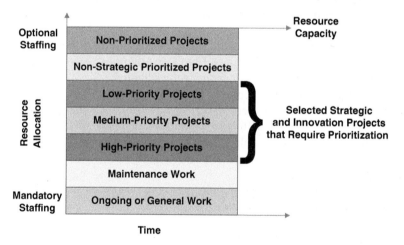

Figure 5-19. Prioritized Resource Utilization.

find it necessary to add resources to an apparently healthy project that has greater opportunities if successful. If the resources must be removed from another project, then the other project may have schedule delays and miss windows of opportunity. With a fixed manpower base, decisions must be made based on the best interest of the entire portfolio rather than a single project.

Identifying the resources needed is part of the challenge. The other part is how the resources are allocated. Usually, there is a priority system for resource assignment, as shown in Figure 5-19.

Optimal resource capacity planning and staffing may be unrealistic. Some people, such as Murro et al. (2016), believe that having organizational slack in resource assignments will increase the opportunities for creative behavior and contribute to a competitive advantage. We can define three types of organizational slack from which we can obtain resources:

1. *Absorbed slack.* These are resources that are absorbed throughout the company but can become available as the organization becomes more efficient.

2. *Unabsorbed slack.* These are resources that are available immediately and can be assigned quickly to an innovation project.
3. *Potential slack.* This is the ability of the firm to obtain extra resources as needed through hiring practices, partnerships, joint ventures, or co-created teams.

There are pros and cons for each category of organizational slack. In one company that prided itself on innovation, management created a culture whereby all workers were expected to spend at least 10 percent of their time on existing projects looking for ideas for new products and services for the firm. While this had the favorable effect of creating new products, it destroyed the budgets that project managers had for existing projects and was accompanied by significant cost overruns. Although we discuss organizational slack in terms of human resources, there can also be slack in physical resources and financial resources.

It should be noted that many companies, even those with good capacity-planning systems, have had to assign more of their already scarce resources needed for innovation activities to potential problems resulting from regulations and legislation with respect to such items as:

- Product liability
- Environmental matters
- Health issues
- Safety issues
- Energy supplies

Making the most out of highly talented people is often difficult, especially if they are prima donnas. Some resource utilization issues common to innovation include:

- How do we leverage underutilized resources?
- How do we redeploy and recombine resources if necessary?
- How do we handle highly technical people that prefer working independently but are not as innovative as they would be if working with others?
- How do we handle workers who are perfectionists and want to exceed rather than meet the requirements and specifications?

The importance of the human resources department is often hidden, but it does have an impact on creating a corporate image and reputation that promotes innovation. This is accomplished by attracting talented technical people, giving them the opportunity to be creative, and ultimately increasing the public's confidence in the value and quality of the innovations.

IMPLICATIONS AND ISSUES FOR PROJECT MANAGERS AND INNOVATION PERSONNEL

Experienced project managers will have to change the way they use traditional project management tools and processes when managing innovation. Some of the significant issues that PMs must deal with include:

- Not enough detailed information about the requirements, thus mandating the use of rolling wave or moving window planning for the WBS, schedule, and budgets.

- Continuous updates to budgets and schedules.
- The need for a great deal of information on consumers to support project decision making, thus having to learn how to use the firm's knowledge management system.
- The assumptions and enterprise environmental factors will change over the life of the project and must be closely monitored.
- Different life-cycle phases may be used based on the type of innovation.
- Ongoing work may be of a higher priority than the innovation project and this could affect project staffing.

REFERENCES

Bodenheimer, T. and Sinsky, C. (2014). From triple to quadruple aim: Care of the patient requires care of the provider. *Annals of Family Medicine* 12 (6), 574–575. Available at www.annfammed.org/content/12/6/573.full. Accessed April 7, 2019.

Calabretta, G. and Gemser, G. (2016). Integrating design into the fuzzy front end of the innovation process. In M. G. Luchs, K.S. Swan, and A. Griffin (ed.). *Design Thinking: New Product Development Essentials from the PDMA*. Hoboken, NJ: John Wiley and Sons, 107–126.

Drucker, P.F. (1999). Knowledge-worker productivity: The biggest challenge. *California Management Review* 1, 79–94.

Hanley, S. (2014). Measure what matters: A practical approach to knowledge management metrics. *Business Information Review* 31 (3), 154–159. DOI: 10.1177/0266382114551120.

He, W., Goodkind, D. and Kowal, P. (2016 March). *An Aging World: 2015. International Population Reports* U.S. Census Bureau, International Population Reports, P95/16-1, Washington, DC: U.S. Government Publishing Office. p. 6. Available at www.fiapinternacional.org/wp-content/uploads/2016/10/An-Aging-World-2015.pdf.

Ihrig, M., Boisot, M., and MacMillan, I. (2011). Forget IP. Mine strategic knowledge instead. *Harvard Business Review*, May 6, 2011.

Kaplan, J. M. and Warren, A. C. (2009). *Patterns of Entrepreneurship Management* (3rd ed.). Hoboken, NJ: John Wiley and Sons.

Kayworth, T. and Leidner, D. (2003). Organizational culture as a knowledge resource. In C. W. Holsapple (ed.). *Handbook on Knowledge Management. Volume 1: Knowledge Matters*. Heidelberg: Springer-Verlag, 235–252.

Martin, M. G. (2010). *Delivering Project Excellence with the Statement of Work*. Management Concepts Incorporated. 2e, Management Concepts Press, Virginia

Melik, R. (2007). *The Rise of the Project Workforce*. Hoboken, NJ: John Wiley & Sons.

Murro, E. V. B., Teixeira, G. B., Beuren, I. M. et al. (2016). Relationship between organizational slack and innovation in companies of BM&FBOVESPA. *Revista de Administração Mackenzie* 17 (3), 132–157. DOI: 10.1590/1678-69712016.

Nagji, B. and Tuff, G. (2012). Managing your innovation portfolio. *Harvard Business Review (May)* 90 (5), 66–74.

O'Connor, G. C. (2008). Major innovation as a dynamic capability: A systems approach. *Journal of Product Innovation Management* 25, 313–330.

Verzuh, E. (2016). *The Fast Forward MBA in Project Management*. Hoboken, NJ: John Wiley and Sons.

Wenger, E. and Snyder, W. (2000). Communities of practice: The organizational frontier. *Harvard Business Review (January–February)* 78 (1), 139–145. Available at https://hbr.org/2000/01/communities-of-practice-the-organizational-frontier.

Wenger, E., Trayner, B. and de Laat, M. (2011). Open Universiteit, Ruud de Moor Centrum. *Promoting and assessing value creation in communities and networks: a conceptual framework* (Rapport 18). Available at http://www.bevtrayner.com/base/docs/Wenger_Trayner_DeLaat_Value_creation.

World Economic Forum. (2017). *Value in Healthcare: Laying the Foundation for Health System Transformation*. Insight Report, April 2017. Geneva, Switzerland: World Economic Forum. Available at http://www3.weforum.org/docs/WEF_Insight_Report_Value_Healthcare_Laying_Foundation.pdf. Accessed April 7, 2019.

Innovation Management Software

Learning Objectives for Project Managers and Innovation Personnel

To understand the need for innovation management software

To understand how innovation management software supports an information warehouse

To understand how innovation management software supports innovation decision making

INTRODUCTION

So far, we have discussed the importance of assigning a professional managerial person dedicated to the management of new ideas that could be commercialized into products or services. This person, the *innovation project manager*, is not the person who would necessarily create something new, but the one who knows all the processes needed to encourage the birth of an idea and to turn it into reality or, better, into *business value*. To better perform this task, it is necessary for him/her to have a profound awareness about the tools that can help make it happen.

Over the past two decades, innovation project managers have recognized the importance of creating an information warehouse for data to support innovation activities. The marketplace has responded with the creation of *innovation management software*. The main/basic idea behind such software is that the greatest heritage to create innovation is already inside the company, the issue being how to better allow those new ideas to come out. This goal is reached by creating an innovation platform in the form

Innovation Project Management: Methods, Case Studies, and Tools for Managing Innovation Projects,
Second Edition. Harold Kerzner.
© 2023 John Wiley & Sons, Inc. Published 2023 by John Wiley & Sons, Inc.

of a digital cloud that collects, filters, develops, and implements idea. The possibility to provide an idea is mainly socialized in the private network of the company, but in some cases can be also opened to the public.

In the following sections, the working principles of the innovation software are discussed; then, to give a clear example about the application of the innovation software philosophy, case studies are presented. The cases selected have been provided by two companies in the field of innovation management software, namely, *IdeaScale* and *HYPE Innovation*.

The services provided by the innovation software companies are not limited to sell "only" the software packages; being innovation experts/strategists, if needed and required, they can customize, develop the software best suited to the company, and even, through a scouting activity, help the assisted company to find possible partners to perform the desired task. In this way, the innovation software companies tend to create the so-called "open innovation" environment. When open innovation is applied permanently, it is a source of innovation in most high-tech companies and a necessity.

ORIGIN AND BENEFITS OF INNOVATION SOFTWARE

Innovation software programs are usually conceived in a way that there is a common platform where all the users (basically employees of the company) have access and can freely leave their proposals or opinions about a possible new idea. The information can be collected anonymously if necessary. Then, each new proposal generates an online debate or discussion with the effect to improve it. Once a certain number of ideas are reached, the selection phase starts. This phase is conducted by *innovation project managers* with the support of sector experts and business unit people with the intent of evaluating the feasibility from a technical and business point of view, respectively. Finally, this committee selects the ideas that are worthy of an investment. The ideas that are not selected are not thrown away; they are archived because there exists the possibility that they could be implemented sometime later perhaps due to the development of a more appropriate technology.

Figure 6-1 outlines the overall workflow in the application of innovation management software.

It is interesting to point out that innovation management software is basically the last evolution of the so-called *suggestion box* introduced more than 100 years ago. The suggestion box had an early and sometimes successful history. Usually, it was run by the then-named personnel department, was aimed primarily at cost savings, and was a passive system that collected ideas (often complaints), which were occasionally reviewed by a committee. While suggestion systems were often successful initially, most eventually fell into disuse through apathy or the fact that submitters often received no feedback on their ideas and therefore stopped providing them. Most of these systems were paper-based and unwieldy (Shockley 2006).

Figure 6–1. Innovation Management Software Process.

Part of this chapter was prepared by Luigi Morsa, Ph.D., aerospace engineer and project manager. ©2022 by Luigi Morsa, Ph.D. All Rights Reserved. Reproduced by permission.

By the 1990s, the Internet provided a medium for a new model for idea gathering. Companies started building web-based pages where employees may post their ideas. But once again, these web-based pages were still managed by the personnel department and were most often built by the company IT department. Ideas were still treated in the same fashion as the suggestion box, and eventually fell into the same problems that faced the suggestion box before it: frequent complaints, slow feedback and review, and a nontransparent backend system to how the ideas were handled (El Sherbiny and Abdel Aziz Hadia 2014).

Almost all of these limitations have been overcome by the modern innovation management software. Nowadays, they find application basically in each sector; more in detail the companies specialized in the innovation management software offer solutions for enterprise, government, banking, finance, health care, nonprofit organizations, small business and so on.

The main benefits derived by the use of the innovation management software can be summarized as follows:

- *Improve employee engagement.* Innovation management software helps employees to capture their ideas that otherwise would be lost. The employees have the perception that they have a voice in the organization's improvement efforts, they feel more connected to the success of the business, and therefore they develop a sense of belonging to the company.[1]
- *Encourage collaboration.* The ideas are usually improved through an online chat discussion because the comments/critiques made by other people with different points of view or background provide new inputs. Then, the author of an idea can return to the system later to add details to its creation. The whole process therefore becomes strongly cross-functional and collaborative (Millard 2014).
- *Simplify employee recognition.* Innovation management software makes it easier for managers and executives to recognize the employees that have good ideas. They can, in a more transparent way, acknowledge and reward the efforts of employees who contribute to business performance improvement through ideas generation or by helping with the ideas fulfillment process (Millard 2014).
- *Help companies increase their speed to market.* Innovation management software helps companies take advantage of the best ideas to commercialize them in the marketplace as new "products/ services" before the competitors (InnovationTools.com 2013). It is possible, in fact, that thanks to the innovation management software the employees or in general the stakeholders with access to the software can very quickly launch an idea once they have recognized an opportunity for new trends or needs in the marketplace.
- *Provided contributors with a sense of accomplishment even if their ideas are not selected.* People understand that not all ideas will be selected, but they know that they did contribute.

There are four critical components that innovation software should possess. According to Jessica Day, vice president at IdeaScale, they are:[2]

- Security, especially when you are partnering with other companies, schools or the general public
- Customization that can conform to your innovation initiatives

---

1. InnovationTools.com, "An Overview of Idea Management Systems," www.innovationmanagement.se/imtool-resources/an-overview-of-idea-management-systems; Millard (2014).

2. Adapted from Jessica Day, *Innovation Management Software: 4 Essential Components*, IdeaScale Newsletter, October 3, 2019.

- Accessible to everyone you want to participate
- Integration such that it can break down barriers between functional silos

Innovation software is more than just brainstorming and recording ideas for new products and services. It is also used as part of customer value management programs to document customer "value-in-use" experiences with your products and services. The information obtained can then be used not only for new or improved products but for improvements in customer service.

Value-in-use is most frequently determined by observing the customer using your products/services and asking for feedback. The feedback you receive should also be based upon how the products/services were advertised, marketed, sold, the speed by which you helped them resolve issues, your willingness to provide warrantees and repairs, and the way you manage customer communications.

Feedback on the total customer experience can then generate ideas for improvements and innovations in customer service. By documenting the feedback, you are showing the customers that you are listening to their concerns.

To provide examples about the potentials of such kind of software and its versatile application, in the following sections, cases studies from two leading companies in the field of innovation management software are presented.

SOFTWARE INNOVATION IN ACTION: IDEASCALE

In 2009, IdeaScale was launched in tandem with President Barack Obama's Open Government Initiative. In its first year, IdeaScale was adopted by 23 federal agencies. It served many organizations, including the Executive Office of the President of the United States. The IdeaScale's software allows organizations to involve the opinions of public and private communities by collecting their ideas and giving users a platform to vote. The ideas are then evaluated, routed, and implemented. As of 2016, IdeaScale has maintained its bootstrapped status and profitability and has offices in Washington, DC, Japan, and Germany with headquarters in Berkeley, California.

The following two cases studies from IdeaScale have been selected:

1. Magneti Marelli is a good example of software application in a high technology field where the ideas have been obtained not by soliciting the employees, but rather university students and fans of motorsport technology.
2. Redwood Credit Union represents an attempt to give voice to the customers through the company's employees, that (especially in case of banks, insurances and so on) collect/listen to customer's feedback.

Magneti Marelli Case Study: Speeding Toward the Competitive Edge

Magneti Marelli is an international company founded in Italy in 1919, committed to the design and production of hi-tech systems and components for the automotive sector, based in Italy (Corbetta, Milan). With more than 38,000 employees, 85 production units, 12 R&D centers, and 26 application centers, the group has a presence in 19 countries and supplies all the most important car makers in Europe, North and South America, and Asia.

When the company partnered with Open Knowledge, an international consulting firm specializing in social business transformation, they developed LapTime Club. LapTime Club is an innovation community built specifically for motorsport engineers and experts, but also for technology and electronics enthusiasts. The objective of the LapTime Club is to stimulate creativity and innovation, which promotes the development of ideas, products, and services that are effective for the world of racing.

The team at Magneti Marelli promoted this new online community using the complete digital toolkit: blogging, email announcements, news articles in relevant publications, digital advertising campaigns on Facebook and Google, and more. Moreover, a team of experts was set up to manage conversations and ensure the proper level of competence to interact in the community. Additionally, as the program matured, so did the engagement of students and universities achieved through ad hoc initiatives, including offline materials to be posted on campuses that directed interested individuals to the community. The team also used the hackathon[3] format to engage the community—inviting other parties to join a technical competition at the 2014 Motor Show in Bologna where four groups of participants were invited to create and develop a motorsport dashboard using 3D printing and other technologies.

Each month, the innovation team at the Magneti Marelli met to review new ideas and contact the idea authors for more details to further develop the most promising ideas. And in the first six months of the project, the team reported that:

- LapTime Club has collected nearly 100 ideas from all over the world through a crowd-sourced[4] effort.
- The top 20 ideas became idea finalists that were being evaluated by Magneti Marelli managers and technical experts.
- Two winning ideas were honored and considered for development by Magneti Marelli, including a Google Glass integration and a new method for optimizing a pilot's decision making during a race.

"We surveyed numerous tools and IdeaScale combined flexible functionalities with a high level of service," said Ilaria, project manager for LapTime Club; "The program has resulted in an incredible mindset shift that has opened up the process of innovation to make it more collaborative."

With close to 100 ideas that originated from more than 600 members (85% of which were external to the company), Magneti Marelli plans to continue to invite global collaboration in their LapTime Club, which will drive motorsport innovation into the future.

Redwood Credit Union Case Study: Capability Improving Customer Experience with Employee Ideas

Founded in 1950, Redwood Credit Union is a full-service financial institution providing personal and business banking to consumers and businesses in the North Bay and San Francisco. Their services include everything from checking and savings accounts, auto and home loans, credit cards, online and mobile

---

3. The word "hackathon" is a combination of the word "hack" and "marathon," where "hack" is used in the sense of exploratory programming, not its alternate meaning as a reference to computer security. A hackathon is a design sprint-like event in which computer programmers and others involved in software development, including graphic designers, interface designers, project managers, and others, often including subject-matter-experts, collaborate intensively on software projects.

4. Crowdsourcing is the practice of obtaining information or input into a task or project by enlisting the services of many people, typically via the Internet.

banking, and beyond. And as part of their member-centric approach, Redwood Credit union is committed to providing exceptional service to member-owners, and to each other.

One of the things that sets Redwood Credit Union apart is its dedication to constantly improving the member experience. It has always rigorously collected feedback and ideas from employees on ways to improve the customer experience, but in 2016 Brett Martinez wanted to enhance the system by using software that would make the process transparent and collaborative.

Redwood Credit Union promoted the use of the tool in a multichannel outreach campaign that included reminders to participate at the monthly company all-hands meeting, launch emails and digest notifications to consistently reengage employees, and send messages from leadership about the importance of participation.

The team also pre-populated the member experience campaign with suggestions that they'd received in the past to encourage engagement when the program launched. Awards were given not just for the ideas that delivered the most impact (the Voyager award) but also for the groups with the most engaged participants (the TME award).

The team recreated the existing customer experience improvement process within the IdeaScale tool using stages functionality. Ideas are reviewed on a monthly basis using the following processes:

1. There is a three-week voting and commenting period.
2. The Idea Administration Team meets to discuss top ideas and triages promising ideas to experts or asks for additional information from the idea author.
3. Experts assign an owner to the idea who rates the idea based on specific departmental criteria.
4. The team then reviews the idea using the five-star assessment (criteria can include things like "innovative," "viable," "impact to member experience," "effort," and so on).
5. Top ideas are selected and passed to the relevant team for implementation.

In order to maximize the number of ideas that are implemented each year, the implementation team works first to find existing in-development programs and projects that align to promising ideas and attaches the idea to the project. This is one of the key reasons that the team has reported successful results in less than a year:

- Changes include multiple enhancements to the member experience, including mobile thumbprint ID, changes to customer receipts, new statements, and much, much more.
- In their first year, over 70 percent of the staff has engaged on the platform and worked to improve the member experience.
- Redwood Credit Union's goal was to implement 50 new customer experience ideas in their first year, and the company exceeded that goal by implementing more than 85 (and counting).
- The team has also noted an improvement to the credit union's overall Net Promoter Score and attributes that success (in part) to the member experience improvements that began as IdeaScale suggestions.

"The tool has taken our existing process and given it so much more power," says Andy Ramos, SVP/Member Experience, "The flexibility of the tool, the ability to easily collaborate and manage ideas, has been critical to implementing so many new ideas in so short a time."

Redwood Credit Union will continue optimizing the member experience by leveraging the power of employee ideas.

SOFTWARE INNOVATION IN ACTION: HYPE INNOVATION _____

Founded in 2001, HYPE Innovation started out as a spin-off from DaimlerChrysler[5] (today Daimler AG). HYPE Innovation produces software to help innovation managers to collect, manage, vet, and turn ideas into concepts with business cases ready for prototyping and implementation. HYPE Innovation has its Headquarter in Bohn (Germany), but there is also an office in Cambridge, Massachusetts.

The Airbus case study presented next describes the key components needed to create an innovation management platform.

AIRBUS Case Study: Creating a Core Innovation Capability

Airbus is one of the world's foremost aerospace companies, with 133,000 employees, manufacturing sites in France, Germany, Spain, the United Kingdom, United States, and China, with revenues of €66.8 billion in December 2017.[6] In 2010, Tom Enders, CEO at the time, initiated an effort to increase and structure innovation activities around an end-to-end innovation process.[7] This led to the creation of the Airbus Innovation Cell, a team dedicated to fueling the innovation engine with ideas, deploying an efficient process, and delivering results through innovation.

Platform Goals and Alignments

As one of the first actions, the Airbus Innovation Cell wanted to offer an open platform for all employees to engage in collaboration and idea sharing. This platform became the digital space for innovation management and helped to promote the spirit of innovation across organizational boundaries. Like many large organizations, document and knowledge management tools such as SharePoint and Wiki's were already in place, with sporadic adoption and use. But a global system, with a defined process and workflow for managing innovations, did not exist. Markus Durstewitz, corporate innovation manager at Airbus, began searching for a tool that could scale to support all Airbus employees over time. After looking at several platforms, they decided to run a series of trials with different vendors. Finally, HYPE Innovation's Enterprise platform was selected, based on its scalability and high degree of flexibility, which would be needed to support the ambitions of the Innovation Cell over time. In 2010, HYPE Innovation's platform was branded as IdeaSpace and launched to a select group within the engineering area only.

The Airbus case study included in this section has been adapted from *Markus Durstewitz 2022*.

5. Daimler AG is a German multinational automotive corporation headquartered in Stuttgart. As of 2014, Daimler owned or had shares in several car, bus, truck and motorcycle brands including Mercedes-Benz, Mercedes-AMG, Smart Automobile, and Detroit Diesel. By unit sales, Daimler is the thirteenth-largest car manufacturer and is the largest truck manufacturer in the world.

6. Airbus, *Annual Report 2017*, available at www.airbus.com/content/dam/corporate-topics/financial-and-company-information/AIRBUS_Annual_Report_2017.pdf.

7. End-to-end is a term used to describe products or solutions that cover every stage in a process, often without any need for anything to be supplied by a third party. End-to-end process is a process that comprises all the work that should be done to achieve the process goal. Therefore, end-to-end means "from the very beginning to the very end" Investopedia.com, "End-to-end definition" www.investopedia.com/terms/e/end-to-end.asp; Anatoly Belaychuk, "What Is End-To-End Process," 2015. https://bpm.com/bpm-today/blogs/968-what-is-end-to-end-process.

The Innovation Cell team aimed to create a self-growing system, where employees would virally spread the message about the tool, and bring more departments on board. To achieve this, they needed to ensure the platform was not seen as a side project, but rather a tool that helps you deliver better results in your day job. They looked at the strategic priorities set out by the Airbus board and went searching for sponsors who had key challenges to solve in support of those priorities.

Idea campaigns were launched with sponsors who had a clear need, and a budget to fund the follow-up and implementation of selected ideas. This helped employees to see that activities on the platform were linked to real needs, and ideas were taken seriously. Initially, there was no direct promotion of IdeaSpace, but only the specific idea campaigns, which helped to foster an action-oriented approach for using the tool.

Since launching with just 50 users, IdeaSpace grew rapidly across the Commercial Division, with approximately 50,000 users now having access. In 2013, the Airbus Innovation Cell was expanded to become Airbus Corporate Innovation. The intention was to broaden the focus beyond engineering, R&D, and emerging technology, to other functions such as sales and marketing, ultimately creating a more business centered innovation mindset. Today, the next step for the IdeaSpace platform is to go group-wide, including the other divisions, Airbus Helicopters, Airbus Defense and Space, and Airbus Headquarters (which includes central functions), totaling around 133,000 employees.

As well as focused, time-bounded idea campaigns, the platform now also supports the concept of idea channels. Each primary business function has an always-open idea channel, where related ideas can be submitted, and designated caretakers will manage the ideas through an end-to-end process. Table 6-1 shows the growth in the idea generation process. The Corporate Innovation team has also provided many supporting resources, including physical spaces for workshops, prototyping labs, recommended methods and tools, a catalyst network, and workshops for sprints, bootcamps, and other formats to help employees mature their ideas and foster collaboration.

The Collaborative Innovation Canvas

The Collaborative Innovation Canvas is a simple way to map out the key components of an innovation management platform. It focuses on three main aspects: alignment (with the larger strategic goals around innovation); people (the stakeholders, advocates, and general audience); and process (selecting, funding, and tracking ideas). The canvas captures the big picture, and the crucial elements needed for success. It allows everybody involved to easily understand and share the big picture. Therefore, it lends itself well as a frame for exploring the development of an innovation program.

TABLE 6–1.   GROWTH IN THE IDEA GENERATION PROCESS

Year	Participants	Ideas	Comments
2010	180	217	484
2011	1,112	599	1,307
2012	3,395	1,089	2,687
2013	5,705	1,921	4,793
2014	7,080	2,505	6,425
2015	17,584	3,523	8,753
2016	23,735	4,459	10,654

Strategy

The innovation management program is aligned with overall company strategy goals for innovation. The strategy for Airbus Corporate Innovation can be defined under three points:

1. *Focus*. Provide focus for what is important in terms of value for customers. Every year the company will issue the top priorities, which the team will then use as the hunting grounds for innovation, and the definition of challenges for IdeaSpace campaigns, thus linking corporate strategy directly to the activities within IdeaSpace. It's important to have the direct backing of the CEO for this kind of initiative, as it provides the authority to challenge different departments about their innovation activities and increase their focus on the core strategy.
2. *Engage*. Provide a place to foster collaboration and raise awareness in relation to corporate challenges. The key is to build engagement between people beyond individual departments and organizational boundaries. A digital hub like IdeaSpace has the scalability to support this aim.
3. *Accelerate*. The process for innovation should itself be designed for speed—limiting the number of phases and gates—but the mindset of the people involved is the most important factor for Airbus. Corporate Innovation provides resources and support throughout the end-to-end workflow, which help to foster the entrepreneurial mindset. Acceleration will then come from the empowerment of individuals and teams and creating a sense of ownership for their innovations.

Top-down versus Bottom-up Support

A bottom-up approach can work, up until a certain point and a process must be simple to be effective. As stated by Durstewitz:

> To keep a big enterprise platform moving, you need top-down support. When it becomes an objective for senior management, then the rest will follow. For the team running the platform, reporting directly to the CEO's office gives you the necessary level of visibility and a certain amount of authority to go out there and get things moving. This in itself is crucial for innovation at a large organization. Large organizations establish complex processes over time due to growing complexity of their business. New fresh ideas do not comply with these processes and tend to be killed from the start. Therefore, innovation at an early stage needs a fast track process providing the flexibility to try out things beyond the obvious.

Success for IdeaSpace is determined by the impact of the end-to-end process. Engagement and adoption of the platform has always been good, but it is equally important that ideas are going all the way through to implementation, and innovation is visibly happening throughout the company. IdeaSpace is the hub where innovation activity is recorded and made transparent to the organization, which, in turn, builds belief in the innovation team's capability, the innovation community, and the IdeaSpace platform itself. Furthermore, if business leaders are requesting to run more campaigns, it means the process is helping to solve their challenges and meet their goals. Additionally, the introduction of Idea Channels has helped to grow usage beyond the campaigns, creating an always-on place to go for ideation and collaboration. Growing usage and impact of both campaigns and channels is a further measurement of success for the program.

Need for Physical Space

There comes a point where the resources, methods, physical spaces, and budgets must come together to support the program. As stated by Konstantin Gänge, corporate innovation manager:

> If you only use a virtual space, it will be quite hard to really implement innovations. At some point you need to make your ideas tangible, and you need to put people together.

Airbus Corporate Innovation is a central team dedicated to providing Airbus with support for innovation. There are four components to that support: the physical space for innovation; the community platform; methods and tools for innovation; and the resources of the team itself:

1. *Physical space.* When ideas are developed into concepts, it is necessary to bring people together physically to work on the idea. There are various physical spaces to support the different stages of idea development, for example: a business space to host innovation projects, and work collaboratively on methods such as the business model canvas; and a prototyping lab, complete with 3D printers; a rapid architecture lab; and ideation spaces.
2. *Community platform.* IdeaSpace is the virtual home for innovation, acting as the repository to store both the online and offline activities. The platform is adapted overtime as new use cases arise, so it always meets the needs of changing innovation practices. Idea Channels—always-open spaces for ideas relevant to particular departments—were implemented, for example, because departments saw a need to handle ideas that arose outside of the focused remit of idea campaigns.
3. *Methods and tools.* Airbus Corporate Innovation wanted to provide standardized methods and tools, to make it easy for employees to practice innovation. It took around two years for the team to research, experiment with, and determine the best tools for the job together with the users. This shortlist of methods and tools were then refined and made more applicable for Airbus employees. For example, the use of design thinking personas is one element that helps the engineers to build an idealized customer since they typically do not have access to users in the operational environment. Nevertheless, human-centered design and co-innovation is of growing importance. Gänge says:Sometimes you have consultants come in and pitch their tools. They then go away, and the employees find it hard to work with these tools as they are too abstract and too far away from their actual working environment. So it's important that we adapt any method ourselves to make them more relevant and easier to use for our employees in their specific working environment.
4. *The corporate innovation team.* Altogether, there are around 25 people in the Airbus Commercial Corporate Innovation Team (henceforth Airbus Corporate Innovation). These are divided into three primary groups, which align to stages of the innovation process:

   - Approximately 10 people working on culture change, the methods and tools, and support for innovators. This group also contains the team which manages the Idea-Space platform (see below). Their background is change management, and expertise in innovation methods.
   - Approximately 10 people working as project leaders, helping to prototype and proof of concept ideas. Their background is mostly from engineering and project management.
   - Approximately 5 people working with startups, focusing on the back-end implementation side, helping to bring ideas to market. Their background is mostly business and marketing, with project management and lean experience.

IdeaSpace itself has three to five people managing the operations of the platform, with the following roles and characteristics:

- A platform and process architect, who oversees the program, manages the team, and refines the process. This individual is also responsible for managing stakeholders.
- A campaign manager dedicated to supporting and facilitating idea campaigns and providing knowledge of methods and tools.
- A community manager, providing training and awareness sessions, and continuously looking to stimulate the network. The role is closely aligned with communications and change management.
- A platform administrator, who focuses on the IT aspects of IdeaSpace, such as further configuration and development of capabilities based on user feedback.
- Communications are a key skillset. The campaign manager has a communications background, and the core Innovation team has links to the corporate communications department, making use of their skills and reach.

Gänge states:

If you cannot put headcount behind an initiative like this, then you should leave it alone. Otherwise you will quickly build up momentum, and then quickly build up frustration when nothing happens.

Stakeholders

The key individuals involved in supporting the program and innovation in general, including campaign sponsors and management stakeholders. The IdeaSpace platform is there to support the goals of the sponsors. Sponsors can request idea campaigns, and each one is treated like an individual project, which Airbus Corporate Innovation will manage. There is a checklist for sponsors to complete before a campaign can be launched. The sponsor must provide one person fully dedicated to facilitating the campaign, evaluation criteria must be predefined, and the problem statement must be clearly stated. At the end of a campaign, a lesson learned document is written up, and it is used to improve future campaigns.

Although it only takes a few minutes to set up and launch an idea campaign in the software, the preparation work behind the campaign can be much more significant. For sponsors running their first campaign, it can seem like a lot of work. But the steps are in place to ensure high-quality output that benefits the business and maintains belief in the system and the process. After running campaigns a few times, it becomes more of a routine for sponsors and a trusted mechanism for solving challenges or seizing opportunities.

The Airbus Corporate Innovation team reports directly to the chief innovation officer, who reports to the CEO. The team believes this is a critical factor in the success of their program. It immediately lends credibility, helps to raise the profile of the activities and get others involved, and can make communications easier. Continuous adoption of the platform has also contributed to senior management providing more support.

As stated by Durstewitz:

It's all about connecting people and ideas. Thus, it is important to get all stakeholders on board of a campaign by (a) reaching out to the community to gain a good level of interest and participation and (b) getting buy-in of the specialists and the business owners to ensure follow-up and implementation of selected ideas. The good balance of the team makes the difference.

The innovation team developed a series of checklists to ensure a consistent approach to running campaigns. Some examples of the checklist items are given below.

Checklist for Campaign Sponsors
- Define scope, objectives, and the campaign question.
- Identify the potential customers for the ideas that will be submitted.
- You and your boss understand that you will spend at least 12 hours per week working on the campaign (with peaks at launch and closure).
- Arrange a kick-off meeting with the main stakeholders.

Campaign Leaders Launch Checklist
- Campaign overview and audience teaser
- Campaign objectives
- Seed idea owners
- Campaign moderators
- Set the date for the evaluation briefing session
- General background information (What should the audience know?)
- Basis for ideas to be selected
- Next steps after campaign (What is going to happen with the ideas?)

Campaign Leaders Closure Checklist
- Provide a summary about the campaign was published in the IdeaSpace blog.
- Send highlights of the campaign, including top ideas and next steps, to all invitees.
- Get a final statement from the sponsor to be used for communications.
- Organize an evaluation session no later than two weeks after closing the campaign.
- Provide the IdeaSpace team with the communication material (including emails) that were used during the campaign (for best practice collection).
- Provide your personal feedback and lessons learned to the IdeaSpace team so they can improve the tool and support.

Audience

Who is invited to use the platform, whether it's internal only or also open to externals? Who can help you expand the success of the program, such as innovation advocates?

IdeaSpace was initially open to 50,000 employees in the Airbus Commercial division but rolled out to the whole Airbus Group during 2016, totaling around 133,000 employees. Sponsors can choose to make their idea campaigns private to only selected groups or individuals. However, while Airbus Corporate Innovation recommend to direct communications to those you specifically want to invite, they strongly advise to keep campaigns visible and open for everybody to participate. Campaigns often benefit from having employees in other areas bring their perspectives and add to the collaboration. This is the essence of innovation at large organizations (i.e., to connect the dots).

The Airbus Corporate Innovation team knows that it cannot build a culture of innovation alone. It must have the help of people who promote and drive culture change and others who support innovators and help to move innovation projects forward throughout the company. They fall into the two following groups:

Caretakers

- Experts in different areas of the business, who are able to review ideas in their field, take responsibility for pushing those ideas to the right people and seeing that a decision is made on whether to progress or not.
- Caretakers operate mostly in the Idea Channels, rather than Idea Campaigns. Managing ad-hoc idea submissions.
- The Airbus Corporate Innovation team works closely with caretakers, reviewing the activity and impact of their channel (see measurements), and sharing best practices with all caretakers.
- It is also possible to be a caretaker for just a single idea.

Catalysts

- A network of around 150+ employees who spend part of their job working on innovation, act as promoters and enablers for innovation initiatives.
- There are three levels of catalysts: advocate, agent, or facilitator.
- When nominated a catalyst, they will benefit from a specific training and education program organized by corporate innovation and the catalyst network in place.
- There is one person dedicated to working full-time on orchestrating the catalyst network. Here, IdeaSpace is used as the bridge between idea owners and the catalysts who can help develop their ideas.

Gänge says:

IdeaSpace is really a big part of the catalyst story—it keeps the network alive. It allows us to manage all of the local initiatives they are running, and it enables innovators to connect with the catalyst network.

Communications

How to communicate effectively, create momentum, and build trust with your audience and stakeholders is critical. Gänge states:

I would say that the communications aspect is something that goes across everything. It's important for all the areas of the innovation program. You have to communicate on the strategy, the resources, the stakeholders, the process. You have to communicate about all the elements to be successful.

Elements of communications include:

- When communicating with employees at Airbus, the Innovation team takes the approach of communicating the specific activities, such as idea campaigns, rather than a generic push for the platform. This focuses attention on how employees can contribute immediately, rather than generally promoting an innovation platform.
- A monthly newsletter is compiled by the Innovation team, which provides information about measurements, latest activity, and lessons learned. The newsletter is primarily aimed at stakeholders, caretakers, and a selection of senior management.
- A campaign guide booklet, which serves as a comprehensive guide to understanding the benefits of idea campaigns. It contains practical tips for the campaign leader on how to frame the challenge, how to launch it effectively, what to do when in submission mode, how to set up evaluation

sessions, when and how to organize an award ceremony, celebrate success, and finally, how to wrap-up the campaign and document lessons learned.

- Airbus Corporate Innovation runs an annual IdeaSpace user convention, which brings the IdeaSpace community together. Special attention is given to testimonies, best practice sharing, and improvement proposals of IdeaSpace lead users, experienced campaign leaders and sponsors. One part of the user convention is to look ahead and propose ways how to further improve the platform. HYPE Innovation actively takes part in the event, an occasion to provide insights about the tool evolution roadmap and to get direct user feedback.

- Airbus has deployed lean methods across engineering and manufacturing. It uses SQCDP boards (safety, quality, cost, delivery, people) to monitor and steer daily operations. IdeaSpace is now listed on the SQCDP board of the head of engineering, helping to raise the awareness and health of the platform at a very prominent level.

- A webinar is run monthly to introduce the platform to newcomers. These webinars are open for everyone but are targeted specifically at new catalysts, caretakers, or sponsors. The Innovation team is often asked, "Can you tell me more about IdeaSpace?" The webinar is an ideal way to inform all of those who are interested in learning about the program in more depth.

- A further detail that has proven important is to personalize the email templates in the platform. The emails are automatically sent to inform people of changes to their ideas or projects, or if an update is required on their progress. The emails have a lot of useful information and are specific to the context. They have proven to be useful in nudging people to update and take action.

Decision Making

Decision making includes how ideas will be judged, selected, and improved; also, who is involved, and what criteria and process should be used.

Idea Campaigns

- A community graduation feature, which allows the crowd to promote the best ideas to management, is sometimes used for campaigns, if the volume is high. However, it is less useful when the ideas are of a highly technical nature. In this case, an expert panel of evaluators is required to judge the ideas fully.

- Online evaluation tools are seen as crucial to the process, because they help to avoid groupthink, or following the sponsor's opinion, which are significant challenges when reviewing in person.

- After an evaluation session is completed, it is recommended that the team sits together to discuss the results and decide.

- There are some cases where the innovation team asks that the sponsors stay out of the process, because their opinion is too strong and can skew the results. The sponsor still has the final say, but the goal is to let the team make a compelling recommendation.

- It's also important that the sponsor agree up front what the decision-making criteria should be. This helps participants understand what is being looked for, and how evaluations will work.

- There is the possibility to play a "wildcard," for example, if a sponsor finds an idea very attractive and wants to provide budget and resources to follow-up and implement it.

Idea Channels
- Each channel will appoint their own pool of experts to review ideas.
- Because ideas are submitted at any time, the process for handling them is more ad-hoc. Each channel works in a slightly different way. For example, the Cabin & Cargo department meets every two weeks to go through all recent ideas, making a decision whether to proceed. This ensures a timely response to every idea and allows promising ones to move through the process quickly. Other departments do it differently, but the important factor is that IdeaSpace is used to track the decisions and status changes, so there is one single source of truth for innovation activity.

Bootcamps
- Bootcamps are one of the formats used to accelerate ideas through the back-end process, offering a fast track to build a team and turn ideas into concepts.
- Bootcamps typically last from three days up to one week. At the end of the bootcamp, the teams have the opportunity to pitch their concept to potential sponsors from senior management.

Execution
- Execution involves how ideas are iterated upon and developed toward implementation:
- Initially, the innovation team went looking for ideas that are targeting incremental innovations, which could quickly be implemented. This approach allowed them to build momentum and credibility. But now, the focus has been switched to 10X projects with big impact if not disruptive innovations. In 2016, Airbus ran a dedicated campaign to find potential 10X project candidates.
- Because of the iterative nature, a design-thinking approach has become central to the whole process for Airbus. It helps to closely observe and understand user needs. Herein, iterative prototyping is a key enabler. It is encouraged at every stage. Some engineers see a prototype as something tangible, but in the context of the innovation process, it's communicated as anything from a slide deck, a paper figure, or a 3D printed design. The point is to focus on user insights, gaining feedback and, where necessary, adapting the idea to meet the nature of the problem.

Measurements
- Measurements determine what key performance indicators (KPIs) are important to measure, and how you can track and judge success over time.
- The innovation team is aware that they need to measure the performance of the innovation program, even though this may sound paradoxical. However, it's important not to use the same KPIs as for operations, but think carefully about useful innovation-specific.
- KPIs. This means setting incentives for culture change toward accepting and generating new ideas as well as helping the maturation and implementation of these ideas. With the launch of IdeaSpace, it was not clear which KPIs should be used, so the team just let it run for a year to observe and see the reaction from employees and management.

Today, Idea Campaigns and Innovation Channels are measured, where activity is the volume of ideas, comments, and contributors, and impact is a score made up of points based on the progression of ideas through the stages. Initially they had used weighted scoring for impact, but it became too complex and created confusion, so it was reduced for simplicity.

The priority remains on ensuring a good level of activity (Activity = Number of ideas and comments submitted) and the right speed of implementation of ideas (Impact = Number of gates passed or ideas stopped). Although, they track many other indicators, only these two are used to form the monthly Innovation Scorecard: activity and impact.

The scorecards make it easy for the innovation team to monitor global activity; if a channel is showing high scores on impact, they will go and ask why, and what can be learned from that? Similarly, if a channel is showing low activity levels, there might be a problem that needs addressing. In either case, the aim is to find new learnings that can be shared with all channel owners. To maintain trust and credibility in the platform, transparency is key. That's the reason why the scorecards are visible to everybody in the community. Gänge states:

> With IdeaSpace, it is now possible to track the progress of ideas after the implementation stage. But measuring innovation is not easy, and you can end up with many KPIs which don't really make sense. Keeping it simple is really important.

Key Advice for Innovation Project Managers

Gänge and Durstewitz offer 10 points of advice for fellow innovation managers:

1. Set the focus first. What does innovation really mean to you and the organization? What do you/the organization want to achieve with innovation? Create a clear sense of purpose.
2. Define strategic innovation areas and select specific themes to get initial buy-in from potential sponsors.
3. Focus on idea campaigns first. They will deliver immediate results and success stories.
4. Frame the problem and define the challenge together with the business sponsor to create a win-win and meet their needs.
5. See yourself as a service provider. Build your competences and service offer around specific methods and formats supporting culture change and fast track implementation.
6. Define clear governance and clear roles with your process. Identify the campaign leader, channel leader, evaluator, etc.
7. Support, train, and educate them accordingly.
8. Install a community manager to foster and animate the community, to organize network events and trainings.
9. Put special attention on communications to increase reach and motivate employees to take an active part in the community.
10. An innovation scorecard is a good means to create visibility for and to maintain buy-in of top management.

SOFTWARE AND OPEN INNOVATION

The case study about Airbus indicated the importance for an innovation project manager to have awareness and understanding of the use of innovation software in high-tech industries. There are differing views of the importance of innovation software. One view is that it is important to use innovation software because it is a formidable way to encourage the birth of new ideas. Another view, especially with product innovation, is that there can be a long process of research conducted by the company, and most of the time it involves a set of suppliers that consists of research centers, universities, or other highly specialized companies. In a nutshell, the complexity is so great that a simultaneous effort by several entities that work in an integrated way, allowing a free knowledge flow, is required.

This type of environment is defined as open innovation (Chesbrough 2003) and was described in Chapter 2, where an application in the Airbus Company was discussed. More specifically, Chesbrough defines open innovation as cooperation between several companies that share resources, knowledge, and skills in a creative goal. This collaboration is carried out within the framework of a market economy with a free flow of information. The open innovation applies the principle of ODOSOS; open data, open source, and open standards (Allal-Chérif 2015).

It is called open innovation because due to the complexity of the product, it is necessary to share information and knowledge among the main company and its suppliers that constitute its innovation network. In other words, the company cannot carry out the project alone, but needs the collaboration with other entities. There must be productive cooperation with the sharing of knowledge. In such an environment, the supplier does not play a passive role; on the contrary, it is actively part of the development and source of ideas. Also, in an open innovation environment, capturing and evaluating all the information available can be carried out more easily and efficiently using innovation software but with some qualifications:

In the open innovation environment, the application of innovation software is helpful, but due to the sensitive data content, the use of the software may be restricted only to the specialists and, to be effective, it must be extended to the partners,

IMPLICATIONS AND ISSUES FOR PROJECT MANAGERS AND INNOVATION PERSONNEL

The potential of innovation management software as a tool for the innovation project managers has been clearly shown through the six case studies. The playing fields that differentiate each of the case studies have given us an idea about the incredible versatility of the software applications. The applicability of the innovation management software has also been proposed in environments characterized by the "open innovation," where, at first glance, the use of such software could appear more complicated.

As for the evolution innovation management software, we can envision two possible paths for evolution or enhancements and the subsequent implications for the innovation project managers. The first could be more participation by the partners and customers in the innovation process. The engagement of the customers would be in line with the current trend of "the Copernican revolution in management" that puts the customer in the center rather than the firm. During the twentieth century, there was the view that the customers revolved around the stationary "center of the universe," namely, the value chain of the organization. In the new vision, the organization is one of many organizations revolving around the customer, and the organization survives and thrives only so long as it is agile enough to meet the customer's shifting needs and desires (Denning 2013). Therefore, it is possible that, in addition to traditional market research studies, we will see participation by the customers and end users as well as benefits provided for the employees with the introduction of innovation management software. Customers will also benefit. The customer will have the ability to see the impact of a proposal, to check the development, and so on. Obviously, even though each company has its own market research department, it is inevitable that the innovation project manager will develop competences required to interpret the market or the sensitivity to foresee customers' needs.

The second possible evolution for the innovation management software could be its application in high-tech environments. Because collaboration is essential, the idea would be to create a kind of innovation network that encompasses all the entities devoted to innovation. The task of innovation management software should be to create the needed connection to fulfill a given idea. Innovation is often a combination of existing solutions, but in some cases, we may be able to identify a missing element requiring further research. We could name this software as *intelligent innovation management software* because it should not only be able to promote the birth of new ideas but also be able to create or suggest possible ways to achieve the goal. In this case, the implication for the innovation project managers would be to develop a kind of *innovation knowledge* and to cultivate the *innovation network*.

REFERENCES

Allal-Chérif, O. (2015). The way towards open innovation: Airbus multi-functional teams. *European Scientific Journal* Special edition vol. 1 (December). Available at http://eujournal.org/index.php/esj/article/view/6684.

Auriga. (2017). Pros and cons of open source software in healthcare. April 19. Available at https://auriga.com/blog/2017/pros-and-cons-of-open-source-software-in-healthcare.

Chesbrough, H. W. (2003). *Open Innovation: The New Imperative for Creating and Profiting from Technology.* Boston, MA: Harvard Business School Press.

Denning, S. (2013). The Copernican revolution in management. www.forbes.com. Available at www.forbes.com/sites/stevedenning/2013/07/11/the-copernician-revolution-in-management/#6bb5049d108d.

El Sherbiny, K. and Abdel Aziz Hadia, H. (2014). Developing idea management systems: Guidelines for success. *Journal of Advanced Management Science* 2 (4) (December), 279–286.

Millard, M. (2014). 6 big advantages of idea management software. November 13, 2014. https://blog.kainexus.com/employee-engagement/employee-engagement-software/idea-management-software.

Shockley, B. (2006). *A Short History of Idea Management and What Makes It Work (Or Not Work).* Tinton Falls, NJ: Innovation Software Advisors (ISA).

7 Value-Based Innovation Project Management Metrics

Learning Objectives for Project Managers and Innovation Personnel

To understand what is meant by business value

To understand the importance of measuring and reporting business value

To understand that there are many metrics available for reporting innovation value

To understand how to create a value metric based on value attributes

INTRODUCTION

In earlier chapters, we discussed how new versions of project management, such as PM 2.0 and PM 3.0, focused on the creation of more business-oriented metrics for project management and how information warehouses and knowledge management systems now include more supporting data for project management decision making. All of these activities are providing innovation project managers with additional information for creating the business value outcomes expected from innovation. Business value will most likely be the driver for all new forms of project management. Value-in-use may be the driver for all new forms of innovation. We now have the capability of creating and monitoring business value metrics throughout the life of an innovation project.

Any metric can be regarded as a value metric based on how and when it is used. Unlike traditional projects where we often do not question who is assigned, strategic projects involving innovation usually

Innovation Project Management: Methods, Case Studies, and Tools for Managing Innovation Projects,
Second Edition. Harold Kerzner.
© 2023 John Wiley & Sons, Inc. Published 2023 by John Wiley & Sons, Inc.

are staffed with some of the firm's best resources. To make sure resources are not squandered and that the project is on track, rapid decision making is often necessitated requiring getting the right information, in the right format, to the right people, and in a timely manner. Companies are now creating human resource utilization metrics for innovation and view staffing metrics as a type of value metrics. The necessity for significantly more metrics than time, cost, and scope should now be apparent. Most of the newer metrics needed are business oriented, often focusing on operational efficiency and effectiveness, and can be different for each project based upon the decisions that executives and portfolio teams must make.

The number of deliverables produced may not be considered as a value metric in the fuzzy front end of a project, but perhaps so during commercialization. Effective governance can be a value metric if it favorably affects the culture of the organization. Some value metrics, as shown later in this chapter, can be composed of several other metrics that act as attributes of a value metric.

For years, the traditional view of project management for projects that did not include innovation was that, if you completed the project and adhered to the triple constraints of time, cost, and performance (or scope), the project was successful. Perhaps in the eyes of the project manager, the project appeared to be a success. In the eyes of the customer or the stakeholders, however, the project might be regarded as a failure.

Innovation projects must be looked at differently. If the results of the innovation activities were unsuccessful, meeting the budget and financial constraints could be meaningless or just a low level of importance. The only true measure of innovation success is if business value was created and the company gained from it economically. While time, cost, and scope are still important when managing innovation projects, metrics must be established for measuring innovation benefits and value. Time, cost, and scope may be treated as value attributes based on how and when they are used.

Project managers are now becoming more business oriented. Projects are being viewed as part of a business for the purpose of providing value to both the ultimate customer and the parent corporation. Project managers are expected to understand business operations more so today than in the past. As the project managers become more business oriented, our definition of success on a project now includes both a business and value component. The business component may be directly related to value.

Situation: The IT group of a large public utility would always service all IT requests without question. All requests were added to the queue and would eventually get done. The utility implemented a PMO that was assigned to develop a template for establishing a business case for the request, clearly indicating the value to the company if the project were completed. In the first year of using the business case template, one-third of all projects in the queue were tossed out. Value became the driver for both measuring performance and ultimately success.

Projects must provide some degree of value when completed as well as meeting the competing constraints. Perhaps the project manager's belief is that meeting the competing constraints provides value, but that's not always the case. Why should a company work on innovation projects that provide no near-term or long-term value? Too many companies either are working on the wrong projects or simply have a poor project portfolio selection process, and no real value appears at the completion of the projects even though the competing constraints have been met.

Assigning resources that have critical skills that are in demand on other projects to projects that provide no appreciable value is an example of truly inept management and poor decision making. Yet selecting projects that may appear to guarantee the creation of business value or an acceptable ROI is very challenging because some of today's projects do not provide the targeted value until years into the future. This is particularly true for innovation and new product development, where as many as 50 or more ideas must be explored to generate one commercially successful product. Predicting the value at the start and tracking the value during execution is difficult.

There are multiple views of the definition of value. For the most part, value is like beauty; it is in the eyes of the beholder. In other words, value may be viewed as a perception at project selection and initiation based on data available at the time. At project completion, however, the actual value becomes a reality that may not meet the expectations that had initially been perceived.

Another problem is that the achieved innovation value of a project may not satisfy all the stakeholders since each stakeholder may have had a different perception of value as it relates to his/her business model. Because of the money invested in some innovation projects, establishing value-based metrics is essential. The definition of innovation value, along with the metrics, can be industry-specific, company-specific, or even dependent on the size, nature, and business base of the firm. Some stakeholders may view innovation value as job security or profitability. Others might view value as image, reputation, or the creation of intellectual property. Satisfying all stakeholders is a formidable task often difficult to achieve and, in some cases, may simply be impossible. In any event, value-based metrics must be established along with the traditional metrics. Value metrics show whether value is being created or destroyed.

VALUE OVER THE YEARS

Before discussing value-based metrics, it is important to understand how the necessity for value identification has evolved. Surprisingly enough, numerous research on value has taken place over the past 20 years. Some of the items covered in the research include:

- Value dynamics
- Value gap analysis
- Intellectual capital valuation
- Human capital valuation
- Economic value-based analysis
- Intangible value streams
- Customer value management/mapping
- Competitive value matrix
- Value chain analysis
- Valuation of IT projects
- Balanced scorecard

Following are some of the models that have occurred over the past 20 years of research:

- Intellectual capital valuation
- Intellectual property scoring
- Balanced scorecard
- Future Value Management™
- Intellectual Capital Rating™
- Intangible value stream modeling
- Inclusive Value Measurement™
- Value Performance Framework (VPF)
- Value measurement methodology (VMM)

TABLE 7–1. APPLICATION OF VPF TO INNOVATION PROJECT MANAGEMENT

VPF Element	Innovation Project Management Application
Understand key principles of valuation	Working with the project's stakeholders to define innovation value
Identification of key value drivers for the company	Identification of key value drivers for the innovation project
Assessing performance on critical business processes and measures through evaluation and external benchmarking	Assessing performance of whatever enterprise project management methodology and framework is selected and continuous improvement using the PMO
Creating a link between shareholder value and critical business processes and employee activities	Creating a link between innovation project values, stakeholder values, and team member values
Aligning employee and corporate goals	Aligning employee, project, and corporate goals
Identification of key "pressure points" (high leverage improvement opportunities) and estimating potential impact on value	Capturing lessons learned and best practices that can be used for continuous improvement activities and other innovation projects
Implementation of a performance management system to improve visibility and accountability in critical activities	Establish and implement a series or project-based dashboards for customers, co-creation team members, and stakeholder visibility of key performance indicators
Development of performance dashboards with a high level of visual impact	Development of innovation performance dashboards for stakeholder, team, and senior management visibility

The reason why these models have become so popular in recent years is because we have developed techniques for the measurement and determination of value. This is essential in order to have value metrics on projects.

There is some commonality among many of these models such that they can be applied to project management. For example, Jack Alexander (2007, 5–6) created a model titled Value Performance Framework (VPF). The model focuses on building shareholder value, which some consider as the ultimate purpose of innovation, and is heavily biased toward financial key performance indicators (KPIs). However, the key elements of VPF can be applied to innovation project management, as shown in Table 7-1. The first column contains the key elements of VPF from Alexander's book, and the second column illustrates the application to innovation project management.

VALUE AND LEADERSHIP

The importance of value can have a significant impact on the leadership style of project managers. Historically, project management leadership was perceived as the inevitable conflict between individual values and organizational values. Today, companies are looking for ways to get employees to align their personal values with the organization's values. One way of accomplishing this is to create leadership metrics that can measure the leadership performance of innovation project managers.

Several books have been written on this subject, and the best one, in this author's opinion, is *Balancing Individual and Organizational Values* by Ken Hultman and Bill Gellerman (2002, 105–106). Table 7-2, adapted from Hultman and Gellerman, shows how our concept of value has changed over the years. If you look closely at the items in Table 7-2, you can see that the changing values affect more than just individual versus organizational values. Instead, it is more likely to be a conflict among four groups,

TABLE 7–2.   CHANGING VALUES

Moving away from: Ineffective Values	Moving toward: Effective Values
Mistrust	Trust
Job descriptions	Competency models
Power and authority	Teamwork
Internal focus	Stakeholder focus
Security	Taking risks
Conformity	Innovation
Predictability	Flexibility
Internal competition	Internal collaboration
Reactive management	Proactive management
Bureaucracy	Boundaryless
Traditional education	Lifelong education
Hierarchical leadership	Multidirectional leadership
Tactical thinking	Strategic thinking
Compliance	Commitment
Meeting standards	Continuous improvements

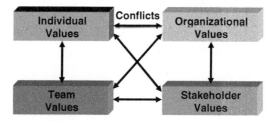

Figure 7–1.   Project Management Value Conflicts.

as shown in Figure 7-1. The team members and stakeholders also include people who are part of the co-creation team.

The needs of each group might be:

Project Manager
- Accomplishment of objectives
- Demonstration of creativity
- Demonstration of innovation

Team Members
- Achievement
- Advancement
- Ambition
- Credentials
- Recognition

Organization
- Continuous improvement
- Learning
- Quality
- Strategic focus
- Morality and ethics
- Profitability
- Recognition and image

Stakeholders
- Organizational stakeholders: Job security.
- Product/market stakeholders: Quality performance and product usefulness.
- Capital markets: Financial growth

There are several reasons why the role of the innovation project manager and the accompanying leadership style have changed. Some reasons include:

- We are now managing our business as though it is a series of projects.
- Project management is now viewed as a full-time profession.
- Project managers are now viewed as both business managers and project managers and are expected to make decisions in both areas. This includes decision making during innovation efforts.
- The value of a project is measured more in business terms, such as business benefits and value, rather than solely in technical terms.
- Project management is now being applied to parts of the business that traditionally haven't used project management such as innovation activities.

COMBINING BENEFITS AND VALUE

Benefits and value are related. A *benefit* is an outcome from actions, behaviors, products, or services that are considered to be important or advantageous to specific individuals, such as business owners, or a group of individuals, such as stakeholders or end-user consumers. Generic benefits might include:

- Improvements in quality, productivity, or efficiency
- Cost avoidance or cost reduction
- Increase in revenue generation
- Improvements in customer service

Benefits, whether they are strategic or nonstrategic, are normally aligned to the organizational business objectives of the sponsoring organization that will eventually receive the benefits. The benefits appear through the *deliverables* or *outputs* that are created by the project. It is the responsibility of the project manager to create the deliverables.

Benefits are identified in the project's business case. Some benefits are tangible and can be quantified. Other benefits, such as an improvement in employee morale, may be difficult to measure and therefore treated as intangible benefits.

There can also be dependencies between the benefits where one benefit is dependent on the outcome of another. As an example, a desired improvement in revenue generation may be dependent on an improvement in quality.

Benefits realization management is a collection of processes, principles, and deliverables to effectively manage the organization's investments. Project management focuses on maintaining the established baselines whereas benefits realization management analyzes the relationship that the project has to the business objectives by monitoring for potential waste, acceptable levels of resources, risk, cost, quality, and time as it relates to the desired benefits.

Project *value* is what the benefits are worth to someone. Project or business value can be quantified whereas benefits are usually explained qualitatively. When we say that the ROI should improve, we are discussing benefits. But when we say that the ROI should improve by 20 percent, we are discussing value. Progress toward innovation value generation is easier to measure than benefits realization, especially during project execution. Benefits and value are generally inseparable; it is difficult to discuss one without the other.

RECOGNIZING THE NEED FOR VALUE METRICS

The importance of the value component in the definition of innovation success cannot be overstated. Consider the following eight postulates:

Postulate #1: Completing a project on time and within budget does not guarantee success if you were working on the wrong project.

Postulate #2: Completing a project on time and within budget is not necessarily success.

Postulate #3: Completing a project within the triple constraints does not guarantee that the necessary business value will be there at project completion.

Postulate #4: Having the greatest enterprise project management methodology in the world cannot guarantee that value will be there at the end of the project.

Postulate #5: Price is what you pay. Value is what you get (Warren Buffett).

Postulate #6: Business value is what your customer perceives as worth paying for.

Postulate #7: Success is when business value is achieved.

Postulate #8: Following a project plan to conclusion is not always success if business-related changes were necessary but never implemented.

These eight postulates lead us to believe that perhaps value may become the dominating factor in the selection of projects for an innovation project portfolio. Project requestors must now clearly articulate the value component in the project's business case or run the risk that the project will not be considered. If the project is approved, then innovation value metrics must be established and tracked. However, it is important to understand that value may be looked at differently during the portfolio selection of projects because the tradeoffs that take place are among projects rather than the value attributes of a single project.

In Postulate #1, we can see what happens when management makes poor decisions during project selection, establishment of a project portfolio, and when managing project portfolios. We end up working on the wrong project or projects. What is unfortunate about this scenario is that we can produce the deliverable that was requested but:

- There's no market for the product.
- The product cannot be manufactured as engineered.
- The assumptions may have changed.
- The marketplace may have changed.
- Valuable resources were wasted on the wrong project.
- Stakeholders may be displeased with management's performance.
- The project selection and portfolio management process are flawed and needs to be improved.
- Organizational morale has diminished.

Postulate #2 is the corollary to Postulate #1. Completing a project on time and on budget:

- Does not guarantee a satisfied client/customer
- Does not guarantee that the customer will accept the product/service
- Does not guarantee that performance expectations will be met
- Does not guarantee that value exists in the deliverable
- Does not guarantee marketplace acceptance
- Does not guarantee follow-on work
- Does not guarantee success

Situation: During the initiation of the project, the project manager, the stakeholders, and members of the co-creation team defined project success and established metrics for each of the competing constraints. When it became obvious that all of the constraints could not be met, the project manager concluded that the best alternative was a tradeoff on value. The stakeholders and the co-creation team members became irate on hearing the news and decided to prioritize the competing constraints themselves. This took time and delayed the project.

Postulate #3 focuses on value. Simply because the deliverable is provided according to a set of constraints is no guarantee that the client will perceive value in the deliverable. The ultimate objective of all projects should be to produce a deliverable that meets expectations and achieves the desired value. While we always seem to emphasize the importance of the competing constraints when defining the project, we spend very little time in defining the value characteristics and resulting metrics that we expect in the final deliverable. The value component or definition must be agreed on jointly by all involved parties during the initiation stage of the project. This can be difficult if using a co-creation team.

Most companies today have some type of project management methodology/framework in place. Unfortunately, all too often there is a mistaken belief that the methodology/framework will guarantee project success. Methodologies and frameworks:

- Cannot guarantee success
- Cannot guarantee value in the deliverables
- Cannot guarantee that the time or cost constraint will be adhered to
- Cannot guarantee that the quality constraint will be met
- Cannot guarantee any level of performance
- Are not a substitute for effective planning
- Are not the ultimate panacea to cure all project ills
- Are not a replacement for effective or ineffective human behavior

Methodologies can improve the chances for success but cannot guarantee success. Methodologies are tools and, as such, do not manage projects. Projects are managed by people and, likewise, tools are managed by people. Methodologies do not replace the people component in project management. They are designed to enhance the performance of people. The methodology used on innovation projects may be different from the methodology used on noninnovation projects.

In Postulate #5, we have a quote from Warren Buffett that emphasizes the difference between price and perceived value. Most people believe that customers pay for deliverables. This is not necessarily true. Customers pay for the value they expect to receive from the deliverable. If the deliverable has not achieved value or has limited value, the result is a dissatisfied customer.

Some people believe that a customer's greatest interest is quality. In other words, "Quality comes first!" While that may seem to be true on the surface, the customer generally does not expect to pay an extraordinary amount of money just for high quality. Quality is just one component in the value equation. Value is significantly more than just quality.

When customers agree to purchase a deliverable, the customer is looking for the value in the deliverable. The customer's definition of success may be "value achieved" or, as we stated previously, value-in-use.

Unfortunately, unpleasant things can happen when the project manager's definition of success is the achievement of the deliverable (and possibly the triple constraint) and the customer's definition of success is value-in-use. This is particularly true when customers want value and the project manager focuses on the profit margins of the project.

Postulate #7 is a summation of Postulates #1 through #6. Perhaps the standard definition of success using just the triple constraints should be modified to include a business component such as value, or even be replaced by a more specific definition of value.

Sometimes the value of a project can change over time, and the project manager may not recognize that these changes have occurred. Failure to establish value expectations or lack of value in a deliverable can result from:

- Market unpredictability
- Market demand that has changed, thus changing constraints and assumptions
- Technology advances or inability to achieve functionality
- Critical resources that were not available or resources who lacked the necessary skills

Establishing value metrics early on can help identify if a project should be canceled. The earlier the project is canceled, the quicker we can assign the resources to those innovation projects that have a higher perceived value and probability of success. Unfortunately, early warning signs are not always present to indicate that the value will not be achieved. The most difficult metrics to establish are value-driven metrics.

THE NEED FOR EFFECTIVE MEASUREMENT TECHNIQUES

Selecting metrics and KPIs is not that difficult, provided they can be measured. This is the major obstacle with the value-driven metrics. On the surface, they look easy to measure, but there are complexities. However, even though value appears in the present and in the future, it does not mean that the value outcome cannot be quantified. Table 7-3 illustrates some of the metrics that are often treated as value-driven KPIs.

TABLE 7–3.   MEASURING VALUE

Value Metric	Measurement
Profitability	Easy
Customer satisfaction	Hard
Goodwill	Hard
Penetrate new markets	Easy
Develop new technology	Moderate
Technology transfer	Moderate
Reputation	Hard
Stabilize work force	Easy
Utilize unused capacity	Easy

Traditionally, business plans identified the benefits expected from the project, and the benefits were the criteria for project selection. Today, portfolio management techniques require identification of the value as well as the benefits. However, conversion from benefits to value is not easy (Phillips et al. 2002, chapter 13).

There are shortcomings in the conversion process that can make the conversion difficult. Figure 7-2 illustrates several common shortcomings.

There are other shortcomings with the measurement of KPIs. KPI are metrics for assessing value. With traditional project management, metrics are established by the enterprise project management methodology and fixed for the duration of the project's life cycle. With value-driven project management, however, metrics can change from project to project, during a life-cycle phase and over time because of:

- The way the customer and contractor jointly define innovation success and value at project initiation
- The way the customer and contractor come to an agreement at project initiation as to what metrics should be used on a given project
- The way the company defines innovation value
- New or updated versions of tracking software
- Improvements to the enterprise project management methodology and the accompanying project management information system
- Changes in the enterprise environmental factors

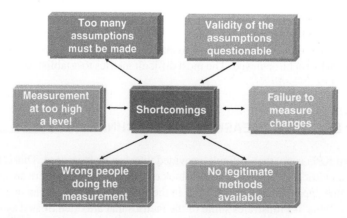

Figure 7–2.   Shortcomings.

TABLE 7–4. TYPICAL FINANCIAL VALUE METRICS

Easy (Soft/Tangible) Value Metrics	Hard (Intangible) Value Metrics
ROI calculators	Stockholder satisfaction
Net present value (NPV)	Stakeholder satisfaction
Internal rate of return (IRR)	Customer satisfaction
Cash flow	Employee retention
Payback period	Brand loyalty
Profitability	Time-to-market
Market share	Business relationships
	Safety
	Reliability
	Goodwill
	Image

TABLE 7–5. PROBLEMS WITH MEASURING VALUE METRICS

Easy (Soft/Tangible) Value Metrics	Hard (Intangible) Value Metrics
Assumptions are often not fully disclosed and can affect decision making.	Value is almost always based on subjective attributes of the person doing the measurement.
Measurement is very generic.	It is more of an art than a science.
Measurement never meaningfully captures the correct data.	Limited models are available to perform measurement.

Even with the best possible metrics, measuring value can be difficult. Benefits less costs indicate the value and determine if the project should be done. The challenge is that not all costs are quantifiable. Some values are easy to measure, while others are more difficult. The easy value metrics to measure are often called soft or are established by the enterprise project management methodology and fixed for the duration of the project's life cycle. The hard values to measure are often considered intangible value metrics. Table 7-4 illustrates some of the easy and hard value metrics to measure. Table 7-5 shows some of the problems associated with measuring both hard and soft value metrics.

Measurement techniques have advanced to the point where we believe that we can measure anything. Projects now have both financial and nonfinancial metrics, and many of the nonfinancial metrics are regarded as intangible metrics. For decades, we shied away from intangibles. As stated by Bontis (2009, 8), "The intangible value embedded in companies has been considered by many, defined by some, understood by few, and formally valued by practically no one." Today, we can measure intangible factors as well as tangible factors that impact project performance.

An intangible asset is nonmonetary and without physical substance. Intangible assets can be the drivers of innovation. Intangibles may be hard to measure, but they are not immeasurable. In an excellent article, Ng et al. (2011) discuss various key intangible performance indicators (KIPIs) and how they can impact project performance measurements. The authors state:

> [T]here are many diverse intangible performance drivers which impact organizational [and innovational] success such as leadership, management capabilities, credibility, innovation management, technology and research and development, intellectual property rights, workforce innovation, employee satisfaction, employee involvement and relations, customer service satisfaction, customer loyalty and alliance, market

opportunities and network, communication, reputation and trust, brand values, identity, image, and commitment, HR practices, training and education, employee talent and caliber, organizational learning, renewal capability, culture and values, health and safety, quality of working conditions, society benefits, social and environmental, intangible assets and intellectual capital, knowledge management, strategy and strategic planning and corporate governance.

Today, there are measurement techniques for these. In dynamic organizations, both KPIs and KIPIs are used to validate innovation performance.

With innovation project management (IPM), we will need significantly more metrics, especially many of the above-mentioned intangibles, to track innovation and business applications. IPM metrics are a source of frustration for almost every firm. There are no standards set for innovation metrics. Companies may have a set of "core" metrics they use and then add in other metrics based on the nature of the project. Metrics for disruptive innovation are probably the hardest to define. However, companies are beginning to develop models to measure innovation (Ivanov and Avasilcăi 2014; Zizlavsky 2016).

The intangible elements are now considered by some to be more important than tangible elements. This appears to be happening on IT projects where executives are giving significantly more attention to intangible values. The critical issue with intangible values is not necessarily in the end result, but in the way that the intangibles were calculated. Phillips et al. (2002) emphasize that the true impact on a business must be measured in business units.

Tangible values are usually expressed quantitatively whereas intangible values may be expressed through a qualitative assessment. There are three schools of thought for value measurement:

School #1: The only thing that is important is ROI.
School #2: ROI can never be calculated effectively; only the intangibles are important.
School #3: If you cannot measure it, then it does not matter.

The three schools of thought appear to be an all-or-nothing approach, where value is either 100 percent quantitative or 100 percent qualitative. The best approach is most likely a compromise between a quantitative and qualitative assessment of value. It may be necessary to establish an effective range, which is a compromise among the three schools of thought.

The timing of value measurement is critical. During the life cycle of a project, it may be necessary to switch back and forth from qualitative to quantitative assessment of the metric, and the actual metrics or KPIs may then be subject to change. Certain critical questions must be addressed:

- When or how far along the project life cycle can we establish concrete metrics, assuming this can be done at all?
- Can value be simply perceived and, therefore, no value metrics are required?
- Even if we have value metrics, are they concrete enough to reasonably predict actual value?
- Will we be forced to use value-driven project management metrics on all projects or are there some projects where this approach is not necessary?
  - Well-defined versus ill-defined projects
  - Strategic versus tactical projects
  - Internal versus external projects
- Can we develop a criterion for when to use value-driven project management, or should we use it on all projects but at a lower intensity level?

For some innovation projects, using metrics to assess value at project closure may be difficult. We must establish a time frame for how long we are willing to wait to measure the final or real value or benefits from a project. This is particularly important if the actual value cannot be identified until sometime after the project has been completed. Therefore, it may not be possible to appraise the success of a project at closure if the true economic values cannot be realized until sometime in the future. As an example, consumers may need to use a project for some time to determine its true value to them.

Some practitioners of value measurement question whether value measurement is better using boundary boxes instead of life-cycle phases. For value-driven projects, which include several forms of innovation projects, the potential problems with life-cycle phase metrics include:

- Metrics can change between phases and even during a phase.
- Inability to account for changes in the enterprise environmental factors.
- Focus may be on the value at the end of the phase rather than the value at the end of the project.
- Team members may get frustrated at not being able to quantitatively calculate value.

Boundary boxes, as shown in Figure 7-3, have some degree of similarity to statistical process control charts and can assist in metric measurements. Upper and lower strategic targets for the value of the metrics are established. As long as the KPIs indicate that the project is still within the upper and lower value targets, the project's objectives and deliverables may not undergo any scope changes or tradeoffs.

Value-driven projects must undergo value health checks to confirm that the project will contribute value to the company. Value metrics, such as KPIs, indicate the current value. What is also needed is an extrapolation from the present into the future. Using traditional project management combined with the traditional enterprise project management methodology, we can calculate the time at completion and the cost at completion. These are common terms that are part of earned value measurement systems. However, as stated previously, being on time and within budget is no guarantee that the perceived value will be there at project completion.

Therefore, instead of using an enterprise project management methodology or framework, which focuses on earned value measurement, we may need to create a value management methodology (VMM), which stresses the value variables. With VMM, time to complete and cost to complete are still used, but we introduce a new term entitled value (or benefits) at completion. Determination of

Upper-value targets

Project's objectives and deliverables

Lower-value targets

Value targets

- Cash flow
- ROI
- Delivery dates
- Performance metrics

Figure 7–3. The Boundary Box.

value at completion, which is critical for innovation projects, must be done periodically throughout the project. However, periodic reevaluation of benefits and value at completion may be difficult because:

- There may be no reexamination process.
- Management is not committed and believes that the reexamination process is unreal.
- Management is overoptimistic and complacent with existing performance.
- Management is blinded by unusually high profits on other projects (misinterpretation).
- Management believes that the past is an indication of the future.

MEASURING INTANGIBLE ASSETS

Companies work on projects, whether traditional or strategic, for the purpose of creating business value which may appear as either a tangible or intangible asset. Metrics are needed to identify, track, measure, and assess the intangible business value and business assets.

The traditional metrics that we use, such as time, cost, and scope, may not capture the true business value of the deliverable of a project if the result is an intangible asset. Today, we live in a world where digitalization is becoming increasingly important. Also, significant advances are being made in measurement techniques that can be applied to projects. As such, the outcomes resulting from intangibles are becoming more important than the tangibles for the business to succeed and develop a sustainable competitive advantage.

There are many types of intangibles that benefit businesses. Examples include:

- Goodwill
- Customer satisfaction
- Our relationships with our customers
- Our relationship with our suppliers and distributors
- Brand image and reputation
- Patents, trademarks, and other intellectual property
- Our business processes
- Executive governance
- The company's culture and mindset
- Human capital, including retained knowledge and the ability to work together
- Strategic decision making
- Strategy execution

Businesses need to understand and create new sets of metrics and key performance indicators (KPIs) that can measure the intangibles and how they impact future decision making and performance.

Making Intangible Become Tangible

For decades, companies have been managing primarily the tangible asset side of their business. Today, companies are realizing that the ability to outperform their competitors is coming from how well they understand and can manage their intangible assets. This is putting pressure on companies to make intangibles become tangible.

The reason for the slow growth and understanding of intangible assets is that standard accounting systems do not measure or track the value of the people, the capabilities of the organization, the effectiveness of the firm's culture and leadership, and the information created. The results of these intangible assets can have a significant effect on the firm's customers, suppliers, distributors, and strategic partnerships.

The two most common intangibles that companies have tried to quantify in the past have been goodwill and intellectual property such as patents and trademarks. For decades, companies have treated "goodwill" as an intangible asset. Economic value was placed upon it even though it was rarely measured. Companies do not often track the cost or value of goodwill but assign a number to it for decision-making purposes.

The cost or perceived value of patents, trademarks, and other intellectual property may appear on executive reports once a year when they see the costs associated with filing. When companies become distresses and need to raise capital, they often try to quantify how much money they can raise by selling or licensing their intellectual property. In this situation, intellectual property is treated as a tangible asset.

Even R&D organizations are sometimes treated as an intangible asset. R&D costs are usually written off as expenses as they occur. The R&D organization appears as a cost center on the balance sheet, but the achievements of the group may not be considered.

Companies are struggling to find ways to appease stakeholders that want to see intangible assets appear on balance sheets. As stated by David Walker:[1]

> Consultancy Brand Finance calculated that at the start of 2016, US$366 billion (or 61%) of Apple's then US$640 billion market capitalization reflected intangibles. Yet just US$9 billion of intangible assets were set out on Apple's balance sheet.

Innovation and Intangible Assets

Innovation activities are an integral part of strategic planning. If a company develops a successful product, we tend to say that their strategic planning activities were successful. However, the real success from an investment in innovation that generates revenue comes from the culture or mindset related to innovation governance effectiveness, the experience of the management team, and how well the innovation team members interacted with each other. These intangibles can have a greater impact on the strategic plans that are created for the future of the business than the outcome of one successful innovation. These intangibles are now being considered as assets.

When executives realize that the way that they manage their innovation projects is an asset, the recognition of the real value of the asset is recognized outside of the organization as well. The "shared" culture or mindset that is created for innovation then becomes a strategic asset. As stated by Ulrich and Smallwood:[2]

> *Shared* implies something common among a group of people that holds them together. A *mindset* represents an enduring thought pattern or framework that you bring to all your activities. When truly and deeply shared, a mindset becomes the enduring identity of the firm not only in the collective mind of the employees, but also of customers and investors. A shared mindset exists when customers and investors outside and employees inside have a common view of the organization's identity.

1. Walker, D. (2019 June/July). Catching up on Intangibles. *Acuity* 6 (3), 14.
2. Ulrich, D. and Smallwood, N. (2003 Spring). *Leader to Leader*, 2003 (28), 25 (Wiley Publication).

The authors then discuss other benefits and intangible assets that can be created from this mindset:[3]

> When a strong and desired shared mindset exists between your firm and its customers, tangible and intangible value is created. Customers are more likely to do repeat business, the right kind of employees are more likely to be attracted to your firm, and investors have greater confidence that the growth plans of the firm will materialize in the future.

Developing a shared mindset is just one example of how an intangible can add value to an organization. When leaders understand how they can build intangible value, they can begin to identify specific actions they can take to strengthen their firm brand and market value.

The Intangible Asset Challenge

There are multiple techniques available to measure and track intangible assets but no agreement. Part of the problem is that there are questions and issues that companies have not resolved yet such as:

- Does measuring intangible assets improve organizational performance and decision making?
- Will intangible assets make it easier for us to achieve project objectives, benefits, and value?
- What resources are needed to support intangible assets?
- Will intangible assets affect the bottom line?
- Should the measurements of intangibles be financial, quantitative, qualitative, or a combination?
- If the outcome of a project requires organizational change, can we determine the impact on the intangible assets?

The answers to these questions can differ for each company and even each project.

CUSTOMER/STAKEHOLDER IMPACT ON VALUE METRICS _____

For years, customers and contractors have been working toward different definitions of project success. The project manager's definition of success was profitability and tracked through financial metrics. The customer's definition of success was usually the quality of the deliverables. Unfortunately, quality was measured at the closure of the project because it was difficult to track throughout the project. Yet quality was often considered the only measurement of success.

Today, clients and stakeholders appear to be more interested in the value they will receive at the end of the project. If you were to ask 10 people, including project personnel, the meaning of value, you would probably get 10 different answers. Likewise, if you were to ask, "Which critical success factor has the greatest impact on value?" you would get different answers. Each answer would be related to the individual's work environment and industry. Today, companies seem to have more of an interest in value than in quality. This does not mean that we are giving up on quality. Quality is part of value. Some people believe that value is simply quality divided by the cost of obtaining that quality. In other words, the less you pay for obtaining the customer's desired level of quality, the greater the value to the customer.

---

3. ibid; p.30.

The problem with this argument is that we assume that quality is the only attribute of value that is important to the client and, therefore, we need to determine better ways of measuring and predicting just quality. Throughout this chapter, when we refer to a "client," the client could be internal to your company, external to your company, or the customers of your external client. You might also consider stakeholders as your clients or members of a co-creation team.

Unfortunately, there are other attributes of value and many of these other attributes are equally as difficult to measure and predict. Customers can have many attributes that they consider as value components, but not all of the value attributes are equal in importance.

Unlike the use of quality as the solitary parameter, value allows a company to better measure the degree to which the innovation project will satisfy its strategic business objectives. Quality can be regarded as an attribute of value along with other attributes. Today, every company has quality and produces quality in some form. This is necessary for survival. What differentiates one company from another, however, are the other attributes, components, or factors used to define value. Some of these attributes might include price, timing, image, reputation, customer service, and sustainability.

In today's world, customers make decisions to hire a contractor based on the value they expect to receive and the price they must pay to receive this value. Actually, it is more of a "perceived" value that may be based on tradeoffs on the attributes of the client's definition of value. *The client may perceive the value of your project to be used internally in their company or pass it on to their customers through their customer value management program.* If your organization does not or cannot offer recognized value to your clients and stakeholders, then you will not be able to extract value (i.e., loyalty) from them in return. Over time, they will defect to other contractors.

Project managers in the future must consider themselves as the creators of value. The definition of a project that is used in project management courses is "a set of values scheduled for sustainable realization." As a project manager, you must, therefore, establish the correct metrics so that the client and stakeholders can track the value that you will be creating. Measuring and reporting customer value throughout the project is now a competitive necessity. If it is done correctly, it will build emotional bonds with your clients.

CUSTOMER VALUE MANAGEMENT PROGRAMS

For decades, many companies believed that they had an endless supply of potential customers. Companies called this the "door knob" approach, whereby they expected to find a potential customer behind every door. Under this approach, customer loyalty was nice to have but not a necessity. Customers were plentiful, often with little regard for the quality of your deliverables. Companies also believed that that either frequent innovation was not necessary or that most of their innovation attempts would be successful. Those days may be gone.

The focus of most CRM programs was to: (1) find the right customers, (2) develop the right relationships with these customers, and (3) retain the customers. This included stakeholder relations management and seeking out ways to maintain customer loyalty. Historically, sales and marketing were responsible for CRM activities. Today, project managers are doing more than simply managing a project; they are managing part of a business. Therefore, they are expected to make business decisions as well as project decisions, and this includes managing activities related to CRM. Project managers soon found themselves managing projects that now required effective stakeholder relations management, as well as customer relations management. Satisfying the needs of both the client and various stakeholders was difficult.

As CRM began to evolve, companies soon found that there were different perceptions among their client base as to the meaning of quality and value. In order to resolve these issues, companies created customer value management (CVM) programs. Customer value management programs address the critical question, *"Why should customers purchase from you rather than from the competition?"* The answer was most often the value that you provided through your products and deliverables. Loyal customers appeared to be more value sensitive than price sensitive. Loyal customers are today a scarce resource and also a source of value for project managers and their organizations. Value breeds loyalty.

There are other items, such as trust and intangibles, that customers may see as a form of value. As stated by a technical consultant:

> The business between the vendor and the customer is critical. It's situational but in technical consulting for instance the customer may really value only the technical prowess of a vendor's team; project management is expected to be competent in this case. If project management itself is adding value, then isn't that really a matter of the customer's view of the project manager providing services above and beyond the normal view of functional responsibility? That would come down to the relationship with the customer. Ask any customer what they truly value in a vendor and they will tell you it is trust because there is a reliance on the customer's business strategy succeeding based on how well the vendor executes.

For example, in answer to the question, Why do you value vendor X?, you could imagine the following answers from customers: "So and so always delivers for me, and I can count on them to deliver a quality (defined however) product on time and at the agreed price," or "Vendor X really helped me be successful with my management by pulling in the schedule by x weeks," or "I really appreciated a recent project done by vendor Y because they handled our unexpected design changes with professionalism and competence."

Now most project management is within the sphere of operations in a vendor's organization. The customer facing business relationship is handled by some company representative in most cases. The project manager would be brought in once the work is underway and typically the direct reporting is to someone underneath the person who authorized the work; so, in this case, the project manager has the opportunity to build value with the underling but not the executive.

We discount the personality of the project managers as though this isn't an issue. It is a major issue and people need to realize that it is. Understanding one's own personality and the personality of the customer is vital to getting a label of value added from a customer. If the project manager isn't flexible in this area, then creating value with the customer becomes more difficult.

Anyway, there are as many variations to this theme as there are projects since personality and other interpersonal relationship nuances are involved. However, so much of successful [innovation] project management is all about these intangibles.

CVM today focuses on maximizing customer value, regardless of the form. In some cases, CVM must measure and increase the lifetime value of the deliverables of the project for each customer and stakeholder. By doing this, the project manager is helping the customer manage their profitability as well.

CVM performed correctly can and will lead to profitability but being profitable does not mean that you are performing CVM correctly. There are benefits to implementing CVM effectively as shown in Table 7-6. CVM is the leveraging of customer and stakeholder business relationships throughout the project. Because each project will have different customers and different stakeholders, CVM must be custom fit to each organization and possibly each project.

If CVM is to be effective, then presenting the right information to the client and stakeholders becomes critical. CVM introduces a value mindset into decision making. Many CVM programs fail because of poor metrics and not measuring the right things. Just focusing on the end result does not tell you if what

TABLE 7–6. BEFORE AND AFTER CVM IMPLEMENTATION

Factor	Before CVM	After CVM (with Metrics)
Stakeholder communications	Loosely structured	Structured using a network of metrics
Decision making	Based on partial information	Value-based informed decision making
Priorities	Partial agreements	Common agreements using metrics
Tradeoffs	Less structured	Structured around value contributions
Resource allocation	Less structured	Structured around value contributions
Business objectives	Projects poorly aligned to business	Better alignment to business strategy
Competitiveness	Market underperformer	Market outperformer

you are doing is right or wrong. Having the correct value-based metrics is essential. Value is in the eyes of the beholder, which is why there can be different value metrics.

CVM relies heavily on customer value assessment. Traditional CVM models are light on data and heavy on assumptions. For CVM to work effectively, it must be heavy on data and light on assumptions. Most successful CVM programs perform "data mining," where the correct attributes of value are found along with data that supports the use of those attributes. However, we should not waste valuable resources calculating value metrics unless the client perceives the value of using the metric. Project management success in the future will be measured by how well the project manager provides superior customer value. To do this, you must know what motivates the customers as well as the customers' customers.

Executives generally have a better understanding of the customers' needs than do the workers at the bottom of the organizational chart where the work takes place. Therefore, the workers may not see, understand, or appreciate the customer's need for value. Without the use of value metrics, we focus on the results of the process rather than the process itself and miss opportunities to add value. Only when a crisis occurs do we put the process under a microscope. Value metrics provide the workers with a better understanding of the customer's definition of value.

Understanding the customer's perception of value means looking at the disconnects or activities that are not value-added work. Value is created when we can eliminate non-value-added work rather than looking at ways to streamline project management processes. As an example, consider the following situation:

Situation: A company had a project management methodology that mandated that a risk management plan be developed on each and every project regardless of the magnitude of the risk. The risk management plan was clearly defined as a line item in the work breakdown structure and the clients eventually paid the cost of this. On one project, the project manager created a value metric and concluded that the risks on the project were so low that risk should not be included as one of the attributes of the value metric. The client agreed with this, and the time and money needed to develop a risk management plan was eliminated from the project plan. On this project, the risk management plan was seen as a disconnect and eliminated so that added value could be provided to the client. The company recognized that the risk management plans might be a disconnect on some projects and made the risk management plan optional at the discretion of the project manager and the clients.

This situation is a clear example that value is created when outputs are produced using fewer inputs or more outputs are created with the same number of inputs. However, care must be taken to make sure that the right disconnects are targeted for elimination.

Project managers must work closely with the customers for CVM to be effective. This includes:

- Understanding the customer's definition of satisfaction and effective performance
- Knowing how the customer perceives your price/value relationship (some clients still believe that value is simply quality divided by price)
- Making sure that the customers understand that value can be expressed in both nonfinancial and financial terms
- Seeing if the client can tell you what your distinctive competencies are and determining if they are appropriate candidates for value attributes
- Being prepared to debrief the customer and stakeholders on a regular basis for potential improvements and best practices
- Validating that the client is currently using or is willing to use the value metrics for their own informed decision making
- Understanding which value attributes are most important to your customers
- Building a customer project management value model or framework possibly unique for each customer
- Making sure that your model or framework fits the customer's internal business model
- Designing metrics that interface with the customer's business model
- Recognizing that CVM can maximize your lifetime profitability with each customer
- Changing from product-centric or service-centric marketing to project management-centric marketing
- Maximizing the economics of customer loyalty

THE RELATIONSHIP BETWEEN PROJECT MANAGEMENT AND VALUE

Companies today are trying to link together quality, value, and loyalty. All of this begins during innovation activities. These initiatives, which many call customer value management initiatives, first appeared as business initiatives performed by marketing and sales personnel rather than project management initiatives. Today, however, project managers are slowly becoming more involved in business decisions, and value has become extremely important.

Quality and customer value initiatives are part of CVM activities and are a necessity if a company wishes to obtain a competitive advantage. Competitive advantages in project management do not come just from being on time and within budget at the completion of each project. Offering something that your competitors do not offer may help. However, true competitive advantage is found when your efforts are directly linked to the customer's value initiatives, and whatever means by which you can show this will give you a step up on the competition. Projects managers must develop value-creating strategies.

Customers today have become more demanding and are requiring the contractor to accept the customer's definition of value according to the attributes selected by the customer. Each customer can, therefore, have a different definition of value. Contractors may wish to establish their own approach for obtaining this value based on their company's organizational process assets rather than having the customer dictate it. If you establish your own approach to obtaining the desired value, do not assume that your customer will understand the approach. They may need to be educated. Customers who recognize and understand the value that you are providing are more likely to want a long-term relationship with your firm.

To understand the complexities with introducing value to project management activities, let's assume that companies develop and commercialize products according to three life-cycle phases; innovation, development, and commercialization. Once the innovation and development phases are completed, the deliverables are turned over to someone in marketing and sales responsible for program management and ultimately commercialization of the product. Program management and commercialization may be done for products developed internally for your own company or they may be done for the client, or even for the client's own customers. In any event, it is during or after commercialization when companies survey their customers as to feedback on customer satisfaction and the value of the product. If the customers are unhappy with the final value, it is an expensive process to go back to the project stage and repeat the project in order to try to improve the value for the end-of-line customers.

The failures often found in these three life-cycle phases can be attributed to:

- Project managers are allowed to make only project technical decisions rather than both project and business decisions.
- Project managers are not informed as to the client's business plans as they relate to what the project manager is developing.
- Customers do not clearly articulate to the project manager, either verbally or through documented requirements, the exact value that they expect.
- Customers fund projects without fully understanding the value needed at the completion of the project.
- Project managers interface with the wrong people on the project.
- No value-based metrics are established in the project management phase whereby informed decision making can take place to improve the final value.
- Tradeoffs are made without considering the impact on the final value.
- Quality and value are considered as synonymous; quality is considered as the only value attribute.

We are now in the infancy stage of determining how to define and measure value. For internal projects, we are struggling in determining the right value metrics to assist us in project portfolio management with the selection of one project over another. For external projects, the picture is more complex. Unlike traditional metrics used in the past, value-based metrics are different for each client and each stakeholder. In Figure 7-4, you can see the three dimensions of values: your parent company's values, your client's

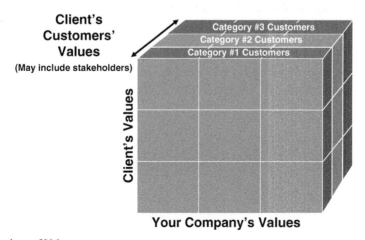

Figure 7–4. Dimensions of Value.

values, your client's customers' values, and we could even add in a fourth dimension, namely, stake-holder's values. It must be understood that the value that the completion of the project brings to your organization may not be as important as the total value that the project brings to the client's organization and the client's customer base.

For some companies, the use of value metrics will create additional challenges. As stated by a global IT consulting company:

> This will be a cultural change for us and for the customer. Both sides will need to have staff competent in identifying the right metrics to use and weightings; and then be able to explain in layman's language what the value metric is about.

The necessity for such value initiatives is clear.

As stated by a senior manager:

> I fully agree on the need for such value initiatives and also the need to make the importance clear to senior management. If we do not work in that direction, it will be very difficult for the companies to clearly state if they are working efficiently enough, providing value to the customer and the stockholders, and in consequence being sufficiently predictive with regard to its future in the market.

The window into the future now seems to be getting clearer. As a guess as to what might happen, consider the following:

- Your clients will perform CVM activities with their clients to discover what value attributes are considered as important. Your client's success is achieved by providing superior value to their customers.
- These attributes will be presented to you at the initiation of the project such that you can create value-based metrics on your project using these attributes if possible. You must interact with the client to understand their value dimensions.
- You must then create value metrics. Be prepared to educate your client on the use of the metrics. It is a mistake to believe that your client will fully understand your value metrics approach.
- Interact closely with your client to make sure you are fully aware of any changes in the value attributes they are finding in their customer value management efforts.
- Since value creation is a series of key and informed decisions, be prepared for value attribute tradeoffs and changes to your value metrics.

Value is now being introduced into traditional project management practices.

Value management practices have been with us for several decades and have been hidden under the radar screen in many companies. Some companies performed these practices in value engineering departments.

CREATING AN INNOVATION PROJECT MANAGEMENT BASELINE

For a project to be able to be controlled, it must be organized as a closed system. This requires that a baseline be established for possibly all competing constraints. Without such a baseline, an innovation project may get out of control and suffer from numerous scope changes that provide little or no value-added opportunities.

The reference point for measuring innovation performance is the value measurement baseline (VMB). It serves as the metric benchmark against which performance can be measured in terms of the competing constraints and the established value expectations.

The primary reasons for establishing, approving, controlling, and documenting the VMB are to:

- Ensure alignment to strategic goals and objectives
- Manage and monitor progress during project execution and commercialization
- Ensure accurate information on the accomplishment of the deliverables and the creation of business benefits and value for the company and its clients
- Establish value measurement criteria including criteria as to when the project should be cancelled

Performance measurement may be meaningless without an accurate baseline as a starting point. Unfortunately, there are numerous examples where project managers in the past had created baselines based upon just those elements of work they felt were important and this may or may not have been in full alignment with customer requirements or the customer's need for identification of value.

A common problem with baselines established on traditional projects was that it often did not account for the value that was expected from the project by people outside of the company. For years, many companies established Value Engineering (VE) Departments that focused on internal value achieved in engineering and manufacturing activities. Later, VE was expanded and called Value Analysis (VA) and included consideration of internal business value. We have now combined VE and VA, and call it Value Management (VM) where VM = VE + VA. Today, we are asking project managers to understand the importance of project value management and its relationship to both the customer's and their consumers' understanding of value. This changes the way we look at VM and is one of the reasons why CVM programs, as discussed previously in this chapter, became important.

Project value management must begin with a clear understanding of the customer's definition of value, and this is usually based upon the customer's value-in-use identification. Value mismatches generally lead to bad results. However, on long-term projects the customer's definition of value-in-use may change.

All baselines are reference points against which a comparison is made between planned and actual progress and are established at a fixed point in time. However, some value baselines must evolve over time. Unlike the traditional baselines for time, cost, and scope, value baselines are highly depended on when the measurements can be made, the measurement intervals, and the fact that value baselines are often displayed as step functions rather than linear functions.

There are several characteristics to the value baseline:

- The value baseline can be composed of attributes from other baselines.
- The value baseline should be shown to the customer. Other baselines may or may not be shown to the customers.
- The value baseline may or may not be a contractual obligation.
- Unlike other baselines, the value baseline can change during the project's life cycle.
- Stakeholders must understand the differences between actual and planned value, whether favorable or unfavorable.
- Baseline changes may require modifying or reworking the project plan, or even result in project cancellation.
- The value baseline can change without any changes occurring in other baselines.

- On some projects, monitoring the value baseline in the early life-cycle phases may provide no meaningful data.
- It is important to determine how often you need to update the value baseline.
- Value baselines may need to be continuously explained to the viewer. This may not be the case with other baselines.
- An increase of say 5 percent in the value baseline does not necessarily mean that the actual value has increased by 5 percent.
- Performance measurements for value may need to be customized rather than off-the-shelf techniques. This may need to be agreed upon upfront on the project.

Getting agreement on project value at the beginning of a project may be difficult. Even with an agreement, each stakeholder can still have their own subjective agenda on what value means to them and their definition is subject to change.

SELECTING THE RIGHT METRICS

Because of innovations in measurement techniques, companies are now tracking a dozen or more metrics on projects. While this sounds good, it has created the additional problem of potential information overload. Having too many performance metrics may provide the viewers with more information than they actually need, and they may not be able to discern the true status or what information is really important. It may be hard to ascertain what is important and what is not, especially if decisions must be made. Providing too few metrics can make it difficult for the viewers to make informed decisions. There is also a cost associated with metric measurement, and we must determine if the benefits of using this many metrics outweigh the costs of measurement. Cost is important because we tend to select more metrics than we actually need.

There are three generic categories of metrics:

1. *Traditional metrics.* These metrics are used for measuring the performance of the applied project management discipline more so than the results of the project and how well we are managing according to the predetermined baselines (e.g., cost variance and schedule variance). These metrics are common to all types of projects, including innovation.
2. *Key performance indicators (KPIs).* These are the few selected metrics that can be used to track and predict whether the project will be a success. These KPIs are used to validate that the critical success factors (CSFs) defined at the initiation of the project are being met (e.g., time-at-completion, cost-at-completion, and customer satisfaction surveys). These KPIs can be unique to a particular project such as innovation.
3. *Value (or value reflective) metrics.* These are special metrics that are used to indicate whether the stakeholders' expectations of project value are being or will be met. Value metrics can be a combination of traditional metrics and KPIs (value-at-completion and time to achieve full value).

Each type of metric has a primary audience, as shown in Table 7-7.
There can be three information systems on a project:

- One for the project manager
- One for the project manager's superior or parent company
- One for the each of the stakeholders or members of a co-creation team

TABLE 7–7. AUDIENCES FOR VARIOUS METRICS

Type of Metric	Audience
Traditional metrics	Primarily the project manager and the team, but may include the internal sponsor(s) as well
Key performance indicators	Some internal usage but mainly used for status reporting for the client and the stakeholders
Value metrics	Can be useful for everyone but primarily for the client as well as members of the co-creation team

There can be a different set of metrics and KPIs for each of these information systems.

Traditional metrics, such baselines as the cost, scope, and schedule, track and can provide information on how well we are performing according to the processes in each knowledge area or domain area in the *PMBOK® Guide*. Project manager must be careful not to micromanage their project and establish 40–50 metrics where most of them may not provide useful information.

Typical metrics on traditional projects may include:

- Number of assigned versus planned resources
- Quality of assigned versus planned resources
- Project complexity factor
- Customer satisfaction rating
- Number of critical constraints
- Number of cost revisions
- Number of critical assumptions
- Number of unstaffed hours
- Percentage of total labor hours on overtime
- Cost variance
- Schedule performance index
- Cost performance index

This is obviously not an all-inclusive list. These metrics may have some importance for the project manager but not necessarily the same degree of importance for the client and the stakeholders.

Clients and stakeholders are interested in critical metrics or KPIs. These chosen few metrics are reported to the client and stakeholders and provide an indication of whether or not innovation success is possible; however, they do not necessarily identify if the desired value will be achieved. The number of KPIs is usually determined by the amount of real estate on a computer screen. Most dashboards can display 6–10 icons or images where the information can be readily seen with reasonable ease.

To understand what a KPI means requires a dissection of each of the terms:

Key: A major contributor to success or failure
Performance: Measurable, quantifiable, adjustable, and controllable elements
Indicator: Reasonable representation of present and future performance

Obviously, not all metrics are KPIs. There are six attributes of a KPI, and these attributes are important when identifying and selecting the KPIs.

Predictive: Able to predict the future of this trend
Measurable: Can be expressed quantitatively
Actionable: Triggers changes that may be necessary

Relevant: The KPI is directly related to the success or failure of the project
Automated: Reporting minimizes the chance of human error
Few in number: Only what is necessary

Applying these six attributes to traditional metrics is highly subjective and will be based on the agreed-on definition of success, the critical success factors (CSFs) that were selected, and possibly the whims of the stakeholders. There can be a different set of KPIs for each stakeholder based on each stakeholder's definition of project success and final project value. This could significantly increase the costs of measurement and reporting, especially if each stakeholder requires a different dashboard with different metrics.

THE FAILURE OF TRADITIONAL METRICS AND KPIS

While some people swear by metric and KPIs, there are probably more failures than success stories. Typical causes of metric failure include:

- Performance being expressed in traditional or financial terms only
- The use of measurement inversion; using the wrong metrics
- No link of performance metrics to requirements, objectives, and success criteria
- No link to whether the customer was satisfied
- Lack of understanding as to which metrics indicate project value
- No feedback from customers on value-in-use

Metrics used for business purposes tend to express all information in financial terms. Project management metrics cannot always be expressed in financial terms. Also, in project management we often identify metrics that cannot effectively predict project success and/or failure and are not linked to the customer's requirements.

Perhaps the biggest issue today is in which part of the value chain metrics are used. Michael Porter, in his book *Competitive Advantage* (1985), used the term *value chain* to illustrate how companies interact with upstream suppliers, the internal infrastructure, downstream distributors, and end-of-the-line customers. While metrics can be established for all aspects of the value chain, most companies do not establish metrics for how the end-of-the-line customer perceives the value of the deliverable. Those companies that have developed metrics for this part of the value chain are more likely doing better than those that have not. These are identified as customer-related value metrics.

THE NEED FOR VALUE METRICS

In project management, it is now essential to create metrics that focus not only on business (internal) performance but also on performance toward customer satisfaction. For innovation projects, this is critical. If the customer cannot see the value in the project, then the project may be canceled and repeat business will not be forthcoming. Good value metrics can also result in less customer and stakeholder interference and meddling in the project.

The need for an effective metrics management program that focuses on value-based metrics is clear:

- There must be a customer/contractor/stakeholder agreement on how a set of metrics will be used to define innovation success or failure; otherwise, you have just best guesses. Value metrics will allow for more confidence in the ability to track and report value.
- Metric selection must cover the reality of the entire project; this can be accomplished with a set of core metrics supported by a value metric.
- A failure in effective metrics management, especially value metrics, can lead to stakeholder challenges and a loss of credibility.

We need to develop value-based metrics that can forecast stakeholder value, possibly shareholder value, and most certainly project value. Most models for creating this metric are highly subjective and are based on assumptions that must be agreed on upfront by all parties. Traditional value-based models that are used as part of a business intelligence application are derivatives of the QCD model (quality, cost, and delivery).

CREATING VALUE METRICS

The ideal situation would be the creation of a single value metric that the stakeholders can use to make sure that the project is meeting or exceeding the stakeholder's expectation of value. The value metric can be a combination of traditional metrics and KPIs. Discussing the meaning of a single value metric may be more meaningful than discussing the individual components; the whole is often greater than the sum of the parts.

There must be support for the concept of creating a value metric. According to a global IT consulting company:

> There has to be buy-in from both sides on the importance and substance of a value metric; it can't be the latest fad—it has to be understood as a way of tracking the value of the project.

Typical criteria for a value metric may be:

- *Every project will have at least one value metric or value KPI.* In some industries, it may not be possible to use just one value metric.
- *There may be a limit, such as five, for the number of value attributes that are part of the value metric.* As we mature in the use of value metrics, the number of attributes can grow or be reduced. Not all attributes that we would like to have will be appropriate or practical.
- *There will be weighting factors assigned to each component.* The weighting factors and the component measurement techniques will be established by the project manager and the stakeholders at the onset of the project. There may be company policies on assigning the weighting factors.
- *The target boundary boxes for the metrics will be established by the project manager and possibly the project management office (PMO).* If a PMO does not exist, then there may be a project management committee taking responsibility for accomplishing this, or it may be established by the funding organization.

To illustrate how this might work, let's assume that you are using innovation project management for creating a new product for consumers, and the agreed-on value attributes will be:

- Quality (of the final product)
- Cost (of commercialization)
- Safety protocols (for product liability concerns)
- Features (functionality)
- Schedule or timing (time-to-market)

These attributes, which can be unique for each project, are agreed to by you, the client, and the stakeholders at the onset of the project. The attributes may come from your metric/KPI library or may be new attributes. Care must be taken to make sure that your organizational process assets can track, measure, and report on each attribute. Otherwise, additional costs may be incurred, and these costs must be addressed up front so that they can be included in the contract price.

Time and cost are generally attributes of every value metric. However, there may be special situations where neither time, nor cost, nor both are value metric attributes:

- The project must be completed by law, such as environmental projects, where failure to perform could result in stiff penalties.
- The project is in trouble, but necessary, and we must salvage whatever value we can.
- We must introduce a new product to keep up with the competition regardless of the cost.
- Safety, aesthetic value, and quality are more important than time, cost, or scope.

Other attributes are almost always included in the value metric to support time and cost.

The next step is to set up targets with thresholds for each attribute or component. This is shown in Figure 7-5. If the attribute is cost, then we might say that performing within ±10 percent of the cost baseline is normal performance. Performing at greater than 20 percent over budget could be disastrous, whereas performing at more than 20 percent below budget is superior performance. However, there are cases where a +20 percent variance could be good and a −20 percent variance could be bad.

The exact definition or range of the performance characteristics could be established by the PMO if company standardization is necessary or through an agreement with the client and the stakeholders. In any event, targets and thresholds must be established.

The next step is to assign value points for each of the cells in Figure 7-5, as shown in Figure 7-6. In this case, two value points were assigned to the cell labeled "Performance Target." The standard approach is to then assign points in a linear manner above and below the target cell. Nonlinear applications are also possible, especially when thresholds are exceeded.

In Table 7-8, weighting factors are assigned to each of the attributes of the value metric. As before, the weighting percentages could be established by the PMO or through an agreement with the client (i.e., funding organization) and the stakeholders. The use of the PMO might be for company standardization on the weighting factors. However, it sets a dangerous precedence when the weighting factors are allowed to change indiscriminately.

Now, we can multiply the weighting factors by the value points and sum them up to get the total value contribution. If all of the value measurements indicated that we were meeting our performance targets, then 2.0 would be the worth of the value metric. However, in this case, we are exceeding performance with regard to quality, safety protocols, and time-to-market, and therefore the final worth of the value metric is 2.7. This implies that the stakeholders or consumers are receiving additional value that is most likely meeting or exceeding expectations.

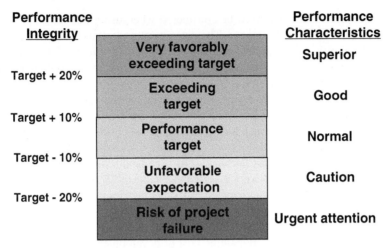

Figure 7–5. The Value Metric/KPI Boundary Box.

Performance Characteristics	Value Points
Superior	4
Good	3
Normal	2
Caution	1
Urgent attention	0

Figure 7–6. Value Points for a Boundary Box.

TABLE 7–8. VALUE METRIC MEASUREMENT

Value Component	Weighting Factor	Value Measurement	Value Contribution
Quality	10%	3	0.3
Cost	20%	2	0.4
Safety protocols	20%	4	0.8
Features	30%	2	0.6
Time-to-market	20%	3	0.6
			TOTAL = 2.7

There are still several issues that must be considered when using this technique. We must clearly define what is meant by normal performance. The users must understand what this means. Is this level actually our target level or is it the minimal acceptable level for the client? If it is our target level, then having a value below 2.0 might still be acceptable to the client/consumers/stakeholders if our target were greater than what the requirements asked for.

The users must understand the real meaning of the value metric. When the metric goes from 2.0 to 2.1 how significant is that? Statistically, this is a 5 percent increase. Does it mean that the value increased 5 percent? How can we explain to a layman the significance of such an increase and the impact on value?

Value metrics generally focus on the present and/or future value of the project and may not provide sufficient information as to other factors that may affect the health of the project. As an example, let's assume that the value metric is quantitatively assessed at a value of 2.7. From the customer's perspective, they are receiving more value than they anticipated. But other metrics may indicate that the project should be considered for termination. For example,

- The value metric is 2.7, but the remaining cost of development or commercialization is so high that the product may be overpriced for the market.
- The value metric is 2.7, but the time-to-market will be too late.
- The value metric is 2.7, but a large portion of the remaining work packages have a very high critical risk designation.
- The value metric is 2.7, but significantly more critical assumptions are being introduced.
- The value metric is 2.7, but the project no longer satisfies the client's needs.
- The value metric is 2.7, but your competitors have introduced a product with a higher value and quality.

In Table 7-9, we reduced the number of features in the deliverable, which allowed us to improve quality and safety as well as accelerate the time-to-market. Since the worth of the value metric is 2.4, we are still providing additional value to the stakeholders and customers.

In Table 7-10, we have added additional features as well as improving quality and safety. However, to do this, we have incurred a schedule slippage and a cost overrun. The worth of the value metric is now 2.7, which implies that the stakeholders are still receiving added value. The stakeholders/customers may be willing to incur the added cost and schedule slippage because of the added value.

Whenever it appears that we may be over budget or behind schedule, we can change the weighting factors and overweight those components that are in trouble. As an example, Table 7-11 shows how the weighting factors can be adjusted. Now, if the overall worth of the value metric exceeds 2.0 with the adjusted weighting factors, the stakeholders may still consider the continuation of the project. Sometimes, companies identify minimum and maximum weights for each component, as shown in Table 7-12. However, there is a risk that management may not be able to adjust to and accept weighting factors that

TABLE 7–9.   A VALUE METRIC WITH A REDUCTION IN FEATURES

Value Component	Weighting Factor	Value Measurement	Value Contribution
Quality	10%	3	0.3
Cost	20%	2	0.4
Safety protocols	20%	4	0.8
Features	30%	1	0.3
Time-to-market	20%	3	0.6
			TOTAL = 2.4

TABLE 7–10. A VALUE METRIC WITH IMPROVED QUALITY, FEATURES, AND SAFETY

Value Component	Weighting Factor	Value Measurement	Value Contribution
Quality	10%	3	0.3
Cost	20%	1	0.2
Safety protocols	20%	4	0.8
Features	30%	4	1.2
Time-to-market	20%	1	0.2
			TOTAL = 2.7

TABLE 7–11. CHANGING THE WEIGHTING FACTORS

Value Component	Normal Weighting Factor	Weighting Factors If We Have a Significant Schedule Slippage	Weighting Factors If We Have a Significant Cost Overrun
Quality	10%	10%	10%
Cost	20%	20%	40%
Safety protocols	20%	10%	10%
Features	30%	20%	20%
Time-to-market	20%	40%	20%

TABLE 7–12. WEIGHTING FACTOR RANGES

Value Component	Minimal Weighting Value	Maximum Weighting Value	Nominal Weighting Value
Quality	10%	40%	20%
Cost	10%	50%	20%
Safety protocols	10%	40%	20%
Features	20%	40%	30%
Time-to-market	10%	50%	20%

can change from project to project, or even during a project. Also, standardization and repeatability of the solution may disappear with changing weighting factors.

Companies are generally reluctant to allow project managers to change weighting factors once the project is under way and may establish policies to prevent unwanted changes from occurring. The fear is that the project manager may change the weighting factors just to make the project look good. However, there are situations where a change may be necessary:

- Customers and stakeholders are demanding a change in weighting factors possibly to justify the continuation of project funding.
- The risks of project have changed in downstream life-cycle phases and a change in weighting factors is necessary.
- As the project progresses, new value attributes are added into the value metric.
- As the project progresses, some value attributes no longer apply and must be removed from the value metric.

- The enterprise environment factors have changed requiring a change in the weighting factors.
- The assumptions have changed over time.
- The number of critical constraints has changed over time.

We must remember that project management metrics and KPIs can change over the life of a project and, therefore the weighting factors for the value metric may likewise be susceptible to changes.

Sometimes, because of the subjectivity of this approach, when the information is presented to the client, we should include identification of which measurement technique was used for each target. This is shown in Table 7-13. The measurement techniques may be subject to negotiations at the beginning of the project.

The use of metrics and KPIs has been with us for decades, but the use of a value metric is relatively new, especially on innovation projects. Therefore, failures in the use of this technique are still common and may include:

- Is not forward looking; the value metric focuses on the present rather than the future
- Does not go beyond financial metrics and, thus, fails to consider the value in knowledge gained, organizational capability, customer satisfaction, and political impacts
- Believing that value metrics (and the results) that other companies use will be the same for your company
- Not considering how the client and stakeholders define value
- Allowing the weighting factors to change too often, to make the project's results look better

As with any new technique, additional issues always arise. Typical questions that we are now trying to answer in regard to the use of a value metric include:

- What if only three of the five components can be measured, for example, in the early life-cycle phases of a project?
- In such a case where only some components can be measured, should the weighting factors be changed or normalized to 100 percent, or left alone?
- Should the project be a certain percentage complete before the value metric has any real meaning?
- Who will make decisions as to changes in the weighting factors as the project progresses through its life-cycle phases?
- Can the measurement technique for a given component change over each life-cycle phase or must it be the same throughout the project?
- Can we reduce the subjectivity of the process?

TABLE 7–13. WEIGHTING FACTORS AND MEASUREMENTS

Value Component	Weighting Factor	Measurement Technique	Value Measurement	Value Contribution
Quality	10%	Sampling techniques	3	0.3
Cost	20%	Direct measurement	2	0.4
Safety protocols	20%	Simulation	4	0.8
Features	30%	Observation	2	0.6
Time-to-market	20%	Direct measurement	3	0.6

INDUSTRY EXAMPLES OF INNOVATION VALUE METRICS _____

This section provides examples of how various companies use innovation value metrics. The number of companies using value metrics is increasing each year. The hard part in using innovation metrics is in determining the attributes as well as the weighting factors innovation. Examples of value attributes commonly used appear in Table 7-14.

What is important to recognize in Table 7-14 is that several of the entries are intangibles rather than tangibles. Intangibles, and their accompanying importance to innovation, may be tough to measure in some firms, but they are not immeasurable. Measuring intangibles is dependent on management's commitment to the measurement techniques used. Measuring intangibles does improve performance as long as we have valid measurements free of manipulation.

The value of intangibles can have a greater impact on long-term considerations than short-term factors. Management support for the value measurements of intangibles can also prevent short-term financial considerations from dominating decision making. Intangibles are long-term measurements and most companies focus on the short-term results.

There is resistance to measuring intangibles:

- Companies argue that intangibles do not impact the bottom line.
- Companies are fearful of what the results will show.
- Companies argue that they lack the capability to measure intangibles.

When managing innovation using co-creation, selecting the value attributes can be difficult because the attribute may have a difference to the customers and the customers' customers. This is shown in Table 7-15.

TABLE 7–14. CATEGORIES OF VALUE ATTRIBUTES

Traditional Value Attributes	Advanced Value Attributes	Leadership Value Attributes	Innovation Value Attributes
Time	Teamwork	Commitment	Innovation management
Cost	Conditions of satisfaction	Culture and values	Intellectual property rights
Quality	Effective communications	Cooperation and collaboration	Workforce skills
Technology and scope	Process adherence	Knowledge management	Organizational capacity
Client satisfaction	Time-to–market	Governance	Sustainability
Risks	Features, usability, and functionality	Strategic planning	Teamwork
Financial Value Attributes	**Human Resources Value Attributes**	**Marketing Value Attributes**	**Social Responsibility Value Attributes**
ROI, NPV, and IRR	Employee talent	Customer satisfaction	Worker safety
Cash flow	Employee morale	Brand loyalty	Worker health
Payback period	Employee retention	Company image	Environmental issues
Market share	Employee stress level	Company reputation	Sustainability
Profitability	Training and education	Goodwill	Community social benefits
Ability to raise funds	Renewal capability	Strategic alliances	Stakeholder and stockholder satisfaction

TABLE 7–15.   INTERPRETATION OF ATTRIBUTES

Generic Value Attribute	Project Manager's Value Attribute	Customer's Value Attribute	Consumer's Value Attribute
Time	Project duration	Time-to-market	Delivery date
Cost	Project cost	Selling price	Purchase rice
Quality	Performance	Functionality	Usability
Technology and scope	Meeting specifications	Strategic alignment	Safe buy and reliable
Satisfaction	Customer satisfaction	Consumer satisfaction	Esteem in ownership
Risks	No future business from this customer	Loss of profits and market share	Need for support and risk of obsolescence

If the definition of innovation success is based on the customer's recognition of value in use, then the consumer's value attributes in Table 7-15 may be more important during project execution than the project manager's value attributes.

ALIGNMENT TO STRATEGIC BUSINESS OBJECTIVES

Because of advances in metric measurement techniques, models have been developed by which we can show the alignment of all projects, including innovation, to strategic business objectives. One such model appears in Figure 7-7. Years ago, the only metrics we would use were time, cost, and scope. Today, we can include metrics related to both strategic value and business value. This allows us to evaluate the health of the entire portfolio of projects as well as individual projects such as those in innovation.

Since all metrics have established targets or forecasted expectations, we can award points for each metric based on how close we come to the targets. Figure 7-8 shows that the project identified in Figure 7-7 has received thus far 80 points out of a possible 100 points. Figure 7-9 shows the alignment of projects to

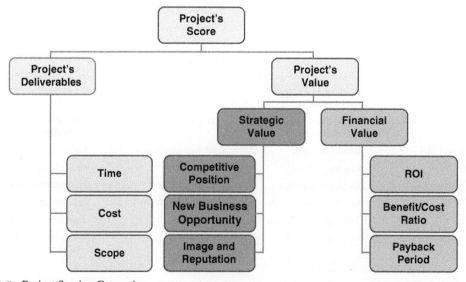

Figure 7–7. Project Scoring Categories.

strategic objectives. If the total score in Figure 7-8 is 0–50 points, we would assume that the project is not contributing to strategic objectives at this time, and this would be shown as a zero or blank cell in Figure 7-9. Scores between 51 and 75 points would indicate a "partial" contribution to the objectives and shown as a one in Figure 7-9. Scores 76–100 points would indicate fulfilling the objective and shown as a two in Figure 7-9. Periodically, we can summarize the results in Figure 7-9 to show management Figure 7-10, which illustrates our ability to create the desired benefits and final value.

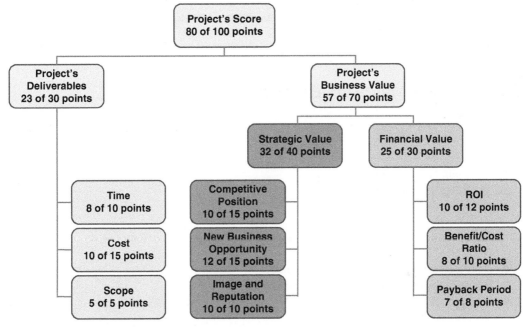

Figure 7–8. Examples of a Project's Score.

	Projects								
Strategic Objectives:	Project 1	Project 2	Project 3	Project 4	Project 5	Project 6	Project 7	Project 8	**Scores**
Technical superiority	2		1			2		1	6
Reduced operating costs				2	2				4
Reduced time to market	1		1	2	1	1		2	8
Increase business profits			2	1	1	1		2	7
Add manufacturing capacity	1		2	2		1		1	7
Column scores	4	0	6	7	4	5	0	6	

	No contribution
1	**Supports objective**
2	**Fulfills objective**

Figure 7–9. Matching Projects to Strategic Objectives.

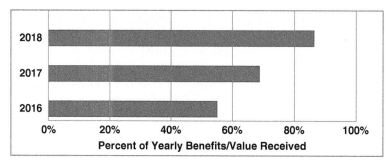

Figure 7–10. Benefits or Value Achieved.

METRICS FOR INNOVATION GOVERNANCE

Governance personnel managing the innovation portfolio of projects need to address three important questions:

1. Are we doing the right things?
2. Are we doing the right things right?
3. Are we doing enough of the right things?

These three questions can then be broken down in more detailed questions:

- Is project and portfolio value being created?
- What are the risks and are they being mitigated?
- When should the innovation portfolio PMO (IPPMO) or other governance personnel intervene in any project decision making?
- How will innovation performance affect future corporate strategy?
- Are the projects still aligned to strategic objectives?
- Do we need to perform resource reoptimization?
- Do we have any weak investments that need to be canceled or replaced?
- Must any of the projects be consolidated?
- Must any of the projects be accelerated or decelerated?
- Do we have the right mix of projects in the portfolio?
- Does the portfolio have to be rebalanced?

A simple classification for innovation metrics is product, service, and transformational metrics, which can then be broken down further into categories such as process measures, growth measures, and profitable growth measures.

Some typical innovation metrics that the governance personnel might use include:

- Percentage of projects in radical innovation
- Percentage of projects in incremental innovation
- Percentage of workers with the required competencies
- Revenue generated by new products over a given period
- Profit growth rate

- Profit and loss impact of innovation projects
- Profit and loss impact per customer
- Percentage of projects in various life-cycle phases
- Project success rate
- Speed-to-market if applicable
- Number of innovation projects in the pipeline
- Number of patents
- Number of ideas generated
- Number of ideas killed (i.e., kill rate)
- Time to go from idea generation to project approval
- Process improvements such as in time-to-market

There are also portfolio PMO metrics. Typical portfolio metrics might include:

- Percentage of employees assigned full-time or part-time to innovation projects
- Percentage of time the assigned employees work on innovation projects
- Percentage of time executives spend on strategic innovation governance rather than day-to-day operations
- Number of ideas submitted over the past year
- Percentage of submitted ideas that were approved as innovation projects
- Percentage of approved projects that were completed and commercialized
- Average amount of time from approval to start of commercialization
- Average amount of time for commercialization
- Percentage of commercialized projects that were considered as partially successful and totally met expectations

Measuring the success of innovation project management is more than just measuring the financial success of the outcome of an individual project. As shown above, there must be a set of metrics specifically for the innovation process that will measure the number of ideas submitted, number of ideas that were selected, and number of ideas that eventually were commercialized. There must also be metrics that relate to the activities, tools, and techniques that are utilized during project execution.

INNOVATION METRICS IN ACTION: INNOVATIONLABS

"Measure what is measurable and make measurable what is not so."

— Galileo

Like everything in business that involves the investment of capital and time, innovation should be a disciplined process that has to be measured so that it can be genuinely managed. This isn't news, but

Material in this section, "Innovation Metrics in Action: InnovationLabs," has been provided by Langdon Morris, senior partner at Innovation Lab Consulting and Training Company, LLC and is excerpted by permission from *The Innovation Master Plan* by Langdon Morris, FutureLab Press, 2011, 2017, and 2020. © 2011 and 2017, and 2020 by Langdon Morris. All rights reserved. Reproduced with permission.

it is nevertheless problematic, because measuring innovation in the wrong way, or measuring the wrong aspects of it, can be a genuine detriment to its progress.

Further, there are a lot of ways to measure innovation productivity so choosing the right metrics requires some selectivity. Process-oriented metrics typically consider the means, such as the number of new ideas proposed, or new ideas introduced. They also consider organizational outcomes such as increased capabilities with existing or new technologies, which makes them potentially useful as indicators. Financial metrics are focused on ends, the results, and include ROI-based models to track financial performance, or the proportion of sales or profits from new products. Given the many possibilities, it takes some effort to sort it all out, which is my purpose in this section.

The Perils of ROI

Among the many measurement tools available, it's become a reflex among business leaders to apply the marvelously useful concept of ROI to just about everything. This is generally a healthy thing, and as innovation is indeed a form of investment that should absolutely generate a better-than-market-rate return (or why bother?), ROI is a natural part of the innovation discussion. But it does present certain problems that we have to be aware of.

ROI discussions make a lot of sense when we're evaluating incremental ideas that will be applied in existing, well-understood markets, using existing, well-understood business processes such as established manufacturing and distribution systems.

But when we're considering ideas that aren't incremental, and when they are in the early stages of development, a huge danger suddenly appears, because ascertaining ROI early on drives us to try to assess what the completed innovation could return to us when we're unlikely to have a realistic idea of what its worth could really be. So, we are sometimes forced to guess. If we like the idea then we may be inspired to make wildly optimistic predictions of revenues; or if we don't like it, we may default to drastically pessimistic ones. And if we then make decisions based on our optimistic or pessimistic predictions, although our spreadsheets are still no more than assumptions, we often forget that, and treat them as real. So, the entire edifice of our thinking process is built on nothing but air, bits, and bytes.

Innovation thrives in environments of 'what if,' 'how about?' and 'it might…' but it can be very difficult to achieve when there is an insistence on certainties, especially when they don't exist. This reinforces something we already discussed about innovation, which is that it's a process that is suffused with ambiguity. But the ROI conversation is entirely intolerant of ambiguity, and when introduced at the wrong time it is an innovation killer.

The other problem with ROI is that discussing it almost always forces us to try to relate a new idea to an existing market to have some basis for comparison. This drives us back to incrementalism even when an idea contains the seeds of a potential breakthrough. Since breakthroughs take us to new territory, comparisons to existing models can be self-defeating.

And then there are the chicken-and-egg discussions that go like this:

Question: "What's the value of this idea?"
Answer: "We don't know."
Response: "We can't fund it if we don't know what's going to be worth."
Counter: "We won't know what it will be worth until we get some funding to develop it…"

So around and around you go.

Discerning the intent behind the dialog is an important aspect of figuring out what the conversation actually means. Many executives use the "ROI question" as a zinger or a gotcha, a trick question through which they wish to discredit the idea or the innovator. They know perfectly well that an accurate assessment of ROI is generally impossible at the early stages, so when they play the ROI card in this setting it's an accepted truism in the research and development community that the term *ROI* really stands for restraint on innovation.

Because of all these factors, ROI-based assessments tend to favor short-term thinking and to disfavor the development of long-term, breakthrough, and discontinuous ideas and projects. Premature use of ROI to measure innovation thus endangers the very life of the thing you want to measure and makes it less likely to achieve the end goal of the process, which is better innovations.

All of this presents difficult problems for R&D and innovation managers who are obliged to look after their portfolios diligently, and to manage their resources effectively, and to provide accurate measurements of their progress. This was evident during a recent meeting at HP Labs when a manager commented that he couldn't even look at a project that didn't have the potential to become at least a $50 million business. The problem, of course, was that he was forced to guess just how big a business every idea that was proposed to him could become. And how could he know?

So, what do you include in your research plan, and what do you put aside? Did the researcher whose work led to the creation of HP's multi-billion-dollar inkjet printing business know what he was getting the company into when he became curious about the burned coffee, he noticed on the bottom of a coffee pot? Could he have said that his idea about superheated ink would be worth $50, much less $50 million?

Unless he was inspired by an awe-inspiring fit of hubris, certainly not. Yet today HP sells $25 *billion* per year of inkjet printers and inks.

Measuring the effectiveness of your innovation process is a lot easier to do when the process itself is mature, and you can look back and see tangible evidence of your accomplishments and failures (both intelligent and no so intelligent). At the early stages, which could be anywhere in the first year, or two, or even three, measuring your progress is more difficult because you may not have as much to show for your efforts as you would like to have.

Which is of course ironic, because it's in the first years that most people want reassurance that they're doing it well enough to continue with the effort, and encouragement that the investment they're making will indeed generate that coveted ROI. Convincing proof, however, will usually only come later, when more results are in. Therefore, please be patient.

Twelve Particularly Useful Innovation Metrics

In exploring the measurement of innovation, we found that across the seven stages of the agile innovation process (see Figure 7-11 later in this section) there are at least 92 metrics. About a third of the total are qualitative, or conceptual, and the rest are quantitative. Since 92 is of course a ridiculous number, far too many for any organization to use, you'll have to choose the ones that will serve you best and leave the others aside.

Before we look at the full set, however, I'll highlight the 12 that we've found to be most consistently useful for our clients.

External Metrics: Impact on Brand and Image

1. The outputs of the innovation system significantly enhance the brand. They accelerate the acquisition of new customers, contracts, and/or clients, as measured by the "rate of new customer acquisition." This is evident in new sales to new customers.
2. The opinion that customers have of our company, as indicated through brand image surveys, customer feedback, and analyst rankings, improves consistently and significantly.

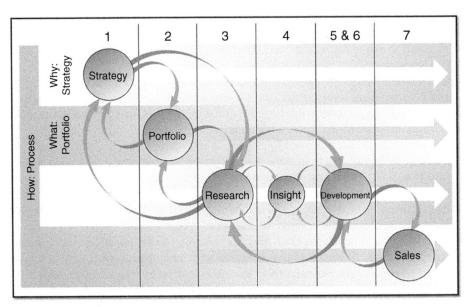

Figure 7–11. The Seven Steps of the Agile Innovation Process.

External Metrics: Impact on Ecosystem

3. The innovation system engages a large and growing set of external partners, customers, suppliers, and others, creating a broad, comprehensive, and thriving open innovation ecosystem.

Internal Metrics: Impact on Growth and Revenue

4. The innovation system results in a significant increase in the number of attractive, new, internally sourced investment opportunities that are available for consideration by senior managers and the board of directors.
5. Valuation of the total innovation portfolio increases significantly compared to prior period, year over year. Financial valuation methods would include NPV, asset valuation, and /or option value. Incremental innovation metrics would include percent of products/services revenue attributable to innovation within existing product/services lines.
6. The net portfolio valuation increase is at least 5x to 10x greater than the capital invested. Financial valuation methods would include NPV, asset valuation, and /or option value.
7. The number and percentage of projects that are in the innovation pipeline that are judged to be high quality increases steadily.
8. The proportion of projects in the pipeline that are not incremental projects (i.e., these are breakthroughs and new business model innovations), increases significantly year over year.
9. The number of nonincremental projects delivered as innovations to the market increases significantly year over year.

People Metrics: Impact on Culture

10. Speed of innovation project completion increases year over year.
11. The number of people who are participating in all aspects of innovation efforts increases significantly year over year.

12. The quality of the contribution by each person increases steadily, and over time more people are contributing more valuable ideas and efforts in the innovation process.

In summary, successful development of the innovation process will steadily enhance your company's overall capability in many areas of performance including innovation, and the innovation results themselves will also get better and better.

These 12 perspectives are mutually reinforcing, so, for example, because of more breakthroughs and new business model innovations being developed and brought to market (#8), the opinion that customers have of the company should improve (#2), etc.

Since at root the innovation process is all about learning, improvement of innovation performance over time is to be expected as you invest effort in developing innovations and at the same time you are investing in improving the process itself.

Ninety-Two Innovation Metrics, Qualitative, and Quantitative

The rather massive list below constitutes our complete set. Granted, 92 are already too many, but it's still possible that there are more, and perhaps some of the ones not included here are the right ones for your organization to use.

So please use this list as a thinking starter and be open to additional possibilities that may serve your needs better.

The metrics are listed by step in two categories, qualitative and quantitative, followed by transversal and human resources metrics. Qualitative metrics often take the form of provocative questions, which are intended to instigate people to think deeply and effectively about the work they're doing and its future consequences. These do not lend themselves to a statistical form, but they can open new avenues of discussion which may stimulate new ideas and conceptual frameworks. Most of the metrics suggested for steps 1–3 are qualitative. They can be used in two ways:

1. They are very useful as provocative questions in dialog. When a particular aspect of the innovation process is the subject of your discussion, raising these questions can direct the conversation in a fruitful direction.
2. They can also be used in surveys to gather input from larger numbers of people. To use them this way, you would turn them into statements and then ask people to state their degree of agreement/disagreement, with options such as "strongly agree, agree, neutral, disagree, strongly disagree." This turns a qualitative question into a process that you can use to gather quantitative input, which can be helpful in getting useful feedback from hundreds or even thousands of people in a very effective format.[4]

Conversely, the metrics for steps 4–7 are mostly quantitative, and they're natural for statistical collection and analysis. ROI, of course, epitomizes this category. And sales itself is of course the subject of many critically important quantitative metrics.

The Overall Framework: The Agile Innovation Master Plan

The 92 metrics are organized into seven major categories, which correspond with the overall Agile Innovation Master Plan framework as shown below in Figure 7-11. This framework is intended to organize the pursuit of innovation in a systematic manner, and it's been adopted by organizations all over the world.

---

4. The innovation audit process that we've developed at InnovationLabs often includes large group surveys to explore many of these topics.

The book from which this chapter is excerpted describes the entire framework in detail. As you might expect, its title is *The Agile Innovation Master Plan.*

The looping arrows indicate feed forward loops to help people working downstream to anticipate change, and feedback loops from outputs back to inputs, representing lessons learned now applied to improving results. The arrows are more symbolic than realistic, as there will ideally be continual interaction between people working in various steps of the innovation process as they learn and share with others. Although the sequence of steps from 1 to 7 suggests that the innovation process is linear, the arrows moving from left to right and back indicate that all aspects of the process occur in parallel as multiple projects progress simultaneously.

Metrics for Step 1: Strategic Thinking

Qualitative Metrics and Provocative Questions
1. Are we targeting the right parts of our business with our existing innovation efforts?
2. Do we change as fast as our markets do?
3. Are we flexible enough?
4. Is our strategic goal clear enough such that we can translate it into innovation initiatives?
5. How well do our strategies match with the way the market is evolving? (For example, if the industry is moving rapidly into a particular technology, does our organization have the requisite expertise?)
6. Do we have an effective innovation dashboard so that we know how we're doing? (The dashboard is discussed below.)
7. Are we measuring innovation appropriately and adequately?

Quantitative Metrics
8. How much time do senior managers invest in innovation?
9. What is the average time required from development of a strategic concept to operational implementation as an innovation?
10. How much capital do we invest in innovation?
11. How much money do we invest in each type of innovation?
12. What business growth do we expect from the innovation process, in percent, and in dollars?

Metrics for Step 2: Portfolios and Metrics

You probably won't know if you're using the right metrics for this step until the portfolio starts producing results that you can compare to with your initial expectations. So whatever metrics you start with here are assumptions that will be managed, and adapted, over time.

Qualitative Metrics and Provocative Questions
13. How does our portfolio compare with what we think our competitors may be planning?
14. Do we have the right balance of incremental and breakthrough projects?
15. Are we introducing breakthroughs at a sufficient rate to keep up with or ahead of change?
16. What are our learning brands, the brands that we use for experimentation to push the envelope and track the evolution of the market?
17. Are we developing new brands at an adequate rate?
18. Are our metrics evoking the innovation behaviors that we want from the people in our organization?
19. Are our metrics aligned with our rewards and reward systems? (This topic is discussed in more detail below.)
20. What did we expect our metrics to tell us compared with the actual performance achieved?

Quantitative Metrics

Metrics Related to the Performance of Innovation Portfolios
21. What is the ratio of capital invested in the early stages vs. return earned in the sales stage?
22. What is the actual portfolio composition in the sales stage compared with planned/intended portfolio composition in the planning stage?

Metrics for Step 3: Research

The purpose of research is to address the questions that have come up in the process of developing innovation portfolios, as well as to expose new perspectives, evoke new concepts, uncover new possibilities, and create new knowledge.

Qualitative Metrics and Provocative Questions
23. How well have we designed our business to meet the tacit dimensions of our customers' experiences?
24. How good are our models of customer behavior and motivation?
25. How well do we understand the implications and applications of new technologies?
26. How well do we understand the emerging future?
27. How good have our past predictions been at anticipating change?
28. Is our research helping to target the right innovation opportunities?
29. Do we have a broad enough range of models of technology possibilities, tacit knowledge models, and societal trends?
30. Are the ideas that we're developing reaching across a broad enough range of business needs?
31. How good are we at creating an "open sandbox" that accommodates a wide range of possible concepts and ideas?
32. Are we encouraging people to share their ideas?

Quantitative
33. How many customer groups have we explored?
34. How many instances are there of research results applied in new products, services, and processes?
35. What is the breadth of participation from throughout our organization in the research process (broader is generally better)?
36. How much time has our organization invested in research?
37. How much money has our organization invested in research?
38. How many ideas have we developed through prototyping?
39. How many ideas have been contributed by our staff?
40. What percentage of the new ideas that we work on come from outside?
41. How many people inside the organization are participating in the innovation process?
42. How many people from outside the organization are participating in the innovation/process?
43. How many ideas were collected in the "idea gathering" system?
44. How many collected ideas from the idea gathering were developed further?
45. How many collected ideas from the idea gathering were brought to market?
46. What percentage of the ideas brought to market came through the strategy-portfolio-research pathway, compared with the percent that originated from the open-door idea gathering system?
47. What is the average length of time it takes to get ideas through research and into development?

Metrics for Step 4: Insight

Qualitative Metrics and Provocative Questions

48. Are we getting enough solid insights and concepts?
49. Is our innovation portfolio balanced correctly?
50. Are we using the right management processes for the different types of innovations that we're working on?

Quantitative

51. What is the percent of investment in non-core innovation projects?
52. What is the total amount invested in non-core innovation projects?
53. How much senior management time is invested in growth innovation as compared with incremental innovation?
54. What percentage of ideas were funded for development?
55. What percentage of the ideas in the research process were killed?

Metrics for Step 5: Innovation Development

Qualitative Metrics and Provocative Questions

56. Are the right people involved in innovation development?
57. Do we have enough failures to be confident that we're pushing the envelope sufficiently?
58. Do we have people with sufficiently broad technical competence in all of the relevant explicit and tacit knowledge domains?

Quantitative

59. How fast do we complete and test new prototypes?
60. What is the number of prototypes per new product?
61. How many patents have we applied for in the past year?
62. How many patents were issued in the last year?

Metrics for Step 6: Market Development

Qualitative Metrics and Provocative Questions

63. How well are we balancing our attempts to reach existing customers compared with new ones?
64. How well do we really understand our customers?
65. Are we positioned properly for changes in the attitudes, beliefs, and ideals of our customers?

Quantitative

66. What is the return on our marketing investments?
67. How many new customers did we add in the last year?
68. What is the growth rate of our customer base?

Metrics for Step 7: Selling

Qualitative Metrics and Provocative Questions

69. How well does our sales process match our customers' needs for knowledge?

Quantitative
70. What is the average age of the products/services we are currently selling?
71. What is our gross sales revenue attributable to innovation?
72. What is our gross sales margin attributable to innovation?
73. What is the number of new products/services that we have launched in the past year?
74. How did expected sales results compare with actual results?
75. How many successful results did we achieve per type of innovation?
76. What cost savings were achieved in the organization due to innovation efforts?
77. How many new customers do we have (by number or by product)?
78. What is the average time to market from research through to sales?
79. What is the level of customer satisfaction with new products/services?

Innovation System Metrics: Transversal and Human Resources

There are also useful transversal metrics that help us to assess the overall performance of the innovation process, and some that assess human resources and training activities involved in teaching people to become more effective at innovation-related activities.

Quantitative metrics across the entire innovation process
80. Now we can talk meaningfully about ROI. Did our total innovation investment, managed through portfolios, yield appropriate results in terms of sales growth, profit growth, and overall ROI?
81. What is the performance of our business units as innovators?
82. What is the percentage of revenue in core categories from new products/services?
83. What is the percentage of revenue in new categories from new products/services?
84. What is the overall percentage of profits from new products/services?
85. What is the percentage of new customers from new products/services attributable to innovation?
86. What is the average time to market from research through to sales?
87. What is the level of customer satisfaction with new products/services?
88. What percentage of projects were terminated at each stage?

Human Resources and Training Metrics Related to Innovation
89. How many people participated in innovation training?
90. How many people used our online innovation tools?
91. How effective is the linkage between our innovation metrics, the criteria we use to assess performance, and our reward systems?
92. What is the "contribution to innovation" made by individuals, teams, and departments across the entire organization? And is it improving from year to year?

Gasp. And that's the end of the list.

Aligning Metrics and Rewards

Metric #19 asks the question, are our metrics aligned with our rewards and reward systems? The underlying point, of course, is that people in organizations gradually adjust their behaviors to fit the prevailing systems that they're measured on and rewarded for, so if they're not measured for their contribution to innovation then their contribution will probably be less than it could be.

Hence, aligning the innovation system, the metrics, and the rewards is an important piece of work to accomplish.

But it's rarely easy to measure an individual's contribution to innovation unless that person happens to be uniquely creative or is involved in high-profile projects. Innovation almost always involves the efforts of many people working diligently but perhaps quietly, so setting up an innovation reward structure that recognizes the team element is usually preferable to a process that only acknowledges individuals.

But this remains a controversial topic, as some people believe that the only suitable reward system is one that rewards everyone in the firm. Rewards for individuals can be seen as divisive.

From a broader perspective, the notion of intrinsic vs. extrinsic rewards can be an important element of this conversation as well. Those who are inspired to probe deeply and find real solutions, and to do so to the highest possible standards, are deeply motivated by what they feel inside. Their interest and commitment is entirely intrinsic; they do this work for the inherent rewards that it brings.

On the other hand, when people are working at tasks because of the need or expectation of external rewards, their commitment is generally not as deep, and the results may not be as good.

This is relevant here because if people are participating in an innovation system because they want to receive some sort of extrinsic reward, a cash prize for example, then over time what we would expect is a general decline in the quality of their participation. In other words, they're doing it for the "wrong reason."

Rewards are a challenging topic in many cultures, including in the United States, because a great deal of society is set up based on the pursuit of extrinsic prizes. For example, the grades that students receive in school are extrinsic rewards, and when you study the problem deeply, you find that grades can be counterproductive and demotivating. Genuine learning is not related to grades, it's about increasing knowledge, skill, and competence, but if we focus on the grades and not the underlying accomplishments then we trivialize the efforts of the student by treating the grade as a bribe; and we all know that bribery is a form of corruption (see Kohn 1999).[5]

The same dynamic applies to innovation rewards. In most situations we recommend against cash awards, and in favor of recognition and appreciation.

Dan Ariely explores these issues in his fascinating study of behavior, *Predictably Irrational* (2008), and among the themes he delves into is an important distinction between market norms, exchanges for money, and social norms, exchanges and relationships based on community and empathy. He notes, "Money, as it turns out, is very often the most expensive way to motivate people. Social norms are not only cheaper, but often more effective as well" (p. 94).

We have found this be entirely true in the realm of innovation— people respond well to genuine appreciation honestly earned, as innovation efforts in organizations are social and creative endeavors well before they become financial ones.

The Last Word ... Choosing

If you tried to implement all the metrics listed here, you'd probably die of frustration before you got even half way across the measurement desert, so it's obvious that you've got to choose some, start working with them, and then gradually learn to fit the most useful ones into your own world. Think selectively and remember that metrics are a critical part of the learning process, so learning when to measure and how to measure is part of the conversation as well.[6]

---

5. If you wish to read more about this topic, I recommend Alfie Kohn's *Punished by Rewards* (Kohn 1999). It's very good advice for parents also.

THE DARK SIDE OF INNOVATION METRICS _____

Financial metrics are usually easy to determine because the information is readily available. Most financial metrics generally do not capture all the value to the firm. Value-based or value-reflective metrics are more difficult to determine but there are techniques available (Kerzner 2017; Schnapper and Rollins 2006). Another challenge with value metrics is whether the value can be measured incrementally as the project progresses or only after the project's outcomes or deliverables have been completed (Kerzner 2018).

The dark side of financial metrics is that it is usually looked at assuming linear value creation:

- Financial statements generally report linear value creation.
- Linear value creation is based on investments in plants, equipment, raw material purchases, work-in-progress, finished goods inventories, and product sales.
- Linear value measurement looks only at the short-term effects.
- We tend to ignore measurements of innovation and performance values, which are intangible competencies that influence future value.

Intangible assets are more than just goodwill or intellectual property. They also include maximizing human performance.

All metrics have strengths and weaknesses. As an example, market share is a poor metric because anyone can capture market share if the price is low enough. As another example, looking at the number of patents implies that the firm is creating technology for new products. But how did the number of patents affect the business? "The most important thing to remember is that … innovation is a means to an end, not the end itself, and therefore the most important metric is the contribution innovation and product development make to the business" (Lamont 2015). The timing of the measurement is also important. A common argument is that revenue generating metrics such as sales and profits should be looked at over a predetermined time such as two or three years.

Some metrics may be used as linkages. As an example, there can be a linkage between innovation and compensation. The measurement system that links intangible assets to compensation is often subjective and a judgment call. Because of this subjectivity, and the desire to link intangible assets to compensation and incentive pay, there exists the risk that the numbers can be manipulated.

Some metrics are often ignored such as those related to changes in culture and processes (Linder 2006). Another innovation metric that has been ignored until now is innovation leadership effectiveness. Muller et al. (2005) have created a framework that includes innovation leadership metrics:

- Resource view: allocation of resources
- Capability: company competencies
- Leadership: leadership support for innovation

---

6. Two resources were particularly helpful in preparing this chapter. The first is chapter 10 of Scott Anthony's *The Innovator's Guide to Growth* (Harvard Business School Press, 2008). The other is a study by Boston Consulting Group called *Measuring Innovation*, prepared in 2006. You can download it at: www.bcg.com/publications/files/2006_Innovation_Metrics_Survey.pdf.

The use of innovation metrics has appeared in the literature for more than 15 years, but its acceptance has been quite slow because people tend to resist change especially when it removes them from their comfort zone. People tend to be fearful of using new metrics. We knew decades ago that more metrics than just the triple constraints were needed to determine the health of projects, but measurement techniques were in the infancy stages. We then took the simplest approach and trained everyone on the three metrics that were the easiest to measure and report. With innovation project management, the constraints may be on shareholder value created, technology created, and strategic business fit. This may remove many team members from their comfort zone.

Some firms start out with good intentions but either select the wrong metrics or measurement techniques, use misaligned metrics, or have a poor approach for innovation metric identification. Reasons for the struggle with innovation metrics is attributed to:

- Lack of a consistent definition of innovation
- Poor understanding of metrics and measurement techniques
- Lack of guidelines on how to interpret and use the metrics
- Being unsure about the costs for metric measurement

Kuczmarski (2001) provides additional mistakes often made:

- Too many metrics
- Too focused on outcomes
- Too infrequent usage
- Too focused on cost-cutting
- Too focused on the past

In the future, innovation and business value metrics may become as common as time and cost metrics. However, the IPPMO must guard against "metric mania," which is the selection of too many metrics, most of which may lead to confusion and provide no value. When metric mania exists, people have difficulty discovering which metrics provide the valuable information.

ESTABLISHING A METRICS MANAGEMENT PROGRAM

The future of innovation project management must include metrics management. What many people neglect to consider is that the selection of metrics is often based on the constraints imposed on the innovation team:

- Having too few constraints gives the innovation team too much freedom and management may not be able to track performance
- Having too many constraints may lead to severe limitations
- The imposed constraints must be supported by metrics that are relatively easy to measure
- Constraints (and the accompanying priority) can change over the life cycle of an innovation project thus causing changes in the metrics selected

We can now identify certain facts about metrics management:

- You cannot effectively promise deliverables to a stakeholder unless you can also identify measurable metrics.
- Good metrics allow you to catch mistakes before they lead to other mistakes.
- Unless you identify a metrics program that can be understood and used, you are destined to fail.
- Metrics programs may require change, and people tend to dislike change.
- Good metrics are rallying points for the project management team and the stakeholders.
- There are also significant challenges facing organizations in the establishment of value-based metrics:
- Project risks and uncertainties may make it difficult for the project team to identify the right attributes and perform effective measurement of the value attributes.
- The more complex the project, the greater the difficulty is in establishing a single value metric.
- Competition and conflicting priorities among projects can lead to havoc in creating a value metrics program.
- Added pressure by management and the stakeholders to reduce the budget and compress the schedule may have a serious impact on the value metrics.

Metric management programs must also consider relationships with suppliers and contractors as well, especially if a co-creation approach is being used.

- Suppliers, contractors, and stakeholders must understand the metrics being used.
- The metrics must be in a form that all parties can understand in order to take effective corrective action if needed.
- Some decision-making metrics must be sufficiently detailed rather than high level.
- If possible, the metrics should be real-time metrics such that governance personnel can react rapidly to changing market conditions.
- A sufficient number of metrics must be selected such that changes in the marketplace can be determined.
- A combination of metrics may be necessary to understand the marketplace and competitive positioning. One metric by itself may not suffice.
- For partnerships and joint ventures, knowledge transfer metrics must be established and tracked throughout the project life cycle to validate that the alliance is working well.
- Metrics allow us to validate that we have consensus building and systematic planning cooperation rather than complexity and rigidity.
- Terminating alliances can be costly.

Metric management programs must be cultivated. Some facts to consider in establishing such a program include:

- There must be an institutional belief in the value of a metrics management program.
- The belief must be visibly supported by senior management.
- The metrics must be used for informed decision making.
- The metrics must be aligned with corporate objectives as well as project objectives.
- People must be open and receptive to change.
- The organization must be open to using metrics to identify areas of and for performance improvement.
- The organization must be willing to support the identification, collection, measurement, and reporting of metrics.

There are best practices and benefits that can be identified as a result of using metrics management correctly and effectively. Some of the best practices include:

- Confidence in metrics management can be built using success stories.
- Displaying a "wall" of metrics for employees to see is a motivational force.
- Senior management support is essential.
- People must not overreact if the wrong metrics are occasionally chosen.
- Specialized metrics generally provide more meaningful results than generic or core metrics.
- The minimization of the bias in metrics measurement is essential.
- Companies must be able to differentiate between long-term, short-term, and lifetime value.
- The benefits of metrics include:
  - Companies that support metrics management generally outperform those that do not.
  - Companies that establish value-based metrics are able to link the value metrics to employee satisfaction and better business performance.

IMPLICATIONS AND ISSUES FOR PROJECT MANAGERS AND INNOVATION PERSONNEL

Project managers need to understand that the way we look at projects today has changed significantly. Words such as *project value, value-in-use*, and *customer value management initiatives* are extremely important. Some of the critical issues and challenges that may be new for project managers include an understanding of the following:

- Measuring value is important.
- Time, cost, and scope may not be regarded as important as other value attributes.
- Benefits and value are not the same.
- The type of innovation selected can be regarded as a form of benefits realization management.
- Measuring value is complex, but that there are techniques available for value measurement.
- Financial business metrics are not the only ways of reporting business value.
- The intangible assets may be more important than the tangible assets when predicting long-term business success.
- There are a great many metrics available, and metric selection must be based on how and when the metric will be used.
- There is a need for a corporate metrics management program that includes value metrics.

REFERENCES

Alexander, J. (2007). Performance Dashboards and Analysis for Value Creation. Hoboken, NJ: John Wiley & Sons.

Anthony, S. (2008). The Innovator's Guide to Growth. Boston, MA: Harvard Business School Press.

Ariely, D. (2008). Predictably Irrational. New York: Harper Perennial.

Bontis, N. (2009). Linking human capital investment with organizational performance. *Drake Business Review* 1 (2), 8–14. Available at www.drakeintl.co.uk/drakepulse/linking-human-capital-investment-with-organizational-performance. Accessed May 14, 2019.

Boston Consulting Group. (2006). *Measuring innovation.* www.bcg.com/publications/files/2006_Innovation_Metrics_Survey.pdf.

Ivanov, C. and Avasilcăi, S. (2014). Performance measurement models: An analysis for measuring innovation processes performance. *Procedia—Social and Behavioral Sciences* 124, 397–404.

Ken Hultman and Bill Gellerman. (2002). *Balancing Individual and Organizational Values.* San Francisco: Jossey-Bass, 105–106.

Kerzner, H. (2017). Value-based project management metrics. In Project Management Metrics, KPIs and Dashboards (3rd ed.). Hoboken, NJ: John Wiley and Sons, 173–251.

Kerzner, H. (2018). Benefits realization and value management. In Project Management Best Practices: Achieving Global Excellence (4th ed.). Hoboken, NJ: John Wiley and Sons, 715–737.

Kohn, A. (1999). Punished by Rewards: The Trouble with Gold Stars, Incentive Plans, A's, Praise, and Other Bribes. New York: Mariner Books.

Kuczmarski, T. D. (2001). Five fatal flaws of innovation metrics. *Marketing Management* 10 (1), 34–39.

Lamont, J. (2015). Innovation: What are the real metrics? *KM World* 24 (8), 17–19.

Linder, J. (2006). Does innovation drive profitable growth? New metrics for a complete picture. *Journal of Business Strategy* 22 (5), 38–44.

Muller, A., Välikangas, L. and Merlyn, P. (2005). Metrics for innovation: Guidelines for developing a customized suite innovation metrics. *Strategy & Leadership* 33 (1), 37–45.

Ng, H. S., Kee, D. M. H. and Brannan, M. (2011). The role of key intangible performance indicators for organizational success. In *Proceedings of the 8th International Conference on Intellectual Capital, Knowledge, Management & Organizational Learning (The Institute for Knowledge and Innovation Southeast Asia [IKI–SEA] of Bangkok University, 27–28 October 2011)*, vol. 2, pp. 779–787. Reading, UK: Academic Publishing Ltd.

Phillips, J., Bothwell, T. W. and Snead, L. (2002). How to convert business measures to monetary values. In The Project Management Scorecard. Oxford, UK: Butterworth Heinemann.

Porter, M. E. (1985). Competitive Advantage. New York: Free Press.

Schnapper, M. and Rollins, S. (2006). Value-Based Metrics for Improving Results. Ft. Lauderdale, FL: J. Ross Publishing.

Zizlavsky, O. (2016). Framework of innovation management control system. *Journal of Global Business and Technology* 12 (2), 10–27.

8 Business Models

Learning Objectives for Project Managers and Innovation Personnel

To understand what is meant by a business model

To recognize the skills needed to participate in business model development

To recognize the relationship between the firm's business model and innovation activities

To recognize the types of business models

INTRODUCTION

"The business world is littered with the fossils of companies that failed to evolve. Disrupt or be disrupted. There is no middle ground."

"Disruption causes vast sums of money to flow from existing businesses and business models to new entrants."

> — Jay Samit, *Disrupt You! Master Personal Transformation, Seize Opportunity, and Thrive in the Era of Endless Innovation*

Innovation project management can create products and services that have the potential of producing long-term business value. The way the organization delivers and captures the desired value for economic

Innovation Project Management: Methods, Case Studies, and Tools for Managing Innovation Projects,
Second Edition. Harold Kerzner.
© 2023 John Wiley & Sons, Inc. Published 2023 by John Wiley & Sons, Inc.

gain is through the company's business model, which interacts within the marketplace to take advantage of a commercial opportunity. Simply stated, innovation creates value opportunities and business models deliver and capture the value generally in economic terms. Business model development focuses on how a firm intends to maximize the usage of its resources and core competencies.

In theory and practice, the term *business model* is used for a broad range of informal and formal descriptions to represent core aspects of a business, including purpose, business process, target customers, offerings, strategies, infrastructure, organizational structures, sourcing, trading practices, and operational processes and policies including culture. The process of business model construction is part of business strategy and includes innovation project management processes. Business models are used to describe and classify businesses, especially in an entrepreneurial setting, but they are also used by managers inside companies to explore possibilities for future development and to increase competitiveness.

Business model development is most frequently a trial-and-error process. Business models must be reassessed frequently due to rapidly changing markets and a high degree of uncertainty.

Traditional or rational project management is viewed as a structured environment with well-defined requirements at project initiation and constraints on time, cost, and scope. Innovation for new products and services is often considered as work that is free flow, without boundaries, and with very little pressure from the triple constraints of time, cost, and scope. However, this does not mean that innovation projects run forever. All projects have an end, and it may be difficult to identify this end on an innovation project. Is it when all funds have been expended, a critical date has arrived, technology has changed, the customers' tastes or expectations of value have changed, etc.?

Historically, the words *project management* and *innovation* were not used in the same sentence. If they were used together, it would most likely be for technical innovation in a Department of Defense (DOD) contract to create new products and services based on advanced levels of technology. But even then, innovation was limited because of statement of work requirements that excluded out-of-scope work, thus limiting out-of-the-box thinking needed due to project complexity and uncertainty. Improvements in traditional project management focused on adding in more control, rather than increasing the flexibility of the methodology needed for projects such as innovation.

For business model innovation, project managers may find themselves in a completely unfamiliar environment. As examples:

- There may be no statement of work.
- Project managers are brought on board before a business model business case is developed (assume one is developed) and must interface with the customers and users in the marketplace.
- Project managers may need to participate in market research.
- Project managers may need to perform a great many experiments.
- Project managers may have to build and test numerous prototypes.
- Project managers must understand the organization's core competencies concerning resources and capabilities, and how they fit into the design of a business model.
- Project managers may need a completely diverse set of tools for business model innovation.

Mainstream literature on project management would have us believe that we can equate projects and innovation, and that the principles of project management can be applied to all types of innovation projects. Lenfle (2008) argues that a distinction should be made between the various types of projects where project management practices are well-suited. Lenfle's arguments certainly have merit.

In traditional project management, most projects are somewhat confined and have limitations imposed by the business case, the statement of work, the assumptions, and the constraints. There may be some degree of risk and uncertainty, and this can be managed according to the risk management processes in the *PMBOK® Guide*.[1] Traditional project management practices may be appropriate for some innovation projects, such as incremental product or services innovation that focus on existing or modified technology. But as we get into the more complex types of innovation that may lead to a radically new or disruptive marketplace, such as with new platforms, the number of unknowns and the accompanying risks and uncertainty may not be handled effectively using traditional project management practices.

Another critical issue is that when companies change business models, the way they handled risk management previously may not work as well in the new business model. Boeing's 787 project had a completely different set of risks than Boeing's 777 project.

The project environment gets even worse when companies try to use traditional project management for business processes such as business model innovation where you have the greatest degree of risk and uncertainty, where traditional risk management planning will not work, and where a great deal of flexibility is needed for decision making. Different project management approaches, many requiring a high level of flexibility, will be differentiated by the level of technology, the amount of product versus product changes, and whether the impact is expected to disrupt the markets.

FROM PROJECT MANAGER TO DESIGNER

Business model innovation requires that the project manager assume the lead role as the designer of the model. According to Van Der Pilj et al. (2016, 9):

> Design is fundamentally about enhancing the way you look at the world. It's a learnable, repeatable, disciplined process that everyone can use to create unique and qualified value. Design is not about throwing away the processes and tools you have. In fact, quite the opposite is true. Just as design has enabled countless upstarts to create new business models and markets, design will also help you decide when to use what tools in order to learn something new, persuade others to take a different course, and at the end of the day, make better (business) decisions.

Most of all, design is about creating the conditions by which businesses thrive, grow, and evolve in the face of uncertainty and change. As such, better businesses are ones that approach problems in a new, systematic way, focusing more on doing rather than on planning and prediction. Better businesses marry design and strategy to harness opportunity in order to drive growth and change in a world that is uncertain and unpredictable.

The skills needed for the design effort require imagination and experimentation and testing of a variety of models to identify the best approach. As stated by Kaplan (2012, 142–143):

As a Business Model Designer, you will design for change by:

- Leading and contributing to ethnographic fieldwork to generate powerful customer experience observations and insights
- Leading and contributing to design teams through analysis and synthesis of ethnographic work to distill the most important insights leading to transformational business model concepts
- Developing testable business model concepts and prototypes
- Leading and contributing to real-world business model experiments

---

1. *PMBOK* is a registered mark of the Project Management Institute, Inc.

- Creating and implementing frameworks to measure results and impact of business model experiments
- Crafting and executing compelling multimedia stories that help stakeholders understand and connect with the work
- Capturing and packaging learning from business model experiments to inform other efforts and ensure maximum leverage

BUSINESS MODELS AND VALUE

Business models are often treated as value networks. Innovations can take place in processes within the business model to bring added value in each network step. Included in the business model can be the relationships/partnerships and contractual agreements with the suppliers and buyers. The relationship with the suppliers and buyers can be highly advantageous and bring long-term business value to all parties if each party has similar business value drivers such that the business relationship is mutually beneficial to all. In such situations, it becomes important when evaluating potential business partners to make sure that there are similar interpretations of business value so that the business models of each party are complementary. Effective design and enhancements to a business model can give a company a sustainable competitive advantage.

Value is like beauty; it is in the eyes of the beholder. Highly diversified companies may need different business models for whom they are creating value. Typically, customer segments can be classified as mass markets, niche markets, segmented markets, and diversified markets. Each market segment may require a different business model, and each company within the segment may have a different interpretation of the value being provided through your business models.

BUSINESS MODEL CHARACTERISTICS

"Organizations are not designed for innovation. Quite the contrary, they are designed for ongoing operations."

— Vijay Govindarajan, *The Other Side of Innovation: Solving the Execution Challenge*

Every company has a unique business model based on their core competencies and technologies they use. However, there are some generic commonalities between business models. Business model design, as described by Osterwalder and Pigneur (2010), includes the modeling and description of a company's:

- Value propositions (What value and benefits will the customers receive from the products and services?)
- Target customer segments (What desires and expectations do the customers have when purchasing your products and services?)
- Distribution channels (What are the ways that a company keeps in touch with its clients?)
- Customer relationships (What are the different links that a company can use to maintain relations with various market segments?)

- Value configurations (How have we arranged our resources and activities to bring value to our clients?)
- Core capabilities (What are our core competencies that support our business model?)
- Partner network (What are our partnership agreements with other companies that assist us in providing commercialized value?)
- Cost structure (How have we leveraged our financial investments in the business model to provide commercialized value?)
- Revenue generation model (What are the ways in which the business model supports revenue flows?)

Osterwalder refers to these nine items as the business model canvas, which outlines your business model in the shape of a story to describe how you create, deliver, and capture value. IPMs should not assume that the project team understands the company's business model. By preparing a business model canvas, it is easier to understand the business model attributes.

If you have direct competitors that appear to have a good business model, it may be beneficial to create a business model canvas for their business and see their strengths, weaknesses, opportunities, and threats. This may provide you with ideas about your new business model.

STRATEGIC PARTNERSHIPS

It is unrealistic to expect companies to own all the resources needed to remain competitive. Companies view strategic partnerships as a way of building competitive business models. Osterwalder and Pigneur (2010, 38) identify four types of partnerships:

1. Strategic alliances between noncompetitors
2. Cooperation: strategic partnerships between competitors
3. Joint ventures to develop new businesses
4. Buyer–supplier relationships to ensure reliable supplies

There are several benefits in these relationships. The partners either employ or have access to resources that are critical to your business model. The partners can help reduce risk and uncertainty as well assisting you in identifying and responding to threats. You may be able to access new market segments through the business models of your strategic partners.

In traditional project management activities, project managers are accustomed to working with suppliers and partners for the procurement of materials and components. Quite often, these activities are handled through a contract administrator. With IPM activities, the burden of responsibility falls on the IPM who must interface with the partner's business personnel and make business rather than technical decisions. This mandates an understanding of your own business model as well as those of your strategic partners.

BUSINESS INTELLIGENCE

Business intelligence is information that a company needs to make the best business decisions based on facts and evidence rather than just guesses. This information may be stored in a database or data warehouse. Business intelligence technologies provide historical, current, and predictive views of business operations. Common functions of business intelligence technologies include reporting, online analytical processing, analytics, data mining, process mining, complex event processing, business performance management, benchmarking, text mining, predictive analytics, and prescriptive analytics.

Business intelligence can be used by enterprises to support a wide range of business decisions, from operational to strategic. Basic operating decisions include product positioning or pricing. Strategic business decisions involve priorities, goals, and directions at the broadest level.

Business intelligence tools allow organizations to gain insight into new markets, to assess demand and suitability of products and services for different market segments, and to gauge the impact of marketing efforts. This can result in a competitive market advantage and long-term stability. Business intelligence can identify the following:

- Strategic opportunities for new products and services requiring innovation
- Strategic opportunities for improvements in your company's business model
- Strengths and weaknesses in the business models of your competitors
- Strengths and weaknesses in your company's business model and where competitors may attack

Historically, project managers came out of the engineering ranks, and many of them had advanced degrees in a technical discipline. These individuals were strong technically but often had a poor understanding of how the business functions. Business-related decisions were usually placed in the hands of the project sponsors or governance committees.

It is extremely difficult, if not impossible, for IPMs to be involved with business modeling without business knowledge. Some companies, IBM as an example, are encouraging their project managers to become certified by PMI® and to become internally certified by IBM. IBM's internal certification program focuses on IBM's business practices. Companies are now following IBM's lead because almost every project management methodology, whether flexible or inflexible, contains business processes. Some companies believe that project managers of the future will possess significantly more business knowledge than technical knowledge. The argument provided is that a company can always hire a multitude of highly technical people to assist in project decision making, but making effective project-related business decisions, especially for IPMs, may require a strong understanding of the business model and business operations.

SKILLS FOR THE BUSINESS MODEL INNOVATOR

For more than five decades we have attempted to define the core skills that project managers should possess. All of this was done while thinking about the traditional project management approach and the traditional types of projects. For innovation projects, there are additional skills needed. Van Der Pilj et al. (2016, 12–13) list the following (and explain them in detail in their book):

- Keep close contact with the customer (understand your customer not just their transactions with you).
- Think and work visually (on how your business create value).
- Rely on others who possess more information than you have.
- Tell stories and share experiences.
- Keep it simple.
- Set up small experiments.
- Embrace uncertainty.

Developing the right skills implies that you also have the right tools. Van Der Pilj et al. (2016, 265) identify 20 tools that innovation project managers need as part of business model design activities:

1. Screenplays
2. Team charter
3. Vision of five bold steps
4. Vision of cover story
5. Design criteria
6. Storytelling canvas
7. Customer journey
8. Value proposition
9. Context canvas
10. Business model canvas
11. Creative matrix
12. Business model ideation
13. Wall of ideas
14. Innovation matrix
15. Sketching
16. Paper prototype
17. Riskiest assumption
18. Experiment canvas
19. Validation canvas
20. Investment readiness

The traditional tools that are identified in the *PMBOK® Guide* may no longer be appropriate by themselves but may have value in combination with other tools such as these 20 tools.

In traditional project management, the project manager may rely on the business case for the identification of the assumptions. Some project managers may mistakenly believe that the assumptions remain constant for the duration of the project, regardless of the length of the project.

Today, project managers are tracking the assumptions over the full life cycle of the project. For business model design, even small changes in the assumptions regarding consumer behavior, consumer expectations of value, and activities of your competitors can lead to major changes in the design of a business model. Metrics, such as shown in Figure 8-1, can be used to track the assumptions.

Kaplan (2012, 52–53) identifies 15 fundamental principles that define the DNA of business model innovators:

● Connect: Business model innovation is a team sport
  1. Catalyze something bigger than yourself.
  2. Enable ransom collisions of unusual suspects.
  3. Collaborative innovation is the mantra.
  4. Build purposeful networks.
  5. Together, we can design our future.
● Inspire: We do what we are passionate about
  6. Stories can change the world.
  7. Make systems-level thinking sexy.
  8. Transformation is itself a creative act.
  9. Passion rules—exceed your own expectations.
  10. Be inspirational accelerators.

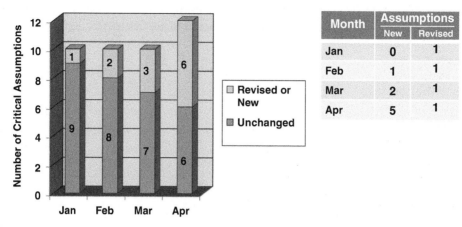

Figure 8–1. Critical Assumptions that Have Been Changed.

- Transform: Incremental change isn't working
  11. Tweaks won't do it.
  12. Experiment all the time.
  13. Get off the whiteboard and into the real world.
  14. It's a user center world; design for it.
  15. A decade is a terrible thing to waste.

Kaplan (2012, 136–137) also identifies 10 behavioral characteristics he uses to recognize someone as a potential innovator:

1. Innovators always think there is a better way.
2. Innovators know that without passion there can be no innovation.
3. Innovators embrace change to a fault.
4. Innovators have a strong point of view but know that they are missing something.
5. Innovators know that innovation is a team sport.
6. Innovators embrace constraints as an opportunity.
7. Innovators celebrate their vulnerability.
8. Innovators openly share their ideas and passions, expecting to be challenged.
9. Innovators know that the best ideas are in the gray areas between silos.
10. Innovators know that a good story can change the world.

BUSINESS MODEL ENHANCEMENTS

Companies invest a great deal of time and effort for innovation for products and services. Unfortunately, considerably less effort is applied to the firm's business model until a threat appears. As stated by Jim Collins (2009, 5):

I've come to see institutional decline like a staged disease: harder to detect but easier to cure in the early stages, easier to detect but harder to cure in the later stages. An institution can look strong on the outside but already be sick on the inside, dangerously on the cusp of a precipitous fall.

Most firms are relatively slow in identifying threats and even when they see them, there is often a complacency attitude and a slow response time in deciding whether enhancements are needed to the existing business model or if a totally new model is needed. The competition between most companies today is between business models, not with the products and services provided (Gassmann et al. 2013). Products and services can be duplicated whereas business models are usually unique to a firm because they tap into the firm's specialized strengths.

Several factors can act as triggers indicating that the business model processes must be reevaluated:

- Changes in consumers' needs for your products and services
- New competitors entering the marketplace
- New suppliers entering the marketplace
- Changing relationships with your strategic partners in the business model
- Significant changes in your firm's core competencies
- Significant changes in the assumptions made about the enterprise environmental factors

Lüttgens and Diener (2016) looked at the threats to a business model using Porter's five forces that describe the competitive forces within an industry. Porter defined the five factors as the bargaining power of buyers, bargaining power of suppliers, competitive rivalry, threats of new entrants, and threats of substitutes. Changes in these five forces can be used as early warning signs or triggers that there are threats to the business model.

In traditional project management, where companies adopt an enterprise project management methodology, the project managers assigned to the PMO perform process improvements on the methodology and monitor the enterprise environmental factors as outlined in the *PMBOK® Guide*. For business model process improvement, the assigned project manager must have a line of sight to senior management, and especially marketing personnel, to monitor the enterprise environmental factors that can impact the business models. The innovations necessary to make changes to a business model and its accompanying processes must be fast and can be more complex than product or service innovations.

The purpose of a business model is to create business value in a profitable manner. Therefore, enhancements must focus on the processes associated with the five dimensions of value (Abdelkafi et al. 2013; Baden-Fuller and Morgan 2010; Beinhocker 2007):

- Value proposition
- Value creation
- Value communication
- Value in distribution channels
- Value capture

The result of process innovations can be either added value or cost reductions.

Core competencies are the building blocks for many forms of business value and serve as the basis for the firm's competitive posture. The core competencies are the combination of the firm's resources, knowledge, and skills, as shown in Figure 8-2, that create core products for the end users. These core products contribute to the competitiveness of the firm by accessing a wide variety of markets and making

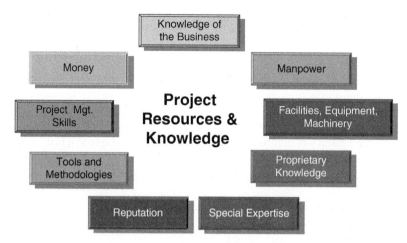

Figure 8–2. Typical Enterprise Resources and Core Competencies.

it difficult for competitors to imitate your products and the accompanying value perceived by the customers. Management must look for ways of improving the core competencies to create new products and new markets.

TYPES OF BUSINESS MODELS

In the 1950s, new business models came from McDonald's restaurants and Toyota. In the 1960s, the innovators were Wal-Mart and hypermarkets. The 1970s saw new business models from FedEx and Toys "R "Us; the 1980s from Blockbuster, Home Depot, Intel, and Dell Computer; the 1990s from Southwest Airlines, Netflix, eBay, Amazon.com, and Starbucks.

Today, the types of business models might depend on how technology is used. For example, entrepreneurs on the Internet have created new models that depend entirely on existing or emergent technology. Using technology, businesses can reach many customers with minimal costs.

The following examples provide an overview for various business model types that have been in discussion since the invention of term *business model*:

- *Bait and hook business model.* This involves offering a basic product at a very low cost, often at a loss (the "bait"), then charging compensatory recurring amounts for refills or associated products or services (the "hook"). Examples include: razor (bait) and blades (hook); cell phones (bait) and air time (hook); computer printers (bait) and ink cartridge refills (hook); and cameras (bait) and prints (hook).

- *Bricks and clicks business model.* Business model by which a company integrates both offline (bricks) and online (clicks) presences. One example of the bricks-and-clicks model is when a chain of stores allows the user to order products online but lets them pick up their order at a local store.
- *Collective business model.* Business system, organization, or association are typically composed of relatively large numbers of businesses, tradespersons or professionals in the same or related fields of endeavor, which pool resources, share information, or provide other benefits for their members.
- *Cutting out the middleman model.* The removal of intermediaries in a supply chain: cutting out the middleman. Instead of going through traditional distribution channels, which had some type of intermediate (such as a distributor, wholesaler, broker, or agent), companies may now deal with every customer directly, for example via the Internet.
- *Direct sales model.* Direct selling is marketing and selling products to consumers directly, away from a fixed retail location. Sales are typically made through party plan, one-to-one demonstrations, and other personal contact arrangements.
- *Distribution business model various fee in, free out.* The business model works by charging the first client a fee for a service, while offering that service free of charge to subsequent clients.
- *Franchise business model.* Franchising is the practice of using another firm's successful business model. For the franchisor, the franchise is an alternative to building 'chain stores' to *distribute* goods and avoid investment and liability over a chain. The franchisor's success is the success of the franchisees. The franchisee is said to have a greater incentive than a direct employee because he or she has a direct stake in the business.
- *Sourcing business model.* Sourcing business models are a systems-based approach to structuring supplier relationships. A sourcing business model is a type of business model that is applied to business relationships where more than one party needs to work with another party to be successful.
- *Freemium business model.* This business model works by offering basic web services, or a basic downloadable digital product, for free, while charging a premium for advanced or special features.
- *Pay what you can (PWYC).* This nonprofit or for-profit business model does not depend on set prices for its goods, but instead asks customers to pay what they feel the product or service is worth to them. It is often used as a promotional tactic but can also be the regular method of doing business. It is a variation on the gift economy and cross-subsidization, in that it depends on reciprocity and trust to succeed.
- *"Pay what you want" (PWYW).* This is sometimes used synonymously with the previous model, but "pay what you can" is often more oriented to charity or socially oriented uses, based more on *ability* to pay, while "pay what you want" is often more broadly oriented to perceived value in combination with willingness and ability to pay.
- *Value-added reseller model.* Value-added reseller (VAR) is a model where a business makes something that is resold by other businesses but with modifications that add value to the original product or service. These modifications or additions are mostly industry specific in nature and are essential for the distribution. Businesses going for a VAR model have to develop a VAR network. It is one of the latest collaborative business models that can help in faster development cycles and is adopted by many technology companies, especially software.

Other examples of business models are:

- Auction business model
- All-in-one business model
- Chemical leasing
- Low-cost carrier business model
- Loyalty business models
- Monopolistic business model
- Multilevel marketing business model
- Network effects business model
- Online auction business model
- Online content business model
- Online media cooperative
- Premium business model
- Professional open-source model
- Pyramid scheme business model
- Servitization of products business model
- Subscription business model

BUSINESS MODELS AND STRATEGIC ALLIANCES

Companies frequently develop close relationships and strategic alliances with companies that are part of the supply chain during innovation activities such as new product development. The result is usually a win–win situation for all parties with the expectation that these relationships will continue for some time into the future. If a new incremental innovation is necessary, the impact on the relationships is usually minor. But if the company is focusing on a disruptive innovation that will result in a new business model, the relationships with the supply chain suppliers can be destroyed if the suppliers believe that the new business model will provide them with fewer benefits than before. As such, the suppliers may not wish to provide support for the disruptive innovation or new business model development if they believe it is not in their best interest.

When a company seeks to disrupt a market by introducing a new product, or responding to disruptions caused by a competitor, the company may need to replace its core competencies with new ones and likewise develop other supply chain relationships. If the company's core competencies are rigid and the company depends heavily on the core competencies of their suppliers, the company may wish to reconsider innovation activities that could result in a new business model that would destroy existing relationships. Characteristics of strategic alliances, adapted from Spekman et al. (2000) include:

- *Trust*. Based on established norms, values, past experiences, and reputation
- *Commitment*. Sharing critical and proprietary information over the long term
- *Interdependence*. Partnership cooperation and dependence on one another for the long term
- *Cultural compatibility*. Trying to align cultures that support a close working relationship
- *Planning and coordination*. A joint effort focusing on the future of the relationship

Most business model designs are impacted by partnerships and alliances in the supply chain. Therefore, any decision to alter a business model without considering the impact on supply chain relationships might be a mistake.

IDENTIFYING BUSINESS MODEL THREATS

There is an old adage that experienced project managers often follow; hope for the best but plan for the worst. The failure of a business model can have catastrophic consequences for a company. When developing a business model, innovators must always ask themselves, what can go wrong? Simply stated, the company must perform risk management and determine the threats to their business model. Sometimes, the threats are not apparent during the development stage. Periodically, companies must therefore reassess all possible threats in time to react appropriately.

There is no standard approach for assessing business model threats. One way to assess threats is by using Porter's five forces, namely (1) entry barriers, (2) exit barriers, (3) bargaining power of suppliers, (4) bargaining power of buyers, and (5) substitute products. As an example, some companies are highly dependent on suppliers for components and materials. We should then assess the threat of what could happen if the supplier is late, refuses to work with us, want to increase their prices, and other such situations.

Another way is to continuously look for triggers or early warning indicators that can lead to discontinuities in the performance of a business model. Examples are shown in Table 8-1.

TABLE 8–1. EXAMPLES OF DISCONTINUITIES AND THEIR TRIGGERS

Triggers/Sources of Discontinuity	Explanation	Problems Posed	Examples of Good and Bad Experiences
New market emerges	Conventional market research/ analytical techniques fail to detect new market.	Established players focused on their existing markets and disregard the threat.	Market that actually emerged was not the one expected or predicted by originators
New technology emerges	Step change occurs either through convergence of several streams or through a single breakthrough.	Occurs beyond periphery of the selection environment. Involves a completely new field or approach.	Ice harvesting to cold storage; valves to solid-state electronics and photos to digital images
New political rules emerge	Political conditions shift dramatically.	Rules of the game, etc. are challenged and established firms fail to understand or learn new rules.	Post-apartheid South Africa and free trade/globalization
Running out of road	There is diminishing space for product and process innovation.	Current system is embedded in a trajectory and subject to steady-state innovation.	Kodak and Encyclopedia Britannica
Sea change in market sentiment or behavior	Public opinion or behavior shifts slowly and then tips over.	Cognitive dissonance.	Apple, Napster, Dell, Microsoft vs. traditional music industry
Deregulation/ shifts in regulatory regime	Political and market pressures lead to shifts in the regulatory framework, resulting in new rules—e.g., liberalization, privatization, or deregulation.	New rules of the game but old mindsets persist and existing player is unable to move fast enough or see new opportunities opened up.	Old monopolies dismantled and new players and/ or /combinations of enterprises emerge
Unthinkable events	Unforeseen events change the world, establishing new rules of the game.	Existing players disempowered/ competencies rendered unnecessary.	9/11
Business model innovations by competitors	New entrant challenges established business models, redefining the problem and, hence, the "rules of the game."	New entrants see a product/service opportunity via a new business model; existing players have to be fast followers.	Amazon.com, Charles Schwab, Southwest and other low-cost airlines

Adapted from W. Phillips et al. 2006 / John Wiley & Sons.

BUSINESS MODEL FAILURE

Senior management must have a vision on how they want the company to compete, now and in the future. This information must be provided to the IPMs responsible for creating or enhancing a business model. Most executives understand that they must compete through business models rather than just products and services, but they lack an understanding of how to do it. The result is usually a doomed business model.

Kaplan (2012, 40–49) identifies 10 reasons and attitudes that cause companies to fail at business model innovation:

1. CEOs don't really want a new business model.
2. Business model innovation will be the next CEO's problem.
3. Product is king—nothing else matters.
4. Information technology is only about keeping the trains moving and lowering costs.
5. Cannibalization is off the table.
6. Nowhere near enough connecting with unusual suspects.
7. Line executives hold your pay card.
8. Great idea; what's the ROI?
9. They shoot business model innovators, don't they?
10. You want to experiment in the real world; are you crazy?

There are seven common mistakes made by senior management:

1. Not realizing that good business models lead to a sustainable competitive advantage
2. Not viewing your business model through the eyes of your customers
3. Building a business model in isolation without considering how your competitors might react and potential threats
4. Building a business model in isolation without considering how you will interact with the business models of your competitors
5. Refusing to build a business model that is new to your firm regardless of whether the competitors have a similar model
6. Believing that your current business model does need to undergo continuous improvement efforts
7. Not understanding that business models are more than just products and services, and must include such items as sales and marketing activities, procurement practices, strategic partnerships, opportunities for vertical integration, and compensation practices

BUSINESS MODELS AND LAWSUITS

When we think about lawsuits involving innovation, we normally consider patent infringement regarding products and technology. Unfortunately, there can also be lawsuits on how a firm decides to implement its business model and its relationships with its clients. The success or failure of most firms is based on how they respond to competition and the strength of the competition. Companies can create superior products and services that give them a competitive advantage and still incur regulatory and litigation issues in the way that it implements its business model. As an example, consider the following regulatory and litigation issues that Intel was faced with.[2]

Patent Infringement Litigation (2006–2007)

In October 2006, a lawsuit was filed by Transmeta Corporation against Intel for patent infringement on computer architecture and power efficiency technologies. The lawsuit was settled in October 2007, with Intel agreeing to pay US$150 million initially and US$20 million per year for the next five years. Both companies agreed to drop lawsuits against each other, while Intel was granted a perpetual nonexclusive license to use current and future patented Transmeta technologies in its chips for 10 years.

Antitrust Allegations and Litigation (2005–2009)

In September 2005, Intel filed a response to a lawsuit by Advanced Micro Devices (AMD), disputing AMD's claims, and claiming that Intel's business practices are fair and lawful. In a rebuttal, Intel deconstructed AMD's offensive strategy and argued that AMD struggled largely as a result of its own bad business decisions, including underinvestment in essential manufacturing capacity and excessive reliance on contracting out chip foundries. Legal analysts predicted the lawsuit would drag on for a number of years since Intel's initial response indicated its unwillingness to settle with AMD. In 2008 a court date was finally set, but in 2009, Intel settled with a $1.25 billion payout to AMD.

On November 4, 2009, New York's attorney general filed an antitrust lawsuit against Intel Corp., claiming the company used "illegal threats and collusion" to dominate the market for computer microprocessors.

On November 12, 2009, AMD agreed to drop the antitrust lawsuit against Intel in exchange for $1.25 billion. A joint press release published by the two chip makers stated, "While the relationship between the two companies has been difficult in the past, this agreement ends the legal disputes and enables the companies to focus all of our efforts on product innovation and development."

Allegations by Japan Fair Trade Commission (2005)

In 2005, the local Fair Trade Commission found that Intel violated the Japanese Antimonopoly Act. The commission ordered Intel to eliminate discounts that had discriminated against AMD. To avoid a trial, Intel agreed to comply with the order.

Allegations by the European Union (2007–2008)

In July 2007, the European Commission accused Intel of anticompetitive practices, mostly against AMD. The allegations, going back to 2003, include giving preferential prices to computer makers buying most or all of their chips from Intel, paying computer makers to delay or cancel the launch of products using AMD chips, and providing chips at below standard cost to governments and educational institutions. Intel responded that the allegations were unfounded and instead qualified its market behavior as consumer-friendly. General counsel Bruce Sewell responded that the Commission had misunderstood some factual assumptions as to pricing and manufacturing costs.

In February 2008, Intel stated that its office in Munich had been raided by European Union regulators. Intel reported that it was cooperating with investigators. Intel faced a fine of up to 10 percent of its

---

2. Adapted from *Wikipedia*, "Intel," https://en.wikipedia.org/wiki/Intel.

annual revenue, if found guilty of stifling competition. AMD subsequently launched a website promoting these allegations. In June 2008, the EU filed new charges against Intel. In May 2009, the EU found that Intel had engaged in anticompetitive practices and subsequently fined Intel €1.06 billion (US$1.44 billion), a record amount. Intel was found to have paid companies, including Acer, Dell, HP, Lenovo, and NEC, to exclusively use Intel chips in their products, and therefore harmed other companies including AMD. The European Commission said that Intel had deliberately acted to keep competitors out of the computer chip market and in doing so had made a "serious and sustained violation of the EU's antitrust rules." In addition to the fine, Intel was ordered by the Commission to immediately cease all illegal practices. Intel has stated that they will appeal against the Commission's verdict. In June 2014, the General Court, which sits below the European Court of Justice, rejected the appeal.

Allegations by Regulators in South Korea (2007)

In September 2007, South Korean regulators accused Intel of breaking antitrust law. The investigation began in February 2006, when officials raided Intel's South Korean offices. The company risked a penalty of up to 3 percent of its annual sales, if found guilty. In June 2008, the Fair Trade Commission ordered Intel to pay a fine of US$25.5 million for taking advantage of its dominant position to offer incentives to major Korean PC manufacturers on the condition of not buying products from AMD.

Allegations by Regulators in the United States (2008–2010)

New York started an investigation of Intel in January 2008 on whether the company violated antitrust laws in pricing and sales of its microprocessors. In June 2008, the Federal Trade Commission also began an antitrust investigation of the case. In December 2009, the FTC announced it would initiate an administrative proceeding against Intel in September 2010.

In November 2009, following a two-year investigation, New York Attorney General Andrew Cuomo sued Intel, accusing the company of bribery and coercion, claiming that Intel bribed computer makers to buy more of their chips than those of their rivals, and threatened to withdraw these payments if the computer makers were perceived as working too closely with its competitors. Intel has denied these claims.

On July 22, 2010, Dell agreed to a settlement with the US Securities and Exchange Commission (SEC) to pay $100M in penalties resulting from charges that Dell did not accurately disclose accounting information to investors. In particular, the SEC charged that from 2002 to 2006, Dell had an agreement with Intel to receive rebates in exchange for not using chips manufactured by AMD. These substantial rebates were not disclosed to investors but were used to help meet investor expectations regarding the company's financial performance: "These exclusivity payments grew from 10 percent of Dell's operating income in FY 2003 to 38 percent in FY 2006 and peaked at 76 percent in the first quarter of FY 2007." Dell eventually did adopt AMD as a secondary supplier in 2006, and Intel subsequently stopped their rebates, causing Dell's financial performance to fall.

IMPLICATIONS AND ISSUES FOR PROJECT MANAGERS AND INNOVATION PERSONNEL

Project managers have traditionally managed innovation activities related to products and services. But now, as project managers get more actively involved in process innovation activities, they need to understand the most important process innovation, the company's business model. Some of the critical issues and challenges that may be new for some project managers include understanding the following:

- Innovation is impacted by the business model, and vice versa.
- Business model innovation may require more experimentation and prototypes than with product and services innovation.
- Significant market research and knowledge of competitors' business models is necessary.
- New skills will be required for business model development.
- Strategic alliances are important in building some business models.
- There are different types of business models.

REFERENCES

Abdelkafi, N., Makhotin, S. and Posselt, T. (2013). Business model innovations for electric mobility – What can be learned from existing business model patterns? *International Journal of Innovation Management* 17 (1), 1–41.

Baden-Fuller, C. and Morgan, M. (2010). Business models as models. *Long Range Planning* 43 (2), 156–171.

Beinhocker, E. D. (2007). *The Origin of Wealth: The Radical Remaking of Economics and What It Means for Business and Society*. Cambridge: Harvard Business School Press.

Collins, J. (2009). *How the Mighty Fall*. New York: HarperCollins.

Gassmann, O., Frankenberger, K. and Csik, M. (2013). *Geschäftsmodelle Entwickeln: 55 Innovative Konzepte mit dem St. Galler Business Model Navigator*. St. Gallen: Carl Hanser Verlag GmbH Co KG.

Kaplan, S. (2012). *The Business Model Innovation Factory*. Hoboken, NJ: John Wiley & Sons.

Lenfle, S. (2008). Exploration and project management. *International Journal of Project Management* 26 (5), 469–478.

Lüttgens, D. and Diener, K. (2016). Business model patterns used as a tool for creating (new) innovative business models. *Journal of Business Models* 4 (3), 19–36.

Osterwalder, A. and Pigneur, Y. (2010). *Business Model Generation: A Handbook for Visionaries, Game Changers, and Challengers*. Hoboken, NJ: John Wiley & Sons.

Spekman, R. E., Isabella, L. A. and MacAvoy, T. C. (2000). *Alliance Competence: Maximizing the Value of Your Partnerships*. New York: John Wiley & Sons.

Van Der Pilj, P., Lokitz, J. and Solomon, L. K. (2016). *Designing a Better Business: New Tools, Skills and Mindset for Strategy and Innovation*. Hoboken, NJ: John Wiley & Sons.

Disruptive Innovation

Learning Objectives for Project Managers and Innovation Personnel
To understand what is meant by disruptive innovation
To recognize the types of disruptive innovation
To recognize the skills needed to work on disruptive innovation projects

INTRODUCTION

In today's business environment, we are faced with challenges and crises due to competition, unstable economies, and sustainability. "Business as usual" is no longer an option for survival, nor is the idea that "we will build it and they will come." Innovations will occur, and many newcomers will disrupt how incumbents conduct their business.

There are many forms of disruptive innovation. Not all disruptive innovations are destructive. Each form may require a different strategic approach and the use of different tools. Failing to understand these differences reduces the chances of success.

There are several categories of innovation, as discussed in Chapter 2. Christensen (1997) classified innovation in two categories:

Innovation Project Management: Methods, Case Studies, and Tools for Managing Innovation Projects,
Second Edition. Harold Kerzner.
© 2023 John Wiley & Sons, Inc. Published 2023 by John Wiley & Sons, Inc.

- *Sustaining innovation.* An innovation that does not significantly affect existing markets. It may be either:
  - Evolutionary: An innovation that improves a product in an existing market in ways that customers are expecting
  - Revolutionary (discontinuous, radical): An innovation that is unexpected, but nevertheless does not affect existing markets
- *Disruptive innovation.* An innovation that creates a new market by providing a different set of (business) values, which ultimately (and unexpectedly) overtakes an existing market

While most people seem to understand what is meant by sustaining innovation and agree to its definition, there are several interpretations of disruptive innovation. Authors who publish papers on disruptive innovation usually provide their definition in the beginning of their work.

The term *disruption* seems to be treated as a buzzword to mean just about anything that leads to a change. As such, the term appears to be meaningless because of the many ways it is being used. There must be a company agreed-on definition of disruptive innovation if the project managers are expected to make business decisions that are aligned with corporate business objectives and in the best interest of the company.

EARLY UNDERSTANDING OF DISRUPTION

"Disruptors don't have to discover something new; they just have to discover a practical use for new discoveries."

— Jay Samit, *Disrupt You!: Master Personal Transformation, Seize Opportunity, and Thrive in the Era of Endless Innovation*

The term *disruptive technologies* was first used by Joseph Bower and Clayton Christensen (Bower and Christensen 1995) and introduced in their 1995 article titled *Disruptive Technologies: Catching the Wave.* The article targeted management executives who made the funding or purchasing decisions in companies, rather than the research community. Christensen then described the term further in his book *The Innovator's Dilemma* (Christensen 1997). *The Innovator's Dilemma* explored the disk drive industry. In his sequel with Michael E. Raynor, *The Innovator's Solution*, (Christensen and Raynor 2003), Christensen replaced the term *disruptive technology* with *disruptive innovation* because he recognized that few technologies are intrinsically disruptive or sustaining in character; rather, it is the business model that the technology enables that creates the disruptive impact. Simply stated, technology by itself is not disruptive. It is how you use the technology that determines its disruptive nature and whether you should follow a disruptive or sustaining path. With both paths there can be an impact on a firm's business model and how and when a firm should interact in the market or industry.

In today's environment, disruptive innovation is used to define a situation that shakes up an industry. This occurs when new entrants challenge incumbent firms that may have superior resources. The new entrants may focus on market segments overlooked by the incumbents or create a market whereby non-consumers become consumers.

Quality and cost are not the only characteristics of a disruptive innovation. There are usually other performance characteristics or functionality that may be deemed important by mainstream customers. The innovation can take place in products, services, and processes. We must remember that many process innovations may alter how we conduct our business but have no impact on sales. In this case, the disruption can occur in how we manage our business.

Nagy et al. (2016) identify three questions that people must address to understand disruptive innovation: "First, what is a disruptive innovation? Second, how can a disruptive innovation be disruptive to some and yet sustaining to others? Third, how can disruptive innovations be identified before a disruption has occurred in an organization?" Even though there are a multitude of articles published on disruptive innovation, there does not exist a universally agreed on answers to these questions. Managers who seem to understand the answers to these questions are more likely to respond favorably to disruptive innovations that affect their firm and turn a potential disaster or business disruption into an opportunity.

Much of the literature on innovation uses the terms disruptive innovation and radical innovation interchangeably. Hopp et al. (2018) differentiate between them:

> Radical innovations … stem from the creation of new knowledge and the commercialization of completely novel ideas or products. Research on radical innovation therefore focuses on the types of organizational behavior and structures that explain and predict the commercialization of breakthrough ideas.

INNOVATION AND THE BUSINESS MODEL DISRUPTION

"When rate of problems is greater than rate of solutions, only radical changes can make the difference."
— Sukant Ratnakar

There are numerous business models in industry, and each model is based on types of targeted customers. We identify five types of customers in a business model that may be impacted by innovation:

1. Satisfied customers
2. Unsatisfied customers (not happy with offerings)
3. Wannabe customers (appeals but out of reach)
4. Refusers (aware but cannot see relevance)
5. Unexplored customers (unconsidered audience)

At the high end of the business model are satisfied customers who provide repeat business to incumbent, well-established businesses. The incumbent businesses are generally quite happy with the profit margins and focus mainly on incremental innovation rather than disruptive innovation. Disruptive innovations can occur at this end of the spectrum, especially if there is a major change in technology, but it is more likely that disruptions will occur at the low end.

Incumbents may be fearful of innovations that can cause them to lose the profits from their most demanding customers. As such, there is generally a close working relationship between the incumbents and the existing customers to give them what they want and possibly more. Incremental innovation at the high end often results in a technology overshoot situation, where the incumbents focus on a "featuritis" mentality and provide more features to their products and services than the customers' need or want. The customers may not ever use the added value provided, but they still appear loyal to the incumbent companies.

We have all heard expressions such as "Listen to the voice of the customer," "Give the customers what they want," "Stay close to the customer," and "Let's do better with updates." These expressions drive sustaining or incremental innovation rather than disruptive innovation. While it is true that technology can change and eventually lead to disruptive innovation, incremental changes are more likely. Customers at the high end that are happy with their products and services may want to see just incremental changes rather than radical changes based on a recent technology. These customers may reject certain technological changes in favor of the status quo when, in fact, the rejections could very well replace existing technology sometime later.

Incremental innovation feeds short-term cash flow and revenue generation, often at the expense of forgoing long-term consideration. Incremental innovation may use the company's R&D guidelines or a project management methodology that the project manager must use. The methodology is part of the company's business model and may not encourage project teams to think outside of the box. The larger the company, the greater the difficulty to innovate outside of the existing business model. As such, project managers then staff the projects with resources that have expertise in incremental innovation rather than technological or disruptive innovation.

Disruptive innovation usually begins at the low end of the business model where products and services are created for a new set of customers. Christensen and Raynor (2003) distinguish between "low-end disruption," which targets customers who do not need the full performance valued by customers at the high end of the market, and "new-market disruption," which targets customers who have needs that were previously unserved by existing incumbents.

According to Christensen et al. (2015), *disruption* describes a process whereby a smaller company with fewer resources can successfully challenge established incumbent businesses. Specifically, as incumbents focus on improving their products and services for their most demanding (and usually most profitable) customers, they exceed the needs of some market segments and ignore the needs of others. New entrants to the market begin the disruptive process by successfully targeting those overlooked segments and gaining a foothold by delivering more-suitable functionality—frequently at a lower price. Incumbents, chasing higher profitability in more-demanding segments, tend not to respond vigorously. Entrants then move upmarket, delivering the performance that incumbents' mainstream customers require, while preserving the advantages that drove their early success. When mainstream customers start adopting the entrants' offerings in volume, disruption has occurred.

To be disruptive, a business must first gain acceptance in the low end of the market, the segment by and large ignored by incumbents in lieu of more profitable high-end customers. A prime example is Netflix, which was founded in 1997. In 2008, Jim Keyes, CEO of Blockbuster, commented, "Neither Redbox or Netflix are even on the radar screen in terms of competition." In 2011, Blockbuster went bankrupt. As summarized by Hopp et al. (2018):

> The initial mail-order movie rental business was not appealing to a large group of Blockbuster customers. It appealed to a niche of film nerds. Only with the rise of technology, including eventually the ability to stream over the Internet, was Netflix able to grow its business and eventually offer on-demand movies and TV to a huge audience, conveniently and cost-effectively. It was the initial encroachment from the low-end of the market that made Netflix disruptive. A focus on a larger market segment initially might have induced a fighting response by Blockbuster. Gaining a low-end foothold allowed Netflix to move upmarket with a completely different business model that was eventually attractive to Blockbuster's core customers. The Netflix case also shows that disruption may take time…. Now, Netflix is targeting other entertainment providers and is set to disrupt yet another part of its industry.

Many of the companies that were hurt by disruptive innovations were well-managed companies that had excellent research and development departments and were responsive to the needs of their customers.

The mistake they made was ignoring those parts of the market that were most susceptible to disruptive innovations because they were too small to provide an acceptable growth rate that the larger firm desired, the profits margins were lower than expected, or simply there were no apparent competitive threats forecasted in the industry. As stated by Mark Parker, CEO Nike, "Companies fall apart when their [business] model is so successful that it stifles thinking that challenges it." This is often referred to as the failure of success.

Disruption can be beneficial if a firm responds rapidly, has the right vision about the future, and can modify its business model in a timely manner. The launch of the Internet disrupted the traditional newspaper industry by eliminating advertising revenue from clients that could expose themselves to a greater market over the Internet and at a lower cost. Book stores and travel agencies also suffered, and many never recovered. Retailers also suffered but those that saw the benefits of Internet marketing quickly converted to a catalog retailer environment.

CATEGORIES OF DISRUPTIVE INNOVATIONS

There are categories of disruption the same way there are categories of innovation. The simplest forms of disruptive innovations are viewed as being either "low-end disruptions" or "high-end disruptions."

Low-end disruption occurs when the rate at which products improve exceeds the rate at which customers can adopt the new performance. Therefore, at some point the performance of the product no longer underperforms on product attributes important to the customers and overshoots the needs of certain customer segments even though these attributes may not be highly valued by the customers. At this point, a disruptive technology may enter the market and provide a product that has lower performance than the incumbent but that exceeds the requirements of certain segments, thereby gaining a foothold in the market.

In low-end disruption, the disruptor is focused initially on serving the least profitable customer, who is happy with a good enough product. This type of customer is most likely price-sensitive and not willing to pay a premium for enhancements in product functionality. Once the disruptor has gained a foothold in this customer segment, it seeks to improve its profit margin. To get higher profit margins, the disruptor needs to enter the segment where the customer is willing to pay a little more for higher quality. To ensure this quality in its product, the disruptor needs to innovate. The incumbent will not do much to retain its share in a not-so-profitable segment and will move up-market and focus on its more attractive customers. After several of such encounters, the incumbent is squeezed into smaller markets than it was previously serving. And then, finally, the disruptive technology meets the demands of the most profitable segment and drives the established company out of the market.

High-end disruptive innovations, on the other hand, are generally more technologically radical in nature. Their appeal is based on technological advancements or added functionality and not limited to the price-sensitive customer.

The term *disruptive innovation* tends to be misleading because people use it to refer to a product or service at one fixed point, such as low-end or high-end, rather than to the evolution of that product or service over time. Innovation may not have anything to do with technology. Innovation may simply be the impact that a new product or service has on changing a firm's business model to capture untapped markets.

Part of the section "Categories of Disruptive Innovations" has been adapted from Wikipedia, "Disruptive Innovation," https://en.wikipedia.org/wiki/Disruptive_innovation.

Dru (2015) focuses on the path to destructive innovation rather than what occurs at a fixed point in time related to technology or product price. Dru discussed 15 paths:

1. Open disruption
2. Structural disruption
3. Asset-based disruption
4. Reverse disruption
5. Sustainability-driven disruption
6. Revival-based disruption
7. Data-driven disruption
8. Usage-based disruption
9. Price-led disruption
10. Added-service disruption
11. Partnership-led disruption
12. Brand-led disruption
13. Insight-driven disruption
14. Business model disruption
15. Anticipation-driven disruption

There are three reasons why Dru's approach is important to innovation project managers. First, project managers are responsible for managing the paths that lead to innovation. Second, because each path chosen is directly related to changes in the company's business model, marketing's involvement is mandatory especially in developing the business case for the selected path. Third, Dru reinforces the understanding that there is a strong bond between innovation and marketing. Peter Drucker (1954) stated in his book *The Practice of Management*, "Because the purpose of business is to create a customer, the business enterprise has two—and only two—functions: marketing and innovation. Marketing and innovation produce results: all the rest are costs." Most innovations are marketing-driven innovations.

The marketing-innovation bond is critical for success. There are four steps in disruptive innovation that are common to most of the paths:

1. Identify the market segments overlooked, add more functionality and features to your products and services, and then be prepared to sell the products and services at a lower price than the competitors.
2. Improve quality such that you can differentiate your products from your competitors. This is the step where you begin attracting customers and disrupt the market.
3. Sales volume increases and disruption is in full force.
4. Customers see the value in your products and services and are willing to switch over.

THE DARK SIDE OF DISRUPTIVE INNOVATION

Disruptive innovation generally addresses how a new product or service can disrupt new and existing customers in the marketplace. Unfortunately, in the process of developing new products and services, a company might find that the disruption to its own business model has occurred.

As an example, a company decided that it could speed up the delivery of its products to its customers by creating several software programs that could be used as part of their logistics and supply chain management activities, which were currently labor-intensive. This would speed up order entry, order preparation, and billing. Everyone understood that this innovation would generate more customers and increase profitability.

As the company began implementation and testing of the newly created software, workers recognized that the new system would eliminate several of their jobs. Workers began sabotaging the system to remain employed. It took the company almost six months to correct the damage that was created.

Internal disruption can occur while companies are attempting to disrupt the marketplace. Companies must proceed cautiously and understand the impact that their actions will have on their own business and business model.

USING INTEGRATED PRODUCT/PROJECT TEAMS

"High Performance Teams create cultures of caring, connection, commitment, collaboration and clear consistent communication."

—Tony Dovale

A team must be assembled to either cause market disruption or to respond to a disruption that has occurred. Making the decision to launch a new product or service and disrupt the marketplace is a lot easier than being able to do it. If the change is incremental, then the members of the team may be part-time. If the change is disruptive or radical, then the team members would probably be assigned on a full-time basis. Most companies seem to prefer full-time assignments for staffing innovation teams because one of the questions that has challenged scholars for decades involves how innovative workers can be on a part-time basis.

The team may be responsible just for the launch of the new product or service rather than also having to develop the technology. The technology may already exist or is being developed by an R&D group.

In recent years, there has been an effort to substantially improve the formation and makeup of teams required to develop a new product or implement a new practice. These teams have membership from across the entire organization and are called integrated product/project teams (IPTs), venture teams, or entrepreneurial teams.

The IPT consists of a sponsor, a program/project manager, and the core team. If the technology already exists, and the team's mission is disruptive innovation, the sponsor most likely would come from marketing because of their knowledge of the target market and how companies may respond. As stated by Reinhardt and Gurtner (2015):

> Customer value, customer satisfaction, customization and many other central management concepts have one joint premise—acquiring knowledge about customers. The process of understanding why consumers become customers of a firm becomes particularly important when firms develop new products and services.

For the most part, members of the core team are assigned full-time to the team but may not be on the team for the duration of the entire project. The membership of the team can change as we go from low-end to high-end market disruption. Team members should possess at least a cursory understanding about disruptive innovation.

The skills needed to be a member of the core team to focus on disruptive innovation include:

- Self-starter ability
- Work without supervision

- Good communications skills
- Cooperative
- Technical understanding
- Willing to learn backup skills if necessary
- Able to perform feasibility studies and cost/benefit analyses
- Able to perform or assist in market research studies
- Able to evaluate asset utilization
- Willingness to make decisions in a timely manner
- Knowledgeable in risk management
- Understand the need for continuous validation

IPTs must be staffed with creative thinkers and be able to think out of the box. They must have the freedom to explore, within limits, and test their ideas. Therefore, traditional R&D guidelines may be inappropriate, too conventional, and restrictive.

Each IPT is given a project charter that identifies the project's mission and the assigned project/program manager or innovation leader. However, unlike traditional charters, the IPT charter can also identify the key members of the IPT by name or job responsibility.

All IPT members must understand the business model and how value is created and distributed through the model. Even though the team has a specific customer targeted for the innovation, there could be tangential customers that may be directly or indirectly affected by the disruptive innovation. As stated by Kumar (2013, 197):

> An innovator in the U.S. healthcare, for example, needs to think not only in terms of the valuable offerings for patients or doctors, but also the opportunities to create value for other stakeholders in the system such as hospitals, pharmacies, insurance companies, and drug-makers—all players with a huge financial stake in the system. Even a good mental model to imagine how value flows between all the stakeholders in the system can be a good diagnostic tool for finding out where the most valuable opportunities for innovation might be.

IPTs that are involved with new product development activities may need legal representation on the team because of patents, copyrights, trademarks, and potential risks such as from product tampering. Corporate legal may provide this support as needed rather than having full-time legal representatives assigned.

Unlike traditional project teams, the IPT thrives on sharing information across the team and collective decision making in a timely manner. IPTs eventually develop their own culture and, as such, can function in either a formal or informal capacity. However, companies seem to prefer the creation of a separate functional group for these ventures.

Since the concept of an IPT is well suited to large, long-term projects, it is no wonder that the Department of Defense has been researching best practices for an IPT.[1] The government looked at four projects, in both the public and private sectors, which were highly successful using the IPT approach and four government projects that had less than acceptable results. The successful IPT projects are shown in Table 9-1. The unsuccessful IPT projects are shown in Table 9-2. The government research indicated that the greater the number of times decisions must be made by executives or stakeholders outside of

---

1. *DoD Teaming Practices Not Achieving Potential Results*, Best Practices Series, GOA-01-501, Government Accounting Office, April 10, 2001. Available at www.gao.gov/products/GAO-01-510.

TABLE 9–1. EFFECTIVE IPTS

Program	Cost Status	Schedule Status	Performance Status
Daimler-Chrysler	Product cost was lowered	Decreased development cycle months by 50%	Improved vehicle designs
Hewlett-Packard	Lowered cost by over 60%	Shortened development schedule by over 60%	Improved system integration and product design
3M	Outperformed cost goals	Product deliveries shortened by 12–18 months	Improved performance by 80%
Advanced Amphibious Assault Vehicle	Product unit cost lower than original estimate	Ahead of original development schedule	Demonstrated fivefold increase in speed

TABLE 9–2. INEFFECTIVE IPTS

Program	Cost Status	Schedule Status	Performance Status
CH-60S Helicopter	Increased cost but due to additional purchases	Schedule delayed	Software and structural difficulties
Extended Range Guided Munitions	Increases in development costs	Schedule slipped 3 years	Redesigning due to technical difficulties
Global Broadcast Service	Experiencing cost growth	Schedule slipped 1.5 years	Software and hardware design shortfalls
Land Warrior	Cost increase of about 50%	Schedule delayed 4 years	Overweight equipment, inadequate battery power, and design

the team, the more likely it is that the time, cost, and performance constraints will not be achieved. The research confirmed that if the IPT has the knowledge necessary to make decisions and the authority to make the decisions, then the desired performance would be achieved, and schedule slippages would be less likely to occur.

The success of the IPT or venture team is heavily dependent on the corporation's attitude toward the ventures that allows the product/program managers to take the necessary steps to be competitive (Crockett et al. 2013). The corporation must give the team some degree of autonomy to make high-level decisions, resolve conflicts, and take risks. The corporation must give the team access to superior human and financial resources. All the support, which includes insulating the team from political battles, must be visible and real rather than lip service.

DISRUPTIVE INNOVATION IN ACTION

One of the key success factors in disruptive innovation is that ideas and solutions tend to come from those not weighed down by what went before. IPTs must be willing to challenge everything using what-if scenarios.

Project managers are now recognizing that the assumptions made at the beginning of a project may change throughout the life of the project and that all the assumptions must be tracked and challenged frequently. If the assumptions change, you could be making the wrong decisions or working on the wrong project. Kumar (2013) provides examples shown in Table 9-3 of what happens when assumptions are challenged. Kumar states:

TABLE 9–3. EXAMPLES OF CHALLENGING ASSUMPTIONS

Organization	From Assumptions...	To New Ways...
Amazon	Mass-market book advertising	Personalized reading recommendations based on your navigation history
Apple	MP3 players	Managing personal music collections
Netflix	Brick-and-mortar movie rentals on daily rates	Online managed library and home delivery (mailing DVD and instant streaming) on a subscription basis
Nike	Shoes	Supporting runners in meeting goals

It is normal for organizations to follow the norms that their industry has established for years. But is it possible to recognize those norms as assumptions and find out if they are still relevant in these rapidly changing times? Are there other ways, new ways, to provide something new, even if they mean disrupting the industry behaviors? And is it possible to do this without losing sight of the core fundamental objectives of meeting peoples' needs and fitting well with their context? (p. 197)

Organizations that create disruptive innovations and become successful are often leaders in exercising this mindset—abandoning conventional models and adopting new ways of thinking. Table 9-3 shows a few examples of organizations that challenged assumptions in a timely manner and reframed their solution space, opening up dramatically new opportunities for products and services.

When disruptive innovation is effective, significant rewards and future opportunities occur. For the incumbents that were unable to see the forest for the trees, their next step may be the need for crisis-driven innovations just to survive. As stated by Gibson (2015, 100):

This is why disruptive innovation newcomers have a big advantage. The come into an existing industry without having any of the preconceptions that blind incumbents to revolutionary opportunities. They have no attachment to the established industry molds that have been long producing the same products and services. Instead, they feel free to break those molds and set up their own unique approach to things. They typically leverage an innovative technology, a fresh product idea, a truly novel service concept, or a game-changing business model to reinvent a stagnant industry and often seize the dominant position away from some sleepy incumbent.

...Suddenly an organization [i.e., an incumbent] is forced fundamentally to rethink what it is doing and where it is going when there is probably no longer enough time to make the changes necessary for survival. When you're going full speed ahead in what turns out to be the wrong direction, it can be almost impossible to quickly and radically turn a company around without having a fatal or near-fatal crash.

When companies cannot react rapidly to an attack on their business, disaster can occur, as shown in Table 9-4.

IMPLICATIONS AND ISSUES FOR PROJECT MANAGERS AND INNOVATION PERSONNEL

Project managers are often placed in charge of innovation projects that are designed to either create disruption in the marketplace or respond to disruption caused by competitors. These types of projects occur

TABLE 9–4.   DISRUPTION WINNERS AND LOSERS

Winner	Loser
Apple	Record companies (i.e., Tower records)
Amazon	Bookstores (i.e., Borders)
Google	Encyclopedias and libraries
Craigslist	Local newspapers
Online education	Colleges and universities
Email	United States Postal Service

less frequently than others, and some project managers may feel uncomfortable being involved in these projects. Most PMs therefore may possess a poor understanding about disruption activities. Some of the critical issues and challenges that may be new for some project managers include an understanding of the following:

● Know what disruptive innovation really means.
● Understand why disruption occurs.
● Identify the relationship between disruptive innovation and business models.
● Identify the categories of disruptive innovation.
● The skills needed to work with disruptive innovation may be different than the skills needed for other forms of innovation.
● Integrated project teams will be needed for some forms of disruptive innovation.

REFERENCES

Bower, J. L. and Christensen, C. M. (1995). Disruptive technologies: Catching the wave. *Harvard Business Review* 73 (1), 43–53.

Christensen, C. (1997). *The Innovator's Dilemma: When New Technologies Cause Great Firms to Fail*. Boston: Harvard Business School Press.

Christensen, C. and Raynor, M. (2003). *The Innovator's Solution: Creating and Sustaining Successful Growth*. Boston: Harvard Business School Press.

Christensen, C., Raynor, M. and McDonald, R. (2015). What is disruptive innovation? Harvard Business Review, December, 44–53.

Crockett, D. R., McGee, J. E. and Payne, G. T. (2013). Employing new business divisions to exploit disruptive innovations: The interplay between characteristics of the corporation and those of the venture management team. *Journal of Product Innovation Management* 30 (5), 856–879.

Dru, J. (2015). *The Ways to New: 15 Paths to Disruptive Innovation*. Hoboken, NJ: John Wiley and Sons.

Drucker, P. (1954). *The Practice of Management*. New York: Harper & Brothers.

Gibson, R. (2015). *The 4 Lenses of Innovation*: A Power Tool for Creative Thinking. Hoboken, NJ: John Wiley & Sons.

Hopp, C., Antons, D., Kaminski, J. and Salge, T. O. (2018). What 40 years of research reveals about the difference between disruptive and radical innovation. *Harvard Business Review* (April 9). Available at https://hbr.org/2018/04/what-40-years-of-research-reveals-about-the-difference-between-disruptive-and-radical-innovation.

Kumar, V. (2013). *101 Design Methods: A Structured Approach for Driving Innovation in Your Organizatio*n. Hoboken, NJ: John Wiley and Sons.

Nagy, D., Schuessler, J. and Dubinsky, A. (2016). Defining and identifying disruptive innovations. *Industrial Marketing Management* 57, 119–126.

Reinhardt, R. and Gurtner, S. (2015). Differences between early adopters of disruptive and sustaining innovations. *Journal of Business Research* 68, 137–145.

Innovation Roadblocks

10

Learning Objectives for Project Managers and Innovation Personnel
To understand what is meant by an innovation roadblock
To recognize the underlying causes of the roadblocks and what actions can be taken
To understand that they may need support from the governance team to get through the
  roadblocks

INTRODUCTION

Roadblocks are barriers, barricades, impediments, or obstructions that can prevent a project manager from taking a desired course of action. For some roadblocks, the project manager can create work-around activities to prevent costly delays. On others, such as approvals or legal issues, the PM may not be able to circumvent the roadblock and may have to fight through it with the help of others. There are several roadblocks that can impact innovation success and many of the roadblocks cannot be predicted.

Innovation Project Management: Methods, Case Studies, and Tools for Managing Innovation Projects,
Second Edition. Harold Kerzner.
© 2023 John Wiley & Sons, Inc. Published 2023 by John Wiley & Sons, Inc.

THE FAILURE OF SUCCESS

Past success is no guarantee of future performance. "The failure of success" occurs when companies become so successful that they refuse to challenge results. You can go from "best in class" to "worst in class" with a loss of innovation capability. As stated by Charles E. Sorenson ([1956] 2006):

> It isn't the incompetent who destroy an organization. The incompetent never get into a position to destroy it. It is those who achieved something and want to rest upon their achievements who are forever clogging things up. (p. 51)

Some articles call the failure of success as the competency trap where people argue that the company is doing well and there is no reason to change.

ONE SIZE FITS ALL

This blockage has some of the same characteristics as the failure of success blockage. Some companies spend a great amount of time and effort developing a project management methodology that has been proven to be successful on some types of projects. These traditional methodologies follow linear thinking and the stage-gate approach for monitoring and controlling projects.

But because of the diversity of innovation projects, especially those projects that require free thinking and cannot be accomplished with linear thinking, the company may avoid working on certain types of innovation because it is not a good fit with the methodology they have. Thus, opportunities are lost.

INSUFFICIENT LINE OF SIGHT

In a traditional project management environment, the project manager relies heavily on the information in the business case for the project. In an innovation environment, the business case may be prepared around high-level goals rather than detailed strategic business objectives, and the accompanying assumptions and constraints may be incomplete. Without the correct information, and all the information, the innovation project manager may have a tough time targeting the innovation.

IPMs need a line of sight to the senior echelons of management to ensure that they have all the necessary information. The line of sight needs to include face-to-face communications rather than expecting everything to appear in the business case. There may be additional information that executives do not want to publicly expose in the wording of the business case. These may also be additional assumptions and constraints that are not apparent.

The answers to the following questions, which focus on the strategic target and may not be addressed in the business case, may have a bearing on decisions that must be made during the innovation process:

- Are the goals short-term or long-term?
- Is this a product or service to enter a new market, and is the market global or restricted?
- Is this a product or service to penetrate deeper into an existing market, and is the market global or restricted?
- Is this product or service intended to support an existing product line?

- Is this a further improvement in performance of an existing product or service?
- If this is process innovation, is the intent to improve the business model or for cost-reduction efforts?

FAILING TO SEARCH FOR IDEAS

Some cultures do not know how to take advantage of the talented people in their organization by getting them to contribute ideas for new products or services, or even for continuous improvement efforts. In these cultures, people are rewarded for following instructions and the R&D is expected to come up will all new ideas.

The wrong culture can also stifle creativity if people are not rewarded for coming up with a creative idea that leads to commercialization. There are many ways that employee recognition can be achieved without monetary rewards.

SENSE OF URGENCY

Pressure from stakeholders can have a detrimental effect on innovation. Common stakeholder pressures placed on an innovation team include:

- Shorter product life cycles
- Increase in competitiveness
- Faster time to market
- Execution with fewer resources
- Higher performance requirements
- Better quality

The most common pressure is the acceleration of the schedule. While schedules are important to many stakeholders, deadlines should not be established such that there are significant increases in performance risk or product liability. Schedules usually put people under pressure to excel and to be creative in a timely manner, but there are risks. Time constraints often force companies to launch products with known defects just to placate stakeholders. Innovation will then continue to improve the product and remove the defects. Then the company announces a recall to replace the defective products with a newer version.

There are several examples of this in industry where lives were lost because of the defective products. Because the cost of large recall can be expensive and erode all the profitability that was expected from the product, some companies delay the recall as long as possible, knowing full well that deaths can occur.

WORKING WITH PRIMA DONNAS

If advanced stages of technology are required, innovation often requires staffing the project with the most innovative technical personnel. Most of these people will make decisions in the best interest of the company. However, there are always a few who desire to act and be treated as prima donnas.

These people believe that organizational or technical status and reputation is more important than the outcome of the project. Thus, they often withhold the truth about the status of the project until such a time where disclosure of the status will benefit them personally. These people are not happy with just meeting specifications and requirements. Their motivation is to exceed performance requirements and expectations, often at the expense of the project. The project may have been completed, but their desire to enhance their reputation takes precedence.

LACK OF COLLABORATION

Companies that have an inflexible project management methodology that may have taken years to develop rely heavily on the accompanying forms, guidelines, templates, and checklists as the primary means of communication. Collaboration is only used when there are problems that need to be resolved or action items.

In an innovation environment, lack of collaboration can be costly and time-consuming. Collaboration is needed to overcome roadblocks such as a sense of urgency, line of sight, and working with prima donnas. Innovation outcomes provide greater business value when people collaborate freely.

POLITICS

Politics, if not controlled, can alter the direction of innovation, add complexity to the decision-making processes and destroy team morale. When dealing with external stakeholders, project governance should insulate the innovation teams from politics if possible. With internal stakeholders, the situation can become complex if political intervention is created by the governance committee.

Some stakeholders may view a project as having an impact on their career and opportunities for advancement. Therefore, their personal agenda may become more important than the outcome of the project.

PROJECT WORKLOADS

In a utopian environment where unlimited funding is available for staffing projects and the company's cash flow is good, we can obtain the best resources for the project and assign them on a full-time basis. Unfortunately, in almost all companies, project workloads must be balanced with functional workloads necessary to support the day-to-day operations.

Roadblocks exist when the assigned resources lack the skills needed for the innovation. Sometimes, we do not know what skills are needed until we get well into the project. There is also the argument that people cannot be truly creative on a part-time basis. IPMs would prefer if all the critical resources were assigned full time, perhaps on a venture team, but this may be unrealistic. The greater the skills of the workers, the greater the demand for their services on other projects.

INTELLECTUAL PROPERTY RIGHTS

Creating intellectual property or obtaining licensing rights from a patent holder requires decision making from the firm's legal group. The decisions that the legal group make can significantly alter the direction of the innovation project and the decisions to be made. The legal group may wish to avoid any potential patent infringement situations that could create downstream financial headaches and delay the commercialization and launch of a product or service. Therefore, they may demand that all innovations not be related to the patent.

Taking out a patent for newly created intellectual property is an easy decision to make. But what happens if people on the innovation team want to publish a paper on their results or make a presentation at a conference? Publishing a paper exposes the work you are doing to competitors who may then aggressively conduct their own innovation based on your ideas. You could then be breeding competitors.

When publishing a paper, the information is usually reviewed several times to make sure that no additional information is provided beyond what was disclosed in the patent. However, when innovation personnel present papers at conferences, they are usually quite proud of their accomplishments and may provide additional company proprietary information that was not part of the patent. This can happen if there are extremely knowledgeable people in the audience that may have conducted similar research and know what specific questions to ask during the Q&A session. This is one of the reasons why companies may have restrictions on what information can be presented at conferences by innovation personnel.

Sometimes, the research you are doing requires you to obtain a license from the patent holder. This can speed up the innovation process but may require that royalties be paid based on any products or services using the patent. Without the license, the innovation team will be pressured to develop noninfringing products or services that may be costlier and take longer to commercialize than they would by obtaining a licensing agreement. One of the major benefits of a licensing agreement is that it may contain much-needed information that is not disclosed in the patent. This can motivate the innovation team to further continue their efforts, knowing that what they create may still be protected by the original patent.

There is also a risk in publicizing that you are a licensee because your competitors and downstream innovators will understand that you did not purchase the license and commit funding to innovation without expecting to create profitable products and services. Therefore, publicizing it may increase the competition.

NOT UNDERSTANDING THE RELATIONSHIP BETWEEN CREATIVITY AND INNOVATION

Innovation is the conversion of an idea into a product or service. The roadblock is in the way that a company will handle the ideas that come from brainstorming. Most companies do not have processes in place to effectively plan for, evaluate, and manage the ideas that come from a brainstorming session. Brainstorming does not fail. The failure is in what happens prior to the start of the brainstorming session and after the brainstorming session is over.

The line-of-sight roadblock must be eliminated prior to the start of the brainstorming session. The brainstorming team must have a good understanding of management's expectations concerning the short-term and long-term strategic goals and objectives so that they can come up with the best ideas for the creation of tangible value. People put forth a lot of time and effort coming up with ideas and may develop supporting data when possible. If the ideas are then immediately shot down by management because it was not what they were expecting, the organization may have wasted a lot of time and money as well as lowering morale. When the line-of-sight roadblock is eliminated, executives find it easier to provide feedback and constructive criticism for the ideas, which may then motivate people to introduce even better ideas.

Truly innovative personnel work in the unknown and possibly in unexplored environments. They may come up with an idea and some test data that is on the verge of a potential breakthrough just to have someone pull the plug because of schedule and budgetary constraints. This also creates a roadblock to innovation. Companies must have a reasonable process in place for evaluating ideas in certain stages of development rather than just arbitrarily pulling the plug because of constraints.

TOO MANY ASSUMPTIONS

Previously, we discussed the risk of not tracking assumptions and then, at an inappropriate time, we discover that the assumptions have changed. Because of the amount of ambiguity, uncertainty, and complexity in innovation projects, more assumptions must be made than in most projects that are operational and use traditional project management methods. Many of the assumptions are based on changes in the markets and the enterprise environmental factors. These changes can lead to major shifts in the direction of the project or possibly project cancellation.

All assumptions carry with them some degree of risk. Innovation PMs must closely and frequently validate the assumptions as part of risk-management activities.

INNOVATION FUNDING

Most organizations have impediments that can affect all projects, not just innovation. The impediments that have the greatest impact are those related to how a firm funds and staffs projects. Companies have strict policies on how funds are allocated, especially for innovation activities. There is a great deal of competition for these funds. This is one of the reasons why many innovation projects begin in "stealth mode," at least initially, and may remain under the radar for some time. Sometimes good projects never make it to the surface because of funding limitations.

A solution to overcome this roadblock is to have a sponsor, whether visible or invisible, at the senior levels of management to help you with additional funding. This is important to prevent a project from being canceled when it might be on the verge of a breakthrough.

CASH FLOW AND FINANCIAL UNCERTAINTY

Cash flow and financial uncertainty are like innovation funding roadblocks. Starting an innovation only to cancel it after work has progressed or put it on the back burner is demoralizing for the team. Innovation projects may take years to finally achieve the desired strategic results.

While financing as many innovation projects as possible seems like a good practice, canceling projects and then restarting them can do more harm than good. The impact on the corporate culture can be unfavorable. Companies must weigh the pros and cons. Companies may be better off financing only those projects where they have some degree of confidence that there will be enough funding to complete the project.

CONTROL, CONTROL, AND CONTROL

An organizational factor that often slows down innovation decision making is the number of signoffs needed before any decision can be made. This is associated with complex bureaucracy. Some organizations are obsessed with very tight control over expenditures and decision making, thus making it difficult for innovation personnel to change directions on a project without prior approval even for small changes.

Hidden within this organizational factor is the belief by some managers and executives that information is power and therefore they feel compelled to participate in all decisions. Managers who

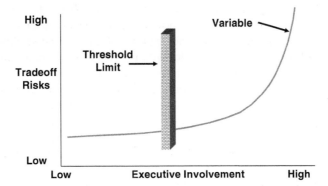

Figure 10–1. Executive Involvement.

believe that they need to see every piece of information, even if it not specifically related to their job, often micromanage the projects beneath them. This, in turn, slows down decision making and may frustrate people working on teams.

One way of controlling meddling and micromanagement is to establish criteria as to when executives should be involved in the project, as shown in Figure 10-1. This assumes, of course, that the executives will abide by the criteria.

ANALYSIS–PARALYSIS

Some organizations find it difficult to make decisions in a timely manner. This is particularly true for some types of innovation where forecasting the future is necessary. The most common analysis–paralysis situation is with the number of assumptions that must be made on innovation projects. The larger the number of assumptions, especially if they are related to long-term projects of the marketplace, the more decision making can be delayed.

Tracking and validating the assumptions, especially those related to financial uncertainty, is the right thing to do but not at the expense of slowing down innovation activities.

INNOVATION IN ACTION: NAVIAIR

Naviair is a state-owned company that provides aviation infrastructure and air navigation traffic control. An air traffic controller at Naviair has a demanding job with the responsibility for separating aircraft from each other, enabling them to safely navigate Danish airspace—aircrafts that carry hundreds of human lives in a thin aluminum tube.

Material in this section, "Innovation in Action: Naviair," has been provided by Mikael Ericsson, Director Development, ATM Projects & Engineering, Naviair. ©2022 by Naviair. All rights reserved. Reproduced with permission.

Air traffic approach controllers are affected by the stress of the job and the technology they must use in a high-tech control center environment. This control center has an advanced technological infrastructure, and is connected to sophisticated surveillance equipment, radios, and satellite signals to monitor traffic and control traffic flows, providing the pilot with information and control the airplane along the flight path. The work environment is strictly regulated, with breaks provided every hour in order for the controller to be in good shape to handle the next traffic peak. Access to this environment is controlled by a supervisor who handles access so the traffic controllers on duty are not disturbed, especially during traffic peaks. An environment like this creates a subculture and a very strong bonds between air traffic controller colleagues and encourages a strong union.

An air traffic controller is well paid due to the responsibility one must perform every day. Like a pilot, an air traffic controller undergoes strict medical checkups every year and is also responsible for declaring himself/herself as fit for service. No alcohol is permitted in Naviair before or during duty hours and there are controls in place, with alcohol breath testing in the air traffic control center.

The academic criteria to apply as an air traffic controller are lower in Denmark compared to some other European countries, where a university degree is required. Because of this, if a controller has been in service for some years and loses his or her job for some reason, it might be very hard to find an equally well-paid position again. This further reinforces the existing subculture among controllers.

Working with these individuals is very interesting indeed. They are strong-minded due to the entrance selection criteria. In our company the saying among controllers is, "If you are in doubt, you are not in doubt," meaning they cannot hesitate when making a decision and they must be sure they are making the right decision. That strong-mindedness is also reflected when they work on projects outside the control room. In many discussions, those strong operational opinions and quick decisions can make it feel like you're working with prima donnas when you are on the administrative side. A decision can change in each meeting, since that is how they are by nature—quick-thinking and adoptable to just that situation right here and now.

What conclusions can you make from the above information? Are air traffic controllers prima donnas? We could argue both yes and no. Yes, in the sense that they are highly specialized and very important people that can be hard to work with; in an organization like this, you may need special attention to lead and manage them. No, because they are not at all arrogant divas.

Project Environment and the Skillset Needed

A business like Naviair, where development of the system support for an air traffic service provider is a cornerstone, tends to create a stream of projects. Projects provide the organization with a good working environment to create an innovative working culture and to shape the future demand in a temporary work situation under temporary governance.

Naviair's portfolio is quite large, with many different types of projects. The skillset needed often includes an operational background, since the air traffic controller typically is the main user for the operational systems.

There are also systems such as new radar installations or wide area network implementations that have more of a need for engineers. In such projects a major objective would be to ensure validation criteria. For the air traffic controller, a system only needs to work and meet the performance criteria, but *how* it is done is, for them, less important. For systems with greater interaction with air traffic controllers, their competence and participation throughout the project is mandatory.

The air traffic controller participates during every phase of such a project. They are a vital part, defining the needs and demands for the future system. They are needed to review and participate in the system engineering phase to ensure that the suppliers understand the operational demands and the operational concept that the functionality must support. This is not something that comes easily for every air traffic controller. Some parts of the system engineering tend to be very detailed, and depending on the supplier's ability to demonstrate and iterate the developed functionality in steps, the demonstrations might be sufficient or the controller or might need to read very complex system descriptions.

During factory acceptance the controllers need to be involved. They have typically already been involved in producing a test procedure book. This phase is more in their comfort zone, since the system is quite mature at this point, even if the test is performed in an artificial environment in a factory.

The operational skillset of the controller is most important during the integration and deployment test. We need to verify that the supplier has met the contractual criteria, and we must be able to validate that the system performs well with the defined operational procedures and the trained air traffic controllers. System, procedures, and controllers must work well together as a homogeneous unit.

Not every air traffic controller can meet these demands or is interested in being part of projects like this. Those who can meet these challenges are often in high demand.

Thus, we have had a very positive experience involving air traffic controllers in complex, change projects across two countries and three control centers. How did we succeed in doing this?

A Unique Constellation to Cope with Change Complexity

A Joint Program Office was set up in 2015 to ensure a more harmonized and efficient air navigation service within the Denmark–Sweden Functional Airspace Block. Swedish LFV, Danish Naviair, and the cross-border NUAC operational alliance launched the program office to support the global harmonization targets for Europe. Three organizations joining forces across national air traffic service providers is a unique constellation never seen before in the world.

The Joint Program Office's main aim is increasing efficiency while reducing costs, ultimately leading to more efficient deployment of technical initiatives. By focusing on a "one system concept" that enables a cost-efficient, state-of-the-art air navigation service for its customers, the Joint Program Office's task is to optimizes deployment of the air traffic system and operational procedures at the three control centers while focusing on increased efficiency by using common configurations, procedures, rules, training, and future joint technical investment plans.

To run the ambitious harmonization and optimization projects, the Joint Program Office introduced new, agile ways of working within each project team, using a sprint methodology. The projects directly involved 90 people—many of them air traffic controllers, engineers, and system experts. The changes affect the 700 air traffic controllers' daily tools and methods.

Project Management Mindset

Change management starts with the project manager's mindset. The most successful project managers are not always the ones with the most experience or competency level but the ones that want the project the most. In the end, the purpose of project management is to create project impact. And that is a very complex matter, as we must consider the views of multiple stakeholders and the fact that they do not always agree on the why, what, how, and who.

How many project managers start their projects by setting a framework of strategic project objectives on how to run the project? In Naviair, we did. The purpose of the strategic project objectives was to support the right mindset in a large change program where three control centers' ways of working are being harmonized—across national borders and in a very conservative environment where change is often considered a bad thing or a risk.

The strategic project objectives were defined to challenge the classical—and conservative—way of running projects. The strategic project objectives were:

- We perform project pulse checks in all the project teams and in the program office every second month. We monitor the project participants' satisfaction level and also project impact.
- Every project manager uses visual project plans instead of using complex project management tools and planning.
- Every month the project manager reports in a simple, visual, and semi-automatized reporting tool—meaning that not much time is spent on project reporting that nobody reads.
- We do not use "watermelon" reporting. Watermelon reporting is to hide the facts that the project is in difficulties by claiming everything is fine—green on the outside, but actually fiery red on the inside. Our reporting is based on a high level of trust and support that it is okay to make mistakes.
- Every time the Programme Office or the project teams is physical together, we used some kind of workshop format to secure a high level of energy and productivity. Sometimes we even conduct workshops together and across the Programme Office and project teams.
- The complex project elements are divided into small and very focused sprints with a sprint coordinator that is trained in change, facilitation, and team dynamics. We would rather serve many "small, tasty cupcakes" than big and overwhelming "wedding cakes."

In our projects, the project manager takes responsibility for progressing of the tasks and activities but also the purpose, energy, meeting facilitation, satisfaction level, and team dynamics.

We work within a certain framework and methodology. We call it Half Double—striving for the double effect and impact in half the time.

Half Double Works

Half Double emphasizes stakeholder satisfaction instead of fixed deliverables as the ultimate success criterion. We ensure stakeholder satisfaction by leading and focusing on the impact case—both cost, revenue, and the behavioral change needed to create successful project.

The question is: How can you accelerate the lead time and enhance the impact of your projects? We need innovative thinking and a new mindset for running our projects. The Half Double methodology is a new and radical methodology that can result in projects achieving double the impact in half the time. There are three core elements in a Half Double design, as shown in Figure 10-2.

Focus on Impact Creation

The Half Double methodology encourages a change of focus. Forget the triple constraints of scope, time, and budget, and focus on impact instead. The idea is to realize the benefits continuously throughout the project, thereby reducing the time to impact and boosting the overall effect.

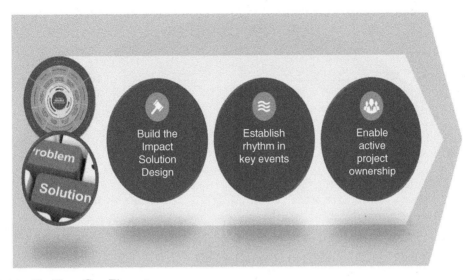

Figure 10–2. The Three Core Elements.
Source: John Ryding, Karoline Thorp Adland, Michael Ehlers, Niels Ahrengot, "Projects in half the time with double the impact." Implement Consulting Group, 2018.

Flow in Your Projects

The Half Double methodology is a change of mindset from resource optimization to progression of the projects impact. Half Double focuses on visual planning, but it is designed to visualize the impact realization and not on the progression in deliverables. Our attention is also directed on the importance of +50 percent allocation of the core people needed to drive the project; we define what we call a *project heartbeat*—a fixed rhythm in events—and specifically design it to ensure high stakeholder involvement and satisfaction. This enables us to achieve the necessary behavioral change to make real business impact.

Project Ownership

Half Double is a shift from management focus to leadership. This means less focus on contract management and compliance and more focus on building trust and commitment. In traditional project management, changes cause resistance and frustration. In the Half Double approach, changes mean new opportunities and chance to discuss scenarios.

Leading a project is not about the management of deliverables but the leadership of people. In traditional project management, top management delegates responsibility for execution to the project manager. In Half Double, key executives take the role of being active project owners—hence, they become highly involved in the project life cycle together with the project leader.

The Half Double methodology elements are shown in Figure 10-3, and at www.halfdouble.dk all tools are accessible.

The Half Double framework helped the Joint Programme Office projects by focusing on the right things and the importance of better dialogues in the various project teams and management involvement. In 2016 and 2017, the project delivered the double benefit realization as budgeted (a savings of 21,000 operational hours in the deployment phase of new air traffic management releases).

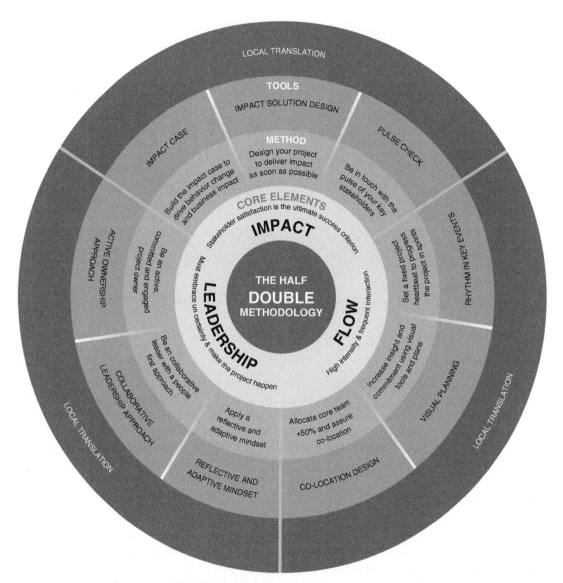

Figure 10–3. The Half Double Elements.
Source: John Ryding, Karoline Thorp Adland, Michael Ehlers, Niels Ahrengot, 2018, "Projects in half the time with double the impact." Implement Consulting Group, p. 65.

The Why behind the Why

We focused on the strategic need/objective instead of the end result or deliverable. The compelling *why* story of harmonization was crucial to define in the beginning of the project. We worked with the why story at many organizational levels as the why meant different things in top management, among the air

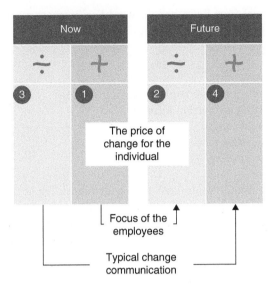

Figure 10–4. The Double-Entry Model.
Source: Implement Consulting Group.

traffic controllers, and the operational management. Simon Sinek's TED talk "Starts with Why" inspired us. Another tool we used was the double-entry model shown in Figure 10-4.

The double-entry tool was used to discuss the current situation and future state with both positive and negative perspectives:

- What is working well today?
- What will be challenging on our journey to our desired future?
- What is not done sufficiently well today?
- What will be better in our desired future?

This gives a framework for structured and trustworthy change communication and supports having facilitated dialogue between management and employees. It also minimizes the risk that management communicate a "pretty picture" of the future state and critique of the current situation.

Avoid the Expert Trap

In the Naviair case, the sprint team coordinators were air traffic controllers and a part of the system expert areas. The task was to harmonization three control centers as a way of working with the air traffic management system. It was a tough task to ensure that all the representatives from each control center were willing to seek compromises and conduct constructive dialogues.

The process of running the sprint teams and facilitation was very important. Therefore, all the sprint team coordinators received training in facilitation and change management.

The word *facilitation* comes from Latin, and the word *Facilis* means move freely or make something easier. But who hasn't tried to participate in meetings like this?

- No agenda
- Lack of focus or purpose
- Key persons are not present or are working on their devices
- Participants are not being involved or heard
- Conflicts are not being managed
- No decisions are made or no results are achieved
- The timeboxing of the meeting is lacking

To coordinate colleagues from three different sites with three different approaches to air traffic management with the object of finding harmonized concepts is not at all easy. Therefore, the planning and mindset of the facilitator makes a great difference. The task of the sprint coordinators was to create an atmosphere of trust with everybody eager to participate and contribute with a focus on the right content and results.

If you want to be a facilitator of a meeting, you must formally take on the facilitator's role. The sprint team coordinators knew their control center by heart. But being the ones both asking and answering the questions would jeopardize the meeting and the workshop quality and experience for the participants.

The potato model was used to highlight the difference between the expert-role and the facilitator role (Figure 10-5).

The analyst and advisor roles are about being an expert in your field. You take responsibility for the created content, not so much for the process (dark gray areas). In the trainer role, you are focused on both the process and the content and on creating a safe learning environment. In the role of facilitator, you are

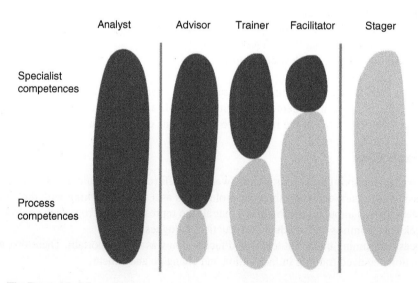

Figure 10–5. The Potato Model.
Source: Henrik Horn Andersen, Line Larsen, and Cecilie Van Loon, 2017, "Facilitation – Create results through involvement," p. 26.

responsible for the process and for moving the participants toward the goal and purpose of the meeting or workshop. This is about the process focus (light gray areas). As a facilitator, you provide more questions than answers.

Great facilitation is often on the edge of chaos—can we deliver the results we need, will the participants disagree, will the timeboxes be realistic? A good facilitator therefore needs to be well prepared. The design star, as shown in Figure 10-6, is a tool to help focus on key elements before the meeting or workshop.

Participants must be able to trust that the facilitator has all the best intensions and clear motives. To be trusted in the role there are four parameters to consider, as shown in Figure 10-7 (Maister et al. 2001).

The Trust Equation is a deconstructive, analytical model of trustworthiness that can be easily understood and used to help yourself and your organization. As a facilitator and sprint coordinator, it is important to reflect on the participants view of you:

- To what degree am I credible?
- What behavior leads others to believe that I am reliable (or not reliable)?
- To what degree do they know me as a person?
- What behaviour leads to believing that I have their best interests at heart?

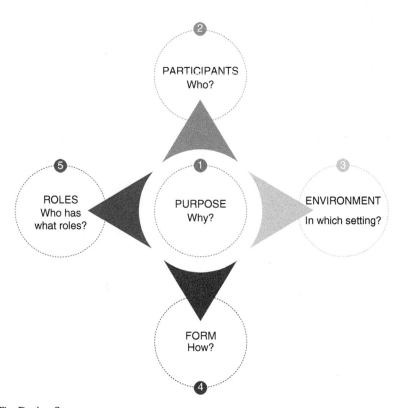

Figure 10–6. The Design Star.

Source: Henrik Horn Andersen, Line Larsen, and Cecilie Van Loon, 2017, "Facilitation—Create results through involvement," p. 49.

The Drivers of Trust

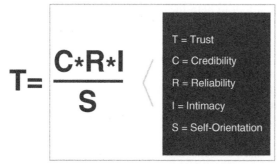

- **Credibility:** Demonstrate competence and expertise, personal integrity, and expert insight.

- **Reliability:** Keep your promises, always be there for the customer, be proactive and always within reach.

- **Intimacy:** Build a personal relationship, understand personal drivers and motives and emphasize listening.

- **Limit your self-orientation:** Listen, treat your customers' problems as your own and help them to be successful; be motivated to help your customer.

Figure 10–7. The Four Parameters of Trust.
Source and inspiration from: David H. Maister, Charles H. Green, and Robert M. Galford. (2001). *The Trusted Advisor.* New York: Simon and Schuster.

The Cycle of Change

Air traffic controllers like being in control. And we are all happy for that, as we can feel secure and safe when we're airborne. But what happens if we change the controllers' primarily tools and affect their routines?

Humans are designed with a super-fast brain, allowing us to unconsciously and quickly react to any situation, when facing danger, changes, or people. One of the pioneers in the field he calls "neuroleadership," David Rock, has created the SCARF model, shown in Figure 10-8, to describe the factors we scan for in order to survive socially.

If any factor or domain goes down, we tend to disengage in the situation, and if the factor goes up, we tend to engage in the task. If we are aware of the emotional reactions to change, we can cope with them in our projects and change implementation. The sprint team coordinators and members of the Joint Programme Office received training on the typical reactions to change and the specific pattern that a cycle of change follows. We used an ActeeChange simulator to exercise and train. It is based on Rick Maurer's book and theories *Beyond the Wall of Resistance* (Maurer 2010) and also his ebook from 2009, *Introduction to Change without Migraines* as shown in Figure 10-9.

We used a digital training platform (www.Actee.com) in which the participants were responsible for implementing changes in an organization and handling the typical reactions to change according to Maurer (2010, 38–41) (See Figure 10-10):

"I don't get it" (cognitive reaction)
"I don't like it" (emotional reaction)
"I don't like you!" (relational reaction)

Status is about relative importance to others

Certainty concerns being able to predict the future

Autonomy provides a sense of control over events

Relatedness is a sense of safety with others

Fairness is a perception of fair exchanges between people

Figure 10–8. The SCARF Model.
Source and inspiration from: David Rock and Implement Consulting Group.

"I don't get it…!" resistance is about:

- Lack of information
- Disagreement with the idea in itself
- Lack of communication about the idea/foundation for the idea
- Confusion about messages

"I don't like it…!" resistance is about:

- Loss of power, control, status
- Losing face or respect
- Belief that the idea will be ineffective
- Fear of isolation or abandonment
- Sense that they cannot take on anything else (too much change)

"I (don't) like you…!"-resistance:

- Is based on the history of the relationship
- Is a response to cultural, ethnic, gender, or power differences
- May reflect significant disagreement over values

Effect of Methods under the Half Double Methodology Elements

Naviair has been very successful using the described methodology and tools. The impact on the teams has been surprising. The effect of exploring the why has paid off well. The tools for ensuring a good team

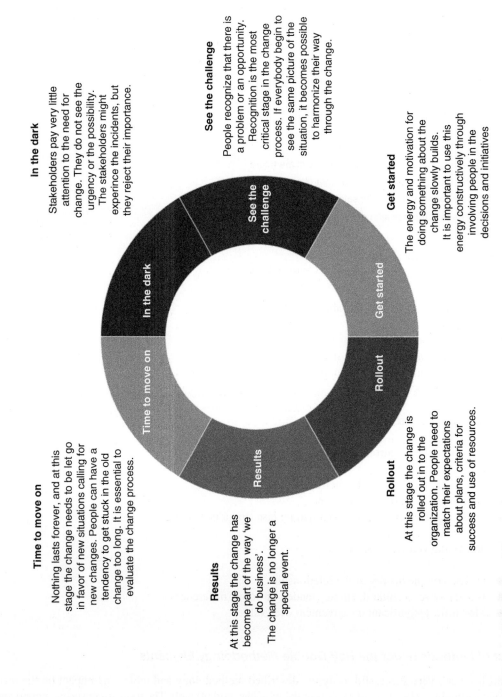

In the dark

Stakeholders pay very little attention to the need for change. They do not see the urgency or the possibility. The stakeholders might experince the incidents, but they reject their importance.

See the challenge

People recognize that there is a problem or an opportunity. Recognition is the most critical stage in the change process. If everybody begin to see the same picture of the situation, it becomes possible to harmonize their way through the change.

Get started

The energy and motivation for doing something about the change slowly builds.
It is important to use this energy constructively through involving people in the decisions and initiatives

Rollout

At this stage the change is rolled out in to the organization. People need to match their expectations about plans, criteria for success and use of resources.

Results

At this stage the change has become part of the way 'we do business'.
The change is no longer a special event.

Time to move on

Nothing lasts forever, and at this stage the change needs to be let go in favor of new situations calling for new changes. People can have a tendency to get stuck in the old change too long. It is essential to evaluate the change process.

Figure 10–9. Components of Change Management.
Adapted from Maurer, R. (2009).

Figure 10–10. Digital Training Platform.

spirit have had a tremendous effect. Not only have we been able to create high-performance teams, but it has also increased speed. The sprint teams were ready in a very short time, often ahead of schedule, allowing problems to carry over to the line organization quickly for implementation. This has been a learning experience for us, to be better to secure the result from this new type of agile project work.

Naviair has concluded that, when working with highly specialized people with their own subculture, such as air traffic controllers, you can maximize the result by using these tools. Not do they meet today's need for speed but they also maximize the impact of high performance teams that focus on achievement.

INNOVATION IN ACTION: OVERCOMING THE ROADBLOCKS _____

In the recent past, *innovation* has developed an image—just say the word, and magic happens. It seems to be the answer to all the worldly problems of a lot of executives, educators, politicians, and even student leaders. And yet, organizational innovation and success seem elusive. While it has been identified that the challenges that organizations face now are very different from those faced in the past and that innovation

Material in this section, "Innovation in Action: Overcoming the Roadblocks," has been provided by Sid Thatham, utility energy meter engineer, assistant professor (adjunct), University of Cincinnati, and Dr. Shaaban Abdallah, Professor of Aerospace Engineering, University of Cincinnati. ©2022 by Sid Thatham and Shaaban Abdallah. All rights reserved. Reproduced with permission.

is necessary, there are several roadblocks that organizations need to overcome to truly be innovative and successful. The following is a perspective on some of these roadblocks to innovation from the point of view of a student organization at the University of Cincinnati:

- *Project.* Research, design, build, and test a high-risk multidisciplinary engineering system.
- *Team.* Full-time students and a faculty advisor to innovate in management, marketing, and raising funds.
- *Motivation.* Adventure to go where no one has gone before, to do something that has never been done before.

Our student organization includes full-time students from various classes/academic levels working toward various degrees while working on a project that only a very few teams in the world are also working on. This group is mostly composed of master's and PhD students but also has several undergraduate students, from freshmen to upperclassmen. Most of the students also work part time (20 to 30 hours a week) to pay for school. Their academic and extracurricular pursuits together demand close to 100 hours or more from these students. Oftentimes, increasing workloads demand more effort and more work, which results in a higher output. However, contrary to popular belief, a higher workload decreases the ability of an individual to think creatively, which diminishes the ability to do innovative work (Kellogg 2002).

One of the major challenges that student groups of any kind face is funding. The ability of students (who themselves must spend a significant chunk of their waking hours working toward paying tuition) to raise funds for their organization determines the kind of innovative work they can do. This challenge is especially pronounced when the task at hand is something new, something that only a handful of teams in the world are working toward. Because the project premise is not proven, because there is uncertainty with respect to the returns on investment, fundraising becomes a massive roadblock to innovation. Our organization started with a funding of a few thousand dollars, but after some much-deserved success and breakthroughs, the budget shot up to upward of six figures. Who'd trust a group of students and invest six-figure-amounts in their endeavors? How did you find these investors? How do convince them that it's worth it? If you do end up raising a little bit of money, you might find yourself in a "turf war" situation, because a certain unit of your organization might seemingly have more immediate need, but allocating your funding toward these efforts may not be the best possible approach in the long run.

Understanding Student Diversity

Diversity and inclusion have become buzzwords these days. While these are important for a variety of reasons, if not dealt with appropriately, they may impede innovation and hence the success of the organization. Our organization has representation from seven countries, student members whose primary languages are very different from others', folks from different cultural backgrounds with different work ethics, and students from various educational backgrounds in terms of academic levels and programs of study. It is imperative for the senior leaders of the team to understand that one style of approach in a diverse team will not be a 100 percent effective, and that they will have to create an atmosphere in which all members of the organization feel important and valued, and not neglected. Something as simple as talking in a common language that everyone on the team can understand can go a long way in building camaraderie. Oftentimes, people resort to talking to their peers from the same country in a local language and this creates a disconnect among the members who cannot understand the conversation. Senior leaders should intentionally take steps to ensure as much as possible that no one on the team feels left out. It is important to ensure that all team members, regardless of their background, have a realistic attitude concerning time; the senior leaders should ensure that the team's priorities come before an individual's. A member's cultural understanding of work ethics may interfere in his/her prioritization of work and this may slow down folks from other cultures. It is also important to understand that different work cultures accept and handle power in an organization in different ways. There may be varied levels of expectations for explanation and a justification for everyone's place in the group. These expectations set the tone for the supervisor or leader's relationship with team members and determine how directive supervision must be. For instance, in contrast with an Indian student member, an American student is likely to perform better independently rather than with a directive approach.

Role of the Advisor/Advisory Board

The role of the advisor and a board of advisors in a student organization is advisory, not managerial. Our faculty advisor for students encouraged the students to invent and test their ideas without overruling their decisions even if they rejected his recommendations. For the first time the students were talking, and the advisor was listening and sometimes learning. The advisor also had to have long sleepless nights to meet unreasonable deadlines and redo failed attempts to solve problems. The students and advisor were one team without a head and had one goal, to succeed.

Given the relative inexperience of the student members of the organization and the project complexity, time was of the essence. Due to lack of time and internal politics, along with the pressure to get things done quickly, the senior leaders decided to not ask for much technical help; reaching out to the board of advisors for their expertise was skipped. In addition to that, there was a lack of delegation of tasks from advisors to the working teams. This signaled a lack of trust between the working teams and the advisors, which led to resources not being available when needed. Lack of collaboration between experts and novices hurt the organization's ability to complete timely, innovative work.

Creating a support team in the early stages of organizational development is essential. It is also important to communicate the culture of the organization to this support team to make them aware of how things are done. Conveying when and where the group needs help establishes boundaries for both parties and increases the chances of maintaining a cordial relationship while ensuring that neither party offends the other. This also helps to avoid unnecessary politics and drama. Burning bridges, especially at the very inception of an organization, may have an adverse effect on the future of the organization at a time when it needs the most support.

The urgency of the situation demanded building the team in a short period. Given the hype around the project, the team faced an issue regarding enthusiasm versus technical knowledge. Senior members needed to be cognizant of availability versus capability as well. Such a situation required that the team leaders create an environment that encouraged the team members to channel their enthusiasm and learn to contribute more technically. Asking folks to show up only to find work that is more technically complex than they were prepared for requires initiative that not all team members may possess.

Senior leaders in an organization, regardless of the level of the organization, need to understand that innovation can't happen overnight. They have to commit to it on a long-term basis and must understand that little things go a long way in achieving true innovation and success.

Implications and Issues for Project Managers and Innovation Personnel

Regardless of what type of innovation project you are working on, there are always roadblocks that can prevent you from taking the actions you believe are correct. Some of the critical issues and challenges that may be new for some project managers include the following:

- There are different types of roadblocks.
- Know what they can do to overcome or circumvent the roadblocks.
- There are resources and support available to help get through the roadblocks.

REFERENCES

Kellogg, K. (2002). When less is more: Exploring the relationship between employee workload and innovation potential. CGO Insights, Briefing Note Number 11 (April). Available at www.simmons.edu/~/media/Simmons/About/CGO/Documents/INsights/Insights-11.ashx?la=en. Accessed April 22, 2019.

Maister, D. H., Green, C. H. and Galford, R. M. (2001). *The Trusted Advisor*. New York: Simon and Schuster.

Maurer, R. (2009). *Introduction to Change without Migraines*. Arlington, VA: Maurer and Associates. www.changewithoutmigraines.com/OpenSourceProject.htm.

Maurer, R. (2010). *Beyond the Wall of Resistance: Why 70% of All Changes STILL Fail—And What You Can Do about It*. Austin, TX: Bard Press.

Sorenson, C. E. (2006). *My Forty Years with Henry Ford*. Detroit, MI: Wayne State University Press. With Samuel T. Williamson, Introduction by David L. Lewis. Originally published New York: Norton, 1956.

Defining Innovation Success and Failure

Learning Objectives for Project Managers and Innovation Personnel

To understand that there are several different meanings for innovation success and failure
  and that the meanings can change in each life cycle or phase

To be able to identify the attributes of innovation success

To understand the difference between operational and strategic success

To understand the importance of establishing success and failure criteria

INTRODUCTION

Project managers believe that they are being paid to produce deliverables and outcomes. This notion is correct and most likely will not change. But what is changing now is how we measure the success of the deliverable or outcome produced. There is more than one way to define innovation success.

Historically, project managers made primarily technical decisions related to project performance. Today, project managers are expected to make both project-related and business-related decisions. Business processes are now integrated into enterprise project management methodologies and/or frameworks to assist the project managers with business-related decisions and to validate that strategic business objectives are being or will be met.

Innovation Project Management: Methods, Case Studies, and Tools for Managing Innovation Projects,
Second Edition. Harold Kerzner.
© 2023 John Wiley & Sons, Inc. Published 2023 by John Wiley & Sons, Inc.

Project managers are now being transformed into strategic leaders thanks to the growth in portfolio management practices and the establishment of a variety of business-related project/program management offices (PMOs). Companies are now asking project managers to establish business-related metrics that can be measured throughout the life cycle of the project and validate that the projects maintain their alignment to strategic goals and objectives. This is causing us to rethink our definition of success and failure.

THE BUSINESS SIDE OF TRADITIONAL PROJECT SUCCESS

Every company has projects. These projects, many of which require innovation, must be successful if the firm is to be competitive in today's business environment. Traditionally, success was measured in terms of the three constraints that composed the *iron triangle*, namely time, cost, and scope or technology. But what was missing was the business side of project success.

Simply because a deliverable has been created does not mean that the right deliverable was produced, even though we met the constraint criteria. Any company can design a product that may not work correctly. Any company can manufacture a product that no one will purchase. Any company can build an attraction that people will not attend. Any company can produce a deliverable, perhaps based solely on the whims of management, that adds no value to the business. All these deliverables could have been produced within time, cost, and scope, but were they really successes? They could be technical successes but, at the same time, business failures.

Without some sort of success criteria, defining success is treated in the same context as beauty; it is defined through the eyes of the beholder. There are many definitions of success, and each definition may have one or more technical and business components. This is true for almost all innovation projects whether the outcomes are for new products, services, or processes. Innovation success for products and services generally is defined in strategic success terms whereas process innovation is defined in operational success terms.

Every innovation project can have multiple definitions of success (and failure) based upon the size and nature of the project. As an example, shown in TABLE 11-1, the same innovation project may have the following definitions of success based upon who is looking at the project:

TABLE 11–1.   CATEGORIES OF INNOVATION PROJECT/PRODUCT SUCCESS

Type of Success	Characteristics
Operational success	Effective use of the methodology or framework selected and the accompanying forms, guidelines, templates, and checklists
Strategic commercialization success	Recognized value by the customers; time-to-market for product launch; reasonable selling price compared to the competition; speed of delivery; minimum warrantee guarantee or repairs needed after delivery
Strategic business success	Long-term and short-term benefits and value that generate sustainable profits; future opportunities; compliance to government regulations; organizational acceptance of the change management activities needed
Innovation success	Intellectual property created; product functionality; development cost and timing; business owners and stakeholders understood their roles and responsibilities; effective use of functional resources

A project could be viewed as an innovation success but a business failure. Under each category of success there can be subcategories of success such as complete and partial success or failure. This will be discussed later in the chapter.

Innovation success could mean different things to different people. Over the years, there has been research on how to define success (Baccarini 1999; Cooper and Kleinschmidt 1987; Freeman and Beale 1992), but the conclusion is still that "one size does not fit all."

Project managers tend to define and measure project success in day-to-day terms as to the manner in which the project is being executed. Their mindset, which focuses on an operationally rather than strategically managed project, is to finish the project according to established success criteria, which is usually the triple constraints, hand off the result or deliverable to a business owner, and then move on to the next project. The business or strategic side of success may not be measurable until well into the future based on market feedback or some other criteria such as efficiency or impact on the customers. The correlation between operational and strategic business success metrics is difficult because of the long time frames between them. Sometimes, what appears to be a troubled project and is finally completed late and over budget can turn out to be great business success. The Sydney Opera House came in 10 years late and cost 14 times its original budget. The design and development of Boeing 787 Dreamliner was originally budgeted for $6 billion and ended up costing close to $40 billion. Both projects are now viewed as business successes.

Success cannot be defined in a few words or with just a couple of metrics. The definition of success is complicated and can involve the interaction of several metrics. The definition can become even more complex based on the industry or the type of project. The timing of the success measurement is also critical especially if the innovation was required for launching a new product into a highly competitive market. In this case, true success may not be able to be measured without seeing the marketplace's reaction to the product. Simply stated, innovation project management is the means to the end. The end result is the impact that it has on the business.

Innovation projects may very well be the most difficult projects in which to measure true success. The goal of innovation is to create long-term business value. The technical components of innovation success may be measurable when the outcome or deliverable of the project is created. But the business component of innovation success may not be known until months or even years after the outcome or deliverable was created. Because of the business component of innovation success, there will be more than one way to define innovation success and the definition may change over the complete life cycle of the project.

Defining innovation project success is now a component of strategic management because of its alignment with long-term and short-term strategic business objects. This is one of the reasons why project managers are now more actively involved in business decisions. Companies are now defining dimensions of success where measurements can be made quantitatively or qualitatively over the entire investment life cycle of the project. Typical dimensions of success include:

- Efficiency by which the project was managed
- Impact on the customers
- Customer satisfaction
- Impact on the business
- Preparation for future business opportunities
- Creation of new business opportunities
- Financial performance
- Market/industry impact

DEFINING PROJECT SUCCESS: THE EARLY YEARS _____

Rather than going back to the construction of the great pyramids, we will start in the 1960s with the development of the Earned Value Measurement System (EVMS). The Department of Defense (DOD) created the EVMS with the intent of standardizing the reporting of project performance from the thousands of contractors, the majority of which were involved in innovation activities. In the eyes of DOD, the EVMS was never intended to be used to predict success. The intent was to measure performance against a few metrics for standardized reporting and control.

The private sector interpreted the EVMS as a way of predicting project success; however, even though the EVMS focused heavily on just time and cost, people believed that success could be determined using the same two metrics. Unfortunately, time and cost were being defined during the competitive bidding stage, at a time when we knew the least about the project. We knew at that time that success measurements for all types of projects including innovation projects needed more metrics than just time and cost, but metric measurement techniques were in the infancy stages. Companies adopted the "rule of inversion," which stated that project performance (and success) should be determined using those metrics that were the easiest to measure and report, namely time and cost.

We knew that other metrics were needed, but there were disagreements on what they were. The private sector wanted to focus on the triple constraints, as shown in Figure 11-1, where the third constraint related to meeting performance requirements. The critical question was, "What is performance?" Should performance be defined as scope, meeting specifications, technology, adhering to the quality acceptance criteria, or other elements? Each company had its own definition of performance.

> While the DOD and the EVMS did discuss performance, emphasis was mainly on time and cost. Most of the DOD contracts in the early years were awarded to high-technology companies for creating advanced high-technology products for military use. Many of the engineers managing these projects defined success as not just meeting the specifications but exceeding them, regardless of the cost. And if the DOD kept paying for the cost overruns, and allowed some schedules to slip, this cycle continued and soon became the norm. The president of one aerospace and defense contractor working on government contracts commented that "When working on DOD contracts, the only true definition of project success is customer acceptance of the deliverables."

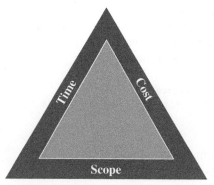

Figure 11–1.   Traditional Triple Constraints.

Figure 11–2. Modified Triple Constraints.

The triple constraints shown in Figure 11-1 were then modified as shown in Figure 11-2 to contain a constraint for customer acceptance. But even if the customer accepted the deliverable, customers had "degrees of success" that the project managers never knew. In some situations, marketing was knowledgeable about the customer's view of success, but that information never made it into the hands of the project managers.

On some government projects, the final cost could be more than two or three times the original budget because of the desire to exceed innovation specifications and demonstrate the contractor's technical abilities. The private sector looked at these cost overruns and demonstrated little interest in accepting project management because project management appeared as an acceptable cost overrun situation, perhaps by as much as 300–400 percent. Therefore, the belief at that time was that success on projects may not be achievable without significant cost overruns.

REDEFINING PROJECT SUCCESS: APPROACHING THE TWENTY-FIRST CENTURY

By the end of the last century, the use of project management practices had spread to virtually every industry in the private sector and every government agency in the public sector. Organizations began to realize that there were many definitions of success, and that success was not simply the point where we met the time and cost constraints. Because completing a project at the exact values of the time and cost constraints was an unrealistic expectation, the definition of success began to change. Success was now being defined as a cube as shown in Figure 11-3. The center point in the cube is where we have the targeted budget, schedule, and scope. But because the definition of a project is usually a grouping of activities that we may not have done before and may never do again, meeting the center point would be difficult. Therefore, we needed an acceptable range of values surrounding the constraints.

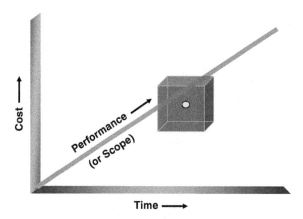

Figure 11–3. Triple Constraints with Boundary Boxes.

Companies began establishing success criteria for projects including tolerance thresholds for the cube. As an example, success criteria could include the following:

- Staying within ±10 percent of the targeted budget is success
- Staying within ±15 percent of the allocated time is acceptable
- Meeting 95 percent of the scope and specifications are acceptable and perhaps the remaining 5 percent will be completed using a follow-on contract or project

We knew that other success metrics were needed, but we did not know at that time how to measure them, or in many cases, how to identify them. Companies began revisiting groundbreaking articles that identified the use of critical success factors (Boynton and Zmud 1984; Rockart 1979). Critical success factors (CSFs) were defined as those few things or activities that had to go well for the company or an organization to be successful.

Unfortunately, companies were trying to identify CSFs as project success criteria. CSFs are elements that identify the achievements of an organization for its strategy to be successful whereas a project's success criteria are best defined by key performance indicators (KPIs), which can quantitatively measure on an ongoing basis the ability to achieve a project's objectives.

DEGREES OF SUCCESS AND FAILURE

"Success doesn't teach as many lessons as failure does."
— Jay Samit, *Disrupt You!: Master Personal Transformation, Seize Opportunity, and Thrive in the Era of Endless Innovation*

Projects get terminated for one of two basic reasons; project success or project failure. Project success is considered as a natural cause for termination and is achieved when we meet the success criteria established at the onset of the project. Project failure is often the result of unnatural causes such as a sudden change in the business base, loss of critical resources, significant changes in the enterprise environmental factors, or inability to meet certain critical constraints. There are numerous reasons why a project can get terminated due to failure. Canceling a project is a critical business decision and can have a serious impact on people, processes, materials, and money within the company. Depending on when it is canceled, it can also impact customer and partner relationships.

In an ideal situation, the business case for a project would contain a section identifying the criteria for success and for early termination. Identifying cancellation criteria is important because too many times a project that should be canceled just lingers on and wastes precious resources that could be assigned to other more value-opportunistic projects.

There are degrees of project success and failure. For example, a project can come in two weeks late and still be considered as a success. A project over budget by $100,000 can also be considered a success if the result provides value to the client and the client accepts the deliverables.

Defining success is easier than defining failure. As an example, a vice president commented how upset he was that less than 20 percent of his R&D projects were considered as a success and made it into the product commercialization phase. He commented that the other 80 percent were failures. In the audience was the director of the PMO. She stood up and argued that the other 80 percent were not failures because that provided the company with intellectual property that was being used to create other successful projects. Her argument was that the only true project failure is when no information or intellectual property is discovered.

Projects can be partial successes and partial failures. One way of classifying project results, as shown in Figure 11-4, can be:

- *Complete success.* The expected business value is achieved within all the competing constraints.
- *Partial success.* Some or all of the expected business value is achieved, but not within all the competing constraints.
- *Partial failure.* The only achievable business value is some intellectual property that may be useful on future projects.
- *Complete failure.* The project may have been canceled or simply not completed and has no recognizable business value, benefits, or intellectual property. Also, the result may not have performed correctly.

In the future, we can expect to have more than three constraints on our projects. It is important to understand that it may not be possible to meet all the competing constraints, and therefore, partial success may become the norm.

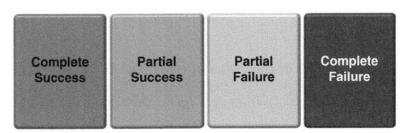

Figure 11–4. Categories of Success and Failure.

DEFINING SUCCESS AT THE BEGINNING OF THE PROJECT _____

Who is responsible for defining project success at the start of a project? Historically, the definition of success has been meeting the customer's expectations on time, cost, and scope, regardless of whether the customer is internal or external. Unfortunately, customers and contractors can have different definitions of project success that go beyond consideration of only the constraints. Customers and contractors must come to an agreement on the definition of success at the start of a project. A project manager was managing a large project for a government agency. The project manager asked one of the vice presidents in his company, "What's our company's definition of success on the project for this government agency?" The vice president responded, "Meeting the profit margins we stated in our proposal." The project manager then responded, "Do you think the government agency has the same definition of project success as we do?" The conversation then ended.

The definition of success can vary according to who the stakeholder is. For example, each of the following can have his or her own definition of success on a project:

- Consumers: safety in its use
- Employees: guaranteed employment
- Management: bonuses
- Stockholders: profitability and dividends
- Government agencies: compliance with federal regulations

When the customer and the contractor are working toward different definitions of success, decision making becomes suboptimal and each party makes decisions in its own best interest. In an ideal situation, at the beginning of a project the customer and the contractor will establish a mutually agreed on definition of success that both parties can live with.

While it is possible that no such agreement can be reached, a good starting point is to view the project through the eyes of the other party. As stated by Rachel Alt-Simmons (2016, 33):

> All too often, we take an inside-out perspective. What this means is that we see a customer's journey from how we engage with them as a company, not how they engage with us as a consumer. A helpful tool in identifying how customers engage with us is by creating a customer journey map. The journey map helps identify all paths customers take in achieving their goal from start to finish. By looking at your organization through your customers' eyes, you can begin to better understand the challenges that a customer faces in doing business with your organization. The team sees the customer outside or product or functional silos and helps link pieces of a customer process across the organization. Often, teams find out that potential solutions for problems that they're identifying extend outside of their functional realm—and that's okay!

THE ROLE OF MARKETING IN DEFINING INNOVATION SUCCESS _____

> *"Being right keeps you in place. Being wrong forces you to explore."*
> — Steven Johnson, *Where Good Ideas Come From:*
> *The Natural History of Innovation*

If the goal of the innovation project is to create products and services for sale to customers, then marketing must be involved in the definition of innovation success. The innovation project manager must have a reasonable idea concerning the definition of success right at the start of the project because it may impact the decisions he/she must make. The innovation project manager's initial definition of success might be technical, whereas the business portion of the success definition may have to be provided by marketing because of their knowledge of the markets and consumer behavior.

Innovation is an investment, and many companies are expanding the traditional life-cycle phases into an investment life-cycle approach, as shown in Figure 11-5. The two arrows under "Execution" labeled "Project Planning" and "Delivery" can be expanded to include the five domain areas of the *PMBOK®* *Guide*, namely initiation, planning, scheduling, monitoring and controlling, and closure.

The true definition of success may be made up of multiple measures, and each measure may have to be made at a different time along the entire investment life cycle. There can also be differences in the definition of business success based on whether we are designing a new product for market entry or a product that will enhance an existing product line.

Kakati (2003) defines seven categories of success that include technical and business components:

1. Characteristics of entrepreneurs
2. Resource-based capability
3. Competitive strategy
4. Product characteristics
5. Market characteristics
6. Financial consideration
7. Performance measures

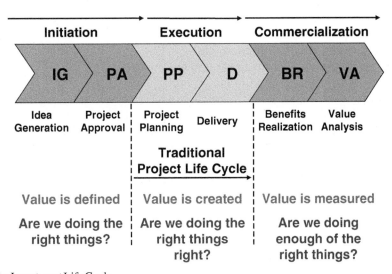

Figure 11–5. The Investment Life Cycle.

There can also be differences between long-term and short-term success definitions. Typical success indicators that can be used for the long term and short term include (Hultink and Robben 1995):

- Customer satisfaction
- Customer acceptance
- Met quality guidelines
- Product performance level
- Launched on time
- Speed to market
- Meeting revenue goals
- Meeting unit sales goals
- Revenue growth
- Attaining margin goals
- Attaining profitability goals
- IRR/ROI
- Development cost
- Breakeven time
- Meeting market share goals
- Percentage of sales by new products

Perhaps the most difficult decision facing the IPM and the governance personnel is in deciding whether to pull the plug on a project. The decision may rest upon the validity of the items defined in an established success (or failure) criteria for the project or from innovation metrics. Some firms prefer to group the innovation metrics used to measure success into categories such as:

- Technology used or created
- Strategic fit
- Customer acceptance
- Financial value created over a given period
- Market growth potential (if the innovation were a product)

These same categories can also be used in templates or checklists defining the success/failure criteria.

There can be different innovation success criteria established on each project based on the interpretation by the customer, contractor, stakeholders, and end users. The success definition can be different for an incremental innovation project as opposed to a disruptive innovation project. Each metric included in the success criteria may be measured at a different time in the life cycle. Commercialization efforts are costly. It is important that the success criteria be reevaluated for validity prior to the decision to commercialize. The definition of innovation success can also change over time based on changing enterprise environmental factors and how well the customers accept the products or services.

The differences between short-term and long-term success can be significant. As an example, a company develops a new product and quickly introduces it into the marketplace. Profitability in the short term may be difficult to assess because the company must first recover its product development and market introduction costs. In another example, a company incurs debt and constructs an attraction or a theme park. Short-term success may be the ability to service the debt, whereas long-term success may be paying off or reducing the debt load.

While customer acceptance may be measurable quickly, financial success criteria require long-term measurements. Many companies tend to focus on short-term profits, speed to market, and immediate customer satisfaction, at the expense of long-term growth. Long-term elements are usually financial performance measurements such as recovering innovation development costs and market-launch expenditures. Most studies do not distinguish between short-term and long-term innovation project success.

THE BUSINESS SIDE OF INNOVATION SUCCESS

The true definition of the business component of innovation success is the creation of deliverables that bring sustainable business value to the firm, can be measured in economic terms, and can be accomplished this within the competing constraints. This requires successfully completed innovation projects. Selecting the right innovation projects is critical, as is having the right definitions of innovation success throughout the project. We must question why any firm would agree to work on an innovation project where the outcome was not to create business value. Success on an innovation project should be measured by the amount of business value created, and we may not be able to make the measurement immediately after the deliverable is produced. Consumer response may be necessary.

Innovation success for products and services is measured by value-in-use determined during the commercialization phase in Figure 11-5. When customers or end users tell you that they see the value in using your product or services, success is identified as the way you can express their value-in-use in economic or financial terms. Value-in-use is critical for defining true business innovation success.

When an innovation project creates a product or service, what you have is an outcome or a deliverable, accompanied by "perceived" value and benefits. Executives and governance personnel want to know if the promised innovation benefits and value have been realized. This may take time, especially if we must first identify the end user's value-in-use. Someone other than the innovation team may have to take ownership for commercialization and/or harvesting the benefits and managing the transition period that leads to success. Innovation is the means to the end, whereas sustainable business value is the end. As an example, you may have created an excellent product, but marketing and sales must now take the responsibility for commercialization to harvest the benefits and value.

Is success defined when the product has been developed or after a certain revenue stream has been achieved? You have created a new software package, but who will take the responsibility for the "go live" phase and train people in the use of the new software? Is success defined when the software package was created or after it has been deployed and used successfully for some time?

As seen in Figure 11-6, a company wishes to go from its current business value position to a new business value position that is based on successful innovation. The company then authorizes funding for several innovation projects. When the projects are completed, the firm has outcomes or deliverables. Someone or some group must now take responsibility for harvesting business value that will define success.

The harvesting period, which may include product commercialization, can become quite long if organizational change management is necessary, resulting from innovation. Old products may be replaced with newer products. New manufacturing facilities may need to be constructed. People may need to learn new skills.

People may have to be removed from their comfort zone because of the changes. There may also be an impact on the business model. If organizational change is necessary, people responsible for benefits harvesting need to consider the following:

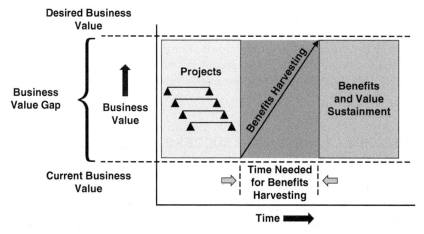

Figure 11–6. Benefits of Harvesting Value Extraction.

- Organizational restructuring
- New reward systems
- Changing skills requirements
- Records management
- System upgrades
- Industrial relations agreements

During value harvesting, habits, processes, and technology may all change. Value extraction and full value realization may face resistance from managers, workers, customers, suppliers, and partners because they may be removed from their comfort zones. There is also an inherent fear that change will be accompanied by loss of promotion prospects, less authority and responsibility, and loss of respect from peers.

There can be costs associated with value harvesting if change management is needed. This happens frequently when new business models are created. Typical costs, which may not have been included when estimating the cost of the innovation project, may be:

- Hiring and training new recruits
- Changing the roles of existing personnel and providing training
- Relocating existing personnel
- Providing new or additional management support
- Updating computer systems
- Purchasing new software
- Creating new policies and procedures
- Renegotiating union contracts
- Developing new relationships with suppliers, distributers, partners, and joint ventures

Also shown in Figure 11-6 is a sustainment period where we try to extend the life of the business value we extracted. The real problem in many companies is not innovation that creates value but the inability to sustain it. Sustainment may be a necessity to increase long-term shareholder value. If change management was necessary to extract the value, then the sustainment period is used to make sure that people do not revert to their old habits that could cause a potentially successful project to be a failure. Unlike traditional project management practices where the project team is disbanded once the deliverables are produced, in sustainment members of the innovation project management team may have a relationship with marketing and may still be actively involved in the project looking for product improvements, spinoffs, and future opportunities.

PRIORITIZATION OF THE SUCCESS FACTORS

Today, we live in an environment where we can have several competing constraints on an innovation project. Innovation success may be defined by a multitude of technical and business-related constraints and other components. It may be impossible to meet all the success criteria. When tradeoffs are needed, the innovation team must know which constraints are the most important.

Companies often solve this problem by identifying primary and secondary constraints. The priority of each constraint can change over the life of a project. Disney's theme park attractions, which are examples of innovation at work, have six constraints; time, cost, scope, safety, aesthetic value, and quality. At Disney, safety is the most important constraint, never to undergo tradeoffs. The next two important constraints appear to be aesthetic value and quality. Therefore, tradeoffs, if necessary, will most likely occur on time, cost, and scope.

Table 11-2 provides some common examples of prioritized constraints. The primary definitions of success are seen through the eyes of the customers. The secondary definitions of success are usually internal benefits, as prioritized by marketing. If achieving 86 percent of the specification is acceptable to the customer and follow-on work is received, then the original project might very well be considered a success.

It is possible for a project management methodology to identify primary and secondary success factors. This could provide guidance to a project manager for the development of a risk management plan and for deciding which risks are worth taking and which are not.

TABLE 11–2. SUCCESS FACTORS

Primary	Secondary
Within time	Follow-on work from this customer
Within cost	Using the customer's name as a reference on your literature
Within quality limits	Commercialization of a product
Accepted by the customer	With minimum or mutually agreed on scope changes
	Without disturbing the main flow of work
	Without changing the corporate culture
	Without violating safety requirements
	Providing efficiency and effectiveness in operations
	Satisfying OSHA/EPA requirements
	Maintaining ethical conduct
	Providing a strategic alignment
	Maintaining a corporate reputation
	Maintaining regulatory agency relationships

INNOVATION PROJECT SUCCESS AND CORE COMPETENCIES

The creation of a deliverable or outcome may appear on the surface as a success and, at the same time, create havoc to an organization. As an example, a company makes a technical breakthrough and creates a new product for its customers. But the new technology changes many of core competencies of the firm that were based on the older technology. The result of an innovation involving technology may enhance or destroy existing competencies that a firm uses to implement its day-to-day operations and execution of its strategy. This is shown in Table 11-3. Core competencies are made up of multiple subsystems but perhaps not all the subsystems are affected by the innovation. Simply stated, the success of a project could cause organizational disruption or even failure. The impact that a project may have on the subsystems that compose the core competencies is critical in when and how we can define success. This is important when selecting and authorizing innovation projects as seen in the following:

- Before fully investing in any innovation project, the firm must decide if the innovation will be built on existing core competencies and subsystems or if new ones must be created that may have a disruptive effect. The result of an innovation, especially successful innovations, can be an enhancement or destruction of existing competencies that are composed of subsystems. Determining true success may take time.
- Innovation that will build new competencies that enhance existing competencies is often the best approach.
- Building new competencies that are technically different can destroy existing technology competencies. Innovations based on peripheral (i.e., external to the company) subsystems are usually less disruptive to the firm because they are not coupled to the core competencies that can impact corporate strategy.
- Complex product innovations require more time-to-market as well as commercialization unless they can be built around existing core competencies and subsystems. Innovation projects that disrupt core competencies usually require a longer time-to-market.
- Even if the innovation is not disruptive, the result may be that workers will need new skills, a great deal of new training will be required, and there can be major changes to the knowledge management system.

The definition of innovation project success could be based on how we classify the levels of technology and their subsystems, such as:

- Use of existing technology and prior skills
- Small adjustments to existing technology subsystems

TABLE 11–3. ENHANCING AND DESTROYING COMPETENCIES

Changing Positions	Competency Enhancing	Competency Destroying
Technology	Modification of existing technology and simple adjustments	New technology which may render older technology as obsolete and to be replaced
Competencies	Perhaps same training and updates to knowledge management system	Probably extensive training and major updates to knowledge management system
New product development	Working with fewer existing subsystems and possibly creating one new subsystem	Creating significantly new subsystems, possibly rendering older subsystems as obsolete and complexities in the integration of the new subsystem(s)

- Use of some new rather than existing technology
- Need to replace existing technology subsystems
- Use of existing subsystems with perhaps the addition of one new subsystem
- Must create additional or new subsystems that make integration of subsystems more complex

INNOVATION PROJECT SUCCESS AND BUSINESS MODELS

There are numerous articles published that discuss innovation success and failure regarding technology creation, products, and services; however, there is another category that does not receive as much attention, namely business process innovations. Innovation in processes, as well as products and services, can force an organization to change its business model.

The construction of a business model describes the organization's business strategy related to how the organization will create, capture, and deliver business value. The literature has diverse interpretations and definitions of a business model which makes it difficult to define business model success.

New products and services can bring changes to a company's business model the same way as with process changes. As an example, a company may create a new product that changes the customer base, the channels of distribution, and the accompanying revenue stream.

CAUSES OF INNOVATION PROJECT FAILURE

> *"Remember the two benefits of failure. First, if you do fail, you learn what doesn't work; and second, the failure gives you the opportunity to try a new approach."*
> — Roger Von Oech, *A Whack on the Side of the Head:*
> *How You Can Be More Creative*

Previously, we stated that projects are usually terminated for one of two reasons. The best reason for termination is the result of project success. The second reason is total innovation project failure. However, there may be a third reason when a spin-off from the existing innovation project that offers significant promise for added business value.

There has been a great deal published on the numerous causes of project failure, whether a partial or complete failure, and most failures are a result of more than one cause. Some cause may directly or indirectly lead to other causes. For example, business case failure can lead to planning and execution failure. For simplicity's sake, project failures, for all types of projects rather than just innovation projects, can be broken down into the following categories:

Planning/Execution Failures
- Business case deterioration
- Business case requirements changed significantly over the life of the project
- Technical obsolescence has occurred
- Technologically unrealistic requirements
- Lack of a clear vision

- Plan asks for too much in too little time
- Poor estimates, especially financial
- Unclear or unrealistic expectations
- Assumptions, if they exist at all, are unrealistic
- Plans are based on insufficient data
- No systemization of the planning process
- Planning is performed by a planning group
- Inadequate or incomplete requirements
- Lack of resources
- Assigned resources lack experience or the necessary skills
- Resources lack focus or motivation
- Staffing requirements are not fully known
- Constantly changing resources
- Poor overall project planning
- Established milestones are not measurable
- Established milestones are too far apart
- The environmental factors have changes causing outdated scope
- Missed deadlines and no recovery plan
- Budgets are exceeded and out of control
- Lack of replanning on a regular basis
- Lack of attention provided to the human and organizational aspects of the project
- Project estimates are best guesses and not based on history or standards
- Not enough time provided for estimating
- No one knows the exact major milestone dates or due dates for reporting
- Team members working with conflicting requirements
- People are shuffled in and out of the project with little regard for the schedule
- Poor or fragmented cost control
- Weak project and stakeholder communications
- Poor assessment of risks if done at all
- Wrong type of contract
- Poor project management; team members possess a poor understanding of project management, especially virtual team members
- Technical objectives are more important than business objectives
- Assigning critically skilled workers, including the project manager, on a part-time basis
- Poor performance tracking metrics
- Poor risk management practices
- Insufficient organizational process assets

Governance/Stakeholder Failures
- End-user stakeholders not involved throughout the project
- Minimal or no stakeholder backing; lack of ownership
- New executive team in place with different visions and goals
- Constantly changing stakeholders
- Corporate goals and/or vision not understood at the lower organizational levels

- Unclear stakeholder requirements
- Passive user stakeholder involvement after handoff
- Each stakeholder uses different organizational process assets, which may be incompatible with each other
- Weak project and stakeholder communications
- Inability of stakeholders to come to an agreement

Political Failures
- New elections resulting in a change of power
- Changes in the host country's fiscal policy, procurement policy, and labor policy
- Nationalization or unlawful seizure of project assets and/or intellectual property
- Civil unrest resulting from a coup, acts of terrorism, kidnapping, ransom, assassinations, civil war, and insurrection
- Significant inflation rate changes resulting in unfavorable monetary conversion policies
- Contractual failure such as license cancelation and payment failure

Technical failure can also be industry-specific such as IT failure or construction failure. Some failures can be corrected, while other failures can lead to bankruptcy.

If we look at just innovation projects, the most common categories of failure are:

- Technical failure
- Market failure
- Performance failure
- Failure to finish on time
- Research failure
- Development failure
- Production failure
- Leadership failure

If we perform a root cause analysis in each of the innovation project failure categories, we could identify the following as common causes of innovation failure:

- Poor definition of goals
- Poor alignment to goals
- Poor monitoring of results
- Unexpected outcomes
- Inadequate know-how
- Poor team participation
- User acceptance failure (i.e., prototypes)
- Unforeseen events
- Insurmountable technical obstacles
- Having the wrong or unqualified resources
- Legal/liability/regulatory uncertainties
- Poor communication and access to needed information
- Critical decisions dictated from the top down

Regardless how good an organization's innovation community might be, some failures are expected. Any organization that always makes the right decisions is not making enough decisions. Any organization where all their innovation projects are completed successfully probably is not taking enough risks.

IDENTIFYING THE SUCCESS AND FAILURE CRITERIA

Failure is an inevitable part of any innovation process. The greater the degree of innovation desired, the greater the need for effective risk management practices to be in place. Without effective risk management, it may be impossible to "pull the plug" on a project that is a cash drain and with no likelihood of achieving success.

Innovation project teams are often so wrapped up with technical innovation that they may not know what constitutes innovation success and failure. Without understanding innovation success, the team may keep adding in bells and whistles that overprice the product in the marketplace. Without understanding innovation failure, the team may keep working on a project that no longer can create business value and resources are being squandered.

Organizations can help alleviate these issues by creating success and failure criteria. Success criteria usually begin during the project selection process. Some innovation projects are selected because of their suitability to the firm's business model. Suitability criteria might include:

- Similar technology
- Similar marketing and distribution channels
- Can be sold by current sales force
- Purchased by existing customer base
- Fits company philosophy, profit goals, and strategic plan
- Fits current production facilities

From the suitability criteria, we can identify innovation success criteria in categories such as:

- Developments in and use of technology
- Strategic fit
- Customer acceptance
- Market growth opportunities if applicable
- Financial factors (profit margins, ROI, payback period, net present value, return on investment, and internal rate of return)

The success criteria provide us with some guidance as to what innovation metrics should be used to validate that the project is meeting the success criteria.

The failure criteria are usually the negative mirror image of the success criteria, and heavily biased toward the firm's business model and market acceptance. Typical innovation failure criteria elements might include:

- Insurmountable obstacles (business or technical)
- Inadequate know-how and/or lack of qualified resources

- Legal/regulatory or product liability uncertainties
- Too small a market or market share for the product; dependence on a limited customer base
- Unacceptable dependence on some suppliers and/or specialized raw materials
- Unwillingness to accept joint ventures and/or licensing agreements
- Costs are excessive, and the selling price of the deliverable will be noncompetitive
- Return on investment will occur too late
- Competition is too stiff and not worth the risks
- The product life cycle is too short
- The technology is not like that used in our other products and services
- The product cannot be supported by our existing production facilities
- The product cannot be sold by our existing sales force and is not a fit with our marketing and distribution channels
- The product/services will not be purchased by our existing customer base

Projects do not go from "green" to "red" overnight. By establishing the right metrics based on the success and failure criteria, a company can identify innovation readjustment triggers that provide opportunities for tradeoffs. Typical triggers might be:

- Loss of market for the product
- Major changes in market conditions
- Loss of faith, enthusiasm, and interest by the innovation team, marketing, and/or top management
- Major changes in the technical difficulty and complexity
- Decrease in the likelihood of success

Without readjustment triggers, a project can get way off track. The cost of recovery can then be huge, and vast or even new resources may be required for corrections. The ultimate goal for tradeoffs during the recovery process is no longer to finish on time, but to finish with reasonable benefits and value-in-use for the customers and the stakeholders. The project's requirements may change during recovery to meet the new goals if they have changed. Regardless of what you do, however, not all troubled innovation projects can be recovered.

POST-FAILURE SUCCESS ANALYSIS

All projects run the risk of failure. This includes traditional projects that have well-defined requirements based upon historical estimates as well as innovation projects that may begin with just an idea. The greater the unknowns and uncertainties, such as with innovation projects, the greater the risk of failure.

When innovation projects appear to be failing, there is a tendency for project teams to walk away from the project quickly in hopes of avoiding potential blame and trying to distance themselves from the failure. Project team members usually return to their functional areas for other assignments and project managers move on to manage other projects. Companies most often have an abundance of ideas for new projects and seem to prefer to move forward without determining if failures can be turned into successes.

Part of the problem is with the expression that many project managers follow, namely "Hope for the best, but plan for the worst." Planning for the worst usually means establishing project failure criteria as to when to exit the project and stop squandering resources. When the failure criteria point is reached, all project work tends to cease. Unfortunately, post-failure success may still be possible if the organization understands and implements the processes that can turn failure into success.

There are many sources for innovation failure. The most common cause of perceived failure is not meeting performance expectations. However, failure can also be the result of using the wrong processes, poor project, and/or organizational leadership, making the wrong assumptions, unrealistic expectations, poor risk management practices, and focusing on the wrong strategic objectives. Many of these activities that were seen as the causes of failure can be overcome by reformulation of the innovation project such that post-failure success may be attainable. Successful innovation project management practices must focus on more than just creating deliverables. They must also focus on processes needed for converting failures into successes. Unfortunately, these practices are seldom taught in project management courses.

SENSEMAKING

Sensemaking is the process of making sense out of something that was novel, heavily based upon uncertainties or ambiguities, and failed to meet expectations. Sensemaking is one of the commonly used techniques that may be able to convert failures into potential successes. Sensemaking cannot guarantee successful recovery but can improve the chances of success.

Turning failure into success requires first, a culture of normalizing of failures when innovating, and second, a process of problem formulation characterized by sensemaking that is both retrospective and prospective (Morais-Storz et al. 2020). Retrospective sensemaking addresses the issue of *what happened*, looks at the causes that led up to the potential failure and tries to make sense out of the results. Prospective sensemaking addresses *what to do now* and envisions what the future might look like if we construct and implement a plausible new path. (Figure 11-7)

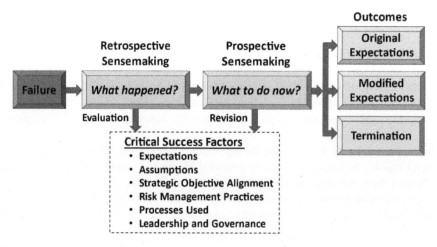

Figure 11–7. Post-Failure Success Analysis.

The leadership style that the project manager selects determines whether retrospective or prospective sensemaking will be emphasized as well as the approach to reformulating the project, if necessary. The outcome from sensemaking can be a reformulation of the original problem or the development of new plans that focus on somewhat different outcomes. Reformulation may be necessary if the team did not fully understand the way that the problem was initially presented to them, decision making was being made based upon guesses rather than facts, or if significant changes occurred in the enterprise environmental factors. The knowledge gained from sensemaking may indicate that the original expectations are still valid, but that project must be reformulated. If the original expectations are no longer valid, then a new trajectory with perhaps modified expectations may be necessary.

THE NEED FOR NEW METRICS

Sensemaking requires more information than may be available in earned value measurement systems. When implementing traditional projects using the Waterfall Methodology and accompanied by well-defined requirements, decision making is centered around the time, cost, and scope metrics.

On traditional projects, the focus is on just time, cost, and scope metrics that show performance. Unfortunately, these three metrics alone do not identify the cause of problems that may have occurred. On innovation projects, given the high probability of failure, additional metrics may be required to determine the impact of variables that may have changed from the original problem formulation and resulted in a need for post-failure analysis. Some of the new metrics include:

- The number of new assumptions made over the project's life cycle
- The number of assumptions that changed over the project's life cycle
- Changes that occurred in the enterprise environmental factors
- The number of scope changes approved and denied
- The number of time, cost, and scope baseline revisions
- The effectiveness of project governance
- Changes in the risk level of the critical work packages

LEARNING FROM FAILURE

Many project management educators advocate that the only true project failures are those from which nothing is learned. The cost for not examining failures can be very expensive if mistakes are repeated. Examination of a failed innovation project usually results in the discovery of at least some intellectual property that can be used elsewhere as well as processes that may or may not have been effective.

Organizations have looked at project failures for the purpose of capturing best practices so that mistakes are not repeated. Some people believe that more best practices can be found from failures than from successes if people are not hesitant to discuss failures. Unfortunately, the best practices discovered from both success and failure analyses are usually related to changes in the forms, guidelines, templates, and checklists. Very little effort is usually expended at post-project reviews to identify behavioral best practices which may very well have been the root cause of the failure.

Sensemaking allows organizations to address the psychological barriers that may have led up to the failure (Sitkin 1992). As stated by Morais-Storz et al. (2020):

> Failure is important for effective organizational learning and adaptation for several reasons. Failure helps organizations discover uncertainties, which are difficult to predict in advance [Sitkin (1992)], creates learning readiness and motivates learning and adaptation [Cyert and March (1992)], increases risk-seeking behavior [Kahneman and Tversky (1979)], and act as a shock trigger to draw organizational attention to problems [Van de Ven, Polley, Garud, and Venkataraman (2008)].

Learning from failures can disrupt an organization if the outcome indicates that a significant change is needed such as in the organization's culture, business model, or processes. Innovation projects are generally not formulated with the same delicacy as traditional projects. The problem is further compounded by the fact that most innovation project managers are not brought on board the project until after organizational management has approved and possibly prioritized the project, identified the constraints, and stated the assumptions the team should follow. The innovation project manager therefore begins implementation with a project formulation that neither he/she nor the team participated in. Sensemaking usually occurs in a collaborative setting, perhaps involving most of the team members. Initial problem formulation, on the other hand, may be accomplished with just a few people, most of whom have never had to manage an innovation project.

The literature discusses various ways to formulate projects, but usually traditional or operations projects rather than innovation projects. There is a lack of literature on the link between failure and how the knowledge gained during retrospective sensemaking can benefit project reformulation on innovation-type projects by challenging complacency, the use of existing processes, and ineffective leadership in dealing with ambiguity.

THE FAILURE OF SUCCESS

Perhaps the greatest psychological barrier to innovation is when an organization becomes complacent and refuses to challenge their assumptions, business model(s), and the way they conduct business. The organization is usually financially successful and believes that they will remain financially successful for years to come. As such, profitability and market share become more important than innovation, and this can create a significant psychological barrier for innovation teams. Eventually, the marketplace will change, profitability will be eroded, and innovation will become the top priority. But by this time, the failure of success may have taken its toll on the company to a point where the company may never recover.

Characteristics of a potential failure of success environment include:

- Maintaining the status quo is essential
- Most decisions are made in favor of short-term profitability
- Maintaining the present market share is more important than investing in opportunities
- Senior management positions are filled by financial personnel rather than from marketing and sales personnel whose vision created the favorable growth
- Executives refuse to challenge any of the business assumptions for fear of changing the status quo

- The guiding principles that led to success are not challenged
- The VUCA environment is expected to remain stable
- The company maintains a very low risk appetite
- No changes are needed in the organization's business model
- The company will continue using the same suppliers and distributors
- No changes are necessary in organizational leadership
- No plans are made for future generations of managers
- The organizational culture is based upon command-and-control from the top floor of the building to the bottom and not depersonalized to support an innovation and free-thinking environment.
- No changes are needed in the organization's reward systems which most likely are not based upon risk-taking
- Changes or continuous improvement efforts for project management processes are at a minimum
- There is not adequate funding for the needed innovation projects, other than perhaps small incremental innovation activities
- The failure of an innovation project is brushed aside if it has no immediate impact on profitability
- The use of sensemaking practices is nonexistent

The critical issue facing innovation teams in successful companies is that all of the above characteristics create complex interrelations that team members must deal with. As stated by James O'Toole (1983):

- "Innovation requires the ability to read changes in the environment, and to create policies and strategies that will allow the organization to capitalize on the opportunities those changes create. Ironically, the most successful companies are likely to ignore environmental signals because it seems wildly risky to tamper when things are going well."
- "Corporate reward systems also encourage behavior that is short-term, safe and conservative. The 'punishments' for entrepreneurial failures, even when they are beyond a manager's control, are much greater than the rewards for successful risk taking. Additional sources of discouragement for the innovator are the hurdles and delays associated with too many levels of approval needed for developing a new product or implementing a change in manufacturing processes or administrative practices."

Overcoming the failure of success may require companies to painstakingly change their management systems, culture, business models, and reward systems. Not all companies respond favorably to the risks associated with change management initiatives, even if the necessity exists. The greatest risk is when a change in the organization's business model may be needed, and people may be removed from their comfort zones. Some companies then perform innovation activities in a stealth mode for fear of upsetting the status quo.

A company that manufactured home products maintained an R&D group that maintained the status quo and focused heavily upon incremental innovation rather than radical innovation efforts. Marketing wanted the R&D group to address several radical innovation projects. The R&D group assigned low priorities to the projects requested by marketing for fear of alienating senior management. Marketing then appointed workers from within the marketing organization to act as innovation project managers and perform the work in a stealth mode.

CONCLUSION

If an organization wishes to excel at innovation project management, they must understand the processes that can turn failures into successes. Discovery is essential. In addition, organizations must foster leadership styles that support failure analyses and accompanying change management efforts needed for retrospective and prospective sensemaking practices.

REFERENCES

Cyert, R. M. and March, J. G. (1992). *A Behavioral Theory of the Firm.* Cambridge, MA: Wiley-Blackwell.Kahneman, D. and Tversky, A. (1979). Prospect theory: An analysis of decision under risk. *Econometrica* 47 (2), 263–291.

Morais-Storz, M., Nguyen, N. and Sætre, A. S. (2020). Post-failure success: Sensemaking in problem representation reformulation. *Journal of Product Innovation Management* 37 (6) (November), 483–505.

Sitkin, S. B. (1992). Learning through failure: the strategy of small losses. *Research in Organizational Behavior* 14, 231–266.

Van de Ven, A. H., Polley, D., Garud, R. and Venkataraman, S. (2008). *The Innovation Journey.* Oxford: Oxford University Press.

IMPLICATIONS AND ISSUES FOR PROJECT MANAGERS AND INNOVATION PERSONNEL

Project managers must understand that there is no single approach for defining innovation project success on any type of innovation project. There must be multiple measures of success factors and the timing of the measurements is critical. Projects can appear to be successful once the deliverables or outcomes are completed, but real success may occur later when the desired business value is achieved. And lastly, effective project management practices, many of which are regarded as intangibles, are contributors to success and must undergo continuous improvements. Some of the other critical issues and challenges that may be new for some project managers include an understanding of the following:

- There are multiple definitions of success.
- There are multiple components of success, including both a business and technical component.
- The true definition of innovation success is the long-term impact innovation has on the business.
- There can be a significant difference in how we define operational versus strategic success.
- There are degrees of success and failure, and they can change over the innovation project's life cycle.
- True success may not be known until we approach the sustainment period or even later.
- The components or attributes of success may need to be prioritized.
- Success and failure can have a favorable or unfavorable impact on the firm's core competencies.
- There is a need for success and failure criteria.

REFERENCES

Alt-Simmons, R. (2016). *Agile by Design*. Hoboken, NJ: John Wiley & Sons.

Baccarini, D. (1999). The logical framework method for defining project success. *Project Management Journal*, 25–32.

Boynton, A. C. and Zmud, R. W. (1984). An assessment of critical success factors. *Sloan Management Review* 25 (4), 17–27.

Cooper, R. G. and Kleinschmidt, E. J. (1987). New products: What separates winners from losers. *Journal of Product Innovation Management* (4), 169–184.

Freeman, M. and Beale, P. (1992). Measuring project success. *Project Management Journal* (1), 8–17.

Hultink, E. J. and Robben, H. S. J. (1995). Measuring new product success: The difference that time perspective makes. *Journal of Product Innovation Management* 12, 392–405.

Kakati, M. (2003). Success criteria in high-tech new ventures. *Technovation* (23), 447–457.

O'Toole, J. (1983). Declining innovation: The failure of success. *Human Resource Planning* 6 (3), 125–141.

Rockart, J. F. (1979). Chief executives define their own data needs. *Harvard Business Review* (2), 81–93.

12 Innovation in Action

Learning Objectives

To identify some of the different techniques some successful companies use for innovation activities

To understand that not all companies use the same innovation techniques

INTRODUCTION

There is no clear-cut template for all the activities that an organization must do for continuous innovation to occur. Even though there might be commonly used innovation tools or an innovation canvas, every company has their own business plan, organizational structure, and culture for innovation.

All of the companies discussed in this chapter have different approaches to innovation. They all have innovation strengths and weaknesses. For each company, only a few of their innovation attributes related to their unique strengths are being discussed as examples of information presented in earlier chapters.

INNOVATION IN ACTION: APPLE

> *"Was [Steve Jobs] smart? No, not exceptionally. Instead, he was a genius. His imaginative leaps were instinctive, unexpected, and at times magical. [...] Like a pathfinder, he could absorb*

Innovation Project Management: Methods, Case Studies, and Tools for Managing Innovation Projects,
Second Edition. Harold Kerzner.
© 2023 John Wiley & Sons, Inc. Published 2023 by John Wiley & Sons, Inc.

information, sniff the winds, and sense what lay ahead. Steve Jobs thus became the greatest busi-
ness executive of our era, the one most certain to be remembered a century from now.

History will place him in the pantheon right next to Edison and Ford. More than anyone else
of his time, he made products that were completely innovative, combining the power of poetry and
processors. With a ferocity that could make working with him as unsettling as it was inspiring, he
also built the world's most creative company. And he was able to infuse into its DNA the design
sensibilities, perfectionism, and imagination that make it likely to be, even decades from now, the
company that thrives best at the intersection of artistry and technology."

—Walter Isaacson, *Steve Jobs*

When people think about companies that have a history of continuous innovation, they usually start with Apple. But what many people do not recognize is that the path leading to continuous innovation success may be strewn with some failures, roadblocks, challenges, and possibly lawsuits such as Apple encountered with Microsoft and Samsung.

Background

Some of Apple's successes include the Macintosh computer, iPod, iPhone, iPad, Apple Watch, Apple TV, HomePod, Software, electric vehicles, and Apple Energy. But there is also a dark side of unsuccessful consumer products that were launched during the 1990s, such as digital cameras, portable CD audio players, speakers, video consoles, and TV appliances. The unsuccessful consumer products were not the result of an innovation failure but from unrealistic market forecasts.

Successful innovations increase market share and stock prices, while unsuccessful products have the opposite effect. Apple was highly successful with the Macintosh computer from 1984 to 1991. From 1991 to 1997 Apple struggled financially due to limited innovation. Apple returned to profitability between 1997 and 2007. In 2007, Apple's innovations in mobile devices were a major part of its astounding success.

Innovation often creates legal issues over the ownership and control of intellectual property. The growth of the Internet created a problem of piracy in the music industry. Steve Jobs commented on Apple's success in the music business, stating that "Over one million songs have now been legally purchased and downloaded around the globe, representing a major force against music piracy and the future of music distribution as we move from CDs to the Internet."

Apple used and continues to use several different types of innovation. Some products use incremental innovation, such as updated versions of cell phones, whereas other products appear as radical innovation. Apple also uses both open and closed innovation. For open innovation activities, Apple has created a set of Apple Developer Tools to make it easier for the creation of products to be aligned to Apple's needs.

Apple also created innovations in its business model, which was designed to improve its relationship with its customers. Apple created a retail program that used the online store concept and physical store locations. Despite initial media speculation that Apple's store concept would fail, its stores were highly successful, bypassing the sales numbers of competing nearby stores, and within three years reached US$1 billion in annual sales, becoming the fastest retailer in history to do so. Over the years, Apple has expanded the number of retail locations and its geographical coverage, with 499 stores across 22 countries worldwide as of December 2017. Strong product sales have placed Apple among the top-tier retail stores, with sales over $16 billion globally in 2011.

Apple created an innovation culture that gave people the opportunity to be creative. Unlike other cultures where executives assign people to innovation projects and then sit back waiting for results to appear, Steve Jobs became an active participant in many of the projects. Numerous Apple employees have stated that projects without Jobs's involvement often took longer than projects with it.

At Apple, employees are specialists who are not exposed to functions outside their area of expertise. Jobs saw this as a means of having "best-in-class" employees in every role. Apple is also known for strictly enforcing single-person accountability. Each project has a "directly responsible individual," or "DRI" in Apple jargon. In traditional project management, project managers often share the accountability for project success and failure with the functional managers who assign resources to the project.

To recognize the best of its employees, Apple created the Apple Fellows program, which awards individuals who make extraordinary technical or leadership contributions to personal computing while at the company. This is becoming a common practice among companies that have a stream of innovations. Disney created a similar society called "Imagineering Legends" to recognize innovation excellence.[1]

Conclusion

Continuous successful innovation is possible if the firm has a tolerance for some failures and recognition that the marketplace may not like some of the products. Also, the company's business model may change, as happened with the opening of Apple stores.

INNOVATION IN ACTION: FACEBOOK

Some companies boast of the size of their user base for their innovations in the thousands or hundreds of thousands. But other companies, such as Facebook, must satisfy the needs of possibly hundreds of millions of end users. To do this successfully, and remain innovative, open source innovation practices are essential.

Background

Many of Facebook's innovations come from open source innovation, crowdsourcing and the use of platforms. Facebook launched the Facebook Platform on May 24, 2007, providing a framework for software developers and other volunteers to create applications that interact with core Facebook features. A markup language called Facebook Markup Language was introduced simultaneously; it is used to customize the "look and feel" of applications that developers create. Using the Platform, Facebook launched several new applications, including Gifts, which allows users to send virtual gifts to each other, Marketplace, allowing users to post free classified ads, Facebook events, giving users a means to inform their friends about upcoming events, Video, which lets users share homemade videos with one another, and a social network game, where users can use their connections to friends to help them advance in games they are playing. Many of the popular early social network games would eventually combine capabilities.

---

1. See Disney (A) Case Study in Chapter 13.

Material in this section ("Innovation in Action: Facebook") was derived from the Wikipedia entry, "Facebook." Available at https://en.wikipedia.org/wiki/Facebook. Accessed May 15, 2019.

For instance, one of the early games to reach the top application spot, Green Patch, combined virtual Gifts with Event notifications to friends and contributions to charities through Causes.

Third-party companies provide application metrics, and several blogs arose in response to the clamor for Facebook applications. On July 4, 2007, Altura Ventures announced the "Altura 1 Facebook Investment Fund," becoming the world's first Facebook-only venture capital firm.

Applications that have been created on the Platform include chess, which allows users to play games with their friends. In such games, a user's moves are saved on the website allowing the next move to be made at any time rather than immediately after the previous move.

By November 3, 2007, seven thousand applications had been developed on the Facebook Platform, with another hundred created every day. By the second annual developers conference on July 23, 2008, the number of applications had grown to 33,000, and the number of registered developers had exceeded 400,000. Facebook was also creating applications in multiple languages.

Mark Zuckerberg said that his team from Facebook is developing a Facebook search engine. "Facebook is pretty well placed to respond to people's questions. At some point, we will. We have a team that is working on it," said Mark Zuckerberg. For him, the traditional search engines return too many results that do not necessarily respond to questions. "The search engines really need to evolve a set of answers: 'I have a specific question, answer this question for me.'"

Conclusion

Facebook appears to have successfully managed open source innovation and developed strategic partnerships with application providers given the fact that it has more than 400,000 providers.

INNOVATION IN ACTION: IBM

Background

According to the *Incumbents Strike Back—19th C-Suite study* from IBM Institute for Business Value, in order for organizations to compete in today's rapid-fire world, they are pressured to bring high-quality, differentiated products and services to market quickly. But the push to "get something out there" can lead to experiences that aren't relevant to real customer needs. If you miss the mark, you may not get a second chance. Traditionally, designers and developers have had to operate within isolated functional areas. By building multidisciplinary teams and combining a design thinking approach with agile methodologies, you can release efficiently and increase the likelihood that a customer's first impression will be a good one.

> Across a growing number of industries, solution discussions are becoming centered on customer experience as opposed to the traditional product focused lens.

Jim Boland, IBM's Project Management Global Center of Excellence Leader, is clear that IBM's project managers need to be front and center in these discussions. Their role is expanding, and the need to continuously adapt is the new norm. The traditional way of thinking—understanding your deliverables, your time to deliver and the budget you have—although still critical, may not be sufficient to ensure success.

Collaboration and agility need to sit comfortably with proven practices such as scope and financial management.

If you think about this statement, it presents quite a challenge—we are asking our project managers to be flexible enough to continuously listen and collaborate to our customers changing needs and adapt the solution accordingly, while in parallel continue managing the deliverables (including scope, time, and budget). Augmenting traditional project management skills with skills such as collaboration, agility, design thinking, and resilience become paramount.

Establishing a high level of trust throughout the journey is critical, not just trust across teams and stakeholders, but trust in the process and the journey itself.

IBM has implemented a set of tools, techniques, learnings, and methods to enable their project managers and set them up for success in this new environment. An example of this was the establishment of academies within IBM such as the agile and design thinking academies, supported by IBM's global on-demand learning platform, YourLearning, enabling a personalized learning journey for everyone in the company.

IBM is also taking this to our clients through the establishment of the IBM Garage, which is a new way of working where IBM experts, including project managers, co-create with clients in a customizable space. It's a place where you can experiment with big ideas, acquire new expertise and build new enterprise-grade solutions with modern and emerging technologies.

Case Study #1

This IBM case study, provided by Galen K. Smith, Cognitive Supply Chain Accelerator and IBM-certified executive project manager at IBM, demonstrates how innovation can and should be a part of project management. In this case, the project team chose to follow some of the agile and design thinking principles mentioned already, orchestrated by project managers in leadership roles facilitating the learning and implementation throughout the project life cycle.

Requirements-gathering started with user interviews, which resulted in the identification of three personas—supply chain specialist/buyer, operational commodity manager, and supply chain leaders. These personas defined the user groups that would participate in determining the deliverables for the minimum viable product (MVP) and first release. It was these three personas that the team focused on to understand their user experience and pain points and how to deliver a better user experience and achieve the business objective.

With the user groups defined, the next step was a design thinking workshop with key members of the project team—product owner, UX (user experience) designer, business lead, and executive sponsor attending along with 13 actual users from each of the personas. The facilitator was an agile project manager who led them through a day of design thinking practices designed to fully understand the current situation for each persona and their pain points along with ideation of ideas for a better UX. These ideas were prioritized, and the team moved into storyboarding, which applies the ideas into a new to-be scenario. The day ended with attendees creating their own paper prototype that envisioned how the UI (user interface) would look and feel, what data is needed and how to show it, and how the screens interact to deliver their vision of the desired user experience.

This approach was run in an open environment that fostered engagement by all, ignored rank, and ensured every attendee's input was heard. The workshop included creativity exercises that targeted opening the creative side of the brain, which, along with the method of collaboration and inclusion, resulted in elevating the overall creativity of the work. This creativity provided dramatically more innovative results, as seen in the wealth of ideas portrayed in the paper prototype designs.

The project managers involved played the roles of product owner, business analyst, and user SME lead and continued this innovative atmosphere after the workshop by infusing creativity, experimentation, user engagement, and feedback in the regular calls with users (twice/week), management (monthly), and the executive sponsor (weekly). With the support of the executive sponsor and management team, the project managers cultivated a cultural change in the organization and sustained it with fun events that focused on users. These events included running innovation jams, Ideation blogs, user engagement games surrounding tool learning and utilization, celebrating experiments, and recognizing folks who contributed the ideas for new function when it gets deployed.

"How is this managing innovation?" asks Smith who summarizes by stating that ideas generate innovation, and ideas flow strongly only when users feel their ideas are being heard and executed. Many avenues were opened to bring in ideas both initially and on an ongoing basis and the project leaders—product owner (PM), user lead SME (PM), and business lead—purposely communicated back to all users where the ideas came from and when they were deployed to ensure users could see how their ideas influenced the design and deliverables of the project.

Case Study #2

In this case study, Gary Bettesworth, a CICS (customer information control system) project manager at IBM, explains how a similar approach was so successful in transforming a traditional software development process.

CICS transaction server (TS) is a powerful mixed language application server, which runs on the IBM Z platform. It is used extensively in the finance and retail sectors for business-critical services, providing online transaction management and connectivity. It can process incredibly high workloads in a scalable and secure environment.

This software, which celebrates its 50th anniversary in 2019, was developed using a traditional waterfall process for most of its life. However, the waterfall development process and long development lifecycles can sometimes be slow and inflexible.

In addition, customer demands to be more agile and to consume software faster, due to the need to respond to constantly changing and competitive marketplaces, driven by technological innovation, required a transformation of the team's software development and management process.

Over the last 10 years, the project team have been on a journey culminating in the use of project management and delivery process and tools, which support the concepts of agile, DevOps, and Enterprise Design Thinking.

According to Bettesworth, the Enterprise Design Thinking method helps the team validate that they are building the right software by implementing activities like as-is and to-be scenario mapping, empathy mapping and interviews, to fully engage with users and understand their personas and needs. This combined with agile practices (time-boxed iterations, frequent code delivery and feedback, code demonstrations/playbacks, small multidisciplined subteams, story points and burndown charts, prioritized backlogs) and supporting agile tooling has completely changed the culture of the CICS TS project team. The whole project team is empowered and self-directed, which supports innovation during the software development process, with project management taking on a servant leadership role to help and guide where necessary. Plans are no longer fixed, with adjustments or pivots being made regularly based on stakeholder feedback and a continuous assessment of the market. Changes to the delivery process are also made by project team members continuously throughout the project.

Innovation has also been essential to enable the team to modernize all its tooling and create a DevOps end-to-end automation pipeline built in a modular manor. This continuous integration pipeline enables code to be rapidly built, deployed and tested as soon as it has been developed. The ability to quickly build and test software has been essential to frequently deliver new capability to project stakeholders. Live dashboards enable code delivery and project status to be viewed by internal stakeholders, including the project manager, and are used as the basis for project status meetings.

These are just two out of thousands of examples of projects being run across IBM where project managers are changing their approach to how they launch, manage and close projects.

Case Study #3

Carlos Carnelós, IBM's Technical Support Services Delivery Transformation Lead in Latin America, and who has been working in the area of IT Automation for the past four years, states that innovation lies in the project deliverables, the technologies deployed and the newer ways we are doing business. In his experience, project management techniques are becoming a mix of traditional and agile and use design thinking as a methodology for defining scope and prioritizing what and when functions get delivered.

Conclusion

In summary, Jim Boland's opinion is that good project managers are equal parts project managers, consultants, change agents, and innovators. As the term *hybrid job* becomes more and more standard practice in the future, our project managers will have to mix their traditional PM skills with new age skills such as design thinking, data analytics, and so on. This statement holds through for many job roles and it's just as important for employees who are not project managers to learn project management skills. Innovation will be a constant in this new hybrid world.

INNOVATION IN ACTION: TEXAS INSTRUMENTS

When companies recognize the need for continuous innovation, they are often at a loss as to where to begin. Some companies tend to focus on technology and organizational restructuring. Texas Instruments quickly identified that starting with people and an organizational culture that supports innovation can accelerate the process.

Background

Most people seem to believe that innovation project management begins with the development of a project management methodology. Furthermore, they often make the fatal mistake of believing that the development of a project management methodology is the solution to all their ailments for traditional and innovation projects. While this may be true in some circumstances, companies that appear to be excellent in project management realize that people execute methodologies and that the best practices in innovation and traditional project management might be achieved quicker if the focus initially is on the people rather than the tools. Therefore, the focus should be on the culture.

One way to become good at project management is to develop a success pyramid. Every company has their own approach as to what should be included in a success pyramid. Texas Instruments recognized the importance of focusing on people as a way to accelerate innovation project success. Texas Instruments developed a success pyramid for managing global innovation projects. The success pyramid is shown in Figure 12-1.

A spokesperson at Texas Instruments describes the development and use of the success pyramid for managing global projects at Texas Instruments:

> By the late 1990s, the business organization for sensors and controls had migrated from localized teams to global teams. I was responsible for managing 5–6 project managers who were in turn managing global teams for NPD (new product development). These teams typically consisted of 6–12 members from North America, Europe, and Asia. Although we were operating in a global business environment, there were many new and unique difficulties that the teams faced. We developed the success pyramid to help these project managers in this task.
>
> Although the message in the pyramid is quite simple, the use of this tool can be very powerful. It is based on the principle of building a pyramid from the bottom to the top. The bottom layer of building blocks is the *foundation* and is called "understanding and trust." The message here is that for a global team

Figure 12–1. The Success Pyramid.
Source: VICUSCHKA / Getty Images, NDABCREATIVITY / Adobe Stock, barisonal / Getty Images, barisonal / Getty Images.

to function well, there must be a common bond. The team members must have trust in one another, and it is up to the project manager to make sure that this bond is established. Within the building blocks at this level, we provided additional details and examples to help the project managers. It is common that some team members may not have ever met prior to the beginning of a project, so this task of building trust is definitely a challenge.

The second level is called *sanctioned direction*. This level includes the team charter and mission as well as the formal goals and objectives. Since these are virtual teams that often have little direct face time, the message at this level is for the project manager to secure the approval and support from all the regional managers involved in the project. This step is crucial in avoiding conflicts of priorities from team members at distant locations.

The third level of the pyramid is called *accountability*. This level emphasizes the importance of including the values and beliefs from all team members. On global teams, there can be quite a lot of variation in this area. By allowing a voice from all team members, not only can project planning be more complete but also everyone can directly buy into the plan. Project managers using a method of distributed leadership in this phase usually do very well. The secret is to get people to transition from attitude of obligation to a willingness of accepting responsibility.

The next level, called *logistics*, is where the team lives for the duration of the project and conducts the day-to-day work. This level includes all of the daily, weekly, and monthly communications and is based on an agreement of the type of development process that will be followed. At Texas Instruments, we have a formal process for NPD projects, and this is usually used for this type of project. The power of the pyramid is that this level of detailed work can go very smoothly, provided there is a solid foundation below it.

Following the execution of the lower levels in the pyramid, we can expect to get good *results*, as shown in the fifth level. This is driven in the two areas of internal and external customers. Internal customers may include management or may include business center sites that have financial ownership of the overall project.

Finally, the top level of the pyramid shows the overall *goal* and is labeled "team success." Our experience has shown that a global team that is successful on a one- to two-year project is often elevated to a higher level of confidence and capability. This success breeds added enthusiasm and positions the team members for bigger and more challenging assignments. The ability of managers to tap into this higher level of capability provides competitive advantage and leverages our ability to achieve success.

Conclusion

At Texas Instruments, the emphasis on culture not only benefited their innovation initiatives but also resulted in best practices that supported other initiatives. It is unfortunate that more companies do not realize the importance of this approach.

INNOVATION IN ACTION: 3M

Companies often struggle with how to bring the workforce into the innovation process. In some companies, workers believe that only the R&D group or any other innovation groups are responsible for coming up with innovation ideas and exploiting them. 3M took a different approach and set the standard on how to involve the entire company.

Background

Companies that are highly successful at innovation use innovation as the driver for sustained corporate growth. 3M Corporation is prime example of innovation in action. Most researchers agree that 3M's success emanates from their corporate culture that fosters an innovation mindset. As stated by Irving Buchen (2000):

> 3M announced that all employees were free to spend up to 15 minutes each working day on whatever ideas they wanted to work on. The only restriction was that it could not be at the expense of their regular assignments. They did not have to secure approval for their project. They did not have to tell anyone what they were working on. They could bunch their l-minute segments if they needed more solid blocks of time. They did not have to produce anything to justify or pay back the time taken. What was the result? There was electricity in the air. Employees came earlier and stayed later to extend their innovation time. Many walked around with a weird smile of mischief and even fun across their face; some even began to giggle. But they were also enormously productive. Scotch tape came out of this ferment; so did Post-its. Perhaps equally as important, morale was given an enormous lift; general productivity was higher; teams seemed to be closer and working better together; the relationships between middle-level managers of different divisions seemed to improve. In short, it was a win-win situation. The innovative gains were matched by a new spirit that changed the entire culture.

Companies such as Google and Hewlett-Packard have programs similar to 3M's 15 percent time program. 3M's program was initiated in 1948 and has since generated many of the company's best-selling products, 22,800 patents, and annual sales of over $20 billion.

There are several distinguishing characteristics of the 3M culture, beginning with employee encouragement for innovation. Employees are encouraged to follow their instincts and take advantage of opportunities. 3M provides forums for employees to see what others are doing, to get ideas for new products, and to find solutions to existing problems. The culture thrives on open communication and the sharing of information. Employees are also encouraged to talk with customers about their needs and to visit 3M's Innovation Centers.

Strategic direction is another characteristic of the 3M culture. Employees are encouraged to think about the future but not at the expense of sacrificing current earnings. Using the "Thirty Percent Rule," 30 percent of each division's revenues must come from products introduced in the last four years. This is tracked almost religiously and forms the basis for employee bonuses.

Funding sources are available to employees to further develop their ideas. Seed money for initial exploration of ideas can come from the business units. If the funding requests are denied, employees can request corporate funding.

Rewards and recognition are part of 3M's innovative culture. A common problem facing many companies is that scientists and technical experts believe that the "grass is greener" in management than in a technical environment. 3M created a dual ladder system whereby technical personnel can have the same compensation and benefits as corporate management by remaining on a technical ladder. By staying on the technical ladder, people are guaranteed their former job even if their research project fails.

Similar to Disney and Apple, 3M created the Carlton Society, named after former company president Richard P. Carlton, which recognizes the achievements of 3M scientists who develop innovative new products and contribute to the innovation culture.

One of the most significant benefits of the 3M culture is in recruiting. Workers with specialized skills are sought after by most companies and the culture at 3M, which offers a significant amount of "freedom" for innovation, helps them attract talented employees.

Conclusion

3M's success set the standard that others have copied on how to involve the entire organization into innovational thinking. All employees must be made aware of the notion that they can contribute to innovation and their ideas will be heard.

INNOVATION IN ACTION: MOTOROLA

For more than 90 years, Motorola has been recognized as a synonym for innovation. Motorola's strength has been in technical innovations in the communications and semiconductor industries but has been expanded to other industries. Motorola set the standard for getting close to the end users during innovation activities and the need to understand the business model of the customers.

Background

In previous chapters, we discussed the importance of getting too close to the customers to understand their needs. In most companies, innovation research is simply asking customers what their needs might be now and in the future. Motorola carries their research much further. Motorola conducts "deep" customer research using their design research and innovation teams to articulate not only how users work with Motorola's products but also how customers run their business processes and what their needs will be in the future. Motorola also observes how customers use their products.

Motorola's research goes beyond simply understanding how the product is being used. It also includes an understanding of why the product is essential to the customer's business success and how the product fits into the customer's business model. This allows Motorola to perform targeted innovation. Customer knowledge is not based on just the end user's requirements. Understanding the business aspects of a product solution can give industrial design groups the opportunity to drive product development direction.

Motorola's generative research is driven by customer and partner interviews as well as observational research. As stated by Graham Marshall:

> Based on the first round of customer visits and generative research, the team identifies specific customers to revisit during the product definition phase. At this time the researcher will bring sample models that demonstrate form, features, and functionality. The product definition phase helps the team clearly define and test the right product fit before there is a commitment to development.
>
> We use model toolkits and storyboards to communicate potential design directions with our customers. We can better see the complexity of the customer's needs by posing specific questions: "What information do you need to display? How much information do you need to key in? How well lighted is your space? Is the product used in the storeroom or the storefront, or both? How far do you need to carry or move the product or the device to complete a transaction?"

The section "Innovation in Action: Motorola" has been adapted from Graham Marshall, "At Motorola, Design Research Becomes a Strategic Asset," *Design Management Journal*. 2009, Vol. 4, Issue 1, pp. 61–67. DOI: 10.1111/j.1942-5074.2009.00007.x.

Motorola also performs validation to ensure that the focus is on a customer solution. As stated by Marshall:

> During the course of the development program, the Innovation and Design team needs to validate the integrity of the gathered information, product direction, and development trade-offs. This ensures that, as product development progresses, the design remains targeted on the customer's needs.

Conclusion

By understanding the customer's business and maintaining close customer contact, Motorola has demonstrated the benefits that can be derived from innovative customer-focused solutions. Simply stated, Motorola has evolved into a targeted business solution provider.

INNOVATION PROJECT MANAGEMENT: THE CASE OF KAUST SMART _____

About KAUST

King Abdullah University of Science and Technology (KAUST) is an international graduate research university situated on the shores of the Red Sea in Saudi Arabia. A relatively young university, with over a decade old since its founding, KAUST is renowned by global benchmarks and is an ascending star of academic and research excellence. KAUST's focus is on advancing science and technology through distinctive and collaborative research integrated with graduate education. (MS and PhD). KAUST acts as a catalyst for innovation, economic development, and social prosperity for Saudi Arabia, the region, and the world.

KAUST presents a unique campus with unique opportunities. It's a "small city" with limitless boundaries for experimentation and a culture that pushes the boundaries of innovation. The campus is 17 sq. miles of land that is divided into academic and research facilities, a community of on-campus houses, villas, and apartments, recreational facilities, retail and dining, K-12 schools, and an industrial park for startups and industry partners. The campus is a microcosm of "smart cities" but with the advantage of being under a flat management structure and governance which makes decision making and experimentation easier than traditional models seen in public cities.

The KAUST campus is well connected in terms of information technology and digital services. The private fiber optic network spans every building, home, and apartment offering high speed data and voice communications to all residents and employees. Externally, KAUST is connected via super-fast subsea cables enabling high speed and high volume research data sharing between KAUST faculty and their international collaboration as well as general internet traffic including growing demand for TV and movie streaming services. WiFi is pervasive everywhere, classrooms are designed to enable in-person and remote teaching, and K-12 school students all utilize laptop devices and smart boards for their class curriculums.

One of KAUST's uniqueness is the diversity of its people. The community of KAUST is composed of over 120 nationalities that make up its student body, faculty, staff, spouses, children, and contractors'

Material in this section, "Innovation Project Management: The Case of KAUST Smart," was provided by Samara S. Barhamain, Program Manager, KAUST Smart and Mohamed Abdel-Aal, Director, Digital Experience and Innovation. ©2022 by KAUST. All rights reserved. Reproduced with permission.

workforce. This diversity offers an extraordinary chance for ideation, differing perspectives, and cultural awareness. At the same time, it poses some challenges for project execution and management styles given the divergent cultures and backgrounds.

About "KAUST Smart"

"KAUST Smart" is the brand for a digital experience and transformation initiative that was kick started in 2019 with a goal to allow KAUST to utilize its smart city for rapid experimentations, and innovations. These experimentations and innovations should ultimately provide a unique experience frictionless experience for visitors, employees, residents, and community members. KAUST Smart also serves to enhance the KAUST identity and its ecosystem by demonstrating to the world KAUST's capabilities which helps attract talent. KAUST Smart also serves to align some of the university's goals with Saudi Arabia's own strategic goals and priorities.

KAUST Smart builds on the campus's autonomy to push the boundaries of innovation and to establish and position KAUST as a living laboratory for digital transformation, research and testing. Some of the activities that KAUST Smart undertakes include idea generation and collection from the community of KAUST to enhance an experience that has the potential to make an impact on people's life while leveraging new solutions or emerging technologies. KAUST Smart also utilizes design thinking techniques to conduct its experiments while staying focused on human-centric principles. Ultimately KAUST Smart is driven by pragmatic approach to results which is done through the execution of pilots and proof of concepts to test ideas and to generate feedback.

KAUST Smart acts a facilitator to execute this mission by cutting across the organizational structure in a horizontal fashion and working jointly with functions and areas that have the subject matter expertise and the operational capabilities to support these ideas and pilots. Therefore, KAUST Smart focuses on building partnerships and engagement with all KAUST departments, industry players, technology vendors, and other universities and government bodies to support co-development and co-design of such concepts and ideas.

KEY CHARACTERISTIC OF KAUST SMART PROJECTS (WHAT MAKES KAUST SMART PROJECTS UNIQUE)

Looking at what makes the KAUST Smart innovation projects unique and what characteristics they share in common, we identified seven aspects that differentiate them from other projects.

Exploration, Pilot Projects, and Proof of Concept Projects

The nature of innovation projects carried under KAUST Smart is very dynamic. These projects don't often start with an intention to buy, implement, and operate a stable service. Instead, they start with the intention to answer a question or more of how does this capability add to a smart city experience? Is

Material in this section, "Key Characteristic Of Kaust Smart Projects (What Makes Kaust Smart Projects Unique)," was provided by Samara S. Barhamain, Program Manager, KAUST Smart and Mohamed Abdel-Aal, Director, Digital Experience and Innovation. ©2022 by KAUST. All rights reserved. Reproduced with permission.

there a place for this in a smart city? How can it improve the experience of the resident and user? How can the ecosystem be ready to adopt this smart capability? How can it be adopted in a scalable and sustainable way?

Majority of the projects carried under KAUTS Smart are "Proof of Concept" or "Pilot" projects in nature. They are unique as they start with curiosity. Many times, they are done in collaboration with external partners who share the same curiosity and business interest to improve certain experiences and explore new capabilities.

Exploration and pilot projects require clarity on the questions we are trying to answer or the problems we are trying to solve. In some cases, they also require criteria-based matrix and evaluation to be conducted to understand how certain smart capabilities can perform in the context of a smart city.

Exploration and pilot projects in context of KAUST Smart share some common attributes including a defined limited timespan, iterative nature, acceptance of failure, cross sector nature, high level of stakeholder management and involvement.

Methodology

The unique value-add and special flavor of KUAST Smart is its methodology. The methodology sets the work culture and defines the common terminology.

The main stages in the KAUST Smart methodology include: Idea, Alignment, Design Thinking, Hackathon, Minimal Viable Product, Pilot/ Proof of Concept, and User Feedback. Sometimes the pilot or proof of concept materializes into a rollout or implementation by the relevant operational entity in KAUST. However, this is not always the objective of these innovative pilot projects.

This methodology is circular and iterative in nature. In addition, marketing and communication aspects are key to everything we do in KAUST Smart in order to engage the community and partners and also to highlight the pilot projects and outcomes to all interested parties.

Agile and Adaptive Approaches

Another common aspect of innovation projects under KAUST Smart is that they adopt and leverage an agile approach. The methodology as illustrated previously calls for an iterative execution that allows for pivoting and adjusting the course of action according to the user feedback and what works in practice.

In some of our innovation projects in KAUST Smart especially the KAUSTCentral mobile application platform, we went a further step and implemented concepts of Scaled Agile Framework to manage from program increments all the way to team sprints.

Agile and adaptive approaches are best suited for KAUST Smart projects for two reasons: the solutions being explored are often bleeding edge and not fully mature yet, and the user needs and wants are dynamic and evolving. Therefore, the flexibility and agility in responding to these factors is very important.

Design Thinking, User Focus Groups, and Community Engagement

Design Thinking is a key aspect in the KAUST Smart methodology. It plays a major role in defining and understanding the user personas, empathizing with the user needs and wants, designing user journeys, and ideating with the users.

Community engagement is a focus in every project or initiative under KAUST Smart. In addition to Design Thinking sessions, we also run focus groups to understand perceptions, feelings, behaviors, and feedback. These can take place before, during, and/or after any pilot project.

Design Thinking sessions, focus groups, and other community engagement activities are open for participation to the wider KAUST community including high school students and families in addition to staff and academic community in KAUST.

Working with the Ecosystem

Conducting proof of concept projects with partners in the industry, support sectors, governments, and relevant entities can take these pilots to a greater level of impact.

Smart and future technologies and capabilities involve many critical aspects of legal, technical, and operational considerations.

One of the objectives of conducting pilot innovative projects is to elevate the ecosystem as a result of being exposed to the unique challenges and opportunities presented by these new capabilities. Insurance is a great example of this especially in context of smart and autonomous mobility projects. We had to navigate the challenges of finding insurance partners that would offer services and coverage for Autonomous Vehicles. Another example is having trained and skilled personnel to operate and maintain self-driving vehicles in a way that also provides service continuity in the future.

Startups also form another component of the KAUST Smart ecosystem that is often engaged and participant in many innovation projects.

Building the Capabilities of the Future

Another common characteristic of KAUST Smart projects is that they aim to build and develop capabilities and local talent. This includes the technical capabilities as well as the framework and methodology knowledge. Through partnerships with key players in the ecosystem and startups, this development aspect is also extended to these partners.

Engaging research community around KAUST Smart initiatives creates additional opportunities for discussions with Research and Development functions within leading industry partner entities about problems of the future that labs and universities can help solve and address.

Measuring Impact

One of the key challenges in digital innovation projects and programs, such as KAUST Smart, is how to apply KPIs and measurements. Standard project management KPIs such as time, cost, resources, variance … etc. are well established and still applicable to such projects. However, measurement of final outcomes in terms of ROI to the organization is more complex. This measurement typically fits under a more comprehensive governance framework. But for innovation programs, governance frameworks should be designed to balance the exploratory nature of innovation activities. It cannot be too tight to stifle and slow down innovation efforts and jeopardize the opportunities. On the other hand, it cannot be overly relaxed to cause risk or lead to wasted resources.

For KAUST Smart, we are still working on evolving a measurement model that balances the unique nature of the context which is KAUST being a research university with a small city and community attached to it that also hosts established companies as well startups. The uniqueness stims from the varied personas that are part of this ecosystem. There are students, faculty, staff, entrepreneurs, spouses, school children, labor workers, and more. There are also external stakeholders that have interest in KAUST and how it serves the larger goals of Saudi Arabia.

This measurement model is fundamentally based on measuring value to the organization, to the various personas, and to the country. A potential brand of such a model is to refer to outcomes as "impact credits" where these credits are calculated based on formulas that consider projects and activities that have a direct impact on cost savings, reputation, attractiveness of the institution to hire and retain employees and students, social outreach, intellectual property generated from activities, translation of research into tangible pilots and experiments, and student, faculty, and community member experiences.

RECENT AND ONGOING PROJECT EXAMPLES

Autonomous Shuttles Assessment

KAUST introduced self-driving shuttles on its campus in December 2019 to become the pioneer in adopting autonomous vehicles in the Kingdom of Saudi Arabia. The pilot project incorporates vehicle technology from two global leaders in autonomous mobility and advanced manufacturing.

The launch of the project establishes KAUST as a leader in the fields of future: eco-friendly transportation and mobility research, and makes KAUST a leading smart city in the region.

The shuttles on the KAUST campus use mapping, cognitive response technology, light detection and ranging (Lidar), and obstacle avoidance systems to control, navigate, and drive the vehicles. Both shuttles are fully electric and sustainable, making them not only easily accessible but also environmentally friendly.

Innovation and sustainability are two of KAUST's highest priorities. Implementing autonomous vehicles on campus is an important next step in creating transportation solutions that help reduce emissions, increase mobility, and can help diversify Saudi Arabia's economy.

After the basic infrastructure was set and the vehicles were successfully operational, the project followed an iterative approach of exploration and adding features including the integration with On-Demand bus requesting system.

In 2021, additional vehicle upgrades were carried out including the installation of additional and more advanced sensors and software upgrades. In addition, the autonomous route was expanded to include additional stops and address the higher demand service areas such as Tamimi Supermarket, Harbor walk, and Discovery square. Between July 2021 and February 2022, the autonomous shuttles transported 400+ passengers on their designated routes.

The community engagement was a key success factor in this project. Several sessions took place including focus groups and community townhall meetings.

The project positioned KAUST as a leading pioneer in the Kingdom in the area of Autonomous mobility and paved the way for many rich conversations and collaborations with national entities working in the areas of mobility strategy, urban planning, and giga projects.

Material in this section, "Recent and Ongoing Project Examples," was provided by Samara S. Barhamain, Program Manager, KAUST Smart and Mohamed Abdel-Aal, Director, Digital Experience and Innovation. ©2022 by KAUST. All rights reserved. Reproduced with permission.

Autonomous Last Mile Delivery Assessment

KAUST and the National Digital Transformation Unit (NDU) collaborated to conduct joint projects in digital transformation that contribute to realizing Vision 2030 and enable digital adoption in the Kingdom. NDU regards this collaboration with KAUST as strategic for achieving its vision, especially since KAUST provides a unique environment as a living lab that allows advanced technologies and concepts to be tested before launching it in other cities and locations.

Globally, consumer behavior has changed significantly with an increase in online shopping and contactless services. This pilot aims to leverage KAUST as an ideal living lab for testing new package delivery solutions using a self-driving vehicle, called UNO. This project also helps to further establish KAUST as a leader in the field of sustainable future logistics, mobility solutions, and digital innovation.

The vehicle is equipped with light detection and ranging (Lidar) sensors as well as GPS receivers and cameras for objects detection and accurate positioning. The vehicle is fully electric and sustainable, which makes it environmentally friendly.

In the autonomous delivery experience, the residents interact with the vehicle via SMS and the touchscreen user interface on the vehicle.

The pilot was conducted in the Island residential area. During the pilot period, 28+ delivery trips were completed by the self-driving vehicle. 200+ packages were delivered. A total of 565 km distance was travelled by the self-driving vehicle in total. The average vehicle speed was ranging from 10 km to 15 km per hour. There were zero cases of disengagement where the safety operator had to take over the vehicle control due to loss of localization or similar.

The user engagement sessions pre and post pilot reflected the community's enthusiasm and active involvement in this pilot and the feedback was invaluable and helped in improving the pilot as well as create a backlog of additional features to channel into the future iterations of this experiment.

Build Your Own Autonomous Car

KAUST and Brightskies are cooperating to develop a self-driving vehicle (autonomous) proof of concept inside the KAUST Campus where researchers, staff, and startups can utilize the POC as a platform for innovation and experimentation.

The pilot project included installing hardware onto a normal car such as sensors, Lidar, cameras, and GPS receivers. It also included deploying the self-driving software with its different modules: perception, localization, motion control, and path planning. The stops and operational test area was also mapped and tested in different conditions.

The user interaction is carried through a mobile app and an in-vehicle screen. The rider can request the car on demand and chose the destination point.

The pilot project is currently well underway and the expected completion is planned in the second quarter of 2022.

KAUSTCentral

KAUSTCentral is a central mobile platform to access different experiences in KUAST as a resident, student, worker, and visitor.

It aims to build a unique and connected experience where users can access information at their fingertips.

The work on KAUSTCentral started late 2019 by laying down the basic architecture of the platform. The development work and the project followed a Scaled Agile approach with multiple program increment planning cycles. The methodology was further adapted with the maturity of the project and the effective use of backlogs and recurring standup meetings and retrospectives.

The KAUSTCentral platform continues to grow and to incorporate additional features to enhance the experience for KAUST community and visitors.

INNOVATION IN ACTION: SAMSUNG

Some companies focus heavily upon creating new products and hoping for the best, regardless of the value that the customers may see in the product. Samsung recognized that there is a significant difference between introducing a few new innovative products occasionally and becoming a global innovation leader. The main difference, as Samsung has identified, is focusing on value innovation.

Background

Samsung and other companies have adopted a value innovation approach, as discussed in Chapter 2, which allowed them to create a corporate culture for becoming an innovation leader rather than an innovation copier and follower. Some characteristics of Samsung's culture include:

- Innovation-oriented sponsorship and governance from the top of the organizational hierarchy downward
- Line of sight about the executives' vision and the company's strategy and strategic objectives for all employees to see
- Use of open innovation practices as well as seeking out innovation ideas internally
- Establishing strategy and innovation centers as well as open innovation centers for better knowledge management
- Recognizing that knowledge management supports core competencies for storage and reuse of knowledge from R&D activities
- Recognizing that globalization in a turbulent environment requires nontraditional systems
- Maintaining customer-focused product innovations
- A willingness to accept innovation risk-taking
- Flattening of the organizational hierarchy
- Development of speed-focused innovation strategies and execution
- Decisions are being made quicker than before
- A reduction in cycle time from months and years to weeks
- Low-cost manufacturing

Conclusion

These characteristics have allowed Samsung to develop superior core competencies. The results of Samsung's value-driven culture have led to innovations in products, technology, marketing, cost reduction, and global management.[2]

AGILE INNOVATION IN ACTION: INTEGRATED COMPUTER SOLUTIONS, INC

Background

The challenges we face today, and the ones we will be facing in the coming months and years, are due to the exponential pace of technological change that is rapidly transforming our societies and competitive landscapes. As someone that has been involved in the practice and management of technology innovation for over 30 years, I have seen the pace of technological change increase from the steady linear growth in the 1980s to the exponential acceleration in the 2000s, to today's nearly vertical pitch where major open-sourced breakthroughs are compounding each new weekly advance, leading to new products and services and even entirely new markets at a clip that is difficult to comprehend. To ensure their continued existence with the hope of remaining competitive, successful organizations are changing their approach to innovation management to include agile concepts. Those that desire to *shape* the pace of change to their advantage are going further, implementing the holistic "Agile Innovation Master Plan"—a framework created by world-renowned author and innovation thought-leader Langdon Morris of InnovationLabs—which was designed to provide a comprehensive yet extremely agile approach to managing innovation strategy, portfolio, process, culture, and infrastructure. It is my belief that implementing the Agile Innovation Master Plan is not only a good idea for innovative organizations—it may be the only way to ensure their survival.

Five Key Tracks

The Five Key Tracks (Morris 2017, 12), as defined in the Agile Innovation Master Plan, are derived from five simple questions: Why innovate? What to innovate? How to innovate? Who innovates? Where? Answering these simple questions reveals the foundational framework components related to strategy, portfolio, process, culture, and infrastructure, and it is these five components that are utilized in the creation and implementation of a "system for innovation." Langdon Morris captures the importance:

---

2. For additional benefits of Samsung's culture and value innovation approach, see Jung and Chung (2016) and Wolff et al. (2006).

The material in the section "Agile Innovation in Action: Integrated Computer Solutions, Inc." has been provided by Thomas Brazil, chief digital officer, Integrated Computer Solutions, Inc. ©2022 by Integrated Computer Solutions, Inc. All rights reserved. Reproduced with permission. This material is an excerpt from Thomas Brazil's new book *Implementing the Agile Innovation Master Plan*, a how-to guide that describes lessons learned and provides tips and tricks for implementing the "five key tracks" of effective Agile innovation programs. The goal of the book is to help implementers of the framework reach mastery levels in a rapid manner. Graphics in this section were provided by Langdon Morris to Harold Kerzner and Thomas Brazil for inclusion in this book and remain under copyright to Langdon Morris of InnovationLabs.

To innovate consistently, you have to make a distinction between luck and innovation. Either you have a reliable system for innovation that delivers consistent results, or you hope that your people luck into good ideas. Those are the only two options. Which do you prefer?

Since you are reading this, it likely means you desire such a system for your organization. However, it is important to keep in mind that we are discussing a framework for innovation success and understanding the importance of each track—and how the tracks feed and inform each other—is paramount. How you *implement* each track may be quite different than our experience, but the *order* of implementation of each track was crucial for our success. The first step, however, is understanding the agile innovation sprint.

The Agile Innovation Sprint

The agile innovation sprint uses complex thinking, design thinking, and other creative efforts in an iterative sequence of six stages for the implementation of The Agile Innovation Master Plan. The intriguing aspect of this approach is that the same methods you will use for your innovation process are utilized for its implementation, which results in an acceleration of learning in preparation for your innovation efforts. Similar to agile software development, where small features are immediately usable as they are implemented, the agile innovation sprints produce usable features and capabilities that further accelerate implementation. In other words, the more tracks you implement, the faster you implement subsequent tracks, while gaining mastery of important concepts and methodologies along the way such that when all five key tracks are complete, you will already have a high level of efficiency in your innovation program. The diagram in Figure 12-2 highlights the general concept. The stages are *understanding*, *divergent thinking*, *convergent thinking*, *simulation and prototyping*, *validation* and the *innospective*. These stages serve to

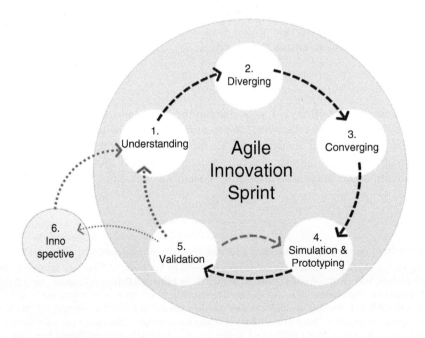

Figure 12–2. Agile Innovation Sprint.

break down the design and implementation of each track into smaller pieces that—when complete—are functionally usable in your innovation efforts.

Part 1. Understanding the Five Parts

You will note that the order of importance of the five key tracks is quite different in terms of *understanding* them than it is for *implementing* them (at least it was for us), and the reason for this is quite simple: You *must be organizationally prepared* to achieve success in your innovation program, and one key prerequisite is having a common language of innovation. This is shown in Figure 12-3.

The point being made is that *once understanding is achieved*, the implementation—which begins with building a culture that supports innovation—becomes much more likely to achieve success as everyone will be swimming in the same direction. Of course, learning is what innovation is all about, but the goal is to let *you* learn from the lessons *we* learned after our time spent in discovery, development and testing of this framework during our implementation. By following this approach, you will be able to *accelerate* your learning curve across your organization, rapidly moving up the levels of the pyramid of mastery (Morris 2017, 320) (Figure 12-4).

Understanding	Implementation
1. Strategy	1. Culture
2. Portfolio	2. Infrastructure
3. Process	3. Process
4. Culture	4. Strategy
5. Infrastructure	5. Portfolio

Figure 12–3.   The order of Understanding and the Order of Implementation.
Source: GEA

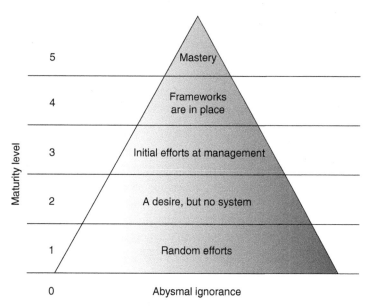

Figure 12–4.   The Pyramid of Mastery Denoting Efforts and Maturity Levels.

It is important to note that our company did not start from scratch: Our CEO understood both the need and the value of innovation for years prior to my arrival, and in fact led efforts that achieved some tangible benefits for both ICS and our customers. However, without a *system* in place, there was no means of ensuring consistent outcomes. Some of the infrastructure was there along with some creative geniuses, but they were lacking just about everything else: an organizational culture to support innovation, a link between strategy and innovation intent, an innovation leader and innovation "champions", and a rigorous process that could produce results in a repeatable, consistent manner. In other words, like so many companies that have a desire—*but no system*—it is easy to get stuck at lower maturity level. As we implemented our own Agile Innovation Master Plan, we rapidly moved from maturity level 2 to a mastery level in less than a year—and it all started with *understanding*—a word you will hear repeatedly due to its importance as the first stage in the agile innovation sprint (Morris 2017, 128).

Understanding the Strategy Track

Most successful organizations will have strategic objectives that support their *raison d'être*—their purpose or reason for their existence—and it is the link (Morris 2017, 25) between strategy and innovation that determines your organization's ability to achieve its objectives while continuously adapting to the frenetic pace of societal and technological change and the resulting uncertainties they introduce (Morris 2018).

Whether you are innovating on behalf of your organization or on behalf of your customers (or both, as is the case for our organization), understanding *why* you are innovating (strategic intent) is necessary before you can determine *what* to innovate (portfolio) to achieve the desired outcomes. In effect, aligning ideas for innovation to at least one (or more) of your strategic objectives is a *risk and opportunity mitigation strategy*: If you focus only on ideas that are aligned with your strategic intent, you will not waste your efforts on ineffective expenditure of time and resources.

Each of the strategic objectives of your organization (or your customer's objectives, if innovating on their behalf) will likely have a weighting—and if they don't, they should. In other words, *some strategic objectives will be more important than others*. For example, one of our DoD customers lists four strategic objectives on its website. One of them—*optimize and reduce costs*—will certainly have a higher priority (or weighting) in peacetime than during a time of war (where cost optimization is less of a concern due to mission requirements). Conversely, it may have an even higher weighting than normal if budget constraints are enacted. There are logical and obvious conclusions that can be drawn from this understanding:

- The strategic objectives themselves can change.
- The weightings of each objective are not necessarily equally balanced.
- The weightings can change dynamically, depending on conditions or events.

The first point will seem obvious to organizations that are mature in their approach to innovation, as the "understanding" stage of an agile innovation sprint requires that management frequently reconsider changes in the technology landscape, competitive landscape, market conditions, and tacit (or hidden) customer needs, which are necessary to remove uncertainty about the strategic direction of the organization and which can result in changes to the strategic objectives in response. This is a logical outflow of the "unpacking" of conditions that identify pain points, problem statements, and trends and opportunities to be addressed by the organization (Morris 2017, 176). However, all of the above considerations have an extremely important role to play in balancing your innovation portfolio and they underscore the importance of agility in adapting to the pace of change.

While your organization may already be structured to do so with its strategic objectives, it is imperative that your innovation portfolio management capabilities be designed such that the entire innovation portfolio can be realigned—or "pivoted"—any time the portfolio evaluation factors and/or their weightings change, to be sure that your innovation efforts remain in direct support of current strategic objectives and weightings.

Understanding the Portfolio Track

A properly balanced innovation portfolio helps an organization align its innovation efforts with its strategic objectives while balancing risk. The kind of risk to be balanced can come in many forms—one such example being in terms of time—over the near, medium, and long-term according to the types of innovation being pursued. Fundamentally it is a strategy for managing risk such that the entire portfolio as a whole can achieve a desired return even when an individual project fails (and they will, or you aren't taking enough risk to explore the world of potentials, nor are you likely learning anything new).

In this section, both ideas and projects are referenced. However, there are times when you can treat the portfolio of *ideas* separately from the portfolio of active *projects*, and times when they need to be treated together. These are important considerations when you get to the implementation phase, but for our purposes, here the important part is understanding that there can be a distinction between the two.

There are a variety of methods to balance a portfolio and maintain an acceptable risk profile:

- Scoring each idea or project's orientation toward the strategic objective weightings
- Scoring each idea or project according to the *type* of innovation it represents, such as incremental, business model, breakthrough, or new venture
- Scoring each idea or project using risk and/or reward factors aligned to your strategic intent
- If technology-related, scoring the idea or project by its technology classification such as AI, Machine Learning, Cloud, etc., depending on strategic focus in each area
- Any combination of methods

One of the standard methods referenced in the Agile Innovation Master Plan is a risk/reward evaluation, which is a very useful method that can apply to any organization. Consider the following example reward factors:

- Benefit to customers
- Revenue potential
- Competitive advantage
- Enhances our digital presence
- Enhances our brand

Similar to strategic objective weightings, the desired reward factors (or opportunity factors) can be assigned a weighting by management (a level of strategic importance on a scale of values), and then each

Project #: 126	Innovation Portfolio Evaluation	Idea or Project Name: Big Idea Project	
Reward Factors: What are the key external, strategic benefits affecting our business?	Weight (1, 2, 3, 5, 8)	Rating (1, 2, 3, 5, 8)	Score (Weight x Rating)
1. Benefit to Customers	8	5	40
2. Revenue Potential	5	8	40
3. Competitive Advantage	3	2	6
4. Enhances our Digital Presence	5	3	15
5. Enhances our Brand	3	5	15
6.			
7.			
Total			116 Reward
Risk Factors: What are the key risks with this idea?	Weight (1, 2, 3, 5, 8)	Rating (1, 2, 3, 5, 8)	Score (Weight x Rating)
1. Financial Risk	5	5	25
2. Failure Risk	2	1	2
3. Technology Risk	5	8	40
4. Distribution Risk	1	2	2
5. Market Risk	3	5	15
6.			
7.			
Total			84 Risk

Reward Factors · Risk Factors · Totals

Figure 12–5. Example Risk/Reward Evaluation.

idea or project can be *rated* for closeness of fit (again, on a scale) by interested parties[3] at the time of its introduction. On the opposite end, risk factors (financial risk, technology risk, market risk, or other risks recognized by your organization) can be managed in an identical manner: Weightings are applied by management, and individual ideas or projects can be rated for closeness of fit.

Using a simple form as shown in the following example, illustrated in Figure 12-5, both cumulative reward and cumulative risk factors can be generated.

In this example, the "fixed"[4] weights for each reward factor (assigned by management) are multiplied by their associated rating, and the products for all reward factors are summed to obtain a cumulative reward score.

3. Our Executive Leadership assigns weighting values to our strategic objectives and the factors related to portfolio balancing, but we empower our Innovation Council members—all IAOIP-Certified Innovation Managers ("Champions")—to perform the rating of individual ideas and projects for closeness-of-fit.

4. Not rigidly fixed, as we have learned in the prior section "Understanding the Strategy Track," but "fixed" in the sense that they stay the same until management changes the factors and/or their weightings.

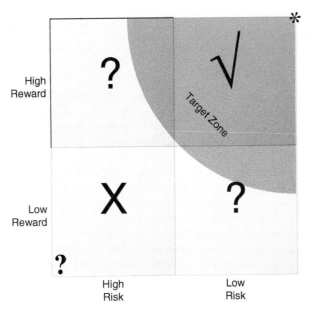

Figure 12–6. Risk/Reward Matrix.

The weights for each risk factor (again, assigned by management[5]) are multiplied by their associated rating, and the products for all risk factors are summed to obtain a cumulative risk score.

Together, these scores can be used in a data visualization exercise to align ideas or projects on a risk/reward matrix. In the matrix shown in Figure 12-6, the "Target Zone" reflects the region with the optimal balance between the computed risk and reward factors (lowest risk and highest reward.)

With a scale factor applied to the axes, it is possible to visualize each scored idea or project in comparison to all others, such as in the Risk/Reward Matrix shown in Figure 12-6.

Note that this approach even allows for investment thresholds to help determine the dividing line for inclusion in the active portfolio.

As mentioned in the prior section on strategy, it was noted that the strategic objectives and their weightings can change due to conditions or events. The same is true for risk and reward factors and their weightings if using that approach. If the appetite for a particular type of risk is changed by management, it could impact the evaluation of every active project (as they may no longer be in alignment.) The same is also true for ideas—whether in the active portfolio or not—as they may not have "made the cut" the *last* time but may *this* time under different evaluation criteria.

When evaluation *criteria* change, all ideas and projects that could be impacted *must* be evaluated under the new conditions. See Figure 12-7. Also, if an evaluation factor is *added or removed*, all ideas or projects must *first* be rerated *and then* reevaluated to ensure that the portfolio of ideas or projects are in alignment with current strategic objectives and priorities. In these scenarios, active projects can be abandoned, deferred, or even killed.

---

5. The importance of having the weightings assigned by management cannot be overstated, as it ensures regular involvement by executive leadership, promotes an understanding of how innovation outcomes are directly tied to strategic objectives, and enhances the cultural alignment required for an effective innovation program.

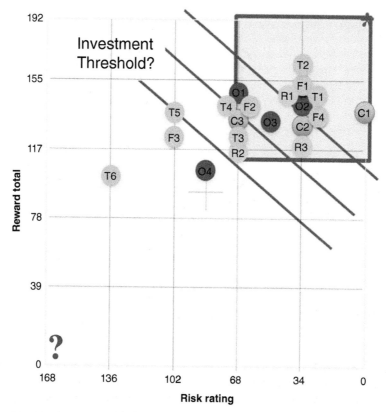

Figure 12–7. The Ideal Risk/Reward Portfolio.

Conclusion

Agile Portfolio Management is the most important aspect of your innovation management practice. You may have great ideas aligned with strategic intent, a culture to support innovation, and a rigorous process with the proper infrastructure and tools to develop and implement them, but unless your innovation *outcomes* are in alignment with your organization's current strategic intent you won't be exploiting the right opportunities.

INNOVATION IN ACTION: COMAU

Introduction

COMAU is a worldwide leader in the manufacture of flexible, automatic systems and integrating products, processes and services that increase efficiency while lowering overall costs. With an international

Material in this section has been provided by Roberto Guida, COMAU Project Management Vice President, Riccardo Bozzo, COMAU Contract Management, Francesca Gaschino, COMAU Risk Manager, and Paolo Vasciminno, COMAU Project Management Excellence. ©2022 by COMAU. All rights reserved. Reproduced with permission.

network that spans 13 countries, COMAU uses the latest technology and processes to deliver advanced turnkey systems and consistently exceed the expectations of its customers. COMAU specializes in body welding, powertrain machining and assembly, robotics and automation, electromobility as well as digital initiatives, consultancy and education for a wide range of industrial sectors. The continuous expansion and improvement of its product range enables COMAU to guarantee customized assistance at all phases of a project—from design, implementation and installation to production start-up and maintenance services.

COMAU innovation is based on manufacturing's digital transformation, added-value manufacturing and human-robot collaboration; these key pillars allow COMAU to reach new heights in leading the culture of automation.

COMAU Project Management

In 2007, COMAU established a contract and project management corporate function, with the aim to create a stronger link between leading roles and project management and to ensure coherence between execution and company strategy. Over time, the contract and project management function grew in responsibility (as shown in Figure 12-8) and modified its structure to reach a configuration based on the coordinated sharing of knowledge and activities between Project Management Excellence, Risk Management and the COMAU PM Academy. Another foundation element that sustains COMAU Project Management framework is represented by the PMI® standard set, recognized as the best practice standard in the Project and Portfolio Management landscape.

1. Project Management Excellence (PME)

In recent years, COMAU started thinking about the industry in a new way, developing new scenarios, designing innovative products, creating ways to streamline production processes, and defining new trends in digital manufacturing, creating a new paradigm to balance collaboration between people and machines.

We call it HUMANufacturing, the innovative COMAU vision that places mankind at the center of business processes within a manufacturing plant, in full cooperation with the industrial automation solutions and new digital technologies that surround them. The above vision needed changes and innovation in all company organization roles to be sustained.

Figure 12–8. COMAU Contract and Project Management Office.

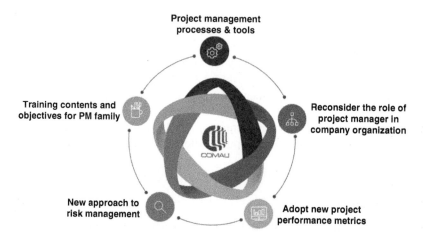

Figure 12–9. COMAU PME Innovation Pillars.

The COMAU PME is therefore innovating, expanding its landscape from traditional industrial project portfolio to new forms of projects, such as new product development, digitalization, and industry4.0 projects.

The COMAU PME through the innovation in each of the five pillars (see Figure 12-9) is now positioned within the organization as a valuable business partner that sharpened its capacity to be adaptive for different forms of projects within the company.

Scenario Analysis

The current context of market evolution highlights new disrupting evidences:

- The degree of innovation is becoming predominant in all COMAU projects
- The size of traditional EPC projects is continuously decreasing
- The development of new, innovative, digital products and solutions is more and more expected by our customer base (traditional automotive, and new customer base: new automotive, general industry, electric vehicle)

Consequently, COMAU began a deep analysis of the current project execution course of action (process, organization, and tools) and of the project management methodologies adopted, to verify the alignment to market needs.

COMAU redesigned its project management process to make it scalable to the degree of innovation typical of each project and adopting where applicable Lean and agile solutions.

Guidelines

The main guidelines followed:

- Profile the process based on project classification criteria. From the well-established COMAU PM process, optimization is achieved by selecting the appropriate activities/tasks/milestones that fit each different project, maximizing the business added-value.

- Empower project managers and encourage team co-location to improve the integration and communication within the team members, and of the project team itself with functions and finally with the customer.
  - Team co-location has introduced a work space re-layout, the integration of the planning activities, and the introduction of a platform organization.
- Digitalization of the project management process, realizing a paperless process in order to achieve a faster and more user-friendly utilization and optimize time/cost of process management.
- Encourage visual management, and exploit the potential of mobile applications (see Figure12-10). The benefits obtained with these operations have been a reduced complexity, reduced time and lower effort for milestones and activities/tasks execution and, in general the reduction of "not value added" operations, maximizing effectiveness and efficiency as requested by the current business scenario.

2. COMAU Contract Management

Considering the "fixed price" and "turn-key" nature of the most part of the contractual agreements that COMAU establishes with the Customers, the Contract Management competences applied both in the Contract acquisition and administration phases are deemed crucial by COMAU to sustain its business model.

Project Contracts include Contractual agreements made with Customers but also those executed with Major turn-key Suppliers and, if any, Partners under a consortium or Joint-venture.

The COMAU Contract Management Function is responsible to ensure an effective life cycle management of Project Contracts from creation, administration, changes and claim management to close-out, during the entire value chain process including Business Development, Order Acquisition and Operation.

Based on the early evaluation of the complexity rate of a Project, the Contract Management is assigned to the Project team starting from the proposal phase and continues to be engaged during the execution. (See Figure 12-11)

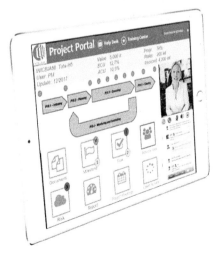
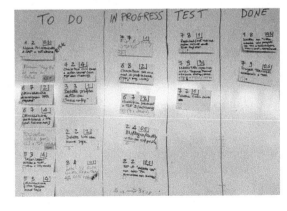

Figure 12–10. COMAU Project Management Digital Process & New Tools (i.e., Agile Visual Management).

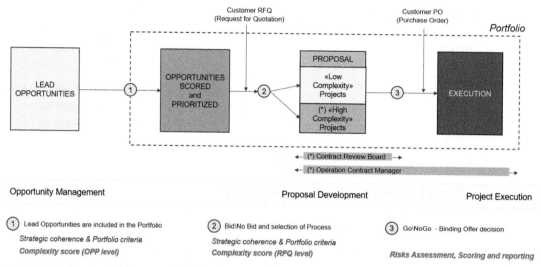

Figure 12–11. Contract Management Life Cycle.

Contract Managers are working closely with Sales & Proposal team as well as Project Management team to provide support on the following main activities:

During Contract Acquisition:
- Analyzing Contracting documents to identify ambiguities, conflicts and risks (e.g. Force Majeure Clauses and others) and providing ongoing guidance on risks and negotiation strategies.
- Organizing and leading Contract Reviews and Reports preparatory for go/no go decision
- Ensuring that Contractual documents and information are effectively handed over from the Sales phase to the Project Execution Team (for example, through dedicated contract-induction sessions).

During Contract Execution:
- Identifying opportunities for customer changes (revenue, cash and profit enhancement), schedule relief, and claim management.
- Collaborating with Legal when disputes with Clients, Suppliers and Partners are likely to result in litigation proceedings.
- Identifying the Customer contractual provisions which must be back-to-back transferred to suppliers and sub-contractors.
- Preparing Contract Review reports in an appropriate way for different audiences: Project Reviews, Portfolio Reviews and Contract Review Board.

In addition to the direct involvement on Projects, the Contract Management function is leading initiatives aimed to keep the appropriate level of awareness on Contract Management, including the delivery of Contract Management courses based on concrete business experience, lesson learned and business case studies.

3. COMAU Risk Management

History and Achievement

In 2006, COMAU began to address risk management with a more focused, strategic approach, recognizing it as an essential part of the successful completion of projects. With the increase of organizational complexity and global presence it was necessary to find more structured and refined tools for managing uncertainties. Consequently, in 2010, a Risk Management Office as part of the project management organization was created.

Specific responsibilities of the risk management office included the definition of a framework (methods, processes, tools) for the management of projects and portfolio risks as well as improve the concrete application throughout the entire project life cycle.

Beginning in 2015, COMAU decided to make a further maturity step, launching an initiative aimed to reinforce and better integrate risk management practices at different company levels (contract sales, project execution, and portfolio management) with a global perspective (see Figure 12-12).

The completion of the initiative provided COMAU with the adequate risk management approach and tools needed to manage the turnkey projects portfolio composed by fixed-price EPC contracts, each characterized by a high degree of complexity and a fixed scope for which a traditional project management predictive approach is to be adopted.

Risk Management for Innovative Projects

The acceleration impressed by the digitalization era required changes to business model for many companies included COMAU. Risk management as all other functions within companies is required to change as well and to approach new models to cover new forms of projects, those that might be named innovation projects (see Figure 12-13).

Innovation projects such as new product or solution development and digitalization projects have peculiarities that need new risk management approaches. To fit with this requirement, COMAU developed a first "concept" to extend and integrate the well-established traditional risk management.

The concept is based on the following guidelines:

- Risk management is a primary vehicle to reinforce PM "strategic thinking" into project execution. New risk management approach might bridge the project management perspective from tactic to strategic as it focuses on pursuing a wider business-value objective.

  Project managers are now expected to master company business processes in addition to the PM process and to be than able to anticipate the implications of project decisions on the different functional objectives, communicate them, and collaborate with functions to set up counteractions.

Sales Management   Projects Management   Portfolios Management

Risk Management Process   Risk Management Process

Figure 12–12. The COMAU Risk Management Initiative.

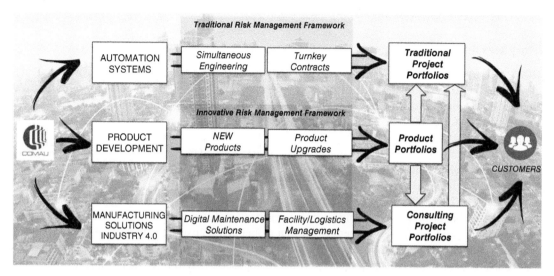

Figure 12–13. New frontiers for Risk Management.

- New company functions and customers are involved in project risk management.

  Accepting that perimeter of project risk management is widening, there are a number of people/structures within the company (i.e., innovation, marketing, sales functions) that become important stakeholders, bearers of interests and objectives that, differently from the past, might be subjected to redefinition while the project is ongoing (agile approach).
- New metrics to measure project risks.

  The value expected and created by innovation projects goes beyond the end of the project itself. The project constraints to be taken into account when assessing the risks are not only limited to scope-time-costs as in a traditional predictive approach. New metrics for the qualitative and quantitative analysis of risks that could include also a wider, more strategic measure of long-term risk impacts are needed. COMAU's new approach to project risk management is therefore based on a hybrid of predictive and adaptive components.

4. COMAU PM Academy

Developing Innovation Project Managers

The PM Academy in COMAU is responsible to ensure people involved in projects are technically skilled and behaviorally prepared to participate in and manage projects. In front of the need of innovation PM Academy challenge is to support project manager transformation in the company—from a person strongly plan and process oriented to a person more and more aware of its strategic role in the creation of value for the company. And what do we need to reach it? Essentially a project manager must be very flexible, culturally sensitive, political-driven, business-oriented, and a master in communication and leadership.

In this new context PM Academy continues its efforts to provide valuable international project management best practices and support the certification process; but this is integrated with agile and Lean concepts and methodologies, and enriched leadership models.

To be an effective PM in the innovation environment, you cannot focus only on certifications. Certifications remain a good method to enlarge people's awareness and knowledge, but now the objective is higher. "New" project managers have to function as part influencers, part psychologists, and part politicians. Not only do they themselves need these soft skills, but they also need to drive teams and stakeholders to a new level of effectiveness in their own soft skills.

PM Academy New Domains

PM Academy started to work on two additional objective areas:

1. The strategic vision of project managers
2. The ability of project managers to inspire others

The first domain was developed in parallel with the gradual redefinition of the role of a COMAU project manager, who was becoming central in driving innovation. The second objective is achieved by developing practical tools for soft skill development. But—this is the novelty—these tools are not designed to develop the project manager's soft skills but to provide the PM with tools they can apply to develop soft skills in teams and stakeholders in their projects. In this way, PMs become actors in the process of changing the "culture-of-involvement-in-projects" (in fact, success is strongly associated with the level of engagement in the project and in the team).

Using these tools, team members can:

- Communicate more and better.
- Learn about one another differences.
- Share values and contribute to the definition of "shared values."
- Analyze conflicts ant try to solve them.
- Tell their emotions and listen to the other's ones.
- Respect an appreciate differences.
- Feel more satisfied.
- Understand better their role in projects.

In conclusion, the goal is to create PMs that, although they continue to be valuable project management professionals, are at the same time strategic business partners, integration managers, inspirers, and coaches. In order to fulfill this objective, the COMAU PM Academy has enriched its catalog with training in agile and Lean project management, project management leadership, and train-the-PM-coach.

INNOVATION IN ACTION: TOKIO MARINE AND NICHIDO SYSTEMS _____

In recent years, the importance of stakeholder management has increased in system development projects. Due to the need to smoothly carry out the project while maintaining a good relationship with the stakeholders, the interpretation of success or failure of the project is often divided. On the other hand, at the site of the project, the current belief is that success depends on individual competence, such as the ability of each member to communicate.

As one solution, Tokio Marine and Nichido Systems use the Future Center (FC) systematically. The company often collaborates with both company employees and IT vendor employees when implementing system development projects. However, it is often difficult to gain mutual trust because of their different positions, and therefore we utilize the Future Center for that purpose. According to a survey conducted by the company, 95 percent of respondents said that the distance between the two groups would be reduced by utilizing the Future Center. In addition, as additional responsibilities suitable for the Future Center became apparent, there were several approaches looked at such as fostering a sense of unity, sharing of tacit knowledge, and as a development process suitable for other knowledge sharing.

Definition and Positioning the Future Center

The company defines the Future Center as "a specially designed space/environment to imagine the future and to solve difficult problems through dialogue." Specifically, it is used as a place for stakeholders to talk about problems that are difficult to solve by conventional means, and to devise meaningful solutions. The aim is to create new ideas by discussing the issues in a "free" atmosphere in a space away from everyday life. Future Center sessions are held during business hours.

Four Elements

In establishing the Future Center at the company, four elements were established: space, facilitator, administrative office, and theme-setting.

Space: The company has a room dedicated to the Future Center. Paintings and audio sets are placed in the room. Once the participants enter the room, the participants are in a relaxed atmosphere created to give them the feeling that "I came to a place different from usual."

Facilitator: The company currently has 13 facilitators. The facilitator is an employee who raises an issue and encourages people to freely discuss their opinions. At the Future Center, this facilitator plays an important role.

Administrative office: The administrative office designs the workshop according to the theme brought by employees. There is great value in this design because, unlike regular conferences, the focus is in bringing out tacit knowledge. The company calls the administrative office the director, and currently two are assigned.

Theme-setting: The theme to be discussed is part of a system in which each organization or team within the company voluntarily brings up the problem to be solved. In other words, the theme is not determined by the company or superiors, but it is based on the motivation and free thinking of each employee.

Session Management

Depending on the theme, the time required for the session may be three hours per session, while some sessions may take two full days.

The session operates according to the following agenda:

- Check-in
- Orientation
- Idea analysis using design thinking
- Story-telling supporting the ideas
- Presentation
- Checkout

Secret of Session Success

The company believes that the secret to making the session successful is by establishing ground rules. The ground rules are as follows:

- Take off the "armor" you are normally wearing (such as belonging to a specific group, or reputation, or status; refer to people as just individuals).
- Positive behavior (let's not deny people's opinions, whether good or bad; let's hear every person's opinion; let's develop their ideas further).
- Do not be afraid of mistakes (any and all ideas will be considered; let's say it first).
- Everyone participates (Let's do it together; let's talk with a smile).

Performance

Since establishing the Future Center in 2009, the company has steadily accumulated achievements. Sessions were held nine times in FY 2009, but in FY 2013, 130 sessions were held. As the number of achievements increases, the operational know-how of the Future Center accumulates, and a virtuous circle is created that enables higher-quality sessions.

Issues of the Company

When conducting 130 sessions a year, the biggest challenge is securing and fostering facilitator time. The facilitator is an employee who is identified through an in-house open recruitment process, even though all of us have system development and operational work as our main business. We function as a facilitator at intervals between our workloads. It is a so-called "in-house volunteer position." Therefore, the burden on the facilitator is great. For many of them, the priority of the core business is of greater importance. Sometimes, participation in the session is difficult. Under such circumstances, there is concern that core business activities will hinder the continuous existence and success of the Future Center. In addition, since facilitators are required to have unique skills, their training requires a certain period of learning and experience. At the beginning of the launch in FY2009, the employees self-educated themselves autonomously. Today this is supported with a standard training curriculum.

Conclusion

As for the future direction of utilization of the Future Center, it is possible to expand the scope of coverage. Stakeholder management is primarily concerned with establishing good relations with outsiders; in the future it is expected that the target participants will be further expanded and will include users and managers of information systems.

INNOVATION IN ACTION: GEA _____

About GEA

GEA is one of the largest suppliers of process technology for the food industry and a wide range of other industries. The international technology group focuses on process technology and components for sophisticated production processes in various end-user markets.

In 2021, GEA generated consolidated revenues of about EUR 4.7 billion. The food and beverages sector, which is a long-term growth industry, accounted for around 70 percent. GEA employs nearly 18,000 people globally. By a multitude of merger and acquisition activities in the past, the company structure was highly fragmented. With strategic initiatives in the past, the company has integrated the activities in a new structure oriented on major technological competences.

Innovation Management at GEA – General Challenges

For GEA, Innovations act as a major lever for sustainable growth. The new organizational structure enables the company to develop and drive new developments across locations and functional areas. The management of innovations was developed and implemented in a stepwise approach and rolled out to the overall company. Within 2019 and 2021 a series of cross-company innovation activities have been driven and lessons learned workshops showed a small set of improvements to make the Front-End of innovation lean and simple. Furthermore, open innovation activities such as Hackathons, Makeathons, collaboration projects with startups and enterprises have been intensified.

In our global acting company with broad customer and market scopes as well as technological competencies, there are still remaining challenges to bring new results and technologies across the organizational borders. A simple measure is to motivate the development experts to regularly share the good things they are doing.

Innovation Management at GEA – The Technical Aspects

The key aspects of the Innovation Management Framework are the Innovation Process, the InnoVate platform and the Innovation Organization (see Figure 12-14):

Innovation Process

The GEA Innovation Process consists mainly of four phases divided into two major clusters (see Figure 12-15):

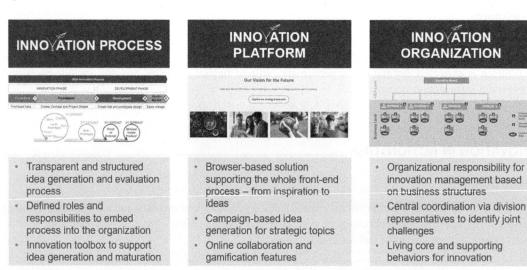

Figure 12–14. The three key aspects of GEAs Innovation Management System.

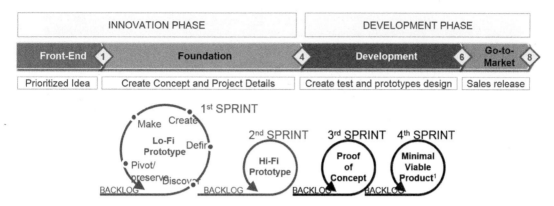

Figure 12–15. The GEA Innovation Process.

- *Innovation Phase*
  1. **Front-End** Idea generation via Idea Generation Campaigns, looking for opportunities, identify major uncertainties (market, technical)
  2. **Foundation** Identify major skills and next evaluation steps, prepare development project plan and business case, identify major risks (market, technical), conduct feasibility studies
- *Development Phase*
  3. **Development** Create tests and prototypes design, feasibility tests with customers or customers products, preparation of series production
  4. **Go-To-Market** Sales release, market entry planning, handover to target business unit

To reduce (pre-)development time and to foster cross-business collaboration there is additional opportunity to setup agile teams besides the daily development business and maturate ideas that address new markets or new technologies. This can be oriented as well in the overall Innovation Process and fed back to a standard product development in a later stage.

InnoVate Platform

To represent the Innovation Process, GEA has set up an IT platform which covers the major parts of the Idea Campaigns, Idea Generation and Front-End activities (Figure 12-16). In this process phase, the focus is much on finding the right experts for given challenges. The platform provides access to all GEA employees and enables finding the right expertise in a small amount of time. Furthermore, it acts as an exchange platform for inspirations – may it be market-wise (e.g. new products, new business models) or technically (e.g. new technologies such as 3D-printing). Platform users can enter new ideas and inspirations and are invited to comment on existing ideas. A powerful search functionality ensures that also stopped ideas (including know-how that has been entered) in the past can be found again via keywords.

Besides specific call for ideas and jointly maturating on the solutions, there are further functions to improve inspirations and information exchange:

- **Trends**

  Trends are regarded as collections of market or technology developments. Typical contents of trends are the maturity level (typically done by market activities extended by expert interviews) and real life examples substantiating the trend maturity.

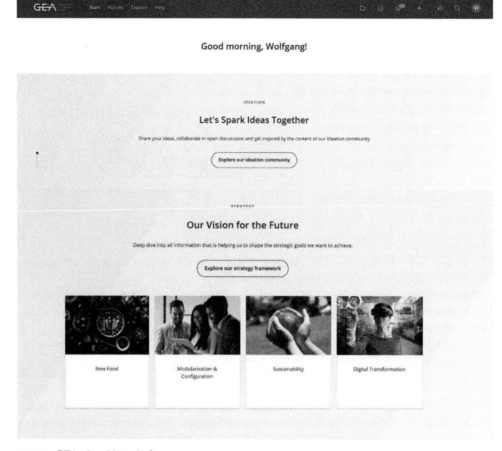

Figure 12–16. GEAs InnoVate platform.

- **Technology Insights**
  New developments launched by enterprises or startups that could act as solution to the ideas and inspire solution finding within ideation campaigns.
- **Partners**
  Database of existing and potential external development partners. This is especially relevant if a business unit is looking for outside partners to complement their product portfolio. As GEA is improving the open innovation activities, we regularly looking outside which potential new customers we find for new market and product trends or which potential partners could act as collaboration partner for providing new technological solutions and complement our product portfolio.
- **Community**
  Recent discussions on ideas, trends, technologies, etc. are being discussed in a "WhatsApp"- or "Yammer"-like manner. The discussion entries and linkage to the platform functions are also part

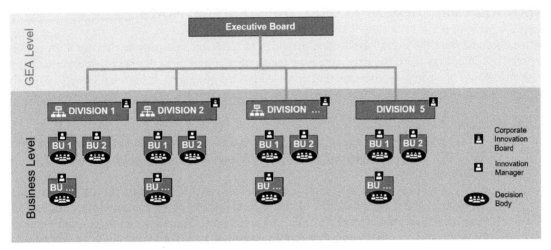

Figure 12–17. GEAs decentralized Innovation Organization (BU: Business Unit).

of the search function within the platform – so whenever is looking for specific keywords, also the discussion entries will be found and leads to the right experts.

● **News**
Linked to the intranet news, here specific Innovation news are being transported across the community worldwide. On the landing page of each person, the news have a good visible position and quickly lead the user to the recent activities and news that could be relevant.

Those functions are typically linked to the ideation campaigns during preparation of them to give ideators impulses in which directions the solution spaces can go or are being expected.

Innovation Organization

To live the Innovation Process, it needs organizational parts to drive Idea Generation and execute decision making. As for the very different businesses GEA is active in, it wouldn't make much sense to have one central unit or decision board to quote on ideas. GEA has set up a two-fold organization whereas the major part deals with product-near innovations (but not only restricted "Incremental Innovations") and which is organizationally located within the Divisions and the Business Units of GEA. Typically, there is a decision board for the Gate decisions within the Innovation Process and an Innovation Manager role to facilitate the decision making process. The business responsibility stays completely within the business units.

Each division sends a representative to the regular Corporate Innovation Board which aligns crossdivisional developments and drives information exchanges across the company. Furthermore, the quarterly Innovation Dashboard is being prepared and discussed. The Innovation Dashboard sums up the key innovation activities and launches that are linked to the strategic targets of the company.

Last but not least, informal networks for expert linkage and exchange are driven and supported (Figure 12-17).

INNOVATION MANAGEMENT AT GEA – THE STRATEGIC PARTS

To measure and steer the overall Innovation activities of GEA, the company has set up a set of Key Performance Indicators (KPI). As only increasing the number of new ideas does not reflect perfectly the innovative power of a company, there are further measurements necessary. At the GEA Group we use **six strategic KPIs** – Key measurements for applying steering measures are

- *"Turnover with new products"*
  As global markets are changing more and more, the companies portfolio has to be renewed regularly. This can be measured by the share of new products against the overall turnover.
- *"Development Time"*
  Especially in the first two phases "Front-End" and "Foundation" the preparation of new development projects is done in parallel to daily business tasks by development experts. Data evaluations show that some ideas in the Front-End or Foundation take long time to be mature enough to be decided on. On the other hand: if decisions take too long (especially in an early phase), motivation of employees can drop significantly and Idea Maturation or content quality suffer.
  Quick decisions, transparent feedback and (if possible) personal feedback for the Idea Owner facilitated by strong Innovation Managers and a powerful innovation community ensure fast idea handling and highly motivated people.
- *"Amortization"*
  Each organization has to proof that it creates value to the company. Especially Innovation Organizations face the challenge that their measurable return is outside one fiscal year. A more virtual but pragmatic value shows the Amortization value which gives a good indication of how efficient an Innovation Management System works.

Furthermore to get a more general overview and developments we use the following three KPIs:

- *"Ideas and Projects per Innovation Phase"*
  This is just an overview how many ideas or projects are in the respective Innovation Phase (Front-End, Foundation, Development, Go-To-Market). This gives an impression on how many ideas you have to create in the Front-End to get a final product launched in the market.
- *"FTE in R&D"*
  Via the units controlling departments we create an overview on the number of Full-Time-Equivalents working on R&D topics.
- *"R&D spend"*
  Similar to the above number this is a collection how many budget is spend on development works. Most of them are covered by unit-related specific R&D-budgets.

Beside the top level KPIs (strategic) the company has setup six further KPIs to identify measures of the **operative part** of Innovation Management. Key measurements for the operative part are:

Material in the section "Innovation Management at GEA - The Strategic Parts" has been provided by Dr. Wolfgang Deis, head of Innovation Management, GEA Group AG, Germany, and Miguel Antonio Martínez Carrizo, group manager, Project Management Office APC Dairy, GEA Process Engineering, Spain. ©2022 by GEA. All rights reserved. Reproduced with permission.

- *"Sales potential in pipeline"*
  As the pure number of ideas is not guaranteeing a successful innovation work we have to regard the sales potential in the funnel. Furthermore, there is a systemic trap one might fall into when purely regarding these numbers as sales potential in EUR (or any other currency): ideas in the Front-End or Foundation phase are often still linked to an uncertainty. Ideas may not technically work in real scale or the market informations are not reliable or just not available. In these cases, you have to calculate an additional factor of uncertainty to your sales potential of the respective ideas. Two major pitfalls could occur:
  1. Underestimation of market potential leads to stop of an idea (which might have a good chance for success).
  2. Overestimation of sales potential leads to focus on high risk ideas which might not fulfill the promises once made.

Generally, it has to be ensured during the overall Innovation Process, that the underlying data are well challenged and evaluated.

A specific measure of feasible challenging the data given for the ideas is to ensure, that also financial and market experts have had a look on the numbers given.

- *"Workout and Processing Time of Ideas and Projects"*
  The duration of ideas in the specific Innovation phases is not only consisting of the pure work on ideas such as conducting workshops for maturation, problem solving, solution finding, testing, etc. It is also a matter of how long it takes or decision making: as soon as the Idea Owner posts its idea to the process owner, he wants to get a decision as soon as possible to further workout the solution. The longer it takes for this decision making, the less motivation, endurance and persistence you get for the further workout of the idea. This also leads to less quality and in the end the idea may be stopped. Especially in the Front-End phase it is necessary not to over-engineer deliverables: who really believes in complete business cases in such an early stage? A way out is to focus on the next step of reducing uncertainty or simply: risk. It might happen that the idea will be stopped in the next phase (e.g. Foundation) if the results are not as expected but: especially for very new things you have to go the first trials.

  Specific measures can be to check regularly the processing times for decision making. With the InnoVate platform at GEA it is easy to check this automatically on a regular basis and evaluate what the hurdles for decision making are. Second, regarding the pure working time of ideas it is feasible to create local support networks to identify, how to support Idea Teams (or Idea Originators) to manage the next steps.

- *"Number of new patents"*
  Similar to the pure number of ideas it might not be a string measurement of innovative power if you only regard the number of new patents. As patent applications and the regionalization can be quite cost intensive, a company would spend some thoughts on how important the application for a specific solution will be. If there is no doubt that filing the patent is important then also the overall number of newly generated patents has some validity. Therefore, it is mainly for identifying and applying measures within your own company how to improve. As a benchmark number with other companies this might not be feasible as each company faces different strategies for Intellectual Property.

- *"Number of Ideas per Innovation Field"*
  Overview of ideas per innovation cluster. There are a set of innovation clusters, called "Innovation Fields" such as "Digitalization", "Sustainability" and "Product Safety". Those Innovation Fields summarize a larger set of ideas with common challenges where groundbreaking work is being done before deployment into the different areas. With the operational dashboard we detect if such an Innovation Field runs dry.
- *"Ratio submitted vs. Realized Ideas"*
  These ratios are already mentioned in the strategic dashboard ("Number of ideas per Innovation Phase"). This gives us an insight on how healthy the feeding part of the innovation funnel looks like.
- *"R&D spend vs. Budget"*
  This is a high level measurement or comparison on how many budget is spend for R&D works in relation to the overall budget.

Innovation Management at GEA – The Enabling Parts

The above section was mainly explaining the technical parts of GEAs Innovation Management System consisting of process, platform and organization as well as regarding several KPIs and defining measures around it.

Besides the technical aspects there are further success factors to ensure effectiveness and efficiency of the Innovation Management System. GEA has therefore started to create internal networks to support process, ideas and solution finding. The network consists not only of management people who act as Innovation ambassadors and often act in the roles of Innovation Managers and Decision Bodies – it also consists of engineers and people on the working level who are ambitious and sometimes do not want to play a management role. But: they are open minded, interested in new things, hands-on in solution finding and willing to share new findings. This community is called the VIBE network whereas VIBE stands for Vital Innovation Behaviour Engagement.

VIBE consists of people from nearly all levels of responsibility, different locations and different units. When starting to reach out for experts, starting new (company-wide) Idea Campaigns the VIBE network is always included to identify, where the experts for a specific topic are and how they can be approached. Two times a year we try to bring the community physically together with the Innovation Managers to exchange learnings, new findings and also meet for problem solving sessions.

Summary and Outlook

After introduction of the Innovation Management Framework in 2017 and rollout until 2018, GEA has refined and extended innovation activities in the last years. Processes and IT-platforms are no more in focus and run smoothly across the company. Focus is now on exploiting open innovation opportunities and extending competence exchange across the divisions and business units.

Identifying joint challenges of a multiple of business units and leveraging measures for co-development are organizational challenges to approach. In the next years, GEA will focus on its strategic measurable targets it has settled in 2021 for the upcoming five years. The transformation to new business models and digital solutions will be as well business challenges as technological challenges to meet the future food and pharma markets.

INNOVATION IN ACTION: WÄRTSILÄ ENERGY SOLUTIONS _____

Project Fox: Project Management and Innovation

The fox is often associated with the figure of the con artist. But as a spirit animal, it can also be a teacher providing guidance on how to swiftly finding your way around obstacles. If you follow the fox, you may be called on to use or develop quick thinking and adaptability.

Project Fox was a sales origination initiative focused on the US real-time energy market with a clear goal to capture order intake. The project was initiated in 2015 and managed by a project manager and a cross-functional team. When the project ended in 2017, the outcome was not only concrete sales cases, a pipeline of leads, and new offerings, but also, and even more valuable, insight on the energy transition toward a renewable energy system. However, let's take it from the start.

Project Fox: Making of a Value Proposition

We strongly believed that there needs to be value in the activities we do and that it is important to be able to showcase and follow up tangible results. Project Fox was initiated as a strategic initiative to develop the existing market in the United States. The ambition was to find new customers and pitch the offering to a different segment of consumers and increase sales.

We started by addressing the four main steps we considered to be important when developing a market:

1. Make a value proposition.
2. Get organized – set up a team for the task and agree on a plan.
3. Develop relationships with the target customers and find a role for the offering to meet their strategy and business.
4. Support customers decision making and develop leads and deals.

Value proposition is about showcasing customer value and not talking about offering features. To simplify this through an example in Project Fox, one offering feature could be high efficiency. The customer benefit in this case would be saving fuel, and customer value would be to save money and the environment.

The overview of the different steps is shown in Figure 12-18. To create a value proposition in Project Fox, we needed to understand the electricity market and develop tools to quantify the values. In addition,

Figure 12–18. Overview of the Different Steps.

we needed to understand the market mechanism and compare market similarities. To be able to compare different markets, the team developed an Excel-based modelling tool. The result from the modelling needed to be verified, and that was done through customer visits and discussions. The result was turned into a value position that was presented to the customers, and together with them the tool was fine-tuned to meet specific customer cases. This co-created input was later turned into business cases. The modeled tool could later be used for other customer cases on the market to showcase the value and expand it to different parts of the US market.

Concrete tools that could also support the value position creation could be the business model canvas and the value proposition canvas innovation tools developed by Alexander Osterwalder. These are good tools to help business developers to understand the customer and how to deliver value. One concrete way of summarizing a sales story is the "elevator pitch." The idea is that you can explain your idea in one 30-second elevator ride, for (target customer), who has (customer problem), our (solution) that gives (key function), unlike (competition), the product (competitive advantage) is a good indication of whether you understand the topic well enough. If you can't explain something in an easy way, then you might not understand the topic well enough.

Project Fox: Placing the Customer in Focus

In a project like Project Fox, one must establish a formal project organization but also a matrix organization to implement needed actions. The roles of the team had to be clarified, including the project manager, sales, marketing and offering development. The work was kicked off by a face-to-face meeting, and we saw that it would be crucial throughout the journey to have regular follow-up meetings and continuous communication about the initiative.

For this big project, there needed to be a plan, but the key was to iterate the plan along the project based on needs. One of the most frequently used buzz words in innovation today is *agile*. Agile is used especially for software development, and it means to divide tasks into short phases and frequent adaptation of plans. Project Fox was a great example of agile in action. This is illustrated through two concrete examples. One of the key insights of learning through this process was the journey that the customer goes through. Through modeling, we in the Project Fox team had found that the offering we provided was more feasible than that of the competitors, and we were confident that our customers would readily accept the value model. This did not turn out to be the case. We visited the customers, and even though we could showcase facts and figures, they did not buy into the topic.

We realized that one of the reasons behind this was that the customer's current understanding did not support the new findings and that the customer had its own set of strategies and plans that were not easy to change. The reasoning behind this can also be found in psychology, where it is natural behavior to first deny new information that is not supported by the current knowledge. It was necessary to gain more insight and look at the facts; i.e., to gain understanding. This new understanding creates inner acceptance and transforms into self-confidence that can result into action.

To explain the value, we agreed to write a book about the transition to demonstrate the value, called *Goodbye to Deerland: Leading Your Utility through the American Energy Transition.*

> Let's state the obvious: coal isn't coming back. Ask any energy utility executive in America today and they'll tell you that the days of coal-based power are over—regardless of shifting politics—and that the time to invest in wind and solar is now. Electric utilities in conservative states like Texas and Oklahoma are at the epicenter of this great transition, where the shift from coal to renewables is already happening today.

As I describe in my book *Goodbye to Deerland*, the transition from coal to wind won't happen overnight, but an honest examination of the economics will show that utilities today cannot afford to wait and hold their breath. They must act now, or they risk losing out to competitors and falling behind in the market.

Goodbye to Deerland: Leading Your Utility Through the American Energy Transition is the story of a utility CEO facing the crisis of his life, and how he overcame it. It is also, more importantly, a roadmap to transform your electric utility and succeed in the fast-changing US energy landscape. Something new is happening across America: a new way of powering communities, a new way of doing business, a new way of thinking.[6]

The other example of an agile way of working came from the offering development side. Much of our offering development follows a stage-gate model, where the projects are prioritized according to a set metrics. Through the customer visits we found the need for low load optimization. The development started by analyzing the customer's needs and preparing a waterfall model of the key metrics. This waterfall model was then used to showcase the different values that the offering development cases would have. For the product development organization this was of great value, as it gave clear prioritisation resulting in a record short time to market. In big corporations, there are usually several divisions; these might sometimes have different priorities. However, when we were able to showcase the value for the customer, this created a good basis for collaboration and working together toward a common goal.

To support in understanding the customer's experience and feelings, one could do a Customer Journey Mapping that is a good innovation tool for stepping into the customer's shoes to gain understanding. These customer journeys are also a great way of visualizing the customer and telling their story for stakeholders in the company. Having a process and way of working for how to engage with customers is important. If you work in a company that may have several functions, there may be a need for each function to address the same customer and it is therefore important that these activities are synchronized.

Project Fox: Telling the Story and Envisioning the Future

The ambition with the project was to build a portfolio of leads and sales, and that was achieved. As the project evolved, there were a lot of learning experiences that emerged as best practices for future initiatives such as the need for clear prioritization and how showcasing customer value can speed up development. However, the greatest learning from the project was the transition towards renewable energy. The transition into the United States was an eye-opener for what will happen in other markets. The message is that world is in transition towards 100 percent renewable energy sources, not because they are green, but because it makes financial sense. This was the starting point for a new vision on how to lead the organization for future generations.

CRITICAL ISSUES _____

Every company has its own set of critical issues that it must consider. The issues can include such topics and the type of innovation, technical competence of its work force, competitive factors, and life expectancy of its existing products.

---

6. www.smartpowergeneration.com/content-center/books/goodbye-to-deerland.

As seen in this chapter, some companies have business units dedicate to innovation activities, whereas other expect all employees to support innovation. The conclusion is therefore: one size does not fit all for innovation. Each company must develop an approach that works well for them.

REFERENCES

Buchen, H,(2000), *National Productivity Review*, Wiley, 19 (2), 33–36. 4p.

Jung, U. and Chung, B. D. (2016). Lessons learned from the history of Samsung's SCM innovations: Focus on the TQM perspective. *Total Quality Management* 27 (7), 751–760.

Morris, L. (2017). *The Agile Innovation Master Plan*. Mill Valley, CA: FutureLab Press.

Morris, L. (2018). *The Big Shift: The 83 Most Important Changes that Everyone Should Know About, and the Big Shift that Changes Everything*. Mill Valley, CA: FutureLab Press.

Wolff, M. F., Jones, T. and Lee, D. (2006). Samsung, others adopting value innovation. *Research Technology Management* 49 (5), 5–7.

13 CASE STUDIES

DISNEY (A): INNOVATION PROJECT MANAGEMENT SKILLS AT DISNEY

Synopsis

All Disney's theme parks and the attractions within the parks can be viewed as innovation in action. Part of Disney's success can be attributed to the Imagineers that understand the skills they must possess to work in this type of innovation environment. The culture at Disney is truly an innovation culture.

Introduction

Not all project managers are happy with their jobs, and they often believe that changing industries might help. Some have delusions about wanting to manage the world's greatest construction projects, while others want to design the next generation cell phone or mobile device. However, the project managers that are probably the happiest are the Imagineering project managers that work for the Walt Disney Company

Innovation Project Management: Methods, Case Studies, and Tools for Managing Innovation Projects,
Second Edition. Harold Kerzner.
© 2023 John Wiley & Sons, Inc. Published 2023 by John Wiley & Sons, Inc.

even though they could possibly earn higher salaries elsewhere on projects that have profit and loss statements. Three of their Imagineering project managers (John Hench, Claude Coats, and Martin Sklar) retired with a combined 172 years of Imagineering project management work experience with the Walt Disney Company. But how many project managers in other industries truly understand what skills are needed to be successful as an Imagineering project manager? Is it possible that many of the Imagineering project management skills, which are core innovation skills, are applicable to other industries and we do not recognize it?

The *PMBOK® Guide* is, as the name implies, just a guide. Each company may have unique or specialized skills needed for the projects they undertake above and beyond what is included in the *PMBOK® Guide*.* Even though the principles of the *PMBOK® Guide* still apply to Disney's theme park innovation projects, there are other skills needed that are significantly different from a lot of the material taught in traditional project management courses. Perhaps the most common skills among all Imagineering project managers are brainstorming, problem solving, decision making, and thinking in three rather than two dimensions. While many of these skills are not taught in depth, or even at all, in traditional project management programs, they may very well be necessities for all project managers. Yet most of us may not recognize this fact.

Walt Disney Imagineering

Walt Disney Imagineering (also known as WDI or simply Imagineering) is the design and development arm of The Walt Disney Company, responsible for the creation and construction of Disney theme parks worldwide. Founded by Walt Disney to oversee the production of Disneyland Park, it was originally known as WED Enterprises, from the initials meaning "Walter Elias Disney," the company founder's full name (Wright 2005, 6).

The term *Imagineering* was introduced in the 1940s by Alcoa to describe its blending of imagination and engineering, and used by Union Carbide in an in-house magazine in 1957, with an article by Richard F. Sailer called BRAINSTORMING IS IMAGINation engINEERing. Disney filed for a copyright for the term in 1967, claiming first use of the term in 1962. Imagineering is responsible for designing and building Disney theme parks, resorts, cruise ships, and other entertainment venues at all levels of project development. All activities require some form of innovation. Imagineers possess a broad range of skills and talents, and thus over 140 different job titles fall under the banner of Imagineering, including illustrators, architects, engineers, lighting designers, show writers, graphic designers, and many more (Wright 2005, 3). It could be argued that all Imagineers are project managers and all project managers at WDI are Imagineers. Simply stated, the culture is that virtually everyone has innovation skills. Most Imagineers work from the company's headquarters in Glendale, California, but are often deployed to satellite branches within the theme parks for long periods of time.

Project Deliverables

Unlike traditional projects where the outcome of a project is a hardware or software deliverable, Imagineering project outcomes for theme park attractions are visual stories created through innovation. The entire deliverable is designed to operate in a controlled environment where every component of the

---

Parts of the section "Walt Disney Imagineering" have been adapted from Wikipedia: "Walt Disney Imagineering." https://en.wikipedia.org/w/index.php?title=Walt_Disney_Imagineering&oldid=895667497.
*PMBOK is a registered mark of the Project Management Institute, Inc.

deliverable has a specific meaning and contributes to part of telling a story. It is visual storytelling. Unlike traditional movies or books, which are two-dimensional, the theme parks and the accompanying characters come to life in three dimensions. Most project managers, including innovators, do not see themselves as storytellers.

The intent of the theme park attraction is to remove people from reality once they enter the attraction and make them believe that they are living out a story and possibly interacting with their favorite characters. Theme park visitors are made to feel that they are participants in the story, rather than just observers, and this includes visitors of all ages.

While some theme parks are composed of rides that appeal to just one of your senses, Disney's attractions appeal to several of the senses thus leaving a greater impact when people exit the attraction, allowing guests "to see, hear, smell, touch and taste in new ways" (Hench and van Pelt 2008, 6). Everything is designed to give people an experience. In the ideal situation, people are made to believe that they are part of the story. When new attractions are launched, Imagineers pay attention to the guests' faces as they come off of a ride. This is important for continuous improvement efforts.

> All I want you to think about is when people walk through or have access to anything you design, I want them, when they leave, to have smiles on their faces. Just remember that. It's all I ask of you as a designer. (Walt Disney, quoted in Disney Book Group 1996, 18)

The Importance of Constraints

Most project management courses emphasize that there are three constraints on projects, namely time, cost, and scope. While these constraints exist for Imagineering projects as well, there are three other theme park constraints that are often considered as more important than time, cost, and scope. The additional constraints are safety, quality, and aesthetic value.

Safety, quality, and aesthetic value are all interrelated constraints. Disney will never sacrifice safety. It is first and foremost the primary constraint. All attractions operate every few minutes 365 days each year and must therefore satisfy the strictest of building codes. Some rides require special effects such as fire, smoke, steam and water. All of this is accomplished with safety in mind. Special effects include fire that actually does not burn, simulated fog that one can breathe safely, and explosions that do not destroy anything. Another special effect is the appearance of bubbling molten lava that is actually cool to the touch.

Reliability and maintainability are important quality attributes for all project managers but of critical importance for the Imagineers. In addition to fire, smoke, stream, and water, there are a significant number of moving parts in each attraction. Reliability considers how long something will perform without requiring maintenance. Maintainability discusses how quickly repairs can be made. Attractions are designed with consideration given to component malfunctions and ways to minimize the downtime. Some people may have planned their entire vacation on the desire to see specific attractions, and if these attractions are down for repairs for a lengthy time, park guests will be unhappy.

Brainstorming

With traditional projects, brainstorming may be measured in hours or days. Members of the brainstorming group are small in number and may include marketing for the purpose of identifying the need for a new product or enhancement to an existing product, and technical personnel to state how long it takes and the approximate cost. Quite often, these innovation project managers may not be assigned and brought on board until after the project has been approved, added into the queue, and the statement of work is well defined. At Disney's Imagineering organization, brainstorming may be measured in years and a multitude of Imagineering personnel will participate, including the innovation project managers.

Attractions at most traditional amusement parks are designed by engineers and architects. Imagineering brainstorming at Disney is done by storytellers that must visualize their ideas in both two and three two dimensions. Brainstorming could very well be the most critical skill for an Imagineer. Brainstorming requires that Imagineers put themselves in the guests' shoes and think like kids as well as adults in order to see what the visitors will see. You must know your primary audience when designing an attraction. This is similar to what marketing personnel must do in new product development.

Brainstorming can be structured or unstructured. Structured brainstorming could entail thinking up an attraction based on a newly released animated or non-animated Disney movie. Unstructured brainstorming is usually referred to as "blue sky" brainstorming. Several sessions may be required to come up with the best idea because people need time to brainstorm. Effective brainstorming mandates that we be open-minded to all ideas. And even if everyone agrees on the idea, Imagineers always ask, "Can we make it even better?" Unlike traditional brainstorming, it may take years before an idea comes to fruition at the Imagineering division.

Imagineering brainstorming must focus on a controlled themed environment where every component is part of telling the story. There are critical questions that must be addressed and answered as part of Imagineering brainstorming:

- How much space will I have for the attraction?
- How much time will the guests need to feel the experience?
- Will the attraction be seen on foot or using people movers?
- What colors should we use?
- What music should we use?
- What special effects and/or illusions must be in place?
- Does technology exist for the attraction or must new technology be created?
- What landscaping and architecture will be required?
- What other attractions precede this attraction or follow it?

Before brainstorming is completed, the team must consider the cost. Regardless of the technology, can we afford to build it? This question must be addressed whether it is part of a structured or blue sky brainstorming session.

Guiding Principles

Imagineers are governed by a few key principles when developing new concepts and improving existing attractions. Often new concepts and improvements are created to fulfill specific needs and to make the impossible appear possible. Many ingenious solutions to problems are Imagineered in this way, such as the ride vehicle of the attraction Soarin' Over California. The Imagineers knew they wanted guests to experience the sensation of flight but weren't sure how to accomplish the task of loading the people on to a ride vehicle in an efficient manner where everyone had an optimal viewing position. One day, an Imagineer found an Erector set in his attic, and was able to envision and design a ride vehicle that would effectively simulate hang gliding (Scribner and Rees 2007).

Imagineers are also known for returning to ideas for attractions and shows that, for whatever reason, never came to fruition. It could be years later when they revisit the ideas. These ideas are often reworked and appear in a different form—like the Museum of the Weird, a proposed walk-through wax museum that eventually became the Haunted Mansion (Scribner and Rees 2007).

Finally, there is the principle of "blue sky speculation," a process where Imagineers generate ideas with no limitations. Many Imagineers consider this to be the true beginning of the design process and operate under the notion that if it can be dreamt, it can be built (Marling 1997). Disney believes that everyone can brainstorm and that everyone wants to contribute to the brainstorming process. No ideas are bad ideas. Effective brainstorming sessions neither evaluate nor criticize the ideas. They are recorded and may be revisited years later.

Imagineers are always seeking to improve on their work—what Walt called "plussing." He firmly believed that "Disneyland will never be completed as long as there's imagination left in the world," meaning there is always room for innovation and improvement (Scribner and Rees 2007). Imagineering also has created many ideas that have never been realized, although some, such as Country Bear Jamboree, do take form in one way or another later. Ideas and eventually future attractions can also come from the animated films produced by the Walt Disney Company or other film studios.

> The brainstorming subsides when the basic idea is defined, understood, and agreed upon by all group members. It belongs to all of us, keeping strong a rich heritage left to use by Walt Disney. Teamwork is truly the heart of Imagineering… . In that spirit, though Imagineering is a diverse collection of architects, engineers, artists, support staff members, writers, researchers, custodians, schedulers, estimators, machinists, financiers, model-makers, landscape designers, special effects and lighting designers, sound technicians, producers, carpenters, accountants, and filmmakers—we all have the honor of sharing the same unique title. Here, you will find only *Imagineers*. (*Walt Disney Imagineering*, 2)
>
> If I could pick any job here, I'd move my office to the Imagineering building and immerse myself in all that lunacy and free-thinking.[1]

Imagineering Innovations

Over the years, Walt Disney Imagineering has been granted over 115 patents in areas such as ride systems, special effects, interactive technology, live entertainment, fiber optics, and advanced audio systems.[2] WDI is responsible for technological advances such as the Circle-Vision 360° film technique and the FastPass virtual queuing system.

Imagineering must find a way to blend technology with the story. Imagineering is perhaps best known for its development of Audio-Animatronics, a form of robotics created for use in shows and attractions in the theme parks that allowed Disney to animate things in three dimensions instead of just two dimensions. The idea sprang from Disney's fascination with a mechanical bird he purchased in New Orleans, which eventually led to the development of the attraction The Enchanted Tiki Room. The Tiki Room, which featured singing Audio-Animatronic birds, was the first to use such technology. The 1964 World's Fair featured an Audio-Animatronic figure of Abraham Lincoln that actually stood up and delivered part of the

---

1. Quoted in *Walt Disney Imagineering* (1996, 28), citing the *Wall Street Journal*, January 6, 1986
2. The Imagineering website, https://disneyimaginations.com, discusses this creative force behind Walt Disney World Parks and Resorts.

Gettysburg Address (which was incidentally just past its centennial at the time) for the "Great Moments with Mr. Lincoln" figure exhibit, the first human Audio-Animatronic.[3]

Today, Audio-Animatronics are featured prominently in many popular Disney attractions, including Pirates of the Caribbean, The Haunted Mansion, The Hall of Presidents, Country Bear Jamboree, Star Tours: The Adventures Continue, and Muppet Vision 3D. Guests also have the opportunity to interact with some Audio-Animatronic characters, such as Lucky the Dinosaur, WALL-E, and Remy from *Ratatouille*. The next wave of Audio-Animatronic development focuses on completely independent figures, or "Autonomatronics." Otto, the first Autonomatronic figure, is capable of seeing, hearing, sensing a person's presence, having a conversation, and even sensing and reacting to guests' emotions.

Storyboarding

Most traditional project managers may be unfamiliar with the use of the storyboarding approach as applied to projects. At Disney Imagineering, it is an essential part of the innovation project. Ideas at Imagineering begin as a two-dimensional vision drafted on a piece of white paper. Storyboards assist the Imagineers in seeing the entire attraction. Storyboards are graphic organizers in the form of illustrations or images displayed in sequence for the purpose of pre-visualizing the relationship between time and space in the attraction. Storyboards have also been used in motion pictures, animation, motion graphics, and interactive media. The storyboard provides a visual layout of events as they are to be seen by the guests. The storyboarding process, in the form it is known today, was developed at Walt Disney Productions during the early 1930s, after several years of similar processes being in use at Walt Disney and other animation studios.

A storyboard is essentially a large comic of the attraction produced beforehand to help the Imagineers visualize the scenes and find potential problems before they occur. Storyboards also help estimate the cost of the overall attraction and save development time. Storyboards can be used to identify where changes to the music are needed to fit the mood of the scene. Often storyboards include arrows or instructions that indicate movement. When animation and special effects are part of the attraction, the storyboarding stage may be followed by simplified mock-ups called *animatics* to give a better idea of how the scene will look and feel with motion and timing. At its simplest, an animatic is a series of still images edited together and displayed in sequence with a rough dialogue and/or rough soundtrack added to the sequence of still images (usually taken from a storyboard) to test whether the sound and images are working together effectively.

The storyboarding process can be very time-consuming and intricate. Today, storyboarding software is available to speed up the process.

Mock-ups

Once brainstorming has been completed, mock-ups of the idea are created. Mockups are common to some other industries, such as construction. Simple mock-ups can be made from paper, cardboard, Styrofoam, plywood, or metal. "The model-maker is the first Imagineer to make a concept real. The art of bringing a two-dimensional design into three dimensions is one of the most important and valued steps in the Imagineering process. Models enable the Imagineer to visualize, in miniature, the physical layout and dimensions of a concept, and the relationships of show sets or buildings as they will appear" (Disney Book Group 1996, 72).

---

3. Ibid.

As the project evolves, so too do the models that represent it. Once the project team is satisfied with the arrangements portrayed on massing models, small-scale detailed-oriented study models are begun. This reflects the architectural styles and colors for the project.

Creating a larger overall model, based on detailed architectural and engineering drawings, is the last step in the model-building process. "This show model is the exact replica of the project as it will be built, featuring the tiniest of details, including building exteriors, landscape, color schemes, the complete ride layout, vehicles, show sets, props, figures and suggested lighting and graphics" (Disney Book Group 1996, 72).

Computer models of the complete attraction, including the actual ride, are next. They are computer generated so that the Imagineers can see what the final product looks like from various positions without actually having to build a full-scale model. Computer models, similar to CAD/CAM modeling, can show in three dimensions the layout of all of the necessary electrical, plumbing, HVAC, special effects, and other needs.

Aesthetics

Imagineers view the aesthetic value of an attraction in a controlled theme environment as a constraint. This aesthetic constraint is more of a passion for perfection than the normal constraints that most project managers are familiar with.[4]

Aesthetics are the design elements that identify the character and the overall theme and control the environment and atmosphere of each setting. This includes color, landscaping, trees, colorful flowers, architecture, music, and special effects. Music must support the mood of the ride. The shape of the rocks used in the landscape is also important. Pointed or sharp rocks may indicate danger whereas rounded or smooth rocks may represent safety. Everything in the attraction is there for the purpose of reinforcing a story. Imagineers go to highly detailed levels of perfection for everything needed to support the story without overwhelming the viewers with too many details. Details that are contradictory can leave the visitors confused about the meaning of the story.

A major contributor to the aesthetics of the attraction are the special effects. Special effects are created by "Illusioneering," which is a subset of Imagineering. Special effects can come in many different forms. Typical projected special effects can include:[5]

- Steam, smoke clouds, drifting fog, swirling effects
- Erupting volcano, flowing lava
- Lightning flashes and strikes, sparks
- Water ripple, reflection, waterfall, flows
- Rotating and tumbling images
- Flying, falling, rising, moving images
- Moving images with animated sections
- Kaleidoscopic projections

4. Some argue that the aesthetics focus more on creating a controlled environment than on reality, thus controlling your imagination.

5. See Rubin (2010). The paper provides an excellent summary of various special effects used by Illusioneers. In addition to the projected special effects, the paper also describes laser effects, holographic images, floating images, mirror gags, gas discharge effects, and fiber optics.

- Liquid projections, bubbles, waves
- Aurora borealis, lumia, abstract light effects
- Twinkling stars (when fiber optics cannot be used, such as on rear-projection screen)
- Spinning galaxies in perspective, comets, rotating space stations, pulsars, meteor showers, shooting stars and any astronomical phenomena
- Fire, torches, forest fire
- Expanding rings
- Ghosts, distorted images
- Explosions, flashes

Perhaps the most important contributor to the aesthetic value of an attraction is color. Traditional project managers rely on sales or marketing personnel to select the colors for a deliverable. At Imagineering, it is done by the Imagineers. Color is a form of communications. Even the colors of the flowers and the landscaping are critical. People feel emotions from certain colors either consciously or subconsciously. Imagineers treat color as a language. Some colors catch the eye quickly and we focus our attention on it. "We must ask not only how colors work together, but how they make the viewer feel in a given situation.... . It is the Imagineer's job to understand how colors work together visually and why they can make guests feel better" (Hench 2008, 104).

> White represents cleanliness and purity, and in many European and North American cultures ... is the color most associated with weddings, and with religious ceremonies such as christenings. Silver-white suggest joy, pleasure and delight. In architecture and interior design, white can be monotonous if used over large areas (Hench 2008, 135).
>
> ... We have created an entire color vocabulary at Imagineering, which includes colors and patterns we have found that stir basic human instincts—including that of survival. (Disney Book Group 1996, 94).

Aesthetics also impacts the outfits and full-body costumes of the cast members that are part of the attraction. The outfits that the cast members wear must support the attraction. Unlike animation where there are no physical limitations to a character's identity or mobility, people may have restricted motion once in the costume. Care must be taken that the colors used in the full body costumes maintain the character's identity without conflicting with the background colors used in the attraction. Even the colors in the rest rooms must fit the themed environment.

Imagineers also try to address queue design by trying to make it a pleasant experience. As people wait in line to see an attraction, aesthetics can introduce them to the theme of the attraction. The aesthetics must also consider the time it takes people to go from attraction to attraction, as well as what precedes this attraction and what follows it. "For transition to be smooth, there must be a blending of themed foliage, color, sound, music, and architecture. Even the soles of your feet feel a change in the paving explicitly and tell you something new is on the horizon" (Disney Book Group 1996, 90).

The Art of the Show

Over the years, Imagineering has conceived a whole range of retail stores, galleries, and hotels that are designed to be experienced and to create and sustain a very specific mood—for example, the mood of Disney's Contemporary Resort could be called "the hello futuristic optimism," and it's readily apparent given the resort's A-frame structure, futuristic building techniques, modern décor, and the monorail gliding quietly through the lobby every few minutes. Together, these details combine to tell the story of the hotel (Marling 1997).

Imagineering is, first and foremost, a form of storytelling, and visiting a Disney theme park should feel like entering a show. Extensive theming, atmosphere, and attention to detail are the hallmarks of the Disney experience. The mood is distinct and identifiable, the story made clear by details and props. Pirates of the Caribbean evokes a "rollicking buccaneer adventure," according to Imagineering Legend John Hench, whereas the Disney Cruise Line's ships create an elegant seafaring atmosphere. Even the shops and restaurants within the theme parks tell stories. Every detail is carefully considered, from the menus to the names of the dishes to the Cast Members' costumes (Hench and van Pelt 2003, 29, 58). Disney parks are meant to be experienced through all senses—for example, as guests walk down Main Street, USA, they are likely to smell freshly baked cookies, a small detail that enhances the story of turn-of-the-century, small-town America.

The story of Disney theme parks is often told visually, and the Imagineers design the guest experience in what they call "The Art of the Show." John Hench (one of Disney's Imagineering Legends) was fond of comparing theme park design to moviemaking, and often used filmmaking techniques in the Disney parks, such as the technique of forced perspective (Hench and van Pelt 2003, 13, 14, 74, 76, 96). Forced perspective is a design technique in which the designer plays with the scale of an object (i.e., a prototype) in order to affect the viewer's perception of the object's size. One of the most dramatic examples of forced perspective in the Disney Parks is Cinderella's Castle. The scale of architectural elements is much smaller in the upper reaches of the castle compared to the foundation, making it seem significantly taller than its actual height of 189 feet (Wright 2005, 24).

The Power of Acknowledgment

Project managers like to be told that they have done a good job. It is a motivational force encouraging them to continue performing well. However, acknowledgment does not have to come with words; it can come from results. At Disney's Imagineering Division, the fact that more than 132,500,000 visitors passed through the gates of the 11 Disney theme parks in 2013 is probably the greatest form of acknowledgment. The Walt Disney Company does acknowledge some Imagineers in other ways. Disney established a society entitled "Imagineering Legends." Three of their most prominent Imagineering Legends are John Hench (65 years with Disney), Claude Coats (54 years with Disney), and Martin Sklar (53 years with Disney). The contributions that these three Imagineers have made appear throughout the Disney theme park attractions worldwide. The goal of all Imagineers at Disney may very well be the acknowledgment of becoming an Imagineering Legend.

The Need for Additional Skills

All projects have special characteristics that may mandate a unique set of project management skills above and beyond what we teach using the *PMBOK*® *Guide*. Some of the additional skills that Imagineers may need can be summarized as:

- The ability to envision a story
- The ability to brainstorm
- The ability to create a storyboard and build mock-ups in various stages of detail
- A willingness to work with a multitude of disciplines in a team environment
- An understanding of theme park design requirements
- Recognizing that the customers and stakeholders range from toddlers to senior citizens
- An ability to envision the attraction through the eyes and shoes of the guests

- An understanding of the importance of safety, quality, and aesthetic value as additional competing constraints
- A passion for aesthetic details
- An understanding of the importance of colors and the relationship between colors and emotions
- An understanding of how music, animatronics, architecture, and landscaping must support the story

Obviously, this list is not inclusive of all skills. But it does show that not everyone can fulfill their desire to be an Imagineer for Disney. But these skills do apply to many of the projects that most project managers are struggling with. Learning and applying these skills could very well make all of us better innovation project managers.

Discussion Questions

1. Is there a difference between Imagineering and innovation?
2. What do you believe is the most important reason why Disney's Imagineering Division has been so successful and for so long?
3. Why is it that most project managers do not recognize that they either need or can use the skills required to perform as an Imagineering project manager?
4. What's the fundamental difference between a ride and an attraction?
5. What are some of the differences between traditional brainstorming and Imagineering brainstorming?
6. How many project constraints are there on a traditional theme park attraction?
7. How would you prioritize the constraints?
8. Why is it necessary to consider cost before the Imagineering brainstorming sessions are completed?
9. What is Audio-Animatronics?
10. What is storyboarding, and how is it used on Disney projects?
11. What is meant by project aesthetics, and how might it apply to projects other than at Disney?
12. How does Disney determine the customer's perception of value-in-use?

Further Reading

- Alcorn, Steve, and David Green, *Building a Better Mouse: The Story of the Electronic Imagineers Who Designed Epcot* (Themeperks Press, 2007).
- Ghez, Didier, and Alain Littaye, translated into English by Danielle Cohn, Disneyland Paris from Sketch to Reality (Nouveau Millénaire Editions, 2002).
- Hench, John, with Peggy Van Pelt. Designing Disney: Imagineering and the Art of the Show (Disney Editions, 2003), ISBN 0–7868-5406–5.
- The Imagineers, *Walt Disney Imagineering: A Behind the Dreams Look at Making More Magic Real* (Disney Editions, 2010).
- The Imagineers, *The Imagineering Way: Ideas to Ignite Your Creativity* (Disney Editions, 2003), ISBN 0–7868-5401–4.
- The Imagineers, (as "The Disney Imagineers"). The Imagineering Workout: Exercises to Shape Your Creative Muscles (Disney Editions, 2005).
- The Imagineers, *The Imagineering Field Guide to Disneyland* (Disney Editions, 2008).
- The Imagineers, *The Imagineering Field Guide to Animal Kingdom at Walt Disney World* (Disney Editions, 2007).

- The Imagineers, *The Imagineering Field Guide to Epcot at Walt Disney World* (Disney Editions, 2006).
- The Imagineers, *The Imagineering Field Guide to Magic Kingdom at Walt Disney World* (Disney Editions, 2005).
- Kurtti, Jeff. *Walt Disney's Legends of Imagineering and the Genesis of the Disney Theme Park* (Disney Editions, 2006), ISBN 0–7868-5559–2.
- Surrell, Jason. *The Disney Mountains: Imagineering at Its Peak* (Disney Editions, 2007).
- Surrell, Jason. *Pirates of the Caribbean: From the Magic Kingdom to the Movies* (Disney Editions, 2007).
- Surrell, Jason. *The Haunted Mansion: From the Magic Kingdom to the Movies* (Disney Editions, 2003).

DISNEY (B): CREATING INNOVATION: DISNEY'S HAUNTED MANSION _____

Introduction

The Haunted Mansion attraction opened to the public August 9, 1969. One week after opening, more than 82,000 guests had seen the attraction. During the first busy season, the time to stand in the queue to see the attraction was three to four hours. Eventually, an army of die-hard fans claimed that the Haunted Mansion was their favorite attraction. Today, there are stores and websites dedicated to the selling of souvenirs of the Haunted Mansion and its inhabitants.

Why Study the Haunted Mansion?

Some projects can have unique characteristics that can make them more difficult to manage than other projects. Projects that involve imagination and creativity fall into this category. Years ago, we believed that, if you understood the concepts of project management, you could work in just about any industry. But today, we recognize the importance of these unique characteristics, especially those related to innovation activities, that may make changing industries more complex.

Disney's Haunted Mansion opened to guests in 1969, the same year that the Project Management Institute (PMI) was formed. The Haunted Mansion attraction was completed without either the use of the *PMBOK® Guide* or PMP credential holders, since these did not appear until the mid-1980s. Many of the individuals assigned to the Haunted Mansion project were some of the most creating and inventive people in the world. So, how did innovation project management take place on such an endeavor as the Haunted Mansion? What were some of the unique characteristics needed for the Haunted Mansion project?

In the Disney (A) Case Study, we identified some of the characteristics that differentiated Imagineering project managers from traditional project managers. We will now look more closely at Imagineering project management in action using Disney's Haunted Mansion Project.

The literature abounds with both authorized and unauthorized stories of Walt Disney's Haunted Mansion. The Haunted Mansion is considered part of Disney's heritage and has attracted research by numerous Disney historians, creating both authorized and unauthorized versions of the attraction. Unfortunately, all of the versions do not directly discuss project management, thus mandating some assumptions and interpretation. The comparison of Imagineering project management with traditional project management, and the accompanying conclusions, are solely the author's interpretation and may not necessarily represent Disney's conclusions. The material in this case study was extracted from numerous sources that are referenced throughout this case study.

Constraints

All projects have constraints. For almost 50 years, we taught project managers to focus on the triple constraints of time, cost, and scope. But for the projects at the Disney theme parks, we must also include the constraints of safety, quality, aesthetic value, and others such as customer satisfaction.

The *PMBOK® Guide* did not begin discussing the importance of competing constraints until the fourth edition was released in 2008. Prior to that time, only the importance of the traditional triple constraints was emphasized. Yet even as early as the 1950s, with the design of the Disneyland theme park, Disney understood the importance of competing constraints and the fact that they must be prioritized.

The most important constraint at Disney was, and still is, the safety of the guests. This constraint is never sacrificed at Disney. In the author's opinion, quality and aesthetic value were probably tied for second and third behind safety. If tradeoffs had to be made on certain attractions, it appears that the tradeoffs took place on time, cost, and scope, but not safety, aesthetic value, or quality. Safety, aesthetic value, and quality are today attributes of the Disney image. The importance of these constraints will be discussed further in this case study.

Life Cycle Phases

When companies strive for some degree of project management maturity, they usually begin with the creation of an enterprise project management methodology developed around required life-cycle phases. The literature does not identify any project management methodology, nor does it identify any life-cycle phases for Disney's theme park attractions. However, the literature does identify many of the various steps in creating an attraction. From these steps, we can assume that typical life-cycle phases might appear such as shown in Figure 13-1. Some of the detailed steps that are performed in each life-cycle phase are described in the Disney (A) Case Study.

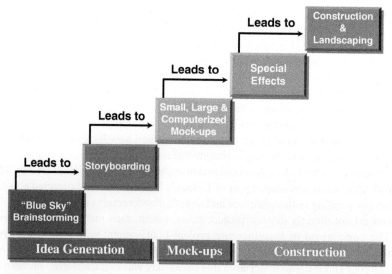

Figure 13–1. Typical Life-Cycle Phases.

The life-cycle phases shown in Figure 13-1 appear as sequential phases. However, in reality, many of the phases can overlap. As an example, special effect activities can take place in any or all of the life-cycle phases, including construction.

The Scope Constraint

Most project managers are accustomed to having a well-defined statement of work (SOW) at the onset of a project. The SOW serves as the scope constraint. Even though the SOW may be highly narrative, the accompanying work breakdown structure (WBS) and specifications can provide significant detail to support the narrative SOW.

Well-defined SOWs are based on a well-defined business case where the concept for the project is understood. If the concept is not well understood, then the SOW may not appear until the end of the concept development or idea generation life-cycle phase in Figure 13-1.

On a project such as the Haunted Mansion, we must remember that, first of all, it is an Imagineering project and Imagineering efforts will continue throughout the life of the project and beyond due to continuous improvement efforts. Expecting a well-defined SOW at the beginning of the project, and having it remain unchanged throughout the project, is highly unlikely on a project such as the Haunted Mansion. The SOW is most likely a constantly evolving document, possibly finalized as we approach the opening day of the attraction.

To understand the complexity of creating a formal SOW, we must first look at the questions that had to be addressed during the concept development phase of the Haunted Mansion Project. Typical questions include:

- Should the attraction be based on a single ghost story concept or several stories?
- Should it be a scary or humorous attraction?
- What should the Haunted Mansion look like?
- What colors and type of landscaping should be used?
- Should it be a walk-through attraction or a ride using a people mover?
- If it is a ride, how many people can we have in the people mover at one time?
- How long should it take to go through the attraction?
- How many ghostly special effects will be needed?
- Will a script be needed to accompany some of the special effects?
- Will we need a host to guide people through the ghostly attraction?
- If a host is needed, will it be a live person or a ghost doing the hosting?
- Will there be eerie music to accompany the special effects?
- Does technology exist for the ghostly images or must new technology be created?
- How much should be budgeted for the attraction?

The answers to the questions were not easy to determine at the onset of the project and were also influenced by who was working on the project at that time and the innovative technology available for special effects. Walt assigned some of his seasoned veterans to this project. Many of the team members had been working with Walt for decades and had been highly creative on other projects. They brought with them their own unique ideas that often created ego problems. If people were reassigned during the Haunted Mansion Project, which they were, their replacements came with their own ideas and then the answers for many of the above questions could then change.

To understand the complexities of creating a SOW for the Haunted Mansion, many of these questions could not be answered until the project was well under way. The questions were, as expected, interrelated and not always easy to answer even in later life-cycle stages. The answer to one question could cause the answers to several other questions to change. If the answers to some of these questions could not be made until well into the project, then there could be a significant amount of scope changes.

Scope Changes

To understand the interrelatedness of the questions and how scope changes can occur even near the completion of the project, consider The Hatbox Ghost special effect. The Hatbox Ghost was a character that was planned for the Haunted Mansion at Disneyland but was removed shortly after the attraction's debut. Located formerly in the ride's attic scene, the figure was described as "an elderly ghost in a cloak and top hat, leaning on a cane with a wavering hand and clutching a hatbox in the other"[6]

> The idea behind The Hatbox Ghost was for his head to vanish from atop his shoulders and reappear alternately inside his hatbox, in time with an adjacent bride figure's beating heart. According to Imagineer Chris Merritt in an interview with DoomBuggies.com, the effect was never completely successful due to the illusion's close proximity to the ride vehicles: "The gag was based purely on lighting. The ghost's head was illuminated by black lighting. A light inside the hatbox he held would rhythmically illuminate and hide the head in the hatbox, while, in tandem, the actual head on the ghost's shoulders would be hidden by extinguishing the black lighting."[7]

The Hatbox Ghost illusion was installed inside the Haunted Mansion and in place for cast member (park employee) previews on the nights of August 7 and 8, 1969 (Surrell 2009, 86). Almost immediately, it became apparent that the effect had failed, as ambient light in the attraction's attic scene prevented the specter's face from disappearing fully, despite the turning off of its designated spotlight. Attempts were made to remedy technical problems, but the effect wasn't convincing enough, and the ghost was decommissioned after a few months. This was just one example of how things can change well into the project.

The Time Constraint

Walt thought up the idea for the Haunted Mansion in the early 1950s. It took almost 18 years for the idea to become reality. To understand the time constraint and complexity of the project, including the interrelatedness of the questions asked previously, we should look at a brief history of the attraction.

The Haunted Mansion is a haunted house dark ride located at Disneyland, Magic Kingdom (Walt Disney World), and Tokyo Disneyland. Phantom Manor, a significantly re-imagined version of the Haunted Mansion, is located exclusively in Disneyland Paris. Another Disney attraction involving the supernatural and set in a mansion, Mystic Manor, recently opened at Hong Kong Disneyland. The Haunted Mansion features a ride-through tour in Omnimover (or people mover) vehicles called "Doom Buggies," preceded by a walk-through show in the queue. The attraction utilizes a range of technology, from centuries-old theatrical effects to modern special effects and spectral Audio-Animatronics.

---

6. Hats Off: The Secret of the Attic—DoomBuggies.com; http://www.doombuggies.com/myths2.php.

7. "Haunted Mansion Hatbox Ghost," https://www.davelandweb.com/hauntedmansion/hbg.html, accessed May 9, 2019.

The attraction predates Disneyland, to when Walt Disney hired the first of his Imagineers. The first known illustration of the park showed a Main Street setting, green fields, western village and a carnival. Disney Imagineering Legend Harper Goff developed a black-and-white sketch of a crooked street leading away from Main Street by a peaceful church and graveyard, with a run-down manor perched high on a hill that towered over Main Street.

Disney assigned Imagineer Ken Anderson to create a story around Goff's idea. Plans were made to build a New Orleans–themed land in the small transition area between Frontierland and Adventureland. Weeks later, New Orleans Square appeared on the souvenir map and promised a thieves' market, a pirate wax museum, and a haunted house walk-through. Anderson studied New Orleans and old plantations and came up with a drawing of an antebellum manor overgrown with weeds, dead trees, swarms of bats, and boarded doors and windows topped by a screeching cat as a weather vane.

Walt, however, did not like the idea of a run-down building in his pristine park. He visited the Winchester Mystery House in San Jose, California, and was captivated by the massive mansion with its stairs to nowhere, doors that opened to walls and holes, and elevators. When the decision was made to begin full-scale development of the Haunted Mansion, Imagineer Marc Davis asked Walt if he wanted the house to look scary. At a panel discussion celebrating the fortieth anniversary of the Haunted Mansion, Davis's widow, Disney costume designer Alice Estes Davis, described their conversation:

> [Marc] said that he had a talk with Walt in regard to how he wanted the outside of the house done.... Marc said, "do you want it like Charles Addams," and Walt said no, he said, "No, I want the lawn beautifully manicured. I want beautiful flowers. I want the house well-painted and well cared for so that people would know that we took care of things in the park," that is was a clean, good park for families to come and have a good time. And he said also "I want them to know that the haunted house is not scary. You can put all the spider webs or whatever else you want inside, I don't care about that… but the outside has to be pristine and clean at all times."[8]

Anderson came up with several possible stories for the mansion. Some of the stories included:

- A wedding gone awry when a ghost suddenly appears and kills the groom. The man that eventually appears hanging from the ceiling in the attic could be the bride's husband.
- Similar to the above story, a ghost appears and kills the groom. The bride then commits suicide and she appears hanging in the attic.
- A newly married bride discovers that her husband is really a blood thirsty pirate. The pirate kills his bride in a jealous rage, but her ghost returns to haunt him. He could not live with himself for what he did to his true love, so he hangs himself in the attic rafters.
- Another story focused on calling the Haunted Mansion "Bloodmere Manor," which may have involved more bloody scenes and body parts. People would appear as having been violently murdered. The story would end with the Headless Horseman in the graveyard.

The number one rule in Imagineering is that the attraction must tell a story. Unfortunately, no one could agree on what the story should be or whether the attraction could be described by just one story. In the meantime, other Imagineers were developing illusions for the Haunted House without

---

8. Alice Davis, panel discussion, Haunted Mansion 40th Anniversary Imagineer panel at The Haunted Mansion 40th Anniversary Event, September 9, 2009, Disneyland. Uploaded to YouTube October 18, 2009, available at www.youtube.com/watch?v=9VCPRp6YJ4A, accessed May 10, 2019.

having any story to go by. It appeared that no firm statement of work existed other than the fact that the Haunted House attraction would eventually be built. There were still too many questions that were unanswered.

In 1961, handbills announcing a 1963 opening of the Haunted Mansion were given out at Disneyland's main entrance. Construction began a year later, and the exterior was completed in 1963. The Haunted Mansion was actually a replica of a pre-existing building. Even though the façade of the Haunted Mansion was completed, the project was put on hold because of Disney's involvement in the 1964–1965 New York World's Fair. Similar to what happens in most companies when priorities change, all of the resources that were assigned to the Haunted Mansion project were reassigned to efforts to support the World's Fair. Work on the Haunted Mansion came and went over the years due to changes in priorities.

In 1963, Inspired by Walt, Marty Sklar, former vice chairman and principal creative executive at Walt Disney Imagineering, created a sign inviting ghosts to continue practicing their trade in active retirement in the Haunted Mansion. The sign is shown in Figure 13-2.[9] The intent of the sign was to keep people focused on the fact that the Haunted Mansion would eventually be built even though the sign hung for many years in front of an empty building. The public's perception of the abandoned construction project took on a life of its own, even though there was still no story line to accompany the abandoned building.

Notice!

All Ghosts and Restless Spirits. Post-lifetime leases are now available in this HAUNTED MANSION. Don't be left out in the sunshine! Enjoy active retirement in this country club atmosphere, the fashionable address for famous ghosts trying to make a name for themselves... and ghosts afraid to live by themselves! Leases include license to scare the daylights out of guests visiting the Portrait Gallery, Museum of the Supernatural, graveyard and other happy haunting grounds. For reservations, send resume of past experience to:

Ghost Relations Dept.

Disneyland

Please! Do not apply in person.

Figure 13–2. The Invitation.

9. The actual sign was not on a tombstone as depicted here. For a picture of the actual sign, see Baham 2014, p. 44.

The popularity of the sign began to grow. Some of Disney's literature stated:

The world's greatest collection of "actively retired" ghosts will soon call this Haunted Mansion "home." Walt Disney and his "Imagineers" are now creating 1001 eerie illusions. Marble busts will talk. Portraits that appear "normal" one minute will change before your eyes. And, of course, ordinary ghost tricks (walking through solid walls, disappearing at the drop of a sheet) will also be seen... and felt. Here will live famous and infamous ghosts, ghosts trying to make a name for themselves... and ghosts afraid to live by themselves![10]

When the project started up again in 1966, a new team of Imagineers were assigned. This was the fourth different Imagineering team that worked on the Haunted Mansion Project. Marc Davis and Claude Coats were responsible for the continuity of the ride and the backgrounds. The responsibility for the special effects was placed in the hands of two Imagineers that were also referred to as Illusioneers, Rolly Crump and Yale Gracey. Rolly Crump was an artist who loved stage magic and illusions, and Yale Gracey was an animator, mechanical genius, and considered the father of Illusioneering. Walt had an army of talented people in various organizations that he could select from. He had a knack of putting people "in conflict" together and telling them to work as a team, knowing full well that the results would be exceptional even with the ego problems that can typically exist with highly talented teams.

Following Walt's death in 1966, many of the Imagineers clashed over the direction of the project. Imagineer Xavier Atencio was brought on board to put together a coherent story. Without having a coherent story for direction, there was a fear that the Haunted Mansion would simply be a multitude of special effects and illusions. Even with Atencio's focus, there was still the decision of whether or not the Haunted Mansion should be a scary attraction.

Walt's original dream was to scare people, but in a pleasant sort of way. That meant that there would be no oozing of blood, missing eye sockets, gory body parts, or horrifying decaying bodies that might be seen as offensive to some. The decision was made that the animation should focus on the lighter or cartoon-like tone of a Haunted Mansion rather than the scarier tone. The Imagineers also decided that, instead of looking like an "old spook house" that may have been Ken Anderson's original thoughts, the Haunted Mansion would be full of illusions.

The Haunted Mansion's long development was rife with repeatedly discarded story concepts, disagreement on the type of scenes and effects to be used, conflicts over how many viewers should be carted through the attraction per hour—even as basic an idea as whether the attraction should be scary or not. Egos were bruised, tempers flared, and at the end of the day, it just seemed that there were "too many cooks in the kitchen," as Imagineer Marc Davis would often recall. (Baham 2014, xiv)

Making the attraction cartoon-like rather than scary, and having the outside of the Haunted Mansion pristine, was certainly in line with Walt's original idea for the attraction. But how do you then make the Haunted Mansion structure look somewhat scary? Imagineering Legend John Hench was regarded as the color expert at Disney's Imagineering Division. According to John Hench (2008, 116):

We wanted to create an imposing southern-style house that would look old, but not in ruins. So, we painted it a cool off-white with dark, cold blue-grey accents in shadowed areas such as the porch ceilings and wrought iron details. To accentuate the eerie, deserted feelings, I had the underside of exterior details painted the

---

10. Baham (2014, 69) quoting a 1996 Disney souvenir book.

same dark color, creating exaggerated, unnaturally deep cast shadows, since we associate dark shadows with things hidden, or half-hidden. The shadow treatment enhanced the structure's other-worldliness.

There was still another critical decision that had to be made. Should the attraction be a walk-through or a ride? There were pros and cons to each approach. With a walk-through, it would be easier to create a single storyline for the entire attraction. Believing that Ken Anderson's approach in the 1950s of a single story-line and a walk-through attraction would be selected, the Imagineers created some illusions where the guests could be more actively involved with the ghosts. However, walk-throughs required a live host as a tour guide, the speed of the tour may then be difficult to control, and there would always be the risk of vandalism or damage to props and equipment in the attraction.

The decision was made to go with a ride. This meant that, instead of a single storyline that would work with a walk-through, the ride would have several stories. Storylines would be needed for each of the ghosts. The tour guide could now be one of the dastardly ghosts. The total attraction, and each individual story, had to be unique and with some degree of weirdness.

Additional Time Constraints

For most project managers, time management refers to the duration of the project, which for the Haunted Mansion would be 18 years from Walt's original concept to the date when the attraction was opened to the public. But for the Imagineers, there were two other time management issues once the decision was made that this would be a ride rather than a walk-through:

- How much time will people need to view each of the scenes?
- How many people can we service each hour?

Writer Bob Thomas wrote an article in which he interviewed Carl Walker from Disneyland, and Dick Irvine, representing WED (Thomas 1969):[11]

> "Then there was the matter of how to conduct people through the ride," said Walker. "At first, it might be a walk-through, with 30 on a conducted tour. But that was difficult to manage, and besides, people don't scare as easily in crowds. So, we made it a ride-through, with three people in a car—their crypt so to speak," said Irvine. "The cars could be programmed to face the right direction, tilt back and keep moving. They provided the capacity we need for rides at Disneyland—2,300 [people] per hour."

The people-mover system was called the "Doom Buggies." It was a modification of the Omnimover system that Disney used in the 1964 New York World's Fair. Since the people were seated, the Imagineers could force the viewers to watch precisely what was intended. The Doom Buggies were programmed to control the angle (i.e., line of sight) by which the guests would see the set without being able to see the supporting animatronics. It also kept the guests at a distance where they could not touch any of the props used in the scenes. Like other attractions at Disney's theme parks, the Haunted Mansion had now become a controlled environment for the guests.

This concept also allowed the designers to be able to place infrastructure elements of the attraction, such as lighting and projectors, behind, above or below the vehicles without concern for having the illusions of the attraction revealed to the riders. The system consists of a chain of vehicles operating on a

---

11. WED stood for Walt Elias Disney. This was previously the name of the Imagineering Division.

track, usually hidden beneath the floor. The chain of vehicles maintains constant motion at a specific speed, thus controlling the viewing time. The duration of the rides varies from 5:50–8:20 minutes, at a maximum speed of three miles per hour.[12]

One of the features that differentiates this system from other people-mover systems is the ability of the vehicle to be rotated to a predetermined orientation. In addition to the main ride rails, each vehicle also has two control rails attached to a wheel. One rail controls the swiveling, allowing the vehicle to face in any direction at any point on the track. The other rail allows the vehicle to tilt in relation to the inclining and declining portions of the track.

Because the entire attraction is in a controlled environment, the Imagineers can control what the guests see. The Imagineers can make it appear that one of the ghosts is in the doom buggy with them.

The Cost Constraint

The Haunted Mansion was completed at a cost of $7 million. In today's dollars, that would be equivalent to more than $50 million. When the Haunted Mansion was built, mainframe computers were just entering the marketplace. Cost control software did not exist, and all cost control was done manually.

There is a misbelief that, when imagination and creativity are allowed to run wild on projects, budgets must be unlimited. That certainly is not the case. Disney monitors all costs. Budgets for each attraction are established during the idea/conceptual phase.

The larger the project, the greater the chance for scope changes and increases in the budget. Unfortunately, the literature does not provide any information related to the original budget or the number of scope changes. The cost of each attraction at Disney's theme parks is generally regarded as proprietary knowledge.

The Safety Constraint

Safety is the main concern at Disney. Walt wanted the Haunted Mansion to be scary but in a pleasant sort of way. The term "scared to death" could lead to wrongful death lawsuits.

Since the Haunted Mansion was a controlled environment, repeat visitors recognized the predictability of the attraction. An attempt was made to have some cast members dress up in a knight's armor suit and wielding an axe (actually made of rubber). This eventually scared the heck out of some people, and there were complaints. Disney discontinued this practice.

The Aesthetics Constraint

Aesthetics and quality go hand-in-hand. All Disney theme park attractions must be aesthetically appealing to the guests. The Haunted Mansion was no exception. The Imagineers converted ideas into reality. Imagineers, and especially Illusioneers, are often equated as dreamers, inventors and even mad scientists. They must have an obsessive commitment to detail and quality.

Nightly maintenance takes place in the Haunted Mansion to make sure that every prop is in place. All of the props are real. Some of the props, such as the pipe organ, was used in the film *20,000 Leagues under the Sea*.

---

12. The doom buggies at Walt Disney World can handle 3,200 guests per hour traveling at about 1.4 miles per hour. At Disneyland, because of the shorter track, only 2,618 guests can be handled.

Even the cobwebs and dust must be aesthetically in place. The cobwebs are made by a liquid cobweb spinner. There must also be a proper amount of dust (which is actually a rubber cement that cannot induce allergies in guests).

A tour of the Haunted Mansion includes:

- The Grounds
- The Foyer
- The Stretching Room
- The Portrait Corridor
- The Library and Music Room
- The Endless Staircase
- The Endless Hallway
- The Conservatory
- The Corridor of Doors
- The Séance Circle
- The Grand Hall
- The Attic
- The Graveyard
- The Crypt

When the decision was made to have a not-so-scary Haunted Mansion, the two Imagineers/Illusioneers, Yale Gracey and Rolly Crump, read ghost stories and watched ghost movies to decide what type of ghosts they could create. The two created numerous effects and often left the special effects running all night long. The night cleaning crew were often spooked and complained to the management, who, in turn, asked the Imagineers not to scare off the cleaning crew.

But instead of leaving the lights on and the special effects off, the two Imagineers decided to connect their special effects to a motion-detector switch. When the duo came to work in the morning, they found a broom hastily left in the middle of their studios. The Imagineers had to clean their studios by themselves from that point on, as management told them that the night cleaning crew were never coming back.

In each location are special effects to support the aesthetic constraint. Some of the special effects include:

- Digital projections
- Computer-controlled effects
- Audio-Animatronics
- Holograms (although they were not used)
- Special lighting
- Real props

Many of the special effects and illusions are based on Pepper's Ghost, an illusion that dates back to the 1800s. Pepper's Ghost is an illusion technique used in theatres, haunted houses, dark rides, and magic tricks. It uses plate glass, Plexiglas, or plastic film and special lighting techniques to make objects seem to appear or disappear, become transparent, or to make one object morph into another. It is named after John Henry Pepper, who popularized the effect in the 1800s.

For the illusion to work, two rooms are required. The viewer must be able to see into the main room, but not into the hidden room. The edge of the glass separating the rooms is sometimes hidden by a cleverly designed pattern in the floor.

The hidden room may be an identical mirror-image of the main room, so that its reflected image matches the main rooms; this approach is useful in making objects seem to appear or disappear. This illusion can also be used to make one object or person reflected in the mirror appear to morph into another behind the glass (or vice versa). The hidden room may instead be painted black, with only light-colored objects in it. In this case, when light is cast on the room, only the light objects reflect the light and appear as ghostly translucent images superimposed in the visible room.

In the Haunted Mansion at Disneyland, Walt Disney World, and Tokyo Disneyland, the glass is vertical to the viewer as opposed to the normal angled position, reflecting animated props below and above the viewer that create the appearance of three-dimensional, translucent "ghosts" that appear to dance through the ballroom and interact with props in the physical ballroom. The apparitions appear and disappear when the lights on the animations turn on and off.

Some of the special effects created for the Haunted Mansion include:

- A ghost host
- Exploding ghosts
- Talking and singing statues
- Furniture that comes to life
- A man made of dripping wax
- A grandfather clock that looks like a coffin
- A graveyard band of ghosts playing music
- A pet cemetery
- An invisible ghost horse with only a saddle and reins
- A ghost poetess creating a poem
- Dancing ghosts
- Ghosts that fade in and out
- Ghosts that suddenly become headless
- A ghost playing a piano
- Portraits that change from reality to the supernatural
- Wallpaper patterned with monster faces
- Hanging ghosts
- A crypt that plays music if you touch the instruments

Some of the above special effects are discussed below in more detail.[13]

Ghost Host

The Ghost Host is one of the first characters that guests to the Mansion meet, so to speak. He remains invisible throughout the tour, guiding "foolish mortals" with an ominous voice. The voice is that of Paul Frees, a popular Disneyland announcer and vocal talent (well-known as the voice of the Pillsbury Doughboy, Ludwig von Drake, and Boris Badenov in the popular TV series *The Adventures of Rocky and Bullwinkle*) was called on to provide the voice of the unseen "Ghost Host." Frees's gleefully sardonic narration often features death-related puns and maniacal laughter. In the Stretching Room scene near the beginning of the tour, it is revealed that he committed suicide by hanging himself from the rafters in the cupola.

---

13. For more information on the special effects, see *Wikipedia, the Free Encyclopedia* "The Haunted Mansion," https://en.wikipedia.org/w/index.php?title=The_Haunted_Mansion&oldid=895866367, accessed May 10, 2019.

Aging Man

Above the fireplace in the foyer of the Walt Disney World and Tokyo Haunted Mansions is a portrait of a former owner of the house. The painting gradually changes from a handsome blue-eyed and black-haired young man to a withered, balding old man and finally, to a decaying skeleton. This portrait can also be found in the changing portrait hallway of the Disneyland Haunted Mansion, but it morphs from the young man to the skeleton with flashes of lightning.

Changing Portrait Characters

Lightning flashes transform these paintings (at the Disneyland and Walt Disney World Haunted Mansions) from benign to frightening. The portraits consist of:

- A beautiful young princess reclining on a couch who changes into a werecat
- A gallant knight (identified as "The Black Prince" in concept art) atop a rearing horse, who both become skeletal
- A handsome young man who decays into a ghastly corpse
- The beautiful, red-haired Medusa, who becomes a hideous Gorgon

Stretching Portrait Characters

The following characters are depicted in the portraits of the Stretching Room:

- A balding man with a brown mustache and beard, dressed in a black tailcoat, a white shirt, a red sash, and a black bowtie. When the portrait stretches, it is revealed that he is not wearing pants (only red and white-striped boxer shorts), and he is standing atop a lit keg of dynamite. In an early attraction script, which gave the names of the characters in the stretching portraits, he was an ambassador named Alexander Nitrokoff, who came to the Mansion one night "with a bang."
- Constance Hatchaway, an old woman holding a rose and smiling. When the portrait stretches, it is revealed that she is seated on top of the tombstone of her late husband, George Hightower, who is depicted as a marble bust with his head split by an axe. The ghost of Constance as a young woman is later seen in the attic.
- A brown-haired man with his arms crossed, dressed in a brown suit and wearing a brown derby hat. When the portrait stretches, it is revealed that he is sitting on the shoulders of another man, who is sitting on the shoulders of another man who is waist-deep in quicksand.
- A pretty young brunette holding a pink parasol. When the portrait stretches, it is revealed that she is balancing on a fraying tightrope above the gaping jaws of an alligator.

Coffin Occupant

In the center of the Conservatory is a large coffin occupied by a possessed corpse attempting to break out. He calls for help in the voice of a feeble old man, and his skeletal hands can be seen attempting to pry open the nailed-down coffin lid. He is voiced by Xavier Atencio, who wrote the attraction's script.

Madame Leota

Madame Leota is one of the iconic characters of the ride. She is the spirit of a psychic medium, conducting an otherworldly séance in an attempt to summon spirits and assist them in materializing. Her ghostly head appears within a crystal ball on a table in the middle of her dark chamber, from which she speaks her incantations. Musical instruments and furniture levitate and make noises in response. Imagineer Leota Toombs was chosen for the face of the medium in the crystal ball. Leota Toombs also played the Ghost Hostess who appears at the end of the attraction, though it is unknown whether or not she and Madame Leota are meant to be the same character.

In 2002, a tombstone for Madame Leota debuted at Walt Disney World's Mansion. The epitaph reads: "Dear sweet Leota, beloved by all. In regions beyond now, but having a ball."

Madame Leota summons the Mansion's restless spirts and encourages them to appear by reciting suitable surreal incantations:

> "Serpents and spiders, tail of a rat. Call in the spirts, wherever they're at!"
> "Rap on a table, it's time to respond, Send us a message from somewhere beyond!"
> "Goblins and ghoulies from last Halloween, Awaken the spirits with your tambourine!"
> "Creepies and crawlies, toads in a pond, Let there be music from regions beyond!"
> "Wizards and witches wherever you dwell, Give us a hint by ringing a bell!"

Duelists

The ghosts of two top-hat-wearing gentlemen emerge from paintings of themselves and shoot each other.

Hitchhiking Ghosts

The Hitchhiking Ghosts—"The Prisoner," "The Skeleton," and "The Traveler"—are often considered to be the mascots of The Haunted Mansion. They have the most merchandise, including pins, stuffed toys, action figures, and bobbleheads. The Hitchhiking Ghosts are a tongue-in-cheek send-up of urban legends involving phantom hitchhikers. They are seen standing together inside a crypt, thumbs extended. They hitch a ride with guests traveling in Doom Buggies and appear alongside them in mirrors. "They have selected you to fill our quota, and they'll haunt you until you return," says the Ghost Host. In 2011 at Walt Disney World's Haunted Mansion, the mirror scene was updated with digital effects that enable the ghosts to interact with the guests.

The Hitchhiking Ghosts are often referred to by fans as "Gus" (Prisoner), "Ezra" (Skeleton), and "Phineas" (Traveler). These names first appeared in fan fiction created by Cast Members who worked at the Walt Disney World Haunted Mansion. Since then, the names have become so well known that they have appeared on merchandise for the characters and in various media licensed by Disney.

Referenced Characters

On numerous tombstones and crypts at the Disneyland, Walt Disney World, and Tokyo Haunted Mansions (and in the Servants Quarters of Walt Disney World's Haunted Mansion) are the names of characters who may or may not appear in the attraction. Most of the names are actually tributes to Imagineers who were involved in the creation of the attraction.

Outside of each Mansion are crypts labeled with pun-based names. At Tokyo, they are identified as "Restless Spirits."

- **As**her T. Ashes (Ashes to ashes)
- Bea Witch (Bewitch)
- Clare Voince (Clairvoyance)
- C. U. Later (See you later)
- Dustin T. Dust (Dust to dust)
- G. I. Missyou (Gee, I miss you)
- Hail N. Hardy (Hale and hearty)
- Hal Lusinashun (Hallucination)
- Hap A. Rition (Apparition)
- Harry After (Hereafter)
- Hobb Gobblin (Hobgoblin)
- L. Beback (I'll be back)
- Emma Spook (I am a spook)
- M. Mortal (I am mortal) or (immortal)
- M. Ready (I am ready)
- Trudy Departed (I truly departed)
- Trudy Dew (I truly do)
- Levi Tation / Lev Itation (Levitation)
- Love U. Trudy (Love you truly)
- Manny Festation (Manifestation)
- Metta Fisiks (Metaphysics)
- M. T. Tomb (Empty tomb)
- Paul Tergyst (Poltergeist)
- Pearl E. Gates (Pearly gates)
- Ray. N. Carnation (Reincarnation)
- Rustin Peece (Rest in peace)
- Rusty Gates (Rusty gates)
- Theo Later (See you later)
- U. R. Gone (You are gone)
- Wee G. Bord (Ouija board)

The Special Effects and Music

The special effects were groundbreaking for the time. This included an attic with the ghost of a spurned bride, a crypt and a cemetery, halls that appear endless, and a mystical fortuneteller named Madame Leota who appears as a disembodied head inside a crystal ball with musical instruments floating in the air around her. Finally, the guests are shown that a "hitchhiking ghost" has hopped into the Doom Buggy with them.

Though the setting is spooky, the mood is kept light by the upbeat "Grim Grinning Ghosts" music that plays throughout the ride. The music was composed by Buddy Baker and the lyrics written by Xavier

Atencio. The deep voice of Thurl Ravenscroft sings as part of a quartet of singing busts in the graveyard scene. Ravenscroft's face is used as well as it is projected onto one of the busts, specifically one with a detached head.

Continuous Improvements

All theme park attractions undergo continuous improvement efforts. According to Bob Zalk, Walt Disney Imagineer and show producer (Veness 2009, 24):

> The idea of going back into an iconic attraction and adding, changing, adjusting, removing elements—the standards are extremely high when you reach the finish line. We have to deliver. Unlike new attractions, re-imagining an established attraction carries with it its own sense of history and tradition that the entire team has to take into account. It's a big challenge, but an exciting one.

Discussion Questions

1. What are the primary differences between traditional projects and the Haunted Mansion Project?
2. What are typical deliverables on an innovation project compared to the deliverables on the Haunted Mansion Project?
3. Why aren't all the project's constraints of equal importance and can the importance change over the life of a project?
4. Who defines the constraints on an innovation project?
5. Can egos affect innovation?
6. Why was it impossible to prepare a clearly defined statement of work at the beginning of the Haunted Mansion Project?
7. In the list of questions that needed to be addressed at project initiation, which three questions are probably most critical for SOW preparation? (*Note*: There can be several answers to this question. What is important is the justification behind the three answers selected.)
8. Why did the Haunted Mansion Project take 18 years from concept to completion?
9. Why did Disney not want the exterior of the Haunted Mansion to appear as a traditional haunted house?
10. Most Disney attractions tell a story. Why was it so difficult to create a single story for the Haunted Mansion?
11. Why do some people, such as Imagineers, often have ego issues?
12. Why was the Haunted Mansion attraction created as a "controlled" ride?

Further Reading

- Cunningham, James D. *The Legend of The Haunted Mansion* (CreateSpace, 2002).
- Wasko, Janet. (2001). *Understanding Disney*. Cambridge, UK: Polity Press.
- Wilson, C. McNair. (2012). *Hatch! Brainstorming Secrets of a Theme Park Designer*. Colorado Springs, CO: Book Villages.

DISNEY (C): IMPACT OF CULTURE ON GLOBAL INNOVATION OPPORTUNITIES

PMI first began promoting the term "enterprise environmental factors" in 2004 with the third edition of the *PMBOK® Guide*. This was twelve years after Euro Disney had opened. It is interesting to look first at the launch of Euro Disney, now called Disneyland Paris, by analyzing the enterprise environmental factors that existed at that time even though they were not referred to as enterprise environmental factors. The enterprise environmental factors can have a serious impact on the design of a business model.

Creating a Business Model

For some people, there is a belief, or rather a misconception, that the Walt Disney Company can simply build or duplicate an existing theme park on foreign soil. Thus, they can use their existing business model and very little innovation is necessary.

Each new country poses new challenges that must be addressed in the business model development. Enterprise environmental factors play a critical role. The following is list of questions that needs to be considered during the business model innovation process:

- How will the host country react to an American theme park on their soil?
- Will there be cultural factors that need to be considered?
- Will the cultural factors influence the design of the rides, products for sale in the gift shops, and type of food served in restaurants?
- Will there be political intervention, and if so, of what magnitude?
- Are there laws in the host country that can impact the design and operation of the park?
- Are there religious considerations that must be addressed and well as dress codes?
- Will the host government serve as a financial stakeholder in the project?
- Will the other financial stakeholders be banks or companies located in the host country?
- Which stakeholders will have the greatest influence in decisions on how the park will be run?
- Should Disney focus on just the theme park or a larger effort such as a Disney Vacation Resort in the host country that involves other amenities?
- Will the weather in the host country be an issue?
- How much of a risk should Disney take concerning other amenities such building Disney-themed hotels, golf courses, shopping malls, etc.?
- How much financial exposure should Disney accept?
- Should Disney focus on a joint venture with partners or a licensing agreement?
- Should Disney consider the risk to the Disney brand name if the theme park is a failure?
- Can a financial failure of this theme park prevent other countries from wanting to host a Disney theme park on their soil?
- Can a failure or unfavorable risks lead to stockholder interference?
- If we have a successful business model in one country, can the same business model be replicated for another country?

Understanding Enterprise Environmental Factors

Enterprise environmental factors are conditions that exist now or in the future and may or may not have an impact on the project. If there is an impact, it can occur any time over the life of the project. The enterprise environmental factors can influence how the project will be managed, whether changes in scope or quality are required and whether the project is viewed as a success. These factors can include the state of the economy, present and future legislation, politics, influence of labor unions, competitive forces in play, and cultural issues. The factors can also change after the project is completed and turn an initially successful project into a failure. They can also have an impact on the design of future business models.

Project planning is generally based on history, especially past successes. Enterprise environmental factors are assumptions and predictions about both the present and the future and are therefore directly related to risk management activities. These assumptions impact the design of innovative business models.

It is generally the responsibility of senior management, the project sponsor or the governance committee to identify the enterprise environmental factors. The factors may be listed as enterprise environmental factors in the project's business case or they may appear as assumptions concerning the business environment. The enterprise environmental factors are generally an interpretation by one person or a consensus of several people including experts. One person may see a factor as having a favorable impact on the project, whereas another person may see it as an unfavorable condition. Simply stated, enterprise environmental factors are subject to interpretation as well as misinterpretation by the people requesting and funding the project. The impact can be devastating unless corrections and changes can be done quickly. Even some of the best managed companies, such as the Walt Disney Company, can be impacted by unanticipated changes in the enterprise environmental factors.

Enterprise Environmental Factors and Culture

Perhaps the most important enterprise environmental factor to be considered in Disney's decision to expand globally was the impact of multinational cultures. Expanding onto foreign soil (i.e., outside of the United States) would be a challenge. Disney's theme parks would have to be integrated culturally and socially with that of the host country and its surrounding neighbors.

Disney understood the American culture and foreign visitors that came to Disneyland and Disney World understood that they were visiting an American theme park. But how would people react to an American theme park that was on foreign soil? What might happen if Disney does not adhere to the cultural and social norms of the host country? How much of a change would be necessary from the way that theme parks are managed in the United States?

Enterprise Environmental Factors and Competing Constraints

Before discussing Euro Disney, it is important to understand competing constraints. There are actions that project managers and executives can take to alleviate to some degree the impact of unfavorable enterprise environmental factors. Although we cannot eliminate the enterprise environmental factors, we may have options available to us to lessen the impact. The actions we take almost always mandate tradeoffs on the competing constraints, thus perhaps making it impossible to meet all the constraints. In such a case, the constraints may have to be prioritized to provide guidance in the order of the tradeoffs. The tradeoff may result in a schedule elongation or significant cost overrun.

While most companies focus on the triple constraints of time, cost, and scope, Disney's theme parks in the United States have six constraints; time, cost, scope, safety, aesthetic value, and quality. Although not discussed in the literature, it appears that safety is understandably the most important constraint at Disney, followed by aesthetic value and quality. These three important constraints very rarely undergo tradeoffs because they have a direct bearing on Disney's image and reputation. All tradeoffs appear to be on time, cost, and scope.

When expanding onto foreign soil, the enterprise environmental factors may also impose constraints on culture and even social behavior. Cultural and social constraints can involve designing the settings for attractions to be more aligned to local architecture, serving foods preferred by the population of the host country and dress codes that are acceptable to the general population. Host countries may not want a theme park on their soil that tries to "Americanize" the guests.

All the constraints may be interrelated when tradeoffs are necessary. For example, Disney maintains blueprints for attractions erected at Walt Disney World and Disneyland. Having to modify the attraction to be more aligned with the local architecture of the host country can require the creation of new blueprints, thus possibly increasing the project's cost and elongating the schedule.

The Decision to Build Euro Disney

In 1984, Disney made the decision to build a theme park in Europe by 1992. Disney wanted to build a large, state-of-the-art theme park, a decision which eventually led to "budget breaker" scope changes. Many of the changes were last-minute changes made by Michael Eisner, Disney's chief executive officer.

History has shown that large projects, especially those designed around state-of-the-art technology, are prone to large cost overruns. The baggage-handling system at Denver International Airport and the Iridium Project, which was designed to create a worldwide wireless handheld mobile phone system with the ability to communicate anywhere in the world at any time, are two examples where the cost overruns were in the billions of dollars.

Highly optimistic financial projections were established for Euro Disney based on the expectation of 11 million visitors the first year and 16 million visitors yearly after the turn of the century. Nine years earlier, when Tokyo Disneyland opened on April 15, 1983, more than 13,000 visitors entered the park. Within the same year, Tokyo Disneyland broke the attendance record for theme parks with a one-day attendance of 93,000 visitors. Within four years, they again broke the one-day record with 111,500 visitors.

Disney created a low-risk business model for Disney Tokyo. From the literature, Disney believed that the same type of business model could be used in Euro Disney. However, this time Disney was willing to accept a greater risk because of the potential rewards. The focus was more toward creating a Disney vacation resort than a Disney theme park.

Disney viewed the Euro Disney theme park as a potentially profitable revenue generator for decades in as much as Disney would have a monopoly in leisure and entertainment in Europe. The definition of a monopoly is when you have no rivals and there are high barriers, especially financial, preventing someone from entering the same market.

Site Selection

Approximately 1,200 locations in Europe were considered and everyone wanted to host Euro Disney. The locations included Portugal, Spain, France, Italy, and Greece. Part of Disney's selection criteria included a warm climate, good weather, a centralized location, and available land for further growth. The list was narrowed down to four locations: two in Spain and two in France. Spain had better weather, but France had a denser population. The final decision was to build Euro Disney in the eastern suburbs of Paris in a new town, Marne-la-Vallee. The theme park would be 20 miles from the heart of Paris. This meant that there were 17 million people less than a two-hour drive from Euro Disney, 68 million people within a four-hour drive, 110 million people within a six-hour drive, and another 310 million people less than two hours by air. In addition, Paris was frequently visited by tourists from around the world.

In line with this belief of having a monopoly and the success of the smaller $1.4 billion theme park in Tokyo Disneyland, Disney decided to build a much larger state-of-the-art theme park in Europe, expecting the same financial success as in Tokyo. Disney needed approximately $5 billion to build Euro Disney. More than $1 billion was provided by the French government in the belief that Euro Disney would create 30,000 jobs. Europe was in a recession. France had an unemployment rate near 14 percent. Also, France expected a large percentage of the projected 11 million visitors to the theme park each year to come from outside France, thus bringing revenue into the country.

The French were willing to make concessions to acquire the theme park. The land was provided at a low price of $7,500 per acre. Euro Disney would be built in a plot of 1,945 acres in the center of a 4,400-acre site. The French would pay for new road construction and provide water, sewage, gas, electricity, and other necessary services such as a subway and train system.

Project Financing

To satisfy the French government's legal requirements, and to limit the financial exposure to the Walt Disney Company, a new company was formed: Euro Disney S.C.A. Unlike Tokyo Disneyland, where Japan's Oriental Land Company owned and operated the park, and paid Disney royalties, Euro Disney S.C.A. would be a publicly held company. Disney would own a maximum of 49 percent of the new company and at least 51 percent would be owned by Europeans. For Disney, this was new business model unlike the business models for the US-based parks and Tokyo Disneyland.

Euro Disney S.C.A. was set up using a project financing model. Project financing involves the establishment of a legally independent project company, Euro Disney S.C.A., where the providers of funds are repaid out of cash flow and earnings, and where the assets of the new company, and only the new company, are used as collateral for the loans. Debt repayment would come from Euro Disney S.C.A. rather than from any other entity. In case of a default on the bank loans, lenders could take legal action against Euro Disney S.C.A., but not the Walt Disney Company.

A risk with project financing in the new business model is that the capital assets may have a limited life. The potential limited life constraint often makes it difficult to get lenders to agree to long-term financial arrangements. With Euro Disney, the attractions in the park would have to undergo continuous improvement and new attractions added. If there is insufficient cash flow to fund the growth, the company would have to incur additional debt.

Another critical issue with project financing especially for high-technology projects is that the projects are generally long term. It may be several years before service will begin, and in terms of technology, this can be an eternity. Project financing is often considered a "bet on the future." And if the project were to fail, the company may be worth nothing after liquidation.

European banks, looking at the financial success of Disneyland, Walt Disney World, and Tokyo Disneyland, rushed in to provide Disney with whatever funding was necessary in the way of construction loans. More than 60 banks entered into loan agreements. Disney negotiated a deal whereby Disney's total investment was $160 million to help fund a $5 billion theme park. Disney would collect hundreds of millions of dollars each year in royalty payments even if the theme park lost money. Following a royalty agreement like that for Tokyo Disneyland, Disney would receive 10 percent royalties on admissions; 5 percent royalties on food, beverage, and merchandise sales; a management fee equivalent to 3 percent of revenue; a licensing fee for using the Disney name and characters; 5 percent of gross revenues of themed hotels; and 49 percent of the profits.[14] Disney also received royalties from companies that sponsored specific rides. For Disney's $160 million investment, Disney estimated that their expected profits would be $230 million to $600 million the first year and $300 million to $1 billion in the second year. In exchange for royalty payments, Disney provided expertise in theme park management and allowed Euro Disney to use the trademarked Disney characters and Disney Imagineering's intellectual property. The business model seemed realistic.

The total price of $5 billion for a theme park would certainly serve as an impediment to prevent rivals from entering the market. The quality and aesthetic value of Disney's products and services, their reputation as one of the world's leaders in leisure and entertainment, and their uniqueness characterized by their brand name made it appear on the surface to be a monopoly. Disney believed that the attendance projections were correct, namely 11 million visitors the first year rising to 16 million per year by the turn of the century.

Much of Disney's thinking was predicated on their phenomenal past success with Disneyland (1955), Disney World (1970), and Tokyo Disneyland (1983). With all three theme parks, Disney adapted correctly to most of the enterprise environmental factors they considered and the impact they might have on project success. The latest theme park, Tokyo Disneyland, was owned and operated by the Oriental Land Company. The construction cost was $1.4 billion and the debt, which was 80 percent of the construction cost, was paid off in three years. The question, of course, was whether these same enterprise environmental factors and assumptions considered in Tokyo Disneyland were transferable to and appropriate for the European marketplace.

Unlike Disneyland and Disney World locations, weather in Tokyo was an issue for Disney. When people in Tokyo showed that they were willing to brave the cold and snow to enjoy the theme park, Disney was convinced that the Europeans would follow suit.

Disneyland and Disney World were based on an American Disney philosophy. The Japanese wanted an American-style theme park like Disneyland and Disney World, and not customized to the Japanese culture. The younger Japanese wanted American-style food. However, some Japanese-style restaurants were built for the adult patrons who preferred traditional Japanese meals.

Blinded by the success of Tokyo Disneyland, Disney believed that the same American Disney philosophy that was part of the Tokyo business model could be introduced into Europe without necessitating any significant changes. However, would the enterprise environmental factors related to culture be the same for the European marketplace? Would the Europeans accept being Americanized once inside the park?

Understanding Cultural Differences

Perhaps Disney's greatest mistake was not fully understanding the cultural differences between the Japanese and the Europeans, primarily the French. This would have a significant impact on Euro Disney's expected revenue stream when the park opened. Some of the critical differences are shown in Table 13-1. These are the differences based on the year when the parks were opened.

---

14. Tokyo Disneyland was a licensing agreement between Disney and the Oriental Land Company. Disney received royalty payments but did not share in the profits. Euro Disney was more of a joint venture, where Disney would receive royalty payments and a percentage of the profits. These agreements will be discussed in the "Disney (D) Case Study".

TABLE 13–1.   CULTURAL DIFFERENCES BETWEEN JAPAN AND FRANCE

Factor	Japan	France
Economy	Booming	In a recession
Per capita income	Increasing	Decreasing
Time spent on leisure activities	Increasing	Decreasing
Frequency of vacations	Several short week-long vacations	One vacation in August lasting 4–5 weeks
Spending	Cannot leave the park empty-handed; gift-giving is important	Gift-giving is unnecessary
Acceptance of US products	High	Low
Size of the park	Unimportant	Important
Attachment to Disney characters	Very high	Scorn American fairytale characters
Appeal of Disney entertainment	High	Low
Disneyland theme park	Symbol of new lifestyle	Seen as an American lifestyle
Tolerance for long queues	Very tolerant; used to crowds and lines	Intolerant
Acceptance of dress codes	Very high; part of the culture is wearing uniforms	Very low; seen as an attack on individualism
Clean-cut grooming	Part of the culture	Attack on individualism
Politeness to strangers	Part of the culture	Not always
Enjoy being part of a team	Part of the culture	Not always
Follow instructions of one's superiors	Always	Sometimes questions authority

In defense of Disney's actions, which some people argue weren't enough to effectively manage the cultural differences, it is important to recognize that Euro Disney is an American theme park and Disney's actions were designed to protect its image, brand names, and reputation. Expecting Disney to make major cultural changes and alter the image of the park would be a mistake.

Land Development

Euro Disney eventually opened in April of 1992. In his opening remarks at its dedication, Disney's CEO Michael Eisner said:

> To all who come to this happy place, welcome. Once upon a time… A master storyteller, Walt Disney, inspired by Europe's best loved tales, used his own special gifts to share them with the world. He envisioned a Magic Kingdom where these stories would come to life and called it Disneyland. Now his dream returns to the lands that inspired it. Euro Disneyland is dedicated to the young, and the young at heart… with a hope that it will be a source of joy and inspiration for all the world.

Disney wanted to develop the commercial and residential property it had purchased surrounding the theme park and then sell off the properties while maintaining ownership and control over its commercial use. Real estate sales were expected to supply 22 percent of Euro Disney's revenue beginning in 1992, climbing to 45 percent of revenue by 1995.

The revenue from land development was expected to help pay down Euro Disney's massive debt of $3.5 billion. But when the park opened, Europe was in a recession and it became obvious that Euro Disney had severely miscalculated the French real estate market, which was quite depressed. When Tokyo Disneyland opened in 1983, the Japanese economy was booming, and the Japanese were spending a large portion of their discretionary income on leisure and entertainment. Tokyo Disneyland reaped the benefits. But in Europe, the recession caused people to cut back on leisure and entertainment. Euro Disney suffered. Disney miscalculated the impact of the recession in Europe.

Euro Disney also miscalculated how Europeans would take vacations. Disney hoped that people would take one-week excursions to Euro Disney throughout the school the year. Instead, the Europeans preferred to save up their vacation until August and take a vacation lasting four to five weeks. The cost of spending one week at Euro Disney was almost the same cost as renting a vacation home in Europe for a month. Once again, Euro Disney suffered from a loss of revenue. Disney expected labor costs to be about 13 percent of total revenue. Instead, it was 24 percent of total revenue in 1992 and climbed to 40 percent in 1993.

Disney's Integrated Services

Disney's integrated services, which made up the revenue portion of their business model, generate revenue from four sources: (1) admission to the theme parks and other attractions, (2) food, (3) shopping, and (4) accommodations. Disney's business model for Disneyland and Disney World did not recognize the potential for significant profits through accommodations. In Disneyland and Disney World, Disney allowed others to build money-making hotels around the theme parks. This was now seen as a mistake that Disney regretted. At Disneyland, Disney owned only 1,000 hotel rooms out of 20,000. At Disney World, only 5,700 hotel rooms out of a possible 70,000 were owned by Disney. Disney also generates revenue from the sale of cruise vacation packages and the rental of vacation club properties.

In Tokyo, Disney believed that it again made a mistake in the business model by not investing heavily in accommodations. When the decision to build Tokyo Disneyland was made, Disney was worried about making a heavy investment in a new cultural environment. The decision was made to limit its financial risk with a small investment in accommodations surrounding the park. This put limitations on profit generation in exchange for a perceived reduction in risk and uncertainty. The result was a small investment in accommodations. The risks were further reduced because the theme park was not owned or operated by Disney. Disney received a predefined royalty.

It is important to understand that an increase in daily park attendance does not necessarily translate into a significant increase in profits unless the average stay in a hotel is lengthened, which, in turn, would generate revenue from the high-profit-margin businesses such as hotels, restaurants, and shops. Admission to the theme parks is not a high-margin business.

Because of the success in Tokyo, Disney took an overly optimistic position with Euro Disney, believing that what worked in Japan could be transplanted into Europe. Disney did not want Euro Disney or any of its other theme parks to be just a theme park. Instead, it wanted Euro Disney to be viewed as a vacation resort or a destination vacation where visitors would stay for four to five days or longer. Disney wanted people to see Disney theme parks as a source of family and adult-oriented high-quality entertainment. Therefore, Disney included in the Euro Disney plans a 27-hole golf course, 5,800 hotel rooms (which is more hotel rooms than the city of Cannes), shopping malls, apartments, and vacation homes. Disney also planned on building a second theme park next to Euro Disney to house an MGM Film Tour site, at a construction cost of $2.3 billion. There was even talk of building a third theme park by 2017. This would help fill the large number of hotel rooms. By the year 2017, Euro Disney, under the terms specified in its contract with the French government, was required to complete construction of a total of 18,200 hotel rooms at varying distances from the resort. All of this assumed that Euro Disney would follow in the same steps as did Disneyland, Disney World, and Tokyo Disneyland. Disney believed that they had a firm grasp on the enterprise environmental factors and set higher standards for Euro Disney than even the theme parks in the United States.

Disney University

Just as it had in the United States, Euro Disney set up a Disney University to train approximately 20,000 employees and cast members who applied for jobs at Euro Disney. Training was designed to enforce the Disney culture as well as Disney's policies and procedures that had worked well for decades. The training had to be completed well before the opening of the park. Employees were expected to be bilingual or even trilingual and were required to attend training sessions conducted by Disney University on behavior codes and how to talk to park guests. The company stressed that all visitors should be treated as guests rather than customers.

Disney also established rules related to facial hair such as beards and mustaches (none were allowed), dress codes, covering of tattoos, limited jewelry and makeup, no highlighting or streaking of the hair, limitations on the length of fingernails, and the wearing of appropriate undergarments. The French saw this as an attack on their individual liberties.

Euro Disney, as well as all other Disney theme parks, had very strict rules on the hiding of behind-the-scenes Disney. Photography and filming were strictly forbidden in backstage areas. The edges of the parks were lined with ride buildings and foliage to hide areas that were not for the public to see. Numerous gates allowed entrance into the park for cast members, parade cars, etc. When gates around the park were opened, anything that could be seen through them was considered part of the Disney magic. Therefore, from the second the gates are opened, all of the crew must be in character and in place to "perform." Since the complex was so big, shuttle buses were needed to take cast members to different parts of the park via roads behind the parks.

Anti-American Sentiment Grows

According to the literature, it appears that the Walt Disney Company understood the sociocultural and economic issues but perhaps did not give them enough attention. Disney did launch an aggressive public relations program targeting young children and government officials. Even with the community relations program, Disney was still viewed as being insensitive to the French culture, the people's need for privacy, and individualism. French labor unions were opposed to the dress code. All this created an anti-American climate that eventually led to deviations from the original plan for Euro Disney.

Some enterprise environmental factors concerning culture were addressed through behavior modification. Others required changes in the design of the attractions. Disney wanted the park to show that many of the Disney characters had a European heritage. This was a necessity because Euro Disney was competing against the historical architecture and sights of Paris. Simply changing the restaurant menus to serve more European food was not enough. When possible, attractions had to show a European flavor. For example, the attraction showing Snow White and the seven dwarfs was located in a Bavarian village. Cinderella was located in a French Inn. Discoveryland featured storylines from the French author, Jules Verne. Castles in the attractions closely resembled the architecture of castles in Europe.

While the Walt Disney Company did the best that it could to address the enterprise environmental factors related to culture without altering its image and reputation, it could not adequately address the factors related to politics. For example, since many visitors were staying at the Euro Disney just for a one-day excursion, the traffic through the town and the accompanying noise irritated many of the local residents. The communities surrounding Euro Disney were mainly farming communities that had opposed the construction of Euro Disney. The French government had to step in to ease tension. Shortly after Euro Disney opened, French farmers used Euro Disney as a site for a protest, driving their tractors to the entrance and blocking it. This globally televised act of protest was aimed not at Disney but at the US government, which had been demanding that French agricultural subsidies be cut. This protest was televised worldwide. Also, Euro Disney encountered several disputes with French labor unions that believed that Disney was attacking the civil liberties of their union members.

Anti-American sentiment increased even more when tensions grew surrounding America's war in Iraq and France's refusal to back it. The drop in the number of American tourists to France was drastic and was felt by the tourism industry especially in Paris. One worker at the restaurant atop the Eiffel tower noted the replacement of American tourists with Spanish and Italian tourists. Other factors that affected tourism was the harsh weather in Europe, a series of transportation strikes, and the outbreak of severe acute respiratory syndrome in Asia.

Underestimating the Impact of Culture

It appeared that, even though Disney took steps to address almost all the cultural differences, Disney had underestimated the magnitude of the differences in culture between the United States and Europe. The impact could be clearly seen through the enterprise environmental factors, as shown in Table 13-2.

There were other mistakes that were made:

- At various locations in the park, there was an insufficient number of restrooms.
- Park staffing assumed that Friday would be a busy day and Monday a light day when, in fact, the reverse was true.
- Park management underestimated the success of the convention business and had to increase convention facilities.

Missing the Targets

On opening day, Euro Disney had expected that as many as 500,000 visitors and 90,000 cars might try to enter the park, even though the capacity of the park was estimated at slightly above 50,000 visitors. Approximately 50,000 visitors showed up, and only 3 out of every 10 visitors were native French. Attendance figures were disappointing. Some people argued that the low attendance was due to Disney's insensitivity to the French culture. Others believed it was due in part to economic conditions in Europe at that time. As the year progressed, Euro Disney lowered their daily projection from 60,000 to 25,000 visitors. The Walt Disney stock plunged, eventually losing one third of its value.

In the first two years of operations, Euro Disney's losses were estimated at $2 billion. Euro Disney also had a debt load of $3.5 billion, with some interest payments as high as 11 percent. The 22 percent operating profit from land development, which was planned to pay down the debt, never materialized. Hotel occupancy was 55 percent rather than the expected 68 percent. Some hotels were shutting down for the winter season. Operating expenses had risen from an expected 60 percent of revenue to 69 percent of revenue. The MGM Film Studio theme park project was put on hold.

TABLE 13–2.   IMPACT OF CULTURE ON THE EURO DISNEY ENTERPRISE ENVIRONMENTAL FACTORS

Enterprise Environmental Factor	Projected Impact	Actual Impact
Monopoly	Euro Disney would be a monopoly. Europeans would be willing to pay the above-market admission fees. Prices for Euro Disney were set at a higher level than all other European theme parks and the Disney theme parks in the United States.	It is difficult to define leisure and entertainment as a monopoly. Unlike necessities such as water or electricity, which are often monopolies, most people can find other, less expensive forms of entertainment and leisure activities. Euro Disney functioned more so as an oligopoly that has few suppliers with either similar or dissimilar products or substitute products.
Vacation resort	Europeans would see Euro Disney as a vacation resort and stay for 4–5 days or longer.	Europeans saw Euro Disney as a one-day short excursion. This meant that accommodations were not seen as a necessity and Euro Disney was not seen as a resort.
Alcoholic beverages	Disney believed that the Europeans would accept the fact that no alcoholic beverages would be allowed in the theme park.	Europeans wanted wine and alcoholic beverages with their meals. The ban on alcohol demonstrated insensitivity to the French culture. The French are the biggest consumers of wine worldwide. People therefore refused to eat in the theme parks. Some brought wine coolers in their cars and had tailgating parties. Also, cigarettes were not sold in the theme parks.
Integrated services	Europeans would stay 4–5 days at the theme park.	Europeans would stay just one day, spend the entire time on the rides, and thus very little time remained for shopping. High admission fees also led to less money spent on shopping. The actual revenues from shopping, food, accommodations, and admission fees was significantly below target levels.
Cost for a family of four	Based on data from Tokyo Disneyland, the cost for a family of four at Tokyo Disneyland was approximately $600 per day excluding accommodations. Disney assumed the Europeans would pay the same prices.	The Europeans believed that $280 per day was too much.
Per capita spending	Euro Disney assumed that per capita spending in the park would be $33 per person.	Actual spending was revised down to $29 per person. This was significantly less than Disneyland and Disney World in the United States, and almost 50 percent less than Tokyo Disneyland.
Mealtime seating capacity	Based on Disneyland and Disney World data, Americans would "graze" all day on snacks and fast foods. The Europeans would do the same, thus implying that restaurant seating capacity at Euro Disney could duplicate other theme park seating.	Expecting 60,000 visitors a day, Disney built 29 restaurants capable of feeding 14,000 visitors each hour. However, Europeans appear to eat healthier than Americans. Most Europeans prefer to eat a healthy lunch at exactly 12:30 p.m. Many of the restaurants could not handle the number of customers arriving at the same time. Europeans are intolerant of long queues.
Park staffing	Euro Disney employees would accept the standards and codes that were set at other Disney theme parks.	Park employees and guests felt that they were being "Americanized." In the first nine months, 1,000 of the 10,000 workers quit.

While project management seemed to be successful regarding construction of the park, the miscalculation of the impact of the enterprise environmental factors was quite apparent. Euro Disney was seen as a project management success, Imagineering and innovation at its best, but possibly a business failure. The possible causes of failure were because Disney:

- Failed to recognize competitive leisure and entertainment offerings
- Failed to recognize the sociocultural and economic issues
- Had a wrong assessment of market conditions, which led to strategic and financial miscalculations
- Took on an overly ambitious $3.5 billion debt load that was hard to pay off
- Overdeveloped the property and land
- Failed to recognize guest awareness of pricing

There were also communication issues. Park executives were not returning phone calls to the media resulting in a failed reputation with the media.

Three interesting comments about the Walt Disney Company appeared in articles and newspapers. In one article, Euro Disney was viewed as "a cultural Chernobyl." In another article, a European banker stated that "Euro Disney is a good theme park married to a bankrupt real estate company and the two can't be divorced." A former Disney executive stated that during Euro Disney financing negotiations, "We were arrogant. It was like we're building the Taj Mahal and people will come—on our terms."

People were even attacking the name of the park. People outside of Europe often viewed "Euro" as being synonymous with fashion, glamor, and even high society. As Michael Eisner, Disney's CEO, stated:

As Americans, we had believed that the word "Euro" in front of Disney was glamorous and exciting. For Europeans, it turned out to be a term they associated with business, currency, and commerce. Renaming the park "Disneyland Paris" was a way of identifying it not just with Walt's original creation but with one of the most romantic and exciting cities in the world. (Eisner and Schwartz 1998, 292)

Changing the name was Disney's attempt to decommercialize the theme park.

In addition to changing the name of the theme park in October of 1994, Disney also took additional steps to overcome the impact of the enterprise environmental factors. Previously, energetic visitors could cover all the rides in about five hours. There were not enough attractions to convince people to stay overnight. Euro Disney eventually:

- Enhanced theme park areas such as Frontierland, Space Mountain, and Animal Kingdom
- Added new attractions, bringing the total number of attractions to 29, including:
  - Zorro
  - Mary Poppins
  - Aladdin
  - Cinderella's Castle
  - Temple of Peril
  - Nautilus
- Stressed the European heritage of many of the Disney characters
- Cut park admission prices by 33 percent
- Cut hotel room costs by 33 percent
- Offered discount prices for winter months
- Offered cheaper meals in the hotels
- Allowed restaurants to serve wine and beer; however, the French never forgot the mistake that Disney made
- Offered more foods from around the world
- Changed the marketing and advertising strategy to include:
  - "California is only 20 miles from Paris"
  - "Fairytales can come true"

- Lowered their projected daily attendance from 60,000 to 25,000 people per day
- Offered package deals that were affordable to everyone. (However, this did not include the entrance fees to the park which were still higher than in the United States.)

Disney wanted to make people believe that, once they entered Disneyland Paris, they had escaped the real world. They would be in "a kingdom where dreams come true." To do this, Disney had to recognize that the European culture was not the same as the culture in the United States or Japan. Disney would not be able to "Americanize" some cultures.

Debt Restructuring

In the fall of 1993, optimism and euphoria over the park came to an end and Euro Disney was in financial distress with a $3.5 billion debt load. If the Walt Disney Company pulled the plug on Euro Disney, there would have been a bankrupt theme park and a massive expanse of virtually worthless real estate. This would certainly blemish Disney's image globally and could significantly hamper Disney's plans for the construction of other theme parks outside of the United States.

The Walt Disney Company developed a rescue plan for Euro Disney that initially was rejected by the French banks. Disney fought back by imposing a deadline for agreement by March 31, 1994, and even threatened with the possible closure of Euro Disney if debt restructuring did not take place. Eisner believed that the French already had so much money invested in the park that they would be forced to restructure the debt. By mid-March, Disney's commitment to support Euro Disney had risen to $750 million. When the banks refused to consider Disney's refinancing plan, Eisner announced to the shareholders that the park might be closed by the end of March, and this would be announced at the annual shareholders' meeting on March 15.

On March 14, the banks capitulated, fearing a huge financial loss if Euro Disney closed. A new preliminary deal was struck whereby Euro Disney's lead banks were required to contribute an additional $500 million. The aim was to cut the park's high-cost debt in half and make Euro Disney profitable by 1996, a date considered unrealistic by many analysts.

Part of the deal stated that Disney would spend about $750 million to buy 49 percent of the new rights offering that was estimated at $1.1 billion. The banks agreed to forgive 18 months of interest payments on the outstanding debt and would defer all principal payments for three years. The banks would also underwrite the remaining 51 percent of the rights offering. For its part, in addition to its $750 million, Disney agreed to eliminate for five years its lucrative management fees (3 percent of revenue), royalties on the sale of tickets (10 percent), and concession sales (5 percent). Disney's management fees were approximately $450 million per year regardless if Euro Disney lost money. Royalties would gradually be reintroduced at a lower level. The capital infusion was not well received by the shareholders, even though then they recognized that, if the park went into receivership, further expansion and the image of the company could be hurt. Some believed that this debt restructuring was just a temporary Band-Aid and that unfavorable changes in the economy or the enterprise environmental factors could require future debt refinancing.

Prince al-Waleed, nephew of King Fahd of Saudi Arabia, purchased 24 percent of Euro Disney S.C.A. for $500 million. After the restructuring, Disney's stake in Euro Disney S.C.A. dropped from 49 percent to 39 percent. The remaining 37 percent was held by a collection of more than 60 banks, mostly French, and individual shareholders primarily from the European community.

The debt restructuring, which included debt payment forgiveness and deferral of some principal payments, was a desperately needed lifeline for Euro Disney and gave it some financial breathing room to change its marketing strategy and attract more visitors. By 1995, with debt refinancing and some theme park enhancements in place, Euro Disney had its first quarterly profit of $35.3 million. However, there was no guarantee that Euro Disney's financial headaches would completely disappear.

By 1996, attendance at Disneyland Paris was more than the Louvre Art Museum, the Eiffel Tower, and Buckingham Palace. At the same time, Tokyo Disneyland was having remarkable attendance success. In 1999, Tokyo Disneyland had 17.5 million visitors. This was more than any other theme park worldwide.

Walt Disney Studios Park

Initial plans for a second theme park, the $2.3 billion MGM Film Studio Tour, was scheduled to open in 1996, though these plans were canceled around mid-1992 due to the resort's financial crisis at the time. After the resort began to make a profit, these plans were revived on a much smaller scale. The new theme park included a history of films, including cinema, cartoons, and how films are made. The new budget was $600 million. The MGM Studio theme park was renamed Walt Disney Studios Park and opened on March 16, 2002. It was dedicated to show business, themed after movies, production, and behind-the-scenes. In 2013, the park hosted approximately 4.4 million guests, making it the third-most visited amusement park in Europe and the twenty-first-most visited in the world though it has the lowest attendance figures of all eleven Walt Disney theme parks.

> To all who enter this studio of dreams…welcome. Walt Disney Studios is dedicated to our timeless fascination and affection for cinema and television. Here we celebrate the art and the artistry of storytellers from Europe and around the world who create magic. May this special place stir our own memories of the past, and our dreams of the future.[15]
>
> — Michael D. Eisner, CEO, the Walt Disney Company, March 16, 2002

The Walt Disney Company had planned to open a third park in Disneyland Paris by 2017, but this plan was pushed into 2030.

Another Debt Restructuring

By 2000, Euro Disney's restructured debt load had risen to $2 billion. With the opening of the Disney Studios Park, Disneyland Paris now included seven hotels, two convention centers, 68 restaurants and 52 boutiques. But Europe's economy was struggling. The slowdown in the European travel and tourism industry had negatively affected Euro Disney's operations and cash flow. The company was strapped for cash. Once again, the word "bankruptcy" raised its ugly head. Euro Disney's financial difficulties forced it to focus on short-term cash flow rather than expansion, enhancing rides and building new attractions.

In response to the cash flow situation, Euro Disney S.C.A. initiated discussions with its lenders and Disney to obtain waivers of its fiscal 2003 loan covenants and to obtain supplemental financing to address Euro Disney's cash requirements. Because of an agreement entered into on March 28, 2003, the Walt Disney Company did not charge Euro Disney royalties and management fees for the period from January 1, 2003, to September 30, 2003. Additionally, the Disney Company agreed to allow Euro Disney to pay its royalties and management fees annually in arrears for fiscal 2004, instead of quarterly.

---

15. From his comments at the dedication of the park, reproduced on a welcome plaque at the entrance to Disneyland Paris.

In fiscal 2005, Euro Disney S.C.A. completed a financial restructuring, which provided for an increase in capital and refinancing of its borrowings. Pursuant to the financial restructuring, the Walt Disney Company agreed to conditionally and unconditionally defer certain management fees and royalties and convert them into long-term subordinated debt and provide a new 10-year line of credit for liquidity needs.

Jeffrey Speed, the chief financial officer (CFO) of Euro Disney, said that the modified agreement would provide "significant liquidity."

2007–2013

By the end of 2007, Disneyland Paris had more than 14 million visitors. The theme park had 54 attractions, 54 shops, and 68 themed restaurants. In 2008, Disneyland Resort Paris welcomed its 200 millionth guest since the opening in 1992. Table 13-3 shows the attendance figures for 2008–2013.

A study done by the Inter-Ministerial Delegation reviewing Disneyland Resort Paris's contribution to the French economy was released in time for the Resort's 20th anniversary in March 2012. It found that despite the Resort's financial hardships, it has generated "37 billion euros in tourism-related revenues over twenty years," supports on average 55,000 jobs in France annually, and that one job at Disneyland Paris generates nearly three jobs elsewhere in France.[16]

In 2012, Disney announced that it would again refinance the debt of Disneyland Paris with a loan of $1.6 billion and a credit facility of $120 million. Disneyland Paris had not been profitable in 12 of the first 20 years of operations.

Disney's 2013 Form 10-K Report

The following information was extracted from Disney's 2013 Form 10-K Report:

Parks and Resorts revenues increased 9%, or $1.2 billion, to $14.087 billion due to an increase of $1.1 billion at our domestic operations and an increase of $112 million at our international operations. Domestic theme park revenue was $11.394 billion and international theme park revenue was $2.693 billion.

TABLE 13–3.   ATTENDANCE FIGURES FOR 2008–2013

Year	Disneyland Europe Theme Park	Disney Studio Park
2008	12,688,000	2,612,000
2009	12,740,000	2,655,000
2010	10,500,000	4,500,000
2011	10,990,000	4,710,000
2012	11,500,000	4,800,000
2013	10,430,000	4,470,000
World Ranking	6	21

16. Inter-Ministerial Delegation for the Euro Disney Project, *Economic and Social Impact of Disneyland Paris (1992–2012)*. For a summary of the findings of the report, see the March 14, 2012 press release from the Delegation archived at http://corporate. disneylandparis.com/CORP/EN/Neutral/Images/uk-2012–03-14-twenty-year-review-of-economic-and-social-impact.pdf, accessed May 10, 2019.

TABLE 13–4. 2013 FORM 10-K SUPPORTING DATA

		Domestic	International
Parks and Resorts	Attendance	4%	(2%)
	Per capita guest spending	8%	4%
Hotels	Occupancy rate	79%	81%
	Available room nights (in thousands)	10,558	2,466
	Per room guest spending	$267	$309

Table 13-4 shows some additional information relative to the theme parks and resorts. Numbers in parentheses show a decrease from the previous fiscal year.

October 2014

For the year ending September 30, 2014, the revenue from Disneyland Paris had dropped by 3 percent from the previous year and loss was estimated between $110 million and $120 million euros. The loss from the previous year was $78 million euros.

Some Disney investors wanted Disney to "pull the plug" on cash-hemorrhaging Disneyland Paris and close the park. On the other end of the spectrum was a petition written in six languages and signed by more than 8000 people, titled "Save Disneyland Paris." The petition cited several problems that needed to be addressed at the theme park—namely, poor maintenance and upkeep of the grounds, a need for better food choices, and a need for newer and upgraded attractions. Upgrades were also needed at the Walt Disney Studios park, where some believed that attractions should be added based on some recent movies such as *The Avengers* and *Iron Man 3*.

Walt Disney Company understood that the survival of Disneyland Paris depended on repeat visitors and, thus, decided to toss Disneyland Paris a lifeline of $1.3 billion ($1 billion euros) over 10 years for improvements to the theme park and Walt Disney Studios Park. In addition, Disney would postpone principal payments on its debt until 2024.

February 2017

Disney's $1.3 billion cash infusion in 2014 was partially used to make improvements and renovations. Revenue began to rebound until the Paris terrorist attacks in 2015. For the fiscal year ending September 30, 2016, Disney Europe lost about $260 million.

On February 10, 2017, Disney announced that it would make its second cash infusion in three years. This time, Disney would invest $1.6 billion and buy out all other shareholders in Disney Europe. The money would also be used for improvements, new attractions, reducing debt, and increasing liquidity at the resort (Martin 2017).

February 2019

In February 2019, Disney announced another investment of $2.47 billion for expansions due to begin in 2021.[17]

---

17. https://www.cnbc.com/2018/02/27/walt-disney-to-invest-2-billion-euros-in-disneyland-paris.html.

Conclusions

Improper assumptions about the enterprise environmental factors can wreak havoc on any project, including innovation. Not all the impacts created by the enterprise environmental factors can be controlled or managed effectively. Disney did what was expected of a company of its stature to correct the impact of the enterprise environmental factors while protecting its name, image, and reputation. While the factors might not have had a direct impact on the way the theme park projects were managed, especially the quality and aesthetic aspects, the factors can and did have a direct bearing on how people define the success and failure of a project.

It is important to understand that theme parks must continuously grow. They must add more rides, update existing attractions, and improve other aesthetic elements as necessary. To do this requires capital, often making it difficult to pay down a large debt load.

Disney demonstrated "Imagineering" at its best, not only in the design and construction of the theme park attractions but also in the way that it handled necessary changes due to cultural issues. Disneyland Paris is an American theme park. Disney maintained its brand name and image. Cultural issues can never be resolved in a manner where everyone is 100 percent pleased. But if I am ever in such a conflicting position, I would want Disney in my corner.

Discussion Questions

1. Should culture be considered as part of business model innovation?
2. Did Disney spend enough time and effort initially to understand the impact of the enterprise environmental factors as related to culture?
3. What steps did Disney take to address the cultural issues?
4. How should Disney have defended itself from French labor unions that argued that what was being taught to the 20,000 workers at Disney University was a violation of their individual rights?
5. What lessons were learned from the Tokyo Disneyland business model?
6. What could Disney have done in the first two years of operations at Euro Disney to get a higher occupancy rate?
7. Do you believe that Disney should have allowed Euro Disney to close in 1994 because of its financial headaches?
8. Can executives or project managers ever really control the enterprise environmental factors?
9. How can we prevent last-minute scope changes caused by executive meddling assuming there will be a major impact on cost?
10. Euro Disney had a major debt restructuring three times between 1993 and 2013. Why was the debt restructuring necessary? What was the driving force that caused the debt restructuring?
11. Should enterprise environmental factors be tracked the same way that we track and report budgets and schedules?

Further Reading

- Borden, Lark. Euro Disneyland: In Paris, when it drizzles, it sizzles. *Gannett News Service, March* **11**, 1992.
- Chu, Jeff, and Marne-La-Vallee Monday. Happily ever after? *Time, March* **18**, 2002, http://content.time.com/time/magazine/article/0,9171,218398,00.html.
- Corliss, Richard, and Marne-La-Vallee. Voila! Disney invades Europe. Will the French resist? *Time,* April 20, 1992.

- "Disney Magic Spreads across the Atlantic; Popular US Theme Park Prepares for Opening of Euro Disneyland Resort near Paris in April 1992." Nation's Restaurant News. October 28, 1991, 3.
- "Disney's $1.7 Billion French Birthday Gift." *Time*. September 19, 2012.
- Disneyland Paris. Come and join Disneyland Paris! The search for recruits continues around the UK. Press release, October 29, 2009. *Euro Disney S.C.A. Archived at* http://corporate. disneylandparis.com/CORP/EN/Neutral/Images/uk-2009-10-29-recruitment-england.pdf, accessed May 14, 2019.
- Disneyland Paris. Disneyland Paris launches a unique "pop-up" office concept for its European recruitment drive. Press release, March 11, 2011. *Euro Disney S.C.A. Archived at* http://corpo rate.disneylandparis.com/CORP/EN/Neutral/Images/uk-2011-03-08-recruitment-pop-up-office. pdf, accessed May 14, 2019.
- Disneyland Paris. European recruitment tour: Launching the new season at Disneyland Paris. Press release, January 25, 2010. *Euro Disney S.C.A. Archived at* http://corporate.disneylandparis.com/ CORP/EN/Neutral/Images/uk-2010-01-25-european-recruitment.pdf, accessed May 14, 2019.
- Disneyland Resort Paris. Disneyland Resort Paris celebrates its 200 millionth visit. Press release, August 12, 2008. Archived at https://web.archive.org/web/20131105162910/http://corporate. disneylandparis.com/CORP/EN/Neutral/Images/uk-2008-08-12-visiteur-200millionieme.pdf, accessedMay 14, 2019.
- Euro Disney S.C.A Euro Disney S.C.A. announces net profit in fiscal year 2008. Archived at http://corporate.disneylandparis.com/CORP/EN/Neutral/Images/uk-2008-10-21-euro-disney-sca-reports-annual-results-for-fiscal-year-2008.pdf, accessed May 14, 2019.
- Euro Disney S.C.A. Disneyland resort Paris launches new European advertising campaign: "*Believe in Your Dreams*." Press release, March 3, 2006. Euro Disney S.C.A. Archived at http://cor porate.disneylandparis.com/CORP/EN/Neutral/Images/uk-2006-03-03-disneyland-resort-paris-launches-new-european-advertising-campaign-believe-in-your-reams.pdf, accessed May 14, 2019.
- Euro Disney S.C.A Euro Disney S.C.A. reports annual results for fiscal year 2007. Press release, November 8, 2007. Euro Disney S.C.A. Archived at https://web.archive.org/web/20141024030130/ http://corporate.disneylandparis.com/CORP/EN/Neutral/Images/uk-2007-11-8-euro-disney-sca-reports-annual-results-for-fiscal-year-2007.pdf, accessed May 14, 2019.
- Euro Disney S.C.A. Disneyland resort Paris partners with the TGV East European Line. Press release, April 19, 2006. *Euro Disney S.C.A. Archived at* http://corporate.disneylandparis.com/ CORP/EN/Neutral/Images/uk-2006-04-19-disneylandresort-paris-partners-with-the-tgv-est-european-line.pdf, accessed May 19, 2019.
- Euro Disney S.C.A. Effective launch of share consolidation. Press release, January 11, 2005. Archived at https://web.archive.org/web/20141023222343/http://corporate.disneylandparis.com/ CORP/EN/Neutral/Images/uk-2005-01-11-euro-disney-sca-reports-first-quarter-revenues-for-fiscal-year-2005.pdf, accessed May 14, 2019.
- Euro Disney S.C.A Euro Disney S.C.A. reports annual results for fiscal year 2005. Press release, November 16, 2005. Archived at http://corporate.disneylandparis.com/CORP/EN/Neutral/Images/uk-2005-11-16-euro-disney-scareports-annual-results-for-fiscal-year-2005.pdf, accessed May 14, 2019.
- Euro Disney S.C.A Euro Disney S.C.A. reports fiscal year 2009 results. Press release, November 12, 2009. Archived at https://web.archive.org/web/20120916020800/http://corporate.disneyland paris.com/CORP/EN/Neutral/Images/uk-2009-11-12-euro-disney-sca-reports-annual-results-for-fiscal-year-2009.pdf, accessed May 14, 2019.
- Euro Disney S.C.A Euro Disney S.C.A. reports fiscal year 2010 results. Press release, November 10, 2010. Archived at https://web.archive.org/web/20111027032419/http://corporate.disneylandparis.

com/CORP/EN/Neutral/Images/uk-2010-11-10-euro-disney-sca-reports-annual-results-for-fiscal-year-2010.pdf, accessed May 14, 2019.

- Euro Disney S.C.A. Euro Disney group improves its debt profile with the 1.3 billion refinancing of the group's debt by the Walt Disney Company. Press release, September 18, 2012. *Euro Disney S.C.A. Archived at* http://corporate.disneylandparis.com/CORP/EN/Neutral/Images/uk-2012-09-18-debt-Press-release.pdf, accessed May 14, 2019.
- "Euro Disneyland," case study. Thunderbird, The American Graduate School of International Management, TB0195, June 15, 1999. Available for download at www.academia.edu/31430890/Eurodisneyland_TB0195_PDF_ENG.
- Ferguson, Anne. *Maximizing the mouse. Management Today*, September 1989, p. 60.
- Graves, Nelson. *Euro Disney attendance in upturn but woes persist. Renter European Business Report*, September 4, 1992.
- The Good Life France. *Disneyland Paris—The main rides and attractions*. March 27, 2013. www.thegoodlifefrance.com/disneyland-paris-the-main-ridesand-attractions
- Hopkins, Nic. Saudi Prince in talks with Euro Disney over rescue. *Times* (London), September 6, 2003.
- Joce, Will. Five fun facts about Disneyland Paris. Venere Travel Blog. Venere.com, January 10, 2011. www.venere.com/blog/disneyland-paris-facts-9818.
- Kleege, Stephen. Magic of Disney wins backers for Paris theme hotels. *American Banker*, March **26**, 1991, p. 11.
- Kraft, Scott. Disneyland Paris is staging a comeback. But long-term prospects hinge on the region's economic improvement. *Los Angeles Times*, February 4, 1996
- Loveman, Gary W., Leonard A. Schlesinger, and Robert Anthony. Euro Disney: The first 100 days. Harvard Business School Case 693-013, August 1992. (Revised June 1993).
- Mathiason, Nick. *The magic dims in Walt's Kingdom. Observer*, August 10, 2003, p. 4.
- McGrath, John. *The lawyers who rebuilt Euro Disney. International Financial Law Review*, August 10, May 1994, p. 10.
- New York Times, "COMPANY NEWS: Euro Disney Park." *February* 5, 1991.
- *New York Times*. Euro Disney adding alcohol. *June* 12, 1993.
- O'Brien, Tim. Walt Disney Studios makes Paris debut. *Amusement Business*, March 25, 2002, p. 3.
- Rawsthorn, Alice. Poisoned apple within the Magic Kingdom. *Financial Times*, November 25, 1993, p. 23.
- Rawsthorn, Alice, and Michael Skapinker. Empty pockets hit imported dream. *Financial Times*, July 9, 1993, p. 23.
- Taylor, Charles Foster, and Stephen Richardson. *Focus on leisure—Euro Disneyland. Estates Gazette*, April 7, 1990, p. 85.
- Thompson, Kevin. Euro Disneyland: *Disney's attempt at foreign corporate expansion. Yahoo Contributor Network*, December 20, 2006.
- Telegraph Media Group. Disneyland Paris top attractions. *The Telegraph*. Telegraph Media Group Limited, May 13, 2011.
- Walt Disney Co DIS (NYSE). Reuters.com. Stocks.us.reuters.com.
- Webster, Paul. *Red carpet rolled out for Euro Disney. Guardian*, May 3, 1991, p. 27.
- White, Christina. Hollywood on the Seine. *Business Week*, March 25, 2002.
- Wise, Deborah. Will Euro Disneyland be able to overcome two main obstacles? The Guardian, March 1, 1991, p. 26.
- Wrubel, Robert. *Le defi Mickey Mouse. Financial World*, October 17, 1989, p. 21.

DISNEY (D): THE PARTNERSHIP SIDE OF GLOBAL BUSINESS MODEL INNOVATION

In the late 1970s, Disney made the decision to begin expanding internationally. Tokyo Disneyland was to be the first Disney theme park built outside of the United States. While Disney understood the enterprise environmental factors surrounding Disneyland and Disney World, there were unknowns with opening a theme park in Tokyo. First, Japan has a winter season that could impact attendance. Second, Disney was unsure as to whether the Japanese would embrace the Disney characters. Having an American theme park in the middle of Japan was seen as a risk. Third, there would be new legal and financial considerations. Disney would need a new business model for theme parks built outside of the United States.

Although several globalization options (i.e., business models) were available to Disney, only three of the options will be considered in this case study. Each option requires some sort of contractual agreement and each type of agreement is impacted by the assumptions and associated risks made concerning the enterprise environmental factors. First, Disney could assume the cost for constructing a theme park wholly owned by Disney. The cost of doing this would require expenditures in the billions of dollars. Disney would have to work directly with foreign governments, labor unions, and stakeholders. While it could be done, the risks and costs involved in doing this were considered as prohibitive especially for the first theme park built outside of the United States. Therefore, the remaining two options were licensing agreements and joint ventures.

Licensing Agreements

A licensing agreement is a legal contract between two parties, known as the licensor and the licensee. In a typical licensing agreement, the licensor, such as the Walt Disney Company, grants the licensee the right to produce and sell goods, apply a brand name or trademark, or use patented technology owned by the licensor. Legal restrictions often mandate that the licensee must be a company in the host's country that is willing to accept such an arrangement with the licensor. In exchange, the licensee usually submits to a series of conditions regarding the use of the licensor's property and agrees to make payments known as royalties.

Licensing agreements cover a wide range of well-known situations. For example, a retailer in the theme park might reach agreement with Disney to develop, produce, and sell merchandise bearing Disney characters. Or a construction company might license proprietary theme park design technology from Disney to gain a competitive edge rather than expending the time and money trying to develop its own technology. Or a greeting card company might reach an agreement with Disney to produce a line of greeting cards bearing the images of popular Disney animated characters.

One of the most important elements of a licensing agreement covers the financial arrangement between the two parties. Payments from the licensee to the licensor usually take the form of guaranteed minimum payments and royalties on sales. Royalties typically range from 6 to 10 percent, depending on the specific property involved and the licensee's level of experience and sophistication. Not all licensors require guarantees, although some experts recommend that licensors get as much compensation up front as possible. In some cases, licensors use guarantees as the basis for renewing a licensing agreement. If the licensee meets the minimum sales figures or theme park attendance figures, the contract is renewed; otherwise, the licensor has the option of discontinuing the relationship.

Another important element of a licensing agreement establishes the time frame of the deal. Many licensors insist on a strict market release date for products licensed to outside manufacturers. This also applies to the time needed to construct the theme park. After all, it is not in the licensor's best interest to grant a license to a company that cannot build the theme park in a timely manner or never markets the products. The licensing agreement will also include provisions about the length of the contract, renewal options, and termination conditions.

Another common element of a licensing agreement covers which party maintains control of copyrights, patents, or trademarks. Many contracts also include a provision about territorial rights, or who manages distribution in various parts of the country or the world. In addition to the various clauses inserted into agreements to protect the licensor, some licensees may add their own requirements. They may insist on a guarantee that the licensor owns the rights to the property, for example, or they may insert a clause prohibiting the licensor from competing directly with the licensed property in certain markets.

There are advantages as well as disadvantages with licensing agreements. The primary advantage is that the licensing agreement can limit Disney's financial exposure. It is entirely possible that Disney may not have to provide any financial support for the construction of the new theme park. Disney would provide expertise in the design, construction, and management of the park and its attractions. Disney can demand that all attractions be identical to those at Disneyland and Disney World. The theme park could be an exact duplication of Disneyland or Disney World.

In exchange, Disney would receive royalty payments based on admission fees and the sale of food, beverages, and merchandise. Disney may also receive royalty payments for the use of Disney characters. This includes use in themed hotels. Disney can also collect a percentage of sponsorship fees. Disney would receive royalty payments regardless of whether the theme park was profitable or lost money.

The disadvantages are limitations on profitability and possibly future opportunities. If the theme park is highly profitable, Disney would receive only royalty payments and would not share in the profitability of the park. All profits may stay with the licensee. The licensee may demand that Disney not be allowed to enter certain markets that could be seen as a competitor for the new theme park. This could limit Disney's ability for future expansion in foreign markets. Since Disney would not be managing the theme park under the licensing agreement, Disney could be faced with a loss of quality control, thus affecting Disney's image and reputation. Licensing agreements therefore can appear as risk minimization for the licensor and risk maximization for the licensee.

Joint Ventures

A joint venture is a business agreement in which the parties agree to develop, for a finite time, a new entity and new assets by contributing shared equity. The theme park would be shared ownership. They both may exercise control over the enterprise and consequently share revenues, expenses, and assets.

A joint venture takes place when two parties come together to take on one project. In a joint venture, both parties are equally invested in the project in terms of money, time, and effort to build on the original concept. While joint ventures are generally small projects, major corporations also use this method in order to diversify or expand their business globally. A joint venture can ensure the success of smaller projects for those firms that are just starting in the business world or for established corporations. Since the cost of starting new projects is generally high, a joint venture allows both parties to share the burden of the project's startup cost, as well as the resulting profits.

Since money is involved in a joint venture, it is necessary to have a strategic plan in place. In short, both parties must be committed to focusing on the future of the partnership, rather than just the immediate returns. For example, it may take years before the theme park arrives at the desired yearly attendance figures. Ultimately, both short-term and long-term successes are important. In order to achieve this success, honesty, integrity, and communication within the joint venture are necessary.

With joint ventures, there can be a dominant partner together with participation of the public. There may also be cases where the public shareholding is a substantial portion of the investment, but the founding partners retain their identity. In such cases, local governments may provide some funding in the way of loans or tax incentives in hope of creating jobs.

Further consideration relates to starting a new legal entity on foreign soil. The licensor may have to abide by legal requirements in the host country related to ownership of shares of stock in the new venture, the use of local labor, abiding by local union contracts, how procurement will be performed and restrictions on land development. Such an enterprise is sometimes called *'an incorporated joint venture'* and can include technology contracts (rights related to knowhow, patents, trademarks, brand use agreements and copyright), technical services, and assisted-supply arrangements.

Joint ventures are profit and risk maximization strategies for the licensor and risk minimization for the licensee. A joint venture does not preclude the licensor such as Disney from collecting royalties. However, it does require that both the licensor and licensee make significant financial contributions. The result is usually a much larger project than each party could afford if they had to do it alone. The main disadvantage is that the licensor and licensee can have different opinions when critical decisions must be made.

The Business Model

For Disney, the decision to expand internationally was inevitable. The business model used for Disneyland and Disney would need to be changed and account for joint venture relationships and/or partnerships. There would most likely be a different business model for each country where a new theme park would open.

The international theme parks and accompanying business models appear on paper as a form of open source innovation. Each business model can be impacted by different enterprise environmental factors such as government requirements, political intervention and culture.

Tokyo Disneyland

Disney's partner for Tokyo Disneyland was the Oriental Land Company. Disney had to decide whether the partnership should be based on a joint venture or a licensing agreement. Unsure about how the enterprise environmental factors would affect the acceptance of the theme park and the fact that this was Disney's first theme park outside of the United States, Disney opted for the risk minimization strategy of a licensing agreement. Under this agreement, Tokyo Disneyland was not partially or wholly owned by Disney. With the licensing agreement, Disney would receive royalty payments of 10 percent of the admission fees and 5 percent of the sales on food, beverages and merchandise. Disney receives its royalty payments even if Tokyo Disneyland loses money. Disney did have a small investment in the theme park of $3.5 million, which amounted to 0.42 percent of the initial construction cost. Because Disney opted for the risk minimization licensing agreement, Disney made the decision not to invest heavily in land development surrounding the theme park.

In April 1979, the first basic contract for the construction of Disneyland in Tokyo was signed. Japanese engineers and architects flocked to California to tour Disneyland and prepare to construct the new operating dreamland in Tokyo. Just one year later, construction of the park began and was covered by hundreds of media reporters as an indication of the high expectations for the park in the future. Though successful in the building process, the final cost of Tokyo Disneyland almost doubled the estimated budget costing 180 billion yen rather than the projected 100 billion yen. Despite this discrepancy, Tokyo Disneyland has been a constant source of pride since opening day over 30 years ago.

With only a few exceptions, Tokyo Disneyland features the same attractions found in Disneyland and Walt Disney World's Magic Kingdom. It was the first Disney theme park to be built outside the United States, and it opened on April 15, 1983. The park was constructed by Walt Disney Imagineering in the same style as Disneyland in California and Magic Kingdom in Florida.

There are seven themed areas in the park: the World Bazaar, the four classic Disney lands—Adventureland, Westernland, Fantasyland, and Tomorrowland—and two mini-lands, Critter Country and Mickey's Toontown. Many of the games and rides in these areas mirror those in the original Disneyland as they are based on American Disney films and fantasies. Fantasyland includes Peter Pan's Flight, Snow White's Scary Adventures, Dumbo the Flying Elephant and more based on classic Disney films and characters. The park is noted for its extensive open spaces, to accommodate the large crowds that visit the park.

The day the park opened, the attendance was 13,200 visitors. On August 13 of the same year, more than 93,000 people visited the park. This was a one-day attendance record surpassing all Disney theme parks. Three years later, Tokyo Disneyland broke the record again with a one-day attendance of 111,500 people.

Euro Disney (Disneyland Paris)

In Tokyo Disneyland's first year of operations, 1983, it was evident that Tokyo Disneyland would be a success. In 1984, Disney made the decision to build a second foreign theme park, this time in Europe. Disney wanted the theme park opened by 1992. Disney wanted to build a state-of-the-art theme park, a decision that eventually led to "budget breaker" scope changes. Many of the changes were last-minute changes made by Michael Eisner, Disney's CEO.

Using the first year's results from Tokyo Disneyland, highly optimistic financial projections were established for Euro Disney based on the expectation of 11 million visitors the first year and 16 million visitors yearly after the turn of the century. When Tokyo Disneyland opened on April 15, 1983, more than 13,000 visitors entered the park.

Disney viewed the Euro Disney theme park as a potentially profitable revenue generator for decades inasmuch as Disney would have a monopoly in leisure and entertainment in Europe. Unlike Tokyo Disneyland, Disney opted for a joint venture that was designed around a profit maximization strategy. Disney would receive 10 percent royalties on admissions; 5 percent royalties on food, beverage, and merchandise sales; a management fee equivalent to 3 percent of revenue, a licensing fee for using the Disney name and characters; 5 percent of gross revenues of themed hotels; and 49 percent of the profits. Disney also received royalties from companies that invested in and endorsed specific rides. If Euro Disney was as successful as Tokyo Disneyland, Disney could receive more than $1 billion in royalties and profit sharing each year.

Part of Disney's decision to use a joint venture relationship was because it realized that they made a serious mistake in Disneyland, Disney World, and Tokyo Disneyland by not investing heavily in property development surrounding the theme parks. With the intent of maximizing its profits, Disney agreed to build 18,200 hotel rooms surrounding Euro Disney by 2017.

Walt Disney Studios Park

Disney recognized that, if you want people to come back to the theme park again and again, you must either add new attractions to the park, build an adjacent theme park on a closely related topic, or do both. Initial plans for a second theme park at Euro Disney, the $2.3 billion MGM Film Studio Tour, was scheduled to open in 1996, though these plans were canceled around mid-1992 due to the resort's financial crisis at the time. After the resort began to make a profit, these plans were revived on a much smaller scale. The new theme park included a history of films, including cinema, cartoons, and how films are made. The new budget was $600 million. The MGM Studio theme park was renamed Walt Disney Studios Park and opened on March 16, 2002. It was dedicated to show business, themed after movies, production, and behind-the-scenes. Just like Euro Disney, the second theme park was part of the original joint venture relationship rather than just a licensing agreement.

In 2013, the park hosted approximately 4.4 million guests, making it the third-most visited amusement park in Europe and the twenty-first-most visited in the world though it had the lowest attendance figures of all eleven Walt Disney theme parks.

Tokyo DisneySea Park

In 1997, Tokyo Disneyland recognized the need for a second theme park. Attendance at the Tokyo Disneyland theme park was levelling off as indicated in Table 13-5.

Between 75 and 80 percent of the visitors to Tokyo Disneyland were repeat visitors. Even with new attractions being built each year, there was apprehension that people might not return to the park after two or three visits. Furthermore, there were expectations that there might be a drop in attendance by as much as 4 percent over the new four years. A new theme park would be needed.

The concepts and designs for a DisneySea park had been in development at Walt Disney Imagineering for more than 20 years. However, for a second theme park in Tokyo, Disney initially recommended that the new theme park be similar to the Walt Disney Studios Park that was in the planning stages for Euro Disney. Disney's partner in Japan, the Oriental Land Company, believed that the Japanese would not be as enamored with movie-making as were the American and the Europeans. Instead, the decision was to build Tokyo DisneySea park for about $3.5 billion. This was based heavily on the knowledge that the Japanese had a love for the sea. Unlike Tokyo Disneyland, the overall intention of the new park was to create a more adult-themed park, including faster, scarier rides, and shows designed more for an older audience.

The success of Tokyo Disneyland made it quite apparent that Disney would have been better off financially had they chosen a joint venture rather than a licensing agreement. However, a sea park was not the same as a Disneyland park. Disney believed that the Tokyo DisneySea park did have some risks. The Oriental Land Company believed that the Tokyo DisneySea park could be just as successful as Tokyo Disneyland. But coming up with $3.5 billion was very risky. The Oriental Land Company would have preferred to minimize its risks by having a joint venture, but eventually negotiated a licensing agreement for the $3.5 billion theme park. The debt for Tokyo Disneyland was paid off in three years after the park

TABLE 13–5. TOKYO DISNEYLAND ATTENDANCE: 1983–1997

Year	Attendance
1983	9,933,000
1984	10,013,000
1985	10,675,000
1986	10,665,000
1987	11,975,000
1988	13,382,000
1989	14,752,000
1990	15,876,000
1991	16,139,000
1992	15,815,000
1993	16,030,000
1994	15,509,000
1995	16,986,000
1996	17,368,000
1997	16,686,000

opened. The Oriental Land Company believed that the Tokyo DisneySea park could also be paid off in a reasonably short period of time as well.

In 2013, Tokyo Disneyland hosted 17.21 million visitors, moving its ranking to the world's second most visited theme park, surpassing Disneyland in California, USA, but falling behind the Magic Kingdom in Florida, USA. However, as seen in Table 13-6, the Tokyo DisneySea park attracted 14.08 million visitors in 2013 making it the world's fourth most visited them park. All 11 of Disney's theme parks totaled 132,549,000 visitors in 2013.

TABLE 13–6. 2013 ATTENDANCE FIGURES FOR SELECTED THEME PARKS

Theme Park	2013 Attendance	2013 Worldwide Ranking
Disney World's Magic Kingdom, Orlando	18,588,000	1
Tokyo Disneyland	17,214,000	2
Disneyland, Anaheim	16,202,000	3
Tokyo DisneySea	14,084,000	4
Disneyland Paris	10,430,000	6
Disney's Animal Kingdom at Disney World	10,198,000	7
Disney's Hollywood Studios, Disney World	10,110,000	8
Ocean Park, Hong Kong	7,475,000	12
Hong Kong Disneyland	7,400,000	13
Walt Disney Studios, Disneyland Paris	4,470,000	21

Future of Tokyo Disneyland

Since the park opened in 1983, Tokyo Disneyland has regularly been the most profitable Disney Resort. By 1994, over 140 million people had entered through the gates of Tokyo Disneyland (the population of Japan is only 127.6 million) and the popularity had increased. Just two years later, it employed 12,390 people, marking Tokyo Disneyland as the biggest workplace in Japan's diversionary outings. Though the attendance trend is similar to that of other Japanese theme parks, the revenue produced by Tokyo Disneyland is larger than all other national theme parks combined, thus greatly profiting the Japanese economy. Many speculate that Tokyo Disneyland is such an economic success due to timing and location; the theme park lies in a metropolitan area with a population of 30 million and opened at the height of a booming economy where hard-working citizens desired a fun escape from reality. One of the main goals of Tokyo Japan was to ever improve the park and grow away from the restrictions of American Disney. Recently Japan had been merging their national identity with the Disneyland Park by adding attractions with distinctly Japanese qualities. Cinderella's Castle displays the classic Disney character and story plot yet presents the story through the eyes of the Japanese. Meet the World, located in World Bazaar, shows true national identity and pride as it embodies Japanese history; instead of classic Disney characters, Meet the World characters wear the traditional Japanese Kimono. Once nominated by Disney Legends, Masatomo Takahashi, the former president of The Oriental Land Company, states this growth and development as one as the primary goals: "We must not just repeat what we receive from Disney. I am convinced that we must contribute to the cultural exchange between Japan and USA."

Hong Kong Disneyland

In 1988–1989, negotiations began to bring the original Disneyland to a new territory, namely Hong Kong. Hong Kong was recognized as an international finance center and the gateway to China. Disney recognized that, even though many countries and cities in Southeast Asia, such as Hong Kong, may be on the cutting edge of technology, they were not familiar with many of the Disney products, including comics of Disney characters such as Mickey Mouse. Because of the potential risk of limited brand awareness, marketing and advertising would be critical. Even with the limited brand awareness, the Hong Kong government recognized significant benefits in the venture:

- Hong Kong Disneyland will attract millions of tourists a year, create thousands of jobs, enrich the quality of life, and enhance Hong Kong's international image.
- The world-class theme park has the potential to provide Hong Kong with a net economic benefit of billions of dollars over 40 years.
- It is estimated that attendance in the park's first year of operation will be over 5 million. This figure will gradually rise to around 10 million a year after 15 years.
- About 18,400 new jobs are expected to be created directly and indirectly on opening, rising to 35,800 over a 20-year period.
- Around 6,000 jobs are expected to be created during the construction of facilities for Phase I of Hong Kong Disneyland. In addition, some 10,000 jobs are expected to be created by the land reclamation and other infrastructural works funded by the government.

The benefits of the base case were based on several assumptions, including:

- The park opens in 2005.
- The park's attendance in its first year of operation is estimated at 5.2 million.
- The park gradually reaches full annual capacity of 10 million after 15 years.

- Nearly all employees at Hong Kong Disneyland will be Hong Kong people. Management of the park will initially be undertaken by about 40 Disney employees from around the world. But eventually about 35 local employees will be trained to take up these management duties.
- Disney would provide master planning, project management expertise, real estate development, design of the attractions, and other such support activities.
- Staff training for key personnel will take place in Hong Kong and the United States. In the United States, trainees will receive hands-on experience at existing Disney theme parks.
- In Hong Kong, the company will develop suitable training packages for a wide spectrum of Hong Kong Disneyland employees. A "Disney University" will be established as part of this process.
- Hong Kong Disneyland will attract 3.4 million incoming tourists in Year 1, rising to 7.3 million after 15 years.

Hong Kong Disneyland is located on reclaimed land in Penny's Bay, Lantau Island. It is the first theme park located inside the Hong Kong Disneyland Resort and is owned and managed by the Hong Kong International Theme Parks. Unlike Disneyland Paris, Disney preferred to be actively involved in the management of the park rather than just being an investor. As part of a negotiated joint venture agreement, the government paid $2.9 billion (US$) to build the park and Disney contributed $314 million (US$).

Risks

Despite Disney's experience with other theme parks, there were several risks that Disney considered. Some of these risks that emanated from the enterprise environmental factors included:

- The Chinese people's willingness to accept an American theme park
- The Chinese culture
- Potential cost overruns that could require that Disney provide additional financial support
- Weather conditions
- Uncertain market conditions
- Hong Kong had another theme park, Ocean Park, which had opened in 1977 (Both parks could be competing for the same tourists.)
- Political uncertainty
- A change in the government's policy for acting as a financial partner
- Legal barriers affecting the joint venture
- Counterfeit products

The park opened to visitors on September 12, 2005. The park consists of five themed areas: Main Street, USA, Fantasyland, Adventureland, Tomorrowland, and Toy Story Land. The theme park's cast members speak in Cantonese, English, and Mandarin. Guide maps are printed in traditional and simplified Chinese as well as English, French, and Japanese.

The park has a daily capacity of 34,000 visitors—the least out of all Disneyland parks. The park attracted 5.2 million visitors in its first year, below its target of 5.6 million. Visitor numbers fell 20 percent in the second year to 4 million, inciting criticism from local legislators. However, the park attendance slightly increased by 8 percent in the third year, attracting a total of 4.5 million visitors in 2007. In 2013, the park's attendance increased to 7.4 million visitors, making it thirteenth in world park attendance.

Feng Shui in Chinese Culture

Disney learned an unpleasant lesson about the importance of culture and the enterprise environmental factors from the negative publicity following the launching of Disneyland Paris. Disney was attacked in the media as being insensitive to the culture of the Europeans and especially the French. Disney attempted to avoid similar problems of cultural backlash by attempting to incorporate Chinese culture, customs, and traditions when designing and building the resort, including adherence to the rules of feng shui. Feng shui is a Chinese geomantic practice in which a structure or site is chosen or configured to harmonize with the spiritual forces that inhabit it.[18] According to the precepts of feng shui, buildings and structures must face in a certain direction, depending on their surroundings. There must be a balance between the elements of earth, wood and fire. For instance, a bend was put in a walkway near the Hong Kong Disneyland Resort entrance so good *qi* (chi) energy wouldn't flow into the South China Sea. Lakes, streams and waterfalls must be strategically placed around the theme park to signify the accumulation of wealth and good fortune.

Disney hired a feng shui expert to assist with the designing of the park and the attractions to focus on practices that would bring the largest amount of good luck. Disney was taking no chance even with the smallest details. Some of the feng shui features that were implemented included:

- September 12 is considered a lucky day for opening a business. Hong Kong Disneyland was officially opened on September 12, 2005.
- Various earthly elements such as wood, fire, earth, metal and water important in feng shui have been carefully balanced throughout the Hong Kong Disneyland Resort according to the rules of feng shui. For example, projections of a rolling fire in one restaurant bar enhances the fire element at that location, while fire is prohibited in other areas.
- Hong Kong Disneyland's main gate and entrance was positioned in a north/south direction for good luck based on feng shui. Another landscaped area was designed east of the Disney theme park to ensure this north–south positioning, also enhanced by large entry portals to the area.
- Hong Kong Disneyland was carefully positioned on Lantau Island in Penny's Bay among the surrounding hills and sea for the best luck. The lucky feng shui hill formations in the area include "white tiger" and "green dragon."
- The actual Hong Kong Disneyland Park entrance was modified to maximize energy and guest flow. This would help the park's success.
- Individual attraction entrances inside the Disney Park have been positioned for good luck as well.
- Large rocks are placed throughout Hong Kong Disneyland Park because they represent stability in feng shui. Two boulders have been placed within the park, and each Disney hotel in the resort has a rock in its entrance and courtyard or pool areas. The boulders also prevent good fortune from flowing away from the theme park or hotels.
- Water features play an important role in the Hong Kong Disneyland landscaping because they are extremely beneficial in feng shui. Lakes, ponds, and streams are placed throughout Hong Kong Disneyland to encourage good luck, fortune, and wealth for the resort, and a large fountain featuring classic Disney characters welcomes guests at the entrance to the park and to provide good luck (and for the taking of pictures).
- The Hong Kong Disneyland Hotel and the Disney's Hollywood Hotel were built in carefully selected locations with water nearby in a southwest direction to maximize prosperity by applying the principles of feng shui.

---

18. *Merriam-Webster Online, s.v.* "feng shui".

- The Hong Kong Disneyland Resort hotels have views of the waterfront onto the ocean and South China Sea. This provides good feng shui.
- The main ballroom at the Hong Kong Disneyland Hotel is 888 square meters, because 888 is a number representing wealth.
- The elevators at Hong Kong Disneyland Resort do not have the number four, and no building (including the Hong Kong Disneyland hotels) has a fourth floor. The number four is considered unlucky in the Chinese culture because it sounds like the Chinese word for death.
- Red is an extremely lucky color in Chinese culture, so it is seen frequently throughout the park, especially on the buildings on Main Street, USA.
- No clocks are sold at the stores in Hong Kong Disneyland because in Chinese the phrase "giving clock" sounds like "going to a funeral."
- No green hats are sold in Hong Kong Disneyland stores because it is said in Chinese culture that a man wearing a green is an indication that his spouse has cheated on him.

Criticisms

Overcrowding Problems

Just before the grand opening, the park was criticized for overestimating the daily capacity limit. The problem became apparent on the charity preview day on September 4, 2005, when 30,000 locals visited the park. The event turned out to be a disaster, as there were too many guests. Wait times at fast-food outlets were at least 45 minutes and wait times at rides went up to two hours.

Although the park's shareholders and the Hong Kong government put pressure on the park to lower the capacity, the park insisted on keeping the limit, only agreeing to relieve the capacity problem by extending the opening time by one hour and introducing more discounts during weekdays. However, the park stated that local visitors tend to stay in the park for more than nine hours per visit, implying that the above-mentioned practices would do little to solve the problem.

During Chinese New Year 2006, many visitors arrived at the park in the morning bearing valid tickets, but were refused entry because the park was already at full capacity. Disgruntled visitors attempted to force their way into the park and climbed over the barrier gates. Disneyland management was forced to revise their ticketing policy and designated future periods close to Chinese public holidays as "special days" during which admission would only be allowed through a date-specific ticket.

Initially, there were only 22 attractions, less than any other theme park. In July 2009, an agreement was reached with the Hong Kong government to add 20 more attractions. Disney would invest $450 million in the expansion as well as providing a loan to the theme park.

Fingerprinting

As at other Disney theme parks, visitors to Hong Kong Disneyland have their finger biometrics scanned at the entry gate. Visitors are not warned of the policy beforehand. Fingerprinting is done of all visitors older than 11 years of age and is used to associate ticket media with the person using it. The company claims that the surface of a guest's finger does not contain sufficient information to recreate a fingerprint image. Nonetheless, forensic specialists note that the data collected are more than adequate to establish a positive identification.

Public Relations

Disney initially refused to release the attendance figures after media reports surfaced, saying the park's attendance numbers might be lower than expected. Disney finally declared on November 24, 2005, that Disney had over 1 million guests during its first two months of operation.

In response to negative publicity locally and to boost visitor numbers, Hong Kong Disneyland offered $50 discounts for admission tickets to holders of Hong Kong I.D. cards in the period before 2005 Christmas. Also, from March to June 2006, the park offered Hong Kong I.D. cardholders the opportunity to purchase a two-day admission ticket for the price of a single-day ticket.

Hong Kong Ocean Park

Hong Kong Ocean Park opened in 1977. The park had a monopoly on theme park entertainment in Honk Kong since it was the only theme park. Being the only park, and owned by the government, it had many outdated attractions and was not under any pressure to add more attractions and grow. But when a deal was reached 1999 to bring Disneyland to Hong Kong, it sounded like a death sentence for Hong Kong Ocean Park because they did not have the financial strength of Disney.

Initially, Ocean Park believed that it might have lost its identity. But Ocean Park's strength was the fact that it seen as an educational park rather than an entertainment park. The park had an aquarium and real animals as well as some attractions. Its ticket prices were significantly less than the proposed admission fees to Hong Kong Disneyland.

Rather than risk closure of the park, a reengineering effort was initiated. A subway line was built into the park and the Chinese government gave the park a pair of pandas, bringing the total to four pandas. Additional hotels were built. The government also acted as guarantor for a loan to the park. The park was successful in fending off the threat of Hong Kong Disneyland and actually received foreign visitors that wanted to visit both parks. In 2012, Ocean Park was the winner of the prestigious Applause Award, the first-ever Asian attraction to be recognized as the best theme park in the world. In 2013, Ocean Park's attendance surpassed Hong Kong Disneyland.

Future Globalization

The future of Disney may very well focus on vacation resorts surrounding theme parks. But to get people to the theme parks, Disney must get young children acquainted with or hooked on Disney characters. In China, Disney is getting children acquainted with its brand name at an early age. Disney operates dozens of English language schools throughout China and where Disney characters and stories are used as teaching aids.

In June 2016, Disney opened another theme park in China, Shanghai Disneyland Park, which is part of Shanghai Disney Resort. In its first half-year of operations, 5.6 million guests were in attendance. Shanghai Disneyland is three times the size of Hong Kong Disneyland and cost $5.5 billion. Two additional theme parks will eventually be attached to Shanghai Disneyland sometime in the future. The park is financed 30 percent with debt and 70 percent with equity. Disney has a 43 percent stake in the joint venture and the remaining 57 percent is controlled by the state-run holding company Shanghai Shendi Group, which is a consortium of three companies owned by the Shanghai government.

> To all who come to this happy place, welcome. Shanghai Disneyland is your land. Here you leave today and discover imaginative worlds of fantasy, romance and adventure that ignite the magical dreams within us all. Shanghai Disneyland is authentically Disney and distinctly Chinese. It was created for everyone,

TABLE 13–7.   2017 ATTENDANCE FIGURES FOR SELECTED THEME PARKS

2017 Rank	Disney Park	Attendance
1	Disney World	20,450,000
2	Disneyland	19,300,000
3	Tokyo Disneyland	16,600,000
5	Tokyo DisneySea	15,500,000
6	Disney's Animal Kingdom at Disney World	10,844,000
7	Epcot at Disney World	12,200,000
8	Shanghai Disneyland	11,000,000
9	Disney Hollywood Studios at Disney World	10,776,000
12	Disneyland Paris	9,660,000
18	Hong Kong Disneyland	6,100,000
22	Disney Hollywood Studios at Disneyland Paris	5,200,000

bringing to life timeless characters and stories in a magical place that will be a source of joy, inspiration, and memories for generations to come.

—Robert A. Iger, CEO Disney, June 16, 2016[19]

In 2017, more than 11 million guests visited the park making it the eighth best attended theme park worldwide. Other theme park attendance figures are shown in Table 13-7.

It is expected that Disney will continue the globalization efforts and expand elsewhere over the next several decades.

Discussion Questions

1. What is the fundamental difference between a licensing agreement and a joint venture as related to Disney's theme parks?
2. Why did Disney opt for a licensing agreement for Tokyo Disneyland?
3. Why did Disney opt for a joint venture agreement with Euro Disney?
4. Does the size of the theme park have a bearing on whether to select a licensing agreement or a joint venture?
5. What is the difference between a theme park and a vacation resort?
6. If the goal is a vacation resort, should Disney negotiate a licensing agreement or a joint venture?
7. Why was it necessary to build the Walt Disney Studios Park as part of Euro Disneyland?
8. Why was it necessary to construct Tokyo DisneySea?
9. For the agreement with Tokyo DisneySea, would Disney have preferred a licensing agreement or a joint venture?
10. What did Disney see as the risks with Hong Kong Disneyland?
11. What is feng shui?

---

19. www.thewaltdisneycompany.com/shanghai-disney-resort-opens-in-mainland-china.Portions of this case have been adapted from "Boeing 787 Dreamliner battery problems," *Wikipedia, the free encyclopedia*, https://en.wikipedia.org/wiki/Boeing_787_Dreamliner_battery_problems, accessed May 14, 2019.

Further Reading

- Disneyland web site, www.tokyodisneyresort.jp.
- Fan, Maureen. *Culture shock. The Standard. Hong Kong.* November 22, 2006.
- Hong Kong Disneyland feng shui secrets and facts. The Disneyland Report.com. Site is no longer active; report is archived at https://web.archive.org/web/20120426001021/http://www.disneylandreport.com/disneysecrets/hong_kong_disneyland_secrets/hong_kong_disneyland_feng_shui_secrets_facts.html, accessed May 14, 2019.
- "Hong Kong Disneyland Posts Record-Breaking Performance in Fiscal Year 2012." Hong Kong Disneyland press release, February 18, 2013. http://news-en.hongkongdisneyland.com/PressReleases/PressReleaseDetail.aspx?AssetId=d609d58f-0913-43d6-90a9-9d45365d58c0, accessed May 14, 2019.
- China Daily, Hong Kong grows its Disneyland. September 28, 2009.
- Misawa, Misuru. Disneyland Tokyo: *Licensing vs. Joint Venture. Asia Case Research Centre*, University of Hong Kong (Case HKU420, Reference no. C106-002–1), 2006.
- "TEA/AECOM 2013 Global Attractions Report." Themed Entertainment Association. 2014.
- *TEA/AECOM 2017 Theme Index and Museum Index. Themed Entertainment Association.*
- Raz, Aviad E. Domesticating Disney: Adaption in Disneyland Tokyo. *Journal of Popular Culture* 33 (4) (2000): 77–99.
- Rishou, Makiya. Disneyland in Tokyo is a 10-year hit. *Los Angeles Times*. April 12, 1994.
- Wikipedia, the Free Encyclopedia; "Tokyo Disneyland."
- Wikipedia, the Free Encyclopedia; "Disneyland Paris."
- Wikipedia, *the Free Encyclopedia*; Joint Ventures.
- Wikipedia, the Free Encyclopedia; Disneyland Shanghai.
- Wikipedia, the Free Encyclopedia; Tokyo Disney Sea Park.

CASE STUDY: BOEING 787 DREAMLINER: MANAGING INNOVATION RISKS WITH A NEW BUSINESS MODEL

Business Model Innovation

Aircraft manufacturers use the concept of platform innovation. The platform is the core structure of the plane from which each airline can then customize the plane according to their needs such as the design of the galley and types of seats. This opportunity for customization encourages the airlines to work with the manufacturer in the design of the platform. Supply chain companies also participate in platform design because, if a plane flies for 30–40 years, each component manufacturer may have a 30- to 40-year production contract for their components.

Companies that focus on platform innovation often prefer to outsource as much work as possible to suppliers without sacrificing the quality, the integrity of the design of the platform, and the accompanying fundamentals. Platform innovators prefer being in the assembly business rather than the manufacturing business. This adds complexities and risks to the design of a new platform but if done correctly, can lower the cost of the platform.

Innovation Using Life-Cycle Cost Analysis

Aircraft manufacturers often use the concept of life-cycle cost analysis (LCCA) when designing a new aircraft. LCCA is a tool to determine the most cost-effective option among competing alternatives to purchase, own, operate, maintain, and dispose of a product. LCCA provides options for innovation activities. Aircraft manufacturers will work with their customers to find more cost-effective and innovative ways of redesigning the galley to service the passengers in flight or reducing the cost of aircraft maintenance.

For a completely new aircraft, manufacturers will partner with their contractors to create innovative products such as more fuel-efficient engines and light-weight composite materials that will result in lowering the operating cost of the plane. Innovation can also take place in developing new working relationships with the suppliers and how much additional responsibilities will be provided to them during innovation activities. However, the greater the number of innovations desired, the greater the risk of unexpected downstream events such as safety issues that may occur due to unknowns. For new product development, innovation risks may not appear until after the product is in use.

The Safety Constraint

When we discuss the triple constraint, we are generally referring to time, cost, and scope. But there are other constraints, and when human life is involved, safety becomes perhaps the most important innovation constraint. There are many forms of safety. On IT projects, safety protocols are installed to make sure that proprietary data is not compromised. Food and health-care products manufacturers worry about product tampering and safety protection for the consumers. Manufacturers worry about consumers using their products in a safe manner. Companies like Disney have safety as the number one constraint for rides and attractions at the theme parks. Most companies would rather allow projects to intentionally fail or be canceled before risking lawsuits over violations of safety. This is particularly true if the there is a chance for loss of human life.

The Boeing 787 Dreamliner Decision

The Boeing 787 "Dreamliner" is a long-range, mid-size wide-body, twin-engine jet airliner that can handle 242–335 passengers in typical three-class seating configurations. It is Boeing's most fuel-efficient airliner and is a pioneering airliner with the use of composite materials (carbon fiber, aluminum, and titanium) as the primary material in the construction of its airframe and an electrical system using lithium-ion batteries. The 787 would reduce airline maintenance costs and replacement costs. The expectation was that the 787 would be 10 percent lower cost-per-seat mile than any other aircraft. The 787 was designed to be 20 percent more fuel efficient than the Boeing 767, which it was intended to replace.

To maximize shareholder value, Boeing decided to outsource 70 percent of the work on the 787 rather than the 35–50 percent outsourcing that was used on the 737 and 747 aircrafts. This was expected to shorten the development time from six to four years and lower development costs from $10 billion to $6 billion. The lowering of Boeing's assembly costs would spread significant financial risk to Boeing's suppliers, which were now responsible for more assembly work. This was a significant change in Boeing's business model.

The longest-range 787 variant can fly 8,000–8,500 nautical miles, enough to cover the Los Angeles to Bangkok or New York City to Hong Kong routes. Its cruising airspeed is Mach 0.85, equivalent to 561 mph at typical cruise altitudes. As of July 2018, the 787 had orders for 1,387 aircraft from its 71 customers and delivered 716 aircraft.

The airline industry spends significantly more than a decade and perhaps as much as $30 billion in designing a new commercial aircraft. But even in the design and manufacturing phases, safety issues and problems can still exist but remain hidden. The only real way to verify that safety issues have been addressed is in the commercial use of the plane. Boeing had to push back the launch date of the 787 seven times, and the first few aircraft were delivered three years late. Boeing has reportedly spent $32 billion on the 787 Program.

Companies like Boeing and Airbus may end up spending billions of dollars after the planes are put in use to resolve any and all safety issues. This is what consumers expect from them. And Boeing and Airbus must comply, as seen in the literature, with the problems with the batteries on the 787 Dreamliner and other issues on the A380.

Innovation Problems

In the Boeing 787 Dreamliner's first year of service, at least four aircraft suffered from electrical system problems stemming from its lithium-ion batteries. Teething problems are common within the first year of any new aircraft design's life:

- November 1, 2011: Landing gear failed to deploy
- July 23, 2012: Corrosion risk identified in an engine component
- December 4, 2012: Leakage in fuel line connectors
- December 4, 2012: A power generator failed
- January 7, 2013: Smoke in the cockpit during an inspection
- January 8, 2013: Faulty left-wing surge tank vent
- January 9, 2013: Indicator falsely reported brake problems
- January 11, 2013: Engine oil leak
- January 11, 2013: Crack developed on the cockpit wide screen

But after a number of incidents, including an electrical fire aboard an All Nippon Airways 787, and a similar fire found by maintenance workers on a landed Japan Airlines 787 at Boston's Logan International Airport, the US Federal Aviation Administration (FAA) ordered a review into the design and manufacture of the Boeing 787 Dreamliner, following five incidents in five days involving the aircraft, mostly involved with problems with the batteries and electrical systems. This was followed with a full grounding of the entire Boeing 787 fleet, the first such grounding since that of DC-10s following the American Airlines Flight 191 disaster in 1979 (Wingfield-Hayes 2013a). It is reported that the plane has had two major battery thermal runaway events in 100,000 flight hours, which substantially exceeded the 10 million flight hours predicted by Boeing, and had done so in a dangerous manner (Hradecky 2013).

In December 2012, Boeing's CEO, James McNerney, told media outlets that the problems were no greater than those experienced by the company with the introduction of other new models, such as the Boeing 777 (Spira 2012). However, on January 7, 2013, a battery overheated and started a fire in an empty 787 operated by Japan Airlines (JAL) at Boston's Logan International Airport (Cooper 2013). On January 9, United Airlines reported a problem in one of its six 787s with the wiring in the same area as the battery fire on JAL's airliner; subsequently, the US National Transportation Safety Board opened a safety probe (Ostrower and Nicas 2013).

On January 11, 2013, the FAA announced a comprehensive review of the 787's critical systems, including the design, manufacture, and assembly of the aircraft. US Department of Transportation secretary Ray LaHood stated the administration was "looking for the root causes" behind the recent issues. The head of the FAA, Michael Huerta, said that so far nothing found "suggests [the 787] is not safe" (Topham 2013). Japan's transport ministry has also launched an investigation in response (Mukai 2013).

On January 16, 2013, an All Nippon Airways (ANA) 787 made an emergency landing at Takamatsu Airport on Shikoku Island after the flight crew received a computer warning that there was smoke inside one of the electrical compartments (Wingfield-Hayes 2013b). ANA said that there was an error message in the cockpit citing a battery malfunction. Passengers and crew were evacuated using the emergency slides.[20] According to the *Register*, there are no fire-suppression systems in the electrical compartments holding batteries, only smoke detectors (Thomson 2013).

US-based aviation regulators' oversight into the 2007 safety approval and FAA certification of the 787 has now come under scrutiny, as a key US Senate committee prepares for a hearing into the procedures of aviation safety certification "in coming weeks." However, an FAA spokesperson defended their 2007 safety certification of the 787 by saying, "The whole aviation system is designed so that if the worst case happens, there are systems in place to prevent that from interfering with other systems on the plane."[21]

On February 12, 2013, the *Wall Street Journal* reported that "Aviation safety investigators are examining whether the formation of microscopic structures known as dendrites inside the Boeing Co. 787's lithium-ion batteries played a role in twin incidents that prompted the fleet to be grounded nearly a month ago."[22]

On January 16, 2013, both major Japanese airlines ANA and JAL announced that they were voluntarily grounding or suspending flights for their fleets of 787s after multiple incidents involving different 787s, including emergency landings. These two carriers operated 24 of the 50 Dreamliners delivered to date (McCurry 2013). The grounding was expected to cost ANA over \$1.1 million a day (Topham and Scott 2013).

On January 16, 2013, the FAA issued an emergency airworthiness directive ordering all US-based airlines to ground their Boeing 787s until yet-to-be- modifications are made to the electrical system to reduce the risk of the battery overheating or catching fire.[23] This was the first time that the FAA has grounded an airliner type since 1979. The FAA also announced plans to conduct an extensive review of the 787's critical systems. The focus of the review was on the safety of the lithium-ion batteries made of lithium cobalt oxide ($LiCoO_2$). The 787 battery contract was signed in 2005[24] when $LiCoO_2$ batteries were the only type of lithium aerospace battery available, but since then newer and safer types (such as LiFePO), which provide less reaction energy during thermal runaway, have become available (Dalløkken 2013; Dudley 2013). FAA approved a 787 battery in 2007 with nine "special conditions" (Scott and Saito 2013).[25] A battery approved by FAA (through Mobile Power Solutions) was made by Rose Electronics using Kokam cells,[26] but the batteries installed in the 787 were made by Yuasa (Brewin 2013).

---

20. BBC News, "Boeing 787 Dreamliner in emergency landing in Japan." January 16, 2013. Available at www.bbc.com/news/av/business-21038307/boeing-787-dreamliner-in-emergency-landing-in-japan, accessed May 29, 2019.

21. Reuters, "Boeing 787's battery woes put US approval under scrutiny," *Business Standard*, January 29, 2013. Available at www.business-standard.com/article/international/boeing-787-s-battery-woes-put-us-approval-under-scrutiny-113012300143_1.html, accessed May 29, 2019.

22. Ibid.

23. FAA press release, January 16, 2013. Available at www.faa.gov/news/press_releases/news_story.cfm?newsId=14233. Retrieved May 14, 2019.

24. "Thales selects GS Yuasa for Lithium ion battery system in Boeing's 787 Dreamliner." Press release, GS Yuasa, June 12, 2005, accessed May 29, 2019.

25. "NM375 Special Conditions No. 25–359–SC," Federal Register vol. 72, no. 196 (Thursday, October 11, 2007), available at www.govinfo.gov/content/pkg/FR-2007-10-11/html/E7-19980.htm, accessed May 29, 2019.

26. Correspondence between Ben Supko, Acting Chief, Standards Development Branch, US DOT (March 15, 2011), and Rod Iverson, Securaplane Technologies, Inc. January 31, 2011. http://cdn.nextgov.com/media/gbc/docs/pdfs_edit/012213bb1b.pdf, accessed May 29, 2019.

On January 20, the NTSB declared that overvoltage was not the cause of the Boston incident, as voltage did not exceed the battery limit of 32 V,[27] and the charging unit passed tests. The battery had signs of short-circuiting and thermal runaway.[28] Despite this, on January 24 the NTSB announced that it had not yet pinpointed the cause of the Boston fire; the FAA will not allow US-based Dreamliners to fly again until the problem is found and corrected. In a press briefing that day, NTSB Chairwoman Deborah Hersman said that the NTSB had found evidence of failure of multiple safety systems designed to prevent these battery problems, and stated that fire must never happen on an airplane (Weld and Mouwad 2013). The Japan Transport Safety Board (JTSB) has said on January 23 that the battery in ANA jets in Japan reached a maximum voltage of 31 V (lower than the 32 V limit like the Boston JAL 787), but had a sudden unexplained voltage drop to near zero (Mitra-Thakur 2013). All cells had signs of thermal damage before thermal runaway (Hradecky 2013). ANA and JAL had replaced several 787 batteries before the mishaps. As of January 29, 2013, JTSB approved the Yuasa factory quality control while the American NTSB continues to look for defects in the Boston battery (Cooper and Matsuda 2013; Tabuchi 2013).[29]

Industry experts disagreed on the consequences of the grounding: Airbus was confident that Boeing would resolve the issue (Keene 2013) and that no airlines would "switch from one airplane type to another because there's a maintenance issue," while other experts saw the problem as "costly" and "could take upwards of a year" (Wall and Rothman 2013; White 2013).

The only US-based airline that operated the Dreamliner at that time was United Airlines, which had six.[30] Chile's Directorate General of Civil Aviation (DGAC) grounded LAN Airlines' three 787s (*La Tercera 2013*). The Indian Directorate General of Civil Aviation (DGCA) directed Air India to ground its six Dreamliners. The Japanese Transport Ministry made the ANA and JAL groundings official and indefinite following the FAA announcement (Upadhyay 2013). The European Aviation Safety Agency had also followed the FAA's advice and grounded the only two European 787s operated by LOT Polish Airlines.[31] Qatar Airways announced that it was grounding its five Dreamliners.[32] Ethiopian Air was the final operator to announce temporary groundings of its four Dreamliners.[33]

As of January 17, 2013, all 50 of the aircraft delivered to date have been grounded (Topham and Scott 2013). On January 18, Boeing announced that it was halting 787 deliveries until the battery problem was resolved (Madslien 2013; Negishi and Kelly 2013; Topham and Scott 2013). On February 4, 2013, the FAA said it would permit Boeing to conduct test flights of 787 aircraft to gather additional data (Freed 2013).

On April 19, 2013, the FAA approved Boeing's new design for the Boeing 787 battery. This would allow the eight airlines that maintained a fleet of 50 787 planes to begin making repairs. The repairs

---

27. NTSB press release, "NTSB Provides third Investigative update on Boeing 787 Battery Fire in Boston." January 20, 2013. www.ntsb.gov/news/press-releases/Pages/Pr20130120.aspx, accessed May 28, 2019.

28. NTSB press release, January 26, 2013. Retrieved January 26, 2013.

29. NTSB press release, "NTSB issues sixth update on JAL Boeing 787 battery fire investigation," January 29, 2013, www.ntsb.gov/news/press-releases/Pages/PR20130129b.aspx, accessed May 30, 2019.

30. "FAA temporarily grounds all Boeing 787s." KIRO TV. January 16, 2013. www.kiro7.com/news/faa-grounding-all-boeing-787s/246413556, accessed May 29, 2019.

31. Reuters, "European safety agency to ground 787 in line with FAA," January 16, 2013. www.reuters.com/article/boeing-787-easa/european-safety-agency-to-ground-787-in-line-with-faa-idUSL6N0AM0E020130117, accessed May 29, 2019.

32. Reuters, "Qatar Airways grounds Boeing Dreamliner fleet," January 17, 2013. www.reuters.com/article/us-qatar-boeing/qatar-airways-grounds-boeing-dreamliner-fleet-idUSBRE90G0D020130117, accessed May 29, 2019.

33. Reuters, "US, others ground Boeing Dreamliner indefinitely." January 16, 2013. www.cnbc.com/id/100385850, accessed May 30, 2019.

would include a containment and venting system for the batteries (Henningan 2013). The new design would add more protection and would also increase the weight of the plane by more than 150 pounds. This was a necessity to ensure safety. The cost of the repairs would be $465,000 per plane. Boeing committed more than 300 people on 10 teams to make the repairs, which would take about five days per plane.[34]

ANA, which operated 17 Dreamliner jets, estimated that it was losing $868,300 per plane over a two-week period and would be talking with Boeing about compensation for losses. Other airlines were also expected to seek some compensation.

Final Results

Boeing was successful in resolving the battery issues and sales of the 787 are doing well. As of July 2018, Boeing had 1387 orders for the Boeing 787 and delivered 716. Boeing's 787 could become Boeing most profitable aircraft program in Boeing's history.

Both Airbus and Boeing understand the importance of customer confidence. If the aircraft customers lose confidence in the aircraft manufacturer's ability to deliver a safe aircraft, significant business will be lost. Aircrafts can have more than 100,000 components. In the cabin area alone on the A380 are more than 23,000 parts. Given the fact that it takes at least 10 years and billions of dollars to design and test these planes, it is impossible to prevent some of these teething problems to have been simulated. Dry runs cannot simulate every possible scenario that could happen. The reliability of every part and every system can be proven only when the aircraft is in operations. The A380 has undergone more testing than any other jet. Yet despite the testing, it may be some time until all the problems are resolved. Because lives may be at stake, Airbus may end up spending billions to correct all of the potential problems that may occur.

There will always be risks with the design and development of new aircraft. Typical risks include:[35]

- *Innovation risks*: dealing with new and unproven technologies
- *Outsourcing risks*: expecting suppliers and partners to take on design and development risks
- *Tiered outsourcing risks*: asking the suppliers and partners to manage and integrate the work of lower tiered suppliers
- *Offshore risks*: having critical components manufactured far away from the final assembly plant
- *Communication by computer risks*: expecting communication by computer to replace face-to-face communication
- *Labor relations risks*: having critical decisions related to outsourcing made by executives without any input from the people doing the work
- *Disengaged C-suite risks*: having executives not wanting to be involved in the day-to-day activities of designing a new plane
- *Project management skills risks*: having a project team that lacks critical skills such as in supply chain management

---

34. Bloomberg News, "ANA's Dreamliner Test Flight Seen as Step in Regaining Customers," April 27, 2013.

35. Adapted from Denning (2013).Material for this case study was adapted from "Sydney Opera House," *Wikipedia*, https://en.wikipedia.org/wiki/Sydney_Opera_House.

Lessons Learned

There are several lessons learned from the Boeing 787 program:

- **Proper testing campaign for new technology.** In the case of 787, the number of tests needed to certify its batteries was not enough.
  - Flaws in manufacturing, insufficient testing, and a poor understanding of an innovative battery all contributed to the grounding of Boeing's 787 fleet (Mouawad 2014).
  - "We advanced the state of the art for testing lithium ion batteries," Mike Sinnett, Boeing's chief engineer for the 787 Program, said at a hearing of the aviation subcommittee of the House Transportation Committee. The hearing was titled "Lessons Learned from the Boeing 787 Incidents" (Reed 2013).
- **Strict quality control on the products provided by the suppliers.** Choice of the supplier based only on the quality.
  - But whatever the outcome, experts said that with so many lives at stake, the design and manufacture of new aircraft should be based solely on legitimate issues of cost and quality, and the selection process for suppliers should be transparent and untainted by other commercial or political concerns.
  - "The greatest enemy of good aircraft is people who interfere with the freedom to shop for the highest quality," Mr. Aboulafia said (Stewart 2013).
  - But these were exacerbated by Boeing's decision to massively increase the percentage of parts it sourced from outside contractors. The wing tips were made in Korea, the cabin lighting in Germany, cargo doors in Sweden, escape slides in New Jersey, landing gear in France. The plan backfired. Outsourcing parts led to three years of delays. Parts didn't fit together properly. Shims used to bridge small parts weren't attached correctly. Many aircraft had to have their tails extensively reworked. The company ended up buying some suppliers, to take their business back in house. All new projects, especially ones as ambitious as the Dreamliner, face teething issues, but the 787's woes continued to mount. Unions blame the company's reliance on outsourcing (Rushe 2013).
- **Careful control and the right attitude by Federal Aviation Administration (FAA).** The Federal Aviation Administration should maintain an attitude toward airplane makers that is intransigent.
  - But the Dreamliner's problems are not just a Boeing issue. They are a lesson in the limits of outsourcing and the all too cozy relationships between regulator and regulated that have caused problems across industries from automotive to food and financial services in recent years (Rushe 2013, 48).
  - Consultant and former airline executive Robert Mann said Boeing's clout put pressure on the Federal Aviation Authority (FAA) to speedily approve the Dreamliner, despite its radical design and manufacturing process.
- **The ultimate goal of designing a new aircraft should be to increase shareholder value**.

  - When the goal focuses more so on maximum shareholder value, especially in the short term, we often take unnecessary risks and turn a good opportunity into a potential disaster.

Discussion Questions

1. Can safety be considered as a constraint on an innovation project and considered to be at a higher priority than even time, cost, and scope?

2. Should the innovation project manager on the 787 Program have the authority on how safety is defined, measured, and reported during innovation activities?
3. What type of innovation did Boeing use?
4. What innovation mistakes did Boeing make?

CASE STUDY: THE SYDNEY AUSTRALIA OPERA HOUSE _____

The Sydney Opera House is a multivenue performing arts center in New South Wales, Australia. It was conceived and largely built by Danish architect Jørn Utzon, opening in 1973 after a long gestation that began with his competition-winning design in 1957. Joseph Cahill's New South Wales Government gave the go-ahead for work to begin in 1958. The government's bold decision to select Utzon's design is often overshadowed by the scandal that followed (Tobias 2011). It is on Bennelong Point in Sydney Harbor, close to the Sydney Harbor Bridge. It sits at the northeastern tip of the Sydney central business district (the CBD), surrounded on three sides by the harbor (Sydney Cove and Farm Cove) and inland by the Royal Botanic Gardens.

Contrary to its name, it houses multiple performance venues. It is among the busiest performing arts centers in the world, hosting over 1,500 performances each year attended by some 1.2 million people. It provides a venue for many performing-arts companies, including the four key resident companies Opera Australia, The Australian Ballet, the Sydney Theatre Company, and the Sydney Symphony Orchestra, and presents a wide range of productions on its own account. It is also one of the most popular visitor attractions in Australia, with more than seven million people visiting each year, 300,000 of whom take a guided tour.[36]

It is administered by the Sydney Opera House Trust, under the New South Wales Ministry of the Arts. On June 28, 2007, it was made a UNESCO World Heritage Site (Braithwaite 2007). It is one of the twentieth century's most distinctive buildings and one of the most famous performing arts centers in the world (Carbone 2011).[37]

It is a modern expressionist design, with a series of large precast concrete "shells," each composed of sections of a sphere of 75.2 meters (246 ft, 8.6 in.) radius, forming the roofs of the structure, set on a monumental podium. The building covers 1.8 hectares (4.4 acres) of land and is 183 m (600 ft) long and 120 m (394 ft) wide at its widest point. It is supported on 588 concrete piers sunk as much as 25 m (82 ft) below sea level.

Although the roof structures are commonly referred to as "shells" (as in this article), they are precast concrete panels supported by precast concrete ribs, not shells in a strictly structural sense. The shells are covered in a subtle chevron pattern with 1,056,006 glossy white- and matte-cream-colored Swedish-made tiles from Höganäs AB, a factory that generally produced stoneware tiles for the paper-mill industry, though, from a distance, the shells appear a uniform white.

Apart from the tile of the shells and the glass curtain walls of the foyer spaces, the building's exterior is largely clad with aggregate panels composed of pink granite quarried at Tarana. Significant interior surface treatments also include off-form concrete, Australian white birch plywood supplied from Wauchope in northern New South Wales, and brush box glulam.

---

36. *Annual Report, Sydney Opera House 2010/11*, "Vision and Goals," p. 10. www.sydneyoperahouse.com/content/dam/pdfs/annual-reports/Annual-Report-2010–2011.pdf. Retrieved April 22, 2019; *Sydney Opera House 08/09 Annual Report*. Available at www.sydneyoperahouse.com/content/dam/pdfs/annual-reports/SOH-Annual-report-2008–2009.pdf. Retrieved April 22, 2019.

37. 3D illuminations light up the Sydney Opera House for Vivid Sydney. *The Independent*. May 9, 2011. https://www.independent.co.uk/travel/news-and-advice/3d-illuminations-light-up-the-sydney-opera-house-for-vivid-sydney-2281271.html, accessed May 30, 2019.

Of the two larger spaces, the Concert Hall is in the western group of shells, the Joan Sutherland Theatre in the eastern group. The scale of the shells was chosen to reflect the internal height requirements, with low entrance spaces, rising over the seating areas up to the high stage towers. The smaller venues (the Drama Theatre, the Playhouse, and The Studio) are within the podium, beneath the Concert Hall. A smaller group of shells set to the western side of the Monumental Steps houses the Bennelong Restaurant. The podium is surrounded by substantial open public spaces, and the large stone-paved forecourt area with the adjacent monumental steps is regularly used as a performance space.

Performance Venues and Facilities

It houses the following performance venues:

- The Concert Hall, with 2,679 seats, the home of the Sydney Symphony Orchestra and used by a large number of other concert presenters. It contains the Sydney Opera House Grand Organ, the largest mechanical tracker action organ in the world, with over 10,000 pipes.
- The Joan Sutherland Theatre, a proscenium theatre with 1,507 seats, the Sydney home of Opera Australia and The Australian Ballet.
- The Drama Theatre, a proscenium theatre with 544 seats, used by the Sydney Theatre Company and other dance and theatrical presenters.
- The Playhouse, an end-stage theatre with 398 seats.
- The Studio, a flexible space with a maximum capacity of 400, depending on configuration.
- The Utzon Room, a small multi-purpose venue, seating up to 210.
- The Forecourt, a flexible open-air venue with a wide range of configuration options, including the possibility of utilizing the Monumental Steps as audience seating, used for a range of community events and major outdoor performances. The Forecourt will be closed to visitors and performances in 2011–2014 to construct a new entrance tunnel to a rebuilt loading dock for the Joan Sutherland Theatre.

Other areas (e.g., the northern and western foyers) are also used for performances on an occasional basis. Venues are also used for conferences, ceremonies, and social functions.

The building also houses a recording studio, cafes, restaurants, and bars and retail outlets. Guided tours are available, including a frequent tour of the front-of-house spaces, and a daily backstage tour that takes visitors backstage to see areas normally reserved for performers and crew members.

Construction History

Planning began in the late 1940s, when Eugene Goossens, the director of the NSW State Conservatorium of Music, lobbied for a suitable venue for large theatrical productions. The normal venue for such productions, the Sydney Town Hall, was not considered large enough. By 1954, Goossens succeeded in gaining the support of NSW Premier Joseph Cahill, who called for designs for a dedicated opera house.

A design competition was launched by Cahill on 13 September 1955 and received 233 entries, representing architects from 32 countries. The criteria specified a large hall seating 3,000 and a small hall for 1,200 people, each to be designed for different uses, including full-scale operas, orchestral and choral concerts, mass meetings, lectures, ballet performances, and other presentations (UNESCO 2018, 6). The winner, announced in 1957, was Jørn Utzon, a Danish architect. According to legend the Utzon design was rescued from a final cut of 30 "rejects" by the noted Finnish architect Eero Saarinen. The prize was £5,000 (Ellis 1992). Utzon visited Sydney in 1957 to help supervise the project (Pearman 2007). His office moved to Sydney in February 1963.

Utzon received the Pritzker Prize, architecture's highest honor, in 2003 (Totaro 2008). The Pritzker Prize citation stated:

> There is no doubt that the Sydney Opera House is his masterpiece. It is one of the great iconic buildings of the 20th century, an image of great beauty that has become known throughout the world—a symbol for not only a city, but a whole country and continent.[38]

Design and Construction

The Fort Macquarie Tram Depot, occupying the site at the time of these plans, was demolished in 1958 and construction began in March 1959. It was built in three stages: stage I (1959–1963) consisted of building the upper podium; stage II (1963–1967) the construction of the outer shells; stage III (1967–1973) interior design and construction.

Stage I: Podium

Stage I commenced on March 2, 1959. The government had pushed for work to begin early, fearing that funding, or public opinion, might turn against them. However, Utzon had still not completed the final designs. Major structural issues still remained unresolved. By January 23, 1961, work was running 47 weeks behind, mainly because of unexpected difficulties (inclement weather, unexpected difficulty diverting stormwater, construction beginning before proper construction drawings had been prepared, changes of original contract documents).[39] Work on the podium was finally completed in February 1963. The forced early start led to significant later problems, not least of which was the fact that the podium columns were not strong enough to support the roof structure and had to be rebuilt (Murray 2004).

Stage II: Roof

The shells of the competition entry were originally of undefined geometry (Arup and Zunz 1969), but, early in the design process, the "shells" were perceived as a series of parabolas supported by precast concrete ribs. However, engineers Ove Arup and Partners were unable to find an acceptable solution to constructing them. The formwork for using in-situ concrete would have been prohibitively expensive, but, because there was no repetition in any of the roof forms, the construction of precast concrete for each individual section would possibly have been even more expensive.

From 1957 to 1963, the design team went through at least 12 iterations of the form of the shells trying to find an economically acceptable form (including schemes with parabolas, circular ribs, and ellipsoids) before a workable solution was completed. The design work on the shells involved one of the earliest uses of computers in structural analysis, in order to understand the complex forces to which the shells would be subjected. In mid-1961, the design team found a solution to the problem: the shells all being created as

---

38. www.pritzkerprize.com/jury-citation-jorn-utzon, accessed May 30, 2019.
39. www.sydneyarchitecture.com/ROC/QUA01.htm, accessed April 22, 2019.

sections from a sphere. This solution allows arches of varying length to be cast in a common mold, and a number of arch segments of common length to be placed adjacent to one another, to form a spherical section. With whom exactly this solution originated has been the subject of some controversy. It was originally credited to Utzon. Ove Arup's letter to Ashworth, a member of the Sydney Opera House executive committee, states: "Utzon came up with an idea of making all the shells of uniform curvature throughout in both directions" (Jones 2006, 199). Peter Jones, the author of Ove Arup's biography, states that "the architect and his supporters alike claimed to recall the precise eureka moment ...; the engineers and some of their associates, with equal conviction, recall discussion in both central London and at Ove's house."

Ove Arup and Partners' site engineer supervised the construction of the shells, which used an innovative adjustable steel-trussed "erection arch" to support the different roofs before completion. On April 6, 1962, it was estimated that the Opera House would be completed between August 1964 and March 1965.

Stage III: Interiors

Stage III, the interiors, started with Utzon moving his entire office to Sydney in February 1963. However, there was a change of government in 1965, and the new Robert Askin government declared the project under the jurisdiction of the Ministry of Public Works. This ultimately led to Utzon's resignation in 1966.

The cost of the project so far, even in October 1966, was still only $22.9 million,[40] less than a quarter of the final $102 million cost. However, the projected costs for the design were at this stage much more significant.

The second stage of construction was progressing toward completion when Utzon resigned. His position was principally taken over by Peter Hall, who became largely responsible for the interior design. Other persons appointed that same year to replace Utzon were E. H. Farmer as government architect, D. S. Littlemore, and Lionel Todd.

Following Utzon's resignation, the acoustic advisor, Lothar Cremer, confirmed to the Sydney Opera House Executive Committee (SOHEC) that Utzon's original acoustic design allowed for only 2,000 seats in the main hall and further stated that increasing the number of seats to 3,000 as specified in the brief would be disastrous for the acoustics. According to Peter Jones, the stage designer, Martin Carr, criticized the "shape, height and width of the stage, the physical facilities for artists, the location of the dressing rooms, the widths of doors and lifts, and the location of lighting switchboards."[41]

Significant Changes to Utzon's Design

The final constructions were modified from Utzon's original designs:

- The major hall, which was originally to be a multipurpose opera/concert hall, became solely a concert hall, called the Concert Hall. The minor hall, originally for stage productions only, had the added function of opera and ballet to deal with and was called the Opera Theatre, later renamed the Joan Sutherland Theatre. As a result, the Joan Sutherland Theatre is inadequate to stage large-scale opera and ballet. A theatre, a cinema and a library were also added. These were later changed to two live drama theatres and a smaller theatre "in the round." These now comprise

---

40. www.sydneyarchitecture.com/ROC/QUA01.htm, accessed April 22, 2019.
41. Ibid.

the Drama Theatre, the Playhouse, and the Studio, respectively. These changes were primarily because of inadequacies in the original competition brief, which did not make it adequately clear how the Opera House was to be used. The layout of the interiors was changed, and the stage machinery, already designed and fitted inside the major hall, was pulled out and largely thrown away.

- Externally, the cladding to the podium and the paving (the podium was originally not to be clad down to the water, but to be left open).
- The construction of the glass walls (Utzon was planning to use a system of prefabricated plywood mullions, but a different system was designed to deal with the glass).
- Utzon's plywood corridor designs, and his acoustic and seating designs for the interior of both major halls, were scrapped completely. His design for the Concert Hall was rejected as it only seated 2,000, which was considered insufficient. Utzon employed the acoustic consultant Lothar Cremer, and his designs for the major halls were later modeled and found to be very good. The subsequent Todd, Hall and Littlemore versions of both major halls have some problems with acoustics, particularly for the performing musicians. The orchestra pit in the Joan Sutherland Theatre is cramped and dangerous to musicians' hearing (Morgan 2006). The Concert Hall has a very high roof, leading to a lack of early reflections onstage—perspex rings (the "acoustic clouds") hanging over the stage were added shortly before opening in an (unsuccessful) attempt to address this problem.

Completion and Cost

The Opera House was formally completed in 1973, having cost \$102 million.[42] H. R. "Sam" Hoare, the Hornibrook director in charge of the project, provided the following approximations in 1973: Stage I: podium Civil & Civic Pty Ltd. approximately \$5.5 million. Stage II: roof shells M.R. Hornibrook (NSW) Pty Ltd. approximately \$12.5 million. Stage III: completion The Hornibrook Group \$56.5 million. Separate contracts: stage equipment, stage lighting and organ \$9.0m. Fees and other costs \$16.5 million.

The original cost estimate in 1957 was £3,500,000 (\$7 million). The original completion date set by the government was January 26, 1963 (Australia Day) (Jones 2006). Thus, the project was completed 10 years late and over budget by more than 14 times.

Jørn Utzon and His Resignation

Before the Sydney Opera House competition, Jørn Utzon had won 7 of the 18 competitions he had entered but had never seen any of his designs built. Utzon's submitted concept for the Sydney Opera House was almost universally admired and considered groundbreaking. The Assessors Report of January 1957, stated:

> The drawings submitted for this scheme are simple to the point of being diagrammatic. Nevertheless, as we have returned again and again to the study of these drawings, we are convinced that they present a concept of an Opera House which is capable of becoming one of the great buildings of the world.

---

42. www.sydneyoperahouse.com/our-story/sydney-opera-house-facts.html, accessed May 30, 2019.

For the first stage, Utzon worked very successfully with the rest of the design team and the client, but, as the project progressed, the Cahill government insisted on progressive revisions. They also did not fully appreciate the costs or work involved in design and construction. Tensions between the client and the design team grew further when an early start to construction was demanded despite an incomplete design. This resulted in a continuing series of delays and setbacks while various technical engineering issues were being refined. The building was unique, and the problems with the design issues and cost increases were exacerbated by commencement of work before the completion of the final plans.

After the election of Robert Askin as premier of New South Wales in 1965, the relationship of client, architect, engineers, and contractors became increasingly tense. Askin had been a "vocal critic of the project prior to gaining office" (Farrelly 2008). His new minister for public works, Davis Hughes, was even less sympathetic. Elizabeth Farrelly (2008), Australian architecture critic, has written that:

> [A]t an election night dinner party in Mosman, Hughes's daughter Sue Burgoyne boasted that her father would soon sack Utzon. Hughes had no interest in art, architecture or aesthetics. A fraud, as well as a philistine, he had been exposed before Parliament and dumped as Country Party leader for 19 years of falsely claiming a university degree. The Opera House gave Hughes a second chance. For him, as for Utzon, it was all about control; about the triumph of homegrown mediocrity over foreign genius.

Differences ensued. One of the first was that Utzon believed the clients should receive information on all aspects of the design and construction through his practice, while the clients wanted a system (notably drawn in sketch form by Davis Hughes) where architect, contractors, and engineers each reported to the client directly and separately. This had great implications for procurement methods and cost control, with Utzon wishing to negotiate contracts with chosen suppliers (such as Ralph Symonds for the plywood interiors) and the New South Wales government insisting contracts be put out to tender (Murray 2004).

Utzon was highly reluctant to respond to questions or criticism from the client's Sydney Opera House executive committee (SOHEC). However, he was greatly supported throughout by a member of the committee and one of the original competition judges, Professor Harry Ingham Ashworth. Utzon was unwilling to compromise on some aspects of his designs that the clients wanted to change.

Utzon's ability was never in doubt, despite questions raised by Davis Hughes, who attempted to portray Utzon as an impractical dreamer. Ove Arup actually stated that Utzon was "probably the best of any I have come across in my long experience of working with architects" and "The Opera House could become the world's foremost contemporary masterpiece if Utzon is given his head."[43]

In October 1965, Utzon gave Hughes a schedule setting out the completion dates of parts of his work for stage III. Utzon was at this time working closely with Ralph Symonds, a manufacturer of plywood based in Sydney and highly regarded by many, despite an Arup engineer warning that Ralph Symonds's "knowledge of the design stresses of plywood, was extremely sketchy" and that the technical advice was "elementary to say the least and completely useless for our purposes." In any case, Hughes shortly after withheld permission for the construction of plywood prototypes for the interiors, and the relationship between Utzon and the client never recovered. By February 1966, Utzon was owed more than $100,000 in fees (Farrelly 2008). Hughes then withheld funding so that Utzon could not even pay his own staff. The government minutes record that following several threats of resignation, Utzon finally stated to Davis Hughes, "If you don't do it, I resign." Hughes replied: "I accept your resignation. Thank you very much. Goodbye."

---

43. https://mashable.com/2015/07/11/building-sydney-opera-house.

Utzon left the project on February 28, 1966. He said that Hughes's refusal to pay him any fees and the lack of collaboration caused his resignation and later famously described the situation as "Malice in Blunderland." In March 1966, Hughes offered him a subordinate role as "design architect" under a panel of executive architects, without any supervisory powers over the House's construction, but Utzon rejected this. Utzon left the country, never to return.

Following his resignation, there was great controversy about who was in the right and who was in the wrong. The *Sydney Morning Herald* initially reported: "No architect in the world has enjoyed greater freedom than Mr. Utzon. Few clients have been more patient or more generous than the people and the Government of NSW. One would not like history to record that this partnership was brought to an end by a fit of temper on the one side or by a fit of meanness on the other." On March 17, 1966, it reported:

> It was not his fault that a succession of Governments and the Opera House Trust should so signally have failed to impose any control or order on the project ... . his concept was so daring that he himself could solve its problems only step by step ... . his insistence on perfection led him to alter his design as he went along.[44]

The Sydney Opera House opened the way for the immensely complex geometries of some modern architecture. It was one of the first examples of the use of computer-aided design to design complex shapes. The design techniques developed by Utzon and Arup for the Sydney Opera House have been further developed and are now used for architecture, such as works of Gehry and blobitecture, as well as most reinforced concrete structures. The design is also one of the first in the world to use araldite to glue the precast structural elements together and proved the concept for future use.

Opening Day

The Opera House was formally opened by Elizabeth II, Queen of Australia, on October 20, 1973. A large crowd attended. Utzon was not invited to the ceremony, nor was his name mentioned. The opening was televised and included fireworks and a performance of Beethoven's Symphony No. 9.

Discussion Questions

1. Who acted originally as the innovation project manager?
2. What type of innovation was used on the project?
3. Did the project demonstrate that an innovation culture was in place?
4. What type of governance was used at the beginning of the innovation project?
5. What's the danger when there is a lack of governance from the business owners?
6. Can scope creep be controlled on a project as this, and if so, how?
7. Was there any process in place for controlling innovation scope creep?
8. What could have been done to control scope creep?
9. Was firing Utzon (or accepting his resignation) the solution for controlling innovation scope creep?
10. Does the end justify the means? Or, how many people today know that the project was completed 10 years late and 14 times its original budget?

---

44. "Mr. Utson's Farewell." *Sydney Morning Herald*, March 17, 1966, p. 4.©2019 by Harold Kerzner."The Iridium System" and "The Terrestrial and Space-Based Network" discuss the operational version of the Iridium system today as described on the Iridium website, www.Iridium.com.

CASE STUDY: AMPORE FAUCET COMPANY: MANAGING DIFFERENT VIEWS ON INNOVATION _____

Background

Ampore Faucet Company had grown into one of the world's largest suppliers of faucets for both commercial and home use. Competition was fierce. Consumers would evaluate faucets on artistic design and quality. Each faucet had to be available in at least 25 different colors. Commercial buyers, such as construction companies erecting apartment buildings, seemed more interested in the cost than the average consumer who viewed the faucet as an object of art, irrespective of price.

Ampore did not spend a great deal of money advertising on the radio or on television. Some money was allocated for ads in professional journals. Most of Ampore's advertising and marketing funds were allocated to regional home and garden trade shows and two annual builders' trade shows. One large builder could purchase more than 5,000 components for the furnishing of one newly constructed hotel or one apartment complex. Missing an opportunity to display the new products at these trade shows could easily result in a 6- to 12-month window of lost revenue.

Culture

Ampore Faucet had a noncooperative culture that had a serious impact on innovation project management. Marketing and engineering would never talk to one another. Engineering wanted the freedom to design new products and explore new technologies whereas marketing wanted to control the design process and have final approval to make sure that what was designed could be sold. Some of the conflicts became so intense that senior management refused to intervene and instead allowed the conflicts to grow. Some executives view this as meaningful conflicts with the mistaken belief that this would increase innovations.

The conflict between marketing and engineering became so fierce that early attempts to implement innovation project management failed. Nobody wanted to be the project manager. Functional team members refused to attend team meetings and spent most of their time working on their own pet projects rather than the required work. Line managers also showed little interest in supporting innovation project management because of the conflicts. This became a serious issue when innovation project managers needed support from workers not in their own functional units.

Each functional unit had its own budget for innovation work, and the person responsible for the innovation project was assigned from the funding functional unit. Each functional unit had its own innovation culture. Marketing wanted innovation in colors, design, and aesthetic characteristics. Its projects were primarily incremental innovation and product improvements. Engineering was interested in new technology development and application as well as improvements in quality. Engineering's focus was on radical innovation.

All previous attempts to develop some standardization for project management, especially for innovation projects, were met with resistance. Each functional unit had its own definition of innovation success. Marketing viewed success in terms of yearly sales, whereas engineering defined success as creating a new design that would eventually become commercialized regardless of the number of units sold. Each functional unit had its own forms, guidelines, templates, and checklists for its projects. Each functional unit had its own way of managing projects. There were no project management offices in Ampore. Most of the workers viewed innovation project management as their secondary rather than their primary job.

The focus of senior management was more on short-term profitability than long-term innovation benefits. As such, senior management did not establish any lists of strategic goals and objectives, nor did senior management provide any list of prioritized strategic needs. Instead, they gave each functional unit the authority and freedom to establish their own strategic innovation objectives, priorities, and supporting budgets.

Project management became so disliked that the procurement manager refused to assign any of her employees to project teams. Instead, she mandated that all project staffing requests for work come through her. She insulated her workers from outside work requests as well as external pressure. She claimed that this would protect them from the continuous conflicts between engineering and marketing.

The Executive Decision

Senior management began to realize that their competitors were becoming more innovative than their firm. The executive council mandated that another attempt to implement good project management practices company-wide must occur quickly. Project management would be needed not only for new product development but also for specialty products and enhancements. The vice presidents for marketing and engineering reluctantly agreed to try and patch up their differences but did not appear confident that any changes would take place. Strange as it may seem, nobody could identify the initial cause of the conflicts or how the trouble actually began. Senior management hired an external consultant to identify the problems, provide recommendations and alternatives, and act as a mediator. The consultant's process would have to begin with interviews.

Engineering Interviews

The following comments were made during engineering interviews:

"We are loaded down with work. If marketing would stay out of engineering, we could get our job done."

"Marketing doesn't understand that there's more work for us to do other than just new product development."

"Marketing personnel should spend their time at the country club and in bar rooms. This will allow us in engineering to finish our work uninterrupted!"

"Marketing expects everyone in engineering to stop what they are doing in order to put out marketing fires. I believe that most of the time the problem is that marketing doesn't know what they want up front. This leads to change after change. Why can't we get a good definition of what we want at the beginning of each project?"

Marketing Interviews

Our livelihood rests heavily on income generated from trade shows. Since new product development is four to six months in duration, we have to beat up on engineering to make sure that our marketing schedules are met. Why can't engineering understand the importance of these trade shows?

Because of the time required to develop new products [4–6 months], we sometimes have to rush into projects without having a good definition of the scope of work required. When a customer at a trade show gives us an idea for a new product, we rush to get the project underway for introduction at the next trade show. We then go back to the customer and ask for more clarification and/or specifications. Sometimes we must work with the customer for months to get the information we need. I know that this is a problem for engineering, but it cannot be helped.

The consultant wrestled with the comments but was still somewhat perplexed. "Why doesn't engineering understand marketing's problems?" pondered the consultant. In a follow-up interview with an engineering manager, the following comment was made:

> We are currently working on 375 different projects in engineering, and that includes those which marketing requested. Why can't marketing understand our problems?

Discussion Questions

1. What are the critical issues that impact innovation?
2. What can be done about solving these issues?
3. Can excellence in innovation project management still be achieved and, if so, how? What steps would you recommend?
4. Given the current noncooperative culture and its impact on innovation, how long will it take to achieve a good cooperative innovation project management culture, and even excellence?
5. What obstacles exist in getting marketing and engineering to agree to a singular methodology for innovation project management?
6. What might happen if benchmarking studies indicate that either marketing or engineering are at fault?
7. Assuming an approach for innovation project management can be implemented and agreed to, should it be accompanied by a process for the prioritization of projects, or should some committee external to the methodology accomplish the prioritization?

CASE STUDY: THE INNOVATION SPONSORS

Background

Two executives worked in a company that focused heavily on incremental innovation. Each executive funded a pet project that focused on radical innovation rather than incremental and had little chance of success. Despite repeated requests by the innovation project managers and team members to cancel the projects, the executives, who were acting as the innovation sponsors, continued their decision to throw away good money after bad money. The sponsors then had to find a way to prevent their embarrassment from such a blunder from becoming apparent to all.

The Story Line

Two vice presidents came up with ideas for pet projects and funded the projects internally using money from their functional areas. Even though there was an R&D group, the projects would be performed within their functional areas. Both projects had budgets close to $2 million and schedules of approximately one year. These were somewhat high-risk radical innovation projects because they both required that a technical breakthrough be made. There was no guarantee that the technical breakthrough could be made at all. And even if the technical breakthrough could be made, both executives estimated that the shelf life of both products would be about one year before becoming obsolete but that they could easily recover their R&D costs.

These two projects were considered as pet projects because they were established at the personal request of two senior managers and without and real business case. Had these two projects been required to go through the formal project selection process, neither project would have been approved. The budgets for these projects were way out of line for the value that the company would receive, and the return on investment would be below minimum levels even if the technical breakthrough could be made. The PMO, which is actively involved in the project selection process, also stated that they would never recommend approval of a project where the end result would have a shelf life of one year or less. Simply stated, these projects existed for the self-satisfaction of the two executives and to gain them prestige from their colleagues.

Nevertheless, both executives found money for their projects and were willing to let the projects go forward without the standard approval process. Each executive was able to get an experienced project manager from their group to manage their pet project.

The Gate Review Meetings

At the first gate review meeting, both project managers stood up and recommended that their projects be canceled and that the resources be assigned to other more promising projects. They both stated that the technical breakthrough needed could not be made in a timely manner. Under normal conditions, both of these project managers should have received medals for bravery in standing up and recommending that their project be canceled. This certainly appeared as a recommendation in the best interest of the company.

But both executives were not willing to give up that easily. Canceling both projects would be humiliating for the two executives that were sponsoring these projects. Instead, both executives stated that the project was to continue on to the next gate review meeting, at which time a decision would be made for possible cancellation of both projects.

At the second gate review meeting, both project managers once again recommended that their projects be canceled. And as before, both executives asserted that the project should continue to the next gate review meeting before a decision would be made.

As luck would have it, the necessary technical breakthrough was finally made, but six months late. That meant that the window of opportunity to sell the products and recover the R&D costs would be six months rather than one year. Unfortunately, the marketplace knew that these products might be obsolete in six months and no sales occurred of either product.

Marketing informed both executives that had they been informed about these two projects, they would have told the executives that the competition was also working on technical breakthroughs that were more advanced than these two projects were attempting. Both executives had to find a way to save face and avoid the humiliation of having to admit that they squandered a few million dollars on two useless R&D projects. This could very well impact their year-end bonuses.

Discussion Questions

1. What type of innovation was used?
2. What innovation mistakes were made?
3. Is it customary for companies to allow executives to have pet or secret innovation projects going on that never follow the normal project approval process?
4. Who got promoted and who got fired? In other words, how did the executives save face?

CASE STUDY: THE RISE, FALL, AND RESURRECTION OF IRIDIUM: WHEN AN INNOVATION BUSINESS MODEL FAILS

The Iridium Project was designed to create a worldwide wireless handheld mobile phone system with the ability to communicate anywhere in the world at any time. Executives at Motorola regarded the project as the eighth wonder of the world. But more than a decade later and after investing billions of dollars, Iridium had solved a problem that very few customers needed solved. What went wrong? How did the Iridium Project transform from a leading-edge technical marvel to a multibillion-dollar blunder? Could the potential catastrophe have been prevented?

> What it looks like now is a multibillion-dollar science project. There are fundamental problems: The handset is big, the service is expensive, and the customers haven't really been identified.
>
> — Chris Chaney, Analyst, A.G. Edwards, 1999

> There was never a business case for Iridium. There was never market demand. The decision to build Iridium wasn't a rational business decision. It was more of a religious decision. The remarkable thing is that this happened at a big corporation, and that there was not a rational decision-making process in place to pull the plug. Technology for technology's sake may not be a good business case (Paterik 2005).
>
> — Herschel Shosteck, Telecommunication Consultant

> Iridium is likely to be some of the most expensive space debris ever (Hiltzik 2000).
>
> —William Kidd, Analyst, C.E. Unterberg, Towbin

In 1985, Bary Bertiger, chief engineer in Motorola's strategic electronics division, and his wife, Karen, were on a vacation in the Bahamas. Karen tried unsuccessfully to make a cellular telephone call back to her home near the Motorola facility in Chandler, Arizona, to close a real estate transaction. Unsuccessful, she asked her husband why it would not be possible to create a telephone system that would work anywhere in the world, even in remote locations.

At this time, cell technology was in its infancy, but was expected to grow at an astounding rate. AT&T projected as many as 40 million subscribers by 2000 (Bird 1985). Cell technology was based on tower-to-tower transmission, as shown in Figure 13-1. Each tower or "gateway" ground station reached a limited geographic area or cell and had to be within the satellite's field of view. Cell phone users likewise had to be near a gateway that would be uplink the transmission to a satellite. The satellite would then downlink the signal to another gateway that would connect the transmission to a ground telephone system. This type of communication is often referred to as bent pipe architecture. Physical barriers between the senders/receivers and the gateways, such as mountains, tunnels, and oceans, created interference problems and therefore limited service to high-density communities. Simply stated, cell phones couldn't leave home. And, if they did, there would be additional "roaming" charges. To make matters worse, every country had its own standards and some cell phones were inoperable when traveling in other countries.

Communications satellites, in use since the 1960s, were typically geo-stationary satellites that orbited at altitudes of more than 22,300 miles. At this altitude, three geosynchronous satellites and just a few gateways could cover most of the Earth. But satellites at this altitude meant large phones and annoying quarter-second voice delays. Comsat's Planet 1 phone, for example, weighed in at a computer-case-sized 4.5 pounds. Geosynchronous satellites require signals with a great deal of power. Small mobile phones, with a one-watt signal, could not work with satellites positioned at this altitude. Increasing the power output of the mobile phones would damage human tissue. The alternative was therefore to move the satellites closer to Earth, such that less power would be needed. This would require significantly more satellites the closer we get to Earth, and additional gateways. Geosynchronous satellites, which are 100 times further away from Earth than low Earth-orbiting (LEO) satellites, could require almost 10,000 times as much power as LEOs, if everything else were the same.

When Bary Bertiger returned to Motorola, he teamed up with Dr. Raymond Leopold and Kenneth Peterson to see if such a worldwide system could be developed while overcoming all of the limitations of existing cell technology. There was also the problem that LEO satellites would be orbiting the Earth rapidly and going through damaging temperature variations—from the heat of the sun to the cold shadow of Earth (Gerding 1996). The LEO satellites would most likely need to be replaced every five years. Numerous alternative terrestrial designs were discussed and abandoned. In 1987, research began on a constellation of low Earth-orbiting (LEO) satellites moving in polar orbits that could communicate directly with telephone systems on the ground and with one another.

Iridium's innovation was to use a large constellation of low-orbiting satellites approximately 400–450 miles in altitude. Because Iridium's satellites were closer to Earth, the phones could be much smaller in size and the voice delay imperceptible. But there were still major technical design problems. With the existing design, a large number of gateways would be required, thus substantially increasing the cost of the system. As they left work one day in 1988, Dr. Leopold proposed a critical design element. The entire system would be inverted whereby the transmission would go from satellite to satellite until the transmission reached the satellite directly above the person who would be receiving the message. With this approach, only one gateway Earth station would be required to connect mobile-to-landline calls to existing land-based telephone systems. This was considered to be the sought-after solution and was immediately written in outline format on a whiteboard in a security guard's office. Thus came forth the idea behind a worldwide wireless handheld mobile phone with the ability to communicate anywhere and anytime.

Naming the Project "Iridium"

Motorola cellular telephone system engineer, Jim Williams, from the Motorola facility near Chicago, suggested the name, Iridium. The proposed 77-satellite constellation reminded him of the electrons that encircle the nucleus in the classical Bohr model of the atom. When he consulted the periodic table of the elements to discover which atom had 77 electrons, he found Iridium—a creative name that had a nice ring. Fortunately, the system had not yet been scaled back to 66 satellites, or else he might have suggested the name Dysprosium.

Obtaining Executive Support

Initially, Bertiger's colleagues and superiors at Motorola had rejected the Iridium concept because of its cost. Originally, the Iridium concept was considered perfect for the US government. Unfortunately, the era of lucrative government-funded projects was coming to an end and it was unlikely that the government would fund a project of this magnitude. However, the idea behind the Iridium concept intrigued Durrell Hillis, the senior vice president and general manager of Motorola's Space and Technology Group. Hillis believed that Iridium was workable if it could be developed as a commercial system. Hillis instructed Bertiger and his team to continue working on the Iridium concept but to keep it quiet (Bennahum 1998):

"I created a bootleg project with secrecy so no one in the company would know about it," Hillis recalls. He was worried that if word leaked out, the ferociously competitive business units at Motorola, all of which had to fight for R&D funds, would smother the project with nay-saying. (p. 194)

After 14 months of rewrites on the commercialized business plan, Hillis and the Iridium team leaders presented the idea to Robert Galvin, Motorola's chairman at the time, who gave approval to go ahead with the project. Robert Galvin, and later his successor and son Christopher Galvin, viewed Iridium as a potential symbol of Motorola's technological prowess and believed that this would become the eighth wonder in the world. In one of the initial meetings, Robert Galvin turned to John Mitchell, Motorola's president and chief operating officer, and said, "If you don't write out a check for this John, I will, out of my own pocket" (Hardy 1996). To the engineers at Motorola, the challenge of launching Iridium's constellation provided considerable motivation. They continued developing the project that resulted in initial service in November 1998 at a total cost of over $5 billion.

Launching the Venture

On June 26, 1990, Hillis and his team formally announced the launch of the Iridium Project to the general public. The response was not very pleasing to Motorola, with skepticism over the fact that this would be a new technology, the target markets were too small, the revenue model was questionable, obtaining licenses to operate in 170 countries could be a problem, and the cost of a phone call might be overpriced. Local phone companies that Motorola assumed would buy into the project viewed Iridium as a potential competitor, since the Iridium system bypassed traditional landlines. In many countries, Postal Telephone and Telegraph (PTT) operators are state owned and a major source of revenue because of the high profit margins. Another issue was that the Iridium Project was announced before permission was granted by the Federal Communications Commission (FCC) to operate at the desired frequencies.

Both Mitchell and Galvin made it clear that Motorola would not go it alone and would absorb the initial financial risk for a hefty price tag of about $3.5 billion. Funds would need to be obtained from public markets and private investors. In order to minimize Motorola's exposure to financial risk, Iridium would need to be set up as a project-financed company. Project financing involves the establishment of a legally independent project company where the providers of funds are repaid out of cash flow and earnings, and where the assets of the unit (and only the unit) are used as collateral for the loans. Debt repayment would come from the project company only rather than from any other entity. A risk with project financing is that the capital assets may have a limited life. The potential limited life constraint often makes it difficult to get lenders to agree to long-term financial arrangements.

Another critical issue with project financing, especially for high-technology projects, is that the projects are generally long term. It would be nearly eight years before service would begin, and in terms of technology, eight years is an eternity. The Iridium Project was certainly a "bet on the future." And if the project were to fail, the company could be worth nothing after liquidation.

In 1991, Motorola established Iridium Limited Liability Corporation (Iridium LLC) as a separate company. In December 1991, Iridium promoted Leo Mondale to vice president of Iridium International. Financing the project was still a critical issue. Mondale decided that, instead of having just one gateway, there should be as many as 12 regional gateways that plugged into local, ground-based telephone lines. This would make Iridium a truly global project rather than appear as an American-based project designed to seize market share from state-run telephone companies. This would also make it easier to get regulatory approval to operate in 170 countries. Investors would pay $40 million for the right to own their own regional gateway. As stated by Flower (1993):

The motive of the investors is clear: They are taking a chance on owning a slice of a de-facto world monopoly. Each of them will not only have a piece of the company, they will own the Iridium gateways and act as the local distributors in their respective home markets. For them it's a game worth playing.

There were political ramifications with selling regional gateways. What if in the future the US government forbids shipment of replacement parts to certain gateways? What if sanctions are imposed? What if Iridium were to become a political tool during international diplomacy because of the number of jobs it creates?

In addition to financial incentives, gateway owners were granted seats on the board of directors. As described by David Bennahum (1998), reporter for *Wired*:

> Four times a year, 28 Iridium board members from 17 countries gather to coordinate overall business decisions. They met around the world, shuttling between Moscow, London, Kyoto, Rio de Janeiro, and Rome, surrounded by an entourage of assistants and translators. Resembling a United Nations in miniature, board meetings were conducted with simultaneous translation in Russian, Japanese, Chinese, and English. (p. 136)

The partner with the largest equity share was Motorola. For its contribution of $400 million, Motorola originally received an equity stake of 25 percent, and 6 of 28 seats on Iridium's board. Additionally, Motorola made loan guarantees to Iridium of $750 million, with Iridium holding an option for an additional $350 million loan.

For its part, Iridium agreed to $6.6 billion in long-term contracts with Motorola that included a $3.4 billion firm-fixed-price contract for satellite design and launch, and $2.9 billion for operations and maintenance. Iridium also exposed Motorola to developing satellite technology that would provide the latter with significant expertise in building satellite communications systems, as well as vast intellectual property.

The Iridium System

The Iridium system is a satellite-based, wireless personal communications network providing a robust suite of voice features to virtually any destination anywhere on Earth.

The Iridium system comprises three principal components: the satellite network, the ground network, and the Iridium subscriber products, including phones and pagers. The design of the Iridium network allows voice and data to be routed virtually anywhere in the world. Voice and data calls are relayed from one satellite to another until they reach the satellite above the Iridium Subscriber Unit (handset) and the signal is relayed back to Earth.

The Terrestrial and Space-Based Network

The Iridium constellation consists of 66 operational satellites and 11 spares orbiting in a constellation of six polar planes. Each plane has 11 mission satellites performing as nodes in the telephony network. The remaining 11 satellites orbit as spares ready to replace any unserviceable satellite. This constellation ensures that every region on the globe is covered by at least one satellite at all times.

The satellites are in a near-polar orbit at an altitude of 485 miles (780 km). They circle the Earth once every 100 minutes traveling at a rate of 16,832 miles per hour. The satellite weight is 1,500 pounds. Each satellite is approximately 40 feet in length and 12 feet in width. In addition, each satellite has 48 spot beams, 30 miles in diameter per beam.

Each satellite is cross-linked to four other satellites; two satellites in the same orbital plane and two in an adjacent plane. The ground network is composed of the System Control Segment and telephony gateways used to connect into the terrestrial telephone system. The System Control Segment is the central management component for the Iridium system. It provides global operational support and control services for the satellite constellation, delivers satellite-tracking data to the gateways, and performs the termination control function of messaging services. The System Control Segment consists of three main components: four Telemetry Tracking and Control sites, the Operational Support Network, and the Satellite Network Operation Center. The primary linkage between the System Control Segment, the satellites, and the gateways is via K-Band feeder links and cross-links throughout the satellite constellation.

Gateways are the terrestrial infrastructure that provides telephony services, messaging, and support to the network operations. The key features of gateways are their support and management of mobile subscribers and the interconnection of the Iridium network to the terrestrial phone system. Gateways also provide network management functions for their own network elements and links.

Project Initiation: Developing the Business Case

For the Iridium Project to be a business success rather than just a technical success there had to exist an established customer base. Independent studies conducted by A.T. Kearney, Booz, Allen & Hamilton, and Gallup indicated that 34 million people had a demonstrated need for mobile satellite services, with that number expected to grow to 42 million by 2002. Of these 42 million, Iridium anticipated 4.2 million to be satellite-only subscribers, 15.5 million satellite and world terrestrial roaming subscribers, and 22.3 million terrestrial roaming-only subscribers.

A universal necessity in conducting business is ensuring that you are never out of touch. Iridium would provide this unique solution to business with the essential communications tool. This proposition of one phone, one number with the capability to be accessed anywhere, anytime was a message that target markets—the global traveler, the mining, rural, maritime industries, government, disaster relief, and community aid groups—would readily embrace.

Also, at the same time of Iridium's conception, there appeared to be another potentially lucrative opportunity in the telecommunications marketplace. When users of mobile or cellular phones crossed international borders, they soon discovered that there existed a lack of common standards thus making some phones inoperable. Motorola viewed this as an opportunity to create a worldwide standard allowing phones to be used anywhere in the world.

The expected breakeven market for Iridium was estimated between 400,000 and 600,000 customers globally, assuming a reasonable usage rate per customer per month. With a launch date for Iridium service established for 1998, Iridium hoped to recover all its investment within one year. By 2002, Iridium anticipated a customer base of five million users. The initial Iridium target market had been the vertical market, those of the industry, government, and world agencies that have defended needs and far-reaching communication requirements. Both industrial and public sector customers also had needs. Often isolated in remote locations outside of cellular coverage, industrial users were expected to use handheld Iridium satellite services to complement or replace their existing radio or satellite communications terminals. The vertical markets for Iridium would include:

● Aviation
● Construction

- Disaster relief/emergency
- Forestry
- Government
- Leisure travel
- Maritime
- Media and entertainment
- Military
- Mining
- Oil and gas
- Utilities

Using their own marketing resources, Iridium appeared to have identified an attractive market segment after having screened over 200,000 people, interviewed 23,000 people from 42 countries, and surveyed over 3,000 corporations.

Iridium would also need regional strategic partners, not only for investment purposes and to share the risks, but also to provide services throughout their territories. The strategic regional partners or gateway operating companies would have exclusive rights to their territories and were obligated to market and sell Iridium services. The gateways would also be responsible for end-user sales, activation, and for deactivation of Iridium services, account maintenance, and billing.

Iridium would need each country to grant full licenses for access to the Iridium system. Iridium would need to identify the "priority" countries that account for the majority of the business plan.

Because of the number of countries involved in the Iridium network, Iridium would need to establish global customer care centers for support services in all languages. No matter where an Iridium user was located, he or she would have access to a customer service representative in their native language. The customer care centers would be strategically located to offer 24-hours-a-day, 7-days-a-week, and 365-days-a-year support.

The "Hidden" Business Case

The decision by Motorola to invest heavily into the Iridium Project may have been driven by a secondary or hidden business case. Over the years, Motorola achieved a reputation of being a first-mover. With the Iridium Project, Motorola was poised to capture first-mover advantage in providing global telephone service via low-Earth-orbiting satellites. In addition, even if the Iridium Project never resulted in providing service, Motorola would still have amassed valuable intellectual property that would make Motorola possibly the major player for years to come in satellite communications. There may have also been the desire of Robert and Christopher Galvin to have their names etched in history as the pioneers in satellite communication.

Risk Management

Good business cases identify the risks that the project must consider. For simplicity's sake, the initial risks associated with the Iridium Project could be classified as follows.

Technology Risks

Although Motorola had some technology available for the Iridium Project, there was still the need to develop additional technology, specifically satellite communications technology. The development process was expected to take years and would eventually result in numerous patents.

Mark Gercenstein, Iridium's vice president of operations, explains the system's technological complexity (Grams and Zerbib 1998, 24):

> More than 26 completely impossible things had to happen first, and in the right sequence (before we could begin operations)—like getting capital, access to the marketplace, global spectrum, the same frequency band in every country of operations.

While there was still some risk in the development of new technology, Motorola had the reputation of being a high-tech, can-do company. The engineers at Motorola believed that they could bring forth miracles in technology. Motorola also had a reputation for being a first-mover (i.e., first-to-market) with new ideas and products, and there was no reason to believe that this would not happen on the Iridium Project. There was no competition for Iridium at its inception.

Because the project schedule was more than a decade in duration, there was the risk of technology obsolescence. This required that certain assumptions be made concerning technology a decade downstream. Developing a new product is relatively easy if the environment is stable. But in a high-technology environment that is both turbulent and dynamic, it is extremely difficult to determine how customers will perceive and evaluate the product 10 years later.

Development Risks

The satellite communication technology, once developed, had to be manufactured, tested, and installed in the satellites and ground equipment. Even though the technology existed or would exist, there were still the transitional or development risks from engineering to manufacturing to implementation, which would bring with it additional problems that were not contemplated or foreseen.

Financial Risks

The cost of the Iridium Project would most certainly be measured in the billions of dollars. This would include the costs for technology development and implementation, the manufacture and launch of satellites, the construction of ground support facilities, marketing, and supervision. Raising money from Wall Street's credit and equity markets was years away. Investors were unlikely to put up the necessary hundreds of millions of dollars on merely an idea or a vision. The technology needed to be developed, and possibly accompanied by the launch of a few satellites, before the credit and equity markets would come on board.

Private investors were a possibility, but the greatest source of initial funding would have to come from the members of the Iridium consortium. While sharing the financial risks among the membership seemed appropriate, there was no question that bank loans and lines-of-credit would be necessary. Since the Iridium Project was basically an idea, the banks would require some form of collateral or guarantee for the loans. Motorola, being the largest stakeholder (and also with the "deepest pockets") would need to guarantee the initial loans.

Marketing Risks

The marketing risks were certainly the greatest risks facing the Iridium membership. Once again, the risks were shared among its membership where each member was expected to sign up customers in their geographic area.

Each consortium member has to aggressively sign up customers for a product that didn't exist yet, no prototypes existed to be shown to the customers, limitations on the equipment were unknown as yet, and significant changes in technology could occur between the time the customer signed up and the time the system was ready for use. Companies that see the need for Iridium today may not see the same need 10 years later.

Motivating the consortium partners to begin marketing immediately would be extremely difficult since marketing material was nonexistent. There was also the very real fear that the consortium membership would be motivated more so by the technology rather than the necessary size of the customer base required.

The risks were interrelated. The financial risks were highly dependent on the marketing risks. If a sufficient customer base could not be signed up, there could be significant difficulty in raising capital.

The Collective Belief

Although the literature doesn't clearly identify it, there was most likely a collective belief among the workers assigned to the Iridium Project. The collective belief is a fervent, and perhaps blind, desire to achieve that can permeate the entire team, the project sponsor, and even the most senior levels of management. The collective belief can make a rational organization act in an irrational manner.

When a collective belief exists, people are selected based on their support for the collective belief. Nonbelievers are pressured into supporting the collective belief and team members are not allowed to challenge the results. As the collective belief grows, both advocates and nonbelievers are trampled. The pressure of the collective belief can outweigh the reality of the results.

The larger the project and the greater the financial risk to the firm, the higher up the collective belief resides. On the Iridium Project, the collective belief originated with Galvin, Motorola's CEO. Therefore, who could possibly function as the person willing to cancel the Iridium Project? Since it most likely should be someone higher up than Galvin, oversight should have been done by someone on the board of directors or even the entire Iridium board of directors. Unfortunately, the entire Iridium board of directors was also part of the collective belief and shirked their responsibility for oversight on the Iridium Project. In the end, Iridium had nobody willing to pull the plug.

Large projects incur large cost overruns and schedule slippages. Making the decision to cancel such a project, once it has started, is very difficult, according to David Davis (1985, 100–101):

> The difficulty of abandoning a project after several million dollars have been committed to it tends to prevent objective review and recosting. For this reason, ideally an independent management team—one not involved in the project's development—should do the recosting and, if possible, the entire review. ... If the numbers do not holdup in the review and recosting, the company should abandon the project. The number of bad projects that make it to the operational stage serves as proof that their supporters often balk at this decision.
>
> ...Senior managers need to create an environment that rewards honesty and courage and provides for more decision making on the part of project managers. Companies must have an atmosphere that encourages projects to succeed, but executives must allow them to fail.

The longer the project, the greater the necessity for the exit champions and project sponsors to make sure that the business plan has "exit ramps" such that the project can be terminated before massive resources are committed and consumed. Unfortunately, when a collective belief exists, exit ramps are purposefully omitted from the project and business plans.

Iridium's Infancy Years

By 1992, the Iridium Project attracted such stalwart companies as General Electric, Lockheed, and Raytheon. Some companies wanted to be involved to be part of the satellite technology revolution, while others were afraid of falling behind the technology curve. In any event, Iridium was lining up strategic partners, but slowly.

The Iridium Plan, submitted to the Federal Communications Commission in August 1992, called for a constellation of 66 satellites, expected to be in operation by 1998, and more powerful than originally proposed, thus keeping the project's cost at the previously estimated $3.37 billion. But the Iridium Project, while based on lofty forecasts of available customers, was now attracting other companies competing for FCC approval on similar satellite systems, including Loral Corp., TRW Inc., and Hughes Aircraft Co., a unit of General Motors Corp. There were at least nine companies competing for the potential billions of dollars in untapped revenue possible from satellite communications.

Even with the increased competition, Motorola was signing up partners. Motorola had set an internal deadline of December 15, 1992, to find the necessary funding for Iridium. Signed letters of intent were received from the Brazilian government and United Communications Co., of Bangkok, Thailand, to buy 5 percent stakes in the project, each now valued at about $80 million. The terms of the agreement implied that the Iridium consortium would finance the project with roughly 50 percent equity and 50 percent debt.

When the December 15 deadline arrived, Motorola was relatively silent on the signing of funding partners, fueling speculation that it was having trouble. Motorola did admit that the process was time-consuming because some investors required government approval before proceeding. Motorola was expected to announce at some point, perhaps in the first half of 1993, whether it was ready to proceed with the next step, namely receiving enough cash from its investors, securing loans, and ordering satellite and group equipment.

As the competition increased, so did the optimism about the potential size of the customer base:

"We're talking about a business generating billions of dollars in revenue," says John F. Mitchell, Vice Chairman at Motorola. "Do a simple income extrapolation," adds Edward J. Nowacki, a general manager at TRW's Space & Electronics Group, Redondo Beach, Calif., which plans a $1.3 billion, 12-satellite system called Odyssey. "You conclude that even a tiny fraction of the people around the world who can afford our services will make them successful." Mr. Mitchell says that if just 1 percent to 1.5 percent of the expected 100 million cellular users in the year 2000 become regular users at $3 a minute, Iridium will breakeven. How does he know this? "Marketing studies," which he won't share. TRW's Mr. Nowacki says Odyssey will blanket the Earth with two-way voice communication service priced at "only a slight premium" to cellular. "With two million subscribers we can get a substantial return on our investment," he says. "Loral Qualcomm Satellite Services, Inc. aims to be the 'friendly' satellite by letting phone-company partners use and run its system's ground stations", says Executive Vice President Anthony Navarra. "By the year 2000 there will be 15 million unserved cellular customers in the world," he says. (Keller 1993, B1)

But while Motorola and other competitors were trying to justify their investment with "inflated market projections" and a desire from the public for faster and clearer reception, financial market analysts were not so benevolent. First, market analysts questioned the size of the customer base that would be willing to pay $3,000 or more for a satellite phone in addition to $3–$7 per minute for a call. Second, the system required a line-of-sight transmission, which meant that the system would not work in buildings or in cars. If a businessman were attending a meeting in Bangkok and needed to call his company, he must exit the building, raise the antenna on his $3,000 handset, point the antenna toward the heavens, and then make the call. Third, the low-flying satellites would eventually crash into the Earth's atmosphere every 5–7 years because of atmospheric drag and would need to be replaced. That would most likely result in high capital costs. And fourth, some industry analysts believed that the start-up costs would be closer to $6 billion to $10 billion rather than the $3.37 billion estimated by Iridium. In addition, the land-based cellular phone business was expanding in more countries, thus creating another competitive threat for Iridium.

The original business case needed to be reevaluated periodically. But with strong collective beliefs and no exit champions, the fear of a missed opportunity, irrespective of the cost, took center stage.

Reasonably sure that 18 out of 21 investors were on board, Motorola hoped to start launching test satellites in 1996 and begin commercial service by 1998. But critics argued that Iridium might be obsolete by the time it actually starts working.

Eventually, Iridium was able to attract financial support from 19 strategic partners:

- AIG Affiliated Companies
- China Great Wall Industry Corporation (CGWIC)
- Iridium Africa Corporation (based in Cape Town)
- Iridium Canada, Inc.
- Iridium India Telecom Private Ltd. (ITIL)
- Iridium Italia S.p.A.
- Iridium Middle East Corporation
- Iridium SudAmerica Corporation
- Khrunichev State Research and Production Space Center
- Korea Mobile TELECOM
- Lockheed Martin
- Motorola
- Nippon Iridium Corporation
- Pacific Electric Wire & Cable Co. Ltd. (PEWC)
- Raytheon
- STET
- Sprint
- Thai Satellite Telecommunications Co. Ltd.
- Verbacom

Seventeen of the strategic partners also participated in gateway operations with the creation of operating companies.

As previously noted, the Iridium board of directors consisted of 28 telecommunications executives. All but one board member was a member of the consortium as well. This made it very difficult for the board to fulfill its oversight obligation effectively given the members' vested/financial interest in the Iridium Project.

In August 1993, Lockheed announced that it would receive $700 million in revenue for satellite construction. Lockheed would build the satellite structure, solar panels, attitude, and propulsion systems, along with other parts and engineering support. Motorola and Raytheon Corp. would build the satellite's communications gear and antenna.

In April 1994, McDonnell Douglas Corp. received from Iridium a $400 million contract to launch 40 satellites for Iridium. Other contracts for launch-services would be awarded to Russia's Khrunichev Space Center and China's Great Wall Industry Corporation, both members of the consortium. The lower-cost contracts with Russia and China were putting extraordinary pressure on US providers to lower their costs.

At the same time, one of Iridium's competitors, the Globalstar system, which was a 48-satellite mobile telephone system led by Loral Corporation, announced that it intended to charge 65 cents per minute in the areas it served. Iridium's critics were arguing that Iridium would be too pricey to attract a high volume of callers (Cole 1994, A4).

Debt Financing

In September 1994, Iridium said that it had completed its equity financing by raising an additional $733.5 million. This brought the total capital committed to Iridium through equity financing to $1.57 billion. The completion of equity financing permitted Iridium to enter into debt financing to build the global wireless satellite network.

In September 1995, Iridium announced that it would be issuing $300 million 10-year senior subordinated discounted notes rated Caa by Moody's and CCC+ by Standard & Poor's, via the investment banker Goldman Sachs Inc. The bonds were considered a high-risk, high-yield "junk" bonds after investors concluded that the rewards weren't worth the risk.

The rating agencies cited the reasons for the low rating to be yet unproven sophisticated technology and the fact that a significant portion of the system's hardware would be located in space. But there were other serious concerns:

- The ultimate cost of the Iridium Project would be much higher than projected, and it was unlikely that Iridium would recover that cost.
- Iridium would be hemorrhaging cash for several more years before service would begin.
- The optimistic number of potential customers for satellite phones may not choose the Iridium system.
- The number of competitors had increased since the Iridium concept was first developed.
- If Iridium defaulted on its debt, the investors could lay claim to Iridium's assets. But what would investors do with more than 66 satellites in space, waiting to disintegrate on reentering the atmosphere?

Iridium was set up as "project financing" in which case, if a default occurred, only the assets of Iridium could be attached. With project financing, the consortium's investors would be held harmless for any debt incurred from the stock and bond markets and could simply walk away from Iridium. These risks associated with project financing were well understood by those who invested in the equity and credit markets.

Goldman Sachs & Co., the lead underwriter for the securities offering, determined that for the bond issue to be completed successfully, there would need to exist a completion guarantee from investors with deep pockets, such as Motorola. Goldman Sachs cited a recent $400 million offering by one of Iridium's competitors, Globalstar, which had a guarantee from the managing general partner, Loral Corp. (Hardy 1995, A5).

Because of the concern by investors, Iridium withdrew its planned $300 million debt offering. Also, Globalstar, even with its loan guarantee, eventually withdrew its $400 million offering. Investors wanted both an equity position in Iridium and a 20 percent return. Additionally, Iridium would need to go back to its original 17-member consortium and arrange for internal financing.

In February 1996, Iridium had raised an additional $315 million from the 17-member consortium and private investors. In August 1996, Iridium had secured a $750 million credit line with 62 banks co-arranged by Chase Securities Inc., a unit of Chase Manhattan Corp. and the investment banking division of Barclays Bank PLC. The credit line was oversubscribed by more than double its original goal because the line of credit was backed by a financial guarantee by Motorola and its AAA credit rating. Because of the guarantee by Motorola, the lending rate was slightly more than the 5.5 percent baseline international commercial lending rate and significantly lower than the rate in the $300 million bond offering that was eventually recalled.

Despite this initial success, Iridium still faced financial hurdles. By the end of 1996, Iridium planned on raising more than $2.65 billion from investors. It was estimated that more than 300 banks around the globe would be involved, and that this would be the largest private debt placement ever. Iridium believed that this debt placement campaign might not be that difficult since the launch date for Iridium services was getting closer.

The M-Star Project

In October 1996, Motorola announced that it was working on a new project, dubbed M-Star, which would be a $6.1 billion network of 72 low-orbit satellites capable of worldwide voice, video, and high-speed data links targeted at the international community. The project was separate from the Iridium venture and was expected to take four years to complete after FCC approval. According to Bary Bertiger, now corporate vice president and general manager of Motorola's satellite communications group, "Unlike Iridium, Motorola has no plans to detach M-Star as a separate entity. We won't fund it ourselves, but we will have fewer partners than in Iridium" (Hardy 1996, B4).

The M-Star Project raised some eyebrows in the investment community. Iridium employed 2,000 people, but M-Star had only 80. The Iridium Project generated almost 1,100 patents for Motorola, and that intellectual property would most likely be transferred to M-Star. Also, Motorola had three contracts with Iridium for construction and operation of the global communication system providing for approximately $6.5 billion in payments to Motorola over a 10-year period that began in 1993. Was M-Star being developed at the expense of Iridium? Could M-Star replace Iridium? What would happen to the existing 17-member consortium at Iridium if Motorola were to withdraw its support in favor of its own internal competitive system?

A New CEO

In 1996, Iridium began forming a very strong top management team with the hiring of Dr. Edward Staiano as CEO and vice chairman. Prior to joining Iridium in 1996, Staiano had worked for Motorola for 23 years, during which time he developed a reputation for being hard-nosed and unforgiving. During his final 11 years with Motorola, Staiano led the company's General Systems Sector to record growth levels. In 1995, the division accounted for approximately 40 percent of Motorola's total sales of $27 billion. In leaving Motorola's payroll for Iridium's, Staiano gave up a $1.3 million per year contract with Motorola for a $500,000 base salary plus 750,000 Iridium stock options that vested over a five-year period. Staiano commented (Hardy 1996, B8):

I was spending 40 percent to 50 percent of my time [at Motorola] on Iridium anyway.... If I can make Iridium's dream come true, I'll make a significant amount of money.

Project Management at Motorola (and Iridium)

Motorola fully understood the necessity of good project management on an effort of this magnitude. Just the building, launching, and positioning of the satellites would require cooperative efforts of some 6,000 engineers located in the United States, Ireland, Italy, Canada, China, India, and Germany. The following were part of Motorola's project management practices on the Iridium Project:

- *Selection of partners.* Motorola had to find highly qualified partners that would be willing to be upfront with all problems and willing to work with teams to find resolutions to these problems as soon as they surfaced. Teamwork and open communications would be essential.
- *Existing versus new technology.* Motorola wanted to use as much existing technology as possible rather than completely "reinvent the wheel." This was critical when considering that the Iridium Project would require upward of 15 million lines of code. Motorola estimated that only about 2 million lines of code would need to be prepared from scratch. The rest would come from existing time-tested legacy software from existing projects.
- *Use of the Capability Maturity Model (CMM).* Each strategic partner was selected and evaluated against their knowledge of the CMM developed by the Software Engineering Institute (SEI) at Carnegie-Mellon University. In many cases, Motorola would offer a crash course in CMM for some strategic partners. In 1995, Motorola had reached level 3 of the 5 levels in CMM and had planned to reach level 4 by 1996.
- *The work breakdown structure (WBS).* The WBS was decomposed into major systems, then subsystems and then products.
- *Scheduling systems.* Primavera Project Planner was the prime tool used for planning, tracking progress, and quickly spotting scheduling bottlenecks. The level 1 schedule on Primavera was a summary schedule for executive-level briefings. Level 2 was a more detailed schedule. Level 3 schedules were for line managers. Level 4 schedules were for the product teams.
- *Tradeoffs.* Scope change control processes were established for tradeoffs on scope, cost, schedule, and risks. Considerable flexibility in product development was provided to the partners and contractors. There was a decentralization of decision making and contractors were empowered to make decisions. These meant that all other product teams that could be affected by a contractor's decision would be notified and provide feedback.

By 1996, 23 out of 47 major milestones were completed on or ahead of schedule and under budget. This was in contradiction to the 1994 Standish Group report that cited that less than 9 percent of large software projects come in on time and within budget.

Satellite Launches

At 11:28 a.m. on a Friday morning the second week of January 1997, a Delta 2 rocket carrying a global positioning system (GPS) exploded on launch, scattering debris above its Cape Canaveral launch pad. The launch, which was originally scheduled for the third quarter of 1996, would certainly have an impact on Iridium's schedule while an industry board composed of representatives from McDonnell-Douglas and the Air Force determined the cause of the explosion. Other launches had already been delayed for a variety of technical reasons.

In May 1997, after six failed tries, the first five Iridium satellites were launched. Iridium still believed that the target date for launch of service, September 1998, was still achievable but that all slack in the schedule had been eliminated due to the earlier failures.

By this time, Motorola had amassed tremendous knowledge on how to mass-produce satellites. As described by Bennahum (1998):

> The Iridium constellation was built on an assembly line, with all the attendant reduction in risk and cost that comes from doing something over and over until it is no longer an art but a process. At the peak of this undertaking, instead of taking 18 to 36 months to build one satellite, the production lines disgorged a finished bird every four and a half days, sealed it in a container, and placed it on the flatbed of an idling truck that drove it to California or Arizona, where a waiting Boeing 747 carried it to a launchpad in the mountains of Taiyuan, China, or on the steppes of Baikonur in Kazakhstan.

An Initial Public Offering (IPO)

Iridium was burning cash at the rate of $100 million per month. Iridium filed a preliminary document with the Security and Exchange Commission (SEC) for an initial public offering of 10 million shares to be offered at $19 to $21 a share. Because of the launch delays, the IPO was delayed.

In June 1997, after the first five satellites were placed in orbit, Iridium filed for an IPO of 12 million shares priced at $20 per share. This would cover about three months of operating expenses, including satellite purchases and launch costs. The majority of the money would go to Motorola.

Signing up Customers

The reality of the Iridium concept was now at hand. All that was left to do was to sign up 500,000–600,000 customers, as predicted, to use the service. Iridium set aside $180 million for a marketing campaign including advertising, public relations, and direct mail effort. Part of the advertising campaign included direct mail translated into 13 languages, ads on television and on airlines, airport booths, and Internet web pages.

How to market Iridium was a challenge. People would certainly hate the phone. According to John Windolph, executive director of marketing communications at Iridium, "It's huge! It will scare people. It is like a brick-size device with an antenna like a stout bread stick. If we had a campaign that featured our product, we'd lose." The decision was to focus on the fears of being out of touch. Thus the marketing campaign began. But Iridium still did not have a clear picture of who would subscribe to the system. An executive earning $700,000 would probably purchase the bulky phone, have his or her assistant carry the phone in their briefcase, be reimbursed by their company for the use of the phone, and pay $3 to $7 per minute for calls, also a business expense. But are there 600,000 executives worldwide that need the service?

There were several other critical questions that needed to be addressed. How do we hide or downplay the $3,400 purchase price of the handset and the usage cost of $7 per minute? How do we avoid discussions about competitors that are offering similar services at a lower cost? With operating licenses in about 180 countries, do we advertise in all of them? Do we take out ads in *Oil and Gas Daily*? Do we advertise in girlie magazines? Do we use full-page or double-page spreads?

Iridium had to rely heavily on its "gateway" partners for marketing and sales support. Iridium itself would not be able to reach the entire potential audience. Would the gateway partners provide the required marketing and sales support? Do the gateway partners know how to sell the Iridium system and the associated products?

The answer to these questions appeared quickly (Cauley 1999, A1):

> Over a matter of weeks, more than one million sales inquiries poured into Iridium's sales offices. They were forwarded to Iridium's partners—and many of them promptly disappeared, say several Iridium insiders. With no marketing channels and precious few sales people in place, most global partners were unable to follow up on the inquiries. A mountain of hot sales tips soon went cold.

Iridium's Rapid Ascent

On November 1, 1998, the Iridium system was officially launched. It was truly a remarkable feat that the 11-year project was finally launched, just a little more than a month late":

> After 11 years of hard work, we are proud to announce that we are open for business. Iridium will open up the world of business, commerce, disaster relief and humanitarian assistance with our first-of-its-kind global communications service… The potential use of Iridium products is boundless. Business people who travel the globe and want to stay in touch with home and office, industries that operate in remote areas—all will find Iridium to be the answer to their communications needs.[45]

On November 2, 1998, Iridium began providing service. With the Iridium system finally up and running, most financial analysts issued "buy" recommendations for Iridium stock with expected yearly revenues of $6 to $7 billion within five years. On January 25, 1999, Iridium CEO Ed Staiano participated in a news conference call to discuss the company's earnings for the fourth quarter of 1998:

> In the fourth quarter of 1998, Iridium made history as we became the first truly global mobile telephone company. Today, a single wireless network, the Iridium Network, covers the planet. And we have moved into 1999 with an aggressive strategy to put a large number of customers on our system, and quickly transform Iridium from a technological event to a revenue generator. We think the prospects for doing this are excellent. Our system is performing at a level beyond expectations.
>
> Financing is now in place through projected cash flow positives. Customer interest remains very high and a number of potentially large customers have now evaluated our service and have given it very high ratings. With all of this going for us, we are in position to sell the service and that is precisely where we are focusing the bulk of our efforts.[46]

Roy Grant, chief financial officer, also participated in the call:

> Last week Iridium raised approximately $250 million through a very successful 7.5 million-share public offering. This offering had three major benefits. It provided $250 million of cash to our balance sheet. It

---

45. Excerpts from the Iridium press release, November 1, 1998.
46. Excerpts from the Iridium conference call, January 25, 1999.

increased our public float to approximately 20 million shares. And it freed up restrictions placed on $300 million of the $350 million of Motorola guarantees. These restrictions were placed on that particular level of guarantees by our bankers in our $800 million secured credit facility.

With this $250 million, combined with the $350 million of additional guarantees from Motorola, this means we have approximately $600 million of funds in excess of what we need to break cash flow break-even. This provides a significant contingency for the company.[47]

December 1998

In order to make its products and services known to travelers, Iridium agreed to acquire Claircom Corporation from AT&T and Rogers Cantel Mobile Communications for about $65 million. Claircom provided in-flight telephone systems for United States planes as well as equipment for international carriers. The purchase of Claircom would be a marketing boost for Iridium.

The problems with large, long-term technology projects were now appearing in the literature. As described by Bennahum (1998):

> "This system does not let you do what a lot of wired people want to do," cautions Professor Heather Hudson, who runs the telecommunications program at the University of san Francisco and studies the business of wireless communications. "Nineteen-nineties technologies are changing so fast that it is hard to keep up. Iridium is designed from a 1980s perspective of a global cellular system. Since then, the Internet has grown and cellular telephony is much more pervasive. There are many more opportunities for roaming than were assumed in 1989. So there are fewer businesspeople who need to look for an alternative to a cell phone while they are on the road.

Additionally, toward the late 1990s, some industry observers felt that Motorola had additional incentive to ensure that Iridium succeeded, irrespective of the costs—namely, protecting its reputation. Between 1994 and 1997, Motorola had suffered slowing sales growth, a decline in net income, and declining margins. Moreover, the company had experienced several previous business mishaps, including a failure to anticipate the cellular industry's switch to digital cell phones, which played a major role in Motorola's more than 50 percent share-price decline in 1998.

Iridium's Rapid Descent

It took more than a decade for the Iridium Project to ascend and only a few months for descent. In the first week of March, almost five weeks after the January teleconference, Iridium's financial woes began to surface. Iridium had expected 200,000 subscribers by the end of 1998 and additional subscribers at a rate of 40,000 per month. Iridium's bond covenants stated a target of 27,000 subscribers by the end of March. Failure to meet such a small target could send investor confidence spiraling downward. Iridium had only 10,000 subscribers. The market that was out there 10 years ago was not the market that was there today. Also, 10 years ago there was little competition for Iridium.

Iridium cited the main cause of the shortfall in subscriptions as being shortages of phones, glitches in some of the technology, software problems and, most important, a lack of trained sales channels. Iridium

---

47. Ibid.

found out that it had to train a sales staff and that Iridium itself would have to sell the product, not its distributors. The investor community did not appear pleased with the sales problem that should have been addressed years ago, not four months into commercial service.

Iridium's advertising campaign was dubbed "Calling Planet Earth" and promised that you had the freedom to communicate anytime and anywhere. This was not exactly true, because the system could not work within buildings or even cars. Furthermore, Iridium underestimated the amount of time subscribers would require to examine and test the system before signing on. In some cases, this would be six months.

Many people blamed marketing and sales for Iridium's rapid descent (Surowieckipp 1999):

> True, Iridium committed so many marketing and sales mistakes that its experiences could form the basis of a textbook on how not to sell a product. Its phones started out costing $3,000, were the size of a brick, and didn't work as promised. They weren't available in stores when Iridium ran a $180 million advertising campaign. And Iridium's prices, which ranged from $3.00 to $7.50 a call, were out of this world.

Iridium's business plan was flawed. With service beginning on November 2, 1998, it was unlikely that 27,000 subscribers would be on board by March of 1999, given the time required to test the product. The original business plan required that the consortium market and sell the product prior to the onset of service. But selling the service from just a brochure was almost impossible. Subscribers want to touch the phone, use it, and test it prior to committing to a subscription.

Iridium announced that it was entering into negotiations with its lenders to alter the terms of an $800 million secured credit agreement due to the weaker-than-expected subscriber and revenue numbers. Covenants on the credit agreement are shown in Table 13-8:

The stock, which had traded as high as almost $73 per share, was now at approximately $20 per share. And, in yet another setback, the chief financial officer, Roy T. Grant, resigned.

April 1999

Iridium's CEO, Ed Staiano, resigned at the April 22 board meeting. Sources believed that Staiano resigned when the board nixed his plan requesting additional funds to develop Iridium's own marketing and distribution team rather than relying on its strategic partners. Sources also stated another issue in that Staiano had cut costs to the barebones at Iridium but could not get Motorola to reduce its lucrative $500 million service contract with Iridium. Some people believed that Staiano wanted to reduce the Motorola service contract by up to 50 percent.

John Richardson, the CEO of Iridium Africa Corp., was assigned as interim CEO. Richardson's expertise was in corporate restructuring. For the quarter ending March, Iridium said it had a net loss of

TABLE 13–8. COVENANTS ON THE CREDIT AGREEMENT

Date	Cumulative Cash Revenue ($ Millions)	Cumulative Accrued Revenue ($ Millions)	Number of Satellite Phone Subscribers	Number of System Subscribers[a]
March 31, 1999	$4	$ 30	27,000	52,000
June 30, 1999	50	150	88,000	213,000
Sept. 30, 1999	220	470	173,000	454,000

Source: Adapted from Iridium World Communications Ltd
[a]Total system subscribers include users of Iridium's phone, fax, and paging services.

$505.4 million, or $3.45 a share. The stock fell to $15.62 per share. Iridium managed to attract just 10,294 subscribers five months after commercial rollout.

One of Richardson's first tasks was to revamp Iridium's marketing strategy. Iridium was unsure as to what business they were in. According to Richardson (Hawn 1999, 60–62):

> The message about what this product was and where it was supposed to go changed from meeting to meeting.... One day, we'd talk about cellular applications, the next day it was a satellite product. When we launch in November, I'm not sure we had a clear idea of what we wanted to be.

May 1999

Iridium officially announced that it did not expect to meet its targets specified under the $800 million loan agreement. Lenders granted Iridium a two-month extension. The stock dropped to $10.44 per share, partly due to a comment by Motorola that it might withdraw from the ailing venture.

Wall Street began talking about the possibility of bankruptcy. But Iridium stated that it was revamping its business plan and by month's end hoped to have chartered a new course for its financing. Iridium also stated in a regulatory filing that it was uncertain whether it would have enough cash to complete the agreement to purchase Claircom Communications Group Inc., an in-flight telephone-service provider, for the promised $65 million in cash and debt.

Iridium had received extensions on debt payments because the lending community knew that it was no small feat transforming from a project plan to an operating business. Another reason why the banks and creditors were willing to grant extensions was because bankruptcy was not a viable alternative. The equity partners owned all of the Earth stations, all distribution, and all regulatory licenses. If the banks and creditors forced Iridium into bankruptcy, they could end up owning a satellite constellation that could not talk to the ground or gateways.

June 1999

Iridium received an additional 30-day extension beyond the two-month extension it had already received. Iridium was given until June 30 to make a $90 million bond payment. Iridium began laying off 15 percent of its 550-employee workforce, including two senior officers. The stock had now sunk to $6 per share and the bonds were selling at 19 cents on the dollar.

> We did all of the difficult stuff well, like building the network, and did all of the no-brainer stuff at the end poorly. (Hawn 1999, 60–62)
>
> **—John Richardson, CEO, Iridium**

> Iridium's major mistake was a premature launch for a product that wasn't ready. People became so obsessed with the technical grandeur of the project that they missed fatal marketing traps...Iridium's international structure has proven almost impossible to manage: the 28 members of the board speak multiple languages, turning meetings into mini-U.N. conferences complete with headsets translating the proceedings into five languages. (Cauley 1999, A1)
>
> **—John Richardson, CEO, Iridium**

We're a classic MBA case study in how not to introduce a product. First we created a marvelous technological achievement. Then we asked how to make money on it.

—John Richardson, CEO, Iridium

Iridium was doing everything possible to avoid bankruptcy. Time was what Iridium needed. Some industrial customers would take six to nine months to try out a new product, but would be reluctant to subscribe if it appeared that Iridium would be out of business in six months. In addition, Iridium's competitors were lowering their prices significantly, putting further pressure on Iridium. Richardson then began providing price reductions of up to 65 percent off of the original price for some of Iridium's products and services.

July 1999

The banks and investors agreed to give Iridium yet a third extension to August 11 to meet its financial covenants. Everyone seemed to understand that the restructuring effort was much broader than originally contemplated.

Motorola, Iridium's largest investor and general contractor, admitted that the project may have to be shut down and liquidated as part of bankruptcy proceedings unless a restructuring agreement could be reached. Motorola also stated that if bankruptcy occurred, Motorola would continue to maintain the satellite network, but for a designated time only.

Iridium had asked its consortium investors and contractors to come up with more money. But to many consortium members, it looked like they would be throwing good money after bad. Several partners made it clear that they would simply walk away from Iridium rather than providing additional funding. That could have a far-reaching effect on the service at some locations. Therefore, all partners had to be involved in the restructuring. Wall Street analysts expected Iridium to be allowed to repay its cash payments on its debt over several years or offer debt holders an equity position in Iridium. It was highly unlikely that Iridium's satellites orbiting the Earth would be auctioned off in bankruptcy court.

August 1999

On August 12, Iridium filed for bankruptcy protection. This was like a dagger to the heart for a company that a few years earlier had predicted financial breakeven in just the first year of operations. This was one of the 20 largest bankruptcy filings up to this time. The stock, which had been trading as little as $3 per share, was suspended from the NASDAQ on August 13, 1999. Iridium's phone calls had been reduced to around $1.40 to $3 per minute and the handsets were reduced to $1,500 per unit.

There was little hope for Iridium. Both the business plan and the technical plan were flawed. The business plan for Iridium seemed like it came out of the film *Field of Dreams* where an Iowa corn farmer was compelled to build a baseball field in the middle of a corn crop. A mysterious voice in his head said, "Build it and they will come." In the film, he did, and they came. While this made for a good plot for a Hollywood movie, it made a horrible business plan.

If you build Iridium, people may come. But what is more likely is, if you build something cheaper, people will come to that first.

—Herschel Shosteck, Telecommunication Consultant, 1992

The technical plan was designed to build the holy grail of telecommunications. Unfortunately, after spending billions, the need for the technology changed over time. The engineers that designed the system, many of whom had worked previously on military projects, lacked an understanding of the word "affordability" and the need for marketing a system to more than just one customer, namely the Department of Defense.

> Satellite systems are always far behind the technology curve. Iridium was completely lacking the ability to keep up with Internet time. (Paterik 2005, D5)
> — Bruce Egan, Senior Fellow at Columbia University's Institute for Tele-Information

September 1999

Leo Mondale resigned as Iridium's CFO. Analysts believed that Mondale's resignation was the result of a successful restructuring no longer being possible. According to one analyst, "If they (Iridium) were close (to a restructuring plan), they wouldn't be bringing in a whole new team."

The Iridium "Flu"

The bankruptcy of Iridium was having a flu-like effect on the entire industry. ICO Global Communications, one of Iridium's major competitors, also filed for bankruptcy protection just two weeks after the Iridium filing. ICO failed to raise $500 million it sought from public-rights offerings that had already been extended twice. Another competitor, the Globalstar Satellite Communications System, was still financially sound (Hardy 1999, 216 217).

> They [Iridium] set everybody's expectations way too high.
> — Anthony Navarro, Globalstar Chief Operating Officer

Searching for a White Knight

Iridium desperately needed a qualified bidder who would function as a white knight. It was up to the federal bankruptcy court to determine whether someone was a qualified bidder. A qualified bidder was required to submit a refundable cash deposit or letter of credit issued by a respected bank that would equal the greater of $10 million or 10 percent of the value of the amount bid to take control of Iridium.

According to bankruptcy court filing, Iridium was generating revenue of $1.5 million per month. On December 9, 1999, Motorola agreed to a $20 million cash infusion for Iridium. Iridium desperately needed a white knight quickly or it could run out of cash by February 15, 2000. With a monthly operating cost of $10 million, and a staggering cost of $300 million every few years for satellite replenishment, it was questionable if anyone could make a successful business from Iridium's assets because of asset specificity.

The cellular-phone entrepreneur Craig McCaw planned on a short-term cash infusion while he considered a much larger investment to rescue Iridium. He was also leading a group of investors who pledged $1.2 billion to rescue the ICO satellite system that filed for bankruptcy protection shortly after the Iridium filing (WSJ 2000, 1).

Several supposedly white knights came forth, but Craig McCaw's group was regarded as the only credible candidate. Although McCaw's proposed restructuring plan was not fully disclosed, it was expected that Motorola's involvement would be that of a minority stakeholder. Also, under the restructuring plan, Motorola would reduce its monthly fee for operating and maintaining the Iridium system from $45 million to $8.8 million (Thurm 2000a, 1).

The Definition of Failure (October 1999)

The Iridium network was an engineering marvel. Motorola's never-say-die attitude created technical miracles and overcame NASA-level technical problems. Iridium overcame global political issues, international regulatory snafus, and a range of other geopolitical issues on seven continents. The Iridium system was, in fact, what Motorola's Galvin called the eighth wonder of the world.

But did the bankruptcy indicate a failure for Motorola? Absolutely not! Motorola collected $3.65 billion in Iridium contracts. Assuming $750 million in profit from these contracts, Motorola's net loss on Iridium was about $1.25 billion. Simply stated, Motorola spent $1.25 billion for a project that would have cost them perhaps as much as $5 billion out of their own pocket had they wished to develop the technology themselves. Iridium provided Motorola with more than 1,000 patents in building satellite communication systems. Iridium allowed Motorola to amass a leadership position in the global satellite industry. Motorola was also signed up as the prime contractor to build the 288-satellite "Internet in the Sky," dubbed the Teledesic Project. Backers of the Teledesic Project, which had a price tag of $15 billion to transmit data, video, and voice, included Boeing, Microsoft's Chairman Bill Gates, and cellular magnate Craig McCaw. Iridium had enhanced Motorola's reputation for decades to come.

Motorola stated that it had no intention of providing additional funding to ailing Iridium, unless, of course, other consortium members followed suit. Several members of the consortium stated that they would not provide any additional investment and were considering liquidating their involvement in Iridium (Thurm 2000b, 1).

In March 2000, McCaw withdrew its offer to bail out Iridium even at a deep discount, asserting that his efforts would be spent on salvaging the ICO satellite system instead. This, in effect, signed Iridium's death warrant. One of the reasons for McCaw's reluctance to rescue Iridium may have been the discontent by some of the investors who would have been completely left out as part of the restructuring effort, thus losing perhaps their entire investment.

The Satellite Deorbiting Plan

With the withdrawal of McCaw's financing, Iridium notified the US Bankruptcy Court that Iridium had not been able to attract a qualified buyer by the deadline assigned by the court. Iridium would terminate its commercial service after 11:59 p.m. on March 17, 2000, and would begin the process of liquidating its assets.

Immediately following the Iridium announcement, Motorola issued the following press release:

> Motorola will maintain the Iridium satellite system for a limited period of time while the deorbiting plan is being finalized. During this period, we also will continue to work with the subscribers in remote locations to obtain alternative communications. However, the continuation of limited Iridium service during this time will depend on whether the individual gateway companies, which are separate operating companies, remain open. In order to support those customers who purchased Iridium service directly from Motorola, Customer Support Call Centers and a website that are available 24 hours a day, seven days a week have been established by Motorola. Included in the information for customers is a list of alternative satellite communications services.

The deorbiting plan would likely take two years to complete at a cost of $50 million to $70 million. This would include all 66 satellites and the other 22 satellites in space serving as spare or decommissioned failures. Iridium would most likely deorbit the satellites four at a time by firing their thrusters to drop them into the atmosphere, where they would burn up.

Iridium Is Rescued for $25 Million

In November 2000, a group of investors led by an airline executive won bankruptcy court approval to form Iridium Satellite Corporation and purchase all remaining assets of failed Iridium Corporation. The purchase was at a fire-sale price of $25 million, which was less than a penny on the dollar. As part of the proposed sale, Motorola would turn over responsibility for operating the system to Boeing. Although Motorola would retain a 2 percent stake in the new system, Motorola would have no further obligations to operate, maintain, or decommission the constellation.

Almost immediately after the announcement, Iridium Satellite was awarded a $72 million contract from the Defense Information Systems Agency, which is part of the Department of Defense (DoD) (Satellite Today 2000, 1):

> Iridium will not only add to our existing capability, it will provide a commercial alternative to our purely military systems. This may enable real civil/military dual use, keep us closer to leading edge technologically, and provide a real alternative for the future.
> — Dave Oliver, Principal Deputy Undersecretary of Defense for Acquisition

Iridium had been rescued from the brink of extinction. As part of the agreement, the newly formed company acquired all of the assets of the original Iridium and its subsidiaries. This included the satellite constellation, the terrestrial network, Iridium real estate, and the intellectual property originally developed by Iridium. Because of the new company's significantly reduced cost structure, it was able to develop a workable business model based on a targeted market for Iridium's products and services (Paterik 2005).

> Everyone thinks the Iridium satellites crashed and burned, but they're all still up there.
> — Weldon Knape, WCC Chief Executive Officer

April 2005

A new Iridium phone cost $1495 and was the size of a cordless home phone. Older, larger models started at $699, or customers could rent one for about $75 per week. Service cost $1 to $1.60 a minute (Paterik 2005).

February 2006

On February 6, 2006, Iridium satellite declared that 2005 was the best year ever. The company had 142,000 subscribers, which was a 24 percent increase from 2004, and the 2005 revenue was 55 percent greater than in 2004. According to Carmen Lloyd, Iridium's CEO, "Iridium is on an exceptionally strong financial foundation with a business model that is self-funding."[48]

---

48. Press release, Iridium, February 6, 2006.

For the year ending 2006, Iridium had $212 million in sales and $54 million in profit. Iridium had 180,000 subscribers and a forecasted growth rate of 14 percent to 20 percent per year. Iridium had changed its business model, focusing on sales and marketing first and hype second. This allowed the company to reach out to new customers and new markets (Jana 2007).

Shareholder Lawsuits

The benefit to Motorola, potentially at the expense of Iridium and its investors, did not go unnoticed. At least 20 investor groups filed suit against Motorola and Iridium, citing:

- Motorola milked Iridium and used the partners' money to finance its own foray into satellite communication technology.
- By using Iridium, Motorola ensured that its reputation would not be tarnished if the project failed.
- Most of the money raised through the IPOs went to Motorola for designing most of the satellite and ground-station hardware and software.
- Iridium used the proceeds of its $1.45 billion in bonds, with interest rates from 10.875 percent to 14 percent, mainly to pay Motorola for satellites.
- Defendants falsely reported achievable subscriber numbers and revenue figures.
- Defendants failed to disclose the seriousness of technical issues.
- Defendants failed to disclose delays in handset deliveries.
- Defendants violated covenants between itself and its lenders.
- Defendants delayed disclosure of information, provided misleading information, and artificially inflated Iridium's stock price.
- Defendants took advantage of the artificially inflated price to sell significant amounts of their own .holdings for millions of dollars in personal profit.

The Bankruptcy Court Ruling

On September 4, 2007, after almost 10 months, the Bankruptcy Court in Manhattan ruled in favor of Motorola and irritated the burned creditors who had hoped to get a $3.7 billion judgment against Motorola. The judge ruled that even though financial experts now know that Iridium was a hopeless one-way cash flow, flawed technology project, and doomed business model, and thus that the capital markets were "terribly wrong" about Iridium's hopes for huge profits, Iridium was "solvent" during the critical period when it successfully raised rather impressive amounts of debt and equity in the capital markets. Even when the bad news began to appear, Iridium's investors and underwriters still believed that Iridium had the potential to become a viable enterprise.

The day after the court ruling, newspapers reported that Iridium LLC, the now privately held company, was preparing to raise about $500 million in a private equity offering to be followed by an IPO within the next year or two.

Epilogue 2011

When Iridium went into bankruptcy, it was considered as a technical masterpiece but a business failure. While many people were willing to write off Iridium, it is alive and doing reasonably well. Following the court ruling in 2007, Iridium announced plans for the second-generation Iridium satellites called Iridium NEXT. Satellite launches for Iridium NEXT would begin in 2015 and be completed by 2017. The original Iridium satellites that were expected to have a life expectancy of 5–7 years after their launch in 1997–1998 were now expected to be fully operational until 2014 through 2020.

Iridium was able to receive new contracts from the US government and also attract new users. Iridium also created a consortium of investors who would provide financial support. On June 2, 2010, Iridium announced the award of a $2.9 billion contract to Thales Alenia Space for satellite procurement. At the same time, a $492 million contract was awarded to Space X for the launch of these satellites from Vandenberg Air Force Base in California.

In 2010, Iridium stock had a high of $11.13 and a low of $6.27. The market capitalization was $656 million and the earnings per share were $.09. But while Iridium was maintaining its growth, there were new risks that had to be considered:

- There are too many satellites in space, and there is a risk that an Iridium satellite will collide with another satellite. (An Iridium satellite did collide with a Russian satellite.) Some people say that this is a defined and acceptable risk.
- There is also the risk of swarms of whirling debris hitting the Iridium satellites.
- Additional spare satellites may be needed and perhaps not every plane will have a spare. Typically, moving satellites can take up to two weeks and consume a great deal of fuel, thus shortening the satellite's life expectancy.
- The original Iridium satellites were manufactured on an assembly line. In its peak during 1997–1998, Iridium produced a satellite every 4.3 days, whereas single satellite development was typically 21 days. Iridium was also able to keep construction costs at about $5 million per satellite. This process would have to be duplicated again or even improved on.
- Some people argue that Iridium's survival is based on the large number of contracts it receives from the US government. If the government reduces its support or even pulls out of Iridium, the financial risks may significantly increase.

Epilogue 2019

On October 29, 2018, Lion Air Flight JT 610 crashed shortly after takeoff from Jakarta, killing all 189 people on board (Tangel and Wall 2018). Less than six months later, on March 10, 2019, an Ethiopian Airlines jet crashed on takeoff, killing 157 aboard (Korte 2019). Both planes were Boeing 737 MAX 8 jetliners.

It can take months to get black box data from plane crashes. But within a week of the Ethiopian Airlines crash, the US Federal Aviation Administration (FAA) was receiving raw data from Aireon LLC, the brainchild of Iridium (Wall 2019):

> Using gear it has placed on satellites, Aireon gathers data such as a plane's speed, heading, altitude, and position. It gets updates every eight seconds or less. Air-traffic-control providers increasingly use the data to track planes from tarmac to tarmac—a capability only made possible with the development of sophisticated satellite networks.

The fact that it was possible traces back about a decade, when Iridium was developing concepts for a new constellation of satellites and recognized that its satellites had excess capacity. CEO Matt Desch and another top executive, Don Thoma, decided to focus on air-traffic control, and thus, in conjunction with

Nav Canada, spun off Aireon as an aircraft-tracking company using Iridium NEXT satellites that carry Aireon flight trackers. Thoma left Iridium to run Aireon (Wall 2019).

Once governments from the United States, Canada, and others started crunching the data provided by Aireon, it was clear that the two crashes had exposed a serious safety issue. A day after declaring the planes safe to fly, the FAA joined other countries in grounding the 737 MAX.

Iridium ended 2018 with 1,121,000 billable subscribers for its payload and other data services:

> Our core business has never been stronger, and momentum in commercial IoT continues to fuel innovation and new applications, which are driving new commercial partnerships and subscriber growth. We achieved our highest revenue growth as a public company and our best OEBITDA growth in seven years.... With the completion of the Iridium(R) NEXT upgrade of our constellation, our financial transformation is well underway. Having now completed an intense period of capital investment, we are turning our attention to a new growth phase for the company that should deliver new sources of revenue and OEBITDA growth, supporting significant free cash flow that can benefit shareholders.[49]

The company continues to be at the front edge of technological breakthroughs, proving that the need for Iridium still exists.

Discussion Questions

1. What type of innovation project was Iridium?
2. Did the innovation project have a sponsor?
3. Did the project require a technical breakthrough?
4. Was there a valid business case for Iridium?
5. Was the project co-creation with its customers?
6. Did the so-called business case change?
7. Why was Iridium a Limited Liability Corporation (LLC)?
8. Did Iridium understand the risks?
9. How is Iridium adapting to a quick-paced technological landscape?

REFERENCES

Arup, O. and Zunz, G. J. (1969). Sydney opera house. *Structural Engineer* 47 (10), (October).

Baham, J. (2014). *The Unauthorized Story of Walt Disney's Haunted Mansion* (2nd ed.). Theme Park Press.

Bennahum, D. S. (1998). The United Nations of Iridium. *Wired* 6 (10), 194. Available at www.wired.com/1998/10/iridium-2. Accessed May 10, 2019.

Bird, J. (1985 October). Cellular technology in telephones. *Data Processing* 27 (8), 37.

Braithwaite, D. (2007). Opera House wins top status. *The Sydney Morning Herald*, June 28.

Brewin, B. (2013). A 2006 battery fire destroyed Boeing 787 supplier's facility. *NextGov*, January 22. Available at www.nextgov.com/emerging-tech/2013/01/2006-battery-fire-destroyed-boeing-787-suppliers-facility/60809.

Carbone, N. (2011). World landmarks go dark in honor of earth hour. *Time*, March 26.

---

49. Press release, "Iridium Announces Record 2018 Results; Company Issues 2019 Outlook," http://investor.iridium.com/2019–02-28-Iridium-Announces-Record-2018-Results-Company-Issues-2019-Outlook, accessed May 30, 2019.

Cauley, L. (1999). Losses in space—Iridium's downfall: The marketing took a back seat to science. *Wall Street Journal (Eastern edition)*, August 18, A1.

Cole, J. (1994). McDonnell Douglas said to get contract to launch 40 satellites for Iridium plan. *Wall Street Journal (Eastern edition)*, New York, April 12, A4.

Cooper, A. (2013). Fire aboard empty 787 Dreamliner prompts investigation. *CNN*, January 8. Available at https://edition.cnn.com/2013/01/07/travel/dreamliner-fire/index.html.

Cooper, C. and Matsuda, K. (2013). GS Yuasa shares surge as Japan ends company inspections. *BusinessWeek*, January 28.

Dalløkken, Per Erlien (2013). Her er Dreamliner-problemet (in Norwegian). *Teknisk Ukeblad. Energy storage technologies—Lithium. Securaplane*, January 17.

Davis, D. (1985). New projects: Beware of false economics. *Harvard Business Review*, March–April, 100–101.

Denning, S. (2013). What went wrong at Boeing? *Forbes*, January 21.

Disney Book Group. (1996). *Walt Disney Imagineering: A Behind the Dreams Look at Making the Magic Real*. Foreword by Michael D. Eisner. New York: Hyperion Books.

Drew, C., Tabuchi, H. and Mouawad, J. (2013). Boeing 787 battery was a concern before failure. *The New York Times*, January 29.

Dudley, B. (2013). Lithium-ion batteries pack a lot of energy—And challenges. *The Seattle Times*, January 17.

Eisner, Michael and Schwartz, Tony. (1998). *Work in Progress: Risking Failure, Surviving Success*. New York: Hyperion.

Ellis, E. (1992). *Interview with Utzon in the Sydney Morning Herald Good Weekend*. October 31. Available at Ericellis.com.

Farrelly, E. (2008). High noon at Bennelong Point. *Canberra Times*, Canberratimes.com.au, December 1. Available at www.smh.com.au/national/high-noon-at-bennelong-point-20081201-gdt4vl.html. Accessed May 30, 2019.

Flower, J. (1993). Iridium. *Wired* 1 (5), (November).

Freed, Joshua. (2013), FAA approves test flights for Boeing 787. *Seattle Times*, February 7. Available at www.seattletimes.com/seattle-news/faa-approves-test-flights-for-boeing-787. Accessed May 29, 2019.

Gerding, B. (1996). Personal communications via satellite: An overview. *Telecommunications* 30 (2) (February), 35, 77.

Grams, P. and Zerbib, P. (1998). Caring for customers in a global marketplace. *Satellite Communications* (October), 24.

Hardy, Q. (1995). Iridium pulls $300 million bond offer; analysts cite concerns about projects. *Wall Street Journal* (Eastern edition), New York, September 22, 1995, A5.

———. (1996a). Motorola is plotting new satellite project—M-Star would be faster than the Iridium System, pitched to global firms. *Wall Street Journal* (Eastern edition), New York, October 14, B4.

———. (1996b). How a wife's question led Motorola to chase a global cell-phone plan. *Wall Street Journal* (Eastern edition), New York, December 16, A1.

———. (1996c). Staiano is leaving Motorola to lead firm's Iridium global satellite project. *Wall Street Journal* (Eastern edition), New York, December 10, B8.

———. (1999). Surviving Iridium. *Forbes*, September 6, 216–217.

Hawn, C. (1999). High Wireless Act. *Forbes*, June 14, 60–62.

Hench, J. (2008). *Designing Disney: Imagineering and the Art of the Show*. New York: Disney Editions.

Hench, J. and van Pelt, P. (2003). *Designing Disney: Imagineering and the Art of the Show*. New York: Disney Editions.

Henningan, W. J. (2013). FAA approves fix for Boeing 787 battery. *Los Angeles Times*, April 19. Available at www.latimes.com/business/la-xpm-2013-apr-19-la-fi-0420-faa-boeing-dreamliner-20130420-story.html. Accessed May 29, 2019.

Hiltzik, Michael A. (2000). McCaw drops Iridium bailout; 50,000 face service loss Monday. *Los Angeles Times*, March 4.

Hradecky, S. (2013). Accident: ANA B787 near Takamatsu on Jan 16th, 2013, battery problem and burning smell on board. *Aviation Herald*, January 16. Available at http://avherald.com/h?article=45c377c5&opt=0.

Jana, R. (2007). Companies known for inventive tech were dubbed the Next Big Thing and then disappeared. Now they're back and growing. Business Week, Innovation, *April 10.*

Jones, P. and Arup, O. (2006). *Masterbuilder of the Twentieth Century*. New Haven, CT: Yale University Press.

Keene, T. (2013). Airbus CEO "confident" Boeing will find fix for 787. *Bloomberg*, January 17. Available at www.bloomberg.com/video/airbus-ceo-confident-boeing-will-find-fix-for-787-b1zkhgggTB6DE6nv47gJNQ.html.

Keller, J. (1993). Telecommunications: Phone space race has fortune at stake. *Wall Street Journal* (Eastern edition), New York, January 18, B1.

Korte, G. (2019). 8 Americans among 157 dead after Ethiopian Airlines flight crashes after takeoff. *USA Today*, March 10. Available at www.wsj.com/articles/aerospace-upstart-changes-how-planes-are-tracked-11552590711.

La Tercera. (2013). LAN suspende de forma temporal la operación de flota Boeing 787 Dreamliner. *La Tercera*, January 16. Available at www.latercera.com/noticia/negocios/2013/01/655-504140-9-lan-suspende-de-forma-temporal-la-operacion-de-flota-boeing-787-dreamliner.shtml. Accessed May 30, 2019.

Madslien, J. (2013). Boeing 787 Dreamliner: The impact of safety concerns. *BBC News*, January 17. Available at www.bbc.com/news/business-21041265. Accessed May 30, 2019.

Marling, K. (1997). *Designing Disney's Theme Parks: The Architecture of Reassurance*. Paris—New York: Flammarion.

Martin, H. (2017). Disney to invest big money on a struggling Euro Disney. *Los Angeles Times*, February 10. Available at www.latimes.com/business/la-fi-euro-disney-20170210-story.html. Accessed May 10, 2019.

McCurry, J. (2013). 787 emergency landing: Japan grounds entire Boeing Dreamliner fleet. *The Guardian*. Retrieved January 16. Available at https://www.theguardian.com/business/2013/jan/16/787-emergency-landing-grounds-787.

Mitra-Thakur, S. (2013). Japan says 787 battery was not overcharged. *Engineering & Technology*, January 23.

Morgan, J. (2006). The phantoms that threaten the opera house. *Sydney Morning Herald*, November 11. Available at www.smh.com.au/national/the-phantoms-that-threaten-the-opera-house-20061111-gdot1e.html.

Mouawad, J. (2014). Report on Boeing 787 Dreamliner battery flaws finds lapses at multiple points. *The New York Times*, December 1.

Mukai, A. (2013). Japan to investigate Boeing 787 fuel leak as FAA reviews. *Bloomberg*, January 15.

Murray, P. (2004). *The Saga of the Sydney Opera House*. London: Spon Press.

Negishi, M. and Kelly, T. (2013). Japanese airlines ground Dreamliners after emergency landing. *Reuters*, January 16, 2013. Available at www.reuters.com/article/us-boeing-ana/japanese-airlines-ground-dreamliners-after-emergency-landing-idUSBRE90F01820130116. Accessed May 29, 2019.

New South Wales Government, Department of Commerce. Available at NSW.gov.au. Accessed December 1, 2008.

Ostrower, J. and Nicas, J. (2013). Fresh jet glitches bedevil Boeing. *Wall Street Journal*, January 9. Available at www.wsj.com/articles/SB10001424127887323482504578229800636659218.

Paterik, S. (2005). Iridium alive and well. *The Arizona Republic*, April 27, D5.

Pearman, H. (2007). Millennium masterwork: Jorn Utzon's Sydney Opera House. Hugh Pearman. *Gabion*.

Reed, T. (2013). *Boeing and FAA: What we learned from 787 problems*. June 12. Available at www.thestreet.com/story/11948417/1/boeing-and-faa-what-we-learned-from-787-problems.html. Accessed May 29, 2019.

Reuters. (2013). European safety agency to ground 787 in line with FAA. *Reuters*, January 16. Available at www.reuters.com/article/boeing-787-easa/european-safety-agency-to-ground-787-in-line-with-faa-idUSL6N0AM0E020130117.

Rubin, Judith (2010). Disney Imagineering: Bill Novey and the business of theme park special effects. *Blooloop.com*. Available at https://blooloop.com/features/disney-imagineering-bill-novey-and-the-business-of-theme-park-special-effects. Accessed April 30, 2019.

Rushe, D. (2013). Why Boeing's 787 Dreamliner was a nightmare waiting to happen. *The Guardian*, January 18.

Satellite Today. (2000). DoD awards $72 million to revamp Iridium. *Satellite Today*. Potomac: December 7, 3 (227), 1.

Scott, A. and Saito, M. (2013). *FAA approval of Boeing 787 battery under scrutiny*. NBCNews.com, January 23. Available at www.nbcnews.com/business/business-news/faa-approval-boeing-787-battery-under-scrutiny-flna1C8087461. Accessed May 29, 2019.

Scribner, G. and Rees, J. (Directors). (2007). *Disneyland: Secrets, Stories, and Magic (DVD)*. Walt Disney Video.

Spira, J. (2012). Boeing: Problems with 787 Dreamliner "normal." *Frequent Business Traveler*, December 16. Available at www.frequentbusinesstraveler.com/2012/12/boeing-problems-with-787-dreamliner-normal.

Stewart, J. B. (2013). Japan's role in making batteries for Boeing. *The New York Times*, January 25 2013.

Surrell, J. (2009). *The Haunted Mansion: From the Magic Kingdom to the Movies* (2nd ed.). New York: Disney Editions.

Tabuchi, H. (2013). No quality problems found at battery maker for 787. *The New York Times*, January 28.

Tangel, A. and Wall, R. (2018). Lion Air crash puts Boeing's popular 737 Max in spotlight. *Wall Street Journal*, October 29. www.wsj.com/articles/lion-air-crash-puts-boeings-popular-737-max-in-spotlight-1540852117?mod=article_inline&mod=article_inline.

Thomas, B. (1969). Dave McIntyre's front row. *San Diego Evening Tribune*, August 19.

Thomson, I. (2013). Boeing 787 fleet grounded indefinitely as investigators stumped. *The Register*, January 25.

Thurm, S. (2000a). Iridium set to get $75 million from investors led by McCaw. *Wall Street Journal*, February 10, p. 1.

———. (2000b). Motorola Inc., McCaw shift Iridium tactics. *Wall Street Journal*, February 18.

Topham, G. (2013). Boeing 787 Dreamliner to be investigated by US authorities. *The Guardian*. Available at www.theguardian.com/business/2013/jan/11/boeing-787-dreamliner-us-investigation. Accessed May 29, 2019.

Topham, J. and Scott, A. (2013). Boeing Dreamliners grounded worldwide on battery checks. *Reuters*, January 17. Available at www.reuters.com/article/us-boeing-dreamliner/boeing-dreamliners-grounded-worldwide-on-battery-checks-idUSBRE90F1N820130117. Accessed May 29, 2019.

Totaro, P. (2008). Joern Utzon dead. *The Sydney Morning Herald*, November 30. Available at www.smh.com.au/world/joern-utzon-dead-20081130-gdt4tv.html. Accessed May 30, 2019.

United Nations Educational, Scientific, and Cultural Organization (UNESCO). (2018). *Joan Sutherland Theatre: Technical and Production Information*. Sydney Opera House. Available at www.sydneyoperahouse.com/content/dam/pdfs/venues/Joan-Sutherland-Theatre/Joan-Sutherland-Technical-Specification.pdf.

Upadhyay, A. (2013). DGCA directs Air India to ground all six Boeing Dreamliners on safety concerns. *Economic Times*, January 17. Available at https://economictimes.indiatimes.com/industry/transportation/airlines-/-aviation/dgca-directs-air-india-to-ground-all-six-boeing-dreamliners-on-safety-concerns/articleshow/18056887.cms. Accessed May 30, 2019.

Veness, S. (2009). *The Hidden Magic of Walt Disney World*. Avon, MA: Adams Media.

Wall, R. (2019). The aerospace newcomer whose data helped make the difference in grounding the 737 Max. *Wall Street Journal*, March 14. Available at www.wsj.com/articles/aerospace-upstart-changes-how-planes-are-tracked-11552590711. Accessed May 29, 2019.

Wall, R. and Rothman, A. (2013). Airbus says A350 design is "lower risk" than troubled 787. *Bloomberg*, January 17. Available at www.bloomberg.com/news/articles/2013-01-17/airbus-says-a350-design-lower-risk-than-troubled-boeing-787. Accessed May 29, 2019.

Wall Street Journal. (2000). *Craig McCaw plans an infusion to support cash-hungry Iridium*. February 7, 2000. Available at www.wsj.com/articles/SB949876087664660171. Accessed May 30, 2019.

Weld, M. and Mouwad, J. (2013). Protracted fire inquiry keeping 787 on Ground. *New York Times*, January 25.

White, M. C. (2013). Is the Dreamliner becoming a financial nightmare for Boeing? *Time*, January 17.

Wingfield-Hayes, R. (2013a). Dreamliner: Boeing 787 planes grounded on safety fears. *BBC News*, January 17. Available at www.bbc.com/news/business-21054089. Accessed May 29, 2019.

———. (2013b). Top Japan airlines ground Boeing 787s after emergency. *BBC News*, January 16. Available at www.bbc.com/news/business-21038128.

Wright, Alex. (2005). *The Imagineering Field Guide to Magic Kingdom at Walt Disney World*. New York: Disney Editions.

CASE STUDY: ZANE CORPORATION: SELECTING AN INNOVATION FRAMEWORK _____

Background

Zane Corporation was a medium-sized company with multiple product lines. More than 20 years ago, Zane implemented project management to be used in all their product lines, but mainly for operational or traditional projects rather than strategic or innovation projects. Recognizing that a methodology would be needed, Zane made the faulty conclusion that a single methodology would be needed and that a one-size-fits-all mentality would satisfy almost all their projects. Senior management believed that this would standardize status reporting and make it easy for senior management to recognize the true performance. This approach worked well in many other companies that Zane knew about, but it was applied to primarily traditional or operational projects.

As the one-size-fits-all approach became common practice, Zane began capturing lessons learned and best practices with the intent of improving the singular methodology. Project management was still being viewed as an approach for projects that were reasonably well-defined, having risks that could be easily managed, and executed by a rather rigid methodology that had limited flexibility. Executives believed that project management standardization was a necessity for effective corporate governance.

The Project Management Landscape Changes

Zane recognized the benefits of using project management from their own successes, the capturing of lessons learned and best practices, and published research data. Furthermore, Zane was now convinced that almost all activities within the firm could be regarded as projects and they were therefore managing their business by projects.

As the one-size-fits-all methodology began to be applied to nontraditional or strategic projects, the weaknesses in the singular methodology became apparent. Strategic projects, especially those that involved innovation, were not always completely definable at project initiation, the scope of work could change frequently during project execution, governance now appeared in the form of committee governance with significantly more involvement by the customer or business owner, and a different form of project leadership was required on some projects. Recognizing the true status of some of the nontraditional projects was becoming difficult.

The traditional risk management approach used on operational projects appeared to be insufficient for strategic projects. As an example, strategic projects require a risk management approach that emphasizes VUCA analyses:

Volatility
Uncertainty
Complexity
Ambiguity

Significantly more risks were appearing on strategic projects where the requirements could change rapidly to satisfy turbulent business needs. This became quite apparent on IT projects that focused heavily upon the traditional waterfall methodology that offered little flexibility. The introduction of an agile methodology solved some of the IT problems but created others. Agile was a flexible methodology or framework that focused heavily upon better risk management activities but required a great deal of collaboration. Every methodology or framework comes with advantages and disadvantages.

The introduction of an agile methodology gave Zane a choice between a rigid one-size-fits-all approach or a very flexible agile framework. Unfortunately, not all projects were perfect fits for an extremely rigid or flexible approach. Some projects were middle-of-the-road projects that fell in between rigid waterfall approaches and flexible agile frameworks.

Understanding Methodologies

Zane's original belief was that a methodology functioned as a set of principles that a company can tailor and then apply to a specific situation or group of activities that have some degree of commonality. In a project environment, these principles might appear as a list of things to do and show up as forms, guidelines, templates, and checklists. The principles may be structured to correspond to specific project life-cycle phases.

For most companies, including Zane, the project management methodology, often referred to as the waterfall approach where everything is done sequentially, became the primary tool for the "command and control" of projects providing some degree of standardization in the execution of the work and control over the decision-making process. Standardization and control came at a price and provided some degree of limitation as to when the methodology could be used effectively. Typical limitations that Zane discovered included:

Type of Project: Most methodologies assumed that the requirements of the project were reasonably well-defined at the onset of the project. Tradeoffs were primarily on time and cost rather than scope. This limited the use of the methodology to traditional or operational projects that were reasonably well-understood at the project approval stage and had a limited number of unknowns. Strategic projects, such as those involving innovation and had to be aligned to strategic business objective rather than a clear statement of work, could not be easily managed using the waterfall methodology because of the large number of unknowns and the fact that they could change frequently.

Performance Tracking: With reasonable knowledge about the project's requirements, performance tracking was accomplished mainly using the triple constraints of time, cost, and scope. Nontraditional or strategic projects had significantly more constraints that required monitoring and therefore used other tracking systems than the project management methodology. Simply stated, the traditional methodology had limited flexibility when applied to projects that were not operational.

Risk Management: Risk management was important on all types of projects. But on nontraditional or strategic projects, with the high number of unknowns that can change frequently over the life of the project, standard risk management practices that are included in traditional methodologies may be insufficient for risk assessment and mitigation practices.

Governance: For traditional projects, governance was provided by a single person acting as the sponsor for the project. The methodology became the sponsor's primary vehicle for command and control and used with the mistaken belief that all decisions could be made by monitoring just the time, cost, and scope constraints.

Selecting The Right Framework

Zane recognized that the future was not simply a decision between waterfall, agile, and Scrum as to which one will be a best fit for a given project. New frameworks, perhaps a hybrid methodology, needed to be created from the best features of each approach and then applied to a project. Zane now believed with a reasonable degree of confidence that new frameworks, with a great deal of flexibility and the ability to be customized, will certainly appear in the future and would be a necessity for continued growth. Deciding which framework is best suited to a given project will be the challenge and project teams will be given the choice of which one to use.

Zane believed that project teams of the future will begin each project by determining which approach will best suit their needs. This would be accomplished with checklists and questions that address characteristics of the project such as flexibility of the requirements, flexibility in the constraints, type of leadership needed, team skill levels needed, and the culture of the organization. The answers to the questions would then be pieced together to form a framework which may be unique to a given project.

Questions

1. What are some of the questions that Zane should ask themselves when selecting a flexible methodology?
2. What issues could arise that would need resolution?
3. What would you recommend as the first issue that needs to be addressed?
4. Was it a mistake or a correct decision not allowing the sales force to manage the innovation projects?
5. Is it feasible to set up a project management methodology for managing innovation projects?

Instructor's Manual

What are some of the questions that Zane should ask themselves when selecting a flexible methodology? Typical questions might include:

How clear are the requirements and the linkage to the strategic business objectives? On some projects, especially when innovation and/or R&D are required, it may be difficult to come up with well-defined objectives for the project even though the line-of-sight to the strategic business objectives is well known. These projects may focus more so on big, hairy, audacious goals (BHAGs) rather than on more well-defined objectives.

When the requirements are unclear, then the project may be tentative in nature and subject to cancellation. You must also expect that changes will occur throughout the life of the project. These types of projects require highly flexible frameworks and a high degree of customer involvement.

How likely is it that changes in the requirements will take place over the life of the project? The greater the expectation of changes, the greater the need for a highly flexible approach. Changes may occur because of changing consumer tastes, needs, or expectations. Allowing for too many changes to take place may get the project off track and result in a failed project that produces no benefits or business value. The size of the project is also important because larger projects are more susceptible to scope changes.

In addition to the number of changes that may be needed, it is also important to know how much time will be allowed for the changes to take place. In critical situations where the changes may have to take place in days or weeks, a fast paced, flexible approach may be necessary with continuous involvement by stakeholders and decision makers.

Will the customer expect all the features and functionality at the end of the project, or will the customer allow for incremental scope changes? Incremental scope changes allow the project to be broken down and completed in small increments that may increase the overall quality and tangible business value of the outcome. This may also provide less pressure on decision making.

Is the team collocated or virtual? Projects that require a great deal of collaboration for decision making may be more easily managed with a collocated team especially when a large amount of scope changes are expected.

If the project requires the creation of features to a product, where will the information come from for determining which features are necessary? The answer to this question may require that the project team interface frequently with marketing and end users to make sure that the features are what the users desire. The ease by which the team can interface with the end users may be of critical importance.

Is there a success (and/or failure) criteria that will help us determine when the project is over? With a poor or lack of a success criteria, the project may require a great deal of flexibility, testing, and prototype development.

How knowledgeable will the stakeholders be with the framework selected? If the stakeholders are unfamiliar with the framework, a great deal of wasted time may be needed to educate the customer on the framework selected and their expected role and responsibility in the framework. This may create a problem for stakeholders that exhibit a resistance to change.

What metrics will the stakeholders and business owner require? Waterfall methodologies focus on time, cost, and scope metrics. Flexible methodologies allow for other metrics such as business benefits and value achieved.

What issues could arise that would need resolution? Selecting the right framework may seem like a relatively easy thing to do. However, as stated previously, all methodologies and frameworks come with disadvantages as well as advantages. Project teams must then hope for the best but plan for the worst. They must understand what can go wrong and select an approach where execution issues can be readily resolved in a timely manner. Some of the questions focusing on "What can go wrong?" that should be addressed before finalizing the approach to be taken include:

Are the customer's expectations realistic?
Will the needs of the project be evolving or known at the onset?
Can the required work be broken down and managed using small work packages and sprints or is it an all-or-nothing approach?
Will the customer and stakeholders provide the necessary support and in a timely manner?
Will the customer and/or stakeholder be overbearing and try to manage the project themselves?
How much documentation will be required?
Will the project team possess the necessary communications, teamwork, and innovation/technical skills?
Will the team members be able to commit the necessary time to the project?
Is the type of contract (i.e., fixed price, cost reimbursable, cost sharing, etc.) well-suited for the framework selected?

What would you recommend as the first issue that needs to be addressed? The corporate culture needs to be addressed first. People need to buy into the new approach and framework. Selecting a highly flexible approach may seem on the surface to be the best way to go since mistakes and potential risks can be identified early, which then allows for faster corrective action to take place and prevent disasters from occurring. But what people seem to fail to realize is that the greater the level of flexibility, more layers of management and supervision may need to be in place. Workers may not like the additional levels of supervision.

Was it a mistake or a correct decision not allowing the sales force to manage the innovation projects? Having the sales force participate in innovation activities is mandatory. However, their involvement should be with customer communication, identifying customer needs, idea generation, and some say in project selection and innovation project portfolio management activities. Allowing the sales force to manage the innovation project could be a mistake.

Is it feasible to set up a project management methodology for managing innovation projects? The answer to this question is argumentative. If there is a great deal of similarity in the innovation projects, such as the type of innovation, some degree of standardization may be workable. But in general, creating a one-size-fits-all approach for innovation activities is not workable.

Conclusions

Today, there are several methodologies and frameworks available for project teams such as "Agile," "Waterfall," "Scrum," "Prince2," "Rapid Application Development," etc. In the future, we can expect the number of methodologies and frameworks available to increase significantly. Some type of criteria must be established to select the best approach for a given project.

CASE STUDY: REDSTONE INC.: UNDERSTANDING INNOVATION CULTURES

Redstone Inc. is a multinational company that has been in business for more than 70 years. Redstone has multiple businesses, the two most profitable being the Aerospace Division and the Commercial Products Division.

The Aerospace Division

The Aerospace Division manufactures components exclusively for the aerospace and defense industry. It maintains its own divisional accounting system and policies and procedures that conform to the government's requirements to participate in competitive bidding for government contracts, most of which are multiyear contracts with follow-on opportunities. The division has its own culture and the workers very rarely interface with any other divisions in Redstone.

The long-term success of the Aerospace Division was largely due to its R&D personnel that had made technical breakthroughs on many of the products that were eventually sold to the government. Almost all the major innovations came from funding on government contracts for R&D activities. Most of the smaller innovations were low-cost incremental changes internally funded by the division and related to quality improvements in their products and looking for ways to lower production costs.

All the contract awards were in the millions of dollars and some multiyear contracts had been in the hundreds of millions. The Aerospace Division developed their own status reporting system aligned to government requirements and using the concepts of earned value reporting for providing status on time, cost, and scope. The status reporting system was used exclusively in the Aerospace Division.

The Commercial Products Division (CPD)

The Commercial Products Division was the most profitable business unit in the company. The success of CPD was largely due to brand recognition and acceptance by their worldwide customer base. Most innovations were incremental, and management was complacent with the success of the firm and CPD's performance. However, this was about to change.

Market research indicated that consumer tastes were changing. CPD's customers were expecting to see next generation products with more advanced features rather than small incremental changes to existing product lines. CPD's profitability and market share were beginning to decline.

Innovation activities in the CPD were highly unstructured. Project management activities were conducted on an informal basis. Anyone who had an idea for an innovation, regardless of the type of innovation, could spend a portion of their time doing stealth or hidden innovation. Their managers would most likely provide any funding needed for experimentation, testing, or prototype development. Senior management was pleased with the results, but because innovation was unstructured, often had no idea how much money or resources were being committed to noncontractual innovation activities. Management also did not know what innovation activities people were working on until an innovation project was officially announced.

Senior management was reluctant to act as sponsors for any critical projects for fear that a project failure could damage their reputation and career. As such, lower- and middle-level managers were forced to assume the role of project sponsors with little if any support from above.

The Challenge

Redstone's management was fearful that, unless some degree of control over the internal innovation processes at the CPD took place, and reasonably soon, there could be a significant downturn in Redstone's financial health. The simplest solution was the decision to try to duplicate the innovation processes that were being performed successfully in the Aerospace Division into the CPD.

First, management transferred two middle-level managers from the Aerospace Division to the CPD. Both managers had more than 20 years of experience working in the Aerospace Division. Second, so as not to have to "reinvent the wheel," the managers were asked to bring with them all of the forms, guidelines, templates, and checklist used in the Aerospace Division along with the earned value software program that tracked and reported time, cost, and scope.

Questions

1. Did Redstone have good intentions in wanting to add structure to the innovation processes in the CPD?
2. Why didn't senior management in the CPD take the lead in adding structure and control to the innovation processes?
3. Was it a good idea to bring two experienced managers from the Aerospace Division to head up the innovation development activities at the CPD?
4. Was it a good idea to use the earned value software program from the Aerospace Division in the CPD?
5. What is your "best guess" as to what most likely happened at the CPD over the next few months with regards to innovation practices?

Instructor's Manual

1. Did Redstone have good intentions in wanting to add structure to the innovation processes in the CPD?

   Redstone had good intentions in wanting to get better control over innovation activities in the CPD. The need was certainly there. However, good intentions do not always lead to good results if the implementation scheme is flawed or based upon the wrong assumptions.

2. Why didn't senior management in the CPD take the lead in adding structure and control to the innovation processes?

Management was reluctant to do their job as sponsors and provide proper governance for fear that any failure would reflect poorly upon them and possibly limit their career path opportunities in Redstone.

3. Was it a good idea to bring two experienced managers from the Aerospace Division to head up the innovation development activities at the CPD?

On the surface, this looks like a good idea. But it is a bad idea. Bringing them on board the project assumes that the innovation practices at the Aerospace Division are transferable to the CPD. This further assumes that one size fits all, and that any type of innovation project at CPD can be managed using the same tools and techniques in the Aerospace Division. This is certainly not the case, especially since the Aerospace Division must conform to government requirements. The transfer also assumes that innovation projects in the CPD would have well-defined statements of work at project onset as they do in the Aerospace Division for government contracts.

4. Was it a good idea to use the earned value software program from the Aerospace Division in the CPD?

The earned value management software provides visibility of status. But it is insufficient in providing information related to other tangible and intangible assets that must be tracked and reported to understand the innovation processes. Also, the software was designed to be used on mega projects, such as those in aerospace and defense, not the smaller type of innovation projects needed in the CPD.

5. What is your "best guess" as to what most likely happened at the CPD over the next few months with regards to innovation practices?

This case study is a disguised case of an actual situation. All attempts to use the Aerospace Division's innovation approach in the CPD failed. The workers continuously complained that their activities in the CPD were not regulated by government requirements that the Aerospace Division must follow.

Senior management finally recognized that the transferability would not be successful and that major changes would be needed. They also recognized that their involvement was mandatory. Senior management accepted their role as leaders of the new culture and mindset that would be needed in the CPD. In less than a year, the CPD had its own approach to innovation activities. The two middle level managers returned to other positions in the Aerospace Division.

CASE STUDY: THE GOVERNMENT THINK TANK: THE FAILURE OF CROWDSOURCING

A government "think tank" had the responsibility for monitoring advances in technology that could be applied to future government needs. One of the critical areas for research monitoring was in the development of high energy solid propellants that could be used in missile development for the manned spaceflight program, launching communication satellites, weaponry, and space exploration. High energy solid propellants were less costly to maintain than cryogenic liquid propellants and had the advantages of possibly lowering project costs, especially missile launch costs, and allowing for additional payload weight for more complex missions.

In the past, whenever a company involved in solid propellant development had an idea for a new type of solid propellant, they would either fund the research internally or submit an unsolicited proposal to their respective government agency seeking contractual governmental funding. Seeking government funding came with risks. If the government paid for the R&D, in whole or in part, then based upon the type of contract, the government could own some or all the rights to the intellectual property and share it with other government contractors. There were government policies in effect whereby the government could not share information provided in a proposal with other companies if the proposal were not followed by the award of a contract. However, with a contract award, all this changed. This is the reason why some companies preferred to fund some R&D activities internally so that their company had complete control over the intellectual property.

The think tank maintained a list of projects that various government agencies deemed necessary for the next several years, and all the projects on this list were predicated upon advances in high energy solid propellant technology. The think tank believed that an open innovation approach using crowdsourcing would bring forth many good ideas that participating companies were willing to share for addressing future projects and the technology needed.[50]

A conference was established for discussing high energy solid propellant technologies. There were nine companies that were government contractors and were known to be performing research on solid propellant technology. All nine companies were invited and asked to bring at least four or five of their high-tech people for a brainstorming session. An agenda was sent out so that everyone understood the intent of the conference.

A senior manager from the think tank opened the session with a discussion of the strategic intent of the conference and the desire to have the participants think up ideas for research on high energy solid propellants based upon what they were now doing in their R&D groups. The government assumed that, although each company represented might be able to contribute ideas to only a part of the problem, the collective gathering of ideas would generate viable alternatives and solutions.

The chairperson for the conference then asked for people to speak up as to what discoveries their companies had made. Nobody volunteered to speak. The chairperson then asked each company to state how they would increase the energy of solid propellants and any research directions they might go in the future. Once again, people were reluctant to speak. Those that did speak, talked about somewhat "outdated" information that everyone in the room knew rather than what the conference was designed to discuss.

The chairperson was becoming upset that nobody in the audience was willing to discuss the topics around which the conference was designed. Finally, one person in the audience spoke up:

> "All of us in the audience are competitors. In simple terms, you are asking us to share our intellectual property and possibly some of our strategic plans with our competitors. This is very difficult for us to do given the potential of long-term lucrative contracts we might receive surrounding out technical expertise. I cannot believe anyone in this conference will provide the information you seek. My company agreed to attend to hear what our competition was doing, not to share critical intellectual property. Now, it appears that everyone here in attendance has shown up for the same reason."

Questions:

1. Was the conference designed as an open innovation crowdsourcing attempt?
2. Why wasn't the conference a success?
3. Could a technical conference on the topic of "advances in high energy solid propellants" have achieved better results?

---

50. Open innovation generally focuses on seeking out information and ideas from reliable sources. Crowdsourcing is an attempt to solve a potential problem and then share the information freely with all contributors.

Instructor's Manual:

1. Was the conference designed as an open innovation crowdsourcing attempt?

   Open innovation generally focuses on idea generation whereas crowdsourcing is an attempt to solve a potential problem and then share the information freely with all contributors. The organizers of the conference intended the conference to be both open innovation and crowdsourcing whereas the participants viewed the conference as just a form of open innovation.

2. Why wasn't the conference a success?

   People are generally willing to participate in these types of events provided they believe that they, or their company, will also benefit. There must be something in it for them. In this case, it appeared to be a one-way street where they are releasing potentially valuable company proprietary information that could eventually be income-generating and perhaps getting nothing in exchange.

3. Could a technical conference on the topic of "advances in high energy solid propellants" have achieved better results?

   In most technical conferences, the information in the presented papers is usually reviewed internally to make sure that no proprietary information is being released. The exception is when the company owns the patent or copyright to the material that is being presented.

CASE STUDY: LEGO: BRAND MANAGEMENT INNOVATION[51] _____

Abstract

Lego is one of the most admired companies in the world. Yet despite their success, they went through a period that put them on the brink of bankruptcy. They eventually changed their corporate culture and reconfigured their product development and innovation processes to turn the company around.[52]

   Although most of the issues discussed in the case can occur in any company, the Lego case illustrates the challenges facing an extraordinarily successful privately held company where innovation was needed to support the growth of the Lego brand.

Understanding Brand Management

One of the most difficult types of innovation projects to manage are those that must support brand management activities. A brand could be the company, a product or family of products, specific services, or people. Successful brands may take years to develop and continuous innovation is necessary to maintain brand awareness, credibility, and consumer loyalty. Companies with strong brand awareness include Apple, Google, Disney, Microsoft, Coca-Cola, Facebook, and Lego.

---

51. ©2020 by Harold Kerzner. All rights reserved. None of the employees at Lego participated in the preparation of this case study.

52. Portions of this case study have been adapted from Wikipedia, the Free Encyclopedia: Lego; The Lego Group; Lego Minifigures; and Lego Mindstorms. The first part of the case study focuses on the products and services provided by Lego, not necessarily in chronological order, so that the reader can understand the interactions with various forms of brand innovation and why cultural changes were necessary. The focus on the case is to gain an understanding of managing projects under a brand, not the effectiveness or ineffectiveness of managerial decisions.

Brand management practices are heavily oriented around marketing activities that focus on the target markets and how the product or family of products look, are priced out, and are packaged. Brand management must also focus on the intangible properties of the brand and the perceived value to the customers. An intangible property might be the value your customers place on your products such that they are willing to pay more than the cost of a generic brand that may function the same.

Almost all brand innovations involve governance by the brand manager whose responsibility is to oversee the relationships that the consumers have with the brand thus increasing the value of the brand over time. Innovations should allow for the awareness and pricing of the brand to grow as well as maintaining or improving consumer brand loyalty.

Unlike other forms of innovation where project teams have the freedom to explore multiple options and ideas and go off on tangents, brand innovation may have restrictions established by brand management. Brand management is responsible for not only managing and promoting the brand, but also deciding what new products or innovations could fall under the brand umbrella. Brand innovation is a marriage between the brand's core values, the target market, and management's vision. The difference between the long-term success and failure of a brand rests with brand innovation.

History

Lego, which conducts business as the Lego Group, is a privately held toy manufacturing company headquartered in Billund, Denmark. It is best known for its flagship product, the manufacturing of colorful interlocking plastic bricks accompanied by an array of gears, figurines called minifigures, and various other parts. There are more than 7,000 different Lego elements. Lego pieces can be assembled and connected in many ways to construct objects, including vehicles, buildings, and working robots. Anything constructed can be taken apart again, and the pieces reused to make new things. As of July 2015, 600 billion Lego parts had been produced.

The history of Lego spans nearly 100 years, beginning with the creation of small wooden playthings during the early 20th century. Manufacturing of plastic Lego bricks began in Denmark in 1947, and since has grown to include factories throughout the world. Movies, games, competitions, stores and Legoland amusement parks have been developed under the Lego brand. Lego has more than 40 global offices. By the turn of the century, Lego was producing more than 20 billion Lego bricks a year and was functioning as both a retailer and entertainer.

The company was founded on 10 August 1932 by Ole Kirk Christiansen (1891–1958). The brand "Lego" is derived from the Danish words "leg godt", meaning "play well". The Lego Group's motto is "det bedste er ikke for godt" which means "only the best is good enough". This motto, which is still used today, was created by its founder to encourage his employees never to skimp on quality, a value he believed in strongly. By 1951 plastic toys accounted for half of the Lego company's output, even though the Danish trade magazine Legetøjs-Tidende ("Toy Times"), visiting the Lego factory in Billund in the early 1950s, felt that plastic would never be able to replace traditional wooden toys. Although a common sentiment, Lego toys seem to have become a significant exception to the dislike of plastic in children's toys.

Lego Bricks

By 1954, Christiansen's son, Godtfred, had become the junior managing director of the Lego Group. It was his conversation with an overseas buyer that led to the idea of a toy system. Godtfred saw the immense potential in Lego bricks to become a system for creative play, but the bricks still had some problems from a technical standpoint; their locking ability had limitations and lacked versatility. In 1958, the modern brick design was developed. It took five years to find the right material for it which was ABS (acrylonitrile butadiene styrene) polymer. The modern Lego brick design was patented on 28 January 1958.

Lego pieces of all varieties constitute a universal system. Despite variations in the design and the purposes of individual pieces over the years, each piece remains compatible in some way with other pieces. Lego bricks from 1958 still interlock with those made today, and Lego sets for young children are compatible with those made for teenagers. Six bricks containing 2 × 4 studs can be combined in 915,103,765 ways.

Each Lego piece must be manufactured to an exacting degree of precision. When two pieces are engaged, they must fit firmly, yet be easily disassembled. The machines that manufacture Lego bricks have tolerances as small as 10 micrometers.

Manufacturing

Manufacturing of Lego bricks occurs at several locations around the world. Molding is done in Billund, Denmark; Nyíregyháza, Hungary; Monterrey, Mexico; and most recently in Jiaxing, China. Brick decorations and packaging are done at plants in Denmark, Hungary, Mexico, and Kladno in the Czech Republic. The Lego Group estimates that in the last five decades it has produced 400 billion Lego bricks. Annual production of Lego bricks averages approximately 36 billion, or about 1140 elements per second. According to an article in Business Week in 2006, Lego could be considered the world's No. 1 tire manufacturer because the factory produces about 306 million small rubber tires a year. The claim was reiterated in 2012.

Lego's Target Consumers

Lego's target consumers were originally boys aged 4–9, although 10%–20% of their total customers were girls. Their consumers were usually members of families that wanted their children to grow up as scientists, architects, designers, and even musicians.

To connect the Lego brand to consumers, Lego had to conduct research and work closely with families to understand how children play and spend their time. In some countries, Lego discovered that parents wanted toys that children could play with by themselves, without supervision, whereas in other countries, parents wanted to sit on the floor and accompany their children playing with the toys. Most families have rules that children must abide by as to how many hours a day they can watch television or play on computers. Although there were several options available for entertainment, Lego believed that children wanted the freedom to show their creativity with the plastic bricks by building something masterful. They could use their imagination to build something they are proud of, and then make up stories using the Lego action figures.

As computers and wireless broadband technology expanded into the children's bedrooms, Lego had to rely upon radical innovation and develop new products to expand their services into the virtual space while remembering that construction rather than technology drives Lego's business. This included videos on large Lego construction projects, videogames, boardgames, movies and the ability to share experiences or play games with other Lego users. The goal was for the consumers to continue purchasing licensed Lego products. Adults were also purchasers of Lego products giving them the chance to relive their childhood. One adult spent two years building a Lego playable harpsichord made with 100,000 bricks.

Lego also developed a strategy for schoolteachers that taught the targeted age groups by developing hands-on kits for teachers. The Lego products were recognized as a compromise between imagination, creativity, and fun for children. However, purchasing the kits was limited by the school's budget. In 2015, an article was published stating that children with autism were improving their long-term social interaction skills using Lego products.[53]

In 1998, Lego suffered its first financial loss. The following year, Lego signed a licensing agreement with Lucasfilm to create Lego kits for the Star Wars movie series. This was a shift in Lego's innovation strategy from just open-ended play kits to branded kits based upon movie themes. It was also a departure from Lego's desire not to make "war toys." Lego's gross sales jumped 30 percent in the first year and sales of the Star Wars kits exceeded expectations by 500 percent. Many of the buyers were adults who purchased the kits for nostalgia reasons.

Lego soon recognized the benefits of targeting adults as well as children. Adults were willing to pay $800 for the Star Wars Millennium Falcon Kit, $500 for the Star Wars Death Star and $400 for Harry Potter's Hogwarts Castle. However, there were some issues. Kids were willing to let their imagination run wild, pretend they were part of the theme, and then quit and disassemble the pieces. Adults needed foolproof assembly instructions because it was the satisfaction of the finished product that motivated them. Some adults even posted time-lapsed videos on YouTube showing how they constructed large Lego buildings and other products.

Another benefit for adults to purchase Lego products was to reduce stress. Many companies had a room with Lego products where employees could reduce stress, meditate, relax, and drowned out noise as they undertook a creative challenge. Lego hired Abbie Headon to write a book focusing on adult usage of Lego products. The book was entitled "Build Yourself Happy: The Joy of Lego Play."

Gender Equality

By the mid to late 1980s, Lego almost trapped themselves with the "failure of success" by not realizing that their market was changing. Even though most of Lego's revenue appeared to be coming from boys, girls were losing interest in Lego's building blocks. In discussions with psychologists, Lego discovered that girls were developing interests other than toys at a much earlier age than boys. However, this was dependent on the area of the world you lived in. Lego also discovered that girls preferred the pastel colors while boys preferred the sharper colors of black, blue, red, yellow, and green.

In 2003, Lego launched Clikits, a product designed specifically for girls six years old and older. It contained arts-and-crafts materials from which girls could design jewelry, accessories for hair and fashion statements, and picture frames. For boys, Lego developed a series of table sports products where they could simulate playing basketball, baseball, and hockey.

In 2012, Lego Friends was launched which was a collection of Lego construction toys designed primarily for girls. The theme introduced the "mini-doll" figures, which were about the same size as the traditional minifigures but were larger, more detailed and realistic. The female mini-doll figures could only sit, stand, or bend over whereas male minifigures used for games for boys had more flexibility and could drive cars, run, and hold tools.

The Lego Friends sets include pieces in many color schemes such as orange and green or pink and purple and depict scenes from suburban life set in the fictional town of Heartlake City. The main characters, one of which appears in every set were: Andrea, Emma, Mia, Olivia, and Stephanie. The sets were usually named after them. In the initial wave of sets, the larger sets included bricks that could build a veterinary clinic, a malt-style café, a beauty salon, and a suburban house; smaller sets included a

53. Barakova, E. I., Bajracharya, P., Willemsen, M., Lourens, T., and Huskens, B. (December 2015). Long-term LEGO therapy with humanoid robot for children with ASD. *Expert Systems*, 32 (6), 698–709.

"cool convertible," a design studio, an inventor's workshop, and a swimming pool. The Friends product replaced previous female-oriented themes.

Following its launch, the girl-friendly Lego Friends was considered by many as offensive and considered as one of the worst toys of the year. But at the same time, plenty of young girls and their families had a different opinion. Despite the criticism by some, Lego Friends was an impressive financial success and honored by the Toy Industry Association as the Toy of the Year in 2013.

In January 2014, a handwritten letter to Lego from a seven-year-old American girl, Charlotte Benjamin, received widespread attention in the media. In it the young author complained that there were "more Lego boy people and barely any Lego girls" and observed that "all the girls did was sit at home, go to the beach, shop, and they had no jobs, but the boys went on adventures, worked, saved people … even swam with sharks".[54]

In June 2014, it was announced that Lego would be launching a new "Research Institute" collection of toys featuring female scientists including a female chemist, paleontologist, and astronomer. The new sets showed women doing intellectually challenging jobs. Lego denied claims that the set was introduced to placate criticism of the company by activists. The Research Institute collections sold out within a week of its online release in August 2014.

Core Values

Over Lego's existence, Lego endured ups and downs in its business. As new products were developed to satisfy changing market conditions, Lego had to revise its business model. Business models also changed due to new partnerships and licensing agreements. But what had not changed in all that time was Lego's strategic vision and core values.

Lego's strategic objectives were to continue to be creative in developing new toys and to reach out to more children each year. The strategic objectives were supported by Lego's core values. Lego's core values focused on the "pride of creation, high quality, a strong hands-on element and fun." All products were designed around these core values. Most of the downturns in their business occurred when they deviated too far from their core values.

These core values were also critical when Lego selected licensing partners. As stated by Jorgen Vig Knudstrop, past CEO of the Lego Group:

> "It's important that the licensing partners we work with provide an experience that is on par with Lego's [core] values."

Licensing Agreements

The Lego Group's licensing agreements fall under two distinct categories: inbound and outbound. Inbound licensing refers to the licensees that grant Lego permission to create licensed themes from such movies (or series of movies) as Star Wars, Winnie the Pooh, Batman, Indiana Jones, Lord of the Rings, Super Heroes (from Marvel comics), Harry Potter and Spider-Man. Outbound licensing refers to examples where a company is given permission to use The Lego Group's intellectual property, such as

---

54. Gander, Kashmira. Lego told off by seven-year-old girl for promoting gender stereotypes, The Independent, 3 February 2014. Also, Alter, Charlotte. Soon There Will Be Female Scientist Legos, Time, June 4, 2014.

for publishing books or Merlin Entertainments use in Legoland theme parks. Outbound licensing also includes apparel, luggage, lunch boxes, electronics, school supplies, media games, clocks, and watches.

Lego's Legacy Of Success

Lego has maintained a legacy of success over its life. Lego's popularity is demonstrated by its wide representation and usage in many forms of cultural works, including books, films, and artwork. Other than the traditional bricks, Lego-branded products included apparel, footwear, backpacks, party goods, greeting cards, children's bedding, Halloween costumes, watches, oral care, board games and publishing.

In 1998, Lego bricks were one of the original inductees into the National Toy Hall of Fame in Rochester, New York. In 1999, Lego bricks was named the "Toy of the Century" by Fortune. In 2011, in a survey by the Research Institute, Lego was the #1 admired brand in Europe, #2 in the United States and Canada, and #5 globally.[55] By the first half of 2015, The Lego Group became the world's largest toy company by revenue, with sales amounting to US$2.1 billion, surpassing Mattel, which had US$1.9 billion in sales. In February 2015, Lego replaced Ferrari as Brand Finance's "world's most powerful brand." In May 2018, the company made it to Forbes top 100 World's Most Valuable Brands 2018, being 97th on the list.

Trademarks And Patents

Since the expiration of the last standing Lego patent in 1989, several companies, including Tyco Toys, Mega Bloks, and Best-Lock, have produced interlocking bricks that were like Lego brand bricks. These competitors' products were typically compatible with Lego brand bricks and were often marketed at a lower cost than Lego sets.

One such competitor was the Chinese company Tianjin Coko Toy Co., Ltd. In 2002, the Lego Group's Swiss subsidiary, Interlego AG, sued the company for copyright infringement. A trial court found many Coko bricks to be infringing. Coko was ordered to cease manufacture of the infringing bricks, publish a formal apology in the Beijing Daily, and pay a small fee in damages to Interlego. On appeal, the Beijing High People's Court upheld the trial court's ruling.

In 2003, The Lego Group won a lawsuit in Norway against the marketing group Biltema for its sale of Coko products, on the grounds that the company used product confusion for marketing purposes. Also, in 2003, a large shipment of Lego-like products marketed under the name "Enlighten" was seized by Finland customs authorities. The packaging of the Enlighten products was like official Lego brand packaging. Their Chinese manufacturer failed to appear in court, and thus Lego won a default action ordering the destruction of the shipment. Lego Group footed the bill for the disposal of the 54,000 sets, citing a desire to avoid brand confusion and protect consumers from potentially inferior products.

Not all patent and trademark lawsuits resulted in favor of the Lego Group. In 2004, Best-Lock Construction Toys defeated a patent challenge from Lego in Oberlandesgericht, Hamburg.

The Lego Group attempted to trademark the "Lego Indicia", the studded appearance of the Lego brick, hoping to stop production of Mega Bloks. On 24 May 2002, the Federal Court of Canada dismissed the case, asserting the design is functional and therefore ineligible for trademark protection. The Lego Group's appeal was dismissed by the Federal Court of Appeal on 14 July 2003. In October 2005, the

---

55. Brad Wieners, Lego Is for Girls, Bloomberg Businessweek, December 25, 2011.

Supreme Court ruled unanimously that "Trademark law should not be used to perpetuate monopoly rights enjoyed under now-expired patents" and held that Mega Bloks can continue to manufacture their bricks.

Because of fierce competition from copycat products, the company has always responded by being proactive in their patenting and has over 600 United States–granted design patents to their name.

Environmental Issues

Lego maintains a corporate social responsibility program that says that it was "our ambition to protect children's rights to live in a healthy environment, both now and in the future."[56] Lego was pressured by environmental groups to acknowledge the impact of its operations on the environment, especially in areas such as climate change, resource, and energy use and waste. All manufacturing sites were certified according to the environmental standard ISO 14001. Lego began seeking alternatives to crude oil as a raw material for its bricks. This resulted in the establishment in June 2015 of the Lego Sustainable Materials Center as a significant step towards the 2030 ambition of finding and implementing sustainable alternatives to current materials.

In 2011, Lego bowed to pressure from the environmental campaigning organization Greenpeace, reportedly agreeing to drop supplier Asia Pulp and Paper, and pledging to only use packaging material certified by the Forest Stewardship Council in future. The environmental group had accused Lego, Hasbro, Mattel and Disney of using packaging material sourced from trees cleared out of the Indonesian rainforest.

Lego partnered with the oil company Royal Dutch Shell in the 1960s, using the company's logo in some of its construction sets. This partnership continued until the 1990s and was renewed again in 2011. In July 2014, Greenpeace launched a global campaign to persuade Lego to cease producing toys carrying the oil company Shell's logo in response to Shell's plans to drill for oil in the Arctic. By August 2014, more than 750,000 people worldwide had signed a Greenpeace petition asking Lego to end its partnership with Shell. In October 2014, Lego announced that it would not be renewing its promotional contract with Royal Dutch Shell. Greenpeace claimed the decision was in response to its campaigning.

Official Website

First launched in 1996, the Lego website provides many extra services beyond an online store and a product catalogue. The website was and still is a social networking site that involves items, blueprints, ranks and badges which are earned for completing certain tasks. There are also trophies called masterpieces which allow users to progress to the next rank. The website has a built-in inbox which allows users to send prewritten messages to one another. By 2013, the Lego websites were attracting more than 20 million visitors a month.

Theme Parks And Discovery Centers

Merlin Entertainments operates eight Legoland amusement parks located in Denmark, England, Germany, California, Florida, Malaysia, United Arab Emirates, and Japan. A ninth is planned to open in 2020

56. Olsen, P. E. (2015 October). Save the whales? A public relations crisis at Lego. *Journal of Critical Incidents* 8, 130.

in New York and a tenth in 2022 in China. Lego had limited experience in running theme parks. In 2005, the control of 70% of the Legoland parks was sold for $460 million to the Blackstone Group of New York while the remaining 30% is still held by Lego Group.

There are also eight Legoland Discovery Centers, two in Germany, four in the United States, one in Japan, and one in the United Kingdom. Two Legoland Discovery Centers opened in 2013: one at the Westchester Ridge Hill shopping complex in Yonkers, New York, and one at the Vaughan Mills in Vaughan, Ontario, Canada. Another opened at the Meadowlands complex in East Rutherford, New Jersey, in 2014.

The target audience for the Legoland Discovery Center is families with young children, normally ages 3 through 12; though a typical location's average guest is about seven years of age. Discovery Centers are located near other family-friendly attractions and dining establishments. In any given year, a single facility can host approximately 400,000 to 600,000 visitors.

A typical Legoland Discovery Center occupies approximately 30,000–35,000 square feet of floor area. Discovery Centers include models of local landmarks rendered in Lego bricks. Visitors can also learn how the Lego bricks are manufactured or partake in building classes taught by a Master Model Builder. Certain locations may also include movie theaters offering multiple showings throughout the day.

A few children's attractions, such as small rides and play fortresses, are also available. The centers can host birthday parties as well as scholastic and group functions and include restaurants and gift shops selling Lego merchandise.

Retail Stores

Lego decided to open its own stores and sell directly to consumers rather than to have to rely upon the limited shelve space they were getting from retailers. Many of the retailers were not providing Lego with enough shelve space to display their brands.

Lego operates 132 so-called "Lego Store" retail shops worldwide. The opening of each store is celebrated with weekend-long events in which a Master Model Builder creates, with the help of volunteers—most of whom are children—a larger-than-life Lego statue, which is then displayed at the new store for several weeks.

The stores are used to introduce entire families to the Lego experience. The stores interact with their customers to bring forth ideas for new Lego products.

Variations On Lego Themes

Since the 1950s, the Lego Group has released thousands of sets with a variety of themes, including space, robots, pirates, trains, Vikings, castles, dinosaurs, undersea exploration, and wild west. Some of the classic themes that continue to the present day include Lego City (a line of sets depicting city life introduced in 1973) and Lego Technic (a line aimed at emulating complex machinery, introduced in 1977).

Over the years, Lego has licensed themes from numerous cartoon and film franchises and even some from video games. These include Batman, Indiana Jones, Pirates of the Caribbean, Harry Potter, Star Wars, and Minecraft. Although some of the licensed themes such as Lego Star Wars and Lego Indiana Jones had highly successful sales, Lego has expressed a desire to rely more upon their own characters and classic themes, and less upon licensed themes related to movie releases. Lego created their own storylines and supporting characters that they believed would appeal to their audiences.

Minifigures

A Lego minifigure, commonly referred to as a minifig, is a small plastic figurine. They were first produced in 1978 and have been a success, with more than four billion produced worldwide by 2006. Minifigures are usually found within Lego sets, although they are also sold separately as collectables or custom-built in Lego stores. While some are named as specific characters, either licensed from film, television, and game franchises, or of Lego's own creation, many are unnamed and are designed simply to fit within a certain theme (such as police officers, astronauts, and pirates). Minifigures are collected by both children and adults. They are highly customizable, and parts from different figures can be mixed and matched, resulting in many combinations.

For the 2012 Summer Olympics in London, Lego released a special Team GB Minifigures series exclusively in the United Kingdom to mark the opening of the games. For the 2016 Summer Olympics and 2016 Summer Paralympics in Rio de Janeiro, Lego released a kit with the Olympic and Paralympic mascots Vinicius and Tom.

One of the largest Lego sets commercially produced was a minifig-scaled edition of the Star Wars Millennium Falcon. It was released in 2007 and contained 5,195 pieces. It was surpassed by a 5,922-piece Taj Mahal. A redesigned Millennium Falcon recently retook the top spot in 2017 with 7,541 pieces.

Robotic Themes

Lego also initiated a robotics line of toys called "Mindstorms" in 1999, and has continued to expand and update this range ever since. The roots of the product originate from a programable brick developed at the MIT Media Lab, and the name was taken from a paper by Seymour Papert, a computer scientist and educator who developed the educational theory of constructionism, and whose research was at times funded by the Lego Group.

The programable Lego brick, which is at the heart of these robotics sets, has undergone several updates and redesigns. The set includes sensors that detect touch, light, sound, and ultrasonic waves.

The intelligent brick can be programmed using official software available for Windows and Mac computers, and is downloaded onto the brick via Bluetooth or a USB cable. There are also several unofficial programs and compatible programming languages that have been made to work with the brick, and many books have been written to support this community.

There are several robotics competitions which use the Lego robotics sets. They focus on middle- and high-school competition like a Lego robotics tournament held at MIT. The tournaments focus on specific age groups such as student ages 6–9 and 9–16. Students form teams and must use Lego-based robots to complete tasks. Students see this as a real-world engineering challenge. In 2010, there were 16,070 teams in more than 55 countries. The competition involved extensive use of Lego Mindstorms equipment which was often pushed to its extreme limits.

There is a strong community of professionals and hobbyists of all ages involved in the sharing of designs, programming techniques, creating third-party software and hardware, and contributing of other ideas associated with Lego Mindstorms. Lego encourages sharing and peering by making software code available for downloading and by holding various contests and events. The overall benefit was that technology was bringing more adults to Lego products.

Integrated Experiences

The toys, minifigs, robotics, books, and accessories allowed customers to develop their own storylines when playing, including roleplaying, rather than just construction activities. This gave customers the opportunity to build a bridge between Lego's traditional toys and the digital world. If the minifigs and robotic themes were based upon TV shows and movies, customers could create their own storylines using their imagination and creativity.

Video Games

Lego has also branched out into the video game market with titles such as Lego Island, Lego Creator, and Lego Racers. Lego developed strategic partnerships to make games like Lego Star Wars, Lego Indiana Jones, Lego Batman, and many more including the very well-received Lego Marvel Super Heroes game, featuring New York City as the overworld and including Marvel characters from the Avengers, the Fantastic Four, the X-Men, and more. More recently, Lego created a game based on The Lego Movie, due to its popularity. By 2013, more than 100 million copies of Lego video games were sold by their licensed partners.

Innovation Management:Plastic Construction Toy

From its inception through the late 1990s, Lego enjoyed a steady growth. In 1998, Lego suffered its first yearly loss and then hired a turnaround specialist as the CEO to get the company back on track. The company had been struggling with poor management, lack of a strategic focus, and a disconnection from their customers. Lego was not responsive to the needs of their customers. There were innovations and some successes, but the innovation management process appeared unstructured. Unable to turn the company around, a new CEO was hired in January 2004. Lego suffered another significant loss in 2004 and was on the verge of bankruptcy.

The marketplace had changed. Children were growing older at a faster rate. Lego's target market of boys aged four to nine were turning to videogames and web-based activities. Other toy manufacturers were working with licensing partners and were becoming serious threats to capture Lego's core customers.

Turning the company around was difficult. Lego had allowed innovation to be uncontrolled and did not know whether the focus should be on sustaining innovation mainly around the Lego bricks, disruptive innovation for new products, or both. It is questionable whether the innovations were linked to strategic business objectives. The number of new products had increased from 6,000 to 14,200. Lego failed to realize that too much innovation can be unhealthy. As stated by Peter Drucker,

> "There is nothing so useless as doing efficiently that which should not be done at all."

Lego was struggling with costs. They did not know the costs of many individual sets and had trouble identifying which products and product lines were profitable.[57]

Lego appeared to have suffered from some of the traits common to many privately held companies regarding innovation. The starting point was with Lego's business model. It is not uncommon for privately held companies to focus on new product development without recognizing that business model innovation may also be necessary. Without having shareholders, the company can lack a financial and operative control system to the point where cost management can get out of control. All ideas for new products may be internally generated, based upon the whims of management, and with no involvement

---

57. Adapted from Ville Kilkku, June 2014. Sustaining innovation and disruptive innovation—case Lego. http://www.kilkku.com/blog/2014/06/sustaining-innovation-and-disruptive-innovation-case-lego, accessed February 2020.

by customers. The company may rush into the launch of new products without proper prototype development and testing. Executives may fall in love with the existing products and refuse to see the benefits of licensing their intellectual property. Executives may not see the benefits of lowering costs by outsourcing production to lower cost organizations.

If Lego were to survive, the effectiveness of its product development process would need to change. Growing the business is the right thing to do, but it must be accompanied by business model transformation if necessary. Only by radically reimagining and speeding up the process could Lego create breakthrough new toy ideas and save the company.[58] There were, of course, other things Lego had to do as well.

The turning point occurred with the launch of Mindstorms. Within three weeks after launching Mindstorms, more than 1,000 advanced users—in a campaign coordinated on the web—had hacked into the software that came with the construction toys to make unauthorized modifications with new functions.[59] The hackers had actually improved the product to the point where more units were being sold. Lego's original thoughts were that the hacking was illegal and done without permission. But Lego soon realized that the product was attractive to customers over the age of 18. Lego was on the verge of finding a new customer base. Lego decided that it would be best not to fight with hackers but instead harness their knowledge and creativity to improve the products.

Lego quickly realized the benefits of open innovation. Lego could tap into the brainpower and imagination of others rather than relying solely upon its own R&D group. The possibilities were endless. Lego was now about to reverse it downward trajectory and return to profitability. Lego's culture and business model were changing. Lego was now listening to their customers. Initially, management feared that this would slow down the product development processes, but soon realized that their fears were unwarranted.

Lego's turnaround strategy came from engaging its expansive customer base. The goal was to generate customer feedback on a small scale before making substantial investments, illustrating Lego's philosophy that, "people don't have to work for us to work with us."[60] To further this practice, the company launched, Lego Ideas, an online crowd-sourcing platform, allowing customers to share and to vote for ideas they wished to see as additions to the product line. Lego Ideas yielded hundreds of suggestions annually, employing social media to generate actionable data. Focusing on products that would sell, Lego was able to reach new audiences through its extensive physical footprint and brand awareness.[61]

Lego introduced several programs to make it easy for consumers to work with the company. Lego launch the Ambassador Program that provided a direct way for the company to access new ideas from its community.[62] A new platform named Lego Cuusoo was launched to allow fans to upload designs. If a design received 10,000 votes from the community members, Lego agreed to consider it for production. This process maximized the possibility that a product would have mass appeal.[63] Another open-source platform was Adult Fans of Lego (AFOL). The consumers could work as lead developers with Lego personnel.

58. Jonathon Ringen, How Lego Became the Apple of Toys, Fast Company, June 15, 2015.

59. Adapted from Lego Success Built on Open Innovation, November 13, 2018. https://www.ideaconnection.com/open-innovation-success/Lego-Success-Built-on-Open-Innovation-00258.html, accessed February 2020.

60. The Leadership Network, "5 Sustainable Innovation Practices that Saved Lego," Innovation Management, November 7, 2016.

61. Adapted from Jaclyn Markowitz, Open Innovation at Lego—The Back Beat in "Everything is Awesome," November 13, 2018. https://digital.hbs.edu/platform-rctom/submission/open-innovation-at-lego-the-back-beat-in-everything-is-awesome, accessed February 2020.

62. Adapted from Bricks & Code: Open Innovation at Lego Group, November 13, 2018. https://digital.hbs.edu/platform-rctom/submission/bricks-code-open-innovation-at-lego-group, accessed February 2020.

63. Antorini, Y. M., Muniz, A. M., Jr., and Askildsen, T. (2012 Spring). Collaborating with customer communities. *MIT Sloan Management Review*.

Lego also created a Future Lab to control internally- and customer-generated innovation ideas at Lego. This innovation lab was tasked with inventing the future of play, a large part of which was identifying growth opportunities and ensuring that Lego stays ahead of the curve. They strived to do things not otherwise done and to introduce radical innovation without jeopardizing the core business and value propositions of the Lego brand.[64] Lego now had design talent spread across the world and all of these new programs created by Lego were focused on connecting the ideas with the product development teams. Lego had changed their business model to become closer to their customers.

Innovation Life Cycle Phases

Primary concept and development work occur at the Billund headquarters, where the company employs product designers. The company also has smaller design offices in the UK, Spain, Germany, and Japan which are tasked with developing products aimed specifically at these markets. Even though Lego has offices dispersed around the world, there is still commonality and interconnectivity among their products whereby all innovation projects appear to contain the same or similar life-cycle phases even though some projects have different phases.

The average development period for a new product is around twelve months, split into three life-cycle phases. The first phase is to identify market trends and developments, including contact by the designers directly with the market. Some designers are stationed in toy shops, especially close to holidays, while others interview children and their parents. The second phase is the design and development of the product based upon the results of the first phase. The design teams use 3D modeling software to generate CAD drawings from initial design sketches. The designs are then prototyped using an in-house stereolithography machine. These prototypes are presented to the entire project team for comment and for testing by parents and children during the "validation" process. Designs may then be altered in accordance with the results from the focus groups. Virtual models of completed Lego products are built concurrently with the writing of the user instructions. Completed CAD models are also used in the wider organization, for marketing and packaging.

The third life-cycle phase is the actual commercialization of the product. After product launch, Lego interacts closely with the consumers for improvements to the products using incremental innovation as well as seeking out ideas for other similar and non-similar products that would require radical innovation.

Creativity and brainstorming are critical innovation skills in all life-cycle phases at Lego. The brainstorm and creativity extend to their user base as well. In May 2011, Space Shuttle Endeavour mission STS-134 brought 13 Lego kits to the International Space Station, where astronauts built models to see how they would react in microgravity, as a part of the Lego Bricks in Space program. In May 2013, the largest model ever created was displayed in New York City and was made of over 5 million bricks; a 1:1 scale model of an X-wing fighter. Other records include a 112-foot tower and a 2.5-mile railway.

Innovation Management Lessons Learned

One of the risks with family-owned businesses is that they tend to become complacent if things are going well financially with the attitude "Let's Leave Well-Enough Alone" or "The Same Old Way Will Work

---

64. Adapted from Michael Fearne, Lego Future Lab—The Rebels of Innovation at Lego, 2019. https://michaelfearne.com/lego-future-lab-the-rebels-of-innovation-at-lego, accessed March 2020. The website contains several good blogs on innovation practices at Lego.

for Years to Come." The only innovation that is considered is then incremental innovation and lessons learned may not be shared across the entire company. Lego did not fall into this trap. Some of the things that Lego appeared to understand was that:[65]

Lego must foster an innovation culture

Innovations may require changes to the firm's business model

Survivability is based upon using multiple forms of innovation even though emphasis is placed upon incremental and radical innovation

Different levels of innovation by different groups must be allowed to improve the product success rate

Radical, incremental, and other forms of innovation may follow different life-cycle phases

Radical innovation is difficult, and control systems, gates, and checkpoints are necessary

Innovation processes must be de-centralized and innovation teams must have some freedom in selecting the best approach such as deciding between using a waterfall or agile project management approach

Innovation teams must have the choice of tools to be used on their projects

All innovation projects must be based upon the firm's core values

Not all Lego's products will be successful

Lego's future must include crowdsourcing practices and maintaining a constant dialogue with its customers

Lego must get close to the customers it serves, not just for idea generation, but to ensure that a market exists for the outcome of projects

Lego must understand the changes that are taking place in the needs and behaviors of its customers

Lego must realize that they have multiple customer bases, especially among older users

Many of Lego's customers want to participate as co-creators if just in providing ideas or actual participation in product development

To maximize ideas, Lego must provide a mechanism whereby customers acting as co-creators can communicate and exchange ideas with one another

New product testing, pilot studies, prototyping, and experimentation will be necessities

Design thinking must be part of innovation processes

Epilogue

The Lego case is an example of the complexities with managing innovation to sustain a global brand. There are numerous challenges such as expanding the brand into new ventures such as games, videos, movies, apparel and accessories, company-owned stores, and licensing agreements. Should the company focus more on incremental or radical innovations? For innovation to be successful, should the company centralize or decentralize operations? Should the entire company realize the strategic vision? How will each innovation impact the firm's business model? These issues must be addressed continuously.

The Lego Group announced on 4 September 2017 its intention to cut 1,400 jobs following reduced revenue and profit in the first half of the year, the first reported decrease in 13 years. The revenue losses appear to be the result of a more competitive environment, where the company has to compete not only

---

65. Some of the lessons learned have been adapted from Divina Paredes, David Gram of Lego: An insider's guide to radical innovation, CIO, June 6, 2017. For a more detailed description of the innovation processes at Lego, see Robertson, David. Brick by Brick: How LEGO Rewrote the Rules of Innovation and Conquered the Global Toy Industry, New York, NY: Random House, 2013.

against its traditional competitors such as Mattel and Hasbro, but also against technology companies such as Sony or Microsoft as more children are using mobile devices for entertainment. However, some insiders at the Lego Group believe that Lego had become complacent due to recent yearly earnings, may have lost its entrepreneurial/innovative spirit, and that it may take a few years to recover. History has shown us that Lego has the capability to overcome these hurdles.

Questions

1. What are some of the innovation project management critical issues that may (or may not) be unique to privately held companies as opposed to publicly held firms?
2. Should project managers participate in market research studies to determine who the customers are?
3. Should project managers participate in follow-up market research studies to determine how well the customers like the products?
4. Do companies have core values and, if so, what might cause them to change as in the Lego case?
5. Should innovation project managers understand licensing agreements?
6. Should project managers be concerned about trademarks, intellectual property, and environmental issues? If so, what depth of knowledge should exist?
7. Can websites be of benefit to innovation project managers?
8. Were the life cycle phases used in the Lego case traditional life cycle phases for innovation projects?
9. What types of innovation were used at Lego?
10. Do brand management activities place limitations on whether innovation practices are centralized or decentralized?

Instructor's Manual

1. What are some of the innovation project management critical issues that may (or may not) be unique to privately held companies as opposed to publicly held firms?

    The objective of the case study is to show not just innovation management practices but also the challenges facing privately held companies where innovation focuses mainly on brand management. The answers to the questions do not necessarily imply that they occurred at Lego, or to show the effective or ineffective management of a firm. The questions and answers are to stimulate classroom discussion.

    Some of the critical issues include:The decision as to where to invest innovation funds rests in the hand of a few, usually family members. This holds true even if a board of directors exists with external membership.Other decision-making, as well, may rest in the hands of a few. Decisions may be made based upon the whims of management or for what is in the best interest of the owners rather than the employees in general.Without having to report financial information to public shareholders, the firm may not possess an adequate cost control system.Innovation activities may be bypassed if they do not support the brand image.Failing to recognize the need for business model transformation.

2. Should project managers participate in market research studies to determine who the customers are?

    This is a necessity for several reasons. First, the age group of the customers might change as well as the gender of the preferred users. In some countries, adults may prefer to play with the children and the toys, thus creating an opportunity for more advanced toys or products designed specifically for the adult community. In other countries, the products must be designed so that the kids can play without supervision. Second, even though the products are used primarily by children, the adults are the purchasers. As such, marketing and advertising information must focus on a compromise between and appeal to children and their parents. Third, it is necessary to determine the frequency of product usage. This could determine the timing of updates to the products.

3. Should project managers participate in follow-up market research studies to determine how well the customers like the products?

   Observing how the customers use the products identifies customer satisfaction and where improvements and updates may be necessary. It can also identify gender inequality situations such as with Lego Friends. Observations and follow-up can provide information on whether the users are interested in just this product or the brand it represents.

4. Do companies have core values and, if so, what might cause them to change as in the Lego case?

   Most companies have core values which can impact their decisions on innovation. However, the core values may not be fully publicized. Some companies publicize their core values related to corporate social responsibility, environmental issues, and natural resource depletion issues.

   Lego's core values focused on the "pride of creation, high quality, a strong hands-on element and fun." Lego was originally averse to making "war" toys. However, the decision to make minifigs for Star Wars changed the core values a bit. Lego's core values focus on the Lego brand image rather than just a specific product.

   When companies come out with new products, they often believe that the existing business model is still workable. In small and privately held companies, there appears to be significant resistance to change the business model hoping that past successes will continue.

5. Should innovation project managers understand licensing agreements?

   The purpose of licensing agreements is to increase revenue. However, the licensing agreements also have a serious impact on product design and cost. As an example, inbound licensing at Lego provided guidance on how Lego products would be designed and used to be compatible with movies such as Star Wars, for example. For outbound licensing, innovation project managers have more freedom during the design of products. In both types, project managers should understand licensing agreements, the impact on product channels of distribution, and how they impact innovation activities.

6. Should project managers be concerned about trademarks, intellectual property, and environmental issues? If so, what depth of knowledge should exist?

   Project managers should be concerned about these elements most frequently as they relate to the design of the product and the materials used. Usually, a representative from the legal staff is a team member, will possess the in-depth legal information, and will participate in making most of the legal decisions.

7. Can websites be of benefit to innovation project managers?

   Websites allow project managers to see the interests that customers have. The websites can also be used to solicit feedback from present or future customers on features they would like to see in the products, or new products. Lego allowed website users to submit product designs and to vote on new designs. When more than 10,000 users voted in favor of a new product, Lego believed that the product would have good market potential and was worth the investment in commercialization.

8. Were the life cycle phases used in the Lego case traditional life cycle phases for innovation projects?

   From the case study, it appeared that there were three life cycle phases: market trends analyses, design & development, and commercialization. While this may have been enough for Lego products, other life cycle phases could have been included such as benefits realization and value determination. These may have been used at Lego, but not identified as such in the case study.

9. What types of innovation were used at Lego?

From the case study, it appears that only incremental and radical innovation were used. However, the problem with the relationship with Royal Dutch Shell implies that sustainable innovation was also considered.

10. Do brand management activities place limitations on whether innovation practices are centralized or decentralized?

In privately held companies, it is possible that innovation practices are centralized. In publicly held companies, centralization may occur by product line rather than at the executive or owner level.

Index

A

ability, 6–8, 78, 83, 142–43,
    151, 157–159, 170–171,
    203–204, 276, 325, 364,
    401, 425, 447, 512–13
  students, 364
  technical, 371
  workers, 163
AC. *See* agile coach
accelerating time-to-market, 173
access to stakeholders, 185
accommodations, 470, 473
accountability, 73, 85, 93, 142,
    150, 239, 266, 395, 401
  actions, 85, 93
  enforcing single-person, 395
  mutual, 85, 91
  project success, 395
accounting system, 194
  divisional, 544
  standard, 277
accuracy, 152, 212–13
acoustics, 504–5
ActeeChange simulator, 360
action, 35, 40–41, 55–56,
    58–61, 63–64, 84–89, 91,

93, 149, 151–52, 203–5,
    228–29, 234–35, 237–38,
    248–49, 251, 257–59, 299,
    341, 351–437
  competitive, 29
  directed, 48
  filter, 143
  legal, 467
  management's, 139
  readjustment, 126–27
actionable, 287
active listening, 141, 165–66
activities/processes, 227
activity workflow, 185
actors, 32–33, 36, 54, 425
  function, 34
adaptability, 103, 435
  proactive, 179
adaptation, 388
adaptive approaches, 406
add-ons, 23–24, 64, 99
administration phases, 421
administrative costs, high, 51
admissions, 468, 470, 485, 491
  above-market, 473
  admission fees, 473, 483, 484, 493

Hong Kong Disneyland, 492
  tickets, 492
adoption, 2, 46, 103, 222, 253
Adult Fans of Lego
    (AFOL), 558
Advanced Management
    Science, 262
Advanced Micro
    Devices. *See* AMD
advanced value attributes, 295
advertising campaign, 525, 528
Advisor/Advisory Board, 365
Aerospace Division, 544–46
Aerospace Engineering, 363
aesthetics, 445–46, 457, 506
  focus, 445
  value, 31, 159, 290, 379, 441,
    445–46, 448, 450, 466, 468
afford-ability, 531
AFOL (Adult Fans of
    Lego), 558
Agile and adaptive
    approaches, 406
agile approach, 38, 40, 200, 231,
    406, 411, 424
Agile by Design, 391

Innovation Project Management: Methods, Case Studies, and Tools for Managing Innovation Projects,
Second Edition. Harold Kerzner.
© 2023 John Wiley & Sons, Inc. Published 2023 by John Wiley & Sons, Inc.

agile coach (AC), 41–43
agile innovation,
    38–40, 217, 411
Agile Innovation in Action,
    40–41, 43, 45, 411,
    413, 415, 417
Agile Innovation Master
    Plan, 303–4, 411–12,
    414–15, 438
agile methodologies,
    396, 540–41
    flexible, 200
agile software development, 412
agile teams work, 39
agility, 234, 397, 406, 415
agreement, 85, 89, 108, 203,
    206, 286, 290, 329–30, 374,
    475–76, 482–84, 491, 493
    contractual, 318, 421, 482
    customer/contractor/stake-
    holder, 289
AIG Affiliated Companies, 521
Airbus, 35–36, 68, 251,
    253–54, 257–60, 262, 496,
    498–99, 539
Airbus and Boeing, 499
Airbus Corporate Innova-
    tion, 252–58
Airbus employees, 251, 254
Airbus Group, 256
Airbus Innovation Cell, 251–52
aircraft, 32–33, 130, 205, 351,
    495–96, 498–500
    components, 33
    customers, 499
    designed, 32
    manufacturers, 494–95
    new, 494–95, 499–500
Aireon, 535–36
    flight trackers, 536
airlines, 32–33, 494, 498–
    500, 525, 533
    low-cost, 327
    maintenance costs, 495
air navigation traffic
    control, 351
air time, 324

air traffic controllers, 351–53,
    357, 360, 363
air traffic management, 358
    new, 355
air traffic management
    system, 357
Aligning Metrics and
    Rewards, 307
alignment, 15–16, 70, 72, 121,
    133–36, 251–52, 285, 296–
    97, 368–69, 417–18, 420
    better, 34, 135, 281
    continuous, 121
    core values, 72
    cultural, 417
    features, 133
    goals, 383
    issues, 135
    market, 420
    metrics, 136
    PMO projects, 136
    strategic issues, 135
allegations, 329–30
Alliance Competence, 331
All-in-one business model, 326
All Nippon Airways. *See* ANA
altitude, 512–13, 515, 535
Amazon, 51, 183–84, 342–43
ambiguity, 18, 24, 68, 125,
    138–40, 155–56, 187–88,
    192, 300, 386, 388
ambition, 223, 226, 251, 267,
    435, 437, 554
AMD (Advanced Micro
    Devices), 329–30
American-based project, 514
American Energy Tran-
    sition, 437
American Graduate School
    of International Man-
    agement, 481
American Productiv-
    ity and Quality Center
    (APQC), 30, 68
American theme park, 464–65,
    469, 479, 482, 489
American tourists, 472

amortization value, 432
Ampore Faucet
    Company, 508–9
ANA (All Nippon Airways),
    32–33, 496–99
analysis, 111, 145, 211–12, 221,
    229, 303, 312–13, 317,
    375, 383, 390
    benefit-to-cost, 114
    competitor, 198
    cost/benefit, 340
    cost-benefit, 210
    creative, 111
    environmental, 101–2
    market-growth, 80
    market-share, 80
    market trends, 562
    post-failure, 387
    value chain, 265
    value gap, 265
analysis for measuring innovation
    processes performance, 313
analysis-paralysis situ-
    ations, 177
analysts, 229, 358, 475,
    512, 531, 537
analytical processing, 320
Analyzing Contracting doc-
    uments, 422
animatics, 444
animation, 444, 446, 455
anticompetitive prac-
    tices, 329–30
Antucheviciene, 124
Apple, 51, 53, 102, 143, 146,
    149, 183–84, 277, 342–43,
    393–95, 402
    developer tools, 394
    employees, 395
    fellows program, 395
    successes, 394
Application Engineering, 96
application providers, 396
applications, 40, 43–47, 50, 52,
    65, 81, 95–96, 98, 147–48,
    192, 194, 246–47, 261–62,
    266, 395–96

cellular, 529
concrete, 423
creating, 396
direct, 98
mind-map, 165
mobile, 50, 421
new, 2, 98, 395, 536
patent, 433
specialized, 81
versatile, 248
Applied research projects, 98
apprehensions, 160, 162, 486
approach, 37, 39, 63, 101–2,
    133, 200–202, 226, 230–32,
    282, 310, 364, 398–401,
    411–13, 417, 540–43
approximate budget, 97
APQC (American Productivity
    and Quality Center), 30, 68
architects, 14, 66, 135, 142,
    146, 440, 442–43, 485, 502,
    504, 506–7
    executive, 507
architecture, 33, 42, 46, 55–56,
    159, 176, 442, 445–46, 448,
    503, 506–7
    customer Reference, 226
    easy-to-remember, 150
    historical, 471
    local, 466
Armed Services, 208
arming employees, 191
art, 95–96, 98, 103, 273,
    444, 446, 448, 500–501,
    506, 508, 537
artificial intelligence, 52,
    182–83, 230
    solutions, 219
artwork, 157, 553
Asia Case Research Centre, 494
assessment, 74, 78, 82, 88, 150,
    180, 198, 301, 382, 391
    qualitative, 274
assets, 19, 37, 40, 50, 84, 115,
    195, 277, 514, 522, 532–33
    knowledge-based, 176
    reconfiguring, 241

shared, 196
ATM Projects & Engi-
    neering, 351
atom, 513
attendance, 91, 125, 476, 478,
    482, 485–88, 492–93, 547
    park's, 488–89
    projected daily, 475
attendance figures, 472, 477,
    487, 492–93
    lowest, 476, 486
    yearly, 484
attention, 45, 85–86, 90–91, 93,
    105, 176, 355, 362, 381–82,
    441, 446–47
attention risk, 291
attractions, 159, 439, 441–53,
    455–57, 461, 463, 466–67,
    470–71, 474, 477–78, 481,
    483, 485, 488–92, 495
    children's, 555
    complete, 445
    favorite, 449
    first-ever Asian, 492
    humorous, 451
    iconic, 463
    new, 441, 463, 467, 474,
        476, 478, 486
    outdated, 492
    popular visitor, 501
    scary, 455
    total, 456
    upgraded, 478
attributes, 120–22, 152, 250,
    264, 279, 281–82, 284–85,
    287–90, 295–96, 337, 367
    common, 406
    correct, 281
    critical, 39, 119
    important quality, 441
    new, 290
    right, 311
    subjective, 273
auction business model, 326
audience, 89, 147, 160, 167,
    252, 256–57, 287, 336,
    349, 547, 555

Audio-Animatronics, 443–
    44, 448, 458
    development, 444
Australia, 7, 501, 507
authority, 8, 59, 125, 135,
    143, 146, 253, 267,
    341, 501, 509
authority relationships, 183
autonomy, 15, 152–53, 341, 361
available risk mitigation
    strategies, 140
aviation safety investigators, 497
awareness
    cultural, 405
    guest, 474
    people's, 424

B
bait and hook business
    model, 324
Balanced Life-Cycle
    Portfolio, 80
balance sheets, 176,
    195, 277, 526
bankruptcy, 383, 476, 529–32,
    534, 548, 557
    Iridium, 531
    protection, 530–31
banks, 50, 60, 248, 464, 467,
    475, 518, 523, 529–30
baselines, 42, 214, 269,
    284–87, 523
    project's schedule, 208
BBC News, 497, 538–39
BCG (Boston Consulting
    Group), 76, 309, 313
    model, 76–78, 81
behavioral change, 354
    necessary, 355
behavioral issues, 34
belief systems, 156
benchmarking, 8–10, 194, 320
    tools, 10, 17
benefit marketing, 105
benefits, 34, 37–39, 44–45,
    58–59, 66–67, 170–72,
    197–99, 206–8, 255–57,

268–69, 272–73, 275–76,
278, 312, 377–78, 402,
415–16, 551, 558, 561–62
Bennelong Point, 501, 537
Berg, 9–10
Bessant, 14, 18, 20, 157, 189
BHAGs (big, hairy, audacious
goals), 200, 205, 542
BI, 154
biases, 70–71, 166–68, 234, 312
Big Data Maturity Model, 72
black box data, 535
Blackstone Group of
New York, 555
Blockbuster, 324, 336
customers, 336
Bloomberg Businessweek, 553
Blue Ocean Strategy, 37
board, 66, 68, 70–71, 122,
171–74, 199–200, 252,
255, 515, 518–19, 521,
528–29, 535, 537
chairman, 214
change control, 214
global, 14
meetings, 515, 528
members, 66, 171–73, 521
preferred, 173
regular Corporate Inno-
vation, 431
smart, 404
white, 15, 163
body costumes, 446
body language, 162, 165–66
person's, 165
Boeing, 7, 32–33, 317, 369,
493–501, 525, 533, 535, 537–39
confident, 538
destroyed, 536
flota, 538
included, 532
permit, 498
boeing-787-dreamliner-us-
investigation, 539
Boeing and FAA, 538
Boeing Co, 497

Boland, Jim, 396
bootlegged innovation, 199
Bootlegged projects, 98, 147
Boston Consulting Group
(BCG), 76, 309, 313
brake problems, 496
brand, 44, 53, 301, 304, 405,
415–16, 548–49, 553,
555, 560, 562
innovation, 53, 548–49
Brand Management Innovation,
548–49, 551–63
manager, 53, 549
practices, 53, 549
Brazil, Thomas, 411
bricks, 325, 528, 549–50, 554,
556, 559–60
produced interlocking, 553
programable, 556
bride, 453
bridge, 7, 178, 257,
423, 500, 557
British Airways, 32–33
budget, 39, 41–44, 46, 200, 207,
234–35, 243–44, 269–70,
290, 371–73, 397, 432, 434,
457, 508–11, 524
constraints, 117, 414
consumption, 43
estimated, 485
financial constraints, 264
new, 476, 486
original, 369, 371, 457, 507
school's, 550
budgeting, 75, 212
Build Euro Disney, 466
Burz, 9–10
business, 3–6, 10–12, 41–42,
93–95, 119–22, 130–32,
149–51, 193–94, 197–200,
237–40, 252–55, 264,
276–81, 316–17, 319–21,
324–25, 333–39, 346,
368–69, 526–27
articulating, 222
assembly, 494

benefit, 276
better, 317
central, 86
chemical, 237
convention, 472
customer's, 404
daily development, 429
deploying social
innovation, 55
existing, 315
family-owned, 559
financial, 62
greatest, 394
high-margin, 470
high-profit-margin, 470
incremental, 132
incumbent, 335–36
land-based cellular
phone, 521
legacy, 142
long-term, 5
multiple, 544
noncyclical, 84
operating, 529
renewal, 224
rental, 336
small, 247
strategic, 120, 145, 541
successful, 73, 531
sustainable, 120
transacting, 222
turbulent, 540
we do, 362
Business Development, 421
Business Model Innovation
Factory, 331
business models, 81–82,
174–75, 315–16, 318–31,
334–40, 381, 388–89, 421,
423, 464–68, 470, 484,
533–34, 552, 558–59
collaborative, 325
companies change, 317
company's, 316, 319–20, 331,
336, 338, 381, 395
competitive, 319

current, 328
customercentric, 50
customer's, 34, 282, 403
doomed, 328, 534
existing, 323, 336, 464, 562
firm's, 53, 71, 141, 153, 315,
   322, 334, 337, 384, 560
for-profit, 325
game-changing, 342
good, 319, 328
innovative, 331, 465
internal, 282
low-risk, 466
network effects, 326
online auction, 326
online content, 326
organization's, 121, 389
premium, 326
pyramid scheme, 326
subscription, 326
successful, 325, 464
traditional, 50
unique, 318
Business Models and
   Lawsuits, 329
business objectives, 6, 99, 121,
   269, 281, 382
corporate, 334
long-term, 70
organizational, 268
BusinessWeek, 537
buzzwords, 334, 364

C
CAD/CAM modeling, 445
California, 248, 440, 442,
   453, 474, 485, 487,
   525, 535, 554
California Management Review,
   17, 188, 244
Canberra Times, 537
Capability Maturity Model
   (CMM), 524
Capability Maturity Model Inte-
   gration (CMMI), 72

capital, 112, 172, 196, 277, 299,
   302, 304–5, 477, 479, 518
   budgets, 83
   expenditures, 112
   investment, 41, 536
   human, 312
   markets, 84, 268, 534
cash, 29, 77, 80, 422, 476, 520,
   526, 529, 531
cash cows, 76–78, 81, 101
cash flow, 22, 28, 37, 81, 84, 97,
   115, 175, 350, 467, 476
   worker safety, 295
Cathay Pacific, 32–33
cause-and-effect rela-
   tionship, 176
CCB (change control
   board), 214
   meeting, 214
CDC, 230, 232
Cecilie Van Loon, 358–59
cell phones, 50, 60, 151, 161,
   324, 394, 512, 527
Cellular technology in telephones, 536
Cengage Learning, 17
CEX, 40–41
   project, 46
CFO (chief financial officer),
   477, 526, 528
CGWIC (China Great Wall
   Industry Corporation), 521
challenges, 11, 13, 48–49, 52,
   67–68, 154, 156, 192,
   228–31, 253, 311–12, 331,
   333, 405, 560–61
   common, 434
   given, 429
   joint, 434
   major, 364
   organizational, 52, 434
   technological, 434
   unique, 407
Chan Kim, 37
Chesbrough, 36, 68, 261–62

China Great Wall Industry Corporation (CGWIC), 521
Chinese culture, 489–91
client and stakeholders, 278–
   80, 287, 294
client base, 280
clients, 24, 278–85, 287, 290,
   292, 294, 301, 318–19, 325,
   328, 373, 397, 506–7
   external, 202, 279
   given, 186
climate change, 554
CMM (Capability Maturity
   Model), 524
CMMI (Capability Maturity
   Model Integration), 72
COMAU, 418–25
   contract management,
   418, 421–22
   innovation, 419
   PME, 420
   project manager, 425
   risk management, 423
communications, 25, 28, 151, 160,
   162, 165, 217–18, 255–57,
   260, 357, 361, 403, 406
   continuous, 436
   direct, 256
   expecting, 499
   external, 217
   face-to-face, 181, 346, 499
   improved organizational, 135
   monthly, 401
   necessary, 201, 543
   open, 73, 89, 184, 402, 524
   rapid, 64
   regular, 89
   virtual, 162
   wireless, 527
Community of Practice,
   224, 228–29
companies, 25–31, 34–40,
   53–57, 69–78, 95–97,
   99–103, 105–15, 142–49,
   158–65, 240–50, 272–86,

315–20, 325–30, 336–40,
346–50, 372–81, 399–403,
423–28, 546–49, 557–63
admired, 548
aerospace, 36, 251
aircraft-tracking, 536
can-do, 518
creative, 394
customer, 96
diversified, 318
forced, 51, 182
gateway, 532
high-tech, 246
high-technology, 370
hundred, 110
incumbent, 335
industrial, 99
innovative, 146
insurance, 340
integrated, 237
international, 248
large, 14, 105
lean, 238, 240
marketing-dominated, 106
medium-sized, 540
multinational, 174, 544
new, 467, 533
operating, 517, 521, 532
performing-arts, 501
pharmaceutical, 108, 148
project-financed, 514
public, 536
rival, 26
single, 36
specialized, 261
stalwart, 520
state-owned, 351
successful, 102, 110, 241, 389
tech, 183
telephone, 514
well-managed, 336
compensation, 148, 309,
402, 482, 499
competences, 249, 260, 280,
308, 352, 358, 360, 425
firm, 68

major technological, 428
technical, 306, 437
competency, 22, 85–95,
152–54, 241, 380
distinctive, 82, 282
establishing new rules, 327
existing, 380
existing technology, 380
firm's, 148, 179
intangible, 309
necessary, 122
new, 380
required, 298
resource, 119
strategic, 7, 16, 49, 185
technological, 428
top, 15
competition, 73, 106–7, 205–6, 280,
282, 328, 330, 333, 349–50,
518, 520, 547, 549, 554, 556
high-school, 556
increased, 520
internal, 143, 157
original, 505–6
robotics, 556
technical, 249
competitive advantage, 21,
25–26, 31–33, 38, 63,
193–95, 229–30, 241–42,
282, 288, 415–16
long-term sustainable, 146
potential sustainable, 73
sustainable, 4, 19, 31, 152,
195, 276, 318, 328
sustained, 73
true, 282
competitive margin, 234
competitive marketplaces, 398
competitiveness, 3–4, 6, 20, 78,
194, 237, 316, 323, 347
company's, 76
long-term, 82
competitive position,
77–80, 83, 97
competitors, 4, 9, 28, 73–75,
82, 96–97, 203, 319–21,

326–28, 330–31, 338, 349,
436, 547, 553
breeding, 349
direct, 319
major, 531
potential, 514
traditional, 561
complexity, 6–8, 24, 65, 137–
40, 152, 185, 187–88, 192,
197–98, 216, 218, 220–21,
226–27, 261, 451–52
defining, 226
growing, 253
low, 220
organizational, 423
reduced, 421
reducing, 229
technological, 518
components, 9–10, 104–5,
139–40, 142–43, 158, 161,
215, 271, 289–90, 292, 294,
440, 442, 515–16
adaptive, 424
central management, 516
critical, 31–32, 247, 499
engine, 496
five, 294, 411
foundational framework, 411
intellectual capital, 195
multiple, 390
outsource, 71
relevant, 167–68
technical, 205, 369, 390
tracks, 175
computer programmers, 249
computers, 50, 58, 60, 182–83,
324, 445, 499, 503, 550
construction, 440, 444, 450–51,
454, 472–73, 475, 479,
483, 485, 488, 503–6,
516, 518
complete, 471
new road, 467
construction activities, 556
Construction Engineering, 18
Construction History, 502

consultants, 5, 103, 119, 241, 254, 399, 500, 510
Consulting Group, 355–56
consumers, 20, 22, 51, 53, 69, 71, 290, 323, 325, 374, 495–96, 549–50, 553, 555, 558–59
  average, 508
  end-product, 63
  end-user, 268
  ultimate, 31
consumer satisfaction, 32, 296
contractors, 122, 125, 213–14, 272, 278–79, 282, 311, 370–71, 374, 376, 506, 524, 530, 532
  selecting potential, 119
contract price, 290
Contract Reviews and Reports, 422
contracts, 107–8, 185, 191, 419, 423, 483, 505–6, 522–23, 532–33, 535, 537, 543, 547
  basic, 485
  compensation, 172
  firm-fixed-price, 515
  fixed-price EPC, 423
  legal, 482
  local union, 484
  long-term, 515
  long-term lucrative, 547
  lower-cost, 522
  multiyear, 544
  new, 535
  outsourcing, 71
  promotional, 554
  sharing, 109
contract sales, 423
contractual failure, 383
contributions, 36–37, 70, 92, 112–13, 161, 164, 218, 222, 297, 303, 307
  evaluating low-quality, 28
  financial, 484
  individual's, 308
  partial, 297

potential profit, 74
total value, 290
control, 17, 25, 28, 42–43, 49–50, 109, 172, 204, 206–8, 350, 360–61, 456–57, 506–8, 541, 545–46
  better, 545
  complete, 547
Coombs, 8–10, 17
Cooper, 369, 391, 496, 498, 537
cooperation, 36, 48, 85, 91, 114, 237, 261, 319, 419
  productive, 261
  systematic planning, 311
copyright infringement, 553
core businesses, 99, 142, 427, 536, 559
core competencies, 22–23, 81–82, 85, 122, 128, 152, 316, 318–19, 323–24, 326, 380
  company's, 152, 326
  correct, 70
  firm's, 122, 323, 390
  operational, 152
  organization's, 316
  superior, 411
core values, 72, 114–15, 121, 552, 561–62
  brand's, 53, 549
  company's, 114, 142
  firm's, 72, 560
corporate culture, 72, 102, 142, 146, 153, 156, 200, 402, 410, 543, 548
  innovative, 66
corporate growth, 145
  sustained, 402
corporation, 25, 76, 99, 105, 149, 238, 341, 343, 402, 512, 517
  failed Iridium, 533
  form Iridium Satellite, 533
  technological, 109
cost, 26, 51–53, 185–86, 192–93, 197–99, 201–3,

208, 210, 213, 264, 275–78, 285–97, 368–72, 378–79, 387, 441–42, 482–83, 504–6, 521–22, 543–45
  approximate, 159, 441
  associated, 179
  correction, 208
  daily, 46
  expected, 178
  final, 371, 485
  high, 101, 158, 210
  indexed, 212
  internal, 107
  life-cycle, 210
  lost, 167
  low, 158, 324
  lower, 30, 83, 97, 101, 205, 337, 525, 553
  lowering, 71, 328, 558
  minimal, 324
  necessary, 210
  opex, 43
  procurement, 203
  projected, 504
  project's, 466, 520
  prototype, 169
  reducing, 71, 169, 353
  replacement, 495
  service, 533
  staggering, 531
  standard, 329
  total, 210, 226, 514
  ultimate, 522
  unit, 176
cost baseline, 290
cost constraints, 270, 371, 457
counterfeit products, 489
countries, 9, 27, 108–9, 217, 219–20, 223, 364–65, 464, 483–84, 502–3, 512, 514–15, 517–18, 550, 561
  developing, 54
  host, 383, 464–66, 484
  host's, 482
  new, 464
  parent, 109

priority, 517
CPD (Commercial Products Division), 149, 544–46
  customers, 545
  performance, 544
  profitability, 545
creation, 10, 53, 56, 114–15, 120–21, 133, 136, 165, 167, 169, 244–45, 247, 263–65, 377, 380
  original, 474
creativity, 2, 4–5, 15–16, 141–42, 145, 147, 155–58, 234–35, 349, 398, 448–49, 550, 557–59
  infusing, 398
  stifle, 347
  stifle innovation, 171
  stimulate, 105, 249
Credera's Growth Life-Cycle Model, 72
credibility, 53, 86, 255, 259–60, 273, 289, 360, 548
credit agreement, 528
credit markets, 522
creditors, 529
crises, 13, 63–64, 71, 138, 140, 187, 281, 333, 437
criteria, 118–19, 143, 145, 162–63, 201–2, 272, 274, 285, 289, 351, 373, 376, 543–44
  constraint, 368
  contractual, 353
  decision-making, 52, 258
  project classification, 420
  success/failure, 66, 376
  suitability, 122, 384
  ultimate success, 354
critical issues, 16, 67, 113, 127, 312, 331, 343, 366, 390, 437, 561
critical skills, 138, 154, 214, 264, 442, 499
  necessary, 199
critical success factors. *See* CSFs
CRM (customer relations management), 31, 194, 279–80

CRM systems, 31
crowdfunding, 50
crowdsourcing, 27–29, 249, 395, 546–48
crypts, 456, 458–59, 461–62
CSFs (Critical success factors), 179, 188, 286, 288, 372, 391
CSR (corporate social responsibility), 53–54, 156, 172, 562
cultural backgrounds, 364
culture, 72–73, 139–42, 144–47, 156, 170–71, 174, 178, 237, 308–9, 347, 365, 393–94, 400–402, 410–11, 413–14, 439–40, 464–81, 490
  aggressive, 178
  correct, 141
  divergent, 405
  multinational, 465
  national-level, 178
  new, 546
  organization's, 178, 388
  project's, 142
  shared, 277
  strong, 142
  unhappy, 173
  wrong, 347
customer base, 30, 84, 133, 194, 208, 306, 381, 420, 516, 519–21
  client's, 284
  end-of-the-line, 193
  expansive, 558
  limited, 122, 197, 385
  new, 420, 558
  worldwide, 544
customer behavior, 152, 156, 305
customer lifecycle, 218, 224–26, 229
customer loyalty, 39, 273, 279, 282
customer management practices, 157

customer relations management. *See* CRM
  replacing, 31
customers, 25–27, 29–35, 37–39, 73–76, 132–33, 154–56, 174–78, 192–94, 207–9, 220, 224–26, 261–62, 269–72, 276–85, 334–40, 373–80, 402–4, 421–22, 424, 435–37, 555–62
  advanced, 33
  approach, 104
  available, 520
  client's, 284
  current, 194
  direct, 29
  disappoint, 133
  dissatisfied, 271
  document, 248
  drive, 130
  end-of-line, 283
  end-of-the-line, 158, 171, 288
  existing, 241, 306, 335, 338
  external, 401
  firm's, 277
  hospital, 220, 226
  idealized, 254
  identifying, 543
  important, 175
  industrial, 530
  intended, 160
  large, 526
  mainstream, 334, 336
  meeting, 73
  ordinary, 33
  ordinary/mainstream, 32–33
  organization's, 82
  potential, 82, 154, 165, 256, 279, 522
  price-sensitive, 337
  profitable, 337
  profitable high-end, 336
  public sector, 516
  real, 396
  repeated, 38
  right, 279
  satisfied, 75, 335

servicing, 226
shifting, 38
single, 120
tangential, 340
target, 198, 316, 336, 435–36
total, 550
ultimate, 264
unhappy, 204, 207
unserved cellular, 520
CVM (customer value management), 68, 280–82
implementation, 281
programs, 280, 285
successful, 281

D

Daikin, 56–57
employees, 57
Group Succession
Committee, 56
plans, 57
values, 57
Daimler, 251
Danish architect Jørn
Utzon, 501
Darmstadt, 234–35
data, 51–52, 57, 74–75, 87,
92–93, 138, 147, 193–94,
209, 211, 228, 232–33, 281,
433, 535–36
actionable, 558
centralized, 194
collected, 57
complicated, 194
correct, 273
filter, 89
historical, 93, 139
insufficient, 382
learned, 204
man-machine-materials, 57
open, 261
proprietary, 177, 495
raw, 535
reliable, 64
satellite-tracking, 516
statistical, 212

structured, 52, 211
time-series, 57
transmit, 532
turning, 55
data algorithms, 50
data analysis, 233
data analytics, 15, 52, 399
databases, 52, 183, 194, 319, 430
large, 52
single, 194
data management, 56
data mining, 154, 281, 320
data warehousing, 194
deadlines, 42–43, 143, 347,
475, 520, 532
hard, 42–43
debt, 376, 467–68, 472, 475,
477–79, 486, 492, 520,
522–23, 529–30, 534
group's, 481
high-cost, 475
debt financing, 522
debt funding, 116
debt refinancing, 475
decision-making processes, 28,
50, 131, 162, 348, 541
complex, 177
rational, 512
decisions, 85–94, 119–24, 138–
39, 141–44, 164–65, 172–73,
179–85, 209–12, 257–59,
278–81, 339–41, 346–52,
374–76, 387–88, 431–33,
455–56, 484–86, 510–12,
541–42, 561–62
business-related, 320, 367
clinical, 220
commercialization, 54
contractor's, 524
controversial, 93–94
critical, 138, 143, 383,
456, 484, 499
daily, 172
delayed, 209
ethical, 177
frame, 87

gate, 431
high-level, 341
important, 46
informed, 184, 219, 282–
84, 286, 311
key, 89
legal, 562
long-term, 99
managerial, 548
marketing's, 103
market-oriented, 179
no-go, 202
pilot's, 249
rapid, 35, 168, 183, 186, 264
recovery, 71
religious, 512
revisit, 92
right, 352, 384
silo, 177
speedy, 167
structured, 206
suboptimal, 75
technical, 210, 283, 319, 367
ultimate, 100
wrong, 140, 193, 341
Dembowski, 9
Denmark, 352–53, 549–50, 554
Department of
Defense. *See* DOD
departments, 191, 215, 229,
247, 252–54, 259, 307, 316,
531, 533, 538
corporate communi-
cations, 255
market research, 261
design, 7–8, 33, 52–53, 130–31,
169–70, 175–76, 208, 225–
27, 248–49, 316–17, 321–
22, 355, 368–69, 439–42,
464–65, 494–96, 499–500,
502–8, 558–59, 562
administrative office, 426
artistic, 508
balanced scorecard, 175
best, 208
changing physical, 16

competition-winning, 501
complete, 170
computer-aided, 507
core, 32
detailed-level, 131
existing, 513
final, 169, 208, 503
human-centered, 254
inclusive, 41
incomplete, 506
industrial, 131
intended, 168–69
interdisciplinary
  leadership, 53
interior, 446, 503–4
modern expressionist, 501
organizational, 220
original acoustic, 504
printed, 259
product's, 208
prototype, 398
queue, 446
radical, 500
responsive web, 44
satellite, 515
terrestrial, 513
two-dimensional, 444
upload, 558
Design and Delivery in Healthcare Business, 219, 221,
  223, 225, 227
design thinking, 52, 152–53,
  155–57, 163–64, 187–88,
  195, 235, 397, 399,
  406–7, 412
  embedding, 156
  necessities, 560
Design Thinking for Strategic
  Innovation, 188
DGCA (Directorate General of
  Civil Aviation), 498
diagnostics, 51–52
Diamond Approach, 68
Digital Experience and Innovation, 404
Directorate General of Civil
  Aviation (DGCA), 498

direct sales model, 325
Discovery & Design, 227
Discovery Centers, 554–55
Disney, 51, 53, 143, 149,
  158–59, 395, 402, 439–93,
  495, 548, 554
  attractions, 452, 463
popular, 444
  behind-the-scenes, 471
  popular, 482
Disney Book Group, 441,
  444–46, 537
Disney brand name, 464
Disney characters, 469, 471,
  474, 482–83, 488, 492
  classic, 488
  trademarked, 468
Disney characters and
  stories, 492
Disney Company, 476
Disney Imagineering,
  444, 468, 538
  Harper Goff, 453
Disney investors, 478
Disneyland, 443, 448, 452–54,
  456–57, 459, 461, 466–71,
  473, 480, 483–87, 492–94
  attraction predates, 453
  original, 485, 488
  surrounding, 482
Disneyland and Disney World,
  465, 468, 470, 473, 483
Disney Legends, 488
Disney royalties, 467
Disney's Imagineering Division,
  159, 447–48, 455
Disney Studios Park, 476–77
  renamed Walt, 476, 486
Disney, Walt, 440–41,
  443–44, 453, 455, 469,
  472, 476, 486
Disney World's Magic
  Kingdom, 487
DOD (Department of Defense),
  191, 215, 316, 340,
  370, 531, 533
  contracts, 370

customers, 414
  teaming practices, 340
Doom Buggies, 452,
  456, 461–62
Dreamliner, 7, 369, 493–
  500, 537–39
  battery problems, 493
  decision, 495
  problems, 500
DSDM methodology, 43
Durstewitz, Markus, 251

E
Earned Value Measurement
  System. *See* EVMS
econometrica, 390
economic issues, 471, 474
economy, 96, 124, 140,
  465, 469, 475
  environment, 53
ecosystem, 32, 53, 220,
  302, 405–8
education, 51, 63–64, 68, 171–
  72, 186, 227, 274, 295, 419
EEFs. *See* enterprise environmental factors
Eisner, 474–75, 537
employees, 19–20, 40, 109,
  113–14, 143–44, 147–48,
  174, 246–48, 250–52, 254,
  256–57, 259–61, 277–78,
  357, 395, 402–5, 426–27,
  471, 548–49
  best-in-class, 395
  company's, 248
  direct, 325
  hired, 103, 241
  innovative, 149
  local, 489
  reengage, 250
  talented, 402
  vendor, 425
end-user stakeholders, 382
energy, 54, 150, 354, 362,
  490, 537, 547
  high, 546–48
  reaction, 497

supplies, 243
engagement, 2, 163, 220, 225, 228, 249–50, 253, 261, 361, 405, 425
engineering, 81, 95, 98, 103, 136, 138, 156, 158, 252, 254, 258, 440, 508–10
  area, 251
  changes, 99, 214
  data, 212
well-defined, 212
  departments, 284
  design, 131, 208
  manager, 510
  resources, 96
  strategy, 96
  system, 364
engineers, 254, 259, 352–53, 434, 440, 442–43, 504, 506, 514, 518, 524, 531
  best development, 96
  cellular telephone system, 513
enterprise, 138, 140, 191–92, 197, 241, 244, 323, 387, 428, 430, 464–66, 468, 471–75, 479, 482–84, 489–90
  changing, 376
  important, 465
  unfavorable, 465
  viable, 534
enterprise environmental factors (EEFs), 125, 138, 140, 191–92, 197, 204, 323, 387, 464–66, 468, 471–75, 479, 482, 484, 489–90
environment, 23, 25–26, 48, 52, 54, 82, 85, 129, 138, 140, 215–16, 261, 352, 389, 518–19
  artificial, 353
  business-as-usual, 20
  catalog retailer, 337
  changing, 241
  cloud, 40
  collaborative, 230–31
  collaborative accelerated exploratory, 230

competitive, 4, 130, 560
complex, 140
conservative, 354
controlled, 46, 440, 445, 456–57
controlled theme, 445
efficient corporate, 238
entrepreneurial, 14, 152
ever-changing, 4, 11, 151
existing hospital, 220
forecasted, 197
free-thinking, 389
healthy, 554
high-tech, 262
high-technology, 518
innovative, 142
multinational, 217
networked, 10
new, 397
non-threating, 141
open, 41, 398
operational, 254
pandemic, 64
political, 125
relevant, 215
right, 228
safe learning, 358
self-directed, 142
static, 39
structured, 316
technical, 402
traditional, 16
turbulent, 410
unexplored, 349
unfamiliar, 316
unique, 409
unstructured, 110
utopian, 348
virtual, 162
virtual working, 220
EPM. *See* enterprise project management
equity, 84, 116, 173, 175, 492, 515, 520, 522, 534
  shared, 483
ERP (enterprise resource planning), 194

ESA (European Space Agency), 215
establishment, 70, 171, 205, 216, 269, 311, 368, 397, 467, 514, 554
estimates, 88, 132, 179, 212, 382, 444
  historical, 385
  original cost, 505
  parametric, 212
  top-down, 212
ethical issues, 172
Ethiopian Airlines, 535, 538
Europe, 10, 35–36, 248, 353, 400, 466–72, 474, 476, 485–86, 553
European Aviation Safety Agency, 498
European Union, 329
euros, 474, 477–78
EVMS (Earned Value Measurement System), 186, 275, 370, 387

F
FAA (Federal Aviation Administration), 496–98, 500, 535–38
  approval, 538
Facebook, 51, 53, 183–84, 249, 395–96, 548
  investment fund, 396
  platform, 395–96
  innovations, 395
facilities
  current production, 10, 384
  existing production, 122–23, 385
  ground support, 518
  recreational, 404
factories, 133, 353, 501, 549–50
  electronic device manufacturing, 60
factors, 2, 4, 23, 26, 63, 115–16, 124–25, 185–86, 279, 281, 360, 416, 465, 472, 479
  competitive, 437

critical, 75, 255
cultural, 464
external, 46, 82
financial, 124, 384
five, 323
hygiene, 64
intangible, 273
internal, 82
organizational, 350
reward, 415–17
scale, 212, 417
short-term, 295
weighing, 115
failure, 10–11, 14–15, 47–49,
    70–71, 126, 142, 147–48,
    211, 228, 271–72, 287–91,
    327–28, 346, 367–91,
    394–95, 464–65, 527, 532
    applauding, 228
    business case, 381
    converting, 386
    decommissioned, 533
    defining, 373
    engineering, 126
    entrepreneurial, 389
    financial, 464
    metric, 288
    payment, 383
    perceived, 386
    potential, 386, 388
    user acceptance, 126, 383
failure analyses, 387
failure criteria, 115, 122, 206,
    367, 384–85, 390
    establishing project, 386
FC. See Future Center
FCC (Federal Communications
    Commission), 514, 520
Federal Aviation Administra-
    tion. See FAA
Federal Communications Com-
    mission (FCC), 514, 520
FFE (fuzzy front end), 120,
    131–32, 156, 188, 193
financial growth, 268
Financial innovation, 50, 62

financial risks, 208, 416, 470,
    495, 514, 518–19, 535
    initial, 514
financial support, 483,
    489, 521, 535
financing, 25, 31, 62, 203, 206,
    350, 514, 526, 529
flexibility, 5, 8, 21, 200–202,
    226, 234–35, 250–51, 253,
    316–17, 540–43, 551
Flexibility Internal compe-
    tition, 267
flexible methodologies, 124,
    186, 201–2, 540, 542–43
    new, 193
frameworks, 136, 150, 162, 176,
    192–93, 200–202, 216–17,
    226, 235, 282, 303–4, 354,
    367–68, 411–13, 540, 542–44
    comprehensive gov-
        ernance, 407
    defined, 235
    dominant, 132
    flexible agile, 200, 541
    implementing, 318
    inflexible, 217
    new, 200, 541
    policy, 10
franchisees, 325
freedom, 98, 138, 141–42, 148,
    154, 208, 213, 500, 507–9,
    549–50, 560, 562
functions, 66–67, 85–87, 91–92,
    142–43, 169, 228, 338, 340,
    399, 401, 423–24, 427,
    429, 431, 437
    central, 252
    cognitive, 182
    commercial intelligence, 74
    contract management, 422
    corporate, 39, 419
    experimental critical, 215
    integrator, 223
    knowledge management, 237
    linear, 285
    major, 94

maps, 163
network management, 516
new, 398, 558
primary business, 252
repetitive, 212
search, 431
social, 502
termination control, 516
total strategic planning, 101
funding, 98, 101, 116, 147, 206–7,
    214–16, 349–50, 364, 465, 467,
    506, 508, 530, 532, 544–45
    contractual governmental, 546
    corporate, 402
    disguised, 147
    initial, 518
    necessary, 520
    unlimited, 348
funds, 77, 81, 106, 295, 300,
    350, 467, 513–14, 523,
    527–28, 546–47
    employee sabbatical, 109
Future Center (FC), 425–27

G
Gaining Strategic Advantage, 68
Galvin, 514, 519
    Robert, 514
games, 25, 64, 327, 395–96, 485,
    515, 549–51, 556–57, 560
    popular early social
        network, 395
    social network, 395
    well-received Lego Marvel
        Super Heroes, 557
Gates, Rusty, 462
GE (General Electric),
    76, 134, 520
GEA, 413, 427–31, 433–34
    employees, 429
    group, 432
    Group AG, 432
    Innovation Management Sys-
        tem, 428, 434
GE Model, 77–78
gender equality, 61, 551

gender stereotypes, 552
General Electric (GE), 76, 134, 520
Geraldi, 8, 17, 65, 68
Germany, 36, 234–35, 248, 251, 427, 500, 524, 554–55, 559
Geschäftsmodelle Entwickeln, 331
Getty Images, 400
Global Broadcast Service, 341
Globalstar Satellite Communi-cations System, 531
goals, 32, 34–35, 134, 136, 159–61, 178–79, 203–5, 253, 255, 374–75, 382–83, 405, 408, 411, 413
  clear, 435
  common, 437
  corporate, 266, 382
  customer's, 165
  defined, 235
  environmental, 54
  final, 238
  formal, 401
  fundamental, 82
  high-level, 138, 346
  long-term, 51
  margin, 376
  new, 385
  often-conflicting, 48
  operational, 175
  original, 523
  primary, 11, 488
  static, 223
  target, 102
  university's, 405
  unrealistic, 91
goods, 32, 118, 131, 291, 325, 327, 482
  consumer, 130
  value metrics, 288
goodwill, 273, 276–77, 295, 309
Google, 51, 53, 138, 146, 183–84, 187, 249, 343, 402, 548
governance, 52–53, 70, 72, 130, 136, 171–74, 181, 184, 404, 507, 540–41, 546, 549

clear, 260
co-creation partners, 180, 206
committee, 185, 540
formalized, 62
innovation portfolio, 175
internal, 188
multi-tiered, 222
necessary, 177
organizational, 171
situational, 174
temporary, 352
government, 47, 108–9, 125, 488–89, 492, 501, 503–5, 507, 513, 516–17, 535–36, 544, 546–47
  agencies, 26, 48–49, 64, 110, 207, 215, 371, 374, 547
respective, 546
  authorities, 59
  contractors, 547
  domestic, 108
  foreign, 108, 482
  funding, 546
  officials, 471
  policies, 108, 197, 204, 547
  local, 484
governor, 61–62
GPS (global positioning system), 524
  receivers, 409
Greenpeace, 554
  environmental campaigning organization, 554
growth, 4, 49–50, 74–75, 77, 79–80, 101, 103, 105, 120–21, 123–24, 162–63, 176–77, 194–95, 252, 466–67
  drive, 317
  profit, 307
  slow, 277
  steady, 557
  subscriber, 536
  sustainable, 428
growth rate, 79, 306, 337
  forecasted, 534
GS Yuasa, 497
Guardian, 123, 481, 538–39

guests, 441–42, 444, 446–47, 449–50, 456–59, 461–62, 466, 471, 473, 476, 486, 491–93
  classic Disney characters welcomes, 490
guide business decisions, 43
guidelines, 8–9, 68, 121, 132, 138, 310, 313, 420, 423, 541, 545

H
habits, 43, 70, 147, 194, 378–79
  new innovative, 16
hack, 249
hackers, 558
Halloween costumes, 553
Hardy, 462, 514, 522–23, 531, 537
Harper Business, 196
Harvard Business Review, 66, 68, 142, 187–89, 236, 244, 343, 391, 537
Harvard Business School Pub-lishing, 68, 189
Hatbox Ghost, 452
haunted house, 453, 458
Haunted Mansion, 443–44, 449, 451–59, 461, 463, 538
  not-so-scary, 458
  the, 459
hazardous materials, 109
health, 52, 54, 63, 84, 108, 149, 177, 208, 219, 292, 296
  consumer, 219
  improving people's, 219
  worker, 295
healthcare, 51–53, 219–20, 244, 262, 340
health issues, 64, 243
health system, 220
Hench, 441, 446–48, 537
  John, 440, 447, 455
Henrik Horn Andersen, 358–59
hierarchical leadership, 267
  traditional, 130
hierarchy, 143–44, 171

organizational, 73, 174, 410
history, 12, 68, 394, 463, 465–66, 476, 486, 507, 517, 526, 549
successful, 246
Hitachi, 55–57
software technologies, 56
portfolio, 56
Hoboken, 17–18, 67–68, 128, 188–89, 244, 312–13, 331, 343–44, 391
holistic approach, 224, 226
Hong Kong Disneyland, 452, 487–94
surpassed, 492
hook business model, 324
Hornibrook Group, 505
hotels, 446, 470, 472, 474, 476, 478, 490, 492
money-making, 470
HPM Business Group, 219
HPOs, 73
HP's multi-billion-dollar inkjet printing business, 301
Hughes, 506–7
Davis, 506
human behavior, 100
Human Resource Management, 84, 187
human resources, 57, 82, 113, 122, 147, 154, 241, 243, 307
limited, 100
Hype's High Involvement Innovation Maturity Model, 72
Hypothesis Research, 233

I

IBM, 183–84, 320, 396–99
business practices, 320
project managers, 396
ICO Global Communications, 531
ICO satellite system, 531–32
Idea Campaigns and Innovation Channels, 259
Idea Management Systems, 247

identification, 32, 35, 119, 123, 125, 132, 171, 175, 195, 198–99, 266, 272
corporate goals, 266
customer's value-in-use, 285
innovation metric, 310
imagination, 158, 317, 394, 440, 443, 445, 449, 457, 550–51, 557–58
imagination and creativity, 449, 457, 557
Imagineering, 158, 440, 443–49, 453, 473, 479, 537
implementation, 5–6, 45, 49, 158, 160, 174–76, 235, 238, 250–53, 255, 259–60, 411–13, 518
corporate-wide, 174
fast track, 260
innovative, 59
operational, 304
policies and models, 238
process, 214
strategy's, 177
successful, 225
improvements, 21, 23, 34, 37–38, 59, 62, 71–72, 120–21, 248, 250, 268–69, 272, 442–43, 478, 559
business model process, 323
continuous process, 227
economic, 481
feature, 22
incremental, 21
indirect ecological, 63
job position, 59
minor, 101
operational, 227
potential, 282
technical, 21
IMS, 113–14
Inazuka, 56–57
Inclusive Value Measurement, 265
Industrial Revolution, 229

industries, 1, 5, 7–10, 58, 75, 78–79, 110–11, 219, 323, 325, 334–37, 369, 371, 419–20, 440
airline, 495
changing, 439, 449
existing, 342
maritime, 516
paper-mill, 501
semiconductor, 403
stagnant, 342
tourism, 472, 476
Industry Pro, 79
information technology, 55–56, 328, 404
information warehouses, 122, 182, 191, 193, 195, 218, 245, 263
company's, 145
developing, 194
infrastructure, 221, 231, 316, 411, 413–14, 418
advanced technological, 352
Initial Public Offering. *See* IPO
initiatives, 56, 63, 145–46, 232, 238, 253, 255, 362, 365, 401, 407, 422–23, 436–37
innovating, 15, 37, 386, 414, 420
innovation, 1–69, 72–77, 99–103, 126–33, 136–50, 153–60, 177–82, 206–12, 237–41, 251–57, 299–304, 306–10, 333–35, 337–40, 346–51, 374–81, 393–99, 401–5, 408–15, 559–63
architectural, 20
better, 301
bridged, 65
classified, 333
competence-destroying, 25
completed, 300
continuous, 4, 20, 53, 142, 177, 393–94, 399, 548
contribution, 309
corporate, 252–53, 257

declining, 391
de-risk, 222
destructive, 338
developing, 303
diamond of, 65
digital, 50, 55, 409
drive motorsport, 249
emphasized internal, 173
expensive, 101
exploitative, 68, 188
exploratory, 62, 68, 188
filters, 143
frequent, 279
greatest, 2
important, 51
influence, 210
joint, 34
large-scale, 172
limited, 394
long-term, 66
marketing, 48, 65, 76
multiple, 6
negative, 158
non-core, 173
operational, 3
patient-oriented, 53
performing, 3
practice, 254
preferred internal, 173
private-sector, 49
product development, 23, 168
product/service, 65
public sector, 68
public-sector, 48–49, 54, 63
state, 327
steady-Britannica, 327
stop, 146
successful, 4, 11–12, 25,
    31, 68, 106, 140, 163,
    172, 377, 380
support, 15–16, 142, 187,
    414, 418, 438
sustainment, 241
system for, 411
technical, 60, 76, 208,
    316, 384, 403
test, 15

true, 25, 365
innovation environment, 25,
    129–30, 137–38, 140, 154,
    170, 197, 203, 240, 346, 348
effective, 184
open, 30, 246, 261
innovation initiatives, 247,
    257, 304, 401
innovation portfolio, 81, 236,
    244, 298, 305–6, 415–16
balanced, 415
efficient, 236
total, 302
innovation portfolio project
    management office.
    See IPPMO
innovation practices, 2, 8–9,
    58, 66, 73, 545–46,
    559, 561, 563
better, 71
changing, 254
open source, 395
open-source, 184
rapid, 64
teaching, 58
traditional, 39
innovation process, 5, 113–14,
    259, 261, 299, 301, 303–5,
    307, 346, 428–29, 431, 433,
    545–46, 548, 560
agile, 301–2
closed, 30
complete, 58
end-to-end, 251
internal, 545
intra-firm, 68
necessary, 560
innovation projects, 3–7,
    65–67, 69–70, 75–78, 122–
    25, 135–36, 138–39, 147,
    171–74, 179–82, 192–94,
    197–200, 263–66, 275–77,
    299, 350–51, 368–70,
    377–81, 383–90, 542–46
authorizing, 380
best, 172
bootlegged, 66

cancel, 173
classroom, 58
companies prioritize, 116
completed, 377
digital, 407
discontinuous, 21
disruptive, 241, 333, 376
existing, 381
failed, 387
funded, 147, 199
given, 200
high-risk radical, 510
host, 254
incremental, 103, 376
large, 116
large-scale, 172
linking, 25
low-risk, 172
managing global, 400
non-core, 306
potential, 114
radical, 389
right, 377
secret, 511
short-term, 31
social, 58
strategic, 146, 177
suggested classifying, 65
troubled, 385
intangibles, 273–74, 276–78,
    280, 295, 390
measuring, 295
values, 273–74, 278, 295
Integrated Computer Solutions,
    411, 413, 415, 417
integrated product/project
    teams. *See* IPTs
integrated solutions, 219
integration, 72, 85, 101–3,
    139–40, 229, 248, 353,
    380, 408, 421
performing solution, 221
successful, 103
Intel, 324, 329–30
intellectual property (IP), 26,
    28–29, 66–67, 114–15,
    157–58, 183, 276–77,

348–49, 373, 515, 517, 547, 558, 561–62
property rights, 34, 172, 273, 295, 348
Inter-Ministerial Delegation, 477
Internet, 16, 50, 55, 58, 151, 230, 247, 249, 324–25, 336–37, 394
Internet of Things. *See* IoT
intimacy, 360
investment, 42, 45, 78, 81, 167, 170, 194, 197–98, 230–31, 299–301, 306, 309, 384–85, 520, 531–32
  financial, 81, 319
  heavy, 76–77, 470
  large, 95
  low-risk, 76
  managing venture, 222
  minimal, 60
  organization's, 269
  small, 470, 484
  technology-related, 232
  total, 467
  weak, 298
investors, 4, 54, 172, 277–78, 330, 364, 514–15, 518, 520–23, 530–35, 539
IoT (Internet of Things), 16, 50, 55, 58, 230
  business ecosystems, 56
  platform, 57
  solution creation, 56
IP. *See* intellectual property
IPM goals, 139
  identifying, 139, 155
  metrics, 274
IPMs (innovation project man-agement), 1–19, 69, 71, 138–39, 147–54, 167, 179–80, 182–83, 206, 266, 274, 310, 315, 319–20, 345–46, 404, 508, 510, 561
IPO (Initial Public Offering), 525, 534

IPPMO (innovation portfolio project management office), 177–79, 298, 310
  function, 179
  Involvement in Innovation, 178
  membership, 178
  roles, 179
IPTs (integrated product/project teams), 339–41
Iridium, 66, 512–38
  ailing, 532
  expected, 530
  firm's, 537
  forced, 529
  granted, 529
  joining, 523
  left, 536
  milked, 534
  original, 533
  permitted, 522
  rescue, 531–32
  revamp, 538
  second-generation, 534
  transform, 526
  viewed, 514
Iridium Africa Corporation, 521
Iridium India Telecom Private Ltd, 521
Iridium International, 514
Iridium Limited Liability Corporation, 514
Iridium Middle East Corporation, 521
Iridium Network, 515–17, 526, 532
ISA (Innovation Software Advisors), 262
Italy, 248, 466, 524
ITIL Maturity Model, 72
IT-platforms, 434
IWB (innovative work behavior), 58
IWB environment, 58

J
JAL (Japan Airlines), 32, 496–98
JAL Boeing, 498
Japan, 55, 57, 469–70, 475, 482, 486, 488, 497–98, 537–38, 554–55, 559
Japan Airlines (JAL), 32, 496–98
Japan Transport Safety Board (JTSB), 498
Joan Sutherland Theatre, 502, 504–5, 539
jobs, 58–59, 70–71, 140, 144, 146, 252, 254, 257, 351–52, 439, 477, 488, 552
  advertised, 47
  better, 49, 112, 161
  creating, 484
  good, 447
  new, 488
  primary, 508
  viewed, 47
Jobs, Steve, 146, 393–95
Joern Utzon, 502, 505, 539
Jones, Peter, 504
Jorn Utzon's Sydney Opera House, 538
JTSB (Japan Transport Safety Board), 498

K
Kanban, 216–17
  board, 216
Kaplan, 175, 188, 198, 244, 317, 321–22, 328, 331
KAUST (King Abdullah University of Science and Technology), 404–10
  community, 404–7
  focus, 404
  Smart Projects, 405–8
Kerzner, 7, 17, 76, 159, 188, 218, 309, 313

Harold, 1, 19, 69, 129, 191, 245, 263, 315, 333, 345, 439
key intangible performance indicators (KIPIs), 273–74, 313
key performance indicator. *See* KPIs
key performance indicators, 47, 184, 259, 266, 276, 286–87, 372, 432
  financial, 266
Khrunichev State Research, 521
King Abdullah University of Science and Technology. *See* KAUST
KIPIs (key intangible performance indicators), 273–74, 313
KM World, 313
knowledge, 36, 78, 98, 127, 134, 152, 171–72, 193–96, 226–28, 261, 323–24, 339, 387–88, 424, 426, 524–25, 561–62
  first-hand, 87
  generated, 195
  good, 95
  increasing, 308
  limited, 192, 199
  methodology, 407
  new, 26, 157, 305, 335
  proprietary, 34, 457
  required, 39
  retained, 276
  scientific, 3, 10, 74
  strategic, 244
  superior, 32–33
  tacit, 196, 426
  technical, 63, 154, 320, 365
  technological, 36, 193
  useful, 194
  worldwide, 20
Koninklijke Philips, 218, 221, 223–25, 227
KPIs (key performance indicator), 47, 184, 238–39,

259–60, 266, 271–72, 274–76, 286–89, 294, 372, 432
Kumar, 157, 188, 340–41, 344

L
labor workers, 408
Langdon Morris, 299, 411
LCC. *See* life-cycle costing
LCCA (life-cycle cost analysis), 210–11, 494–95
leaders, 15, 51, 95–97, 106, 146, 149–52, 167, 170, 174, 277–78, 408–9
  better, 151
  channel, 260
  digital, 40
  effective, 150–51
  emblematic, 146
  executive, 15
  global, 408
  good, 151
  improved, 150
  new strategic, 5
  senior, 39, 364–65
  solid, 151
  student, 363
  successful, 151
  supply chain, 397
  world's, 468
  worldwide, 418
leadership, 82, 85, 146, 149–50, 153, 174, 183, 185, 187, 199–200, 266–67, 273, 355
  competitive, 33
  disciplined, 142
  distributed, 401
  ineffective, 388
  new, 177
  strong, 150, 161
  technical, 34, 107, 179
  transformational, 174
lean manufacturing strategy, 73
Lean Transformation Programs, 237, 239
learning, 20, 22, 60, 175–76, 227–28, 230, 232,

308, 387–88, 390, 397, 412–13, 415
  continuous collective, 237
  distance, 63
  effective innovation, 58
  greatest, 437
  important, 228
  lifelong, 186
  machine, 58, 415
  surrounding tool, 398
  traditional textbook, 58
Lego, 53, 548–63
  case, 557
  action figures, 550
  based robots, 556
  Batman, 557
  boy, 552
  brand, 548–50, 559
  city, 555
  construction toys, 551
  creator, 557
  friends, 551–52, 562
  girls, 552
  launch, 558
  Mindstorms, 548, 556
  Movie, 557
  robotics sets, 556
  success, 558
  theme parks, 553
  toys, 549
  video games, 557
Lego Group, 548–49, 552–53, 555–56, 558, 560–61
LEOs (low Earth-orbiting), 513
LEO satellites, 513
licensing agreements, 29, 123, 241, 349, 464, 468, 482–84, 486, 493, 551–52, 560–62
  risk minimization, 484
life cycle, 29, 74, 78, 124, 136, 168, 176, 182, 197, 367–68, 376
life cycle
  innovation project's, 390
  long product, 97
  profitable, 81
  project's, 119, 144, 186, 272–73, 285, 387

short product, 97, 103, 105
life-cycle phases, 3, 5, 7,
    72, 120, 152, 154, 202,
    206–10, 213, 272, 283, 294,
    450–51, 559–60
  early, 286, 294
life-cycle stages, 187, 214, 452
Lilly Research Laboratories, 85
Limited Liability Corporation
    (LLC), 299, 536
Line Larsen, 358–59
LLC (Limited Liability Corpo-
    ration), 299, 536
Long-term LEGO therapy, 551
Loral Qualcomm Satellite
    Services, 520
Los Angeles Times, 481,
    494, 537–38
low Earth-orbiting (LEOs), 513
Low-Priority Projects, 242

M
Macintosh computer, 394
Madame Leota, 461–62
Magic Kingdom, 449, 452, 469,
    481, 485, 487, 538–39
Magneti Marelli, 248–49
management, 5–7, 20, 67,
    88–89, 92–93, 99–100,
    127–28, 133–37, 142–43,
    153, 170–72, 187–88,
    230–32, 258–59, 261–62,
    276, 357, 413–17,
    543–46, 557–58
  alienating senior, 389
  asset, 50
  bid, 229
  business performance, 320
  claim, 421–22
  conflict, 125
  corporate, 402
  crisis, 140
  customer relationship, 31
  effective life cycle, 421
  financial, 397
  global, 411
  ineffective, 561

inept, 264
lean, 46
mistakes, 146
online transaction, 398
operational, 357
organizational, 113, 157, 388
outcome-based, 53
pharmaceutical projects, 85
project communication, 217
project management
    talent, 222
reactive, 186, 267
stakeholder, 125, 227,
    406, 425, 427
strategic, 76, 369
supply chain, 499
top, 95, 99–100, 108, 114,
    177, 179, 260, 356, 385
traditional innovation
    software, 114
upper, 237
visual, 421
Management & Economic Engi-
    neering, 10
management practices, 139–40
  active innovation, 66
  better customer relations, 35
  corporate-level portfolio, 6
  effective project, 390
  effective resource, 183
  effective risk, 137–38, 384
  good project, 509
  government project, 49
  ineffective risk, 137
  influence knowledge, 194
  new, 135
  normal project, 212
  standardized project, 136
  standard risk, 541
  strategic project, 229
managers, 5, 8, 47, 90–91, 113–
    14, 119, 172–73, 176, 181,
    350, 520, 523–24, 545–46
  agile project, 397
  alert, 175
  assigned project, 323
  assigned project/program, 340

better innovation project, 448
contribution project, 122
corporate innovation, 251, 254
efficient project, 236
equal parts project, 399
functional, 5, 23, 105, 158,
    167, 174, 395
fund, 173
good project, 399
government project, 49
group's, 228
high-technology project, 106
innovation/R&D, 126
middle, 67
middle level, 546
middle-level, 402, 545
multinational project, 217
operational commodity,
    397
pension fund, 173
procurement, 509
product/program, 341
professional project, 154
program/project, 339
regional, 401
remind project, 136
right innovation project, 70
right project, 71
senior, 66, 94, 102, 122,
    241, 284, 302, 304,
    511, 519, 547
successful innovation
    project, 150
successful project, 353
traditional project, 6,
    444, 446, 449
Managing Innovation Risks,
    494–95, 497, 499
Manjón, 9–10
manufacturers, 32, 164, 170,
    251, 483, 494–95, 506
  health-care products, 495
manufacturing, 3, 22, 36,
    96–97, 99–100, 103–5,
    109, 208, 419, 424,
    549–50
  added-value, 419

market, 20–22, 36–37, 72–74, 76–80, 95, 103, 106, 130–31, 151–53, 177–78, 295–97, 302–5, 326–27, 336–38, 346–47, 375–77, 428–29, 435–37, 483, 559–60
advanced, 32
changing, 155, 316
competitive, 369
consortium, 528
dedicated, 236
diversified, 318
electricity, 435
end-user, 427
existing, 20, 22, 64, 300, 327, 334, 346, 435
foreign, 483
fragmented, 97
global, 432
good, 562
growing, 234
mass, 318
mature, 77
niche, 318
perceived, 131
pharma, 434
profitable, 95
public, 514
segmented, 318
stable, 81
vertical, 516
marketing, 12, 74–76, 82–83, 95–96, 98–100, 102–6, 180, 200–203, 205–6, 214, 236–37, 282–83, 338–39, 374–75, 379, 384–85, 388–89, 508–11, 518–19, 526–28
blamed, 528
internet, 337
required, 192, 526
service-centric, 282
marketplace, 35, 37–38, 75, 77, 101, 103, 177, 197, 203, 247, 311, 316, 323, 338–39, 395
disruptive, 317
global, 537
telecommunications, 516

Mark Parker, 337
Mark Zuckerberg, 396
Marshall, Graham, 403
MDR (medical device regulation), 149
measurement of KPIs, 272
measurements, 203, 253, 257, 259, 266, 272–73, 278, 285–86, 288, 301, 309, 311, 407–8
effective, 311
long-term, 295, 377
string, 433
traditional, 176
valid, 295
medical device regulation (MDR), 149
Mega Bloks, 553–54
methodologies, 184, 186, 201–2, 206, 270–71, 323–24, 354, 356, 406, 410, 412, 540–41, 543–44
distinct, 136
execute, 399
hybrid, 541
lean-based, 237
one-size-fits-all, 70, 141, 167, 200, 540
radical, 354
single, 540
singular, 510, 540
sprint, 353
traditional, 346, 541
traditional project delivery, 41
value management, 275
methods, 19–20, 58–59, 116, 127, 129, 133–34, 148, 151, 157, 254–55, 260, 263, 353, 397–98, 415
best, 151
common, 76
deployed lean, 258
dynamic systems development, 42
effective, 75
estimating, 211
formal ideation, 21

good, 424
logical framework, 391
multiple, 120
new, 157, 249
open source, 63
popular, 45
process-based, 46
procurement, 506
recommended, 252
regular, 325
standard, 415
standardized, 254
statistical, 182
statistical sampling, 169
useful, 415
metrics, 72, 135–36, 192–93, 201, 263–65, 270–76, 280–81, 286–89, 292, 296, 298–99, 303–5, 307–13, 369–70, 387, 543
application, 396
business-oriented, 263
business-related, 368
concrete, 274
correct, 279
creating human resource utilization, 264
critical, 216, 287
decision-making, 311
developed, 288
difficult, 271
financial, 278, 294, 300, 309
generating, 309
important, 309
intangible, 115, 273
key, 437
knowledge management, 244
knowledge transfer, 311
life-cycle phase, 275
measurable, 311
misaligned, 310
nonfinancial, 198, 273
portfolio PMO, 299
real, 313
real-time, 311
selected, 286
special, 286

strategic, 121–22, 136
strategic business
    objectives, 186
tracking, 199
transformational, 298
ultimate, 170
unique, 65
useful transversal, 307
value chain, 288
value-reflective, 309
wrong, 288, 310, 312
metrics and KPIs, 287–88, 294
Mexico, 550
Microsoft, 53, 74, 146, 183–84,
    327, 394, 548, 561
middleman model, 325
Mill Valley, 438
mind maps, 141, 157, 163–64
mindset, 5, 144, 191, 234,
    253, 276–78, 331, 342,
    355, 358, 369
  creative, 4
  project manager's, 353
  right, 160, 354
  shared, 277–78
Minimal Viable Product, 406
Minimal Weighting Value, 293
minimizing risks and maxi-
    mizing, 120
minimum viable product
    (MVP), 41, 44, 397
Mobile Power Solutions, 497
mobility strategy, 408
model cars, 164
models, 72, 76, 85, 117,
    123–25, 163–64, 238–40,
    265–66, 296, 305, 317, 325,
    327–28, 335, 444–45
  activity-stage, 65
  analytical, 359
  baseline, 33
  basic, 228
  best competency, 85
  bricks-and-clicks, 325
  classical Bohr, 513
  comprehensive, 17

computer, 445
conversation process, 65
core competency, 85
creative problem-solving, 163
decision-stage, 65
departmental-stage, 65
design workflow, 168
double-entry, 357
effective competency, 85
enriched leadership, 424
existing, 300
flexible project
    management, 8
full-scale, 445
fuzzy, 124
generic, 8
good mental, 340
incomplete, 168
largest, 559
learning loop, 228
linear project management, 7
linear thinking, 5
massing, 445
mathematical, 120
mental, 156
new, 247, 323–24, 423, 496
new data analytics, 50
operating, 238
performance meas-
    urement, 313
potato, 358
product life-cycle, 76
profit, 65
project financing, 467
qualitative, 119
rapid prototype devel-
    opment, 213
response, 65
revenue generation, 319
sample, 403
scale, 559
simulation, 56
small-scale detailed-oriented
    study, 445
stage-gate, 437
tacit knowledge, 305

traditional, 404
type-2 fuzzy optimi-
    zation, 124
validation, 124
Moderate Technology, 272
money, 28–29, 75, 95, 97, 203,
    205, 235–36, 304–5, 308,
    482–84, 508, 510–11,
    524–25, 530, 534
  bad, 510
  good, 510, 530
  lost, 468, 475, 483
  raising, 518
Monopolistic business
    model, 326
monopoly, 327, 466–68,
    473, 485, 492
  de-facto world, 515
Morsa, Luigi, 35, 112, 246
Motorola, 403–4, 512–18,
    520–25, 527–34, 537
  exposed, 515
  facility, 512–13
  guarantees, 527
  service contract, 528
Mousavi, 124
movies, 449, 476, 478, 486,
    538, 549–50, 552, 555,
    557, 560, 562
  non-animated Dis-
    ney, 159, 442
  streaming services, 404
M-Star, 523, 537
  Project, 523
Multi-Criteria Decision
    Analysis, 124
MVP (minimum viable prod-
    uct), 41, 44, 397

N

national market, 21
Natural History of Innova-
    tion, 47, 374
Naviair, 351–61, 363
NDU, 409
Netflix, 324, 336, 342

net present value. *See* NPV
Net Promoter Score and
    attributes, 250
network, 27, 32, 36, 220, 224,
    228–29, 255, 257, 274, 321,
    325, 523, 529
    catalyst, 252, 257
    local support, 433
    new supplier, 21
    partner, 319
    personal communi-
        cations, 515
    strategic knowledge, 196
Network Social Network Pilot
    Learning, 239
new business models, 21,
    50–51, 174, 180–81, 317,
    319, 324, 326, 328, 467,
    494–95, 497, 499
new product development
    (NPD), 23, 78, 130,
    134, 171, 188, 208, 234,
    264, 400, 509
new products, 2–4, 21–24, 64,
    74–78, 97, 100, 102–3,
    105–6, 108, 130, 197, 234,
    236–37, 337–39, 375–76,
    380–81, 508–9, 549–50,
    557–60, 562
    creating, 164, 243, 410
    developing, 338
    innovative, 402
    major, 106
    successful, 111
    support for, 102
New South Wales, 501, 506
    Government, 538
new technologies, 3, 20–24, 36,
    73, 96, 101, 107, 216, 220,
    234–38, 429, 514, 518
    applying, 50
    inserting, 216
New York, 17, 128, 188–89,
    196, 312–13, 329–31, 360,
    366, 537–39, 553, 555, 560
New York City, 495, 557, 559

New York World's Fair, 454, 456
Nichido Systems, 425
Ninety-Two Innovation
    Metrics, 303
Nippon Iridium Corpo-
    ration, 521
Nominal Weighting Value, 293
Nontraditional Life-Cycle
    Phases for Innovation, 209
Norton, 175, 188, 366
    approach, 176
    to strategy maps, 176
NPD. *See* new product
    development
    process, 130–31
    projects, 208, 401
NPV (net present value), 37,
    116, 198, 273, 295, 302, 384
NTSB, 498
number, 8, 27–28, 45, 104–5,
    123–24, 287–89, 294–95,
    299–300, 302–3, 306–7,
    309, 350–51, 387, 396,
    432–34, 491, 495–96,
    515–17, 519, 528
    benchmark, 433
    growing, 396
    high, 541
    insufficient, 472
    maximum, 124
    optimistic, 522
    pure, 433–34
    real, 123
    ridiculous, 301
    small, 169, 175–76
    subscriber, 534
    total, 474
    visitor, 489, 492
NWW, 240

O
objectives, 34–35, 39, 72,
    74–75, 90–91, 102, 120–21,
    126–27, 134–36, 138, 176–
    77, 203–5, 207, 235, 297
    campaign, 256

common, 85, 91
    competing, 22
    customer's, 414
    financial, 54
    functional, 423
    fundamental, 342
    interim, 205
    linked, 176
    operational/traditional, 192
    original, 91
    project's, 70, 135,
        205, 275, 372
    shared, 92
    strategic/business, 192
    ultimate, 207
    valued, 141
    well-defined, 200, 542
obsolete, 21–22, 35, 69, 144,
    380, 511, 521
Ocean Park, 487, 489, 492
OEBITDA growth, 536
OECD (Organisation for Eco-
    nomic Cooperation and
    Development), 65, 68
one-size-fits-all approach, 23,
    540–41, 544
open innovation, 25–27, 35–36,
    63, 68, 154, 158, 246,
    260–62, 547–48, 558
operations, 59–61, 83, 210,
    227, 318, 320, 379–80,
    421, 477, 479, 485, 488,
    492, 518, 520
    manager, 85
    projects, 388
Organisation for Economic
    Cooperation and Develop-
    ment (OECD), 65, 68
organizations, 5–6, 15, 27–29,
    44–48, 71–76, 81–83,
    86, 119–24, 148–52,
    225–27, 229–31, 237–42,
    260–61, 277–80, 303–5,
    342, 349–53, 362–65,
    386–90, 414–16
    client's, 284

collaborative, 238
dynamic, 274
executing, 223
fast-changing, 241
functional, 133
hospital, 220
hosting, 26
innovative, 9, 115,
    230, 411
large, 251, 253, 256
low-performing, 223
manufacturing, 17
mature, 102
military, 210
nonprofit, 41, 247
partner, 16, 30
prestigious, 5
private-sector, 52
public, 49
rational, 519
reference, 8
service, 102
sponsoring, 67, 268
student, 364–65
successful, 411, 414
traditional, 9
vendor's, 280
you/the, 260
Oriental Land Company, 468,
    484, 486–88
OT (operational technol-
    ogy), 55–56

P
parallel project management
    methodologies, 185
paralysis situation, 351
parametric curves, 212
parent company, 27, 33–34, 286
    project manager's, 209
park, 36, 68, 439, 453, 464,
    466–76, 478, 483, 485–93
    adult-themed, 486
    amusement, 476, 486

attendance, 489
educational, 492
good, 453
industrial, 404
new, 486
pristine, 453
sea, 486
traditional amusement, 442
partnerships, 22, 28, 34, 36,
    158, 183, 230, 236, 243,
    326, 331, 484, 554
    continuous, 225
    great, 149
    new, 552
    new commercial, 536
    non-profit, 183
    private, 52
patients, 52, 149, 219–20, 244,
    301, 340, 507
Patterns of Entrepreneurship
    Management, 244
payments, 50–51, 62, 330, 475,
    478, 482, 523
    royalty, 468, 483–84
PDMA (Product Development
    and Management Associa-
    tion), 2, 244
Peer-to-peer lending
    models, 50
People, 59, 113–14, 157–58,
    160–61, 174, 310–12,
    362, 377, 382, 473–74,
    525, 529, 543
    Organization Man-
    agement, 238
    Metrics, 302
perception, 26, 31, 45,
    133, 247, 265, 280, 361,
    407, 409
    customer's, 37, 281, 448
performance, 48–49, 113,
    137, 175–76, 266, 270–71,
    285–88, 291, 295–
    96, 303–4,

307, 336–37, 346–47, 370,
    501–2
    ballet, 502
    drive, 188
    effective, 282
    exceeding, 290
    existing, 276
    financial, 300, 330, 369
    human, 309
    innovative, 188
    lower, 337
    management's, 270
    measuring, 264
    monitoring, 172
    new, 337
    normal, 290, 292
    organizational, 278, 312
    strategic, 176
    superior, 290
    sustained, 7
    team's, 46, 174
    true, 540
personnel, 83, 108–10,
    119, 127, 130, 160,
    206, 439
    department, 247
    existing, 378
    financial, 388
    internal, 30, 32, 67
    partner's business, 319
    qualified, 241
    skilled, 407
    sustaining operational, 210
    trained, 74
Philips Business Group HPM
    Services & Solution Deliv-
    erability, 218
PI software, 113
planes, 36, 494–99, 515,
    535–36, 539
planning, 41, 46, 49, 125–26,
    197, 199, 354, 358, 375,
    381–82, 386, 502, 505
    benefit realization, 185

enterprise resource, 194
market entry, 429
traditional risk man-
   agement, 317
planning process, 92, 382
   strategic, 108, 131
plans, 39, 41, 43, 75–76, 85–90,
   92, 139–40, 143, 145–46, 199,
   201, 382, 435–36, 476, 486
   original, 471
   restructuring, 531–32
   technical, 530–31
Planview's Innovation Management Maturity Model, 72
platform, 32, 46–47, 178, 183,
   248, 250–58, 260, 395–96,
   398, 409–10, 428–31,
   433–34, 494
   advanced intelligence, 219
   central mobile, 409
   common, 113, 246
   digital, 50, 64
   digital training, 360, 363
   enterprise-grade IoT core, 56
   global on-demand
      learning, 397
   internet brokerage house
      trading, 50
   new, 3, 317, 494, 558
   online crowd-sourcing, 558
   open, 47, 251
   open-source, 558
   social media, 164
PMI (Project Management
   Institute), 2, 5, 14, 152,
   183, 220, 226–27, 317,
   320, 440, 449
PMOs (project management
   office), 9, 70–71, 74–75,
   123, 136, 177, 181, 183,
   264, 266, 289–90, 508, 511
point-of-sale, 51, 63
policies and models, 238
policies and strategies, 389
political changes, 49
political risks, 125

mitigating, 125
politics, 124–25, 348,
   365, 465, 472
portfolio, 70, 72, 179, 181,
   236, 239, 242, 298, 301–2,
   304, 307, 411, 413–15,
   417, 423–24
   active, 417
   balanced, 80
   co-creation project, 17
   developing innovation, 305
   growth life-cycle, 78–79
   managing project, 269
   mixed, 76
   product life-cycle, 78
   profit, 78
   robust, 150
   traditional industrial
      project, 420
   turnkey projects, 423
portfolio management
   activities, 235
portfolio management
   process, 270
portfolio metrics, 299
portfolio models, 80
portfolio of customer cases, 55
portfolio PMO, 70–71,
   102, 105, 123
portfolio risks, 423
Postal Telephone and Telegraph
   (PTT), 514
power, 4, 30, 115, 134, 143,
   250, 361, 365, 394,
   401, 512–13
   bargaining, 323, 327
   information is, 119, 135
   innovative, 432–33
practices, 156–57, 183–84, 188,
   218, 224, 228–29, 244, 249,
   338, 343, 406, 411, 490–91
   administrative, 389
   agile, 40, 398
   artificial intelligence, 58
   compensation, 328
   competitive bidding, 120

crisis-management, 140
   defined, 150
   employee motivation, 9
   hiring, 243
   illegal, 330
   improved, 130
   lean, 223
   managerial, 63
   primary, 216
   procurement, 328
   professional, 114
   project schedule optimi-
      zation, 183
   reporting, 136
   standardized, 223
   trading, 316
   updated, 186
   world-class project, 184
price-value analysis, 83
priorities, 15–16, 42–43, 85,
   88, 90–92, 105, 242, 244,
   310–11, 401, 405, 414, 417
prioritization, 115, 117, 133,
   136, 238, 365, 379, 510
   clear, 437
   product/feature, 134
prioritization criteria, 162
private sector, 20, 47–49, 54,
   57, 172, 192, 215–16,
   340, 370–71
processes, 2–3, 5, 8–11, 50–52,
   56–59, 70–72, 81–82, 99,
   129–88, 222–24, 226,
   234–38, 250–53, 257–60,
   300–305, 316–18, 357–59,
   386–88, 413, 423–26
   brazing, 57
   business model, 323
   certification, 424
   clinical, 220
   commercialization,
      22, 71, 221
   complex, 130, 253
   consultant's, 509
   continuous improve-
      ment, 8, 237

costly drilling, 104
creative, 41
creative problem-solving, 163
critical, 71, 87
disciplined, 299, 317
discontinuous, 20
disruptive, 336
distribution, 103
establishing, 143
evolutionary, 19
existing, 250, 388
existing customer experience
    improvement, 250
expedition, 214
extra, 46
fabrication, 169
fast track, 253
firm's production, 103
formal, 401
front-end, 132
gated, 222
ideas fulfillment, 247
innovation audit, 303
internal, 222
iterative, 132
listening, 166
logical, 85, 90
market pull, 234
model-building, 445
multiple, 236
new, 3, 24, 222
new-product evolution, 110
open recruitment, 427
operational, 50, 316
organizational, 140
paperless, 421
permeation, 102
product-evolution, 111
reactive, 71
recovery, 385
reexamination, 276
responsive, 225
right management, 306
scope change control, 524
social, 63
standardized, 8
step-by-step, 214

storyboarding, 444
streamlined, 56
structured, 70, 155
systematic analytical, 210
technology push, 234
traditional, 17
traditional waterfall, 398
trial-and-error, 316
upstream, 229
value chain, 421
well-documented, 223
wrong, 386
Product Development and
    Management Association
    (PDMA), 2, 244
product development process,
    130–31, 159–60, 236, 558
Product Innovation Manage-
    ment, 17, 68, 187–88, 244,
    343, 390–91
products, 20–25, 27–32, 37–39,
    43–47, 53–54, 62–65,
    72–77, 79–83, 95–102,
    130–33, 155–58, 163–65,
    167–72, 192–98, 208–11,
    327–31, 334–38, 374–77,
    556–59, 561–62
advanced, 36
associated, 324, 526
basic, 324
basic downloadable
    digital, 325
best-selling, 402
commercialize, 283
competitive, 22
completed, 32
complex, 188
complex engineered, 130
copycat, 554
creating advanced high-tech-
    nology, 370
defective, 347
defined, 234
developing, 559
develop noninfringing, 349
differentiated, 396
digital, 420

discrete, 219
dissimilar, 473
effective, 20
excellent, 377
expected, 44
final, 25, 44, 131, 168–69,
    208, 290, 432, 445
finished, 551
firm's, 63, 71
flagship, 549
flanker, 97
friends, 552
generation, 545
good enough, 155
improved, 37, 248
incessant, 36
incremental, 68, 236, 317
inferior, 553
launch, 347
managing large-scale complex
    engineering, 130
manufactured home, 389
marketable, 98
market-pull, 234
mature, 47
military aerospace, 35
modified, 162
new digital, 40
next-generation, 24
original, 101, 325
perfect, 207
profitable, 349
question mark, 77
radical, 20
revenue-generating commer-
    cialized, 180
satellite, 529
selling, 325
short, 106
specialty, 509
spinoff, 147
substitute, 327, 473
successful, 101, 110–11,
    193, 265, 277
superior, 328
sustainable, 63
table sports, 551

technology-based
   financial, 50
traditional, 396
troublesome, 81
unsuccessful, 394
unsuccessful consumer, 394
value-in-use, 67
vintage, 23
product sales, 309
products business model, 326
product teams, 524
profitability, 37, 39, 76, 265,
   268, 278, 280, 336, 339,
   374, 376, 388–89, 483
brand loyalty, 273
lifetime, 282
near-term, 74
short-term, 54, 173, 388, 508
profitable growth, 10, 313
long-term, 3
sustainable, 74
profitable improvements, 10, 74
long-term, 3
Profit Life-Cycle Portfolio, 80
profit margins, 271, 335,
   337, 374, 384
profits, 13, 20, 67, 296,
   299–300, 307, 309, 468,
   470, 476, 483–86,
   532, 534
personal, 534
program management, 148–49,
   215, 227, 283
programs, 26, 31, 215–16, 237,
   240, 249–50, 253–56,
   258, 341, 402, 407,
   496, 500–501
aggressive public
   relations, 471
community relations, 471
continuous product
   improvement, 78
existing in-development, 250
global corporate, 238
government innovation/tech-
   nology transfer, 110
large change, 354

manned space-flight, 546
meister, 56
metric management, 311
new, 559
profitable aircraft, 499
pump repair training, 61
retail, 394
salary, 179
salary administration, 181
short-term, 99
telecommunications, 527
unofficial, 556
value software, 545–46
Program Strategic Innovation
   Review, 239
project life-cycle phases, 541
project management, 1–8,
   11, 14–17, 68–69, 72,
   100, 123–25, 135–36,
   182–88, 191–93, 199–200,
   263–64, 268–69, 271–72,
   280, 282, 316, 397–400,
   419–22, 508–9
agile, 184
co-creation innovation, 4
contract R&D, 107
effective, 7, 46
effective innovation, 74, 150
end-to-end, 5
engagement, 156
good, 524
government, 49
implemented, 540
improved innovation, 149
innovational, 146
innovative, 15
international, 424
modern, 191
projects enterprise, 186
rational, 316
socialized, 184
stellar, 221
support innovation, 150
viewed innovation, 508
project management approaches,
   8, 48, 191, 317
flexible, 8, 192

preferred, 42
scalable, 225
traditional, 320
project management
   office. *See* PMOs
project managers, 3–9, 15–16,
   22–24, 70–72, 119–23, 125,
   180–88, 192–93, 199–200,
   203–9, 266–68, 279–83,
   285–87, 316–17, 319–21,
   366–69, 397–401, 423–25,
   439–41, 561–62
project managers and innovation
   personnel, 1, 19, 69, 127,
   129, 191, 243, 245, 261,
   263, 366–67
projects, 4–8, 39–49, 60–71,
   85–94, 114–28, 133–40,
   146–54, 177–87, 197–214,
   264–66, 268–76, 278–94,
   296–99, 350–56, 368–82,
   384–90, 415–26, 447–52,
   503–14, 540–43
abandoned construction, 454
active, 417
agile, 40, 230
aid, 62
autonomous mobility, 407
average, 111
backlogged, 126
bad, 179, 186, 241, 519
bootleg, 514
cancel, 143, 180
canceling, 350
cancelling, 216
close, 399
commercialized, 299
complex, 18, 139, 171, 189
consultancy, 227
correct, 119–20
cost-reduction, 77
critical, 109, 545
customers fund, 283
delay, 48
difficult, 369
digitalization, 423
environmental, 290

execute, 15
execute medium complexity, 227
existing, 243, 524
external, 274, 283
failed, 201, 542
flawed technology, 534
funded, 62, 66–67
giga, 408
given, 15, 200, 202, 272, 541–42, 544
global satellite, 537
good, 350
government-funded, 513
healthy, 242
high complexity, 226–27
higher-priority, 29, 127
high-profile, 308
high-risk, 27
high-technology, 467, 514
history, 15
ill-defined, 274
incremental, 302
industrial, 216
industry4.0, 420
innovation/R&D, 106, 117, 127
innovation-type, 70, 388
internal, 283
interrupting, 123
joint, 409
large, 184, 186, 374, 466, 519
link, 177
long-term, 203, 285, 340, 351
low complexity, 227
managed, 171, 369
managing, 16, 130, 240, 279, 508, 548
mega, 546
middle-of-the-road, 200, 541
military, 531
multibillion-dollar science, 512
multinational, 125

multiple, 124
new satellite, 537
nonincremental, 302
noninnovation, 70, 271
nontraditional, 120, 540
non-traditional, 120
offensive, 64
official, 147
operational, 70, 152, 540–41
organizational leaders champions, 15
original, 379
personal, 61
pet, 508, 510–11
potential, 119–20
prioritize, 49, 105, 122
prioritized, 116
private-sector, 48
public, 49
public-sector, 48–49
right, 17, 119, 135, 188
running, 354
selected, 136
selecting, 122, 264
service-related, 24
single, 242, 269
small, 186, 483
solution implementation, 226
staffs, 350
stalled, 122
stealth, 147
strategic, 70, 81, 121, 135, 177, 263, 540–41
successful, 123, 134, 354, 373, 379, 465
successful IPT, 340
support core, 173
tactical, 5, 274
theme park, 479
traditional EPC, 420
traditional type, 136
transformational, 24
troubled, 369
unsuccessful IPT, 340
value-opportunistic, 373

wrong, 173, 264, 269–70, 341
project selection, 75–76, 95, 102, 112, 114–15, 119–24, 136, 172, 265, 269–70, 272
project success, 108, 125, 152, 154, 192, 278, 288, 368, 370, 372–74, 381
defined, 270
defining innovation, 369, 390
establishing, 115
long-term innovation, 377
predicting, 370
promotions, 83–84, 106
prototype development, 130, 156, 201, 543, 545, 558
prototypes, 38, 42–43, 103, 156–57, 168–70, 207, 210, 229, 231, 233, 254, 316–17, 321
creating, 168
initial, 170
multiple, 171
new, 306
plywood, 506
prototypes design, 429
prototype specialists, 169
prototyping, 103, 156–57, 168, 230, 234, 251, 305, 412, 560
continuous, 181
iterative, 259
linear, 156
nonlinear, 156
rapid, 39, 170
PTT (Postal Telephone and Telegraph), 514
Pyramid of Mastery Denoting Efforts and Maturity Levels, 413

Q

Qatar Airways, 36, 498
QCD model, 289
Qualitative, 303

metrics, 303
  research, 40
quality assurance, 42
  tests, 169
Quality Maturity Model, 72
Quantitative, 303, 305–7
  metrics, 304–5, 307

R
radical collaboration, 234
radical innovation, 17, 21–22,
    24, 33, 37, 76, 78, 131–32,
    335, 508, 510, 559–60, 563
  successful, 22
  innovation outcomes, 21
  outcomes, 21
Rapid Project, 186
R&D, 69, 75, 83, 85, 97–98,
    100, 102–8, 111, 230, 232,
    236–37, 432–34, 542
  collaborative, 36
  team, 236
  worldwide, 181
Redstone Inc, 544–45
  management, 545
Redwood Credit Union, 248–50
Reinventing Project Man-
    agement, 68
Renter European Business
    Report, 481
research, 26, 96, 98–100, 131–
    32, 187–88, 195, 229–32,
    261–62, 265, 301–2, 305,
    307, 349, 407–8, 546–47
  applied, 77, 98–99
  attracted, 449
  basic, 99
  classical, 112
  collaborative, 404
  competitive, 155
  completed, 96
  conduct, 183, 550
  contract, 109
  excellent, 336
  generative, 403
  industrial, 109
  observational, 403

performing, 547
  product-development, 99
  pure, 66, 98, 241
  user, 169
Research Technology Manage-
    ment, 188, 438
resources, 19–20, 31–32, 36–37,
    72, 85–88, 92, 98, 122–24,
    138, 147, 212–14, 241–43,
    252–54, 257–58, 269–71,
    309, 316, 319,
    365–66, 382
  best, 241, 264, 348
  centralized, 220
  changing, 382
  correct, 72
  costly, 37
  critical, 115, 146, 186,
    271, 348, 373
  economic, 195
  existing, 23, 103, 241
  extra, 243
  financial, 243, 341
  firm's, 179, 323
  functional, 368
  innovation-capable, 154
  key, 91
  massive, 520
  new, 385
  nonhuman, 70, 198
  physical, 243
  planned, 287
  pool, 325
  reallocate, 241
  recombine, 243
  renewable, 54
  required, 138
  right, 122
  scarce, 63, 210, 243, 280
  sharing, 49, 241
  superior, 334
  supply, 105
  talented, 24
  technical, 29
  underutilized, 243
  unqualified, 49, 383
  wasted, 407

return-on-investment, 96
revenue, 29–30, 34–35, 298,
    300, 302, 307, 309, 467–70,
    472–73, 475, 478, 485, 488,
    520–21, 528
  advertising, 337
  annual, 330
  division's, 402
  expected yearly, 526
  generating, 531
  gross, 468, 485
  gross sales, 307
  increasing, 71
  international theme
    park, 477
  lost, 137, 508
  products/services, 302
  reduced, 560
  total, 470
  tourism-related, 477
revenue generator, 526
  profitable, 466, 485
revenue growth, 121, 376
  highest, 536
revenue losses, 560
revenue model, 514
review, 143, 150, 187, 196,
    204, 209, 213, 247, 249,
    496–97, 519
  objective, 519
  periodic project, 126
  stage gate, 237
  systematic, 17, 68
RICE Scoring Model, 134
rights, 55, 58, 60, 218, 221,
    223–25, 227, 229, 234,
    237, 425, 427, 479,
    482–84, 547–48
  children's, 554
  exclusive, 517
  new, 475
  patent, 108
  territorial, 483
  worker, 109
risk factors, 158, 416–17
  cumulative, 416
risk level, 24, 387

risk management, 8, 14, 24, 137, 139, 316–17, 327, 340, 419–20, 423–24, 541
  effective, 138, 384
  ineffective, 74
  political, 125
  strategic, 171
  traditional, 423
Risk/Reward Matrix, 417
risks, 11–15, 21–26, 28, 45, 70–71, 122–23, 125–27, 137–44, 147–48, 162, 170–74, 177–78, 198–99, 203–4, 316–17, 349–51, 384–85, 414–17, 517–19, 535–36
  appreciable, 62
  associated, 53, 482
  attendant, 88
  balancing, 415
  clear, 88
  computed, 417
  downside, 147–48, 183
  exposing, 49
  greatest, 24, 35, 66, 389, 519
  initial, 517
  key, 199, 416
  lower, 39, 539
  lowest, 417
  major, 429
  managing, 415
  minimal, 62
  minimizing, 120
  mitigated, 187
  new, 62, 535
  potential, 202, 340, 488, 543
  scientific, 88
  successful, 389
  unacceptable, 122
  unfavorable, 464
roadblocks, 16, 172, 216, 345, 348–50, 363–66, 394
  innovation funding, 350
  line-of-sight, 349
  massive, 364
roadmap, 235, 238, 437
Rogers Cantel Mobile Communications, 527

ROI, 54, 170, 264, 269, 274, 295–97, 300–301, 303, 307, 328, 384
  based models, 300
  objectives, 275
  question, 300
ROM method, 211
royalties, 349, 468, 475–77, 482, 484–85
RUTF innovation, 54
RWD (responsive web design), 44

S
Samsung, 51, 146, 394, 410–11, 438
  culture, 410
  section, 38
  SCM innovations, 438
Satellite Deorbiting Plan, 532
Satellite Network Operation Center, 516
satellite networks, 515, 530, 535
  global wireless, 522
satellite phones, 521–22
satellite procurement, 535
satellite replenishment, 531
satellites, 512–13, 515–16, 518, 520, 522, 524–25, 528, 533–38
  five, 525
  friendly, 520
  geo-stationary, 512
  geosynchronous, 512–13
  launching communication, 546
  launching test, 521
  low-Earth-orbiting, 517
  low-flying, 521
  low-orbit, 523
  low-orbiting, 513
  mission, 515
  moving, 535
  operational, 515
  ordering, 520
  spare, 535
  unserviceable, 515

Saudi Arabia, 404–5, 408, 475
SBU (strategic business unit), 76, 105
Scaled Agile Framework, 406
Scaling Model, 118
Scaling Project Management Innovation, 14–15
SCARF Model, 360–61
Scrum, 38–39, 45, 47, 192, 200, 202, 207, 209, 216, 541, 544
  approaches, 184
  framework, 39
  traditional, 42
  innovation, 39
  technology, 22
secrecy, 147, 179, 514
secrecy agreements, 108
Securaplane Technologies, 497
senior management, 66, 85–87, 89, 92, 94, 119, 121–23, 130–31, 135–36, 206–7, 253, 328, 508–9, 540, 545–46
services, 2–5, 8–10, 20–22, 29–33, 37–40, 50–51, 53–55, 62–65, 74–76, 120–21, 209–11, 213–15, 219–22, 225–26, 245–49, 322–25, 334–39, 346–49, 375–77, 525–28
  business-critical, 398
  commercial, 521, 528, 532
  computer, 119
  contactless, 409
  control, 516
  digital, 404
  digital banking, 50
  efficient air navigation, 353
  exceptional, 250
  existing, 48
  extra, 554
  financial, 50–51, 68, 500
  global communications, 526
  global telephone, 517
  handheld Iridium satellite, 516

initial, 514
integrated, 470, 473
limited, 512
lip, 341
mobile satellite, 516
necessary, 467
new, 48
offering basic web, 325
paging, 528
producing, 62
professional, 40, 222
satellite communications, 532
stable, 405
state-of-the-art air navigation, 353
subscription, 222
technical, 223, 484
telephony, 516
two-way voice communication, 520
Shaaban Abdallah, 363
shareholders, 10, 171–72, 475, 478, 557
annual, 475
park's, 491
public, 561
value, 11, 54, 266, 289, 310, 500
long-term, 2, 66, 378
maximum, 500
sustainable, 10
skill level, 85, 115, 138, 174, 183, 241
skills, 24, 34, 36, 56–57, 123, 150–54, 159, 174, 222, 320–21, 323–24, 343, 348, 439–40, 447–48
backup, 340
brazing, 56–57
common, 440
competition's, 64
educational, 84
entrepreneurship, 102
human, 58
imaginative, 157
important, 155, 217
improving, 223

innovation/technical, 201, 543
major, 429
master, 57
necessary, 12, 203, 271, 382
prior, 380
right, 153, 321
selling, 100
specialized, 153–54, 402, 440
unique, 427
skillset, 352
operational, 353
social innovation, 54–55, 63
Social Innovation in Action, 55
societies, 53, 143, 149, 183, 237, 308, 331, 395, 411, 447
society benefits, 274
sociocultural, 471, 474
software, 113–14, 174, 185–86, 219–21, 245–48, 250–51, 255, 260–62, 339, 341, 394, 398
algorithms, 183
applications, 248, 261
code, 556
creating third-party, 556
developers, 395
development, 216, 249, 436
existing time-tested legacy, 524
idea management, 162–63, 262
modeling, 559
new, 377–78
official, 556
open source, 262
produced, 44
right, 398
self-driving, 409
specialized collaboration, 163
storyboarding, 444
tracking, 272
value management, 546
videoconferencing, 64
working, 44

Software Engineering Institute, 524
SOHEC (Sydney Opera House Executive Committee), 504, 506
SOLiD Design & Delivery Framework, 223
solutions, 24, 27–28, 39, 43–45, 56–58, 61–62, 103, 140–42, 156, 158, 160–62, 168, 220–26, 228–30, 396–97, 423, 425–26, 429–30, 433, 503–4
agile, 420
best, 39, 161
better, 2, 20, 161
bulletproof, 144
changes/potential, 230
collaborative, 229
common, 170
complete, 222
complex, 220
custom-made, 40, 47
existing, 262
expected, 28
final, 115, 156, 158
ingenious, 442
new, 46, 111, 157, 221, 405
novel, 208
off-the-shelf, 40
optimal, 91
partial, 24
potential, 230, 374
real, 308
recruiting, 41
servicing, 224, 229
short-term, 4
unique, 516
Solutions & Services, 224, 229
sources, 19–21, 25–27, 31–32, 87–88, 108–11, 193–95, 274, 280, 355–61, 386, 389, 469–70, 528
constant, 485
external, 107, 110, 195
greatest, 518
internal, 110

major, 88, 514
open, 261
reliable, 547
single, 259
standard, 88
SOW, 119–20, 224, 451–52
  contractual, 120
  well-defined, 241, 451
space, 155, 164, 215–16,
  228, 426, 442, 444, 522,
  533, 535, 537
Space-Based Network, 507,
  515
Spain, 36, 251, 427,
  466–67, 559
special effects, 441–45, 451–52,
  455, 458–59, 462, 538
  projected, 445
special features, 117, 164, 325
sponsors, 40–47, 66–67, 147,
  235–36, 252, 255–56, 258,
  339, 536, 541, 545–46
  executive, 397–98
  internal, 287
  potential, 259–60
sprints, 39, 43–45, 47, 201, 217,
  252, 354, 521, 543
sprint team coordinators,
  357–58, 360
SQCDP boards, 258
stability, 101, 490
  long-term, 320
stakeholder base, 139
  large, 139
stakeholder business relationships, 280
Stakeholder Management
  Knowledge Area, 183
Stakeholder RACI matrix, 221
stakeholder relations management, 125
  included, 279
  required effective, 279
stakeholders, 28, 42–43, 45,
  47–49, 125, 144–45, 154–
  56, 183–85, 201, 255–57,
  264–68, 270, 278–80,

285–90, 292–95, 311, 340,
  382–83, 424–26, 542–43
  appease, 277
  becoming active, 218
  changing, 382
  external, 234, 348, 408
  financial, 464
  important, 424
  internal, 348, 399
  key, 125
  largest, 518
  managing, 255
  minority, 532
  multiple, 49, 139, 353
  placate, 347
  private-sector, 64
  project's, 266
  relevant, 234
standardization, 65, 215, 218,
  223, 229, 293, 508, 541, 544
Star Wars, 551–52, 555, 562
St. Galler Business Model
  Navigator, 331
stockholders, 4, 284, 374
stockholders and stakeholders, 4
stockholder satisfac-
  tion, 273, 295
storyboarding, 163, 397,
  444, 448, 450
storyboarding approach, 444
Strategic, 11, 78, 115,
  274, 296, 320
strategic alliances, 172, 295,
  319, 326, 331
strategic benchmarking, 8–9
strategic business
  goals, 121, 127
strategic business objectives,
  5–6, 16, 23, 38, 121, 176,
  186, 198, 200, 296–97, 542
strategic business unit
  (SBU), 76, 105
  portfolio, 76
  products, 76
strategic goals, 72–73, 102, 135,
  141, 143–44, 155, 197, 241,
  252, 285, 304

corporate, 102
defining, 120
long-term, 349
organizational, 136
primary, 176
shared, 177
strategic innovation, 3, 5, 7, 188
strategic KPIs, 432
Strategic Management Maturity Model, 72
strategy, 5–6, 17, 73–74, 81–82,
  95–97, 102, 127–28,
  134–36, 150–51, 174–77,
  187–88, 234–36, 253,
  302, 316–17, 389–90,
  413–15, 435–36
  advertising, 474
  aggressive, 526
  build-market-share, 81
  company's, 25, 156, 158, 410
  corporate, 132, 135–36,
  253, 298, 380
  deconstructed AMD's
  offensive, 329
  entrepreneurship, 102
  firm's, 8, 140
  follow-the-leader, 97
  functional unit, 135
  initial, 127
  intellectual property protection, 215
  knowledge network, 196
  long-term, 14, 146, 175
  me-too, 97
  negotiation, 422
  organization's, 40
  proactive, 63
  profit maximization, 485
  risk maximization, 484
  risk minimization, 484
  risk mitigation, 204, 215
  self-regulated, 53
  updated, 73
strategy maps, 175–77, 187
strategy sessions, 70
success, 9–10, 14–16, 66–67,
  149–53, 185–86, 191–92,

228–29, 252–53, 264, 269, 271, 278, 286–88, 362–65, 367–77, 379–80, 384–91, 400–402, 425, 543–44
astounding, 394
celebrate, 258
client's, 284
creating, 384
defined, 370
defining, 368, 373–74
digital wallet, 51
early, 336
economic, 488
establishing, 367
firm's, 22
franchisor's, 325
guarantee, 269–71
initial, 523
innovative, 228
judge, 259
long-term, 53, 70, 376, 484, 544, 549
measure business value, 192
much-deserved, 364
new product, 391
new product/service, 30
organizational, 120, 313
organization's, 82
park's, 490
post-failure, 386, 390
potential, 386
real, 37, 277, 390
strategic, 135, 367, 390
technical, 117, 368, 516
true, 369, 380, 390
viewed, 508
suppliers, 30, 32–33, 36, 121–22, 196–97, 261, 276–77, 311, 318–19, 326–27, 353, 378, 422, 494–95, 499–500
existing contracted, 163
expecting, 499
external, 26
largest, 427, 508
lower tiered, 499
new, 323
secondary, 330

supply chain, 326
upstream, 288
supplier's facility, 536
supply chain, 64, 325–26, 338
support, 85–86, 92, 101–2, 105–7, 113–15, 134–35, 140–42, 147, 159–60, 171–72, 194–95, 237–38, 240–41, 251–56, 345–46, 353–54, 435–37, 445–46, 502–4, 516–17
SWAG method, 211
Sydney Australia Opera House, 501, 503, 505, 507
Sydney Opera House Executive Committee (SOHEC), 504, 506
Symonds, Ralph, 506
systems, 57, 75, 195, 215, 219–21, 246–47, 339–40, 352–53, 412–14, 456–57, 497, 505–6, 513, 518–19, 521, 525–28, 531
12-satellite, 520
automatic, 418
aviation, 497
baggage-handling, 466
categorization, 81
closed, 284
commercial, 513
configurable, 220
critical, 496–97
disparate, 194
distribution, 300
electrical, 495–97
fire-suppression, 497
given, 98
global, 251
hi-tech, 248
knowledge-based, 182
major, 524
measurement, 309
military, 533
new, 174, 339, 533
nontraditional, 410
operational, 352
passive, 246

people-mover, 456–57
priority, 242
propulsion, 521
ranking, 133
reliable, 412
reporting, 184, 544
ride, 443
satellite, 520, 531
self-growing, 252
strategic-planning, 75
suggestion, 246
toy, 549
tracking, 541
train, 467
universal, 550
venting, 499
working, 168
worldwide, 513

T
Tamimi Supermarket, 408
target business unit, 429
target markets, 53, 178, 339, 514, 516, 549
initial Iridium, 516
targets, 43, 89, 172, 174, 177, 290–92, 294, 296, 305, 527, 529
measurable, 45
strategic measurable, 434
teachers, 64, 435, 550
team, 15, 39–47, 89–94, 137–39, 148, 150, 154–55, 158–59, 162–63, 180–81, 235–37, 249–51, 253–55, 258–59, 339–41, 364–65, 387–88, 396–403, 425–26, 435–36
adaptive, 16
agile, 39, 429
autonomous, 15
building multidisciplinary, 396
central, 254
co-created, 243
collocated, 15, 201, 542
creating high-performance project, 72

cross-functional, 46, 152, 435
drive, 425
engineering, 158
entrepreneurial, 339
good, 361
high performance, 363
high-performance, 73, 363
improvement, 238
internal, 28
localized, 400
local sports, 54
multi-disciplinary, 222
multidisciplinary Project, 220
multi-functional, 68, 262
new, 455, 531
new-product devel-
    opment, 110
problem-solving, 158
pump mechanic, 61
relevant, 250
right, 137
small, 16, 131
special, 93
sprint, 357, 363
students form, 556
support Idea, 433
sustainment, 180–81
talented, 455
traditional project, 340
vendor's, 280
venture, 339, 341, 348
virtual, 144, 181–82, 217, 401
working, 365
team meetings, 164–
    65, 237, 508
team members, 15–16, 43–45,
    86–94, 154–56, 162–64,
    167–68, 181, 217, 235, 267,
    339, 365, 382, 388–89, 401
assigned, 23
influence, 129
multidisciplinary, 46
open-source, 171
push, 88, 91
technical, 133
virtual, 382

technical skills, 103, 107
    necessary, 241
techniques, 145, 163, 166, 169,
    182, 205, 207, 209, 215,
    292, 294, 309, 312
emotional management, 154
futuristic building, 446
interfunctional, 96
project management exe-
    cution, 135
rapid application devel-
    opment, 170
technological
    advancements, 337
technology, 7–8, 10–13, 24,
    26–27, 36, 49–51, 55–56,
    99–100, 109–10, 131–32,
    154, 182–83, 214–15, 234–
    36, 316–18, 334–39, 380,
    384–85, 442–43, 518–19
advanced, 219, 409
artificial intelligence, 183
blend, 443
blockchain, 50
business intelligence, 319–20
cell, 512
cognitive response, 408
commercial, 56
common, 73
communication, 231
communicational, 52
computer, 29
creating, 309
developing innovative manu-
    facturing, 36
developing satellite, 515
edge, 114
emergent, 324
emerging, 252, 397, 405
existing, 22, 39, 106, 122,
    198, 216, 336, 380–81, 524
improved, 151
innovative, 148, 342, 451
interactive, 443
invented, 65
killer, 36

license proprietary theme park
    design, 482
machine learning, 182
mature, 215
modified, 317
motorsport, 248
patented, 482
patented Transmeta, 329
power efficiency, 329
relevant, 96
required, 103
sensor, 57
solid propellant, 547
state-of-the-art, 466
successful, 151
vehicle, 408
wireless broadband, 550
Technology Management &
    Innovation, 10
Technology Program Manage-
    ment Model, 215
technology readiness
    levels. *See* TRLs
Teledesic Project, 532
Telegraph Media Group, 481
test data, 349
test flights, 537
test software, 399
Texas Instruments,
    102, 399–401
Thai Satellite Telecommuni-
    cations, 521
Thatham, Sid, 363
Themed Entertainment Asso-
    ciation, 494
Theme Park Designer, 463
theme parks, 376, 440–41,
    443, 447, 464–71, 473–79,
    482–93, 495, 538, 554
adjacent, 486
bankrupt, 475
best, 492
building Disney, 440
designing, 158
existing, 464
existing Disney, 489

foreign, 485
good, 474
international, 484
national, 488
new, 476, 483–84, 486
running, 555
state-of-the-art, 466–67, 485
studio, 476, 486
surrounding, 492
world-class, 488
thinking, 37, 43, 62, 159, 162,
    166–67, 170, 175, 435,
    437, 440, 442
creative, 40, 110, 158, 343
innovational, 403
innovative, 57–58, 354
linear, 5, 139, 346
thinking-led approach, 230
Third-party companies, 396
threats, 6, 71, 73, 82–83, 145,
    155, 171, 179–80, 319,
    322–23, 327
competitive, 337, 521
time, 37–39, 41–46, 56–61,
    159–63, 211–14, 269–72,
    294–97, 303–5, 346–50,
    354–56, 364–65, 370–72,
    374–80, 440–42, 449–52,
    464–66, 476–83, 521–25,
    530–33, 541–45
time management, 456
time-to-market, 3–4, 22–23, 30,
    34, 121, 133, 141, 290–94,
    296, 299, 380
fast, 38
timing, 70, 95, 99, 114, 119,
    198, 207–8, 215, 274,
    279, 368–69
Titone, Rick, 58
Tokyo, 55, 462, 467–68, 470,
    473, 482, 485–86, 494
Tokyo business model, 468
tools, 1–2, 71–72, 112–13,
    155–57, 162–64, 175–76,
    183–84, 186–87, 222–23,
    249–52, 254–56, 315–17,

321, 333, 355–57, 359–61,
    397–98, 400, 423, 425
best, 254
better, 30
communication, 168
complex, 185
critical, 213
daily, 353
double-entry, 357
duplicate, 59
effective, 82
efficient, 223
excellent, 80
good, 436
machine, 58–59
measurement, 300
modeled, 436
modeling, 435
political, 515
primary, 541
refined, 423
right, 225, 321
standard, 141
technical, 163
traditional, 191, 321
Total Quality Management, 438
Tough Economic Times, 69
Toyota, 59, 146, 324
track, 93–94, 186, 198–99, 201,
    203, 259–60, 264, 276–79,
    286–87, 289–90, 300,
    412–13, 457
dedicated career, 149
fast, 259
track innovation, 274
track performance, 217, 310
trade, 50, 454, 508–9
trademarks, 114, 276–77, 340,
    482–84, 553, 561–62
tradeoffs, 107, 111, 177, 269–
    70, 275, 279, 281, 283, 379,
    385, 450, 465–66, 524
value attribute, 284
traditional approach to project
    management, 150, 184, 192
Traditional CVM models, 281

traditional metrics, 136, 265,
    276, 283, 286–89
Traditional Project Gates, 202
traditional project management,
    8, 11, 137–39, 146, 149,
    152, 156, 159, 184, 204,
    207, 316–17, 321, 323, 355
traditional projects, 72, 75,
    120, 125, 135, 139, 187,
    285, 287, 385, 387–88,
    440–41, 540–41
implementing, 387
managing, 192
traffic controllers, 352, 357
trained air, 353
trainees, 57, 489
trainer role, 358
training, 56–57, 179, 181, 255,
    257, 260, 357, 360, 378,
    380, 425, 427, 471
Training Metrics, 307
transaction server (TS), 398
transferability, 546
transformation, 2, 68, 238,
    321, 398, 434
cultural, 238, 240
organizational, 14
social business, 249
support project manager, 424
transition, 50, 182, 222, 401,
    436–37, 446
responsible successful tech-
    nology, 215
Translating Strategy, 188
trends, 71, 82, 95, 199, 208,
    220, 235, 287, 414, 429–30
TRLs (Technology readiness
    levels), 214–16
TRLs for weapon system pro-
    curement activities, 215
TRW's Space & Electronics
    Group, 520
TS (transaction server), 398
turf war situation, 364
Turner, 17, 188
Twenty-First Century, 371

two-stage fuzzy approach, 124
types, 2–3, 8, 19–70, 72–73,
    75–76, 81, 97–99, 107–10,
    132–34, 148–54, 184–88,
    196–97, 199–200, 202–3,
    212, 215–17, 241–42,
    324–25, 368–70, 541–48
  airliner, 497
  airplane, 498
  complex, 317
  contract, 109
  difficult, 53, 548
  five, 65, 335
  safer, 497
  secondary, 11
  traditional, 320

U
UATs (user acceptance
    tests), 42–43
UI, 41, 397
Ulrich, 277
unanticipated changes, 465
unanticipated problems, 111
uncertainties and chal-
    lenges, 130
uncertainty, 21–22, 65, 119–20,
    123, 125, 138–40, 177–78,
    187–88, 192–93, 228,
    316–17, 319–20,
    385–86, 414, 433
  major, 429
  managing, 423
  new customer, 23
  perceived, 193
  product liability, 122, 385
  reducing, 433
  technological, 8
  up-front, 156
underinvestment, 329
UNESCO (United Nations
    Educational, Scientific,
    and Cultural Organiza-
    tion), 502, 539
UNESCO World Herit-
    age Site, 501

UNICEF, 54
UNICEF Kid Power, 54
unions, 83–84, 500
United Communications
    Company, 520
United Nations Educational,
    Scientific, and Cultural
    Organization (UNE-
    SCO), 502, 539
United Nations of Iridium, 536
United States, 217, 248, 251,
    435, 437, 465–66, 471, 473,
    475, 482, 484–85, 489, 524,
    527, 554–55
United States Postal
    Service, 343
unit sales, 251
universities, 25, 36, 57–58,
    64, 249, 261, 343,
    405, 407
unrealistic value estimates, 242
unsatisfied customers, 335
unsolved problems, 58
unstructured brainstorm-
    ing, 159, 442
unstructured data, 52
upgrades, 77, 99, 191,
    424, 478, 536
US aviation companies, 36
user acceptance tests
    (UATs), 42–43
users, 33, 37, 42–47, 156–57,
    159–60, 164, 201, 252,
    254, 258–59, 292, 376–77,
    395–98, 405–6, 516,
    543, 554, 562
  advanced, 558
  cell phone, 512
  cellular, 520
  direct, 29
  existing, 48
  heavy, 184
  industrial, 516
  leading-edge, 30
  new, 48, 535
  ordinary, 33

preferred, 561
primary, 184
regular, 520
website, 562
US government, 472,
    513, 515, 535
US market, 436
US National Transportation
    Safety Board, 496
US products, 469
Utzon design, 502
Utzon Room, 502
Utzon's ability, 506
Utzon's Design, 501, 504
UX designers, 42, 44

V
Vacík, 7
valuation, net portfolio, 302
value, 10–11, 30–32, 37–40,
    52–53, 122–23, 158,
    180, 193–95, 205–6,
    225–30, 243–44, 264–92,
    294–96, 309–12, 315–16,
    318–21, 323–26, 375,
    377–79, 435–37
  achieved, 271
  appreciable, 264
  commercialized, 319
  corporate, 237
  creating, 280, 318
  current, 275
  exact, 283, 371
  extract, 279
  final, 283, 297
  forecasted, 144
  forecast stakeholder, 289
  great, 426, 437
  guarantee, 270
  hard, 273
  highest, 151
  highest leadership, 151
  incremental, 23
  innovation project, 266
  internal, 285
  limited, 271

long-term, 264
major, 30
maximize, 144
monetary, 313
numeral, 57
option, 302
organization's, 266
parent company's, 283
perceived, 53, 271, 275, 277,
    279, 325, 377, 549
personal, 162, 266
planned, 285
pragmatic, 432
primary, 11
qualified, 317
real, 158, 264, 275, 277
recognizable, 158
recognized, 279, 368
redefine, 156
secondary, 11
share, 425
shared, 140, 425
stakeholder, 266
stakeholder's, 284
superior, 284
total, 284
true, 194, 275
true economic, 275
unique, 145
weighting, 416
Value-added innovations, 62
value attributes, 263–64, 269,
    279, 282–84, 289, 293,
    295–96, 311–12
  agreed-on, 290
  new, 293
  project manager's, 296
value-based, 31
Value-Based Innovation, 263
Value-Based Innovation Pro-
    ject Management Met-
    rics, 264–312
value-based metrics, 38, 265,
    283–84, 289, 311–12
  correct, 281
  establishing, 38, 265

value chain, 30, 160,
    179, 261, 288
value KPI, 289
Value Management (VM),
    30–31, 68, 100, 186, 248,
    265, 275, 279–82, 284–85,
    312–13, 546
  practices, 186, 284
  measurement, 274–75,
    290–95, 312
value measurement baseline
    (VMB), 285
value measurement methodol-
    ogy (VMM), 186, 265, 275
Value Metric/KPI Bound-
    ary Box, 291
value metrics, 263–66, 269,
    272–75, 278, 281–82, 284,
    286, 288–90, 292–95,
    309, 311–12
  customer-related, 288
  hard, 273
  intangible, 273
  monitoring business, 263
  right, 283
  single, 289, 311
  soft, 273
value mismatches, 285
value model, 436
  customer project man-
    agement, 282
value networks, 318
value outcome, 271
Value Performance Framework.
  See VPF
  titled, 266
value propositions, 178, 318,
    321, 323, 435–36, 559
  social, 54
  unique, 63
variables, 120, 123, 130, 351, 387
vehicles, 211, 408, 445, 452,
    456–57, 549
  autonomous, 407–8
  self-driving, 407, 409
vendor, 194, 196, 251, 280

VIBE, 434
  network, 434
video game market, 557
video projectors, 58
viewpoints, 92, 160
  new, 53
vision, 134, 150, 158, 162, 175,
    204, 226, 237–38, 321, 382,
    388, 409–10
  corporate social responsi-
    bility, 124
  innovative COMAU, 419
  right, 337
  shared, 73
  strategic, 425, 552, 560
visionary, 41–42
visualization, 57, 217
visualize, 141, 183, 209, 216–
    17, 221, 355, 417, 442, 444
visualizing stakeholder
    involvement, 157
Vital Innovation Behaviour
    Engagement, 434
VM. *See* Value Management
VMB (value measurement
    baseline), 285
VMM (Value measure-
    ment methodology),
    186, 265, 275
VPF (Value Performance
    Framework), 265–66
VUCA environment, 125, 145

W
Wall Street Journal, 443,
    497, 537–39
Walt Disney Company, 439–40,
    443, 447, 464–65, 467,
    471–72, 474–78, 481–82
Walt Disney Imagineering, 440,
    443, 448, 454, 485–86, 537
Walt Disney Productions, 444
Walt Disney Studios, 476,
    478, 481, 487
Walt Disney World, 448–49,
    452, 457, 459, 461, 467, 539

Walt Disney World Parks and
  Resorts, 443
Walt Disney World's Magic
  Kingdom, 485
Wärtsilä Energy Solutions, 435
waterfall methodology, 387, 541
  traditional, 540
waterfall model, 437
  traditional, 43
WBS (Work breakdown
  structure), 138, 164, 185,
  192, 211–13, 224, 243,
  281, 451, 524
  high-level, 211
  incremental innovation, 212
WCC Chief Executive
  Officer, 533
WDI, 440, 443
weak project, 382–83
WED Enterprises, 440
Wenger, 228, 244
Wheelwright, 25, 68, 178, 189
Wikipedia, 168, 175, 182–83,
  324, 329, 337, 440, 459,
  493–94, 499, 548
Wiley, John, 1, 17–19, 67–69,
  128–29, 188–89, 191,

244–45, 263, 312–13,
  315, 331, 333, 343–45,
  367, 393, 439
Wingfield-Hayes, 496–97, 539
Withhold, 101, 347
workers, 20–22, 56, 112–13,
  124, 134, 143–44, 146, 148,
  162–63, 243, 281, 339,
  401–2, 508–9, 543–44
  alienate, 113
  appointed, 389
  expecting, 163
  expert, 56–57
  frontline, 143
  hired, 57
  innovative, 339
  internal, 20
  overseas, 57
  plant, 56
  skilled, 26, 122, 382
  train, 56–57
workflow, 216, 219, 246, 251
  activities, 216
  analysis, 221
  clinical, 227
  designed, 220
workforce, 5, 9, 64, 401, 405

550-employee, 529
  company's, 28
  skills, 295
workloads, 92, 364, 427
  balancing, 107
  functional, 348
  high, 398
  internal, 107
Workout and Processing Time
  of Ideas and Projects, 433
workshops, 42–43, 163, 252,
  359, 398, 426, 433
  inventor's, 552
  joint, 43
  learned, 428
World Bazaar, 485, 488
World Economic
  Forum, 219, 244
World Health Organization, 219
World's Fair, 443, 454

Y
Yale Gracey, 455, 458

Z
Zane Corporation, 540–41, 543